15th EDITION

Leading Constitutional Decisions

ROBERT F. CUSHMAN

New York University

PRENTICE-HALL, INC. Englewood Cliffs, New Jersey 07632

Library of Congress Cataloging in Publication Data

CUSHMAN ROBERT FAIRCHILD,
   Leading constitutional decisions.

  First-13th editions by R. E. Cushman.
    1. United States—Constitutional law—Cases.
I. Cushman, Robert Eugene, 1889–1969. Leading
constitutional decisions. II. Title.
KF4549.C83 1977   342'.73'02648   76-41870
ISBN 0-13-527358-7

055286

342.73
@ 986L 15

© 1977 by Robert F. Cushman

Printed in the United States of America

10 9 8 7 6 5 4 3

Prentice-Hall International, Inc., *London*
Prentice-Hall of Australia, Pty. Ltd., *Sydney*
Prentice-Hall of Canada, Ltd., *Toronto*
Prentice-Hall of India Private Limited, *New Delhi*
Prentice-Hall of Japan, Inc., *Tokyo*
Prentice-Hall of Southwest Asia Pte. Ltd., *Singapore*
Whitehall Books Limited, *Wellington, New Zealand*

Contents

iii

Preface

No one can understand fully and clearly how our American national government works, or how it came to be the kind of government it is, unless he is familiar with the way in which the Supreme Court of the United States does its work, and with some of its decisions which are milestones in the growth of our American constitutional system. This collection of cases is intended primarily to serve the needs of students of American government and American history.

The Supreme Court does not work in a vacuum. Its decisions upon important constitutional questions can be fully understood only when viewed against the background of history, politics, and economics out of which they grew. The brief introductory notes attempt to reconstruct this background, to suggest the significance of the cases in our constitutional development, and, to a limited extent, to indicate the relation of the decisions printed to other, and perhaps equally important, ones which could not be included.

In editing the cases and writing the notes the guiding assumptions have, in general, been these: (1) the job of the Supreme Court is to provide reasoned opinions so that lower courts and administrators can apply its rulings intelligently to similar problems; (2) the extent to which the Court supplies such guidance and the skill with which it develops its present reasoning from what has gone before are measures of how well it is doing its job; and (3) students should be encouraged to evaluate this aspect of the Court's work.

For these reasons the emphasis in this edition, as in earlier ones, is on the evolution of the ideas used to explain our Constitution rather than on stating "the law" of any particular moment. And so that students will have ammunition with which to do intellectual battle, some important dissents have been included and a fuller exploration of a few problems has been favored over a more superficial treatment of many. Thus, where old material has had to be omitted to make room for new, it was thought better to drop whole subjects to allow more complete coverage of those that remained. Loyal and valued users of the earlier edition may, like the author himself, find some favorite subject missing. But the preparation of a new edition inevitably involves parting with old friends and it is only hoped that the new ones will be as useful and as much fun to know.

ROBERT F. CUSHMAN

Table of Cases

Bold face capitals (with boldface page numbers) indicate the cases reprinted in this supplement; italics indicate cases commented on in the editor's notes; ordinary type indicates cases quoted or discussed in the opinions. For convenience, all cases in which the United States is plaintiff are also indexed under the name of the defendant.

1

The Judicial Branch

MARBURY v. MADISON
1 Cranch 137; 2 L. Ed. 60 (1803)

Although the election in the autumn of 1800 brought to the Federalists a defeat from which they never recovered, President Adams and his Federalist associates did not retire from office until March, 1801. The Federalists had been for some time considering plans to reform the federal courts by remodeling the Judiciary Act of 1789, and now in the eleventh hour they boldly set themselves to the task with renewed energy in order, undoubtedly, to insure a fortress for Federalist principles which would not easily be broken down. Accordingly they passed the Judiciary Act of February 13, 1801, which relieved the Supreme Court justices of circuit court duty, reduced the size of the Supreme Court from six to five, and created six new circuit courts with 16 new judgeships. Two weeks later Congress passed an act providing that the President might appoint for the District of Columbia for five-year terms as many justices of the peace as he thought necessary. President Adams proceeded during the last 16 days of his administration to fill these newly created vacancies (58 in all) with loyal Federalists; and the task of signing their commissions occupied him until well into the night before the inauguration of Jefferson on March 4, 1801. Among the judicial appointments made by Adams in the closing weeks of his administration was that of John Marshall, a staunch Federalist, to be Chief Justice of the United States.

The federal courts had already incurred the bitter animosity of the Jeffersonians, largely because of the vigor with which they had enforced the obnoxious Alien and Sedition Acts of 1798; and the Republicans were enraged beyond measure at what they deemed the effrontery of the Federalists in enacting the Judiciary Act of 1801. The judiciary was caustically referred to by Randolph as a "hospital for decayed politicians," while Jefferson wrote to a friend, "The Federalists have retired into the judiciary as a stronghold . . . and from that battery all the works of republicanism are to be beaten down and erased." One of the first efforts of the Republican administration was to repeal the Judiciary Act of 1801, and after a long and acrimonious debate this was accomplished, March 8, 1802. The repealing act restored the Supreme Court justices to circuit court duty, restored the size of the Supreme Court to six, and abolished the new circuit judgeships which had been created. The Federalists in Congress bitterly assailed the repealing statute as unconstitutional. Marshall himself apparently adhered to that view, and probably would have held the law void if it had come before him immediately in his judicial capacity. In order to prevent this, however, the repealing act had so altered the sessions of the Supreme Court that it did not convene again for 14 months, by which time acquiescence in the act by the judges affected made a decision of unconstitutionality impracticable.

However, when the Court convened in February, 1803, the case of Marbury v. Madison was on the docket. Marbury was one of those whom President Adams had appointed to a five-year justiceship of the peace in the District of Columbia. His commission, signed and sealed on March 3, was among four that had not been delivered when Jefferson had taken office on March 4. It was, in fact, Marshall, then serving as Secretary of State as well as Chief Justice, who had sealed but had not delivered Marbury's commission. Jefferson immediately ordered his new Secretary of State, James Madison, to withhold the commission; and Marbury filed suit asking the Supreme Court in the exercise of its original jurisdiction to issue a writ of mandamus to compel Madison to give him his commission. The right to issue such a writ had been conferred upon the Court by a provision of the Juciciary Act of 1789, and jurisdiction thereunder had been exercised by the Court twice before Marshall's accession to the bench. When the case came on for argument, it assumed very largely the aspect of a quarrel between the President and the judiciary. Marbury's own interest in it was small, since Jefferson made it fairly clear that he had no intention of giving Marbury his commission even if the Court ordered him to do so. The Republicans seem to have expected that the Court would issue the mandamus asked for, and there were open threats that Marshall and his colleagues would be impeached if that occurred.

Marshall's decision that the Constitution forbade the Court to issue the writ of mandamus asked for by Marbury might have placated the Republicans had he not in their judgment gratuitously gone beyond the necessities of the case. While holding that the Court could not take jurisdiction and decide the case, inasmuch as the statute authorizing it was unconstitutional, he nonetheless pointed out that Marbury was entitled to his commission; that a writ of mandamus was the proper remedy; and that the executive was properly subject to mandamus if the case were started in the proper court. In addition he scolded the administration for not delivering the commission. In the storm of criticism thereby engendered, the judicial review aspect of the case seems largely to have escaped attack; and when, six months later, a circuit court held unconstitutional another act of Congress abolishing fees granted by an earlier law to justices of the peace in the District of Columbia, it evoked no criticism of any kind. The case, not in any offical report, is noted by Charles Warren, The Supreme Court in United States History, Vol. I, 255.

No more vehement argument has ever raged in the field of constitutional law and theory than that over the genesis of the power of judicial review. Did the framers of the Constitution intend to grant the power as part of the checks and balances system in the first three articles? Or did Chief Justice Marshall "usurp" this power for the judiciary in his decision in Marbury v. Madison? Scholars still disagree, and the real intention of the framers will probably never be known. But a number of things are certain. It is certain that this was the first case in which the Supreme Court openly and clearly held unconstitutional an act of Congress. It is equally certain that the idea of judicial review did not originate with Marshall. Most of the arguments which he used in his famous opinion had been presented again and again in the debates in Congress on the Repeal Act of 1802, and the basic theory had been advanced by Hamilton in Number 78 of The Federalist. Moreover, the lower federal courts, without exciting opposition, had held invalid the act of Congress making them, in effect, claims commissioners for pension claims (a fact pointed out by Marshall in his opinion); and a number of earlier state cases have been considered as embodying the principle; see Bayard v. Singleton (1787). That Marshall cited no precedents to bolster his interpretation of judicial power is not particularly surprising. As a jurist he relied heavily on deductive reasoning, and in neither Gibbons v. Ogden nor McCulloch v. Maryland, two of his most famous opinions, did he cite a single case as precedent.

There is evidence that public opinion tended to look upon the power of judicial review as one of the normal incidents of judicial power. The Court considered the constitutionality of the carriage tax in Hylton v. United States (1796); and its refusal to declare it unconstitutional, as well as the refusal of the lower federal courts to hold unconstitutional the Alien and Sedition Acts and the United States Bank Charter, was bitterly con-

demned by the Republicans, who seemed to feel that the courts were neglecting their duty in not sustaining the Constitution against legislative usurpation of power. That Congress itself recognized the power is perhaps evidenced by their alteration of the term of the Supreme Court to prevent the Repeal Act of 1802 from coming to the Court for review for more than a year after its enactment.

The power of the Supreme Court to declare acts of Congress unconstitutional has so long been an integral part of our constitutional system, and Marshall's reasoning in the case of Marbury v. Madison is so impressive, that it is easy to lose sight of the fact that a most cogent argument may be made against the establishment of the power, and that had the Supreme Court never enjoyed it no very calamitous results would have ensued. Jefferson, Marshall's most bitter personal and political adversary, never admitted the paramount authority of the Supreme Court to determine the validity of an act of Congress, but held that each of the three departments of the national government being equal and separate was equally empowered "to decide on the validity of an act according to its own judgement and uncontrolled by the opinions of any other department." This view was shared by many other thoughtful men of the day. In the exercise of its power of judicial review the Court will not pass upon what it terms "political questions," questions the final determination of which has been confided by the Constitution to the discretion of the political departments, that is, the legislative or the executive. According to the view of Jefferson and his followers, all questions involving the constitutionality of acts of Congress which might come before the Court would be "political questions." The statute might conflict with the Constitution, but that fact would not of itself endow the Court with any power to invalidate it; rather it would be the duty of the Court to enforce the statute without questioning its validity. That such a system would not have been followed by any strikingly disastrous results may be inferred from the fact that in most of the constitutional governments of the world the courts do not enjoy the power of judicial review, and that in this country fewer than 100 statutes of Congress have been held unconstitutional, of which only a very few involved problems of any vital or lasting importance. As Mr. Justice Holmes declared, "The United States would not come to an end if we lost our power to declare an act of Congress void." In fact, the power to declare an act of Congress invalid is a power very much less important to the Supreme Court than the power to pass upon the validity of state legislation. This last authority may well be regarded as vital to the preservation of our federal system by providing a necessary method of preventing the state governments from encroaching upon the domain of federal authority or impairing the federal rights and immunities of the individual.

The case of Marbury v. Madison has a certain strategic significance which should not be left out of account. The next case in which an act of

Congress was invalidated by the Supreme Court was the famous Dred Scott case, decided in 1857. By that time nearly 70 years had elapsed from the time of the formation of our constitutional system, and the Court was composed of men holding nationalistic views far less strong than those of Marshall and his associates. Moreover, Marbury v. Madison involved the use of judicial power to protect the Court itself against interference by the legislature, a use reasonably easy to justify in view of the separation of powers; while the Dred Scott case involved the use of congressional power in quite another field. Had the power of judicial review not been exercised and the doctrine established in the case of Marbury v. Madison, one may well conjecture whether our constitutional development would have been the same.

The Supreme Court has always had its critics, and following particularly unpopular decisions invalidating acts of Congress the attacks have been exceedingly bitter. Such decisions as the Dred Scott case, the Income Tax Cases, and a whole series of cases prior to 1937 which invalidated social legislation stirred up opposition which reduced the prestige of the Court and which endured until either a constitutional amendment or the Court itself changed the effect of the ruling. Recognizing the wide latitude left to the judges in interpreting the Constitution, and the manifest political and economic character of many of their decisions, a number of critics have attacked the power of judicial review as an undemocratic instrument of government in an increasingly democratic society, and from time to time some of the justices on the Court itself (usually, it may be said, in dissenting opinions) have appeared to share this view. Against this background, it is interesting to note that at no time in our history has the power of judicial review been seriously endangered. Despite attacks on the Court's decisions, on its personnel, and even on the procedures by which review is exercised, no major political party has ever urged the complete abolition of the power of review itself. The resounding defeat in Congress of the so-called "Court Packing Plan," suggested by President Franklin D. Roosevelt at the height of his popularity, indicates that popular dissatisfaction with the use of the power of judicial review does not necessarily imply a feeling that the Court should be dominated by the political branches of the government.

Mr. Chief Justice Marshall delivered the opinion of the Court, saying in part:

In the order in which the court has viewed this subject, the following questions have been considered and decided.

1st. Has the applicant a right to the commission he demands? . . . [The Court finds that he has.]

2d. If he has a right, and that right has been violated, do the laws of his country afford him a remedy? . . . [The Court finds that they do.]

3d. If they do afford him a remedy, is it a mandamus issuing from this court? . . .

This, then, is a plain case for a mandamus, either to deliver the commission, or a copy of it from the record; and it only remains to be inquired,

Whether it can issue from this court.

The act to establish the judicial courts of the United States authorizes the Supreme Court "to issue writs of mandamus in cases warranted by the principles and usages of law, to any courts appointed, or persons holding office, under the authority of the United States."

The Secretary of State, being a person holding an office under the authority of the United States, is precisely within the letter of the description, and if this court is not authorized to issue a writ of mandamus to such an officer, it must be because the law is unconstitutional, and therefore absolutely incapable of conferring the authority, and assigning the duties which its words purport to confer and assign.

The constitution vests the whole judicial power of the United States in one Supreme Court, and such inferior courts as congress shall, from time to time, ordain and establish. . . .

In the distribution of this power it is declared that "the Supreme Court shall have original jurisdiction in all cases affecting ambassadors, other public ministers and consuls, and those in which a state shall be a party. In all other cases, the Supreme Court shall have appellate jurisdiction." . . .

If it had been intended to leave it in the discretion of the legislature to apportion the judicial power between the supreme and inferior courts according to the will of that body, it would certainly have been useless to have proceeded further than to have defined the judicial power, and the tribunals in which it should be vested. The subsequent part of the section is mere surplusage, is entirely without meaning, . . . the distribution of jurisdiction, made in the constitution, is form without substance. . . .

It cannot be presumed that any clause in the constitution is intended to be without effect; and, therefore, such a construction is inadmissible, unless the words require it. . . .

To enable this court, then, to issue a mandamus, it must be shown to be an exercise of appellate jurisdiction, or to be necessary to enable them to exercise appellate jurisdiction. . . .

It is the essential criterion of appellate jurisdiction, that it revises and corrects the proceedings in a cause already instituted, and does not create that cause. Although, therefore, a mandamus may be directed to courts, yet to issue such a writ to an officer for the delivery of a paper, is in effect the same as to sustain an original action for that paper, and, therefore, seems not to belong to appellate, but to original jurisdiction. Neither is it necessary in such a case as this, to enable the court to exercise its appellate jurisdiction.

The authority, therefore, given to the Supreme Court, by the act establishing the judicial courts of the United States, to issue writs of mandamus to public officers, appears not to be warranted by the constitution; and it becomes necessary to inquire whether a jurisdiction so conferred can be exercised.

The question, whether an act, repugnant to the constitution can become the law of the land, is a question deeply interesting to the United States; but, happily, not of an intricacy proportioned to its interest. It seems only necessary to recognize certain principles, supposed to have been long and well established, to decide it.

That the people have an original right to establish, for their future government, such principles, as, in their opinion, shall most conduce to their own happiness is the basis on which the whole American fabric has been erected. The exercise of this original right is a very great exertion; nor can it, nor ought it, to be frequently repeated. The principles, therefore, so established, are deemed fundamental. And as the authority from which they proceed is supreme, and can seldom act, they are designed to be permanent.

This original and supreme will organizes the government, and assigns to different departments their respective powers. It may either stop here, or establish certain limits not to be transcended by those departments.

The government of the United States is of the latter description. The powers of the legislature are defined and limited; and that those limits may not be mistaken, or forgotten, the Constitution is written. To what purpose are powers limited, and to what purpose is that limitation committed to writing, if these limits may, at any time, be passed by those intended to be restrained? The distinction between a government with limited and unlimited powers is abolished, if those limits do not confine the persons on whom they are imposed, and if acts prohibited and acts allowed, are of equal obligation. It is a proposition too plain to be contested, that the constitution controls any legislative act repugnant to it; or, that the legislature may alter the constitution by an ordinary act.

Between these alternatives there is no middle ground. The constitution is either a superior paramount law, unchangeable by ordinary means, or it is on a level with ordinary legislative acts, and, like other acts, is alterable when the legislature shall please to alter it.

If the former part of the alternative be true, then a legislative act contrary to the constitution is not law: if the latter part be true, then written constitutions are absurd attempts, on the part of the people, to limit a power in its own nature illimitable.

Certainly all those who have framed written constitutions contemplate them as forming the fundamental and paramount law of the nation, and, consequently, the theory of every such government must be, that an act of the legislature, repugnant to the constitution, is void.

This theory is essentially attached to a written constitution, and, is consequently, to be considered, by this court, as one of the fundamental principles of our society. It is not therefore to be lost sight of in the further consideration of this subject.

If an act of the legislature, repugnant to the constitution, is void, does it, notwithstanding its invalidity, bind the courts, and oblige them to give it effect? Or, in other words, though it be not law, does it constitute a rule as operative as if it was a law? This would be to overthrow in fact what was established in theory; and would seem, at first view, an absurdity too gross to be insisted on. It shall, however, receive a more attentive consideration.

It is emphatically the province and duty of the judicial department to say what the law is. Those who apply the rule to particular cases, must of necessity expound and interpret that rule. If two laws conflict with each other, the courts must decide on the operation of each.

So if a law be in opposition to the constitution; if both the law and the constitution apply to a particular case, so that the court must either decide that case conformably to the law, disregarding the constitution; or conformably to the constitution, disregarding the law; the court must determine which of these conflicting rules governs the case. This is of the very essence of judicial duty.

If, then, the courts are to regard the constitution, and the constitution is superior to any ordinary act of the legislature, the constitution, and not such ordinary act, must govern the case to which they both apply.

Those, then, who controvert the principle that the constitution is to be considered, in court, as a paramount law, are reduced to the necessity of maintaining that courts must close their eyes on the constitution, and see only the law.

This doctrine would subvert the very foundation of all written constitutions. It would declare that an act which, according to the principles and theory of our government, is entirely void, is yet, in practice, completely obligatory. It would declare that if the legislature shall do what is expressly forbidden, such act, notwithstanding the express prohibition, is in reality effectual. It would be giving to the legislature a practical and real omnipotence, with the same breath which professes to restrict their powers within narrow limits. It is prescribing limits, and declaring that those limits may be passed at pleasure.

That it thus reduces to nothing what we have deemed the greatest improvement on political institutions, a written constitution, would of itself be sufficient, in America, where written constitutions have been viewed with so much reverence, for rejecting the construction. But the peculiar expressions of the constitution of the United States furnish additional arguments in favor of its rejection.

The judicial power of the United States is extended to all cases arising under the constitution.

Could it be the intention of those who gave this power, to say that in using it the constitution should not be looked into? That a case arising under the constitution should be decided without examining the instrument under which it arises?

This is too extravagant to be maintained.

In some cases, then, the constitution must be looked into by the judges. And if they can open it all, what part of it are they forbidden to read or to obey?

There are many other parts of the constitution which serve to illustrate this subject.

It is declared that "no tax or duty shall be laid on articles exported from any state." Suppose a duty on the export of cotton, of tobacco, or of flour; and a suit instituted to recover it. Ought judgment to be rendered in such a case? ought the judges to close their eyes on the constitution, and only see the law?

The constitution declares "that no bill of attainder or ex post facto law shall be passed."

If, however, such a bill should be passed, and a person should be prosecuted under it, must the court condemn to death those victims whom the constitution endeavors to preserve?

"No person," says the constitution, "shall be convicted of treason unless on the testimony of two witnesses to the same overt act, or on confession in open court."

Here the language of the constitution is addressed especially to the courts. It prescribes, directly for them, a rule of evidence not to be departed from. If the legislature should change that rule, and declare one witness, or a confession out of court, sufficient for conviction, must the constitutional principle yield to the legislative act?

From these, and many other selections which might be made, it is apparent, that the framers of the constitution contemplated that instrument as a rule for the government of courts, as well as of the legislature.

Why otherwise does it direct the judges to take an oath to support it? This oath certainly applies in an especial manner, to their conduct in their official character. How immoral to impose it on them, if they were to be used as the instruments, and the knowing instruments, for violating what they swear to support!

The oath of office, too, imposed by the legislature, is completely demonstrative of the legislative opinion on this subject. It is in these words: "I do solemnly swear that I will administer justice without respect to persons, and do equal right to the poor and to the rich; and that I will faithfully and impartially discharge all the duties incumbent on me as————, according to the best of my abilities and understanding agreeably to the constitution and laws of the United States."

Why does a judge swear to discharge his duties agreeably to the constitution of the United States, if that constitution forms no rule for his government? if it is closed upon him, and cannot be inspected by him?

If such be the real state of things, this is worse than solemn mockery. To prescribe, or to take this oath, becomes equally a crime.

It is also not entirely unworthy of observation, that in declaring what shall be the supreme law of the land, the constitution itself is first mentioned; and not the laws of the United States generally, but those only which shall be made in pursuance of the constitution, have that rank.

Thus, the particular phraseology of the constitution of the United States confirms and strengthens the principle, supposed to be essential to all written constitutions, that a law repugnant to the constitution is void; and that courts, as well as other departments, are bound by that instrument.

The rule must be discharged.

BAKER v. CARR

369 U. S. 186; 82 S. Ct. 691; 7 L. Ed. 2d 663
(1962)

In his opinion in Marbury v. Madison (1803) Marshall grounded his constitutional argument for judicial review upon the language of Article III, which extends to the Supreme Court (and inferior courts) judicial power to be exercised in "all cases, in law and equity, arising under this Constitution. . . ." In short, the reason why the Court occasionally declares an act of Congress unconstitutional is that, according to Marshall, it has to do so in deciding the "cases and controversies" coming before it in the exercise of its "judicial power." Thus Marshall permanently tied judicial review to "cases and controversies." This has meant, over the years, that only when one of the parties in an actual "case" relies for his rights upon a statute will the Court undertake to decide whether or not that statute violates the Constitution; furthermore, it will do so only when such a decision is essential to the disposal of the case. Since Article III also extends judicial power to "such inferior courts as the Congress may from time to time ordain and establish," these lower courts also exercise the power of judicial review. Under the statutes, however, such lower court decisions on constitutional questions are subject to review by the Supreme Court, and almost invariably they are so reviewed. The Supreme Court has the last word.

But what is a "case" or "controversy" within the meaning of Article III? An essential requirement is that there be actual litigants with condition of a foreign government, the acquisition of territory, the determination. Thus the Court held in United States v. Evans (1909) that it would not hear an appeal by the government on a point of law taken from a trial court case in which the defendant had been acquitted, despite an act of Congress giving the government "the same right of appeal as is given to the defendant" but with the proviso that "a verdict in favor of the defendant shall not be set aside." Evans had been tried for murder in the District of Columbia and acquitted, and the government objected to the exclusion by the trial judge of certain evidence. The Court ruled that the acquittal of Evans, in view of the prohibition against double jeopardy, had removed one of the parties to the suit. To decide the question of law involved, since there were no longer two litigants and therefore no case, would be to render an advisory opinion.

An important effect of the Evans decision is to make impossible a Supreme Court review of the constitutionality of a federal penal statute in a case where the lower court acquits the defendant by holding invalid the act under which he was prosecuted. To overcome this difficulty the trial judge is often persuaded to rule on the constitutionality of the indictment, and to quash it if he concludes that it is brought under an invalid criminal statute. Since indicting a person does not put him in jeopardy, the lower court's ruling on the constitutional issues can be appealed directly to the Supreme Court without abridging the rights of the accused. United States v. Classic (1941), testing the constitutionality of federal control of primary elections, was carried to the Supreme Court in this way.

Following the admission to citizenship of the Cherokee Indians, Congress had by law altered the original distribution of tribal property. Since this had the effect of reducing the amount of lands and funds to which certain Indians were entitled, its constitutionality was seriously questioned. To settle the matter Congress passed an act specifically providing that David Muskrat and others might bring suits in the court of claims, with a right of appeal to the Supreme Court, to test the constitutionality of the redistribution statutes. The courts involved were ordered to give preference to these suits; the Attorney General was ordered to defend them; and if Muskrat et al. lost, the government was to pay their attorney's fees. In Muskrat v. United States (1911) the Supreme Court held there was no case or controversy involved and refused jurisdiction. The United States, the Court pointed out, was not claiming Muskrat's land and had no interest adverse to his. "The whole purpose of the law is to determine the constitutional validity of this class of legislation, in a suit not arising between parties concerning a property right necessarily involved in the decision in question, but in a proceeding against the government in its sovereign capacity, and concerning which the only judgment required is to settle the doubtful character of the legislation in question. . : . In a legal sense the judgment could not be executed, and amounts in fact to no more than an expression of opinion upon the validity of the acts in question. "

One other important corollary of the Court's refusal to exercise nonjudicial powers is the doctrine of "political questions." Very early in the exercise of its power of judicial review the Court pointed out that certain powers are vested in the legislative or executive departments of the government to be exercised in a purely discretionary manner, and that whether they have been constitutionally exercised or not is a "political question" which the Court will not undertake to decide. One of the early and very striking instances of this type of question was that which was raised in the famous case of Luther v. Borden.

This case arose out of the following facts: the original constitution of Rhode Island, which was merely the colonial charter with a few minor adaptations, provided for a very restricted suffrage based upon the possession of property; and the right to vote continued to be thus limited long after universal manhood suffrage had been rather generally adopted throughout the country. Many efforts were made to have the constitution amended so as to put the franchise upon a more democratic basis, but all such attempts were defeated by the relatively small group of legal voters. In 1841 the popular feeling regarding the situation ran even higher than before; mass meetings were held throughout the state, and without any semblance of constitutional sanction the citizens were directed to choose by universal manhood suffrage, delegates to a constitutional convention. The convention thus formed duly met and drafted a new state constitution which established adult manhood suffrage and made many other changes. A popular referendum was conducted in which all the adult male citizens of the state were permitted to vote, and the new constitution was approved by a majority of the votes cast. The leader of the whole movement was a young lawyer, Thomas W. Dorr, who was elected governor under the new constitution and immediately attempted to put the new government into operation. The regular charter government, of course, did not recognize the validity of any of these acts. It called out the state militia, declared martial law, and finally appealed to President Tyler to send federal troops to aid in putting down the insurrection. The President took steps to comply with this request and the "Dorr Rebellion" collapsed. Dorr himself was captured, tried for treason, and finally sentenced to life imprisonment. He was later pardoned. He naturally had managed to arouse a good deal of sympathy for his cause outside the state, particularly among the Democrats, and it was felt that it would be desirable to present to the Supreme Court of the United States the question of the legality of the new constitution and the acts done under it. This was tried first by Dorr himself by attempting to sue out a writ of habeas corpus in the Supreme Court, but that tribunal dismissed the petition for want of jurisdiction; see Ex parte Dorr (1845). Under the assumption that the same issue could be raised collaterally the civil controversy between Luther and Borden, relatively unimportant in itself, was pushed through to the Supreme Court. Luther had been a supporter of the Dorr movement; and in an effort to arrest him, Borden and others who were enrolled as members of the militia under the charter government broke into Luther's house. This act they justified upon the ground that martial law had been declared and that they were acting under the orders of their superior officers. Luther, however, sued Borden for trespass, claiming that the act of the legislature establishing martial law was void inasmuch as the Dorr government, elected by the people of the state, was the lawful government. (It should be noted that in January, 1842, the charter government had called a constitutional convention and drafted a new constitution which was ratified by the people in due form and went into effect in 1843. Thus the Dorr movement did not entirely fail in its purposes.)

By the facts as presented in this case, the Court was invited to decide which of the two governments struggling for supremacy in Rhode Island in the year 1842 was the lawful one. But this question, replied the Supreme Court, was a "political question." The President in exercising the power conferred on him by Congress to send federal troops to aid states in suppressing insurrection had indicated that he regarded the charter government as the lawful government, and this decision was binding upon the Court. The Court intimated that Congress itself would also share the power of deciding between the competing governments by deciding which group of rival senators and representatives it would seat in Congress, but it was not asked to make such a decision. The Court declined to decide whether Rhode Island had a republican form of government within the meaning of the guaranty in the United States Constitution, Article IV, Sec. 4, but held that the enforcement of that guaranty was confided to the political departments of the government.

There are, of course, numerous other questions which have been held by the courts to be "political" in character. Such is the question whether there is a sufficient emergency to justify the President, acting under the authority of an act of Congress, in calling out the militia to repel invasion or to put down insurrection; see Martin v. Mott (1827). Such, also, are many of the questions which arise for determination in the course of conducting foreign relations; as, for instance, the recognition of a foreign government, the acquisition of territory, the determination of boundaries, the existence or termination of a treaty, and the like. The question whether or not a state of the Union has a republican form of government within the meaning of that clause of the Constitution guaranteeing such form of *government was squarely raised in 1912 in the case of Pacific States Telephone & Telegraph Co. v. Oregon. In 1902 Oregon had amended her state constitution to establish the initiative and referendum. In 1906 a law was proposed by popular initiative and duly enacted by the people which imposed certain taxes on corporations. The plaintiff corporation resisted the payment of the tax on the ground that the incorporation of the initiative and referendum into the constitutional system of the state destroyed the republican character of its government and thus robbed it of lawful authority. The argument was that republican government means representative government and that representative government is destroyed by the system of direct legislation. The Supreme Court refused to pass on the question whether Oregon had a republican form of government or not, and pointed out that that question was political in character and had been determined by Congress in admitting senators and representatives of the state to their seats in Congress.*

In Coleman v. Miller (1939) the Court held that most of the questions relating to the procedure of federal amendment are "political" in nature. The Court was there asked to rule that the Child Labor Amendment could no longer be validly ratified because it had been before the states for ratification for too long a time, and that a state which had once rejected a proposed amendment could not later ratify it. On each point the Court held that the final decision rested with Congress, not with the Court. But in Powell v. McCormack (1969) the Court rejected the contention of the House of Representatives that the question of Adam Clayton Powell Jr.'s right to his House seat was a political one because the Constitution made each house "the judge of the . . . qualifications of its own members." This power, the Court held, was limited to judging the existence of those qualifications for congressmen explicitly stated in the Constitution—and only those. Powell, it was conceded, met these formal qualifications.

In Colegrove v. Green (1946), relief was sought from the unequal apportionment of congressional seats in the state of Illinois. The Illinois constitution of 1870 provided that the state should be divided into 51 state senatorial districts, from each of which one state senator and three state representatives should be chosen. The legislature, after each census, was to redraw the lines of these districts to meet changes in population. By the turn of the century it was obvious that more than half the population of the state would shortly be concentrated in the metropolitan area of Chicago. Legislators from the down-state rural districts, enjoying a comfortable legislative majority, felt no inclination to yield their political control by reapportioning the state to give the growing metropolis the proportion of the 51 districts to which its population clearly entitled it. The political bitterness created by this inequitable situation had made it impossible for the Illinois legislature to agree upon a revision of its legislative districts since the apportionment of 1901. Attempts were made to invoke court action, but the supreme court of Illinois, itself applying the doctrine of "political questions," held that it had no power to compel the legislature to pass a new and fair redistricting law.

This all bears on the problem of congressional apportionment posed in Colegrove v. Green. When Congress after each census reapportions seats in the House of Representatives among the states, it becomes the duty of each state legislature to carve out such new congressional districts as the new allotments may require. But the Illinois legislature was no more willing to give the Chicago metropolitan area its fair share of seats in Congress than in the state legislature itself. At the time the case arose, it had not reapportioned congressional seats since 1901. Rank inequalities had resulted. One congressional district in Chicago had a population of 914,053, while another in southern Illinois had a population of 112,116. The Court was asked to enjoin the appropriate Illinois state officials from conducting an election in November, 1946, under the provisions of the old congressional apportionment act of 1901. Such an injunction would have compelled the state to elect all of its congressmen on one general ballot, instead of by districts; and this would have given full effect to the political strength of the populous urban areas. Mr. Justice Frankfurter, speaking for himself and Justices Reed and Burton, held this to be a political question which the Court could not decide. This opinion was widely construed as the ruling of the case, although Mr. Justice Rutledge concurred on different grounds.

In the years following Colegrove v. Green (1946), the Court continued to adhere to its stand that state political districting could not be upset by the federal courts. In MacDougall v. Green (1948) the efforts of the Progressive party to get on the ballot in Illinois were defeated by their inability to get petition signatures in the rural counties. While the Court conceded that the "requirement of two hundred signatures from at least fifty counties gives to the votes of the less populous counties . . . the power completely to block the nomination . . ." it held that neither due process nor equal protection "deny a State the power to assure a proper diffusion of political initiative as between its thinly populated counties and those having concentrated masses, in view of the fact that the latter have practical opportunities for exerting their political weight at the polls not available to the former." In South v. Peters (1950) the Court refused to interfere with the "County Unit System" in Georgia, a scheme which assigned to each county from two to six electoral votes which went to the candidate receiving the most votes in the county. Despite the fact that this discriminated heavily against the urban Negro voter, the Court refused to review the case.

The first break in the Court's attitude came in 1960 in the case of

Gomillion v. Lightfoot. There the Court, without passing upon the truth of the alleged discrimination, unanimously rejected the idea that legislative apportionment could never be the subject for judicial review. The issue raised was unique. An Alabama statute of 1957 had redefined the boundaries of the city of Tuskeegee, within which is the well-known Tuskeegee Institute. The city, which had been square in shape, was transformed "into a strangely irregular twenty-eight sided figure," with the intention and result of removing from the city "all save four or five of its 400 Negro voters while not removing a single white voter or resident." The Negroes thus excluded could not, as a result, vote in municipal elections. The lower federal courts, relying in part upon Colegrove v. Green, had dismissed the complaint attacking the validity of the statute. In an opinion by Mr. Justice Frankfurter, eight justices agreed that the plaintiffs had a right to have a court decide whether the weird apportionment denied them the right to vote in violation of the Fifteenth Amendment. Mr. Justice Whittaker, denying that the right to vote was involved "inasmuch as no one has the right to vote in . . . an area in which he does not reside," argued that the discrimination violated both the equal protection and due process clauses of the Fourteenth Amendment.

Baker v. Carr is a landmark in constitutional law in American government and politics. In a majority of states over the past few decades the rural counties have lost, and continue to lose, population to the cities and surrounding metropolitan areas. These rural counties in most states, however, have stubbornly refused to permit the change of the existing apportionment of legislative members which gives them a dominating overrepresentation at the expense of the growing urban centers. Reform could be achieved by constitutional amendment were it not for the fact that the existing legislatures control the amending process. Thus the holding in Colegrove v. Green seemed to make permanent the stranglehold of the rural and sparsely populated areas upon the political destinies of the state. Baker v. Carr holds that the courts may now scrutinize the fairness of legislative apportionments and take steps to assure that serious inequalities are wiped out. The impact of this holding is discussed in connection with the equal protection clause.

Mr. Justice Brennan delivered the opinion of the Court, saying in part:

This civil action was brought . . . to redress the alleged deprivation of federal constitutional rights. The complaint, alleging that by means of a 1901 statute of Tennessee apportioning the members of the General Assembly among the

State's 95 counties, "these plaintiffs and others similarly situated, are denied the equal protection of the laws accorded them by the Fourteenth Amendment to the Constitution of the United States by virtue of the debasement of their votes," was dismissed by a three-judge court. . . . We hold that the dismissal was error, and remand the cause to the District Court for trial and further proceedings consistent with this opinion.

The General Assembly of Tennessee consists of the Senate with 33 members and the House of Representatives with 99 members. The Tennessee Constitution provides in Art. II as follows: . . . [The text of sections 3–6 follows.]

Thus, Tennessee's standard for allocating legislative representation among her counties is the total number of qualified voters resident in the respective counties, subject only to minor qualifications. . . . In 1901 the General Assembly abandoned separate enumeration in favor of reliance upon the Federal Census and passed the Apportionment Act here in controversy. In the more than 60 years since that action, all proposals in both Houses of the General Assembly for reapportionment have failed to pass.

Between 1901 and 1961, Tennessee has experienced substantial growth and redistribution of her population. In 1901 the population was 2,020,616, of whom 487,380 were eligible to vote. The 1960 Federal Census reports the State's population of 3,567,089, of whom 2,092,891 are eligible to vote. The relative standings of the counties in terms of qualified voters have changed significantly. It is primarily the continued application of the 1901 Apportionment Act to this shifted and enlarged voting population which gives rise to the present controversy.

Indeed, the complaint alleges that the 1901 statute, even as of the time of its passage, "made no apportionment of Representatives and Senators in accordance with the constitutional formula . . . , but instead arbitrarily and capriciously apportioned representatives in the Senate and House without reference . . . to any logical or reasonable formula whatever." It is further alleged that "because of the population changes since 1900, and the failure of the Legislature to reapportion itself since 1901," the 1901 statute became "unconstitutional and obsolete." Appellants also argue that, because of the composition of the legislature effected by the 1901 Apportionment Act, redress in the form of a state constitutional amendment to change the entire mechanism for reapportioning, or any other change short of that, is difficult or impossible. The complaint concludes that "these plaintiffs and others similarly situated, are denied the equal protection of the laws accorded them by the Fourteenth Amendment to the Constitution of the United States by virtue of the debasement of their votes." They seek a declaration that the 1901 statute is unconstitutional and an injunction restraining the appellees from acting to conduct any further elections under it. They also pray that unless and until the General Assembly enacts a valid reapportionment, the District Court should either decree a reapportionment by mathematical application of the Tennessee constitutional formulae to the most recent Federal Census figures, or direct the appellees to conduct legislative elections, primary and general, at large. They also pray for such other and further relief as may be appropriate.

I. The District Court's Opinion and Order of Dismissal.
[Here summarized.]

In the light of the District Court's treatment of the case, we hold today only (a) that the court possessed jurisdiction of the subject matter; (b) that a justiciable cause of action is stated upon which appellants would be entitled to appropriate relief; and (c) because appellees raise the issue before this Court, that the appellants have standing to challenge the Tennessee apportionment statutes. Beyond noting that we have no cause at this stage to doubt the District Court will be able to fashion relief if violations of constitutional rights are found, it is improper now to consider what remedy would be most appropriate if appellants prevail at the trial.

II. Jurisdiction of the Subject Matter.

The District Court was uncertain whether our cases withholding federal judicial relief rested upon a lack of federal jurisdiction or upon the inappropriateness of the subject matter for judicial consideration—what we have designated "nonjusticiability." The distinction between the two grounds is significant. In the instance of nonjusticiability, consideration of the cause is not wholly and immediately foreclosed; rather, the Court's inquiry necessarily proceeds to the point of deciding whether the duty asserted can be judicially identified and its breach judicially determined, and whether protection for the right asserted can be judicially molded. In the instance of lack of jurisdiction the cause either does not "arise under" the Federal Constitution, laws or treaties (or fall within one of the other enumerated categories of Art. 3, § 2), or is not a "case or controversy" within the meaning of that section; or the cause is not one described by any jurisdictional statute. Our conclusion that this cause presents no nonjusticiable "political question" settles the only possible doubt that it is a case or controversy. Under the present heading of "Jurisdiction of the Subject Matter" we hold only that the matter set forth in the complaint does arise under the Constitution. . . .

Article 3, § 2, of the Federal Constitution provides that "The Judicial Power shall extend to all Cases, in Law and Equity, arising under this Constitution, the Laws of the United States, and Treaties made, or which shall be made, under their Authority. . . ." It is clear that the cause of action is one which "arises under" the Federal Constitution. The complaint alleges that the 1901 statute effects an apportionment that deprives the appellants of the equal protection of the laws in violation of the Fourteenth Amendment. Dismissal of the complaint upon the ground of lack of jurisdiction of the subject matter would, therefore, be justified only if that claim were "so attenuated and unsubstantial as to be absolutely devoid of merit." ... Since the District Court obviously and correctly did not deem the asserted federal constitutional claim unsubstantial and frivolous, it should not have dismissed the complaint for want of jurisdiction of the subject matter. And of course no further consideration of the merits of the claim is relevant to a determination of the court's jurisdiction of the subject matter. ...

An unbroken line of our precedents sustains the federal courts' jurisdiction of the subject matter of federal constitutional claims of this nature. The first cases involved the redistricting of States for the purpose of electing Representatives to the Federal Congress. When the Ohio Supreme Court sustained Ohio legislation against an attack for repugnancy to Art. 1 § 4, of the Federal Constitution, we affirmed on the merits and expressly refused to dismiss for want of jurisdiction "in view ... of the subject-matter of the controversy and the Federal characteristics which inhere in it. ..." Ohio ex rel. Davis v. Hildebrant [1916]. When the Minnesota Supreme Court affirmed the dismissal of a suit to enjoin the Secretary of State of Minnesota from acting under Minnesota redistricting legislation, we reviewed the constitutional merits of the legislation and reversed the State Supreme Court. Smiley v. Holm [1932]. ...

The appellees refer to Colegrove v. Green [1946], as authority that the District Court lacked jurisdiction of the subject matter. Appellees misconceive the holding of that case. The holding was precisely contrary to their reading of it. Seven members of the Court participated in the decision. Unlike many other cases in this field which have assumed without discussion that there was jurisdiction, all three opinions filed in Colegrove discussed the question. Two of the opinions expressing the views of four of the Justices, a majority, flatly held that there was jurisdiction of the subject matter. Mr. Justice Black joined by Mr. Justice Douglas and Mr. Justice Murphy stated: "It is my judgment that the District Court had jurisdiction. ..." Mr. Justice Rutledge, writing separately, expressed agreement with this conclusion. ...

We hold that the District Court has jurisdiction of the subject matter of the federal constitutional claim asserted in the complaint.

III. Standing.

A federal court cannot "pronounce any statute, either of a State or of the United States, void, because irreconcilable with the Constitution, except as it is called upon to adjudge the legal rights of litigants in actual controversies."

. . . Have the appellants alleged such a personal stake in the outcome of the controversy as to assure that concrete adverseness which sharpens the presentation of issues upon which the court so largely depends for illumination of difficult constitutional questions? This is the gist of the question of standing. It is, of course, a question of federal law. . . .

We hold that the appellants do have standing to maintain this suit. Our decisions plainly support this conclusion. Many of the cases have assumed rather than articulated the premise in deciding the merits of similar claims. And Colegrove v. Green squarely held that voters who allege facts showing disadvantage to themselves as individuals have standing to sue. . . .

These appellants seek relief in order to protect or vindicate an interest of their own, and of those similarly situated. Their constitutional claim is, in substance, that the 1901 statute constitutes arbitrary and capricious state action, offensive to the Fourteenth Amendment in its irrational disregard of the standard of apportionment prescribed by the State's Constitution or of any standard, effecting a gross disproportion of representation to voting population. The injury which appellants assert is that this classification disfavors the voters in the counties in which they reside, placing them in a position of constitutionally unjustifiable inequality vis-à-vis voters in irrationally favored counties. A citizen's right to vote free of arbitrary impairment by state action has been judicially recognized as a right secured by the Constitution, when such impairment resulted from dilution by a false tally, cf. United States v. Classic [1941] or by a refusal to count votes from arbitrarily selected precincts, . . . or by a stuffing of the ballot box, cf. Ex parte Siebold [1880]. . . .

It would not be necessary to decide whether appellants' allegations of impairment of their votes by the 1901 apportionment will, ultimately, entitle them to any relief, in order to hold that they have standing to seek it. If such impairment does produce a legally cognizable injury, they are among those who have sustained it. They are asserting "a plain, direct and adequate interest in maintaining the effectiveness of their votes," . . . not merely a claim of "the right, possessed by every citizen, to require that the Government be administered according to law. . . ." Fairchild v. Hughes [1922]. . . . They are entitled to a hearing and to the District Court's decision on their claims. "The very essence of civil liberty certainly consists in the right of every individual to claim the protection of the laws, whenever he receives an injury."

IV. Justiciability.

In holding that the subject matter of this suit was not justiciable, the District Court relied on Colegrove v. Green, and subsequent per curiam cases. The court stated: "From a review of these decisions there can be no doubt that the federal rule . . . is that the federal courts . . . will not intervene in cases of this type to compel legislative reapportionment." We understand the District Court to have read the cited cases as compelling the conclusion that since the appellants sought to have a legislative apportionment held unconstitutional, their suit presented a "political question" and was therefore nonjusticiable. We hold that this challenge to an apportionment presents no nonjusticiable "political question." The cited cases do not hold the contrary.

Of course the mere fact that the suit seeks protection of a political right does not mean it presents a political question. Such an objection "is little more than a play upon words." . . . Rather, it is argued that apportionment cases, whatever the actual wording of the complaint, can involve no federal constitutional right except one resting on the guaranty of a republican form of government, and that complaints based on that clause have been held to present political questions which are nonjusticiable.

We hold that the claim pleaded here neither rests upon nor implicates the Guaranty Clause and that its justiciability is therefore not foreclosed by our decisions of cases involving that clause. The District Court misinterpreted Colegrove v. Green and other decisions of this Court on which it relied. Appellants' claim that they are being denied equal protection is justiciable, and if "discrimination is sufficiently shown, the right to relief under the equal protection clause is not diminished by the fact that the discrimination relates to political rights." . . . To show why we reject the argument based on the Guaranty Clause, we must examine the authorities under it. But because there appears to be some uncertainty as to why those cases did present political questions, and specifically as to whether this apportionment case is like those cases, we deem it necessary first to consider the contours of the "political question" doctrine.

Our discussion, even at the price of extending this opinion, requires review of a number of political question cases, in order to expose the attributes of the doctrine—attributes which, in various settings, diverge, combine, appear, and disappear in seeming disorderliness. Since that review is undertaken solely to demonstrate that neither singly nor collectively do these cases support a conclusion that this apportionment case is nonjusticiable, we of course do not explore their implications in other contexts. That review reveals that in the Guaranty Clause cases and in the other "political question" cases, it is the relationship between the judiciary and the coordinate branches of the Federal Government, and not the federal judiciary's relationship to the States, which gives rise to the "political question."

We have said that "In determining whether a question falls within [the political question] category, the appropriateness under our system of government of attributing finality to the action of the political departments and also the lack of satisfactory criteria for a judicial determination are dominant considerations." Coleman v. Miller [1939]. The nonjusticiability of a political question is primarily a function of the separation of powers. Much confusion results from the capacity of the "political question" label to obscure the need for case-by-case inquiry. Deciding whether a matter has in any measure been committed by the Constitution to another branch of government, or whether the action of that branch exceeds whatever authority has been committed, is itself a delicate exercise in constitutional interpretation, and is a responsibility of this Court as ultimate interpreter of the Constitution. To demonstrate this requires no less than to analyze representative cases and to infer from them the analytical threads that make up the political question doctrine. We shall then show that none of those threads catches this case. . . .

[Here follows a long summary of cases involving the political question doctrine as they have arisen in the fields of (1) foreign relations, (2) dates of duration of hostilities, (3) validity of enactments, (4) status of Indian tribes, and (5) republican form of government.]

We come, finally, to the ultimate inquiry whether our precedents as to what constitutes a nonjusticiable "political question" bring the case before us under the umbrella of that doctrine. A natural beginning is to note whether any of the common characteristics which we have been able to identify and label descriptively are present. We find none: The question here is the consistency of state action with the Federal Constitution. We have no question decided, or to be decided, by a political branch of government coequal with this Court. Nor do we risk embarrassment of our government abroad, or grave disturbance at home if we take issue with Tennessee as to the constitutionality of her action, here challenged. Nor need the appellants, in order to succeed in this action, ask the Court to enter upon policy determinations for which judicially manageable standards are lacking. Judicial standards under the Equal Protection Clause are well developed and familiar, and it has been open to courts since the enactment of the Fourteenth Amendment to determine, if on the particular facts they must, that a discrimination reflects *no* policy, but simply arbitrary and capricious action. . . .

We conclude that the complaint's allegations of a denial of equal protection present a justiciable constitutional cause of action upon which appellants are entitled to a trial and a decision. The right asserted is within the reach of judicial protection under the Fourteenth Amendment.

The judgment of the District Court is reversed and the cause is remanded for further proceedings consistent with this opinion.

Reversed and remanded.

Mr. Justice Whittaker did not participate in the decision of this case.

Mr. Justice Douglas, concurring, said in part:

While I join the opinion of the Court and, like the Court, do not reach the merits, a word of explanation is necessary. I put to one side the problems of "political" questions involving the distribution of power between this Court, the Congress, and the Chief Executive. We have here a phase of the recurring problem of the relation of the federal courts to state agencies. More particularly, the question is the extent to which a State may weight one person's vote more heavily than it does another's. . . .

I agree with my Brother Clark that if the allegations in the complaint can be sustained a case for relief is established. We are told that a single vote in Moore County, Tennessee, is worth 19 votes in Hamilton County, that one vote in Stewart or in Chester County is worth nearly eight times a single vote in Shelby or Knox County. The opportunity to prove that an "invidious discrimination" exists should therefore be given the appellants. . . .

With the exceptions of Colegrove v. Green, MacDougall v. Green, South v. Peters, and the decisions they spawned, the Court has never thought that protection of voting rights was beyond judicial cognizance. Today's treatment of those cases removes the only impediment to judicial cognizance of the claims stated in the present complaint. . . .

Mr. Justice Clark, concurring, said in part:

One emerging from the rash of opinions with their accompanying clashing of views may well find himself suffering a mental blindness. The Court holds that the appellants have alleged a cause of action. However, it refuses to award relief here—although the facts are undisputed—and fails to give the District Court any guidance whatever. One dissenting opinion, bursting with words that go through so much and conclude with so little, contemns the majority action as "a massive repudiation of the experience of our whole past." Another describes the complaint as merely asserting conclusory allegations that Tennessee's apportionment is "incorrect," "arbitrary," "obsolete," and "unconstitutional." I believe it can be shown that this case is distinguishable from earlier cases dealing with the distribution of political power by a State, that a patent violation of the Equal Protection Clause of the United States Constitution has been shown, and that an appropriate remedy may be formulated.

. . . The widely heralded case of Colegrove v. Green was one not only in which the Court was bobtailed but in which there was no majority opinion. Indeed, even the "political question" point in Mr. Justice Frankfurter's opinion was no more than an alternative ground. Moreover, the appellants did not present an equal protection argument. While it has served as a Mother Hubbard to most of the subsequent cases, I feel it was in that respect ill-cast and for all of these reasons put it to one side. . . .

The controlling facts cannot be disputed. . . .

. . . The frequency and magnitude of the inequalities in the present districting admit of no policy whatever. . . . It leaves but one conclusion, namely that Tennessee's apportionment is a crazy quilt without rational basis. . . .

[Examples are given of the inequalities in apportionment in Tennessee.]

The truth is that—although this case has been here for two years and has had over six hours' argument (three times the ordinary case) and has been most carefully considered over and over again by us in Conference and individually —no one, not even the State nor the dissenters, has come up with any rational basis for Tennessee's apportionment statute.

. . . Like the District Court, I conclude that appellants have met the burden of showing "Tennessee is guilty of a clear violation of the state constitution and of the [federal] rights of the plaintiffs. . . ."

Although I find the Tennessee apportionment statute offends the Equal Protection Clause, I would not consider intervention by this Court into so delicate a field if there were any other relief available to the people of Tennessee. But the majority of the people of Tennessee have no "practical opportunities for exerting their political weight at the polls" to correct the existing "invidious discrimination." Tennessee has no initiative and referendum. I have searched diligently for other "practical opportunities" present under the law. I find none other than through the federal courts. . . .

As John Rutledge (later Chief Justice) said 175 years ago in the course of the Constitutional Convention, a chief function of the Court is to secure the national rights. Its decision today supports the proposition for which our forebears fought and many died, namely, that to be fully conformable to the principle of right, the form of government must be representative. That is the keystone upon which our government was founded and lacking which no republic can survive. It is well for this Court to practice self-restraint and discipline in constitutional adjudication, but never in its history have those principles received sanction where the national rights of so many have been so clearly infringed for so long a time. National respect for the courts is more enhanced through the forthright enforcement of those rights rather than by rendering them nugatory through the interposition of subterfuges. In my view the ultimate decision today is in the greatest tradition of this Court.

Mr. Justice Stewart wrote a brief concurring opinion.

Mr. Justice Frankfurter, whom Mr. Justice Harlan joins, dissenting, said in part:

The Court today reverses a uniform course of decision established by a dozen cases, including one by which the very claim now sustained was unanimously rejected only five years ago. The impressive body of rulings thus cast aside reflected the equally uniform course of our political history regarding the relationship between population and legislative representation—a wholly different matter from denial of the franchise to individuals because of race, color, religion or sex. Such a massive repudiation of the experience of our whole past in asserting destructively novel judicial power demands a detailed analysis of the role of this Court in our constitutional scheme. Disregard of inherent limits in the effective exercise of the Court's "judicial Power" not only presages the futility of judicial intervention in the essentially political conflict of forces by which the relation between population and representation has time out of mind been and now is determined. It may well impair the Court's position as the ultimate organ of "the supreme Law of the Land" in that vast range of legal problems, often strongly entangled in popular feeling, on which this Court must pronounce. The Court's authority—possessed neither of the purse nor the sword—ultimately rests on sustained public confidence in its moral sanction. Such feeling must be nourished by the Court's complete detachment, in fact and in appearance, from political entanglements and by abstention from injecting itself into the clash of political forces in political settlements. . . .

. . . The Framers carefully and with deliberate forethought refused so to enthrone the judiciary. In this situation, as in others of like nature, appeal for relief does not belong here. Appeal must be to an informed, civically militant electorate. In a democratic society like ours, relief must come through an aroused popular conscience that sears the conscience of the people's representatives. In any event there is nothing judicially more unseemly nor more self-defeating than for this Court to make in terrorem pronouncements, to indulge in merely empty rhetoric, sounding a word of promise to the ear, sure to be disappointing to the hope. . . .

[Mr. Justice Frankfurter continued in a long and heavily documented opinion to support the position he had taken in Colegrove v. Green.]

Mr. Justice Harlan wrote a dissenting opinion in which Mr. Justice Frankfurter joined.

EX PARTE McCARDLE
7 Wallace 506; 19 L. Ed. 264 (1869)

A court, in order to be a court and behave like one, must possess two kinds of authority. The first is jurisdiction, which is the power of the court to bring parties before it for the purpose of deciding the kinds of disputes in which those parties are involved. What the court can do about a dispute properly before it depends upon its possession of judicial power. Both jurisdiction and judicial power are provided for the federal courts in Article III of the Constitution.

Article III provides that "the judicial power shall extend to all cases . . ." and then proceeds to enumerate the bases upon which federal jurisdiction may be taken. One class of cases comes to the courts because of the subject matter of the case, and these are cases in which federal questions are raised, i.e., questions of the interpretation of the Constitution, law, or treaties of the United States. A second category is based on the parties to the suit and includes generally cases where impartiality might not be had in the courts of the states. Here are the cases between citizens of different states. Does the phrase "shall extend" mean that any federal court, as soon as it is created by Congress, is fully invested with both kinds of jurisdiction by the Constitution? The answer is no, despite the urging of Federalists who favored a strong independent judiciary. The wording of the Judiciary Act of 1789 creating the courts, and the circumstances surrounding its passage, both indicate a legislative acceptance of the idea that Congress has complete control over the jurisdiction of the lower federal courts; ten years later, in Turner v. Bank of North America (1799), the Supreme Court approved that interpretation. Congress had specifically denied the courts a portion of the jurisdiction based upon diversity of citizenship; and the bank argued that since diversity jurisdiction was given by Article III, Congress had no power to take it away. The Court upheld the congressional limitation and refused to take jurisdiction. Congress has made free use of its power to grant, withhold, or distribute the jurisdiction of the lower federal courts as it has thought wise. Some of the jurisdiction mentioned in Article III, such as diversity jurisdiction in cases involving small sums, has never been conferred on the federal courts at all. It was not until 1875 that the lower federal courts were given jurisdiction over cases involving federal questions.

The Constitution, in providing for the Supreme Court, distinguishes between its original *jurisdiction to decide cases which start in the Supreme Court and its* appellate *jurisdiction to decide cases which come to it on appeal, or by other procedure, from some other court. Article III provides that "in all cases affecting ambassadors, other public ministers, and consuls, and those in which a State shall be a party, the Supreme Court shall have original jurisdiction. In all the other cases before mentioned, the Supreme Court shall have appellate jurisdiction, both as to law and fact, with such exceptions, and under such regulations as the Congress shall make." The Supreme Court held in Marbury v. Madison (1803) that Congress cannot validly enlarge the original jurisdiction of the Court. That portion of the Judiciary Act of 1789 which purported to enlarge the original jurisdiction of the Court to include the power to issue writs of mandamus was held unconstitutional.*

But to what extent and by what means may Congress control the appellate jurisdiction of the Supreme Court? The present case was one of a series of attempts by the Southern states to get from the Supreme Court a clear decision on the validity of the military reconstruction program set up by Congress after the Civil War. The behavior of the Court must to some extent be judged in the light of the bitterness which this conflict engendered. McCardle, a Southern newspaper editor, was arrested for sedition and tried and convicted by a federal military commission. When his petition to the circuit court for a writ of habeas corpus was denied, he appealed directly to the Supreme Court under a statute designed, ironically, to protect the rights of Negroes and federal officers in the South. The Court unanimously agreed that the statute gave it jurisdiction in McCardle's case; and in view of its denunciation of military commissions in Ex parte Milligan two years before (1866), there was a widespread expectation that the Court would hold the Reconstruction Acts unconstitutional because of their establishment of military government throughout much of the South. To prevent possible judicial sabotage of its reconstruction program, the House had already passed a bill providing that the Court could invalidate acts of Congress only by a two-thirds vote, but the Senate had not concurred. Then, with argument in the McCardle case already concluded, Congress undertook to block a decision of the Court by repealing the law by which jurisdiction to hear McCardle's appeal had been conferred. Despite impeachment proceedings against him, the President vetoed the act; but it was repassed over his veto. The Court, which had waited to see whether the repealing statute would pass, put off until the following term the question of the effect of this repeal on its jurisdiction in the McCardle case. Justices Grier and Field bitterly excoriated their brethren for what they regarded as a shameful and cowardly delay in deciding the case.

Over 100 years since Ex parte McCardle, the action by Congress in lopping off part of the appellate jurisdiction of the Supreme Court in order to forestall an unwanted decision has been generally regarded as a regrettable legislative assault upon the independence of the Court—a precedent which it was hoped would not be followed.

If Congress finds itself in conflict with the Supreme Court on constitutional issues, it may always seek to employ the direct and orderly process of constitutional amendment to accomplish its ends. It has done this in three cases. Chisholm v. Georgia (1793) was nullified by the Eleventh Amendment; the Dred Scott case (1857), ruling on the nature and source of citizenship, was nullified by the first section of the Fourteenth Amendment; while the Sixteenth Amendment reversed at least part of the Court's ruling in the Income Tax Cases (1895). Such changes are not easy to accomplish, however, and most efforts to alter or nullify controversial

Court decisions have been unsuccessful. For example, in 1965 and again in 1966, Senator Everett Dirkson of Illinois failed by only seven votes to obtain Senate approval for an amendment to modify the one-man-one-vote rule of Reynolds v. Sims (1964).

Mr. Chief Justice Chase delivered the opinion of the Court, saying in part:

... The first question necessarily is that of jurisdiction; for, if the Act of March, 1868, takes away the jurisdiction defined by the Act of February, 1867, it is useless, if not improper, to enter into any discussion of other questions.

It is quite true, as was argued by the counsel for the petitioner, that the appellate jurisdiction of this court is not derived from Acts of Congress. It is, strictly speaking, conferred by the Constitution. But it is conferred "with such exceptions and under such regulations as Congress shall make."

It is unnecessary to consider whether, if Congress had made no exceptions and no regulations, this court might not have exercised general appellate jurisdiction under rules prescribed by itself. From among the earliest Acts of the first Congress, at its first session, was the Act of September 24th, 1789, to establish the judicial courts of the United States. That Act provided for the organization of this court, and prescribed regulations for the exercise of its jurisdiction.

The source of that jurisdiction, and the limitations of it by the Constitution and by statute, have been on several occasions subjects of consideration here. In the case of Durousseau v. United States [1910]; Wiscart v. Dauchy [1796], particularly, the whole matter was carefully examined, and the court held, that while "the appellate powers of this court are not given by the Judicial Act, but are given by the Constitution"; they are, nevertheless, "limited and regulated by that Act, and by such other acts as have been passed on the subject." The court said, further, that the Judicial Act was an exercise of the power given by the Constitution to Congress "of making exceptions to the appellate jurisdiction of the Supreme Court."

"They have described affirmatively," said the court, "its jurisdiction, and this affirmative description has been understood to imply a negation of the exercise of such appellate power as is not comprehended within it."

The principle that the affirmation of appellate jurisdiction implies the negation of all such jurisdiction not affirmed having been thus established, it was an almost necessary consequence that Acts of Congress, providing for the exercise of jurisdiction, should come to be spoken of as Acts granting jurisdiction, and not as Acts making exceptions to the constitutional grant of it.

The exception to appellate jurisdiction in the case before us, however, is not an inference from the affirmation of other appellate jurisdiction. It is made in terms. The provision of the Act of 1867, affirming the appellate jurisdiction of this court in cases of habeas corpus, is expressly repealed. It is hardly possible to imagine a plainer instance of positive exception.

We are not at liberty to inquire into the motives of the Legislature. We can only examine into its power under the Constitution; and the power to make exceptions to the appellate jurisdiction of this court is given by express words.

What, then, is the effect of the repealing Act upon the case before us? We cannot doubt as to this. Without jurisdiction the court cannot proceed at all in any cause. Jurisdiction is power to declare the law, and when it ceases to exist, the only function remaining to the court is that of announcing the fact and dismissing the cause. And this is not less clear upon authority than upon principle.

Several cases were cited by the counsel for the petitioner in support of the position that jurisdiction of this case is not affected by the repealing Act. But none of them, in our judgment, afford any support to it. . . .

On the other hand, the general rule, supported by the best elementary writers . . . is, that "when an Act of the Legislature is repealed, it must be considered, except as to transactions past and closed, as if it never existed." And the effect of repealing Acts upon suits under Acts repealed, has been determined by the adjudications of this court. The subject was fully considered in Norris v. Crocker [1852], and more recently in Insurance Company v. Ritchie [1867]. In both of these cases it was held that no judgment could be rendered in a suit after the repeal of the Act under which it was brought and prosecuted.

It is quite clear, therefore, that this court cannot proceed to pronounce judgment in this case, for it has no longer jurisdiction of the appeal; and judicial duty is not less fitly performed by declining ungranted jurisdiction than in exercising firmly that which the Constitution and the laws confer.

Counsel seem to have supposed, if effect be given to the repealing Act in question, that the whole appellate power of the court, in cases of habeas corpus, is denied. But this is in error. The Act of 1868 does not except from that jurisdiction any cases but appeals from circuit courts under the Act of 1867. It does not affect the jurisdiction which was previously exercised. . . .

The appeal of the petitioner in this case must be dismissed for want of jurisdiction.

2

The Legislative Branch

BARENBLATT v. UNITED STATES
360 U. S. 109; 79 S. Ct. 1081; 3 L. Ed. 2d 1115
(1959)

The legislative power of Congress is the power to pass laws, and the actual process of lawmaking is not subject to judicial control. The extent to which Congress can, by making laws, enlarge or diminish the powers of the judiciary and executive is discussed in connection with those branches. But may Congress, as a means of performing its own delegated functions, borrow the powers of another branch? The power to subpoena witnesses and punish them for contempt by fine and imprisonment if they do not appear and testify is a vital and inherent judicial power. No court is really a court without it. Can a house of Congress borrow this judicial power as a means of performing its own delegated functions without violating the doctrine of the separation of powers?

This question was effectively dealt with in McGrain v. Daugherty (1927). Early in the Harding administration scandals were uncovered in the federal government, with the result that the Senate created a special committee to investigate the Department of Justice and the possible misconduct in office of Attorney General Harry M. Daugherty. In the course of the investigation the committee subpoenaed Mally S. Daugherty, brother of the Attorney General, to appear before it and testify. This he refused to do. The Senate then issued a warrant ordering McGrain, a deputy sergeant-at-arms, to arrest Mally S. Daugherty and bring him before the Senate to testify. Daugherty challenged the Senate's power to compel him to do this.

The Court upheld the Senate action. Its opinion mentioned that in 1792 the House of Representatives had appointed a select committee to inquire into the ill-fated St. Clair expedition against the Indians; and it then reviewed the legislative practice, congressional enactments, and court decisions bearing on the power of Congress to conduct inquiries and to punish for contempt. The Court concluded "that the power of inquiry—with process to enforce it—is an essential and appropriate auxiliary to the legislative function." However, it is a power which may validly be used only "in aid of the legislative function." Daugherty had alleged, and the lower court had agreed, that the committee was not seeking information to help it in legislation, but was in reality putting the Attorney General on trial. The Supreme Court disagreed. It said, "The only legitimate object the Senate could have in ordering the investigation was to aid it in legislating; and we think the subject-matter was such that the presumption should be indulged that this was the object. An express avowal of the object would have been better; but ... was not indispensable."

The power to investigate and compel the attendance of witnesses may also be used by Congress to facilitate its exercise of nonlegislative congressional powers. In the case of Barry v. United States ex rel. Cunningham (1929) the Court upheld the power of a Senate committee investigating senatorial campaign expenditures in Pennsylvania to punish for contempt a witness who refused to answer relevant questions. There can be no doubt of the similar right of a committee of the House of Representatives to punish recalcitrant witnesses in a hearing on the question of bringing impeachment charges against an officer of the government.

There are two ways in which either house of Congress may exercise its power to punish a stubborn witness for contempt. First, it may pass a resolution holding him in contempt and punishing him summarily. He may be fined, or he may be sent at once to prison. In Anderson v. Dunn (1821) the Supreme Court held that such imprisonment could not, however, extend beyond the adjournment of Congress. While Congress still enjoys this power of direct and summary punishment for contempt, experience early proved it unsatisfactory in a number of ways. Accordingly, in 1857 Congress provided a second method for dealing with the problem. It passed a statute making it a crime for a person to refuse to testify or answer questions before either house of Congress or any congressional committee when subpoenaed to do so. The maximum penalty is a fine of $1000 or a year in prison. The procedure under this statute is as follows: if a witness refuses to testify before a congressional investigating committee, the committee reports this refusal to the House (or Senate), and that body, usually *as a matter of routine, passes a resolution declaring the witness to be in contempt of the House or Senate. This resolution is then sent to the United States attorney in the District of Columbia, who presents the matter to a grand jury for indictment under the statute. If thus indicted, the witness is tried in the federal district court, and at his trial presents any legal or constitutional defenses he thinks he has. Punishment is, of course, imposed by the court.*

The opinion of the Court in McGrain v. Daugherty had very reasonably given Congress and its committees a sense of security from judicial interference with the legislative power to compel testimony. The Court had generously declared that if there was a possible legislative purpose which could be served by a congressional demand for evidence and facts, the Court would presume that that was the purpose of the investigation whether it was or not. What more latitude could Congress and its committees wish? But the McGrain case had not given congressional committees carte blanche. There were two reservations: the investigation must be in aid of a valid congressional duty or power, and the questions asked of witnesses must be relevant to the purpose of the inquiry.

From the time of their origin, congressional committees that were set up to investigate subversive or "un-American" activities were in a number of respects sui generis. They were given by Congress roving commissions to find out what they could about persons, organizations, or movements which were believed to be subversive or unorthodox, and to suggest ways and means of defeating these undermining influences. Very early in the game these committees convinced themselves that their most useful function was the public "exposure" of persons of dubious loyalty. This had been explicitly stated by Congressman Martin Dies when his resolution calling for the creation of the House Committee on Un-American Activities (HUAC) was being debated in the House. He said, "I am not in a position to say whether we can legislate effectively in reference to this matter, but I do know that exposure in a democracy of subversive activities is the most effective weapon that we have in our possession." During the Second World War and the subsequent cold war, House and Senate committees investigating subversion were dominanted by this zeal to "expose" persons or groups whose loyalty was open to question, in the well-grounded belief that an aroused public opinion would inflict its own nonlegal punishments or reprisals. The "exposure" of disloyalty or crime came to be generally accepted as the controlling purpose of such legislative investigating committees. The idea that committee investigations were justifiable only if they aided Congress in its wise consideration of legislation was almost wholly forgotten.

When, in 1957, the Supreme Court in Watkins v. United States held void a conviction for contempt of HUAC, it understandably came as a profound and unwelcome shock to those who regarded our congressional committees on subversive activities as the most useful defenders of our national security and as enjoying unrestricted authority in their investigations. Apparently striking at the very core of the committee, the Court made clear that "there is no congressional power to expose for the sake of exposure," and "investigations conducted solely for the personal aggrandizement of the investigators or to 'punish' those investigated are indefensible." Moreover, questions asked of a witness had to be pertinent to the matter under inquiry, and the vagueness of the term "un-American" and the "excessively broad charter" of HUAC, coupled with the failure of the committee itself to define the "question under inquiry," made it impossible for the witness to judge whether or not the committee had the right to insist that he answer. "Fundamental fairness," said the Court, "demands that no witness be compelled to make such a determination with so little guidance."

The constitutional limitations upon congressional powers of investigation spelled out in the Watkins case were, on the same day, made applicable to state legislative investigations through the medium of the Fourteenth Amendment in the case of Sweezy v. New Hampshire (1957). The legislature of New Hampshire had authorized the attorney general of the state to investigate subversive persons and activities. Sweezy, a university professor, was summoned to testify before the attorney general. He refused to answer questions regarding the content of a lecture he had given at the state university, and also questions concerning the Progressive party and its adherents. The attorney general petitioned the county court to propound the questions to Sweezy; the court did so, and upon Sweezy's continued refusal to answer them, held him guilty of contempt. The Supreme Court held that Sweezy's conviction denied him due process of law. Four justices (Warren, Black, Douglas, and Brennan) held that the legislature in its authorizing resolution had not specified that it desired the information to which the questions asked of Sweezy by the attorney general related, and the attorney general therefore was without authority to ask them. Justices Frankfurter and Harlan agreed that the conviction should be set aside, but on the ground that the questions asked of Sweezy infringed upon his constitutionally protected academic and political freedoms, and therefore denied due process.

The decision of the Court in the Watkins case (1957) was widely hailed by critics of HUAC as a long overdue rebuke, and the language of the opinion suggested that the whole concept of un-Americanism was so vague that the investigation of it could in no way serve a proper legislative purpose. This interpretation was apparently shared by the supporters of the

Committee as well, and bills were immediately introduced in Congress to curb the jurisdiction of the federal courts to review the Committee's work.

The decision in the Barenblatt case, printed below, came as a shock to those who had welcomed the Watkins decision and as a relief to its critics. Not only did the Court not strike dead the HUAC, but it seemed to back away from Chief Justice Warren's statement in Watkins that the Committee could not "expose for the sake of exposure." In Uphaus v. Wyman (1959), decided the same day as Barenblatt, it upheld the contempt conviction of Uphaus for refusing to divulge the names of persons attending a "World Fellowship" camp in New Hampshire. The Court distinguished the case from Sweezy v. New Hampshire (1957) on the ground that (1) no question of academic freedom was involved; (2) it was clear the legislature wanted the questions answered; and (3) the government's interest in "self-preservation" "outweighs individual rights in an associational privacy which . . . were here tenuous at best." Four justices dissented on the ground that not only did the state not have a sufficient interest but the real object of the investigation was "exposure for exposure's sake."

The impression that Barenblatt and Uphaus had in effect overruled Watkins and Sweezy proved to be unwarranted, and in subsequent cases the Supreme Court has both sustained and struck down convictions for contempt of congressional committees. In Braden v. United States and Wilkinson v. United States the Court in 1961 upheld by a five-to-four vote the contempt convictions of the defendants who refused to testify before the HUAC. Although the Committee's investigation was apparently sparked by the opposition these men had expressed to the work of the Committee, the Court held that this did not alter the validity of what, on the basis of Barenblatt, was an otherwise valid investigation. In Deutsch v. United States (1961), on the other hand, the Court held that questions regarding Communist activity at Cornell University were not pertinent to an investigation of Communism in the Albany, New York, labor movement.

The decision of the cases just discussed turned on whether the legislative committee was authorized to investigate a particular activity, and if it was, whether the question asked of the witness was pertinent to such investigation. In 1962 the Court added a new dimension to this last problem. In Russell v. United States, it held that a prosecution for contempt was void unless the indictment by which the charge was brought stated explicitly the purpose of the investigation. The indictment in question had listed as a separate count each question the witness had refused to answer, but had stated merely that they were pertinent without stating what the subject of the inquiry was. This, said the Court, not only made it impossible to make an independent judgment of pertinency on appeal but did not sufficiently clearly indicate to the defendant the exact crime for which he was being tried.

For 25 years the Supreme Court has been asked to hold that there was a constitutional "right to silence" flowing from the First Amendment which would justify a person in refusing to testify before a legislative committee. The Court has never conceded such a right, but in 1963 in Gibson v. Florida Investigation Committee it upheld for the first time against a legislative committee the closely related claim of "associational privacy." The Florida committee, in the course of investigating Communist infiltration of the civil rights movement, subpoenaed the membership lists of the Miami chapter of the NAACP. The Court sustained the chapter's refusal to produce them. Conceding the right of the state to inform itself, the Court held that absent any tie in, or "nexus," between the NAACP and subversion, there was no showing of a "subordinating interest" sufficient to override the right of association. A similar result was reached in De Gregory v. Attorney General (1966), where the New Hampshire attorney general sought to inquire into De Gregory's Communist activities of a decade earlier. Since the record was "devoid of any evidence that there is any Communist movement in New Hampshire," there was no " 'overriding and compelling state interest'. . . that would warrant intrusion into the realm of political and associational privacy. . . ." Justices Harlan, Stewart, and Clark dissented on the ground that the purpose of the inquiry was to find out if there were such a "movement."

In 1975, in Eastland v. United States Servicemen's Fund, the Court held the speech and debate clause, Art. 1, §6, cl. 1, forbade judicial interference with a Senate committee investigation. The Senate Internal Security Subcommittee had subpoenaed bank records showing who had contributed to an organization operating on and near military bases which it considered disruptive and possibly foreign-dominated. The bank agreed to turn over the records and the Fund, arguing that the records were the same as membership lists, sought an injunction against the committee on the basis of the Gibson case, above. Eight members of the Supreme Court agreed that the speech and debate clause was absolute and since the subpoena fell within the sphere of legitimate legislative activity the committee could not be made answerable to the courts by injunction.

Mr. Justice Harlan delivered the opinion of the Court, saying in part:

Once more the Court is required to resolve the conflicting constitutional claims of congressional power and of an individual's right to resist its exercise. The congressional power in question concerns the internal process of Congress in moving within its legislative domain; it involves the utilization of its committees to secure "testimony needed to enable it efficiently to exercise a legislative function belonging to it under the Constitution." McGrain v. Daugherty [1927]. The power of inquiry has been employed by Congress throughout our history, over the whole range of the national interests concerning which Congress might legislate or decide upon due investigation not to legislate; it has similarly been utilized in determining what to appropriate from the national purse, or whether to appropriate. The scope of the power of inquiry, in short, is as penetrating and far-reaching as the potential power to enact and appropriate under the Constitution.

Broad as it is, the power is not, however, without limitations. Since Congress may only investigate into those areas in which it may potentially legislate or appropriate, it cannot inquire into matters which are within the exclusive province of one of the other branches of the Government. Lacking the judicial power given to the Judiciary, it cannot inquire into matters that are exclusively the concern of the Judiciary. Neither can it supplant the Executive in what exclusively belongs to the Executive. And the Congress, in common with all branches of the Government, must exercise its powers subject to the limitations placed by the Constitution on governmental action, more particularly in the context of this case the relevant limitations of the Bill of Rights.

The congressional power of inquiry, its range and scope, and an individual's duty in relation to it, must be viewed in proper perspective. . . . The power and the right of resistance to it are to be judged in the concrete, not on the basis of abstractions. In the present case congressional efforts to learn the extent of a nationwide, indeed world wide, problem have brought one of its investigating committees into the field of education. Of course, broadly viewed, inquiries cannot be made into the teaching that is pursued in any of our educational institutions. When academic teaching-freedom and its corollary learning-freedom, so essential to the well-being of the Nation, are claimed, this Court will always be on the alert against intrusion by Congress into this constitutionally protected domain. But this does not mean that the Congress is precluded from interrogating a witness merely because he is a teacher. An educational institution is not a constitutional sanctuary from inquiry into matters that may otherwise be within the constitutional legislative domain merely for the reason that inquiry is made of someone within its walls.

In the setting of this framework of constitutional history, practice and legal precedents, we turn to the particularities of this case.

We here review petitioner's conviction for contempt of Congress, arising from his refusal to answer certain questions put to him by a Subcommittee of the House Committee on Un-American Activities during the course of an inquiry concerning alleged Communist infiltration into the field of education. . . .

Petitioner's various contentions resolve themselves into three propositions: First, the compelling of testimony by the Subcommittee was neither legislatively authorized nor constitutionally permissible because of the vagueness of

Rule XI of the House of Representatives, Eighty-third Congress, the charter of authority of the parent Committee. Second, petitioner was not adequately apprised of the pertinency of the Subcommittee's questions to the subject matter of the inquiry. Third, the questions petitioner refused to answer infringed rights protected by the First Amendment.

Subcommittee's Authority to Compel Testimony.

At the outset it should be noted that Rule XI authorized this Subcommittee to compel testimony within the framework of the investigative authority conferred on the Un-American Activities Committee. Petitioner contends that Watkins v. United States [1957], nevertheless held the grant of this power in all circumstances ineffective because of the vagueness of Rule XI in delineating the Committee jurisdiction to which its exercise was to be appurtenant. This view of Watkins was accepted by two of the dissenting judges below.

The Watkins Case cannot properly be read as standing for such a proposition. A principal contention in Watkins was that the refusals to answer were justified because the requirement of 2 USC § 192 that the questions asked be "pertinent to the question under inquiry" had not been satisfied. This Court reversed the conviction solely on that ground, holding that Watkins had not been adequately apprised of the subject matter of the Subcommittee's investigation or the pertinency thereto of the questions he refused to answer. In so deciding the Court drew upon Rule XI only as one of the facets in the total mise en scène in its search for the "question under inquiry" in that particular investigation. The Court, in other words, was not dealing with Rule XI at large, and indeed in effect stated that no such issue was before it. That the vagueness of Rule XI was not alone determinative is also shown by the Court's further statement that aside from the Rule "the remarks of the chairman or members of the committee, or even the nature of the proceedings themselves, might sometimes make the topic [under inquiry] clear." In short, while Watkins was critical of Rule XI, it did not involve the broad and inflexible holding petitioner now attributes to it.

Petitioner also contends, independently of Watkins, that the vagueness of Rule XI deprived the Subcommittee of the right to compel testimony in this investigation into Communist activity. We cannot agree with this contention, which in its furthest reach would mean that the House Un-American Activities Committee under its existing authority has no right to compel testimony in any circumstances. Granting the vagueness of the Rule, we may not read it in isolation from its long history in the House of Representatives. Just as legislation is often given meaning by the gloss of legislative reports, administrative interpretation, and long usage, so the proper meaning of an authorization to a congressional committee is not to be derived alone from its abstract terms unrelated to the definite content furnished them by the course of congressional actions. The Rule comes to us with a "persuasive gloss of legislative history," which shows beyond doubt that in pursuance of its legislative concerns in the domain of "national security" the House has clothed the Un-American Activities Committee with pervasive authority to investigate Communist activities in this country. . . .

[The Court here summarizes the history of the Committee, showing the wide range of areas in which it had pursued its search for Communists.]

In the context of these unremitting pursuits, the House has steadily continued the life of the Committee at the commencement of each new Congress; it has never narrowed the powers of the Committee, whose authority has remained throughout identical with that contained in Rule XI; and it has continuingly supported the Committee's activities with substantial appropriations. Beyond this, the Committee was raised to the level of a standing committee of the House in 1945, it having been but a special committee prior to that time.

In light of this long and illuminating history it can hardly be seriously argued that the investigation of Communist activities generally, and the attendant use of compulsory process, was beyond the purview of the Committee's intended authority under Rule XI.

We are urged, however, to construe Rule XI so as at least to exclude the field of education from the Committee's compulsory authority. . . .

[The Court finds Congress was aware of and did not disapprove previous investigations in this field.]

In this framework of the Committee's history we must conclude that its legislative authority to conduct the inquiry presently under consideration is unassailable, and that independently of whatever bearing the broad scope of Rule XI may have on the issue of "pertinency" in a given investigation into Communist activities, as in Watkins, the Rule cannot be said to be constitutionally infirm on the score of vagueness. The constitutional permissibility of that authority otherwise is a matter to be discussed later.

Pertinency Claim.

Undeniably a conviction for contempt under 2 USC § 192 cannot stand unless the questions asked are pertinent to the subject matter of the investigation. Watkins v. United States. But the factors which led us to rest decision on this ground in Watkins were very different from those involved here.

In Watkins the petitioner had made specific objection to the Subcommittee's questions on the ground of pertinency; the question under inquiry had not been disclosed in any illuminating manner; and the questions asked the petitioner were not only amorphous on their face, but in some instances clearly foreign to the alleged subject matter of the investigation—"Communism in labor."

In contrast, petitioner in the case before us raised no objections on the ground of pertinency at the time any of the questions were put to him. . . . We need not, however, rest decision on petitioner's failure to object on this score, for here "pertinency" was made to appear "with undisputable clarity." First of all, it goes without saying that the scope of the Committee's authority was for the House, not a witness, to determine, subject to the ultimate reviewing responsibility of this Court. What we deal with here is whether petitioner was sufficiently apprised of "the topic under inquiry" thus authorized "and the connective reasoning whereby the precise questions asked relate[d] to it." In light of his prepared memorandum of constitutional objections there can be no doubt that this petitioner was well aware of the Subcommittee's authority and purpose to question him as it did. In addition the other sources of this information which we recognized in Watkins leave no room for a "pertinenc" objection on this record. The subject matter of the inquiry had been identified at the commencement of the investigation as Communist infiltration into the field of education. Just prior to petitioner's appearance before the Subcommittee, the scope of the day's hearings had been announced as "in the main communism in education and the experiences and background in the party by Francis X. T. Crowley. It will deal with activities in Michigan, Boston, and in some small degree, New York." Petitioner had heard the Subcommittee interrogate the witness Crowley along the same lines as he, petitioner, was evidently to be questioned, and had listened to Crowley's testimony identifying him as a former member of an alleged Communist student organization at the University of Michigan while they both were in attendance there. Further, petitioner had stood mute in the face of the Chairman's statement as to why he had been called as a witness by the Subcommittee. And, lastly, unlike Watkins, petitioner refused to answer questions as to his own Communist Party affiliations, whose pertinency of course was clear beyond doubt.

Petitioner's contentions on this aspect of the case cannot be sustained.

Constitutional Contentions.

Our function, at this point, is purely one of constitutional adjudication in the particular case and upon the particular record before us, not to pass judgment upon the general wisdom or efficacy of the activities of this Committee in a vexing and complicated field.

The precise constitutional issue confronting us is whether the Subcommittee's inquiry into petitioner's past or present membership in the Communist Party transgressed the provisions of the First Amendment, which of course reach and limit congressional investigations. Watkins.

The Court's past cases establish sure guides to decision. Undeniably, the First Amendment in some circumstances protects an individual from being compelled to disclose his associational relationships. However, the protections of the First Amendment, unlike a proper claim of the privilege against self-incrimination under the Fifth Amendment, do not afford a witness the right to resist inquiry in all circumstances. Where First Amendment rights are asserted to bar governmental interrogation resolution of the issue always involves a balancing by the courts of the competing private and public interests at stake in the particular circumstances shown. These principles were recognized in the Watkins Case. . . .

The first question is whether this investigation was related to a valid legislative purpose, for Congress may not constitutionally require an individual to disclose his political relationships or other private affairs except in relation to such a purpose. See Watkins v. United States.

That Congress has wide power to legislate in the field of Communist activity in this Country, and to conduct appropriate investigations in aid thereof, is hardly debatable. The existence of such power has never been questioned by this Court, and it is sufficient to say, without particularization, that Congress has enacted or considered in this field a wide range of legislative measures, not a few of which have stemmed from recommendations of the very Committee whose actions have been drawn in question here. In the last analysis this power rests on the right of self-preservation, "the ultimate value of any society," Dennis v. United States [1951]. Justification for its exercise in turn rests on the long and widely accepted view that the tenets of the Communist Party include the ultimate overthrow of the Government of the United States by force and violence, a view which has been given formal expression by the Congress. . . .

. . . To suggest that because the Communist Party may also sponsor peaceable political reforms the constitutional issues before us should now be judged as if that Party were just an ordinary political party from the standpoint of national security, is to ask this Court to blind itself to world affairs which have determined the whole course of our national policy since the close of World War II, . . . and to the vast burdens which these conditions have entailed for the entire Nation.

We think that investigatory power in this domain is not to be denied Congress solely because the field of education is involved. Nothing in the prevailing opinions in Sweezy v. New Hampshire [1957] stands for a contrary view. The vice existing there was that the questioning of Sweezy, who had not been shown ever to have been connected with the Communist Party, as to the contents of a lecture he had given at the University of New Hampshire, and as to his connections with the Progressive Party, then on the ballot as a normal political party in some 26 States, was too far removed from the premises on which the constitutionality of the State's investigation had to depend to withstand attack under the Fourteenth Amendment. . . . This is a very different thing from inquiring into the extent to which the Communist Party has succeeded in infiltrating into our universities, or elsewhere, persons and groups committed to furthering the objective of overthrow. Indeed we do not understand petitioner here to suggest that Congress in no circumstances may inquire into Communist activity in the field of education. Rather, his position is in effect that this particular investigation was aimed not at the revolutionary aspects but at the theoretical classroom discussion of communism.

In our opinion this position rests on a too constricted view of the nature of the investigatory process, and is not supported by a fair assessment of the record before us. An investigation of advocacy of or preparation for overthrow certainly embraces the right to identify a witness as a member of the Communist Party . . . and to inquire into the various manifestations of the Party's tenets. The strict requirements of a prosecution under the Smith Act, see Dennis v. United States [1951] and Yates v. United States [1957], are not the measure of the permissible scope of a congressional investigation into "overthrow," for of necessity the investigatory process must proceed step by step. Nor can it fairly be concluded that this investigation was directed at controlling what is being taught at our universities rather than at overthrow. The statement of the Subcommittee Chairman at the opening of the investigation evinces no such intention, and so far as this record reveals nothing thereafter transpired which would justify our holding that the thrust of the investigation later changed. The record discloses considerable testimony concerning the foreign domination and revolutionary purposes and efforts of the Communist Party. That there was also testimony on the abstract philosophical level does not detract from the dominant theme of this investigation—Communist infiltration furthering the alleged ultimate purpose of overthrow. And certainly the conclusion would not be justified that the questioning of petitioner would have exceeded permissible bounds had he not shut off the Subcommittee at the threshold.

Nor can we accept the further contention that this investigation should not be deemed to have been in furtherance of a legislative purpose because the true objective of the Committee and of the Congress was purely "exposure." So long as Congress acts in pursuance of its constitutional power, the Judiciary lacks authority to intervene on the basis of the motives which spurred the exercise of that power. . . . "It is, of course, true," as was said in McCray v. United States [1904], "that if there be no authority in the judiciary to restrain a lawful exercise of power by another department of the government, where a wrong motive or purpose has impelled to the exertion of the power, that abuses of a power conferred may be temporarily effectual. The remedy for this, however, lies, not in the abuse by the judicial authority of its functions, but in the people, upon whom, after all, under our institutions, reliance must be placed for the correction of abuses committed in the exercise of a lawful power." These principles of course apply as well to committee investigations into the need for legislation as to the enactments which such investigations may produce. . . . Thus, in stating in the Watkins Case that "there is no congressional power to expose for the sake of exposure," we at the same time declined to inquire into the "motives of committee members," and recognized that their "motives alone would not vitiate an investigation which had been instituted by a House of Congress if that assembly's legislative purpose is being served." Having scrutinized this record we cannot say that the unanimous panel of the Court of Appeals which first considered this case was wrong in concluding that "the primary purposes of the inquiry were in aid of legislative processes." . . . Certainly this is not a case like Kilbourn v. Thompson [1881], where "the House of Representatives not only exceeded the limit of its own authority, but assumed a power which could only be properly exercised by another branch of the government, because it was in its nature clearly judicial." The constitutional legislative power of Congress in this instance is beyond question.

Finally, the record is barren of other factors which in themselves might sometimes lead to the conclusion that the individual interests at stake were not subordinate to those of the state. There is no indication in this record that the Subcommittee was attempting to pillory witnesses. Nor did petitioner's appearance as a witness follow from indiscriminate dragnet procedures, lacking in probable cause for belief that he possessed information which might be helpful to the Subcommittee. And the relevancy of the questions put to him by the Subcommittee is not open to doubt.

We conclude that the balance between the individual and the governmental interests here at stake must be struck in favor of the latter, and that therefore the provisions of the First Amendment have not been offended.

We hold that petitioner's conviction for contempt of Congress discloses no infirmity, and that the judgment of the Court of Appeals must be

Affirmed.

[Mr. Justice Black, with whom Chief Justice Warren and Mr. Justice Douglas concurred, dissented on grounds that (1) the term "un-American" was so vague as to make the Committee's mandate void for vagueness under the due process clause; (2) the Court's "balancing test" is not the way to determine the scope of freedom of speech, and if it were, the Court should have balanced the interest of society in "being able to join organizations, advocate causes and make political 'mistakes,' " against the government's limited interest in making laws in the area of free speech—an interest which cannot reasonably be equated with "self-preservation"; (3) the chief aim of the HUAC is to "try witnesses and punish them because they are or have been Communists," which constitutes a bill of attainder.]

Mr. Justice Brennan dissented, saying in part:

I would reverse this conviction. It is sufficient that I state my complete agreement with my Brother Black that no purpose for the investigation of

Barenblatt is revealed by the record except exposure purely for the sake of exposure. This is not a purpose to which Barenblatt's rights under the First Amendment can validly be subordinated. An investigation in which the processes of law-making and law-evaluating are submerged entirely in exposure of individual behavior—in adjudication, of a sort, through the exposure process—is outside the constitutional pale of congressional inquiry. Watkins v. United States. . . .

3

The Executive Branch

YOUNGSTOWN SHEET & TUBE COMPANY v. SAWYER
343 U. S. 579; 72 S. Ct. 863; 96 L. Ed. 1153
(1952)

The President exercises the bulk of his policy-making powers under dele-
gations of authority made to him by Congress. But there are important
areas in which he enjoys powers granted not by Congress, but by the
Constitution itself. The conduct of foreign affairs has traditionally been
the concern of the executive branch of government, and the Constitution
of the United States recognizes this fact. The President appoints our for-
eign ambassadors, ministers, and consuls. He alone receives ambassadors
and other public ministers from abroad and thereby "recognizes" the
governments by which such officers are sent. It is he who, usually through
his Secretary of State, negotiates treaties. But Congress has some power
with respect to foreign affairs. Treaties or other agreements which call for
the expenditure of money will be ineffective unless Congress appropriates
that money by statute. The Senate must consent to the appointments of
our diplomatic representatives, and two-thirds of the Senate must give its
approval to a treaty. This latter requirement has tended to limit the use
of the treaty power to fairly formal and important international agree-
ments, among which have been military alliances, the making of peace,
and adherence to international organizations. A substantial proportion of
our international agreements take the form of executive agreements con-
cluded between the President and the executive of a foreign nation. Some
of these, particularly in the field of foreign trade, are specifically autho-

rized by Congress. Others are made solely on the authority of the President as chief executive. While the Constitution provides that treaties shall be the law of the land, and executive agreements made with congressional consent would also have the authority of law, there had long been some doubt about the binding nature of an agreement made by the executive alone.

In 1937, in United States v. Belmont, the Court laid this doubt to rest. The case involved the title to money which a Russian company had on deposit in Belmont's bank. The Soviet government had nationalized the company in 1918 and confiscated its assets, including, presumably, the funds in Belmont's bank. Then in 1933 the President, by receiving the Soviet ambassador, recognized the Soviet government as the legitimate government of Russia. A final settlement of the claims and counter claims between the two countries was concluded in the Litvinov Assignments, and the Belmont deposits were assigned to the United States. The assignments were made by an exchange of diplomatic correspondence between the Soviet government and the United States and were not submitted to the Senate in the form of a treaty. The Supreme Court rejected the argument that the assignments were void since confiscation was against the public policy both of New York and the United States. "The recognition, establishment of diplomatic relations, the assignment, and agreements with respect thereto, were all parts of one transaction, resulting in an international compact between the two governments. That the negotiations, acceptance of the assignment and agreements and understandings in respect thereof were within the competence of the President may not be doubted. Governmental power over internal affairs is distributed between the national government and the several states. Governmental power over external affairs is not distributed, but is vested exclusively in the national government. And in respect of what was done here, the Executive had authority to speak as the sole organ of that government. The assignment and the agreements in connection therewith did not, as in the case of treaties, as that term is used in the treaty-making clause of the Constitution (Article II, § 2), require the advice and consent of the Senate."

Another area in which the President receives direct constitutional powers is found in Article II, which makes the President the Commander in Chief of the Army and Navy. This is clearly not a power merely to command the disposition of the armed forces. But if it is more than that, how much more? A democratic distrust of executive power cannot alter the fact that in times of war a near-dictatorship may be necessary to preserve the nation. In such times Congress has wisely delegated vast areas of authority to the President. But where Congress has not done so, and the President has felt that the emergency justified it, he has often acted on his own authority. The fact that Congress usually gives belated approval to such executive acts *hardly obscures the fact that the crucial policy decisions are made by the executive.*

The Constitution gives Congress the power to declare war; but may the President on his own authority decide that a state of war exists, and on the strength of this decision take action affecting the lives and property of American citizens? Following the firing upon Fort Sumter in 1861, President Lincoln declared the existence of a state of insurrection and called out the militia. Authority to do this had been given him by Congress, and the Court had held in Martin v. Mott (1827) that vesting of this discretion in the President was valid. But a week after Sumter the President, acting wholly on his own authority, declared a naval blockade of the Confederate ports. Pursuant to this proclamation four blockade runners were captured and condemned. The Court sustained this action in the Prize Cases (1863), pointing out that "if a war be made by invasion of a foreign nation, the President is not only authorized but bound to resist force, by force. He does not initiate the war, but is bound to accept the challenge without waiting for any special legislative authority. And whether the hostile party be a foreign invader, or States organized in rebellion, it is none the less a war. . . ." The proclamation of a blockade was held "itself, official and conclusive evidence to the court that a state of war existed which demanded and authorized a recourse to such a measure, under the circumstances peculiar to the case."

Even the most drastic and dictatorial exercises of power by the President acting under his authority as Commander in Chief have usually not resulted in clarifying or determining the actual constitutional scope of pure executive power. This is because Congress in nearly all such cases has hastened to shore up the President's authority by legislative ratification of what he has done. Thus when Congress came into session on July 4, 1861, it underwrote the President's blockade of Southern ports by passing an act "approving, legalizing and making valid all the acts, proclamations, and orders of the President, &c., as if they had been issued and done under the previous express authority and direction of the Congress. . . ." In 1944, following the issue of the executive order creating military districts from which persons of Japanese ancestry were excluded (see the Korematsu case), Congress made it a crime to "enter, remain in, leave, or commit any act in any military area . . . prescribed [by executive order] . . . contrary to the order of the Secretary of War or any such military commander. . . ."

In September, 1940, the President, by executive agreement with Great Britain, traded 50 old destroyers for the right to build air bases on certain British islands in the Caribbean. The constitutionality of this move was widely argued, since it is Congress which possesses the power to dispose of the property of the United States. The action was never challenged in the courts, as indeed it scarcely could have been since no one was "injured," and Congress gave its silent approval by appropriating money to build the air bases. While it is clear that presidential discretion alone initiated the agreement, the implied ratification of the agreement by Congress tends to provide a measure of delegated authority and thus prevents a clear test of inherent presidential power.

The constitutional grants of power over foreign affairs and as Commander in Chief have always been interpreted as being independent grants to the President to make important policy decisions in these two fields, and whatever power Congress has in these areas can be delegated to the President virtually without limit. In contrast to this his duty to "take care that the laws be faithfully executed" seems a requirement that he carry out the laws of Congress. In the case of In re Neagle (1890), the Court interpreted this clause, too, as a grant of policy-making authority. The laws are not merely the laws of Congress, but include independent acts of the President himself. There is, moreover, a peace of the United States, and the President, as chief executive, is protector of that peace with power to prevent violations.

The case arose out of an extraordinary set of circumstances. A long and bitter legal battle involving title to more than a million dollars had culminated in the United States circuit court in California at a time when Mr. Justice Field of the United States Supreme Court was sitting as circuit justice. The disappointed contestant was represented by her husband, a lawyer named Terry who had once been chief justice of the California supreme court. At the close of the case Mrs. Terry accused Mr. Justice Field of selling justice, and the United States marshal was ordered to quiet her. A fight ensued and Terry and his wife went to prison for six months for contempt of court. Upon their release they threatened to kill Mr. Justice Field if he ever came back to California. Since the law at that time required Supreme Court justices to ride circuit, the matter was laid before the Attorney General; and when Field again returned to California, Neagle, a deputy marshal, was detailed to serve as a bodyguard. Terry, following up his threat, tried to make a murderous attack upon the justice in a railroad restaurant where the justice had stopped while traveling on circuit duty. He was about to draw his knife when Neagle shot and killed him. Neagle was promptly arrested by the local authorities and held for murder. He was released from the custody of the state court upon a writ of habeas corpus by the federal circuit court on the ground that he was held in custody for "an act done in pursuance of a law of the United States" within the meaning of the federal statute providing for the issuance of the writ in such cases.

The most significant feature of the case is that the "law of the United States" in pursuance of which Neagle acted was not an act of Congress, *but merely an executive order issued by authority of the President. In sustaining Neagle's release, the Court holds that the President in the exercise of the duty imposed upon him to see that the laws are faithfully executed may, without special statutory authority, appoint an officer to protect the life of a federal judge. It was on the President's power to "take care that the laws be faithfully executed" that Chief Justice Vinson relied in his dissent in the Steel Seizure Case, printed below.*

This case climaxed a long dispute between the steel companies and the steel workers. On December 18, 1951, the United Steel Workers of America, CIO, gave notice that it would strike on December 31. The Federal Mediation and Conciliation Service failed to effect a settlement. The Federal Wage Stabilization Board, to which President Truman referred the dispute on December 22, also failed. The President did not invoke the provisions of the Taft-Hartley Act, which would have set up a "period of waiting" before a strike. On April 4, 1952, the union announced that it would call a nationwide strike on April 9. A few hours before the strike was to begin the President directed Secretary of Commerce Sawyer to seize and operate most of the country's steel mills. The Secretary issued the appropriate orders. The President reported the seizure to Congress on April 9, and again on April 21, but Congress took no action. The steel companies complied under protest with the seizure order, but sought a temporary injunction to restrain the government's action. On April 30, the district court of the District of Columbia issued a preliminary injunction, which was stayed on the same day by the court of appeals.

On May 3, the Supreme Court, bypassing the court of appeals, brought the case to its docket by certiorari. It heard argument on May 12, and decided the case on June 2. These dates indicate the celerity with which the Supreme Court can act when the national interest requires speed.

The difficulty and complexity of the case is shown by the fact that the Court divided six to three, and that seven justices wrote separate opinions totaling 128 pages. The Court did not face here the naked question of the President's power to seize the steel plants in the absence of any congressional enactments or expressions of policy. Congress had provided limited powers of seizure in the Selective Service Act of 1948 and in the Defense Production Act of 1950. Furthermore, in its debates on the Taft-Hartley Act of 1947 Congress had considered an amendment authorizing seizure of plants by the President in case of strike, and had rejected it. In fact, over a period of years, Congress had made it clear that the seizure of private property in time of emergency was a problem to be controlled by congressional policy. For a variety of reasons, the majority of the Court found that this legislative occupation of the field made untenable the President's claim of authority to seize the plants as an exercise of inherent executive power or as Commander in Chief. Congress had set up various procedures for the President to follow in such cases, and he had not followed them.

Mr. Justice Black delivered the opinion of the Court, saying in part:

We are asked to decide whether the President was acting within his constitutional power when he issued an order directing the Secretary of Commerce to take possession of and operate most of the Nation's steel mills. The mill owners argue that the President's order amounts to lawmaking, a legislative function which the Constitution has expressly confided to the Congress and not to the President. The Government's position is that the order was made on findings of the President that his action was necessary to avert a national catastrophe which would inevitably result from a stoppage of steel production, and that in meeting this grave emergency the President was acting within the aggregate of his constitutional powers as the Nation's Chief Executive and the Commander in Chief of the Armed Forces of the United States. . . .

The President's power, if any, to issue the order must stem either from an act of Congress or from the Constitution itself. There is no statute that expressly authorizes the President to take possession of property as he did here. Nor is there any act of Congress to which our attention has been directed from which such a power can fairly be implied. Indeed, we do not understand the Government to rely on statutory authorization for this seizure. There are two statutes which do authorize the President to take both personal and real property under certain conditions. [The Selective Service Act of 1948 and the Defense Production Act of 1950.] However, the Government admits that these conditions were not met and that the President's order was not rooted in either of the statutes. The Government refers to the seizure provisions of one of these statutes (§ 201 (b) of the Defense Production Act) as "much too cumbersome, involved, and time-consuming for the crisis which was at hand."

Moreover, the use of the seizure technique to solve labor disputes in order to prevent work stoppages was not only unauthorized by any congressional enactment; prior to this controversy, Congress had refused to adopt that method of settling labor disputes. When the Taft-Hartley Act was under consideration in 1947, Congress rejected an amendment which would have authorized such governmental seizures in cases of emergency. Apparently it was thought that the technique of seizure, like that of compulsory arbitration, would interfere with the process of collective bargaining. Consequently, the plan Congress adopted in that Act did not provide for seizure under any circumstances. Instead, the plan sought to bring about settlements by use of the customary devices of mediation, conciliation, investigation by boards of inquiry, and public reports. In some instances temporary injunctions were authorized to provide cooling-off periods. All this failing, unions were left free to strike after a secret vote by employees as to whether they wished to accept their employers' final settlement offer.

It is clear that if the President had authority to issue the order he did, it must be found in some provision of the Constitution. And it is not claimed that express constitutional language grants this power to the President. The contention is that presidential power should be implied from the aggregate of his powers under the Constitution. Particular reliance is placed on provisions in Article II which say that "The executive Power shall be vested in a President . . ."; that "he shall take Care that the Laws be faithfully executed"; and that he "shall be Commander in Chief of the Army and Navy of the United States."

The order cannot properly be sustained as an exercise of the President's military power as Commander in Chief of the Armed Forces. The Government attempts to do so by citing a number of cases upholding broad powers in military commanders engaged in day-to-day fighting in a theater of war. Such cases need not concern us here. Even though "theater of war" be an expanding concept, we cannot with faithfulness to our constitutional system hold that the Commander in Chief of the Armed Forces has the ultimate power as such to take possession of private property in order to keep labor disputes from stopping production. This is a job for the Nation's lawmakers, not for its military authorities.

Nor can the seizure order be sustained because of the several constitutional provisions that grant executive power to the President. In the framework of our Constitution, the President's power to see that the laws are faithfully executed refutes the idea that he is to be a lawmaker. The Constitution limits his functions in the lawmaking process to the recommending of laws he thinks wise and the vetoing of laws he thinks bad. And the Constitution is neither silent nor equivocal about who shall make laws which the President is to execute. The first section of the first article says that "All legislative Powers herein granted shall be vested in a Congress of the United States." . . .

The President's order does not direct that a congressional policy be executed in a manner prescribed by Congress—it directs that a presidential policy be executed in a manner prescribed by the President. The preamble of the order itself, like that of many statutes, sets out reasons why the President believes certain policies should be adopted, proclaims these policies as rules of conduct to be followed, and again, like a statute, authorizes a government official to promulgate additional rules and regulations consistent with the policy proclaimed and needed to carry that policy into execution. The power of Congress to adopt such public policies as those proclaimed by the order is beyond question. It can authorize the taking of private property for public use. It can make laws regulating the relationships between employers and employees, prescribing rules designed to settle labor disputes, and fixing wages and working conditions in certain fields of our economy. The Constitution does not subject this lawmaking power of Congress to presidential or military supervision or control.

It is said that other Presidents without congressional authority have taken possession of private business enterprises in order to settle labor disputes. But even if this be true, Congress has not thereby lost its exclusive constitutional authority to make laws necessary and proper to carry out the power vested by the Constitution "in the Government of the United States, or any Department or Officer thereof."

The Founders of this Nation entrusted the lawmaking power to the Congress alone in both good and bad times. It would do no good to recall the historical events, the fears of power and the hopes for freedom that lay behind their choice. Such a review would but confirm our holding that this seizure order cannot stand.

The judgment of the District Court is
Affirmed.

Mr. Justice Frankfurter, concurring with the judgment and opinion of the Court, said in part:

Apart from his vast share of responsibility for the conduct of our foreign relations, the embracing function of the President is that "he shall take Care that the Laws be faithfully executed . . . ." Art. 2, § 3. The nature of that authority has for me been comprehensively indicated by Mr. Justice Holmes. "The duty of the President to see that the laws be executed is a duty that does not go beyond the laws or require him to achieve more than Congress sees fit to leave within his powers" Myers v. United States [1926]. The powers of the President are not as particularized as are those of Congress. But unenumerated powers do not mean undefined powers. The separation of powers built into our Constitution gives essential content to undefined provisions in the frame of our government. . . .

A scheme of government like ours no doubt at times feels the lack of power to act with complete, all-embracing, swiftly moving authority. No doubt a government with distributed authority, subject to be challenged in the courts of law, at least long enough to consider and adjudicate the challenge, labors under restrictions from which other governments are free. It has not been our tradition to envy such governments. In any event our government was designed to have such restrictions. The price was deemed not too high in view of the safeguards which these restrictions afforded. . . .

Mr. Justice Douglas, concurring with the judgment and opinion of the Court, said in part:

There can be no doubt that the emergency which caused the President to seize these steel plants was one that bore heavily on the country. But the emergency did not create power; it merely marked an occasion when power should be exercised. And the fact that it was necessary that measures be taken to keep steel in production does not mean that the President, rather than the Congress, had the constitutional authority to act. The Congress, as well as the President, is trustee of the national welfare. The President can act more quickly than the Congress. The President with the armed services at his disposal can move with force as well as with speed. All executive power—from the reign of ancient kings to the rule of modern dictators—has the outward appearance of efficiency.

Legislative power, by contrast, is slower to exercise. There must be delay while the ponderous machinery of committees, hearings, and debates is put into motion. That takes time; and while the Congress slowly moves into action, the emergency may take its toll in wages, consumer goods, war production, the standard of living of the people, and perhaps even lives. Legislative action may indeed often be cumbersome, time-consuming, and apparently inefficient. But as Mr. Justice Brandeis stated in his dissent in Myers v. United States [1926]

"The doctrine of the separation of powers was adopted by the Convention of 1787, not to promote efficiency but to preclude the exercise of arbitrary power. The purpose was, not to avoid friction, but, by means of the inevitable friction incident to the distribution of the governmental powers among three departments, to save the people from autocracy."

We therefore cannot decide this case by determining which branch of government can deal most expeditiously with the present crisis. The answer must depend on the allocation of powers under the Constitution. That in turn requires an analysis of the conditions giving rise to the seizure and of the seizure itself. . . .

The great office of President is not a weak and powerless one. The President represents the people and is their spokesman in domestic and foreign affairs. The office is respected more than any other in the land. It gives a position of leadership that is unique. The power to formulate policies and mould opinion inheres in the Presidency and conditions our national life. The impact of the man and the philosophy he represents may at times be thwarted by the Congress. Stalemates may occur when emergencies mount and the Nation suffers for lack of harmonious, reciprocal action between the White House and Capitol Hill. That is a risk inherent in our system of separation of powers. The tragedy of such stalemates might be avoided by allowing the President the use of some legislative authority. The Framers with memories of the tyrannies produced by a blending of executive and legislative power rejected that political arrangement. Some future generation may, however, deem it so urgent that the President have legislative authority that the Constitution will be amended. We could not sanction the seizures and condemnations of the steel plants in this case without reading Article 2 as giving the President not only the power to execute the laws but to make some. Such a step would most assuredly alter the pattern of the Constitution.

We pay a price for our system of checks and balances, for the distribution of power among the three branches of government. It is a price that today may seem exorbitant to many. Today a kindly President uses the seizure power to effect a wage increase and to keep the steel furnaces in production. Yet tomorrow another President might use the same power to prevent a wage increase, to curb trade-unionists, to regiment labor as oppressively as industry thinks it has been regimented by this seizure.

Mr. Justice Jackson, concurring in the judgment and opinion of the Court, said in part:

That seems to be the logic of an argument tendered at our bar—that the President having, on his own responsibility, sent American troops abroad derives from that act "affirmative power" to seize the means of producing a supply of steel for them. . . .

I cannot foresee all that it might entail if the Court should indorse this argument. Nothing in our Constitution is plainer than that declaration of a war is entrusted only to Congress. Of course, a state of war may in fact exist without a formal declaration. But no doctrine that the Court could promulgate would seem to me more sinister and alarming than that a President whose conduct of foreign affairs is so largely uncontrolled, and often even is unknown, can vastly enlarge his mastery over the internal affairs of the country by his own commitment of the Nation's armed forces to some foreign venture. . . .

The Solicitor General lastly grounds support of the seizure upon nebulous, inherent powers never expressly granted but said to have accrued to the office from the customs and claims of preceding administrations. The plea is for a resulting power to deal with a crisis or an emergency according to the necessities of the case, the unarticulated assumption being that necessity knows no law.

The appeal, however, that we declare the existence of inherent powers *ex necessitate* to meet an emergency asks us to do what many think would be wise, although it is something the forefathers omitted. They knew what emergencies were, knew the pressures they engender for authoritative action, knew, too, how they afford a ready pretext for usurpation. We may also suspect that they suspected that emergency powers would tend to kindle emergencies. . . .

In the practical working of our Government we already have evolved a technique within the framework of the Constitution by which normal executive powers may be considerably expanded to meet an emergency. Congress may and has granted extraordinary authorities which lie dormant in normal times but may be called into play by the Executive in war or upon proclamation of a national emergency. In 1939, upon congressional request, the Attorney General listed ninety-nine such separate statutory grants by Congress of emergency or war-time executive powers. They were invoked from time to time as need appeared. Under this procedure we retain Government by law —special, temporary law, perhaps, but law nonetheless. The public may know the extent and limitations of the powers that can be asserted, and persons affected may be informed from the statute of their rights and duties.

In view of the ease, expedition and safety with which Congress can grant and has granted large emergency powers, certainly ample to embrace this crisis, I am quite unimpressed with the argument that we should affirm possession of them without statute. Such power either has no beginning or it has no end. If it exists, it need submit to no legal restraint. I am not alarmed that it would plunge us straightway into dictatorship, but it is at least a step in that wrong direction. . . .

But I have no illusion that any decision by this Court can keep power in the hands of Congress if it is not wise and timely in meeting its problems. A crisis that challenges the President equally, or perhaps primarily, challenges Congress. If not good law, there was worldly wisdom in the maxim attributed to Napoleon that "The tools belong to the man who can use them." We may say that power to legislate for emergencies belongs in the hands of Congress, but only Congress itself can prevent power from slipping through its fingers.

The essence of our free Government is "leave to live by no man's leave, underneath the law"—to be governed by those impersonal forces which we call law. Our Government is fashioned to fulfill this concept so far as humanly possible. The Executive, except for recommendation and veto, has no legislative power. The executive action we have here originates in the individual will of the President and represents an exercise of authority without law. No one, perhaps not even the President, knows the limits of the power he may seek to exert in this instance and the parties affected cannot learn the limit of their rights. We do not know today what powers over labor or property would be claimed to flow from Government possession if we should legalize it, what rights to compensation would be claimed or recognized, or on what contingency it would end. With all its defects, delays and inconveniences, men have discovered no technique for long preserving free government except that the Executive be under the law, and that the law be made by parliamentary deliberations.

Such institutions may be destined to pass away. But it is the duty of the Court to be last, not first, to give them up.

Mr. Justice Burton, concurring in the opinion and judgment of the Court, said in part:

... In the case before us, Congress authorized a procedure which the President declined to follow. Instead, he followed another procedure which he hoped might eliminate the need for the first. Upon its failure, he issued an executive order to seize the steel properties in the face of the reserved right of Congress to adopt or reject that course as a matter of legislative policy.

This brings us to a further crucial question. Does the President, in such a situation, have inherent constitutional power to seize private property which makes congressional action in relation thereto unnecessary? We find no such power available to him under the present circumstances. The present situation is not comparable to that of an imminent invasion or threatened attack. We do not face the issue of what might be the President's constitutional power to meet such catastrophic situations. Nor is it claimed that the current seizure is in the nature of a military command addressed by the President, as Commander-in-Chief, to a mobilized nation waging, or imminently threatened with, total war.

The controlling fact here is that Congress, within its constitutionally delegated power, has prescribed for the President specific procedures, exclusive of seizure, for his use in meeting the present type of emergency. Congress has reserved to itself the right to determine where and when to authorize the seizure of property in meeting such an emergency. Under these circumstances, the President's order of April 8 invaded the jurisdiction of Congress. It violated the essence of the principle of the separation of governmental powers. Accordingly, the injunction against its effectiveness should be sustained.

Mr. Justice Clark, concurring in the judgment of the Court, said in part:

... In my view ... the Constitution does grant to the President extensive authority in times of grave and imperative national emergency. In fact, to my thinking, such a grant may well be necessary to the very existence of the Constitution itself. As Lincoln aptly said, "[is] it possible to lose the nation and yet preserve the Constitution?" In describing this authority I care not whether one calls it "residual," "inherent," "moral," "implied," "aggregate," "emergency," or otherwise. ...

I conclude that where Congress has laid down specific procedures to deal with the type of crisis confronting the President, he must follow those procedures in meeting the crisis; but that in the absence of such action by Congress, the President's independent power to act depends upon the gravity of the situation confronting the nation. I cannot sustain the seizure in question because here ... Congress had prescribed methods to be followed by the President in meeting the emergency at hand. ...

... The Government made no effort to comply with the procedures established by the Selective Service Act of 1948, a statute which expressly authorizes seizures when producers fail to supply necessary defense matériel. ...

Mr. Chief Justice Vinson, with whom Justices Reed and Minton joined, dissented, saying in part:

Focusing now on the situation confronting the President on the night of April 8, 1952, we cannot but conclude that the President was performing his duty under the Constitution "to take Care that the Laws be faithfully executed"—a duty described by President Benjamin Harrison as "the central idea of the office."

The President reported to Congress the morning after the seizure that he acted because a work stoppage in steel production would immediately imperil the safety of the Nation by preventing execution of the legislative programs for procurement of military equipment. And, while a shutdown could be averted by granting the price concessions requested by plaintiffs, granting such concessions would disrupt the price stabilization program also enacted by Congress. Rather than fail to execute either legislative program, the President acted to execute both.

Much of the argument in this case has been directed at straw men. We do not now have before us the case of a President acting solely on the basis of his own notions of the public welfare. Nor is there any question of unlimited executive power in this case. The President himself closed the door to any such claim when he sent his Message to Congress stating his purpose to abide by any action of Congress, whether approving or disapproving his seizure action. Here, the President immediately made sure that Congress was fully informed of the temporary action he had taken only to preserve the legislative programs from destruction until Congress could act.

The absence of a specific statute authorizing seizure of the steel mills as a mode of executing the laws—both the military procurement program and the anti-inflation program—has not until today been thought to prevent the President from executing the laws. Unlike an administrative commission confined to the enforcement of the statute under which it was created, or the head of a department when administering a particular statute, the President is a constitutional officer charged with taking care that a "mass of legislation" be executed. Flexibility as to mode of execution to meet critical situations is a matter of practical necessity. . . .

As the District Judge stated, this is no time for "timorous" judicial action. But neither is this a time for timorous executive action. Faced with the duty of executing the defense programs which Congress had enacted and the disastrous effects that any stoppage in steel production would have on those programs, the President acted to preserve those programs by seizing the steel mills. There is no question that the possession was other than temporary in character and subject to congressional direction—either approving, disapproving or regulating the manner in which the mills were to be administered and returned to the owners. The President immediately informed Congress of his action and clearly stated his intention to abide by the legislative will. No basis for claims of arbitrary action, unlimited powers or dictatorial usurpation of congressional power appears from the facts of this case. On the contrary, judicial, legislative and executive precedents throughout our history demonstrate that in this case the President acted in full conformity with his duties under the Constitution. Accordingly, we would reverse the order of the District Court.

UNITED STATES v. NIXON

418 U. S. 683; 94 S. Ct. 3090; 41 L. Ed. 2d 1039
(1974)

In setting up a government based on the separation of powers, the Framers deliberately devised a form in which authority was divided and policies would necessarily be made as a result of compromise rather than by a single man or body. Given what they viewed as a choice between "liberty" and "tyranny," they opted for liberty, but the decision to sacrifice speed and efficiency for debate and compromise was perhaps easier to make then than it would be now. The image of George III and the teachings of Montesquieu were fresh in their minds, government played a minimal role in people's lives, and the slowness of communications made quick decisions less important than they are today.

Since the turn of the century, and especially in the last 40 years, all this has changed dramatically. The role of government has grown until it is the dominant force in people's lives, the world has shrunk until the most distant part is only a few hours away, the spectre of George III has been relegated to the pages of history, and effective policy making power has been steadily shifted to the President. With the new pace of the world and our intimate involvement in the affairs of other countries, the frustration and delays imposed by the separation of powers seem scarcely tolerable. Although given virtually dictatorial powers, presidents like Lincoln and Franklin Roosevelt had not betrayed the public trust and that kind of presidency seemed essential to the effectiveness of the United States in that area of world politics upon which our national safety depended. Demands for more government and more effeciency were inexorable and few people saw in them a threat to essential democratic values. The choice made by the Framers seemed scarcely relevant.

Against this background it is easy to view Watergate as a turn in destiny

—a Gilbert and Sullivan operetta played to awaken us to our danger. For it is hard to imagine a more improbable plot in which to set a crucial test of presidential power. Any competent writer of fiction could do better. On June 17, 1972, seven men were caught breaking into the Democratic National Committee headquarters in the Watergate, a luxury apartment-office complex a few blocks from the White House. (The reasons for the break-in are still obscure.) Instead of immediately admitting White House involvement in the affair with an apology for the enthusiasm of his followers (a course which he could certainly have survived politically), the President and his staff undertook the bizarre and dramatically ill-fated "Watergate cover-up." The outcome was the resignation on August 9, 1974, of the President of the United States.

The burglary itself was the culmination of some three years of White House-directed investigation and harassment of political enemies, sparked in part by leaks to the press of the secret bombing of Cambodia and the "Pentagon Papers," and in part by a growing fear that President Nixon might not be reelected in 1972. A successful entry into the DNC the month before had netted nothing of value, and this entry was apparently for the purpose of placing additional electronic bugging equipment.

Five of the "Watergate Seven" pleaded guilty to the burglary and the other two, both members of the Committee to Reelect the President, were convicted. While the upshot of the trial was to suggest that Watergate was merely the work of a few enthusiastic but misguided underlings whose intense loyalty to the President had led them into illegal activities, something about the trial itself belied this conclusion. At its close the presiding judge, John J. Sirica, stated that in his opinion the entire truth had not come out, and on the day of the sentencing he read in court a letter from James W. McCord, Jr., one of those convicted, stating that others involved in the break-in had not been prosecuted, that there had been perjury during the trial, and that pressure had been brought on him and others to plead guilty and keep silent. . . .

A shocked senate investigating committee heard McCord's story then called John W. Dean III, a former counsel to the President. Dean testified for a week, explaining how the White House staff, and ultimately the President, had congratulated him on successfully limiting the case to the few who had been tried and discussed with him the question of executive clemency and hush money for some of them. He said the President had known of the White House involvement almost from the beginning and had been actively involved in permitting the cover-up to continue. Implicated by Dean's testimony were former Attorney General John Mitchell and top presidential aides H. R. Haldeman and John Erlichman. White House denials raised the question: who was telling the truth?

The present constitutional issue appeared with the startling disclosure that presidential conversations for the previous two years had been recorded on tape including, apparently, those crucial conversations with John Dean. Since it seemed the credibility issue could thus be easily resolved, an immediate demand was made for the tapes; but the President, citing the separation of powers and the absolute right of the President to keep his conversations confidential, refused to release them either to the Senate committee or to Archibald Cox, the Special Prosecutor heading the government's investigation of the matter.

There the issue was joined. Judge Sirica, after hearing argument in August of 1973, ordered the President to turn the tapes over to Cox. (He declined to enforce the Senate committee's subpoena for want of jurisdiction.) He conceded that executive privilege did exist, but denied "that it is the Executive that finally determines whether its privilege is properly invoked. . . . Judicial control over the evidence in a case cannot be abdicated to the caprice of executive officers." Nor was he persuaded by the argument based on the separation of powers. Whatever the merits of Mississippi v. Johnson (1866), it would be unrealistic to argue since Youngstown Sheet and Tube Co. v. Sawyer (1952) that compulsory court process cannot touch the White House. "In all candor," he added, "the court fails to perceive any reason for suspending the power of courts to get evidence and rule on questions of privilege in criminal matters simply because it is the President of the United States who holds the evidence." He ordered the tapes turned over to him for in camera inspection with the understanding that unprivileged portions would be made available to the grand jury. After an abortive effort to get the two parties to compromise, the court of appeals sustained Judge Sirica's order; Nixon v. Sirica, 487 Fed. 2d 700 (1973).

Despite a widespread assumption that the President would seek from the Supreme Court that "definitive decision" by which he had announced he would abide, he instead decided to avoid a "constitutional crisis" by declining to appeal the decision and ordered Cox, as "an employee of the executive branch," not to pursue the matter further. Declining to follow the court's order, he proposed instead providing White House "summaries" of the tapes. Cox rejected the offer, and on October 20, in what has become known as the "Saturday Night Massacre," the President accepted the resignation of Attorney General Elliot Richardson when he refused to fire Cox, fired Deputy Attorney General Ruckelshaus when he refused to fire Cox, and finally persuaded Solicitor General Robert H. Bork to fire Cox and his staff of 90 investigators.

Three days later, bowing to a "fire storm" of public protest and the start of formal impeachment proceedings in the House of Representatives, the President agreed to turn over the tapes themselves. By the end of the week Leon Jaworski, a former head of the American Bar Association, had been chosen the new special prosecutor and assured even more independence than Cox had enjoyed.

Although two of the nine tapes ordered released turned out to be missing, and one had an unexplained 18-minute gap in it, enough was produced to clinch the indictments of seven more conspirators, including Mitchell, Haldeman, and Ehrlichman, on charges of conspiring to obstruct justice. On Jaworski's advice that a sitting president could not be indicted, President Nixon was named merely as an "unindicted co-conspirator." On order of Judge Sirica the grand jury evidence, including what tapes Jaworski had received, was turned over to the House Judiciary Committee for use in its impeachment investigation.

But the constitutional confrontation was not over. The House committee subpoenaed 42 more conversations and Jaworski 64, but the President refused to yield and instead made public some 1200 pages of White House-edited transcripts—some of them those already released under court order. The public response to this brutally candid glimpse of the workings of the Nixon presidency was one of horrified shock, and demands for his impeachment became overwhelming. If he would release this kind of material, the argument ran, what was he concealing?

In a last-ditch stand the President not only elected to carry Jaworski's subpoena to the Supreme Court, but to protest his being named an unindicted co-conspirator (a point later dismissed by the Court). Over the objection of the President, the Court agreed to by-pass the Court of Appeals and hear argument in the closing days of its term. The President, in a series of procedural manoeuvers, argued that no case or controversy existed, since the dispute between the President and Jaworski was entirely within the executive branch and the President could decide what evidence he wanted to present in prosecuting a case. The Court, in the case below, rejected this argument on the ground that Jaworski had been given freedom to ask for just such information, that the President had promised him complete freedom to pursue in court any interference by the executive, and this was, in fact, "the kind of controversy courts traditionally resolve."

It is important to note that President Nixon did not claim executive privilege from the tapes on the ground that they contained material involving either military or diplomatic matters. He claimed, rather, that all personal presidential conversations with his aides were privileged because without the assurance of such confidentiality the President could not get the uninhibited advice he needed and the presidency would thus be weakened. It was, in effect, a claim that the sanctity of the presidency was the highest constitutional value, and it was this claim that the Court rejected in the present case.

The President's last constitutional crisis came in the wake of the Court's decision. In 1832, following the Supreme Court's decision in Worcester v.

Georgia, President Andrew Jackson is reputed to have said "John Mar-shall has made his decision, now let him enforce it." The realization that the court has no enforcement machinery at its command must make such a response a tempting one, and President Nixon, who alone knew what the tapes contained, reputedly agonized a whole day over the question whether or not to defy the Supreme Court. But wiser counsel prevailed and he agreed to comply with the Court's order.

Within a week of the Court's decision, while arguing whether to wait for the contents of the tapes, the House judiciary committee voted three arti-cles of impeachment against the President. And President Nixon, even as he began complying with the Court order to release the tapes, elected to release transcripts of three of them which showed that he had known about the Watergate break-in from the beginning. With his concession that he had from the outset lied not only to his supporters in Congress, but even to his own lawyer, those on the judiciary committee who had argued that the President should not be impeached changed their minds. Next morn-ing three members of the congressional leadership visited the President to tell him he could count on no more than 10 votes in the House against impeachment and no more than 15 votes in the Senate against removal. That night, in a TV broadcast to the Nation, President Nixon resigned his office, effective the following noon.

Mr. Chief Justice Burger delivered the opinion of the Court, saying in part:

IV. The Claim of Privilege

A.

Having determined that the requirements of Rule 17(c) were satisfied, we turn to the claim that the subpoena should be quashed because it demands "confidential conversations between a President and his close advisors that it would be inconsistent with the public interest to produce." The first contention is a broad claim that the separation of powers doctrine precludes judicial review of a President's claim of privilege. The second contention is that if he does not prevail on the claim of absolute privilege, the court should hold as a matter of constitutional law that the privilege prevails over the subpoena duces tecum.

In the performance of assigned constitutional duties each branch of the

Government must initially interpret the Constitution, and the interpretation of its powers by any branch is due great respect from the others. The President's counsel, as we have noted, reads the Constitution as providing an absolute privilege of confidentiality for all Presidential communications. Many decisions of this Court, however, have unequivocally reaffirmed the holding of Marbury v. Madison (1803) that "[it] is emphatically the province and duty of the judicial department to say what the law is."

No holding of the Court has defined the scope of judicial power specifically relating to the enforcement of a subpoena for confidential Presidential communications for use in a criminal prosecution, but other exercises of power by the Executive Branch and the Legislative Branch have been found invalid as in conflict with the Constitution. Powell v. McCormack [1969]; Youngstown Sheet & Tube Co. v. Sawyer (1952). In a series of cases, the Court interpreted the explicit immunity conferred by express provisions of the Constitution on Members of the House and Senate by the Speech or Debate Clause, U.S. Const. Art. I §6. Doe v. McMillan (1973); Gravel v. United States (1972). . . . Since this Court has consistently exercised the power to construe and delineate claims arising under express powers, it must follow that the Court has authority to interpret claims with respect to powers alleged to derive from enumerated powers.

Our system of government "requires that federal courts on occasion interpret the Constitution in a manner at variance with the construction given the document by another branch." Powell v. McCormack. And in Baker v. Carr [1962], the Court stated: "Deciding whether a matter has in any measure been committed by the Constitution to another branch of government, or whether the action of that branch exceeds whatever authority has been committed, is itself a delicate exercise in constitutional interpretation, and is a responsibility of this Court as ultimate interpreter of the Constitution." Notwithstanding the deference each branch must accord the others, the "judicial Power of the United States" vested in the federal courts by Art. III, §1, of the Constitution can no more be shared with the Executive Branch than the Chief Executive, for example, can share with the Judiciary the veto power, or the Congress share with the Judiciary the power to override a Presidential veto. Any other conclusion would be contrary to the basic concept of separation of powers and the checks and balances that flow from the scheme of a tripartite government. . . . We therefore reaffirm that it is the province and duty of this Court "to say what the law is" with respect to the claim of privilege presented in this case. Marbury v. Madison.

B.

In support of his claim of absolute privilege, the President's counsel urges two grounds, one of which is common to all governments and one of which is peculiar to our system of separation of powers. The first ground is the valid need for protection of communications between high Government officials and those who advise and assist them in the performance of their manifold duties; the importance of this confidentiality is too plain to require further discussion. Human experience teaches that those who expect public dissemination of their remarks may well temper candor with a concern for appearances and for their own interests to the detriment of the decision making process.* Whatever the nature of the privilege of confidentiality of Presidential communications in the exercise of Art. II powers the privilege can be said to derive from the supremacy of each branch within its own assigned area of constitutional duties. Certain powers and privileges flow from the nature of enumerated powers;** the protection of the confidentiality of Presidential communications has similar constitutional underpinnings.

The second ground asserted by the President's counsel in support of the claim of absolute privilege rests on the doctrine of separation of powers. Here it is argued that the independence of the Executive Branch within its own sphere, Humphrey's Executor v. United States [1935]; Kilbourn v. Thompson (1881), insulates a President from a judicial subpoena in an ongoing criminal prosecution, and thereby protects confidential presidential communications. However, neither the doctrine of separation of powers, nor the need for confidentiality of high level communications, without more, can sustain an absolute, unqualified Presidential privilege of immunity from judicial process under all circumstances. The President's need for complete candor and objectivity from advisers calls for great deference from the courts. However, when the privilege depends solely on the broad, undifferentiated claim of public interest in the confidentiality of such conversations, a confrontation with other values arises. Absent a claim of need to protect military, diplomatic, or sensitive national security secrets, we find it difficult to accept the argument that even the very important interest in confidentiality of Presidential communications is significantly diminished by production of such material for in camera inspection with all the protection that a district court will be obliged to provide.

---

*There is nothing novel about governmental confidentiality. The meetings of the Constitutional Convention in 1787 were conducted in complete privacy. 1 M. Farrand. The Records of the Federal Convention of 1787, pp. xi–xxv (1911). Moreover, all records of those meetings were sealed for more than 30 years after the Convention. Most of the Framers acknowledged that without secrecy no constitution of the kind that was developed could have been written. C. Warren, The Making of the Constitution, 134–139 (1937).

**The Special Prosecutor argues that there is no provision in the Constitution for a presidential privilege as to the President's communications corresponding to the privilege of Members of Congress under the Speech or Debate Clause. But the silence of the Constitution on this score is not dispositive. "The rule of constitutional interpretation announced in McCulloch v. Maryland [1819] that that which was reasonably appropriate and relevant to the exercise of a granted power was to be considered as accompanying the grant, has been so universally applied that it suffices merely to state it." Marshall v. Gordon (1917).

The impediment that an absolute, unqualified privilege would place in the way of the primary constitutional duty of the Judicial Branch to do justice in criminal prosecutions would plainly conflict with the function of the courts under Art. III. In designing the structure of our Government and dividing and allocating the sovereign power among three co-equal branches, the Framers of the Constitution sought to provide a comprehensive system, but the separate powers were not intended to operate with absolute independence. "While the Constitution diffuses power the better to secure liberty, it also contemplates that practice will integrate the dispersed powers into a workable government. It enjoins upon its branches separateness but interdependence, autonomy but reciprocity." Youngstown Sheet & Tube Co. v. Sawyer. (Jackson, J., concurring). To read the Art. II powers of the President as providing an absolute privilege as against a subpoena essential to enforcement of criminal statutes on no more than a generalized claim of the public interest in confidentiality of nonmilitary and nondiplomatic discussions would upset the constitutional balance of "a workable government" and gravely impair the role of the courts under Art. III.

C.

Since we conclude that the legitimate needs of the judicial process may outweigh Presidential privilege, it is necessary to resolve those competing interests in a manner that preserves the essential functions of each branch. The right and indeed the duty to resolve that question does not free the judiciary from according high respect to the representations made on behalf of the President. United States v. Burr, 25 Fed. Cas. 187 (No. 14,694) (1807).

The expectation of a President to the confidentiality of his conversations and correspondence, like the claim of confidentiality of judicial deliberations, for example, has all the values to which we accord deference for the privacy of all citizens and added to those values the necessity for protection of the public interest in candid, objective, and even blunt or harsh opinions in Presidential decision-making. A President and those who assist him must be free to explore alternatives in the process of shaping policies and making decisions and to do so in a way many would be unwilling to express except privately. These are the considerations justifying a presumptive privilege for Presidential communications. The privilege is fundamental to the operation of government and inextricably rooted in the separation of powers under the Constitution. In Nixon v. Sirica, 487 F. 2d 700 (1973), the Court of Appeals held that such Presidential communications are "presumptively privileged," and this position is accepted by both parties in the present litigation. We agree with Mr. Chief Justice Marshall's observation, therefore, that "[in] no case of this kind would a court be required to proceed against the President as against an ordinary individual." United States v. Burr.

But this presumptive privilege must be considered in light of our historic commitment to the rule of law. This is nowhere more profoundly manifest than in our view that "the twofold aim [of criminal justice] is that guilt shall not escape or innocence suffer." Berger v. United States [1935]. We have elected to employ an adversary system of criminal justice in which the parties contest all issues before a court of law. The need to develop all relevant facts in the adversary system is both fundamental and comprehensive. The ends of criminal justice would be defeated if judgments were to be founded on a partial or speculative presentation of the facts. The very integrity of the judicial system and public confidence in the system depend on full disclosure of all the facts, within the framework of the rules of evidence. To ensure that justice is done, it is imperative to the function of courts that compulsory process be available for the production of evidence needed either by the prosecution or by the defense.

Only recently the Court restated the ancient proposition of law, albeit in the context of a grand jury inquiry rather than a trial, "that 'the public . . . has a right to every man's evidence,' except for those persons protected by a constitutional, common-law, or statutory privilege, United States v. Bryan [1950]; [United States v. Dionisio (1973)]. The privileges referred to by the Court are designed to protect weighty and legitimate competing interests. Thus, the Fifth Amendment to the Constitution provides that no man "shall be compelled in any criminal case to be a witness against himself." And, generally an attorney or a priest may not be required to disclose what has been revealed in professional confidence. These and other interests are recognized in law by privileges against forced disclosure, established in the Constitution, by statute, or at common law. Whatever their origins, these exceptions to the demand for every man's evidence are not lightly created nor expansively construed, for they are in derogation of the search for truth.

In this case the President challenges a subpoena served on him as a third party requiring the production of materials for use in a criminal prosecution; he does so on the claim that he has a privilege against disclosure of confidential communications. He does not place his claim of privilege on the ground they are military or diplomatic secrets. As to these areas of Art. II duties the courts have traditionally shown the utmost deference to Presidential responsibilities. In C. & S. Air Lines v. Waterman Steamship Corp. (1948), dealing with Presidential authority involving foreign policy considerations, the Court said: "The President, both as Commander-in-Chief and as the Nation's organ for foreign affairs, has available intelligence services whose reports are not and ought not to be published to the world. It would be intolerable that courts, without the relevant information, should review and perhaps nullify actions of the Executive taken on information properly held secret." In United States v. Reynolds (1953), dealing with a claimant's demand for evidence in a damage case against the Government the Court said: "It may be possible to satisfy the court, from all the circumstances of the case, that there is a reasonable danger that compulsion of the evidence will expose military matters which, in the interest of national security, should not be divulged. When this is the case, the occasion for the privilege is appropriate, and the court should not jeopardize the security which the privilege is meant to protect by insisting upon an examination of the evidence, even by the judge alone, in chambers." No case of the Court, however, has extended this high degree of deference to a President's generalized interest in confidentiality. Nowhere in the Constitution, as we have noted earlier, is there any explicit reference to a privilege of confidentiality, yet to the extent this interest relates to the effective discharge of a President's powers, it is constitutionally based.

The right to the production of all evidence at a criminal trial similarly has constitutional dimensions. The Sixth Amendment explicitly confers upon every defendant in a criminal trial the right "to be confronted with the witnesses against him" and "to have compulsory process for obtaining witnesses in his favor." Moreover, the Fifth Amendment also guarantees that no person shall be deprived of liberty without due process of law. It is the manifest duty of the courts to vindicate those guarantees, and to accomplish that it is essential that all relevant and admissible evidence be produced.

In this case we must weigh the importance of the general privilege of confidentiality of Presidential communications in performance of his responsibilities against the inroads of such a privilege on the fair administration of criminal justice.* The interest in preserving confidentiality is weighty indeed and entitled to great respect. However, we cannot conclude that advisers will be moved to temper the candor of their remarks by the infrequent occasions of disclosure because of the possibility that such conversations will be called for in the context of a criminal prosecution.**

---

*We are not here concerned with the balance between the President's generalized interest in confidentiality and the need for relevant evidence in civil litigation, nor with that between the confidentiality interest and congressional demands for information, nor with the President's interest in preserving state secrets. We address only the conflict between the President's assertion of a generalized privilege of confidentiality and the constitutional need for relevant evidence in criminal trials.

**Mr. Justice Cardozo made this point in an analogous context. Speaking for a unanimous Court in Clark v. United States (1933), he emphasized the importance of maintaining the secrecy of the deliberations of a petit jury in a criminal case. "Freedom of debate might be stifled and independence of thought checked if jurors were made to feel that their arguments and ballots were to be freely published to the world." Nonetheless, the Court also recognized that isolated inroads on confidentiality designed to serve the paramount need of the criminal law would not vitiate the interests served by secrecy: "A juror of integrity and reasonable firmness will not fear to speak his mind if the confidences of debate are barred to the ears of mere impertinence or malice. He will not expect to be shielded against the disclosure of his conduct in the event that there is evidence reflecting upon his honor. The chance that now and then there may be found some timid soul who will take counsel of his fears and give way to their repressive power is too remote and shadowy to shape the course of justice."

On the other hand, the allowance of the privilege to withhold evidence that is demonstrably relevant in a criminal trial would cut deeply into the guarantee of due process of law and gravely impair the basic function of the courts. A President's acknowledged need for confidentiality in the communications of his office is general in nature; whereas the constitutional need for production of relevant evidence in a criminal proceeding is specific and central to the fair adjudication of a particular criminal case in the administration of justice. Without access to specific facts a criminal prosecution may be totally frustrated. The President's broad interest in confidentiality of communications will not be vitiated by disclosure of a limited number of conversations preliminarily shown to have some bearing on the pending criminal cases.

We conclude that when the ground for asserting privilege as to subpoenaed materials sought for use in a criminal trial is based only on the generalized interest in confidentiality, it cannot prevail over the fundamental demands of due process of law in the fair administration of criminal justice. The generalized assertion of privilege must yield to the demonstrated, specific need for evidence in a pending criminal trial.

D.

We have earlier determined that the District Court did not err in authorizing the issuance of the subpoena. If a President concludes that compliance with a subpoena would be injurious to the public interest he may properly, as was done here, invoke a claim of privilege on the return of the subpoena. Upon receiving a claim of privilege from the Chief Executive, it became the further duty of the District Court to treat the subpoenaed material as presumptively privileged and to require the Special Prosecutor to demonstrate that the Presidential material was "essential to the justice of the [pending criminal] case." United States v. Burr. Here the District Court treated the material as presumptively privileged, proceeded to find that the Special Prosecutor had made sufficient showing to rebut the presumption, and ordered an in camera examination of the subpoenaed material. On the basis of our examination of the record we are unable to conclude that the District Court erred in ordering the inspection. Accordingly we affirm the order of the District Court that subpoenaed materials be transmitted to that court. We now turn to the important question of the District Court's responsibilities in conducting the in camera examination of Presidential materials or communications delivered under the compulsion of the subpoena duces tecum.

E.

Enforcement of the subpoena duces tecum was stayed pending this Court's resolution of the issues raised by the petitions for certiorari. Those issues now having been disposed of, the matter of implementation will rest with the District Court. "[T]he guard, furnished to [the President] to protect him from being harassed by vexatious and unnecessary subpoenas, is to be looked for in the conduct of a [district] court after the subpoenas have issued; not in any circumstance which is to precede their being issued." United States v. Burr. Statements that meet the test of admissibility and relevance must be isolated; all other material must be excised. At this stage the District Court is not limited to representations of the Special Prosecutor as to the evidence sought by the subpoena; the material will be available to the District Court. It is elementary that in camera inspection of evidence is always a procedure calling for scrupulous protection against any release or publication of material not found by the court, at that stage, probably admissible in evidence and relevant to the issues of the trial for which it is sought. That being true of an ordinary situation, it is obvious that the District Court has a very heavy responsibility to see to it that presidential conversations, which are either not relevant or not admissible, are accorded that high degree of respect due the President of the United States. Mr. Chief Justice Marshall sitting as a trial judge in the Burr case was extraordinarily careful to point out that "[i]n no case of this kind would a court be required to proceed against the president as against an ordinary individual." Marshall's statement cannot be read to mean in any sense that a President is above the law, but relates to the singularly unique role under Art. II of a President's communications and activities, related to the performance of duties under that Article. Moreover, a President's communications and activities encompass a vastly wider range of sensitive material than would be true of any "ordinary individual." It is therefore necessary* in the public interest to afford Presidential confidentiality the greatest protection consistent with the fair administration of justice. The need for confidentiality even as to idle conversations with associates in which casual reference might be made concerning political leaders within the country or foreign statesmen is too obvious to call for further treatment. We have no doubt that the District Judge will at all times accord to presidential records that high degree of deference suggested in United States v. Burr and will discharge his responsibility to see to it that until released to the Special Prosecutor no in camera material is revealed to anyone. This burden applies with even greater force to excised material; once the decision is made to excise, the material is restored to its privileged status and should be returned under seal to its lawful custodian.

---

*When the subpoenaed material is delivered to the District Judge in camera questions may arise as to the excising of parts and it lies within the discretion of that court to seek the aid of the Special Prosecutor and the President's counsel for in camera consideration of the validity of particular excisions, whether the basis of excision is relevancy or admissibility or under such cases as Reynolds or Waterman Steamship.

Since this matter came before the Court during the pendency of a criminal prosecution, and on representations that time is of the essence, the mandate shall issue forthwith.

Affirmed.

Mr. Justice Rehnquist took no part in the consideration or decision of these cases.

4

Principles of the Federal System

McCULLOCH v. MARYLAND
4 Wheaton 316; 4 L. Ed. 579 (1819)

Perhaps the most difficult problem faced by the government of a large nation is the reconciliation of local and national interests. To be strong, a country must have a strong central government. To be strong it must also have the support of its people, and this support will come only if the people are allowed to solve at the local level those problems which they regard as local in nature. The American Revolution stemmed from the failure of George III to allow his American colonies sufficient local autonomy, and the framers of the new Constitution knew that they must find a wiser adjustment of these competing interests and loyalties if the country was to endure as a political unit. The solution they worked out was to delegate in Article I, Sec. 8, certain enumerated powers to the national government. The Tenth Amendment declared that those powers not so delegated were left to the states, or to the people, to be later assigned by constitutional amendments.

One of the axioms of American constitutional law is that Congress has only powers that are delegated to it by the Constitution, or are reasonably implied from those so delegated. The origin and history of this theory of national power is as follows: when Randolph proposed the Virginia Plan in the Constitutional Convention of 1787, it contained the only sound principle by which the powers of nation and state could be divided. It stated: ". . . the national legislature ought to be empowered . . . to legislate in all cases to which the separate states are incompetent, or in which the harmony of the United States may be interrupted by the exercise of individual legislation." This stated a principle rather than a method of allocating powers, and as a principle it was received with approval by the Convention. After two months of debate the Convention created a committee of detail to formulate the text of a constitution and gave it various instructions. The instruction with regard to national powers was that: "The national legislature ought to possess the legislative rights vested in Congress by the Confederation; and, moreover, to legislate in all cases for the general interest of the Union, and also in those to which the states are separately incompetent, or in which the harmony of the United States may be interrupted by individual legislation." Acting upon this instruction the committee of detail reported back to the Convention the specific enumeration of the powers of Congress found in Article I, Sec. 8. The committee, adhering, as did the entire Convention, to the principle of delegated powers, thus gave to the new Congress all of the powers then believed to be described in the article of instruction; and by providing for amendments in Article V, it created the means by which those powers could be increased or altered when it seemed desirable to do so.

In spite of this very conclusive evidence to the contrary, it has sometimes been urged that the framers intended that Congress should have the power to deal with any truly national problem whether that power is delegated to it or not. James Wilson, a member of the Convention of 1787 and later a justice of the Supreme Court, is quoted, not too convincingly, as sponsoring this theory. It remained for President Theodore Roosevelt to publicize the doctrine in his forceful discussions of what he called the New Nationalism. He pointed out the awkward consequences of the fact that business combinations had grown to such proportions that they were beyond the legislative reach of any state or states, and yet could not be effectively controlled by Congress since the power of Congress was limited to the interstate commerce aspects of big business. In one of his better phrases he referred to the "twilight zone" in our constitutional system, a zone lying safely between state and federal authority, to which "malefactors of great wealth" might repair and be safe from punishment and restraint. He urged that "whenever the states cannot act, because the need to be met is not one merely of a single locality, then the national government, representing all the people, should have complete power to act."

The Supreme Court rejected this doctrine out of hand in Kansas v. Colorado (1907), a case in which the United States tried to intervene in a dispute over the control of river water on the ground that the problem of reclaiming arid land was "national," since it was beyond the geographical jurisdiction of any one state. The Court emphasized that ours is a government of "enumerated powers" and pointed out that the Tenth

Amendment had been adopted because of a "widespread fear that the national government might, under the pressure of a supposed general warfare, attempt to exercise powers which had not been granted."

Although the Court has never questioned the doctrine that the national government is one of delegated powers, as early as 1819 in McCulloch v. Maryland, printed below, it made clear that the fact that they were delegated did not mean they must be given a narrow or rigid interpretation. When Congress in 1791 chartered the First Bank of the United States, it was only after a most full and bitter argument as to whether it had the power to do so. Hamilton, who had proposed the creation of the bank, had written an elaborate opinion defending it as an exercise of a power reasonably implied from those expressly delegated to Congress. Jefferson and his friends had stoutly maintained that congressional powers must be strictly construed and that the granting of the charter was an act of unwarrantable usurpation. Nevertheless the charter of the First Bank was never attacked in the courts as being unconstitutional, and the institution continued to exist until its charter expired in 1811. The financial conditions ensuing after the War of 1812 made the reestablishment of the bank desirable, and the Second Bank of the United States was accordingly chartered in 1816. Almost immediately it incurred the bitter odium of large sections of the country, especially of the West and South. The bank was largely under the control of the Federalists, who were accused of using it as a political machine and of wielding its great influence for political purposes; its stock was largely held by British capitalists and other foreign investors; and it was accused of being responsible for a period of financial depression which brought ruin to thousands. It is true that the bank had begun operations under corrupt and inefficient management and had encouraged a high degree of inflation of credits. This had resulted in heavy losses to investors; in the state of Maryland the Baltimore branch collapsed with a loss to Maryland investors alone of a sum variously estimated from $1,700,000 to $3,000,000. Wiser counsels prevailed shortly, however, and the bank faced about and embarked upon a financial course as conservative as it had hitherto been headlong. It refused to accept the bank notes of the imprudent state banks and insisted upon the liquidation of its credits. One after another these overinflated state banks failed, and hundreds of reckless speculators were ruined. Money was almost unobtainable. While most of this financial disaster was the inevitable result of the orgies of inflation and speculation in which the frontier communities in particular had been indulging, the Bank of the United States was popularly regarded as the cause of the disaster, as the ruthless "money trust" which was ruining the prosperity of the country. A popular demand for legislative control of the bank was set up, and eight states passed either laws or constitutional amendments restricting the activities of the bank or imposing heavy bur-

dens upon it. The law involved in this case, passed by the legislature of Maryland, which was particularly hostile to the bank because of its earlier debacle, is typical of this legislative onslaught.

The Maryland statute forbade all banks not chartered by the state itself to issue bank notes save upon special stamped paper obtainable upon the payment of a very heavy tax. This requirement could be commuted by the payment of an annual tax to the state of $15,000. A penalty of $500 forfeiture was inflicted for each offense, an amount which in the case of the now large and prosperous Baltimore branch of the Bank of the United States would have come possibly to millions of dollars. McCulloch, the cashier of the branch in Baltimore, issued notes without complying with the state law, and this action was brought on behalf of the state of Maryland to recover the penalties.

The case was argued for nine days before the Supreme Court by the greatest lawyers of the day; William Pinkney, Daniel Webster, and William Wirt defended the bank, while Luther Martin, Joseph Hopkinson, and Walter Jones represented the state of Maryland. The opinion of Marshall in the case is commonly regarded as his greatest state paper.

The announcement of the decision was the signal for a veritable storm of abuse directed against the Supreme Court. Judge Roane, of the Virginia court of appeals, published a series of newspaper attacks upon the decision so bitter that Marshall was led to write a reply in his defense. The Virginia legislature passed a resolution urging that the Supreme Court be shorn of its power to pass upon cases to which states were parties. Ohio, which had previously passed a law taxing each branch of the Bank of the United States within its limits $50,000 a year, defied the Supreme Court and proceeded to collect the tax in spite of its decision, a position from which it was later obligated to withdraw; see Osborn v. The Bank of the United States (1824). The attack upon the Court in this case was directed in large part against the failure of that tribunal to invalidate an act of Congress (incorporating the bank) and not against the exercise of the judicial veto. The decision was peculiarly odious to the strict constructionists because it not only sustained the doctrine of the implied powers of Congress but also recognized the binding effect of an implied limitation upon the states preventing them from interfering with the functioning of federal agencies.

The doctrine of implied powers in Congress was not new in this case. Not only had it been ably expounded by Hamilton, as mentioned above, but in the case of United States v. Fisher (1805), which had been decided 14 years before, Marshall himself had given expression to the doctrine; but as that case did not relate to any such important political issue as did the bank case, the decision at that time had evoked no comment.

Later cases make it clear that the implied powers of Congress may be derived not only from a single delegated power but also from a combina-

tion of such powers taken together. Thus the power to condemn by eminent domain the land for the national cemetery at Gettysburg was sustained upon the theory that it could thus be implied from a group of federal powers combined. This has sometimes been called the theory of "resulting powers." See United States v. Gettysburg Electric Ry. Co. (1896). In Cleveland v. United States (1945) the Court came near to holding that a power of Congress can be implied from an implied power. The Court held that Congress could validly authorize the use of eminent domain for the purpose of securing land for a federal housing development which Congress could constitutionally provide for as a means of exercising its delegated power to spend money, raised by taxation, for the "public welfare."

Mr. Chief Justice Marshall delivered the opinion of the Court, saying in part:

In the case now to be determined, the defendant, a sovereign state, denies the obligation of a law enacted by the legislature of the Union, and the plaintiff, on his part, contests the validity of an act which has been passed by the legislature of that state. The constitution of our country, in its most interesting and vital parts, is to be considered; the conflicting powers of the government of the Union and of its members, as marked in that constitution, are to be discussed; and an opinion given, which may essentially influence the great operations of the government. No tribunal can approach such a question without a deep sense of its importance, and of the awful responsibility involved in its decision. But it must be decided peacefully, or remain a source of hostile legislation, perhaps of hostility of a still more serious nature; and if it is to be so decided, by this tribunal alone can the decision be made. On the Supreme Court of the United States has the constitution of our country devolved this important duty.

The first question made in the cause is, has Congress power to incorporate a bank? . . .

In discussing this question, the counsel for the state of Maryland have deemed it of some importance, in the construction of the constitution, to consider that instrument not as emanating from the people, but as the act of sovereign and independent states. The powers of the general government, it has been said, are delegated by the states, who alone are truly sovereign; and must be exercised in subordination to the states, who alone possess supreme dominion.

It would be difficult to sustain this proposition. The convention which framed the constitution was, indeed elected by the state legislatures. But the instrument, when it came from their hands, was a mere proposal, without obligation, or pretensions to it. It was reported to the then existing Congress of the United States, with a request that it might "be submitted to a convention of delegates, chosen in each state by the people thereof, under the recommendation of its legislature, for their assent and ratification." This mode of proceeding was adopted; and by the convention, by Congress, and by the state legislatures, the instrument was submitted to the people. They acted upon it in the only manner in which they can act safely, effectively, and wisely, on such a subject, by assembling in convention. It is true, they assembled in their several states—and where else should they have assembled? No political dreamer was ever wild enough to think of breaking down the lines which separate the state and of compounding the American people into one common mass. Of consequence, when they act, they act in their states. But the measures they adopt do not, on that account, cease to be the measures of the people themselves, or become the measures of the state governments.

From these conventions the constitution derives its whole authority. The government proceeds directly from the people; is "ordained and established" in the name of the people; and is declared to be ordained, "in order to form a more perfect union, establish justice, insure domestic tranquility, and secure the blessings of liberty to themselves and to their posterity." The assent of the states, in their sovereign capacity, is implied in calling a convention, and thus submitting that instrument to the people. But the people were at perfect liberty to accept or reject it; and their act was final. It required not the affirmance, and could not be negatived, by the state governments. The constitution, when thus adopted, was of complete obligation, and bound the state sovereignties.

It has been said that the people had already surrendered all their powers to the state sovereignties, and had nothing more to give. But, surely, the question whether they may resume and modify the powers granted to government does not remain to be settled in this country. Much more might the legitimacy of the general government be doubted, had it been created by the states. The powers delegated to the state sovereignties were to be exercised by themselves, not by a distinct and independent sovereignty, created by themselves. To the formation of a league, such as was the confederation, the state sovereignties were certainly competent. But when, "in order to form a more perfect union," it was deemed necessary to change this alliance into an effective government, possessing great and sovereign powers, and acting directly on the people, the necessity of referring it to the people, and of deriving its powers directly from them, was felt and acknowledged by all.

The government of the Union, then (whatever may be the influence of this fact on the case), is, emphatically, and truly, a government of the people. In form and in substance it emanates from them. Its powers are granted by them, and are to be exercised directly on them, and for their benefit.

This government is acknowledged by all to be one of enumerated powers. The principle, that it can exercise only the powers granted to it, would seem too apparent to have required to be enforced by all those arguments which its enlightened friends, while it was depending before the people, found it necessary to urge. That principle is now universally admitted. But the question respecting the extent of the powers actually granted, is perpetually arising, and will probably continue to arise, as long as our system shall exist.

In discussing these questions, the conflicting powers of the general and state government must be brought into view, and the supremacy of their respective laws, where they are in opposition, must be settled.

If any one proposition could command the universal assent of mankind, we might expect it would be this—that the government of the Union, though limited in its powers, is supreme within its sphere of action. This would seem to result necessarily from its nature. It is the government of all; its powers are delegated by all; it represents all, and acts for all. Though any one state may be willing to control its operations, no state is willing to allow others to control them. The nation, on those subjects on which it can act, must necessarily bind its component parts. But this question is not left to mere reason; the people have, in express terms, decided it by saying, "this constitution, and the laws of the United States, which shall be made in pursuance thereof," "shall be the supreme law of the land," and by requiring that the members of the state legislatures, and the officers of the executive and judicial departments of the states, shall take the oath of fidelity to it.

The government of the United States, then, though limited in its powers, is supreme; and its laws, when made in pursuance of the constitution, form the supreme law of the land, "anything in the constitution or laws of any state to the contrary notwithstanding."

Among the enumerated powers, we do not find that of establishing a bank or creating a corporation. But there is no phrase in the instrument which, like the articles of confederation, excludes incidental or implied powers; and which requires that everything granted shall be expressly and minutely described. Even the 10th amendment, which was framed for the purpose of quieting the excessive jealousies which had been excited, omits the word "expressly," and declares only that the powers "not delegated to the United States, nor prohibited to the states, are reserved to the states or to the people"; thus leaving the question, whether the particular power which may become the subject of contest has been delegated to the one government, or prohibited to the other, to depend on a fair construction of the whole instrument. The men who drew and adopted this amendment had experienced the embarrassments resulting from the insertion of this word in the articles of confederation, and probably omitted it to avoid those embarrassments. A constitution, to contain an accurate detail of all the subdivisions of which its great powers will admit, and of all the means by which they may be carried into execution, would partake of the prolixity of a legal code, and could scarcely be embraced by the human mind. It would probably never be understood by the public. Its nature, therefore, requires, that only its great outlines should be marked, its important objects designated, and the minor ingredients which compose those objects be deduced from the nature of the objects themselves. That this idea was entertained by the framers of the American constitution, is not only to be inferred from the nature of the instrument, but from the language. Why else were some of the limitations, found in the ninth section of the 1st article, introduced? It is also, in some degree, warranted by their having omitted to use any restrictive term which might prevent its receiving a fair and just interpretation. In considering this question, then, we must never forget that it is a constitution we are expounding.

Although, among the enumerated powers of government, we do not find the word "bank" or "incorporation," we find the great powers to lay and collect taxes; to borrow money; to regulate commerce; to declare and conduct a war; and to raise and support armies and navies. The sword and the purse, all the external relations, and no inconsiderable portion of the industry of the nation, are entrusted to its government. It can never be pretended that these vast powers draw after them others of inferior importance, merely because they are inferior. Such an idea can never be advanced. But it may, with great reason, be contended, that a government, entrusted with such ample powers, on the due execution of which the happiness and prosperity of the nation so vitally depends, must also be entrusted with ample means for their execution. The power being given, it is the interest of the nation to facilitate its execution. It can never be their interest, and cannot be presumed to have been their intention, to clog and embarrass its execution by withholding the most appropriate means. Throughout this vast republic, from the St. Croix to the Gulf of Mexico, from the Atlantic to the Pacific, revenue is to be collected and expended, armies are to be marched and supported. The exigencies of the nation may require that the treasure raised in the north should be transported to the south, that raised in the east conveyed to the west, or that this order should be reversed. Is that construction of the constitution to be preferred which would render these operations difficult, hazardous, and expensive? Can we adopt that construction (unless the words imperiously require it) which would impute to the framers of that instrument, when granting these powers for the public good, the intention of impeding their exercise by withholding a choice of means? If, indeed, such be the mandate of the constitution, we have only to obey; but that instrument does not profess to enumerate the means by which the powers it confers may be executed; nor does it prohibit the creation of a corporation, if the existence of such a being be essential to the beneficial exercise of those powers. It is, then, the subject of fair inquiry, how far such means may be employed. It is not denied that the powers given to the government imply the ordinary means of execution. That, for example, of raising revenue, and applying it to national purposes, is admitted to imply the power of conveying money from place to place, as the exigencies of the nation may require, and of employing the usual means of conveyance. But it is denied that the government has its choice of means; or, that it may employ the most convenient means, if, to employ them, it be necessary to erect a corporation.

. . . The power of creating a corporation, though appertaining to sovereignty, is not, like the power of making war, or levying taxes, or of regulating commerce, a great substantive and independent power, which cannot be implied as incidental to other powers, or used as a means of executing them. It is never the end for which other powers are exercised, but a means by which other objects are accomplished. No contributions are made to charity for the sake of an incorporation, but a corporation is created to administer the charity; no seminary of learning is instituted in order to be incorporated, but the corporate character is conferred to subserve the purposes of education. No city was ever built with the sole object of being incorporated, but is incorporated as affording the best means of being well governed. The power of creating a corporation is never used for its own sake, but for the purpose of effecting something else. No sufficient reason is, therefore, perceived, why it may not pass as incidental to those powers which are expressly given, if it be a direct mode of executing them.

But the constitution of the United States has not left the right of Congress to employ the necessary means for the execution of the powers conferred on the government to general reasoning. To its enumeration of powers is added that of making "all laws which shall be necessary and proper, for carrying into execution the foregoing powers, and all other powers vested by this constitution, in the government of the United States, or in any department thereof."

The counsel for the State of Maryland have urged various arguments, to prove that this clause, though in terms of grant of power, is not so in effect; but is really restrictive of the general right, which might otherwise be implied, of selecting means for executing the enumerated powers.

In support of this proposition, they have found it necessary to contend, that this clause was inserted for the purpose of conferring on Congress the power of making laws. That, without it, doubts might be entertained whether Congress could exercise its powers in the form of legislation.

But could this be the object for which it was inserted? . . . That a legislature, endowed with legislative powers, can legislate, is a proposition too self-evident to have been questioned.

But the argument on which most reliance is placed, is drawn from the peculiar language of this clause. Congress is not empowered by it to make all laws, which may have relation to the powers conferred on the government, but such only as may be "necessary and proper" for carrying them into execution. The word "necessary" is considered as controlling the whole sentence, and as limiting the right to pass laws for the execution of the granted powers, to such as are indispensable, and without which the power would be nugatory. That it excludes the choice of means, and leaves to Congress, in each case, that only which is most direct and simple.

Is it true that this is the sense in which the word "necessary" is always used? Does it always import an absolute physical necessity, so strong that one thing, to which another may be termed necessary, cannot exist without that other? We think it does not. If reference be had to its use, in the common affairs of the world, or in approved authors, we find that it frequently imports no more than that one thing is convenient, or useful, or essential to another. To employ the means necessary to an end, is generally understood as employing any means calculated to produce the end, and not as being confined to those single means, without which the end would be entirely unattainable. Such is the character of human language, that no word conveys to the mind, in all situations, one single definite idea; and nothing is more common than to use words in a figurative sense. Almost all compositions contain words, which, taken in their rigorous sense, would convey a meaning different from that which is obviously intended. It is essential to just construction, that many words which import something excessive should be understood in a more mitigated sense —in that sense which common usage justifies. The word "necessary" is of this description. It has not a fixed character peculiar to itself. It admits of all degrees of comparison; and is often connected with other words, which increase or diminish the impression the mind receives of the urgency it imports. A thing may be necessary, very necessary, absolutely or indispensably necessary. To no mind would the same idea be conveyed by these several phrases. ... This word, then, like others, is used in various senses; and, in its construction, the subject, the context, the intention of the person using them, are all to be taken into view.

Let this be done in the case under consideration. The subject is the execution of those great powers on which the welfare of a nation essentially depends. It must have been the intention of those who gave these powers, to insure, as far as human prudence could insure, their beneficial execution. This could not be done by confiding the choice of means to such narrow limits as not to leave it in the power of Congress to adopt any which might be appropriate, and which were conducive to the end. This provision is made in a constitution intended to endure for ages to come, and, consequently, to be adapted to the various crises of human affairs. To have prescribed the means by which government should, in all future time, execute its powers, would have been to change, entirely, the character of the instrument, and give it the properties of a legal code. It would have been an unwise attempt to provide, by immutable rules, for exigencies which, if foreseen at all, must have been seen dimly, and which can be best provided for as they occur. To have declared that the best means shall not be used, but those alone without which the power given would be nugatory, would have been to deprive the legislature of the capacity to avail itself of experience, to exercise its reason, and to accommodate its legislation to circumstances. . . .

But the argument which most conclusively demonstrates the error of the construction contended for by the counsel for the state of Maryland, is founded on the intention of the convention, as manifested in the whole clause. To waste time and argument in proving that without it Congress might carry its powers into execution, would be not much less idle than to hold a lighted taper to the sun. As little can it be required to prove, that in the absence of this clause, Congress would have some choice of means. That it might employ those which, in its judgment, would most advantageously effect the object to be accomplished. That any means adapted to the end, any means which tended directly to the execution of the constitutional powers of the government, were in themselves constitutional. This clause, as construed by the state of Maryland, would abridge, and almost annihilate this useful and necessary right of the legislature to select its means. That this could not be intended, is, we should think, had it not been already controverted, too apparent for controversy. We think so for the following reasons:

1st. The clause is placed among the powers of Congress, not among the limitations on those powers.

2d. Its terms purport to enlarge, not to diminish the powers vested in the government. It purports to be an additional power, not a restriction on those already granted. No reason has been, or can be assigned for thus concealing an intention to narrow the discretion of the national legislature under words which purport to enlarge it. The framers of the constitution wished its adoption, and well knew that it would be endangered by its strength, not by its weakness. Had they been capable of using language which would convey to the eye one idea, and, after deep reflection, impress on the mind another, they would rather have disguised the grant of power than its limitation. If, then, their intention had been, by this clause, to restrain the free use of means which might otherwise have been implied, that intention would have been inserted in another place, and would have been expressed in terms resembling these. "In carrying into execution the foregoing powers, and all others," etc., "no laws shall be passed but such as are necessary and proper." Had the intention been to make this clause restrictive, it would unquestionably have been so in form as well as in effect.

The result of the most careful and attentive consideration bestowed upon this clause is, that if it does not enlarge, it cannot be construed to restrain the powers of Congress, or to impair the right of the legislature to exercise its best judgment in the selection of measures to carry into execution the constitutional powers of the government. If no other motive for its insertion can be suggested, a sufficient one is found in the desire to remove all doubts respecting the right to legislate on that vast mass of incidental powers which must be involved in the constitution, if that instrument be not a splendid bauble.

We admit, as all must admit, that the powers of the government are limited, and that its limits are not to be transcended. But we think the sound construction of the constitution must allow to the national legislature that discretion, with respect to the means by which the powers it confers are to be carried into execution, which will enable that body to perform the high duties assigned to it, in the manner most beneficial to the people. Let the end be legitimate, let it be within the scope of the constitution, and all means which are appropriate, which are plainly adapted to that end, which are not prohibited, but consist with the letter and spirit of the constitution, are constitutional. . . .

If a corporation may be employed indiscriminately with other means to carry into execution the powers of the government, no particular reason can be assigned for excluding the use of a bank, if required for its fiscal operations. To use one, must be within the discretion of Congress, if it be an appropriate mode of executing the powers of government. That it is a convenient, a useful, and essential instrument in the prosecution of its fiscal operations, is not now a subject of controversy. All those who have been concerned in the administration of our finances, have concurred in representing the importance and necessity; and so strongly have they been felt, that statesmen of the first class, whose previous opinions against it had been confirmed by every circumstance which can fix the human judgment, have yielded those opinions to the exigencies of the nation. . . .

But, were its necessity less apparent, none can deny its being an appropriate measure; and if it is, the degree of its necessity, as has been very justly observed, is to be discussed in another place. Should Congress, in the execution of its powers, adopt measures which are prohibited by the constitution; or should Congress, under the pretext of executing its powers, pass laws for the accomplishment of objects not entrusted to the government, it would become the painful duty of this tribunal, should a case requiring such a decision come before it, to say that such an act was not the law of the land. But where the law is not prohibited, and is really calculated to effect any of the objects entrusted to the government, to undertake here to inquire into the degree of its necessity, would be to pass the line which circumscribes the judicial department, and to tread on legislative ground. This court disclaims all pretensions to such a power. . . .

After the most deliberate consideration, it is the unanimous and decided opinion of this court that the act to incorporate the bank of the United States is a law made in pursuance of the constitution, and is a part of the supreme law of the land. . . .

It being the opinion of the court that the act incorporating the bank is constitutional, and that the power of establishing a branch in the state of Maryland might be properly exercised by the bank itself, we proceed to inquire:

2. Whether the state of Maryland may, without violating the constitution, tax that branch?

That the power of taxation is one of vital importance; that it is retained by the states; that it is not abridged by the grant of a similar power to the government of the Union; that it is to be concurrently exercised by the two governments: are truths which have never been denied. But, such is the paramount character of the constitution, that its capacity to withdraw any subject from the action of even this power, is admitted. The states are expressly forbidden to lay any duties on imports or exports, except what may be absolutely necessary for executing their inspection laws. If the obligation of this prohibition must be conceded—if it may restrain a state from the exercise of its taxing power on imports and exports—the same paramount character would seem to restrain, as it certainly may restrain, a state from such other exercise of this power, as is in its nature incompatible with, and repugnant to, the constitutional laws of the Union. A law, absolutely repugnant to another, as entirely repeals that other as if express terms of repeal were used.

On this ground the counsel for the bank place its claim to be exempted from the power of a state to tax its operations. There is no express provision for the case, but the claim has been sustained on a principle which so entirely pervades the constitution, is so intermixed with the materials which compose it, so interwoven with its web, so blended with its texture, as to be incapable of being separated from it without rending it into shreds.

This great principle is, that the Constitution and the laws made in pursuance thereof are supreme; that they control the Constitution and laws of the respective States, and cannot be controlled by them. From this, which may be almost termed an axiom, other propositions are deduced as corollaries, on the truth or error of which, and on their application to this case, the cause has been supposed to depend. These are, 1st. That a power to create implies a power to preserve. 2d. That a power to destroy, if wielded by a different hand, is hostile to, and incompatible with these powers to create and preserve. 3d. That where this repugnancy exists, that authority which is supreme must control, not yield to that over which it is supreme. . . .

The power of Congress to create, and of course to continue, the bank, was the subject of the preceding part of this opinion; and is no longer to be considered as questionable.

That the power of taxing it by the states may be exercised so as to destroy it, is too obvious to be denied. But taxation is said to be an absolute power, which acknowledges no other limits than those expressly prescribed in the Constitution, and like sovereign power of every other description, is trusted to the discretion of those who use it. . . .

The argument on the part of the state of Maryland is, not that the states may directly resist a law of Congress, but that they may exercise their acknowledged powers upon it, and that the constitution leaves them this right in the confidence that they will not abuse it. . . .

That the power to tax involves the power to destroy; that the power to destroy may defeat and render useless the power to create; that there is a plain repugnance, in conferring on one government a power to control the constitutional measures of another, which other, with respect to those very measures, is declared to be supreme over that which exerts the control, are propositions not to be denied. But all inconsistencies are to be reconciled by the magic of the word confidence. Taxation, it is said, does not necessarily and unavoidably destroy. To carry it to the excess of destruction would be an abuse, to presume which, would banish that confidence which is essential to all government.

But is this a case of confidence? Would the people of any one state trust those of another with a power to control the most insignificant operations of their state government? We know they would not. Why, then, should we suppose that the people of any one state should be willing to trust those of another with a power to control the operations of a government to which they have confided their most important and most valuable interests? In the legislature of the Union alone, are all represented. The legislature of the Union alone, therefore, can be trusted by the people with the power of controlling measures which concern all, in the confidence that it will not be abused. This, then, is not a case of confidence, and we must consider it as it really is.

If we apply the principle for which the state of Maryland contends, to the constitution generally, we shall find it capable of changing totally the character of that instrument. We shall find it capable of arresting all the measures of the government, and of prostrating it at the foot of the states. The American people have declared their constitution, and the laws made in pursuance thereof, to be supreme; but this principle would transfer the supremacy, in fact, to the states.

If the states may tax one instrument, employed by the government in the execution of its powers, they may tax any and every other instrument. They may tax the mail; they may tax the mint; they may tax patent-rights; they may tax the papers of the custom-house; they may tax judicial process; they may tax all the means employed by the government, to an excess which would defeat all the ends of government. This was not intended by the American people. [They] did not design to make their government dependent on the states. . . .

It has also been insisted, that, as the power of taxation in the general and State governments is acknowledged to be concurrent, every argument which would sustain the right of the general government to tax banks chartered by the states, will equally sustain the right of the states to tax banks chartered by the general government.

But the two cases are not on the same reason. The people of all the states have created the general government, and have conferred upon it the general power of taxation. The people of all the states, and the states themselves, are represented in Congress, and, by their representatives, exercise this power. When they tax the chartered institutions of the states, they tax their constituents; and these taxes must be uniform. But, when a state taxes the operations of the government of the United States, it acts upon institutions created, not by their own constituents, but by people over whom they claim no control. It acts upon the measures of a government created by others as well as themselves, for the benefit of others in common with themselves. The difference is that which always exists, and always must exist, between the action of the whole on a part, and the action of a part on the whole—between the laws of a government declared to be supreme, and those of a government which, when in opposition to those laws, is not supreme.

But if the full application of this argument could be admitted, it might bring into question the right of Congress to tax the state banks, and could not prove the right of the states to tax the Bank of the United States.

The court has bestowed on this subject its most deliberate consideration. The result is a conviction that the states have no power, by taxation or otherwise, to retard, impede, burden, or in any manner control the operations of the constitutional laws enacted by Congress to carry into execution the powers vested in the general government. This is, we think, the unavoidable consequence of that supremacy which the constitution has declared.

We are unanimously of opinion that the law passed by the legislature of Maryland, imposing a tax on the Bank of the United States, is unconstitutional and void.

This opinion does not deprive the states of any resources which they originally possessed. It does not extend to a tax paid by the real property of the bank, in common with the other real property within the state, nor to a tax imposed on the interest which the citizens of Maryland may hold in this institution, in common with other property of the same description throughout the state. But this is a tax on the operations of the bank, and is, consequently, a tax on the operation of an instrument employed by the government of the Union to carry its powers into execution. Such a tax must be unconstitutional. . . .

UNITED STATES v. BUTLER

297 U. S. 1; 56 S. Ct. 312; 80 L. Ed. 477 (1936)

While it is clear from Kansas v. Colorado that Congress has no authority in the absence of a delegation of power, are there limits to the way in which Congress can exercise those powers that are clearly delegated? From time to time, and in connection with various powers of Congress, the Court has held that there are. In Ashton v. Cameron County Water Dist. (1936)

Congress was held unable to extend the bankruptcy power to a state agency, since to do so would be to "pass laws inconsistent with the idea of sovereignty," and in Hammer v. Dagenhart (1918) the Court held for the first time that the powers reserved to the states by the Tenth Amendment acted as a limit to the use of congressional power. There the Court struck down the use of the commerce power to control child labor. The philosophy underlying this decision is that the powers of Congress cannot be used to achieve ends which have not been delegated to Congress, and hence, according to the Tenth Amendment, are reserved to the states.

Perhaps the most lucid explanation of this doctrine, dubbed "dual federalism" by Professor E. S. Corwin, is that made by Mr. Justice Roberts in the Butler case below. In an effort to solve the problem of low farm prices and agricultural surpluses, Congress passed the Agricultural Adjustment Act of 1933, part of which provided for paying farmers to limit the growing of certain commodities. The necessary money was raised by a processing tax on those commodities that were raised, and over a billion dollars was collected before the Court held the act void. The Court does not contend that such a processing tax, taken alone, would be void; but when coupled with a clear attempt to regulate agriculture, it was an unconstitutional use of a delegated power.

The doctrine of dual federalism, in the form that appears here, was destined to be short-lived. In the Social Security Act Cases in 1937 the Court sustained an almost identical use of the tax power, and in United States v. Darby in 1941 the Court consciously abandoned it, noting that the Tenth Amendment "states but a truism that all is retained which has not been surrendered." In 1945 the Court held in Cleveland v. United States that Congress could validly condemn land and build low-cost housing under the United States Housing Act, since the purpose of the act was declared to be "to promote the general welfare of the nation by employing . . . funds and credit to assist the states and their political subdivisions to relieve unemployment and safeguard the health, safety and morals of the Nation's citizens by improving housing conditions."

One of the crucial problems of the Depression of the 1930's was the presence of agricultural surpluses so great that the market price often failed to cover the cost of production. So, as a major part of the New Deal recovery program, Congress passed the Agricultural Adjustment Act of 1933. The AAA undertook to restore farm prices, and thus the purchasing power of the farmer, by persuading farmers to reduce their production of certain basic agricultural commodities enough to restore the prewar market prices. Farmers who thus reduced their production were paid enough by the government to make up the difference. The money for these crop-reduction payments was raised by levying processing taxes on the industries which prepared farm products for the market. The program was voluntary in the sense that no farmer was compelled by law to reduce his crops. He was merely well paid if he did so. Butler and others paid the processing taxes under protest and sued to get them back again on the ground that the AAA was unconstitutional.

Mr. Justice Roberts delivered the opinion of the Court, saying in part:

Second. The Government asserts that even if the respondents may question the propriety of the appropriation embodied in the statute their attack must fail because Article 1, § 8 of the Constitution authorizes the contemplated expenditure of the funds raised by the tax. This contention presents the great and the controlling question in the case. We approach its decision with a sense of our grave responsibility to render judgment in accordance with the principles established for the governance of all three branches of the Government.

There should be no misunderstanding as to the function of this court in such a case. It is sometimes said that the court assumes a power to overrule or control the action of the people's representatives. This is a misconception. The Constitution is the supreme law of the land ordained and established by the people. All legislation must conform to the principles it lays down. When an act of Congress is appropriately challenged in the courts as not conforming to the constitutional mandate the judicial branch of the Government has only one duty,—to lay the article of the Constitution which is invoked beside the statute which is challenged and to decide whether the latter squares with the former. All the court does, or can do, is to announce its considered judgment upon the question. The only power it has, if such it may be called, is the power of judgment. This court neither approves nor condemns any legislative policy. Its delicate and difficult office is to ascertain and declare whether the legislation is in accordance with, or in contravention of, the provisions of the Constitution; and, having done that, its duty ends.

The question is not what power the federal Government ought to have but what powers in fact have been given by the people. It hardly seems necessary to reiterate that ours is a dual form of government; that in every state there are two governments,—the state and the United States. Each State has all governmental powers save such as the people, by their Constitution, have conferred upon the United States, denied to the States, or reserved to themselves. The federal union is a government of delegated powers. It has only such as are expressly conferred upon it and such as are reasonably to be implied from those granted. In this respect we differ radically from nations where all legislative power, without restriction or limitation, is vested in a parliament or other legislative body subject to no restrictions except the discretion of its members.

Article I, § 8, of the Constitution vests sundry powers in the Congress. But two of its clauses have any bearing upon the validity of the statute under review.

The third clause endows the Congress with power "to regulate Commerce . . . among the several States." Despite a reference in its first section to a burden upon, and an obstruction of the normal currents of commerce, the act under review does not purport to regulate transactions in interstate or foreign commerce. Its stated purpose is the control of agricultural production, a purely local activity, in an effort to raise the prices paid the farmer. Indeed, the Government does not attempt to uphold the validity of the act on the basis of the commerce clause, which, for the purpose of the present case, may be put aside as irrelevant.

The clause thought to authorize the legislation,—the first,—confers upon the Congress power "to lay and collect Taxes, Duties, Imposts and Excises, to pay the Debts and provide for the common Defense and general Welfare of the United States. . . ." It is not contended that this provision grants power to regulate agricultural production upon the theory that such legislation would promote the general welfare. The Government concedes that the phrase "to provide for the general welfare" qualifies the power "to lay and collect taxes." The view that the clause grants power to provide for the general welfare, independently of the taxing power, has never been authoritatively accepted. Mr. Justice Story points out that if it were adopted "it is obvious that under color of the generality of the words, to 'provide for the common defence and general welfare,' the government of the United States is, in reality, a government of general and unlimited powers, notwithstanding the subsequent enumeration of specific powers." The true construction undoubtedly is that the only thing granted is the power to tax for the purpose of providing funds for payment of the nation's debts and making provision for the general welfare.

Nevertheless the Government asserts that warrant is found in this clause for the adoption of the Agricultural Adjustment Act. The argument is that Congress may appropriate and authorize the spending of moneys for the "general welfare;" that the phrase should be liberally construed to cover anything conducive to national welfare; that decision as to what will promote such welfare rests with Congress alone, and the courts may not review its determination; and finally that the appropriation under attack was in fact for the general welfare of the United States.

The Congress is expressly empowered to lay taxes to provide for the general welfare. Funds in the Treasury as a result of taxation may be expended only through appropriation. (Art. I, § 9, cl. 7.) They can never accomplish the objects for which they were collected unless the power to appropriate is as broad as the power to tax. The necessary implication from the terms of the grant is that the public funds may be appropriated "to provide for the general welfare of the United States." These words cannot be meaningless, else they would not have been used. The conclusion must be that they were intended to limit and define the granted power to raise and to expend money. How shall they be construed to effectuate the intent of the instrument?

Since the foundation of the nation sharp differences of opinion have persisted as to the true interpretation of the phrase. Madison asserted it amounted to no more than a reference to the other powers enumerated in the subsequent clauses of the same section; that, as the United States is a government of limited and enumerated powers, the grant of power to tax and spend for the general national welfare must be confined to the enumerated legislative fields committed to the Congress. In this view the phrase is mere tautology, for taxation and appropriation are or may be necessary incidents of the exercise of any of the enumerated legislative powers. Hamilton, on the other hand, maintained the clause confers a power separate and distinct from those later enumerated, is not restricted in meaning by the grant of them, and Congress consequently has a substantive power to tax and to appropriate, limited only by the requirement that it shall be exercised to provide for the general welfare of the United States. Each contention has had the support of those whose views are entitled to weight. This court has noticed the question, but has never found it necessary to decide which is the true construction. Mr. Justice Story, in his Commentaries, espouses the Hamiltonian position. We shall not review the writings of public men and commentators or discuss the legislative practice. Study of all these leads us to conclude that the reading advocated by Mr. Justice Story is the correct one. While, therefore, the power to tax is not unlimited, its confines are set in the clause which confers it, and not in those of § 8 which bestow and define the legislative powers of the Congress. It results that the power of Congress to authorize the expenditure of public moneys for public purposes is not limited by the direct grants of legislative power found in the Constitution. . . .

We are not now required to ascertain the scope of the phrase "general welfare of the United States" or to determine whether an appropriation in aid of agriculture falls within it. Wholly apart from that question, another principle embedded in our Constitution prohibits the enforcement of the Agricultural Adjustment Act. The act invades the reserved rights of the states. It is a statutory plan to regulate and control agricultural production, a matter beyond the powers delegated to the federal government. The tax, the appropriation of the funds raised, and the direction for their disbursement, are but parts of the plan. They are but means to an unconstitutional end.

From the accepted doctrine that the United States is a government of delegated powers, it follows that those not expressly granted, or reasonably to be implied from such as are conferred, are reserved to the states or to the people. To forestall any suggestion to the contrary, the Tenth Amendment was adopted. The same proposition, otherwise stated, is that powers not granted are prohibited. None to regulate agricultural production is given, and therefore legislation by Congress for that purpose is forbidden.

It is an established principle that the attainment of a prohibited end may not be accomplished under the pretext of the exertion of powers which are granted.

"Should Congress, in the execution of its powers, adopt measures which are prohibited by the constitution; or should Congress, under the pretext of executing its powers, pass laws for the accomplishment of objects not intrusted to the government; it would become the painful duty of this tribunal, should a case requiring such a decision come before it, to say that such an act was not the law of the land." M'Culloch v. Maryland [1819].

"Congress cannot, under the pretext of executing delegated power, pass laws for the accomplishment of objects not intrusted to the Federal Government. And we accept as established doctrine that any provision of an act of Congress ostensibly enacted under power granted by the Constitution, not naturally and reasonably adapted to the effective exercise of such power but solely to the achievement of something plainly within the power reserved to the States, is invalid and cannot be enforced." Linder v. United States [1925].

These principles are as applicable to the power to lay taxes as to any other federal power. Said the court, in M'Culloch v. Maryland:

"Let the end be legitimate, let it be within the scope of the constitution, and all means which are appropriate, which are plainly adapted to that end, which are not prohibited, but consist with the letter and spirit of the constitution, are constitutional."

The power of taxation, which is expressly granted, may, of course, be adopted as a means to carry into operation another power also expressly granted. But resort to the taxing power to effectuate an end which is not legitimate, not within the scope of the Constitution, is obviously inadmissible. . . .

COYLE v. SMITH
221 U. S. 559; 31 S. Ct. 688; 55 L. Ed. 853 (1911)

The power which Congress possesses to admit new states into the Union is a purely discretionary power. No territory has any right to claim statehood, but must wait until it seems wise to Congress to confer that status. It is not surprising, therefore, that it should be assumed that Congress in the exercise of an unquestioned power to grant or withhold such a privilege might make the enjoyment of the right contingent upon the meeting of such conditions by the incoming state as might seem to the congressional mind desirable. This seems to have been the theory upon which Congress proceeded with reference to the admission of states; and as early as 1802 we find Ohio compelled, as the price of admission into the Union, to enter into an agreement, irrevocable without the consent of Congress, not to tax for a period of five years lands within the state which were sold by the United States government. The imposing of conditions of various kinds upon the incoming states became a settled policy of Congress, and the stipulations agreed to covered a considerable range of topics. They related to the disposition of public lands, many of them being much more detailed than the Ohio provision; to the use of navigable waters; to the protection of the rights of citizens of the United States; to slavery; to civil and religious liberty; to the right to vote. When Utah came into the Union in 1894 it was obliged to make an irrevocable agreement that there should be perfect religious toleration maintained in the state, that the public schools should be kept free from sectarian control, and that polygamous marriages should be forever prohibited. In 1910 Arizona was authorized by a congressional enabling act to draw up a state constitution preparatory to entering the Union. The constitution framed contained provisions for the popular recall of judges. While Congress somewhat reluctantly passed a resolution admitting Arizona into the Union, President Taft, being bitterly opposed to the recall of judges, vetoed the resolution. A new resolution was then passed providing that Arizona be admitted on condition that the objectionable provision be stricken out of the constitution. This was done and Arizona became a member of the Union. The state thereupon promptly restored the recall of judges by amending the new state constitution, and has retained the provision ever since.

But if Congress can thus impose conditions upon the new states as they assume statehood, the question arises: are the states equal? Do we actually have states in the Union which do not have the power enjoyed by other states; as, for instance, to decide how judges shall be removed from office, or what shall constitute a lawful marriage? It is a rather curious fact that the question of the binding nature of these restrictions was not brought squarely before the Supreme Court until 1911 in the case of Coyle v. Smith. This case grew out of a congressional restriction imposed upon Oklahoma in the enabling act passed in 1906 which provided (1) that the new state should locate its capital at Guthrie, (2) that it should irrevocably agree not to move it from that place before the year 1913, and (3) that it should not appropriate any unnecessary money for public buildings. This agreement was ratified by the voters of the state at the time that the new constitution was adopted; and, thus bound, Oklahoma entered the Union. In 1910, a bill initiated by the people providing that the state capital should forthwith be moved to Oklahoma City and appropriating $600,000 for public buildings was approved by the voters of Oklahoma. This was, of course, in plain violation of the "irrevocable" agreement which the state *had made, and a proceeding was instituted to test the validity of the law. In sustaining the right of the state to move its capital at its discretion regardless of its agreement, the Supreme Court enunciated the important doctrine of the political equality of the states.*

A distinction, however, should be noted between those conditions imposed upon incoming states which relate to political or governmental authority and which would therefore place the state upon an unequal footing in the Union, and those conditions in the nature of business agreements or contracts which relate to property. Thus, for example, the agreement of a new state to conditions in its Enabling Act that lands given to it by the United States in trust for certain purposes has been held enforceable like any other trust agreement. See Ervien v. United States (1919) in which New Mexico, which was given lands for school purposes, was held properly enjoined from using them for advertising the resources of the state.

It may be said that the vital question whether one of the states of the Union may constitutionally secede was effectively and permanently answered upon the battlefields of the Civil War. Four years after the war had ended, however, the Supreme Court found itself under the necessity of deciding, in the case of Texas v. White (1869), whether the Southern states had at any time during the period of attempting secession been actually out of the Union. Was secession, in point of law, constitutionally possible? The facts in this case were as follows:

In 1850 the United States gave the state of Texas $10,000,000 in 5 percent bonds in settlement of certain boundary claims. Half were held in Washington; half were delivered to the state, and made payable to the state or bearer and redeemable after December 31, 1864. A Texas law was passed providing that the bonds should not be available in the hands of any holder until after their endorsement by the governor. Texas joined the Confederacy at the outbreak of the war, and in 1862 the state legislature repealed the act requiring the endorsement of the bonds by the governor and created a military board to provide for the expenses of the war, empowering the board to use any bonds in the state treasury for this purpose up to $1,000,000. In 1865 this board made a contract with White and others for the transfer of some of the bonds for military supplies. None of the bonds was endorsed by the governor of the state. Immediately upon the close of the war, but while the state was still "unreconstructed" or unrestored to its former normal status as a member of the Union, suit was brought by the governor of the state to get the bonds back and to enjoin White and the other defendants from receiving payment for them from the federal government. The suit was brought by Texas in the Supreme Court of the United States as an original action, and at the very threshold of the case arose the question whether Texas, after her efforts at secession, was

still a "state" within the meaning of Article III, of the Constitution extend-
ing the original jurisdiction of the Supreme Court to those cases "in which
a State shall be party." Texas at this time was still unrepresented in
Congress, and the radical Republicans like Stevens claimed that she was
out of the Union.

The Court held that secession was constitutionally impossible and that
Texas had never ceased to be a state in the Union. Mr. Chief Justice Chase
said the Articles of Confederation created what was solemnly declared to
be a "perpetual Union"; that the Constitution was ordained "to form a
more perfect Union"; and he concluded that: The Constitution, in all of
its provisions, looks to an indestructible union, composed of indestructible
states." The fact that Texas, by her own efforts at secession, had tempo-
rarily given up the rights and privileges of membership in the Union did
not alter the fact that she could not sever the constitutional ties which
bound her to that Union. The Court accordingly took jurisdiction in the
case and decided that Texas was entitled to recover the bonds.

In cases of spectacular importance the Supreme Court faced the issue
of who holds title to the land beneath the sea within the so-called "three-
mile" limit. The discovery of oil off the coasts of California, Louisiana,
and Texas gave this underwater land tremendous value; and the three
states, assuming the land was theirs, leased to various oil companies the
right to drill for offshore oil. The United States, asserting that it was "the
owner in fee simple, or possessed of paramount rights in and powers over"
this land, brought suit to enjoin the states from trespassing upon it. The
Supreme Court, in United States v. California (1947), invoked the "equal
footing" rule to sustain the United States, at least in its claim to "para-
mount rights." A similar question had reached the Court in 1845 in
Pollard v. Hagan. Alabama had been admitted to the Union on an equal
footing with the other states, but in the act of admission it had been
stipulated that Alabama disclaimed title to waste and unappropriated
lands under the navigable waters within the state, and that its navigable
waters should remain public highways and free to the citizens of the state
and of the United States. On the strength of this the United States claimed
title to the submerged lands under the navigable waters within the state
of Alabama. The Court found that all the other states had had common-
law title to these submerged lands when they came into the Union. "Ala-
bama is therefore entitled to the sovereignty and jurisdiction over all the
territory within her limits, . . . to the same extent that Georgia possessed
it before she ceded it to the United States. To maintain any other doctrine,
is to deny that Alabama has been admitted into the Union on an equal
footing with the original states. . . . "

The Court decided the claims of Louisiana (United States v. Louisiana,
1950) on the basis of the California decision. But United States v. Texas

(1950) presented a slightly different problem. Texas had been an independent state prior to its admission to the Union and had had undoubted title to its offshore lands. The Court applied the Pollard argument in reverse: "The 'equal footing' clause, we hold, works the same way in the converse situation presented by this case. It negatives any implied, special limitation of any of the paramount powers of the United States in favor of a State. . . . When Texas came into the Union, she ceased to be an independent nation. She then became a sister State on an 'equal footing' with all the other States. That act concededly entailed a relinquishment of some of her sovereignty. . . . We hold that as an incident to the transfer of that sovereignty any claim that Texas may have had to the marginal sea was relinquished to the United States."

The "tideland's oil" question became an issue in the 1952 presidential campaign, and the victorious Republican Congress redeemed its campaign pledge to cede to the three states the lands which they claimed. Since the acts ceded title to the land extending to the original boundaries of the states, the Gulf states claimed three leagues (nine nautical miles) of marginal sea. Congress' right to make this cession was upheld in Alabama v. Texas in 1954, but in 1960 the Court held that only Texas and Florida were entitled to three leagues. The fact that this apparently leaves these states sticking out some six miles beyond the boundaries of the United States raises potential problems in international law which the Court declined to answer. "It is sufficient for present purposes to note that there is no question of Congress' power to fix state land and water boundaries as a domestic matter. Such a boundary, fully effective as between Nation and State, undoubtedly circumscribes the extent of navigable inland waters and underlying lands owned by the State under the Pollard rule." See United States v. Louisiana (1960).

Mr. Justice Lurton delivered the opinion of the Court, saying in part:

. . . The only question for review by us is whether the provision of the enabling act was a valid limitation upon the power of the state after its admission, which overrides any subsequent state legislation repugnant thereto.

The power to locate its own seat of government, and to determine when and how it shall be changed from one place to another, and to appropriate its own public funds for that purpose, are essentially and peculiarly state powers. That one of the original thirteen states could now be shorn of such powers by an act of Congress would not be for a moment entertained. The question, then, comes to this: Can a state be placed upon a plane of inequality with its sister states in the Union if the Congress chooses to impose conditions which so operate, at the time of its admission? The argument is, that while Congress may not deprive a state of any power which it *possesses,* it may, as a condition to the admission of a new state, constitutionally restrict its authority, to the extent, at least, of suspending its powers for a definite time in respect to the location of its seat of government. This contention is predicated upon the constitutional power of admitting new states to this Union, and the constitutional duty of guaranteeing to "every state in this Union a republican form of government." The position of counsel for the plaintiff in error is substantially this: That the power of Congress to admit new states, and to determine whether or not its fundamental law is republican in form, are political powers, and as such, uncontrollable by the courts. That Congress may, in the exercise of such power, impose terms and conditions upon the admission of the proposed new state, which, if accepted, will be obligatory, although they operate to deprive the state of powers which it would otherwise possess, and, therefore, not admitted upon "an equal footing with the original states."

The power of Congress in respect to the admission of new states is found in the 3d section of the 4th article of the Constitution. That provision is that, "new states may be admitted by the Congress into this Union." The only expressed restriction upon this power is that no new state shall be formed within the jurisdiction of any other state, nor by the junction of two or more states, or parts of states, without the consent of such states, as well as of the Congress.

But what is this power? It is not to admit political organizations which are less or greater, or different in dignity or power, from those political entities which constitute the Union. It is, as strongly put by counsel, a "power to admit states."

The definition of "a state" is found in the powers possessed by the original states which adopted the Constitution,—a definition emphasized by the terms employed in all subsequent acts of Congress admitting new states into the Union. The first two states admitted into the Union were the states of Vermont and Kentucky, one as of March 4, 1791, and the other as of June 1, 1792. No terms or conditions were exacted from either. Each act declares that the state is admitted "as a new and *entire member* of the United States of America." . . . Emphatic and significant as is the phrase admitted as "an entire member," even stronger was the declaration upon the admission in 1796 of Tennessee as the third new state, it being declared to be "one of the United States of America," "on an equal footing with the original states in all respects whatsoever,"—phraseology which has ever since been substantially followed in admission acts, concluding with the Oklahoma act, which declares that Oklahoma shall be admitted "on an equal footing with the original states."

The power is to admit "new states into *this* Union."

"This Union" was and is a union of states, equal in power, dignity, and authority, each competent to exert that residuum of sovereignty not delegated to the United States by the Constitution itself. To maintain otherwise would be to say that the Union, through the power of Congress to admit new states, might come to be a union of states unequal in power, as including states whose powers were restricted only by the Constitution, with others whose powers had been further restricted by an act of Congress accepted as a condition of admission. Thus it would result, first, that the powers of Congress would not be defined by the Constitution alone, but in respect to new states, enlarged or restricted by the conditions imposed upon new states by its own legislation admitting them into the Union; and, second, that such new states might not exercise all of the powers which had not been delegated by the Constitution, but only such as had not been further bargained away as conditions of admission.

The argument that Congress derives from the duty of "guaranteeing to each state in this Union a republican form of government," power to impose restrictions upon a new state which deprive it of equality with other members of the Union, has no merit. It may imply the duty of each new state to provide itself with such state government, and impose upon Congress the duty of seeing that such form is not changed to one anti-republican, . . . but it obviously does not confer power to admit a new state which shall be any less a state than those which compose the Union.

We come now to the question as to whether there is anything in the decisions of this court which sanctions the claim that Congress may, by the imposition of conditions in an enabling act, deprive a new state of any of those attributes essential to its equality in dignity and power with other states. In considering the decisions of this court bearing upon the question, we must distinguish, first, between provisions which are fulfilled by the admission of the state; second, between compacts or affirmative legislation intended to operate *in futuro,* which are within the scope of the conceded powers of Congress over the subject; and third, compacts or affirmative legislation which operate to restrict the powers of such new states in respect of matters which would otherwise be exclusively within the sphere of state power.

As to requirements in such enabling acts as relate only to the contents of the Constitution for the proposed new state, little need[s] to be said. The constitutional provision concerning the admission of new states is not a mandate, but a power to be exercised with discretion. From this alone it would follow that Congress may require, under penalty of denying admission, that the organic law of a new state at the time of admission shall be such as to meet its approval. A Constitution thus supervised by Congress would, after all, be a Constitution of a state, and as such subject to alteration and amendment by the state after admission. Its force would be that of a state Constitution, and not that of an act of Congress. . . .

So far as this court has found occasion to advert to the effect of enabling acts as affirmative legislation affecting the power of new states after admission, there is to be found no sanction for the contention that any state may be deprived of any of the power constitutionally possessed by other states, as states, by reason of the terms in which the acts admitting them to the Union have been framed. . . . [Here follows discussion of a case involving the construction of the act under which Alabama was admitted to the Union.]

The plain deduction from this case is that when a new state is admitted into the Union, it is so admitted with all of the powers of sovereignty and jurisdiction which pertain to the original states, and that such powers may not be constitutionally diminished, impaired, or shorn away by any conditions, compacts, or stipulations embraced in the act under which the new state came into the Union, which would not be valid and effectual if the subject of congressional legislation after admission. . . .

It may well happen that Congress should embrace in an enactment introducing a new state into the Union legislation intended as a regulation of commerce among the states, or with Indian tribes situated within the limits of such new state, or regulations touching the sole care and disposition of the public lands or reservations therein which might be upheld as legislation within the sphere of the plain power of Congress. But in every such case such legislation would derive its force not from any agreement or compact with the proposed new state, nor by reason of its acceptance of such enactment as a term of admission, but solely because the power of Congress extended to the subject, and therefore would not operate to restrict the state's legislative power in respect of any matter which was not plainly within the regulating power of Congress. . . .

No such question is presented here. The legislation in the Oklahoma enabling act relating to the location of the capital of the state, if construed as forbidding a removal by the state after its admission as a state, is referable to no power granted to Congress over the subject, and if it is to be upheld at all, it must be implied from the power to admit new states. If power to impose such a restriction upon the general and undelegated power of a state be conceded as implied from the power to admit a new state, where is the line to be drawn against restrictions imposed upon new states. . . .

. . . If anything was needed to complete the argument against the assertion that Oklahoma has not been admitted to the Union upon an equality of power, dignity, and sovereignty with Massachusetts or Virginia, it is afforded by the express provision of the act of admission, by which it is declared that when the people of the proposed new state have complied with the terms of the act, that it shall be the duty of the President to issue his proclamation, and that "thereupon the proposed state of Oklahoma shall be deemed admitted by Congress into the Union under and by virtue of this act, *on an equal footing with the original states.*" The proclamation has been issued and the Senators and Representatives from the state admitted to their seats in the Congress.

Has Oklahoma been admitted upon an equal footing with the original states?

If she has, she, by virtue of her jurisdictional sovereignty as such a state, may determine for her own people the proper location of the local seat of government. She is not equal in power to them if she cannot. . . .

To this we may add that the constitutional equality of the states is essential to the harmonious operation of the scheme upon which the Republic was organized. When that equality disappears we may remain a free people, but the Union will not be the Union of the Constitution.

Judgment affirmed.

Mr. Justice McKenna and Mr. Justice Holmes dissent.

5

Areas of National Control

GIBBONS v. OGDEN

9 Wheaton 1; 6 L. Ed. 23 (1824)

In 1798 Robert R. Livingston secured from the New York legislature an exclusive twenty-year grant to navigate by steam the rivers and other waters of the state, provided that within two years he should build a boat which would make four miles an hour against the current of the Hudson River. The grant was made amidst the ribald jeers of the legislators, who had no faith whatever in the project. The terms of the grant were not met, however, and it was renewed in 1803—this time to Livingston together with his partner, Robert Fulton—and again for two years in 1807. In August, 1807, Fulton's steamboat made its first successful trip from New York to Albany, and steamboat navigation became a reality. The following year the legislature, now fully aware of the practical significance of Fulton's achievement, passed a law providing that for each new boat placed on New York waters by Fulton and Livingston they should be entitled to a five-year extension of their monopoly, which should, however, not exceed 30 years. The monopoly was made effective by further providing that no one should be allowed to navigate New York waters by steam without a license from Fulton and Livingston, and any unlicensed vessel should be forfeited to them. The business of steamboat navigation developed rapidly. Boats were put in operation between New York and Albany and intervening points, and steam ferries ran between Fulton Street, New York City, and points in New Jersey. In 1811 the partners obtained from the Territory of Orleans (later Louisiana) a monopoly of steam navigation on the waters of Louisiana similar to that granted by New York, thus assuring them a pivotal position in the two greatest ports of the land. Naturally the monopolistic nature of the Fulton-Livingston rights worked hardship on their would-be competitors, and neighboring states began to pass retaliatory laws directed against the New York partners. The New Jersey legislature in 1811 authorized the owner of any boat seized under the forfeiture clause of the Fulton-Livingston charter to capture and hold in retaliation any boat belonging to any New York citizen. Connecticut in 1822 forbade any vessel licensed by Fulton and Livingston to enter the waters of that state, and Ohio passed a somewhat similar law in the same year. Granting such exclusive franchises was a game at which more than one state could play; and such grants were made by Georgia, Massachusetts, Pennsylvania, Tennessee, New Hampshire, and Vermont. With the inevitable increase of feeling created by such policies, retaliatory acts became common. In short, an achievement of science which had seemed destined to enlarge the means of communication and develop the commerce of the nation appeared rather to be embroiling the states in bitter antagonisms and commercial warfare such as prevailed during the dismal period of the Confederation. It is against the background of this intensely acute economic situation that the case of Gibbons v. Ogden must be read.

Ogden had secured a license for steam navigation from Fulton and Livingston. Gibbons had originally been his partner but was now his rival and was operating steamboats between New York and New Jersey under the authority of a coasting license obtained from the United States government. Upon Ogden's petition the New York court had enjoined Gibbons from continuing in business. The great jurist Chancellor James Kent wrote the opinion in this case, upholding the validity of the New York statute establishing the monopoly and repudiating the idea that there was any conflict involved between federal and state authority. An appeal was taken by Gibbons to the Supreme Court of the United States, thus presenting to that tribunal its first case under the commerce clause of the Constitution.

So accustomed are we to the free flow of commerce among the states that it is hard to conceive how the nation might have developed had the arguments in favor of the monopoly prevailed, for it was urged that the powers of state and nation to regulate interstate commerce were concurrent; that in the absence of a conflicting congressional statute the state was free to exercise this concurrent power as it pleased; and that the "commerce" which Congress may regulate was "the transportation and sale of commodities." Had that argument prevailed, the federal coasting license under which Gibbons operated would have given him no protection, since he was carrying passengers, not goods. But the most crucial argument of all was that the New York monopoly law was not a regulation of interstate commerce but was merely a regulation of commerce within the boundaries of the state of New York. "It [the law] does not deny the right of entry into its waters to any vessel navigated by steam; it only forbids such vessel, when within its waters and jurisdiction, to be moved by steam; but that vessel may still navigate by all other means; and it leaves the people of other states, or of New York, in full possession of the right of navigation, by all the means known or used at the time of the passage of the law. [Most early steamboats were also sailboats.] It is, therefore, strictly a regulation of internal trade and navigation, which belongs to the state. This may, indeed, indirectly affect the right of commercial intercourse between the states. But so do all other laws regulating internal trade. . . ."

Webster's argument against the validity of the steamboat monopoly was perhaps his greatest effort before the Supreme Court, and some writers believe that Marshall's opinion invalidating the New York law is his greatest state paper; others would place it second only to the opinion in McCulloch v. Maryland. It was perhaps the only genuinely popular decision which Marshall ever handed down. It was received with widespread expressions of approval, for it was, as one writer has put it, "the first great anti-trust decision." The economic consequences of it in freeing a developing commerce from the shackles of state monopoly can hardly be overestimated; and it established for all time the supremacy of the national government in all matters affecting interstate and foreign commerce.

Mr. Chief Justice Marshall delivered the opinion of the Court, saying in part:

The appellant contends that this decree is erroneous, because the laws which purport to give the exclusive privilege it sustains, are repugnant to the constitution and laws of the United States.

They are said to be repugnant:

1st. To that clause in the constitution which authorizes Congress to regulate commerce.

2d. To that which authorizes Congress to promote the progress of science and useful arts. . . .

As preliminary to the very able discussions of the constitution, which we have heard from the bar, and as having some influence on its construction, reference has been made to the political situation of these states, anterior to its formation. It has been said that they were sovereign, were completely independent, and were connected with each other only by a league. This is true. But when these allied sovereigns converted their league into a government, when they converted their Congress of Ambassadors, deputed to deliberate on their common concerns, and to recommend measures of general utility, into a legislature, empowered to enact laws on the most interesting subjects, the whole character in which the states appear, underwent a change, the extent of which must be determined by a fair consideration of the instrument by which that change was effected.

This instrument contains an enumeration of powers expressly granted by the people to their government. It has been said that these powers ought to be construed strictly. But why ought they to be so construed? Is there one sentence in the constitution which gives countenance to this rule? In the last of the enumerated powers, that which grants, expressly, the means of carrying all others into execution, Congress is authorized "to make all laws which shall be necessary and proper" for the purpose. But this limitation on the means which may be used, is not extended to the powers which are conferred; nor is there one sentence in the constitution, which has been pointed out by the gentlemen of the bar, or which we have been able to discern, that prescribes this rule. We do not, therefore, think ourselves justified in adopting it. What do gentlemen mean by a strict construction? If they contend only against that enlarged construction which would extend words beyond their natural and obvious import, we might question the application of the term, but should not controvert the principle. If they contend for that narrow construction which, in support of some theory not to be found in the constitution, would deny to the government those powers which the words of the grant, as usually understood, import, and which are consistent with the general views and objects of the instrument; for that narrow construction, which would cripple the government and render it unequal to the objects for which it is declared to be instituted, and to which the powers given, as fairly understood, render it competent; then we cannot perceive the propriety of this strict construction, nor adopt it as the rule by which the constitution is to be expounded. As men, whose intentions require no concealment, generally employ the words which most directly and aptly express the ideas they intend to convey, the enlightened patriots who framed our constitution, and the people who adopted it, must be understood to have employed words in their natural sense, and to have intended what they have said. If, from the imperfection of human language, there should be serious doubts respecting the extent of any given power, it is a well-settled rule that the objects for which it was given, especially when those objects are expressed in the instrument itself, should have great influence in the construction. We know of no reason for excluding this rule from the present case. The grant does not convey power which might be beneficial to the grantor, if retained by himself, or which can enure solely to the benefit of the grantee, but is an investment of power for the general advantage, in the hands of agents selected for that purpose; which power can never be exercised by the people themselves, but must be placed in the hands of agents or lie dormant. We know of no rule for construing the extent of such powers, other than is given by the language of the instrument which confers them, taken in connection with the purposes for which they were conferred.

The words are: "Congress shall have power to regulate commerce with foreign nations, and among the several states, and with the Indian tribes."

The subject to be regulated is commerce; and our constitution being, as was aptly said at the bar, one of enumeration, and not of definition, to ascertain the extent of the power it becomes necessary to settle the meaning of the word. The counsel for the appellee would limit it to traffic, to buying and selling, or the interchange of commodities, and do not admit that it comprehends navigation. This would restrict a general term, applicable to many objects, to one of its significations. Commerce, undoubtedly, is traffic, but it is something more; it is intercourse. It describes the commercial intercourse between nations, and parts of nations, in all its branches, and is regulated by prescribing rules for carrying on that intercourse. The mind can scarcely conceive a system for regulating commerce between nations, which shall exclude all laws concerning navigation, which shall be silent on the admission of the vessels of the one nation into the ports of the other, and be confined to prescribing rules for the conduct of individuals, in the actual employment of buying and selling, or of barter.

If commerce does not include navigation, the government of the Union has no direct power over that subject, and can make no law prescribing what shall constitute American vessels, or requiring that they shall be navigated by American seamen. Yet this power has been exercised from the commencement of the government, has been exercised with the consent of all, and has been understood by all to be a commercial regulation. All America understands, and has uniformly understood, the word "commerce" to comprehend navigation. It was so understood, and must have been so understood, when the constitution was framed. The power over commerce, including navigation, was one of the primary objects for which the people of America adopted their government, and must have been contemplated in forming it. The convention must have used the word in that sense, because all have understood it in that sense, and the attempt to restrict it comes too late. . . .

The word used in the constitution, then, comprehends, and has been always understood to comprehend, navigation within its meaning; and a power to regulate navigation is as expressly granted as if that term had been added to the word "commerce."

To what commerce does this power extend? The constitution informs us, to commerce "with foreign nations, and among the several states, and with the Indian tribes."

It has, we believe, been universally admitted that these words comprehend every species of commercial intercourse between the United States and foreign nations. No sort of trade can be carried on between this country and any other, to which this power does not extend. It has been truly said that commerce, as the word is used in the constitution, is a unit, every part of which is indicated by the term.

If this be the admitted meaning of the word, in its application to foreign nations, it must carry the same meaning throughout the sentence, and remain a unit, unless there be some plain intelligible cause which alters it.

The subject to which the power is next applied, is to commerce "among the several states." The word "among" means intermingled with. A thing which is among others, is intermingled with them. Commerce among the states cannot stop at the external boundary line of each state, but may be introduced into the interior.

It is not intended to say that these words comprehend that commerce which is completely internal, which is carried on between man and man in a state, or between different parts of the same state, and which does not extend to or affect other states. Such a power would be inconvenient, and is certainly unnecessary.

Comprehensive as the word "among" is, it may very properly be restricted to that commerce which concerns more states than one. . . . The completely internal commerce of a state, then, may be considered as reserved for the state itself.

But, in regulating commerce with foreign nations, the power of Congress does not stop at the jurisdictional lines of the several states. It would be a very useless power if it could not pass those lines. The commerce of the United States with foreign nations, is that of the whole United States. Every district has a right to participate in it. The deep streams which penetrate our country in every direction, pass through the interior of almost every state in the Union, and furnish the means of exercising this right. If Congress has the power to regulate it, that power must be exercised whenever the subject exists. If it exists within the states, if a foreign voyage may commence or terminate at a port within a state, then the power of Congress may be exercised within a state.

This principle is, if possible, still more clear, when applied to commerce "among the several states." They either join each other, in which case they are separated by a mathematical line, or they are remote from each other, in which case other states lie between them. What is commerce "among" them; and how is it to be conducted? Can a trading expedition between two adjoining states commence and terminate outside of each? And if the trading intercourse be between two states remote from each other, must it not commence in one, terminate in the other, and probably pass through a third? Commerce among the states must, of necessity, be commerce with the states. In the regulation of trade with the Indian tribes, the action of the law, especially when the constitution was made, was chiefly within a state. The power of Congress, then, whatever it may be, must be exercised within the territorial jurisdiction of the several states. . . .

We are now arrived at the inquiry, What is this power?

It is the power to regulate; that is, to prescribe the rule by which commerce is to be governed. This power, like all others vested in Congress, is complete in itself, may be exercised to its utmost extent, and acknowledges no limitations, other than are prescribed in the constitution. These are expressed in plain terms, and do not affect the questions which arise in this case, or which have been discussed at the bar. . . .

The power of Congress, then, comprehends navigation within the limits of every state in the Union; so far as that navigation may be, in any manner, connected with "commerce with foreign nations, or among the several states, or with the Indian tribes." It may, of consequence, pass the jurisdictional line of New York, and act upon the very waters to which the prohibition now under consideration applies.

But it has been urged with great earnestness, that although the power of Congress to regulate commerce with foreign nations, and among the several states, be co-extensive with the subject itself, and have no other limits than are prescribed in the constitution, yet the states may severally exercise the same power within their respective jurisdictions. In support of this argument, it is said that they possessed it as an inseparable attribute of sovereignty, before the formation of the constitution, and still retain it, except so far as they have surrendered it by that instrument; that this principle results from the nature of the government, and is secured by the tenth amendment; that an affirmative grant of power is not exclusive, unless in its own nature it be such that the continued exercise of it by the former possessor is inconsistent with the grant, and that this is not of that description.

The appellant, conceding these postulates, except the last, contends that full power to regulate a particular subject, implies the whole power, and leaves no residuum; that a grant of the whole is incompatible with the existence of a right in another to any part of it. . . .

In discussing the question, whether this power is still in the states, in the case under consideration, we may dismiss from it the inquiry, whether it is surrendered by the mere grant to Congress, or is retained until Congress shall exercise the power. We may dismiss that inquiry, because it has been exercised, and the regulations which Congress deemed it proper to make, are now in full operation. The sole question is, can a state regulate commerce with foreign nations and among the states, while Congress is regulating it? . . .

The act passed in 1803, prohibiting the importation of slaves into any state which shall itself prohibit their importation, implies, it is said, an admission that the states possessed the power to exclude or admit them; from which it is inferred that they possess the same power with respect to other articles.

If this inference were correct; if this power was exercised, not under any particular clause in the constitution, but in virtue of a general right over the subject of commerce, to exist as long as the constitution itself, it might now be exercised. Any state might now import African slaves into its own territory.

But it is obvious that the power of the states over this subject, previous to the year 1808, constitutes an exception to the power of Congress to regulate commerce, and the exception is expressed in such words as to manifest clearly the intention to continue the pre-existing right of the states to admit or exclude, for a limited period. The words are: "The migration or importation of such persons as any of the states, now existing, shall think proper to admit, shall not be prohibited by the Congress prior to the year 1808." The whole object of the exception is to preserve the power to those states which might be disposed to exercise it; and its language seems to the court to convey this idea unequivocally. The possession of this particular power, then, during the time limited in the constitution, cannot be admitted to prove the possession of any other similar power.

It has been said that the act of August 7th, 1789, acknowledges a concurrent power in the states to regulate the conduct of pilots, and hence is inferred an admission of their concurrent right with Congress to regulate commerce with foreign nations, and amongst the states. But this inference is not, we think, justified by the fact.

Although Congress cannot enable a state to legislate, Congress may adopt the provisions of a state on any subject. When the government of the Union was brought into existence, it found a system for the regulation of its pilots in full force in every state. The act which has been mentioned, adopts this system, and gives it the same validity as if its provisions had been specially made by Congress. But the act, it may be said, is prospective also, and the adoption of laws to be made in future, presupposes the right in the maker to legislate on the subject.

The act unquestionably manifests an intention to leave this subject entirely to the states, until Congress should think proper to interpose; but the very enactment of such a law indicates an opinion that it was necessary; that the existing system would not be applicable to the new state of things, unless expressly applied to it by Congress. . . .

These acts were cited at the bar for the purpose of showing an opinion in Congress that the states possess, concurrently with the legislature of the Union, the power to regulate commerce with foreign nations and among the states. Upon reviewing them, we think they do not establish the proposition they were intended to prove. They show the opinion that the states retain powers enabling them to pass the laws to which allusion has been made, not that those laws proceed from the particular power which has been delegated to Congress.

It has been contended by the counsel for the appellant, that, as the word "to regulate" implies in its nature, full power over the thing to be regulated, it excludes, necessarily, the action of all others that would perform the same operation on the same thing. That regulation is designed for the entire result, applying to those parts which remain as they were, as well as to those which are altered. It produces a uniform whole, which is as much disturbed and deranged by changing what the regulating power designs to leave untouched, as that on which it has operated.

There is great force in this argument, and the court is not satisfied that it has been refuted.

Since, however, in exercising the power of regulating their own purely internal affairs, whether of trading or police, the states may sometimes enact laws, the validity of which depends on their interfering with, and being contrary to, an act of Congress passed in pursuance of the constitution, the court will enter upon the inquiry, whether the laws of New York, as expounded by the highest tribunal of that state, have, in their application to this case, come into collision with an act of Congress, and deprived a citizen of a right to which that act entitles him. Should this collision exist, it will be immaterial whether those laws were passed in virtue of a concurrent power "to regulate commerce with foreign nations and among the several states," or in virtue of a power to regulate their domestic trade and police. In one case and the other, the acts of New York must yield to the law of Congress; and the decision sustaining the privilege they confer, against a right given by a law of the Union, must be erroneous. . . .

The questions, then, whether the conveyance of passengers be a part of the coasting trade, and whether a vessel can be protected in that occupation by a coasting license, are not, and cannot be, raised in this case. The real and sole question seems to be, whether a steam machine, in actual use, deprives a vessel of the privileges conferred by a license.

In considering this question, the first idea which presents itself, is that the laws of Congress, for the regulation of commerce, do not look to the principle by which vessels are moved. That subject is left entirely to individual discretion; and, in that vast and complex system of legislative enactment concerning it, which embraces everything that the legislature thought it necessary to notice, there is not, we believe, one word respecting the peculiar principle by which vessels are propelled through the water, except what may be found in a single act, granting a particular privilege to steamboats. With this exception, every act, either prescribing duties, or granting privileges, applies to every vessel, whether navigated by the instrumentality of wind or fire, of sails or machinery. The whole weight of proof, then, is thrown upon him who would introduce a distinction to which the words of the law give no countenance.

If a real difference could be admitted to exist between vessels carrying passengers and others, it has already been observed that there is no fact in this case which can bring up that question. And, if the occupation of steamboats be a matter of such general notoriety that the court may be presumed to know it, although not specially informed by the record, then we deny that the transportation of passengers is their exclusive occupation. It is a matter of general history, that, in our western waters, their principal employment is the transportation of merchandise; and all know, that in the waters of the Atlantic they are frequently so employed.

But all inquiry into this subject seems to the court to be put completely at rest by the act already mentioned, entitled, "An act for the enrolling and licensing of steamboats."

This act authorizes a steamboat employed, or intended to be employed, only in a river or bay of the United States, owned wholly or in part by an alien, resident within the United States, to be enrolled and licensed as if the same belonged to a citizen of the United States.

This act demonstrates the opinion of Congress, that steamboats may be enrolled and licensed, in common with vessels using sails. They are, of course, entitled to the same privileges, and can no more be restrained from navigating waters, and entering ports which are free to such vessels, than if they were wafted on their voyage by the winds, instead of being propelled by the agency of fire. The one element may be as legitimately used as the other, for every commercial purpose authorized by the laws of the Union; and the act of a state inhibiting the use of either to any vessel having a license under the act of Congress, comes, we think, in direct collision with that act.

As this decides the cause, it is unnecessary to enter in an examination of that part of the constitution which empowers Congress to promote the progress of science and the useful arts. . . .

UNITED STATES v. DARBY

312 U. S. 100; 61 S. Ct. 451; 85 L. Ed. 609 (1941)

It used to be said that the federal government has no police power. In a narrow sense this is true, for the police power is defined as the general power to pass regulatory laws for the protection of the health, morals, safety, good order, and general welfare of the community. The Constitution grants no such broad power to Congress, and so, by the operation of the Tenth Amendment, it is reserved to the states. In recent years, however, what may be fairly called a federal police power has come into existence through the use by Congress of certain of its delegated powers to achieve some of the same social objectives which the states achieve through the state police power. Thus Congress has no delegated power to forbid the production of impure food products; but it does have power to forbid the shipping of impure food in interstate commerce. It cannot punish ordinary business swindles; but it may make it a crime to use the mails for purposes of fraud.

In this way Congress has been able to use its power to regulate interstate commerce, to operate the postal service, and to tax, as "constitutional pegs" upon which to hang policies for the national welfare which it has no direct authority to promulgate. By this somewhat indirect method Congress has come to exercise control over an ever-increasing number of social and economic problems. By far the largest part of this growing federal police power is based upon the commerce clause.

The use of commerce power as a peg on which to hang social legislation developed in two somewhat different ways. The first of these involved the doctrine, first announced in the Lottery Case (Champion v. Ames, 1903), that Congress could validly bar from interstate commerce commodities which are dangerous or otherwise objectionable. In 1895 Congress forbade the sending of lottery tickets through interstate commerce or the mails. After holding that lottery tickets are articles of commerce, the Court decided that Congress had the power to guard the people of the United States from the "widespread pestilence of lotteries" by keeping lottery tickets out of the channels of interstate commerce over which Congress has undisputed control. Congress was not slow to exercise the kind of power sustained in the Lottery Case. It has excluded from interstate commerce impure or misbranded food and drugs, meat not properly inspected, obscene literature, and prize fight films (later modified in part), and other injurious or fraudulent commodities. Under a federal statute, if fabrics shipped in interstate commerce are marked "all wool" they must be in fact all wool. It may be noted in passing that the power of Congress over the postal system has enabled it to exercise a wide police power by excluding objectionable articles from the mails, and by forbidding the use of the mails for purposes of fraud.

The Court found no difference in principle between barring objectionable articles from interstate commerce and forbidding the use of the facilities of interstate commerce to aid immoral or criminal activities. In Hoke v. United States (1913), it held valid the Mann Act of 1910 which makes it a crime to transport women across a state line for immoral purposes. The act was not aimed at localized prostitution, but at the organized gangs of white slavers who carried on the interstate traffic in girls and women upon which commercialized vice depends. In 1925 Congress made it a crime knowingly to drive a stolen automobile across a state line, and this was upheld in Brooks v. United States (1925). Under the recent "anti-fence" laws, the same ban was put upon the interstate shipment of stolen goods in general. The so-called Lindbergh Act makes kidnapping a federal crime if the kidnapped person is carried across a state line (held valid in Gooch v. United States, 1936), and it is also a federal crime to use the mails, telephone, telegraph, or any system of interstate communication for purposes of extortion or blackmail. The theory in all these cases is clear and convincing. Congress, which is responsible for interstate commerce, may punish those who use the facilities of that commerce for immoral or criminal purposes.

The federal police power development reviewed thus far had fairly plain sailing constitutionally. All the articles barred from commerce had been "bad" articles, and all the forbidden uses of the facilities of that commerce had been "bad" uses. In 1916, however, Congress pushed the police power theory somewhat further in passing the Child Labor Act of 1916. Congress was well aware that it lacked the power to forbid child labor throughout the country. What it did, therefore, was to forbid the transportation in interstate commerce of the products of mines or factories in which children were employed in violation of the standards set up in this act. In other words, any employer who wished to market his goods through interstate commerce would have to stop employing children. It could not be claimed that the commodities produced in establishments using child labor were "bad" commodities, but merely that the conditions under which they were produced were "bad" conditions. The Supreme Court, split five to four, held the statute invalid in Hammer v. Dagenhart (1918). The majority opinion emphasized that the goods barred from interstate commerce by the act were harmless; that the effect of the act was to regulate, not interstate commerce, but the conditions under which goods entering that commerce were produced, and that it was, therefore, not a bona fide exercise of the commerce power. The Court rejected the argument that Congress could validly prevent those who produce goods under unsatisfactory labor conditions from using the channels of interstate commerce in order to compete with producers in other states who maintain decent labor conditions. It said: "Many causes may cooperate to give one state, by reason of local laws or conditions, an economic advantage over others. The commerce clause was not intended to give Congress a general authority to equalize such conditions." Finally, the act was void under the Tenth Amendment because Congress was using its delegated power over commerce for the purpose of regulating child labor, a power which lies within the range of the powers reserved to the states.

Mr. Justice Holmes dissented in Hammer v. Dagenhart in a strong opinion in which he declared that the Child Labor Act was a clear and direct exercise of the commerce power and that it should not be held void because of its indirect effects upon state authority. "It does not matter," he said, "whether the supposed evil precedes or follows the transportation. It is enough that, in the opinion of Congress, the transportation encourages the evil. The notion that prohibition is any less prohibition when applied to things now thought evil I do not understand. But if there is any matter upon which civilized countries have agreed,—far more unanimously than they have with regard to intoxicants and some other matters over which this country is now emotionally aroused,—it is the evil of premature and excessive child labor. I should have thought that if we were to introduce our own moral conceptions where, in my opinion, they do not belong, this was preeminently a case for upholding the exercise of all its powers by the United States. But I had thought that the propriety of the exercise of a power admitted to exist in some cases was for the consideration of Congress alone, and that this Court always had disavowed the right to intrude its judgment upon questions of policy or morals. It is not for this Court to pronounce when prohibition is necessary to regulation if it ever may be necessary—to say that it is permissible as against strong drink, but not against the product of ruined lives. The act does not meddle with anything belonging to the states. They may regulate their internal affairs and their domestic commerce as they like. But when they seek to send their products across the state line they are no longer within their rights."

Seldom has judicial and professional opinion been more sharply divided than on the issues presented in Hammer v. Dagenhart. It is therefore both interesting and important that in the Darby case printed below the Court overruled Hammer v. Dagenhart. It is equally significant that this reversal met with virtually universal approval. In the 23 years which had intervened, we had reached a clearer and surer understanding of the responsibility which the commerce clause places upon Congress. The early and not uncommon idea that the use by Congress of its commerce power to deal with broad social problems was not quite honest, that it amounted to "covert" or "backstairs" legislation, had been largely forgotten. We had come to realize that serious evils which menace the health, safety, and welfare of the nation are spread and even generated by our vast national system of transportation and communication and by our continent-wide network of interstate markets. It was clear that interstate commerce could be used for the public injury as well as for the public welfare. The commerce clause makes Congress the guardian of interstate commerce—and the only guardian. It was therefore, not only the right of Congress but its clear duty to see to it that the facilities of interstate commerce were not used by any one, in any manner, to do any kind of harm. This is the basic doctrine on which the Darby case rests.

With the overruling of Hammer v. Dagenhart went another long-standing doctrine—the doctrine of "dual federalism" (see United States v. Butler, 1936) under which the reserved powers of the states were held to check the delegated powers of Congress. Congress, by this theory, was forbidden to exercise its delegated powers for "purposes" lying within the range of the reserved powers of the states. Since the reserved powers of the states are those powers which remain after the Constitution delegates powers to Congress, it did seem dubious logic to assert that reserved powers could somehow limit the body of powers from which they were merely leftovers. The Court, in the Darby case, announces that when the Constitu-

tion delegates a power to Congress, the delegation is complete; and no strings running from the Tenth Amendment diminish or restrain the scope or reach of that power.

While important powers have accrued to Congress from the increased use of interstate commerce facilities, Congress has not ordinarily sought to use this new authority to injure the states or subvert their authority. Congressmen, after all, represent the people of the states as well as the people of the nation. Most uses of this growing federal power have resulted from the inability of the states to cope with problems which have spread beyond their jurisdiction. Where states have local policies they wish to preserve, Congress has frequently used its power over commerce to help them. The practical effect of the Darby decision, for example, is that a state may now outlaw child labor and other substandard labor conditions without subjecting their own manufacturers to competition from goods made by such labor in other states. Even more helpful from the standpoint of state policy are the so-called "divesting statutes" which forbid certain shipments into a state if that state wishes to keep them out; see Clark Distilling Co. v. Western Maryland Ry. Co. (1917). Legislation, similar in purpose, is the Federal Black Bass Act of 1926, which makes it illegal to ship fish out of the state if it violates the law of the state to do so; see United States v. Howard (1957).

In 1938 Congress enacted the Fair Labor Standards (Wages and Hours) Act, which provided the first comprehensive regulation of the working standards of persons engaged in interstate commerce or producing goods for that commerce. The act provided (the first year) for a minimum wage of 25 cents an hour and a maximum 44-hour week without overtime pay, and required employers subject to the act to keep records of the hours and pay of their workers. Prohibited, also, was the employment of children under 16 in manufacturing and mining, and under 18 in hazardous occupations. The act not only made it a crime to ship in interstate commerce goods manufactured in violation of these standards but, in addition, made it a crime to employ persons in the manufacture of goods for commerce under conditions which did not meet the prescribed standards. Darby, the president of a lumber company, was indicted for violating the wages, hours, and record-keeping provisions of the act.

Mr. Justice Stone delivered the opinion of the Court, saying in part:

The two principal questions raised by the record in this case are, *first,* whether Congress has constitutional power to prohibit the shipment in interstate commerce of lumber manufactured by employees whose wages are less than a prescribed minimum or whose weekly hours of labor at that wage are greater than a prescribed maximum, and, *second,* whether it has power to prohibit the employment of workmen in the production of goods "for interstate commerce" at other than prescribed wages and hours. A subsidiary question is whether in connection with such prohibitions Congress can require the employer subject to them to keep records showing the hours worked each day and week by each of his employees including those engaged "in the production and manufacture of goods to wit, lumber, for 'interstate commerce.' " . . .

The Fair Labor Standards Act set up a comprehensive legislative scheme for preventing the shipment in interstate commerce of certain products and commodities produced in the United States under labor conditions as respects wages and hours which fail to conform to standards set up by the Act. Its purpose, as we judicially know from the declaration of policy in § 2(a) of the Act, and the reports of Congressional committees proposing the legislation, . . . is to exclude from interstate commerce goods produced for the commerce and to prevent their production for interstate commerce, under conditions detrimental to the maintenance of the minimum standards of living necessary for health and general well-being; and to prevent the use of interstate commerce as the means of competition in the distribution of goods so produced, and as the means of spreading and perpetuating such substandard labor conditions among the workers of the several states. The Act also sets up an administrative procedure whereby those standards may from time to time be modified generally as to industries subject to the Act or within an industry in accordance with specified standards, by an administrator acting in collaboration with "Industry Committees" appointed by him. . . .

The indictment charges that appellee is engaged, in the state of Georgia, in the business of acquiring raw materials, which he manufactures into finished lumber with the intent, when manufactured, to ship it in interstate commerce to customers outside the state, and that he does in fact so ship a large part of the lumber so produced. There are numerous counts charging appellee with the shipment in interstate commerce from Georgia to points outside the state of lumber in the production of which, for interstate commerce, appellee has employed workmen at less than the prescribed minimum wage or more than the prescribed maximum hours without payment to them of any wage for overtime. Other counts charge the employment by appellee of workmen in the production of lumber for interstate commerce at wages [of] less than 25 cents an hour or for more than the maximum hours per week without payment to them of the prescribed overtime wage. Still another count charges appellee with failure to keep records showing the hours worked each day a week by each of his employees as required by § 11(c) and the regulation of the administrator, . . . and also that appellee unlawfully failed to keep such records of employees engaged "in the production and manufacture of goods, to-wit lumber, for interstate commerce." . . .

The case comes here on assignments by the Government that the district court erred in so far as it held that Congress was without constitutional power to penalize the acts set forth in the indictment, and appellee seeks to sustain the decision below on the grounds that the prohibition by Congress of those Acts is unauthorized by the commerce clause and is prohibited by the Fifth Amendment. . . . Hence we . . . confine our decision to the validity and construction of the statute.

The prohibition of shipment of the proscribed goods in interstate commerce. Section 15(a) (1) prohibits, and the indictment charges, the shipment in interstate commerce, of goods produced for interstate commerce by employees whose wages and hours of employment do not conform to the requirements of the Act. Since this section is not violated unless the commodity shipped has been produced under labor conditions prohibited by § 6 and § 7, the only question arising under the commerce clause with respect to such shipments is whether Congress has the constitutional power to prohibit them.

While manufacture is not of itself interstate commerce the shipment of manufactured goods interstate is such commerce and the prohibition of such shipment by Congress is indubitably a regulation of the commerce. The power to regulate commerce is the power "to prescribe the rule by which commerce is governed." Gibbons v. Ogden [1824]. It extends not only to those regulations which aid, foster and protect the commerce, but embraces those which prohibit it. . . . It is conceded that the power of Congress to prohibit transportation in interstate commerce includes noxious articles, Lottery Case (Champion v. Ames) [1903] . . . ; stolen articles, Brooks v. United States [1925]; kidnapped persons, Gooch v. United States [1936] . . . and articles such as intoxicating liquor or convict made goods, traffic in which is forbidden or restricted by the laws of the state of destination. Kentucky Whip & Collar Co. v. Illinois C. R. Co. [1937].

But it is said that the present prohibition falls within the scope of none of these categories; that while the prohibition is nominally a regulation of the commerce its motive or purpose is regulation of wages and hours of persons engaged in manufacture, the control of which has been reserved to the states and upon which Georgia and some of the states of destination have placed no restriction; that the effect of the present statute is not to exclude the prescribed articles from interstate commerce in aid of state regulation as in Kentucky Whip & Collar Co. v. Illinois C. R. Co., but instead, under the guise of a regulation of interstate commerce, it undertakes to regulate wages and hours within the state contrary to the policy of the state which has elected to leave them unregulated.

The power of Congress over interstate commerce "is complete in itself, may be exercised to its utmost extent, and acknowledges no limitations other than are prescribed in the Constitution." Gibbons v. Ogden. That power can neither be enlarged nor diminished by the exercise or nonexercise of state power. . . . Congress, following its own conception of public policy concerning the restrictions which may appropriately be imposed on interstate commerce, is free to exclude from the commerce articles whose use in the states for which they are destined it may conceive to be injurious to the public health, morals or welfare, even though the state has not sought to regulate their use. . . .

Such regulation is not a forbidden invasion of state power merely because either its motive or its consequence is to restrict the use of articles of commerce within the states of destination and is not prohibited unless by other constitutional provisions. It is no objection to the assertion of the power to regulate interstate commerce that its exercise is attended by the same incidents which attend the exercise of the police power of the states. . . .

The motive and purpose of the present regulation are plainly to make effective the Congressional conception of public policy that interstate commerce should not be made the instrument of competition in the distribution of goods produced under substandard labor conditions, which competition is injurious to the commerce and to the states from and to which the commerce flows. The motive and purpose of a regulation of interstate commerce are matters for the legislative judgment upon the exercise of which the Constitution places no restriction and over which the courts are given no control. . . . "The judicial cannot prescribe to the legislative department of the government limitations upon the exercise of its acknowledged power." Veazie Bank v. Fenno [1869]. Whatever their motive and purpose, regulations of commerce which do not infringe some constitutional prohibition are within the plenary power conferred on Congress by the Commerce Clause. Subject only to that limitation, presently to be considered, we conclude that the prohibition of the shipment interstate of goods produced under the forbidden substandard labor conditions is within the constitutional authority of Congress.

In the more than a century which has elapsed since the decision of Gibbons v. Ogden, these principles of constitutional interpretation have been so long and repeatedly recognized by this Court as applicable to the Commerce Clause, that there would be little occasion for repeating them now were it not for the decision of this Court twenty-two years ago in Hammer v. Dagenhart [1918]. In that case it was held by a bare majority of the Court over the powerful and now classic dissent of Mr. Justice Holmes setting forth the fundamental issues involved, that Congress was without power to exclude the products of child labor from interstate commerce. The reasoning and conclusion of the Court's opinion there cannot be reconciled with the conclusion which we have reached, that the power of Congress under the Commerce Clause is plenary to exclude any article from interstate commerce subject only to the specific prohibitions of the Constitution.

Hammer v. Dagenhart has not been followed. The distinction on which the decision was rested that Congressional power to prohibit interstate commerce is limited to articles which in themselves have some harmful or deleterious property—a distinction which was novel when made and unsupported by any provision of the Constitution—has long since been abandoned. Brooks v. United States; Kentucky Whip & Collar Co. v. Illinois C. R. Co.; . . . Mulford v. Smith [1939]. The thesis of the opinion that the motive of the prohibition or its effect to control in some measure the use or production within the states of the article thus excluded from the commerce can operate to deprive the regulation of its constitutional authority has long since ceased to have force. . . . And finally we have declared "The authority of the federal government over interstate commerce does not differ in extent or character from that retained by the states over intrastate commerce." United States v. Rock Royal Co-operative [1939].

The conclusion is inescapable that Hammer v. Dagenhart was a departure from the principles which have prevailed in the interpretation of the commerce clause both before and since the decision and that such vitality, as a precedent, as it then had has long since been exhausted. It should be and now is overruled.

Validity of the wage and hour requirements. Section 15 (a) (2), and §§ 6 and 7 require employers to conform to the wage and hour provisions with respect to all employees engaged in the production of goods for interstate commerce. As appellee's employees are not alleged to be "engaged in interstate commerce" the validity of the prohibition turns on the question whether the employment, under other than the prescribed labor standards, of employees engaged in the production of goods for interstate commerce is so related to the commerce and so affects it as to be within the reach of the power of Congress to regulate it.. . . .

. . . The power of Congress over interstate commerce is not confined to the regulation of commerce among the states. It extends to those activities intrastate which so affect interstate commerce or the exercise of the power of Congress over it as to make regulation of them appropriate means to the attainment of a legitimate end, the exercise of the granted power of Congress to regulate interstate commerce. . . .

. . . A recent example is the National Labor Relations Act for the regulation of employer and employee relations in industries in which strikes, induced by unfair labor practices named in the Act, tend to disturb or obstruct interstate commerce. See National Labor Relations Bd. v. Jones & L. Steel Corp. [1937]. . . . But long before the adoption of the National Labor Relations Act this Court had many times held that the power of Congress to regulate interstate commerce extends to the regulation through legislative action of activities intrastate which have a substantial effect on the commerce or the exercise of the Congressional power over it.

In such legislation Congress has sometimes left it to the courts to determine whether the intrastate activities have the prohibited effect on the commerce, as in the Sherman Act. It has sometimes left it to an administrative board or agency to determine whether the activities sought to be regulated or prohibited have such effect, as in the case of the Interstate Commerce Act, and the

National Labor Relations Act or whether they come within the statutory definition of the prohibited Act as in the Federal Trade Commission Act. And sometimes Congress itself has said that a particular activity affects the commerce as it did in the present act, the Safety Appliance Act and the Railway Labor Act. In passing on the validity of legislation of the class last mentioned the only function of courts is to determine whether the particular activity regulated or prohibited is within the reach of the federal power. . . .

Congress, having by the present Act adopted the policy of excluding from interstate commerce all goods produced for the commerce which do not conform to the specified labor standards, it may choose the means reasonably adapted to the attainment of the permitted end, even though they involve control of intrastate activities. . . . A familiar like exercise of power is the regulation of intrastate transactions which are so commingled with or related to interstate commerce that all must be regulated if the interstate commerce is to be effectively controlled. Shreveport Case [1914]. . . . Similarly Congress may require inspection and preventive treatment of all cattle in a disease infected area in order to prevent shipment in interstate commerce of some of the cattle without the treatment. . . . It may prohibit the removal, at destination, of labels required by the Pure Food & Drugs Act to be affixed to articles transported in interstate commerce. . . . And we have recently held that Congress in the exercise of its power to require inspection and grading of tobacco shipped in interstate commerce may compel such inspection and grading of all tobacco sold at local auction rooms from which a substantial part but not all of the tobacco sold is shipped in interstate commerce. . . .

We think also that § 15(a) (2) now under consideration, is sustainable independently of § 15(a) (1), which prohibits shipment or transportation of the proscribed goods. As we have said the evils aimed at by the Act are the spread of substandard labor conditions through the use of the facilities of interstate commerce for competition by the goods so produced with those produced under the prescribed or better labor conditions; and the consequent dislocation of the commerce itself caused by the impairment or destruction of local businesses by competition made effective through interstate commerce. The Act is thus directed at the suppression of a method or kind of competition in interstate commerce which it has in effect condemned as "unfair," as the Clayton Act has condemned other "unfair methods of competition" made effective through interstate commerce. . . .

The Sherman Act and the National Labor Relations Act are familiar examples of the exertion of the commerce power to prohibit or control activities wholly intrastate because of their effect on interstate commerce. . . .

The means adopted by § 15(a) (2) for the protection of interstate commerce by the suppression of the production of the condemned goods for interstate commerce is so related to the commerce and so affects it as to be within the reach of the commerce power. . . . Congress, to attain its objective in the suppression of nation-wide competition in interstate commerce by goods produced under substandard labor conditions, has made no distinction as to the volume or amount of shipments in the commerce or of production for commerce by any particular shipper or producer. It recognized that in present day industry, competition by a small part may affect the whole and that the total effect of the competition of many small producers may be great. . . . The legislation aimed at a whole embraces all its parts.

So far as Carter v. Carter Coal Co. [1936] is inconsistent with this conclusion, its doctrine is limited in principle by the decisions under the Sherman Act and the National Labor Relations Act, which we have cited and which we follow. . . .

Our conclusion is unaffected by the Tenth Amendment which provides: "The powers not delegated to the United States by the Constitution nor prohibited by it to the states are reserved to the states respectively or to the people." The amendment states but a truism that all is retained which has not been surrendered. There is nothing in the history of its adoption to suggest that it was more than declaratory of the relationship between the national and state governments as it had been established by the Constitution before the amendment or that its purpose was other than to allay fears that the new national government might seek to exercise powers not granted, and that the states might not be able to exercise fully their reserved powers. . . .

From the beginning and for many years the amendment has been construed as not depriving the national government of authority to resort to all means for the exercise of a granted power which are appropriate and plainly adapted to the permitted end. . . . Whatever doubts may have arisen of the soundness of that conclusion they have been put at rest by the decisions under the Sherman Act and the National Labor Relations Act which we have cited. . . .

Reversed.

HEART OF ATLANTA MOTEL v. UNITED STATES
379 U. S. 241; 85 S. Ct. 348; 13 L. Ed. 2d 258
(1964)

In the cases discussed above the Court permitted Congress to close the channels of interstate commerce to commodities and for purposes of which it disapproves. The effect is to permit a certain diversity of policy among the states without fear of out-of-state interference, as well as to aid in the capture of local criminals by helping to reduce their avenues of escape.

A quite different use of the commerce power, however, lies in the power of Congress to keep the channels of interstate commerce open and unimpeded. The development of this aspect of the commerce power into an effective weapon of social control came very slowly. For one hundred years prior to 1887, Congress made no attempt to regulate interstate commerce, and the Supreme Court was left to struggle alone with the question whether a particular activity was local, and hence subject to state control, or was interstate commerce and hence subject to no control at all.

With the passage of the Interstate Commerce Act in 1887 and the Sherman Act in 1890, Congress for the first time moved to regulate transportation and forbid monopoly in interstate commerce—only to find itself faced with a Supreme Court whose members showed little sympathy for government economic regulation of any kind. While the Court conceded Congress' right to provide for the safe movement of goods across state lines, it drew a sharp line between the control of things which had a direct effect on such commerce, and those whose effect was merely indirect. Thus, in United States v. E. C. Knight Co. (1895), it denied the use of the Sherman Act to break up the powerful sugar trust which had been formed to control the manufacture and distribution of refined sugar throughout the United States. The Court held the Antitrust Act did not apply to combinations in restraint of manufacturing. "Doubtless the power to control the manufacture of a given thing involves in a certain sense the control of its disposition, but this is a secondary and not the primary sense; and although the exercise of that power may result in bringing the operation of commerce into play, it does not control it, and affects it only incidentally and indirectly. Commerce succeeds to manufacture, and is not a part of it. The power to regulate commerce is the power to prescribe the rule by which commerce shall be governed, and is a power independent of the power to suppress monopoly." In Oliver Iron Mining Co. v. Lord (1923) the Court held that mining, like manufacturing, was not interstate commerce.

Even where an interstate carrier was clearly involved, the regulation was limited to things directly affecting interstate movement. A federal statute outlawing so-called "yellow-dog contracts" (by which workmen were forced to agree not to join labor unions) was held void in Adair v. United States (1908) on the ground, among others, that there is no "possible legal or logical connection . . . between an employee's membership in a labor organization and the carrying on of interstate commerce. . . ."

In 1914, in the Shreveport Case, the Court abandoned this outmoded concept of two mutually exclusive areas of intrastate and interstate commerce, each clearly and safely under the control of state or federal government, and put in its place as a rule for measuring federal authority in the field of commerce, the realistic test of whether commercial or business activities—even though they be local—so impinge upon or affect interstate commerce as to bring them reasonably within the range of federal control. The Court recognized a functional relationship between local and interstate commerce and permitted the ICC to forbid a railroad to set local rates which discriminated against interstate rates which had been found by the commission to be reasonable.

In 1922 the doctrine of the Shreveport Case was extended to cover local businesses other than common carriers. In 1921 Congress had passed the Packers and Stockyards Act in an effort to break up discriminatory practices resulting from control of the stockyards by the "Big Five" meat packers: Swift, Armour, Cudahy, Wilson, and Morris. Livestock was shipped into Chicago from producers throughout the West and most of the meat, either before or after packing, was shipped to eastern markets. The control of the stockyards by the packers resulted in discrimination against the western shipper as well as other buyers. The act provided an elaborate scheme of regulation, including approval by the Secretary of Agriculture of all rates and charges for services and facilities in the stockyards. In Stafford v. Wallace (1922) the Supreme Court sustained this regulation, rejecting the argument that Congress had no authority to control purely local sales of cattle after they had come to rest in the stockyards. "The stockyards," the Court said, "are not a place of rest or final destination. Thousands of head of live stock arrive daily by carloads and trainload lots, and must be promptly sold and disposed of and moved out to give place to the constantly flowing traffic that presses behind. The stockyards are but a throat through which the current flows, and the transactions which occur therein are only incident to this current from the West to the East, and from one State to another. Such transactions cannot be separated from the movement to which they contribute, and necessarily take on its character. . . ."

Finally, in 1937 in NLRB v. Jones & Laughlin Steel Corp., the last of the serious impediments to the use of the commerce power for police-power purposes was abandoned. In July, less than two months after the National Industrial Recovery Act had been held void in Schechter Poultry Corp. v. United States (1935), Congress passed the National Labor Relations Act (Wagner Act), the first thoroughgoing and genuinely regulatory federal act to deal with the relations between labor and capital. The act was unique both in scope and in method. Its scope included all labor disputes which burdened or obstructed interstate commerce. Such burden or obstruction might take the form (1) of impairing the efficiency or safety of the instrumentalities of commerce, (2) of restraining the flow of raw materials or manufactured goods through interstate commerce, or controlling the prices thereof, (3) of reducing employment and wages sufficiently to reduce substantially the market for goods moving in interstate commerce, or (4) of obstructing directly the actual current of commerce. The method employed by the act was that of defining carefully seven or eight "unfair labor practices" which were forbidden, and of creating a new National Labor Relations Board with power upon investigation to issue "cease and desist orders," enforceable in the courts, against those guilty of these practices. This was the technique employed in the Federal Trade Commission Act under which the commission issued "cease and desist orders" against those found to be engaging in unfair competitive trade practices. The NLRB was, therefore, a very powerful body.

The Wagner Act appeared at first to rest upon precarious footing, since its provisions extended to labor relations in the process of manufacturing goods which were to be moved in interstate commerce. Ever since the E. C. Knight case the Court had insisted that manufacturing was antecedent to and clearly separate from the interstate commerce in which the manufactured goods later move; see Hammer v. Dagenhart (1918). While the Shreveport Case and Stafford v. Wallace indicated that the Court's attitude toward this distinction was becoming less rigid, the emphasis in the Schechter case upon "direct" and "indirect" effects which local activities produce on interstate commerce did not give supporters of the Wagner Act much encouragement. Moreover, in Carter v. Carter Coal Co. (1936), which held the Guffey Coal Act void, the Court said that the relations between employers and workmen in the coal industry did not directly affect interstate commerce in coal and could not therefore be regulated by Congress. The Court might very consistently have held the Wagner Act void in its application to labor relations in the field of manufacturing.

The Wagner Act came before the Court in the Jones & Laughlin Steel case. The NLRB had found that the Jones & Laughlin Steel Corporation had discharged some of its men because of their labor union activities. The board ordered the company to reinstate them and to cease such discrimination. The company was the fourth largest producer of steel in the country. It had 19 subsidiaries which comprised an integrated system. It owned mines, ships, railroads, furnaces, and mills. The board found that the plants in which the labor troubles occurred "might be likened to the heart of a self-contained, highly integrated body. They draw in the raw materials from Michigan, Minnesota, West Virginia, Pennsylvania in part through arteries and by means controlled by the respondent; they transform the materials and then pump them out to all parts of the nation through the vast mechanism which the respondent has elaborated."

The Court brushed aside arguments that the "stream of commerce" was broken, that this was manufacturing, and that its effect on interstate commerce was only indirect. "In view of respondent's far-flung activities, it is idle to say that the effect would be indirect or remote. It is obvious that it would be immediate and might be catastrophic. We are asked to shut our eyes to the plainest facts of our national life and to deal with the

*question of direct and indirect effects in an intellectual vacuum. . . . When
industries organize themselves on a national scale, making their relation
to interstate commerce the dominant factor in their activities, how can it
be maintained that their industrial labor relations constitute a forbidden
field into which Congress may not enter when it is necessary to protect
interstate commerce from the paralyzing consequences of industrial war?"*

Perhaps even more striking than the extension of federal control in the
field of labor relations has been the development of such control in the field
of agriculture. The Agricultural Adjustment Act of 1933, which was held
void in United States v. Butler (1936), had relied for its constitutional
underpinning upon the delegated powers of Congress to tax and to spend
money. The Agricultural Adjustment Act of 1938, which aimed at similar
objectives, was based on the commerce power. The act declared that its
policy (in part) was: *"to regulate interstate and foreign commerce in
cotton, wheat, corn, tobacco and rice to the extent necessary to provide an
orderly, adequate, and balanced flow of such commodities in interstate
and foreign commerce through storage of reserve supplies, loans, marketing quotas, assisting farmers to obtain, in so far as practicable, parity prices
for such commodities and parity of income, and assisting consumers to
obtain an adequate and steady supply of such commodities at fair prices."*

The attack upon the validity of the statute arose under the sections
providing for the establishment of marketing quotas for flue-cured tobacco. There were similar sections dealing with cotton, wheat, corn, and
rice. The act authorized the Secretary of Agriculture, when he found that
the supply of tobacco had increased beyond a certain point, to put into
effect a national marketing quota, provided that not more than one-third
of the previous year's tobacco growers were opposed. The quotas were
allocated in such a way that each grower was given a quota which he must
not exceed. If tobacco in excess of the quota for a particular farm was
marketed through a warehouse man, the latter paid to the Secretary a
penalty equal to 50 percent of the market price of the excess, and might
deduct this amount from the prices paid to the producer. In Mulford v.
Smith (1939) the Supreme Court held the act valid. It was not, the Court
said, a regulation of production but only a regulation of the interstate
commerce in tobacco at the *"throat where tobacco enters the stream of
commerce,—the marketing warehouse."* The fact that not all the tobacco
was sold interstate was considered immaterial since the *"regulation to be
effective, must, and therefore may constitutionally, apply to all sales."*

A more extreme application of the 1938 statute was upheld in Wickard
v. Filburn (1942). Quotas were established for the production of wheat in
order to prevent surpluses and maintain prices. Filburn raised 23 acres of
wheat, none of which was intended for interstate commerce, and all of
which he consumed or fed to his stock. The quota allotted to him, however,

was 11.1 acres; and the Court held him validly liable to the statutory penalties on the wheat produced in excess of this quota. His production of this wheat affected interstate commerce "directly" just as much as though he had farmed 23,000 acres instead of 23.

To a person unfamiliar with our institutions and constitutional history, it must seem strange that the national government, in its efforts to abolish race discrimination, should be forced to act under a grant of power to regulate interstate commerce. Of course, if a state government does the discriminating, either through its laws or its officials, the courts can interfere under the equal protection clause of the Fourteenth Amendment. But as early as 1883 in the Civil Rights Cases the Court made clear that private discrimination was not forbidden by the Fourteenth Amendment, and Congress had no "police power" under which it could outlaw it generally.

The passage of the Civil Rights Act of 1964, Title II of which was sustained in the present cases, brought to an all-time high congressional efforts to abolish race discrimination in the United States. The act itself was remarkable for a number of reasons. First, for the first time since the ill-fated Civil Rights Act of 1875, Congress made a sweeping attack on race discrimination. Second, the act commanded overwhelming bipartisan support. After five months of committee hearings, 2800 pages of testimony, and seven months of debates, the measure passed the House 289 to 126. In an unusual move, the Senate did not even send it to committee, but worked out a bill with informal bipartisan conferences. The House adopted the Senate bill without change. Third, for the first time in history the Senate, with the all-out support of both majority and minority leaders, invoked cloture to stop a Southern filibuster on a civil rights measure.

Mr. Justice Clark delivered the opinion of the Court, saying in part:

This is a declaratory judgment action attacking the constitutionality of Title II of the Civil Rights Act of 1964. . . . Appellees counterclaimed for enforcement under § 206(a) of the Act and asked for a three-judge district court under § 206(b). A three-judge court . . . sustained the validity of the Act and issued a permanent injunction on appellees' counterclaim restraining appellant from continuing to violate the Act. . . . We affirm the judgment.

1. The Factual Background and Contentions of the Parties.

The case comes here on admissions and stipulated facts. Appellant owns and operates the Heart of Atlanta Motel which has 216 rooms available to transient guests. The motel is located on Courtland Street, two blocks from downtown Peachtree Street. It is readily accessible to interstate highways 75 and 85 and state highways 23 and 41. Appellant solicits patronage from outside the State of Georgia through various national advertising media, including magazines of national circulation; it maintains over 50 billboards and highway signs within the State, soliciting patronage for the motel; it accepts convention trade from outside Georgia and approximately 75% of its registered guests are from out of State. Prior to passage of the Act the motel had followed a practice of refusing to rent rooms to Negroes, and it alleged that it intended to continue to do so. In an effort to perpetuate that policy this suit was filed.

The appellant contends that Congress in passing this Act exceeded its power to regulate commerce under Art. I, § 8, cl. 3, of the Constitution of the United States; that the Act violates the Fifth Amendment because appellant is deprived of the right to choose its customers and operate its business as it wishes, resulting in a taking of its liberty and property without due process of law and a taking of its property without just compensation; and, finally, that by requiring appellant to rent available rooms to Negroes against its will, Congress is subjecting it to involuntary servitude in contravention of the Thirteenth Amendment. . . .

2. The History of the Act.

[The Court notes the passage by Congress of earlier civil rights acts, and reviews briefly the struggle to enact the present statute.]

The Act as finally adopted was most comprehensive, undertaking to prevent through peaceful and voluntary settlement discrimination in voting, as well as in places of accommodation and public facilities, federally secured programs and in employment. Since Title II is the only portion under attack here, we confine our consideration to those public accommodation provisions.

3. Title II of the Act.

This Title is divided into seven sections beginning with § 201(a) which provides that:

"All persons shall be entitled to the full and equal enjoyment of the goods, services, facilities, privileges, advantages, and accommodations of any place of public accommodation, as defined in this section, without discrimination or segregation on the ground of race, color, religion, or national origin."

There are listed in § 201 (b) four classes of business establishments, each of which "serves the public" and "is a place of public accommodation" within the meaning of § 201 (a) "if its operations affect commerce, or if discrimination or segregation by it is supported by State action." The covered establishments are:

"(1) any inn, hotel, motel, or other establishment which provides lodging to transient guests, other than an establishment located within a building which contains not more than five rooms for rent or hire and which is actually occupied by the proprietor of such establishment as his residence; (2) any restaurant, cafeteria . . . [not here involved]; (3) any motion picture house . . . [not here involved]; (4) any establishment . . . which is physically located within the premises of any establishment otherwise covered by this subsection, or . . . within the premises of which is physically located any such covered establishment . . . [not here involved]."

Section 201 (c) defines the phrase "affect commerce" as applied to the above establishments. It first declares that "any inn, hotel, motel, or other establishment which provides lodging to transient guests" affects commerce per se. . . .

Finally, § 203 prohibits the withholding or denial, etc., of any right or privilege secured by § 201 . . . or the intimidation, threatening or coercion of any person with the purpose of interfering with any such right or the punishing, etc., of any person for exercising or attempting to exercise any such right.

The remaining sections of the Title are remedial ones for violations of any of the previous sections. Remedies are limited to civil actions for preventive relief. The Attorney General may bring suit where he has "reasonable cause to believe that any person or group of persons is engaged in a pattern or practice of resistance to the full enjoyment of any of the rights secured by this title, and that the pattern or practice is of such a nature and is intended to deny the full exercise of the rights herein described . . . ."

4. Application of Title II to Heart of Atlanta Motel.

It is admitted that the operation of the motel brings it within the provisions of § 201 (a) of the Act and that appellant refused to provide lodging for transient Negroes because of their race or color and that it intends to continue that policy unless restrained.

The sole question posed is, therefore, the constitutionality of the Civil Rights Act of 1964 as applied to these facts. The legislative history of the Act indicates that Congress based the Act on § 5 and the Equal Protection Clause of the Fourteenth Amendment as well as its power to regulate interstate commerce under Art. I, § 8, cl. 3 of the Constitution.

The Senate Commerce Committee made it quite clear that the fundamental object of Title II was to vindicate "the deprivation of personal dignity that surely accompanies denials of equal access to public establishments." At the same time, however, it noted that such an objective has been and could be readily achieved "by congressional action based on the commerce power of the

Constitution.".... Our study of the legislative record, made in the light of prior cases, has brought us to the conclusion that Congress possessed ample power in this regard, and we have therefore not considered the other grounds relied upon. This is not to say that the remaining authority upon which it acted was not adequate, a question upon which we do not pass, but merely that since the commerce power is sufficient for our decision here we have considered it alone. . . .

5. The Civil Rights Cases (1883), and their Application.

In the light of our ground for decision, it might be well at the outset to discuss the Civil Rights Cases, which declared provisions of the Civil Rights Act of 1875 unconstitutional. We think that decision inapposite, and without precedential value in determining the constitutionality of the present Act. Unlike Title II of the present legislation, the 1875 Act broadly proscribed discrimination in "inns, public conveyances on land or water, theaters, and other public places of amusement," without limiting the categories of affected businesses to those impinging upon interstate commerce. In contrast, the applicability of Title II is carefully limited to enterprises having direct and substantial relation to the interstate flow of goods and people, except where state action is involved. Further, the fact that certain kinds of businesses may not in 1875 have been sufficiently involved in interstate commerce to warrant bringing them within the ambit of the commerce power is not necessarily dispositive of the same question today. Our populace had not reached its present mobility, nor were facilities, goods and services circulating as readily in interstate commerce as they are today. Although the principles which we apply today are those first formulated by Chief Justice Marshall in Gibbons v. Ogden [1824], the conditions of transportation and commerce have changed dramatically, and we must apply those principles to the present state of commerce. The sheer increase in volume of interstate traffic alone would give discriminatory practices which inhibit travel far larger impact upon the Nation's commerce than such practices had on the economy of another day. . . .

6. The Basis of Congressional Action.

While the Act as adopted carried no congressional findings the record of its passage through each house is replete with evidence of the burdens that discrimination by race or color places upon interstate commerce. . . . This testimony included the fact that our people have become increasingly mobile with millions of people of all races traveling from State to State; that Negroes in particular have been the subject of discrimination in transient accommodations, having to travel great distances to secure the same; that often they have been unable to obtain accommodations and have had to call upon friends to put them up overnight . . . ; and that these conditions have become so acute as to require the listing of available lodging for Negroes in a special guidebook which was itself "dramatic testimony to the difficulties" Negroes encounter in travel. . . . These exclusionary practices were found to be nationwide, the Under Secretary of Commerce testifying that there is "no question that this discrimination in the North still exists to a large degree" and in the West and Midwest as well. . . . This testimony indicated a qualitative as well as quantitative effect on interstate travel by Negroes. The former was obvious impairment of the Negro traveler's pleasure and convenience that resulted when he continually was uncertain of finding lodging. As for the latter, there was evidence that this uncertainty stemming from racial discrimination had the effect of discouraging travel on the part of a substantial portion of the Negro community. . . . This was the conclusion not only of the Under Secretary of Commerce but also of the Administrator of the Federal Aviation Agency who wrote the Chairman of the Senate Commerce Committee that it was his "belief that air commerce is adversely affected by the denial to a·substantial segment of the traveling public of adequate and desegregated public accommodations.". . . We shall not burden this opinion with further details since the voluminous testimony presents overwhelming evidence that discrimination by hotels and motels impedes interstate travel.

7. The Power of Congress Over Interstate Travel.

The power of Congress to deal with these obstructions depends on the meaning of the Commerce Clause. Its meaning was first enunciated 140 years ago by the great Chief Justice John Marshall in Gibbons v. Ogden, in these words:

[The Court here quotes at length from the opinion concerning the nature of interstate commerce and congressional power over it.]

In short, the determinative test of the exercise of power by the Congress under the Commerce Clause is simply whether the activity sought to be regulated is "commerce which concerns more States than one" and has a real and substantial relation to the national interest. Let us now turn to this facet of the problem.

That the "intercourse" of which the Chief Justice spoke included the movement of persons through more States than one was settled as early as 1849, in the Passenger Cases where Mr. Justice McLean stated: "That the transportation of passengers is a part of commerce is not now an open question." Again in 1913 Mr. Justice McKenna, speaking for the Court, said: "Commerce among the States, we have said, consists of intercourse and traffic between their citizens, and includes the transportation of persons and property." Hoke v. United States. And only four years later in 1917 in Caminetti v. United States, Mr. Justice Day held for the Court:

"The transportation of passengers in interstate commerce, it has long been settled, is within the regulatory power of Congress, under the commerce clause of the Constitution, and the authority of Congress to keep the channels of interstate commerce free from immoral and injurious uses has been frequently sustained, and is no longer open to question."

Nor does it make any difference whether the transportation is commercial in character. In Morgan v. Virginia (1946), Mr. Justice Reed observed as to the modern movement of persons among the States:

"The recent changes in transportation brought about by the coming of automobiles [do] not seem of great significance in the problem. People of all races travel today more extensively than in 1878 when this Court first passed upon state regulation of racial segregation in commerce. [It but] emphasizes the soundness of this Court's early conclusion in Hall v. De Cuir."

The same interest in protecting interstate commerce which led Congress to deal with segregation in interstate carriers and the white-slave traffic has prompted it to extend the exercise of its power to gambling . . . ; to criminal enterprises . . . ; to deceptive practices in the sale of products . . . ; to fraudulent security transactions . . . ; to misbranding of drugs . . . ; to wages and hours . . . ; to members of labor unions . . . ; to crop control . . . ; to discrimination against shippers . . . ; to the protection of small business from injurious price cutting . . . ; to resale price maintenance . . . ; to professional football . . . ; and to racial discrimination by owners and managers of terminal restaurants. . . .

That Congress was legislating against moral wrongs in many of these areas rendered its enactments no less valid. In framing Title II of this Act Congress was also dealing with what it considered a moral problem. But that fact does not detract from the overwhelming evidence of the disruptive effect that racial discrimination has had on commercial intercourse. It was this burden which empowered Congress to enact appropriate legislation, and, given this basis for the exercise of its power, Congress was not restricted by the fact that the particular obstruction to interstate commerce with which it was dealing was also deemed a moral and social wrong.

It is said that the operation of the motel here is of a purely local character. But, assuming this to be true, "[i]f it is interstate commerce that feels the pinch, it does not matter how local the operation which applies the squeeze.". . . As Chief Justice Stone put it in United States v. Darby [1941]:

"The power of Congress over interstate commerce is not confined to the regulation of commerce among the states. It extends to those activities intrastate which so affect interstate commerce or the exercise of the power of

Congress over it as to make regulation of them appropriate means to the attainment of a legitimate end, the exercise of the granted power of Congress to regulate interstate commerce. . . ."

Thus the power of Congress to promote interstate commerce also includes the power to regulate the local incidents thereof, including local activities of both the States of origin and destination, which might have a substantial and harmful effect upon that commerce. One need only examine the evidence which we have discussed above to see that Congress may—as it has—prohibit racial discrimination by motels serving travelers, however "local" their operations may appear.

Nor does the Act deprive appellant of liberty or property under the Fifth Amendment. . . .

We find no merit in the remainder of appellant's contentions, including that of "involuntary servitude." . . .

We, therefore, conclude that the action of the Congress in the adoption of the Act as applied here to a motel which concededly serves interstate travelers is within the power granted it by the Commerce Clause of the Constitution, as interpreted by this Court for 140 years. It may be argued that Congress could have pursued other methods to eliminate the obstructions it found in interstate commerce caused by racial discrimination. But this is a matter of policy that rests entirely with the Congress not with the courts. How obstructions in commerce may be removed—what means are to be employed—is within the sound and exclusive discretion of the Congress. It is subject only to one caveat—that the means chosen by it must be reasonably adapted to the end permitted by the Constitution. We cannot say that its choice here was not so adapted. The Constitution requires no more.

Affirmed.

Justices Black, Douglas, and Goldberg wrote concurring opinions.

KATZENBACH v. McCLUNG
379 U. S. 294; 85 S. Ct. 377; 13 L. Ed. 2d 290
(1964)

Mr. Justice Clark delivered the opinion of the Court, saying in part:

This case was argued with Heart of Atlanta Motel v. United States in which we upheld the constitutional validity of Title II of the Civil Rights Act of 1964 against an attack by hotels, motels, and like establishments. This complaint for injunctive relief against appellants attacks the constitutionality of the Act as applied to a restaurant. . . .

2. The Facts.

Ollie's Barbecue is a family-owned restaurant in Birmingham, Alabama, specializing in barbecued meats and homemade pies, with a seating capacity of 220 customers. It is located on a state highway 11 blocks from an interstate one and a somewhat greater distance from railroad and bus stations. The restaurant caters to a family and white-collar trade with a take-out service for Negroes. It employs 36 persons, two-thirds of whom are Negroes.

In the 12 months preceding the passage of the Act, the restaurant purchased locally approximately $150,000 worth of food, $69,683, or 46% of which was meat that it bought from a local supplier who had procured it from outside the State. The District Court expressly found that a substantial portion of the food served in the restaurant had moved in interstate commerce. The restaurant has refused to serve Negroes in its dining accommodations since its original opening in 1927, and since July 2, 1964, it has been operating in violation of the Act. The court below concluded that if it were required to serve Negroes it would lose a substantial amount of business.

On the merits, the District Court held that the Act could not be applied under the Fourteenth Amendment because it was conceded that the State of Alabama was not involved in the refusal of the restaurant to serve Negroes. . . . As to the Commerce Clause, the court found . . . that the clause was . . . a grant of power "to regulate intrastate activities, but only to the extent that action on its part is necessary or appropriate to the effective execution of its expressly granted power to regulate interstate commerce." There must be, it said, a close and substantial relation between local activities and interstate commerce which requires control of the former in the protection of the latter. The court concluded, however, that the Congress, rather than finding facts sufficient to meet this rule, has legislated a conclusive presumption that a restaurant affects interstate commerce if it serves or offers to serve interstate travelers or if a substantial portion of the food which it serves has moved in commerce. This, the court held, it could not do because there was no demonstrable connection between food purchased in interstate commerce and sold in a restaurant and the conclusion of Congress that discrimination in the restaurant would affect that commerce. . . .

3. The Act As Applied.

Section 201 (a) of Title II commands that all persons shall be entitled to the full and equal enjoyment of the goods and services of any place of public accommodation without discrimination or segregation on the ground of race, color, religion, or national origin; and § 201 (b) defines establishments as places of public accommodation if their operations affect commerce or segregation by them as supported by state action. Sections 201 (b) (2) and (c) place any "restaurant . . . principally engaged in selling food for consumption on the premises" under the Act "if . . . it serves or offers to serve interstate travelers or a substantial portion of the food which it serves . . . has moved in commerce."

Ollie's Barbecue admits that it is covered by these provisions of the Act. The Government makes no contention that the discrimination at the restaurant was supported by the State of Alabama. There is no claim that interstate travelers frequented the restaurant. The sole question, therefore, narrows down to whether Title II, as applied to a restaurant annually receiving about $70,000 worth of food which has moved in commerce, is a valid exercise of the power of Congress. The Government has contended that Congress had ample basis upon which to find that racial discrimination at restaurants which receive from out of state a substantial portion of the food served does, in fact, impose commercial burdens of national magnitude upon interstate commerce. The appellees' major argument is directed to this premise. They urge that no such basis existed. It is to that question that we now turn.

4. The Congressional Hearings.

As we noted in Heart of Atlanta Motel both houses of Congress conducted prolonged hearings on the Act. And, as we said there, while no formal findings were made, which of course are not necessary, it is well that we make mention of the testimony at these hearings the better to understand the problem before Congress and determine whether the Act is a reasonable and appropriate means toward its solution. The record is replete with testimony of the burdens placed on interstate commerce by racial discrimination in restaurants. A comparison of per capita spending by Negroes in restaurants, theaters, and like establishments indicated less spending, after discounting income differences, in areas where discrimination is widely practiced. This condition, which was especially aggravated in the South, was attributed in the testimony of the Under Secretary of Commerce to racial segregation. . . . This diminutive spending springing from a refusal to serve Negroes and their total loss as customers has, regardless of the absence of direct evidence, a close connection to interstate commerce. The fewer customers a restaurant enjoys the less food it sells and consequently the less it buys. . . . In addition, the Attorney General testified that this type of discrimination imposed "an artificial restriction on the market" and interfered with the flow of merchandise. . . . In addition, there were many references to discriminatory situations causing wide unrest and having a depressant effect on general business conditions in the respective communities. . . .

Moreover there was an impressive array of testimony that discrimination in restaurants had a direct and highly restrictive effect upon interstate travel by Negroes. This resulted, it was said, because discriminatory practices prevent Negroes from buying prepared food served on the premises while on a trip, except in isolated and unkempt restaurants and under most unsatisfactory and often unpleasant conditions. This obviously discourages travel and obstructs interstate commerce for one can hardly travel without eating. Likewise, it was said, that discrimination deterred professional, as well as skilled, people from moving into areas where such practices occurred and thereby caused industry to be reluctant to establish there. . . .

We believe that this testimony afforded ample basis for the conclusion that established restaurants in such areas sold less interstate goods because of the discrimination, that interstate travel was obstructed directly by it, that business in general suffered and that many new businesses refrained from establishing there as a result of it. Hence the District Court was in error in concluding that there was no connection between discrimination and the movement of interstate commerce. The court's conclusion that such a connection is outside "common experience" flies in the face of stubborn fact.

It goes without saying that, viewed in isolation, the volume of food purchased by Ollie's Barbecue from sources supplied from out of state was insignificant when compared with the total foodstuffs moving in commerce. But, as our late Brother Jackson said for the Court in Wickard v. Filburn (1942):

"That appellee's own contribution to the demand for wheat may be trivial by itself is not enough to remove him from the scope of federal regulation where, as here, his contribution, taken together with that of many others similarly situated, is far from trivial."

We noted in Heart of Atlanta Motel that a number of witnesses attested the fact that racial discrimination was not merely a state or regional problem but was one of nationwide scope. Against this background, we must conclude that while the focus of the legislation was on the individual restaurant's relation to interstate commerce, Congress appropriately considered the importance of that connection with the knowledge that the discrimination was but "representative of many others throughout the country, the total incidence of which if left unchecked may well become far-reaching in its harm to commerce." . . .

With this situation spreading as the record shows, Congress was not required to await the total dislocation of commerce. . . .

5. The Power of Congress to Regulate Local Activities.

Article I, § 8, cl. 3, confers upon Congress the power "[t]o regulate Commerce . . . among the several States" and Clause 18 of the same Article grants it the power "[t]o make all Laws which shall be necessary and proper for carrying into Execution the foregoing Powers . . . ." This grant, as we have pointed out in Heart of Atlanta Motel "extends to those activities intrastate which so affect interstate commerce, or the exertion of the power of Congress over it, as to make regulation of them appropriate means to the attainment of a legitimate end, the effective execution of the granted power to regulate interstate commerce." . . . Much is said about a restaurant business being local but "even if appellee's activity be local and though it may not be regarded as commerce, it may still, whatever its nature, be reached by Congress if it exerts a substantial economic effect on interstate commerce . . . ." . . . The activities that are beyond the reach of Congress are "those which are completely within a particular State, which do not affect other States, and with which it is not necessary to interfere, for the purpose of executing some of the general powers of the government.". . . This rule is as good today as it was when Chief Justice Marshall laid it down almost a century and a half ago. . . .

Nor are the cases holding that interstate commerce ends when goods come to rest in the State of destination apposite here. That line of cases has been applied with reference to state taxation or regulation but not in the field of federal regulation.

The appellees contend that Congress has arbitrarily created a conclusive presumption that all restaurants meeting the criteria set out in the Act "affect commerce." Stated another way, they object to the omission of a provision for a case-by-case determination—judicial or administrative—that racial discrimination in a particular restaurant affects commerce.

But Congress' action in framing this Act was not unprecedented. In United States v. Darby, this Court held constitutional the Fair Labor Standards Act of 1938. There Congress determined that the payment of substandard wages to employees engaged in production of goods for commerce, while not itself commerce, so inhibited it as to be subject to federal regulation. The appellees in that case argued, as do the appellees here, that the Act was invalid because it included no provision for an independent inquiry regarding the effect on commerce of substandard wages in a particular business. . . . But the Court rejected the argument, observing that:

"[S]ometimes Congress itself has said that a particular activity affects the commerce, as it did in the present Act, the Safety Appliance Act and the Railway Labor Act. In passing on the validity of legislation of the class last mentioned the only function of courts is to determine whether the particular activity regulated or prohibited is within the reach of the federal power."

Here, as there, Congress has determined for itself that refusals of service to Negroes have imposed burdens both upon the interstate flow of food and upon the movement of products generally. Of course, the mere fact that Congress has said when particular activity shall be deemed to affect commerce does not preclude further examination by this Court. But where we find that the legislators, in light of the facts and testimony before them, have a rational basis for finding a chosen regulatory scheme necessary to the protection of commerce, our investigation is at an end. The only remaining question—one answered in the affirmative by the court below—is whether the particular restaurant either serves or offers to serve interstate travelers or serves food a substantial portion of which has moved in interstate commerce. . . .

Confronted as we are with the facts laid before Congress, we must conclude that it had a rational basis for finding that racial discrimination in restaurants have a direct and adverse effect on the free flow of interstate commerce. Insofar as the sections of the Act here relevant are concerned, §§ 201(b) (2) and (c), Congress prohibited discrimination only in those establishments having a close tie to interstate commerce, i.e., those, like the McClungs', serving food that has come from out of the State. We think in so doing that Congress acted well within its power to protect and foster commerce in extending the coverage of Title II only to those restaurants offering to serve interstate travelers or serving food, a substantial portion of which has moved in interstate commerce.

The absence of direct evidence connecting discriminatory restaurant service with the flow of interstate food, a factor on which the appellees place much reliance, is not, given the evidence as to the effect of such practices on other aspects of commerce, a crucial matter.

The power of Congress in this field is broad and sweeping; where it keeps within its sphere and violates no express constitutional limitation it has been the rule of this Court, going back almost to the founding days of the Republic, not to interfere. The Civil Rights Act of 1964, as here applied, we find to be plainly appropriate in the resolution of what the Congress found to be a national commercial problem of the first magnitude. We find it in no violation of any express limitations of the Constitution and we therefore declare it valid.

The judgment is therefore

Reversed.

Justices Black, Douglas, and Goldberg wrote concurring opinions.

UNITED STATES v. CURTISS-WRIGHT EXPORT CORPORATION

299 U. S. 304; 57 S. Ct. 216; 81 L. Ed. 255 (1936)

The theory that the national government has only delegated powers is categorically true only in the realm of domestic affairs. In many decisions the Supreme Court has held that in conducting its relations with foreign nations the United States is a sovereign nation which possesses all the powers that other sovereign nations enjoy, and these powers are not limited to those which are delegated by the clauses of the Constitution. Thus, while the Constitution mentioned none of these powers, Congress has been held to have the power to punish the counterfeiting in this country of foreign money or securities, to annex unoccupied territory, to set up judicial tribunals in foreign countries, and to exclude, deport, or regulate the admission of aliens.

This broad power of Congress in the field of foreign relations was upheld in the case of Fong Yue Ting v. United States (1893), upholding the power of Congress to exclude or deport aliens. Fong Yue Ting was born in China and came to the United States prior to 1879, during a period when the United States and China had a treaty according the rights of domicile in this country to Chinese. In 1892 Congress passed a statute prohibiting further Chinese immigration and providing that all Chinese laborers who were entitled to remain in the country should apply to the proper authorities for a certificate of residence; if they failed to do this they were to be deemed unlawfully in the country and deported. Fong Yue Ting's failure to comply with the statute resulted in deportation proceedings against him, and in resisting such action he set up the unconstitutionality of the statute. The opinion of the Court sustaining the act is a clear exposition of the doctrine of the sovereign authority of Congress with respect to international affairs. The theory as laid down forms the constitutional basis of all our immigration legislation not resting upon treaty provisions.

In 1856 Congress passed an act authorizing the annexation of any unoccupied guano islands which might be discovered by an American citizen. Such an island was discovered in the Caribbean Sea in 1859, was annexed by proclamation, and criminal jurisdiction was extended over it by federal statute. In Jones v. United States (1890) Jones, who had been convicted of murder committed on the island, contended that the statute authorizing the acquisition of the island was invalid and that the court therefore had no jurisdiction to try him. The Supreme Court upheld the statute on the ground that under the law of nations recognized by all civilized states new territory may be acquired by discovery and occupation. This fact fully justified the legislation under which the island was annexed. In Afroyim v. Rusk (1967) the Supreme Court overturned a century of practice and held that the inherent power over foreign affairs did not include the power to deprive a person of his United States citizenship.

In the case printed below the Court re-examines and reaffirms the Fong Yue Ting doctrine. In 1934 Congress passed a joint resolution providing that if the President finds that an embargo on the sale of arms and munitions in the United States to countries at war in the Chaco (Bolivia *and Paraguay) "may contribute to the reestablishment of peace between those countries," he may, after consultation with other American republics, establish such an embargo by proclamation. Violation of such an embargo was made a crime. The joint resolution did not restrict or direct the President's discretion in setting up the embargo. It clearly delegated legislative power without any of the standards which the Court in the Schechter case (1935) had held to be vital if the delegation were to be held valid. The President proclaimed the embargo and the defendant company, convicted of selling guns to Bolivia, challenged the constitutionality of the resolution.*

Mr. Justice Sutherland delivered the opinion of the Court, saying in part:

On January 27, 1936, an indictment was returned in the court below, the first count of which charges that appellees, beginning with the 29th day of May, 1934, conspired to sell in the United States certain arms of war, namely fifteen machine guns, to Bolivia, a country then engaged in armed conflict in the Chaco, in violation of the Joint Resolution of Congress approved May 28, 1934, and the provisions of a proclamation issued on the same day by the President of the United States pursuant to authority conferred by § 1 of the resolution. In pursuance of the conspiracy, the commission of certain overt acts was alleged, details of which need not be stated. The Joint Resolution follows:

"*Resolved by the Senate and House of Representatives of the United States of America in Congress assembled,* That if the President finds that the prohibition of the sale of arms and munitions of war in the United States to those countries now engaged in armed conflict in the Chaco may contribute to the reestablishment of peace between those countries, and if after consultation with the governments of other American Republics and with their cooperation, as well as that of such other governments as he may deem necessary, he makes proclamation to that effect, it shall be unlawful to sell, except under such limitations and exceptions as the President prescribes, any arms or munitions of war in any place in the United States to the countries now engaged in that armed conflict, or to any person, company, or association acting in the interest of either country, until otherwise ordered by the President or by Congress.

"Sec. 2. Whoever sells any arms or munitions of war in violation of section 1 shall, on conviction, be punished by a fine not exceeding $10,000 or by imprisonment not exceeding two years, or both." . . .

Appellees severally demurred to the first count of the indictment on the grounds (1) that it did not charge facts sufficient to show the commission by appellees of any offense against any law of the United States; . . . The points urged in support of the demurrers were, first, that the joint resolution effects an invalid delegation of legislative power to the Executive; second, that the joint resolution never became effective because of the failure of the President to find essential jurisdictional facts; . . .

The court below sustained the demurrers upon the first point, but overruled them on the second and third points. . . . The government appealed to this court under the provisions of the Criminal Appeals Act of March 2, 1907. . . . That act authorizes the United States to appeal from a district court direct to this court in criminal cases where, among other things, the decision sustaining a demurrer to the indictment or any count thereof is based upon the invalidity or construction of the statute upon which the indictment is founded.

First. It is contended that by the Joint Resolution, the going into effect and continued operation of the resolution was conditioned (a) upon the President's judgment as to its beneficial effect upon the reestablishment of peace between the countries engaged in armed conflict in the Chaco; (b) upon the making of a proclamation, which was left to his unfettered discretion, thus constituting an attempted substitution of the President's will for that of Congress; (c) upon the making of a proclamation putting an end to the operation of the resolution, which again was left to the President's unfettered discretion; and (d) further, that the extent of its operation in particular cases was subject to limitations and exception by the President, controlled by no standard. In each of these particulars, appellees urge that Congress abdicated its essential functions and delegated them to the Executive.

Whether, if the Joint Resolution had related solely to internal affairs it would be open to the challenge that it constituted an unlawful delegation of legislative power to the Executive, we find it unnecessary to determine. The whole aim of the resolution is to affect a situation entirely external to the United States, and falling within the category of foreign affairs. The determination which we are called to make, therefore, is whether the Joint Resolution, as applied to that situation, is vulnerable to attack under the rule that forbids a delegation of the law-making power. In other words, assuming (but not deciding) that the challenged delegation, if it were confined to internal affairs, would be invalid, may it nevertheless be sustained on the ground that its exclusive aim is to afford a remedy for a hurtful condition within foreign territory?

It will contribute to the elucidation of the question if we first consider the differences between the powers of the Federal government in respect of foreign or external affairs and those in respect of domestic or internal affairs. That there are differences between them, and that these differences are fundamental, may not be doubted.

The two classes of powers are different, both in respect of their origin and their nature. The broad statement that the Federal government can exercise no powers except those specifically enumerated in the Constitution, and such implied powers as are necessary and proper to carry into effect the enumerated powers, is categorically true only in respect of our internal affairs. In that field, the primary purpose of the Constitution was to carve from the general mass of legislation powers *then possessed by the states* such portions as it was thought desirable to vest in the Federal government, leaving those not included in the enumeration still in the states. Carter v. Carter Coal Co. [1936]. That this doctrine applies only to powers which the states had is self-evident. And since the states severally never possessed international powers, such powers could not have been carved from the mass of state powers but obviously were transmitted to the United States from some other source. During the colonial period, those powers were possessed exclusively by and were entirely under the control of the Crown. By the Declaration of Independence, "the Representatives of the United States of America" declared the United [not the several] Colonies to be free and independent states, and as such to have "full Power to levy War, conclude Peace, contract Alliances, establish Commerce and to do all other Acts and Things which Independent States may of right do."

As a result of the separation from Great Britain by the colonies, acting as a unit, the powers of external sovereignty passed from the Crown not to the colonies severally, but to the colonies in their collective and corporate capacity as the United States of America. Even before the Declaration, the colonies were a unit in foreign affairs, acting through a common agency—namely the Continental Congress, composed of delegates from the thirteen colonies. That agency exercised the powers of war and peace, raised an army, created a navy, and finally adopted the Declaration of Independence. Rulers come and go; governments end and forms of government change; but sovereignty survives. A political society cannot endure without a supreme will somewhere. Sovereignty is never held in suspense. When, therefore, the external sovereignty of Great Britain in respect of the colonies ceased, it immediately passed to the Union. . . . That fact was given practical application almost at once. The treaty of peace, made on September 3, 1783, was concluded between his Britannic Majesty and the "United States of America." . . .

The Union existed before the Constitution, which was ordained and established among other things to form "a more perfect Union." Prior to that event, it is clear that the Union, declared by the Articles of Confederation to be "perpetual," was the sole possessor of external sovereignty, and in the Union it remained without change save in so far as the Constitution in express terms qualified its exercise. . . .

It results that the investment of the Federal government with the powers of external sovereignty did not depend upon the affirmative grants of the Constitution. The powers to declare and wage war, to conclude peace, to make treaties, to maintain diplomatic relations with other sovereignties, if they had never been mentioned in the Constitution, would have vested in the Federal government as necessary concomitants of nationality. Neither the Constitution nor the laws passed in pursuance of it have any force in foreign territory unless in respect to our own citizens . . . ; and operations of the nation in such territory must be governed by treaties, international understandings and compacts, and the principles of international law. As a member of the family of nations, the right and power of the United States in that field are equal to the right and power of the other members of the international family. Otherwise, the United States is not completely sovereign. The power to acquire territory by discovery and occupation (Jones v. United States [1890]), the power to expel undesirable aliens (Fong Yue Ting v. United States [1893]), the power to make such international agreements as do not constitute treaties in the constitutional sense (Altman & Co. v. United States [1912] . . .), none of which is expressly affirmed by the Constitution, nevertheless exist as inherently inseparable from the conception of nationality. This the court recognized, and in each of the cases cited found the warrant for its conclusions not in the provisions of the Constitution, but in the law of nations. . . .

Not only, as we have shown, is the Federal power over external affairs in origin and essential character different from that over internal affairs, but participation in the exercise of the power is significantly limited. In this vast external realm, with its important, complicated, delicate and manifold problems, the President alone has the power to speak or listen as a representative of the nation. He *makes* treaties with the advice and consent of the Senate; but he alone negotiates. Into the field of negotiation the Senate cannot intrude; and Congress itself is powerless to invade it. . . .

It is important to bear in mind that we are here dealing not alone with an authority vested in the President by an exertion of legislative power, but with such an authority plus the very delicate, plenary and exclusive power of the President as the sole organ of the Federal government in the field of international relations—a power which does not require as a basis for its exercise an act of Congress, but which, of course, like every other governmental power, must be exercised in subordination to the applicable provisions of the Constitution. It is quite apparent that if, in the maintenance of our international relations, embarrassment—perhaps serious embarrassment—is to be avoided and success for our aims achieved, congressional legislation which is to be made effective through negotiation and inquiry within the international field must often accord to the President a degree of discretion and freedom from statutory restriction which would not be admissible were domestic affairs alone involved. Moreover, he, not Congress, has the better opportunity of knowing the conditions which prevail in foreign countries, and especially is this true in time of war. He has his confidential sources of information. He has his agents in the form of diplomatic, consular and other officials. Secrecy in respect of information gathered by them may be highly necessary, and the premature disclosure of it productive of harmful results. . . .

In the light of the foregoing observations, it is evident that this court should not be in haste to apply a general rule which will have the effect of condemning legislation like that under review as constituting an unlawful delegation of legislative power. The principles which justify such legislation find overwhelming support in the unbroken legislative practice which has prevailed almost from the inception of the national government to the present day. . . .

Practically every volume of the United States Statutes contains one or more acts or joint resolutions of Congress authorizing action by the President in respect to subjects affecting foreign relations, which either leave the exercise of the power to his unrestricted judgment, or provide a standard far more general than that which has always been considered requisite with regard to domestic affairs. . . .

. . . A legislative practice such as we have here, evidenced not by only occasional instances, but marked by the movement of a steady stream for a century and a half of time, goes a long way in the direction of proving the presence of unassailable ground for the constitutionality of the practice, to be found in the origin and history of the power involved, or in its nature, or in both combined. . . .

We deem it unnecessary to consider, seriatim, the several clauses which are said to evidence the unconstitutionality of the Joint Resolution as involving an unlawful delegation of legislative power. It is enough to summarize by saying that, both upon principle and in accordance with precedent, we conclude there is sufficient warrant for the broad discretion vested in the President to determine whether the enforcement of the statute will have a beneficial effect upon the reestablishment of peace in the affected countries; whether he shall make proclamation to bring the resolution into operation; whether and when the resolution shall cease to operate and to make proclamation accordingly; and to prescribe limitations and exceptions to which the enforcement of the resolution shall be subject.

Second. The second point raised by the demurrer was that the Joint Resolution never became effective because the President failed to find essential jurisdictional facts. . . .

1. The Executive proclamation recites, "I have found that the prohibition of the sale of arms and munitions of war in the United States to those countries now engaged in armed conflict in the Chaco may contribute to the re-establishment of peace between those countries, and that I have consulted with the governments of other American Republics *and have been assured of the cooperation of such governments as I have deemed necessary as contemplated by the said joint resolution.*" This finding satisfies every requirement of the Joint Resolution. There is no suggestion that the resolution is fatally uncertain or indefinite; and a finding which follows its language, as this finding does, cannot well be challenged as insufficient. . . .

The judgment of the court below must be reversed and the cause remanded for further proceedings in accordance with the foregoing opinion.
Reversed.

Mr. Justice McReynolds does not agree. He is of opinion that the court below reached the right conclusion and its judgment ought to be affirmed.

Mr. Justice Stone took no part in the consideration or decision of this case.

EX PARTE MILLIGAN
4 Wallace 2; 18 L. Ed. 281 (1866)

The Constitution gives Congress the power to declare war and to raise and support armies. The war power which has developed from these simple grants staggers the imagination by its scope and variety. This is because, as Chief Justice Hughes put in in Home Building & Loan Ass'n. v. Blaisdell (1934), "the war power of the Federal Government . . . is a power to wage war successfully." In short, what is necessary to win the war Congress may do, and the Supreme Court has shown no inclination to hold void new and drastic war measures. In World War II the war power was invoked to fix price ceilings, to ration food and fuel, to commandeer factories, and to direct the production, distribution, and consumption of commodities. Our entire economy was mobilized for the war effort. A number of specific war powers exercised by Congress have been challenged in the courts, but in every case unsuccessfully.

The power of Congress to draft men into the armed services was attacked during World War I, although the draft had been resorted to sporadically and inefficiently during the Civil War. In 1917 Congress passed the Selective Draft Act, which made all male citizens between the ages of 21 and 30 subject to national military service. Public officers, ministers of religion, and theological students were exempt from the draft, while conscientious objectors who were affiliated with a "well recognized" pacifist religious sect were permitted to engage in noncombatant duty. In Selective Draft Law Cases (Arver v. United States, 1918) the Supreme Court unanimously held the act valid. The power to compel men to serve in the armed forces is reasonably implied from the power to raise and support armies, for a grant of power with no compulsion behind it is no power at all. The exemption of ministers and theological students is not an "establishment of religion" forbidden by the First Amendment; nor does compulsory military service constitute "involuntary servitude" forbidden by the Thirteenth Amendment.

In the Selective Training and Service Act of 1940, Congress changed the exemption rule, making it unnecessary to belong to a pacifist sect if a person's conscientious objection were based on "religious training and belief." The meaning of this phrase was spelled out in more detail in the Selective Service Act of 1948 (renamed in 1951 the Universal Military Training and Service Act): "Religious training and belief," according to the act, was to be defined as "an individual's belief in a relation to a Supreme Being involving duties superior to those arising from any human relation, but [not including] essentially political, sociological, or philosophical views or a merely personal moral code." In United States v. Seeger (1965), the Supreme Court held that this belief in a Supreme Being was not confined to a belief in God, in the traditional sense, but included any "sincere and meaningful belief which occupies in the life of its possessor a place parallel to that filled by the God of those admittedly qualifying for the exemption. . . ." In 1967, following continued bitter and sometimes violent demonstrations against the draft, General Lewis B. Hershey, then head of the selective service system, recommended to the country's draft boards that persons engaged in illegal demonstrations be reclassified if necessary and inducted promptly into the armed service. In 1968 over 500 students who returned their draft cards as a protest against the Vietnam War had their student deferment cancelled and were inducted into the army. The Supreme Court, in Gutknecht v. United States (1970), held that the Selective Service System was not authorized by law to use "immediate induction as a disciplinary or vindictive measure."

Congress, following the Seeger decision, amended the draft act to make explicit that only religiously motivated CO's could be exempted from service, and in United States v. Sisson (297 Fed. Supp. 902, 1969), district judge Charles E. Wyzanski, Jr. of Boston upset the conviction of a nonreligious objector to the Vietnam War both on the ground that the act amounted to an establishment of religion, and that the government's interest in fighting in Vietnam was insufficient to outweigh Sisson's individual rights. The Supreme Court held that Sisson had in effect been ordered acquitted and refused to review the case.

During World War I Congress passed a limited type of rent control act applicable to the District of Columbia. It forbade a landlord to evict a tenant at the expiration of his lease if the latter wished to remain and continued to pay the former rent and observed the other conditions of the lease. In Block v. Hirsh (1921) the Supreme Court held that the housing emergency growing out of the war justified the exercise of this power. In World War II Congress resorted to rent and price controls in earnest. The

Emergency Price Control Act of 1942 gave the Administrator of the Office of Price Administration (OPA) broad authority to fix maximum prices on most commodities and on residential rents. The act created a special Emergency Court of Appeals, manned by federal judges designated by the Chief Justice of the United States, to pass upon the validity of OPA regulations. In Yakus v. United States (1944) the Court held valid the price-fixing provisions of the statute, while in Bowles v. Willingham (1944) it upheld the rent-control sections of the act. In pithy language it rejected Mrs. Willingham's claim that, while the rents fixed might be generally fair, the rents she was allowed to charge were so low as to be a taking of her property without due process of law. "Of course, price control, the same as other forms of regulation, may reduce the value of the property regulated. But . . . that does not mean that the regulation is unconstitutional. . . . A nation which can demand the lives of its men and women in the waging of . . . war is under no constitutional necessity of providing a system of price control on the domestic front which will assure each landlord a 'fair return' on his property." In Woods v. Miller (1948), the Court held that the war power not only supports rent control during the actual war, but during such post-war period as the war-caused housing shortage continued.

It is apparent from the challenges to the draft laws, mentioned above, that one of the evils of war seems frequently to be a certain incompatibility between the demands of military necessity and a punctilious regard for the civil rights of the individual. Certainly in war emergencies the citizen finds his liberty curtailed and his rights abridged in ways that in times of peace would seem intolerable. There is plenty of evidence that President Lincoln, largely supported by public opinion, definitely proceeded during the Civil War upon the theory that questions of constitutional power were to be dealt with in the light of the great objective of preserving the Union. No President has ever invaded private constitutional rights more flagrantly, or from worthier motives, than he. This may be illustrated by the famous case of Ex parte Merryman (1861). Merryman was a Southern agitator residing in Maryland who persisted during the early days of the war in conduct and utterances which in the judgment of the military authorities hindered the success of the Northern cause. He was thereupon arrested and locked up in the military prison at Fort McHenry. Merryman promptly petitioned Mr. Chief Justice Taney for a writ of habeas corpus. Taney issued the writ, directed to the general in command of the fort. The general did not honor the writ, replying that he was authorized by the President to suspend the writ of habeas corpus, but would seek further instructions; and he declined to obey the writ further. Taney thereupon issued a writ of contempt against the general and sent the United States marshal to serve it. The marshal reported that he had not been allowed to enter the outer gate of the fort, although he had sent in his card, and that he had not been able to serve the writ. Taney, while protesting that the marshal had a perfect right to summon a posse comitatus and storm the fort, excused him from that duty. Rather, he contented himself with writing a full account of the entire case which he addressed to President Lincoln and which concluded with the observation that it now remained for the President, acting in fulfillment of his solemn oath of office, to enforce the laws, execute the judgment of the court, and release the prisoner. Lincoln made no answer whatever to this document, but Merryman was later released from military confinement and turned over to the civil authorities.

No case of this kind came to the Supreme Court while the war was in progress, although in 1864 an attempt was made to bring before that tribunal on a writ of habeas corpus the validity of the arrest of the notorious agitator, Vallandigham. The Court held that it was without jurisdiction and dismissed the case; see Ex parte Vallandigham (1864). It is interesting to speculate what the results might have been had the Supreme Court locked horns with the President in such a case; if, for example, the Milligan case had come up for decision during the early part of the war instead of in 1866.

The facts in the Milligan case were as follows: Milligan, a civilian, was arrested by order of General Hovey, who commanded the military district of Indiana; was tried in October, 1864, by a military commission which had been established under presidential authority; was found guilty of initiating insurrection and of various treasonable and disloyal practices; and was sentenced to be hanged on May 19, 1865. This sentence was approved by President Johnson. On May 10, 1865, Milligan sued out a writ of habeas corpus to the United States circuit court in Indiana, alleging the unconstitutional character of the proceedings under which he had been convicted and claiming the right of trial by jury as guaranteed by the Constitution. Thus, for the first time, the Supreme Court faced the question of the right of the President to suspend the writ of habeas corpus and to substitute trial by military authority for trial in the ordinary civil courts in districts outside the actual field of military operations.

The Supreme Court itself found difficulty in agreeing upon the important questions presented. They all held that a military commission set up by the President under such circumstances and without special authority from Congress was unlawful and without any power whatsoever. Five of the judges took the view that neither Congress nor the President had the power to set up military tribunals except in the actual theater of war where the civil courts were no longer functioning. Four judges, while denying such power to the President, held that it could be exercised by Congress. The Court decided, however, that Milligan had been unlawfully convicted and he was released.

The subsequent story of the case is not without interest. Milligan's sentence had been commuted to life imprisonment by the President in June, 1865, and he had been imprisoned by General Hovey in the Ohio penitentiary until his final release on April 10, 1866, as a result of the decision of the Supreme Court. On March 13, 1868, he brought an action of damages against General Hovey for unlawful imprisonment. The case was tried in the federal circuit court and the jury rendered a verdict for Milligan, but awarded only nominal damages inasmuch as the two-year statute of limitations allowed him to recover damages only for his imprisonment between March 13 and April 10, 1866.

The fact that the decision in the Milligan case set up a powerful judicial protection against military and executive invasion of individual constitutional rights was not sufficient to distract contemporary attention from the vital political consequences of the rule regarding congressional power which was laid down. Congress was in the midst of the important work of reconstruction. The radical leaders of the Republican party were committed to a policy of reconstruction which should keep the Southern states under the control of federal military forces until conditions seemed to warrant the adoption of a less drastic policy. But the doctrine of the Milligan case, by condemning military government in peaceful sections where the civil courts were open, was obviously incompatible with any such form of military reconstruction. It looked as though the Court was trying to prevent the carrying out of the congressional policy, and the decision was received with an outburst of anger by the congressional leaders. There was some talk of impeaching the judges; Congress went forward with its plans for military government in the South in contemptuous disregard for the decision, and utterances from prominent men were not lacking to the effect that the Court would come off the loser in any combat over the validity of the reconstruction plan adopted. It is an interesting fact that the constitutionality of these reconstruction acts was never passed upon by the Supreme Court. See the cases of Mississippi v. Johnson (1867), and Ex parte McCardle (1869).

The issues raised by Ex parte Milligan came before the Court again in 1946 in Duncan v. Kahanamoku, a case arising out of the declaration of martial law in the Hawaiian Islands. The day following the Japanese attack on Pearl Harbor the Army established military government and took over legislative, executive, and judicial functions. The administration of criminal justice by the civil courts was completely blacked out. Courtrooms and offices were taken over by the Army; grand jury proceedings, trial by jury, the subpoenaing of witnesses, and the issuance of writs of habeas corpus were all forbidden; and criminal cases of every description were handled by summary military procedure. This continued until

March, 1943, when a partial restoration of authority to the civil officers was ordered, mainly with respect to civil matters. Most classes of civilian crimes were still tried by the Army. Martial law was finally abolished in the islands by a presidential proclamation in October, 1944.

To responsible military leaders this drastic subordination of civilian affairs to Army control undoubtedly seemed imperative, but to the civil officers of the territory it seemed a wanton and unnecessary denial of constitutionally protected civil liberties. It was urged that any active danger of the invasion of the islands was ended by the Battle of Midway in June, 1942. It was also pointed out that there were no known acts of sabotage, espionage, or other disloyal conduct by any of the Japanese in Hawaii either on or after the day of the Pearl Harbor attack. The civil courts of the territory were ready at all times to perform their normal functions had they been allowed to do so, and experienced federal judges testified that there was no good reason why any of the civilian criminal cases handled by Army courts could not just as well have been handled by the courts of the territory. The bitter resentment engendered by this military suppression of civil government finally came to a climax in a dramatic struggle between federal district judge Delbert E. Metzger and Lieutenant General Robert C. Richardson, Commanding General of the Central Pacific Area.

Judge Metzger issued a writ of habeas corpus in the case of two German-American citizens who had been interned by summary military action. General Richardson replied with an order forbidding any judge in the territory to issue a writ of habeas corpus. The judge countered by fining General Richardson $5000 for contempt of court. To break this deadlock an emissary was sent from the Department of Justice in Washington, and a compromise was reached by which the President remitted the fine imposed on General Richardson and the general withdrew his order against Judge Metzger. It was agreed that writs of habeas corpus might be issued, but that prisoners would not be released unless higher courts on appeal so ordered. While in the Duncan case the Court held invalid the military government of the islands, a majority of the Court did not rest their decision on constitutional grounds. They dealt rather with the question whether Congress, in passing the Hawaiian organic act of 1900 under the authority of which military rule in Hawaii had been set up, intended to authorize this complete supplanting of civil government by martial law. In reaching its conclusion that Congress did not so intend, the Court plainly implies, in the final paragraphs of its opinion and particularly in its reference to the Milligan case, that if the organic act did authorize such military domination of civilian life it would be unconstitutional.

Mr. Justice Davis delivered the opinion of the Court, saying in part:

The importance of the main question presented by this record cannot be overstated, for it involves the very framework of the government and the fundamental principles of American liberty.

During the late wicked Rebellion, the temper of the times did not allow that calmness in deliberation and discussion so necessary to a correct conclusion of a purely judicial question. Then, considerations of safety were mingled with the exercise of power, and feelings and interests prevailed which are happily terminated. Now that the public safety is assured, this question, as well as all others, can be discussed and decided without passion or the admixture of any element not required to form a legal judgment. We approach the investigation of this case fully sensible of the magnitude of the inquiry and the necessity of full and cautious deliberation. . . .

The controlling question in the case is this: Upon the facts stated in Milligan's petition, and the exhibits filed, had the Military Commission mentioned in it jurisdiction, legally, to try and sentence him? Milligan, not a resident of one of the rebellious states, or a prisoner of war, but a citizen of Indiana for twenty years past, and never in the military or naval service, is, while at his home, arrested by the military power of the United States, imprisoned and, on certain criminal charges preferred against him, tried, convicted, and sentenced to be hanged by a military commission, organized under the direction of the military commander of the military district of Indiana. Had this tribunal the legal power and authority to try and punish this man?

No graver question was ever considered by this court, nor one which more nearly concerns the rights of the whole people; for it is the birthright of every American citizen when charged with crime, to be tried and punished according to law. The power of punishment is alone through the means which the laws have provided for that purpose, and if they are ineffectual, there is an immunity from punishment, no matter how great an offender the individual may be, or how much his crimes may have shocked the sense of justice of the country, or endangered its safety. By the protection of the law human rights are secured; withdraw that protection, and they are at the mercy of wicked rulers, or the clamor of an excited people. If there was law to justify this military trial, it is not our province to interfere; if there was not, it is our duty to declare the nullity of the whole proceedings. The decision of this question does not depend on argument or judicial precedents, numerous and highly illustrative as they are. These precedents inform us of the extent of the struggle to preserve liberty and to relieve those in civil life from military trials. The founders of our government were familiar with the history of that struggle; and secured in a written Constitution every right which the people had wrested from power during a contest of ages. By that Constitution and the laws authorized by it, this question must be determined. The provisions of that instrument on the administration of criminal justice are too plain and direct to leave room for misconstruction or doubt of their true meaning. Those applicable to this case are found in that clause of the original Constitution which says "that the trial of all crimes, except in case of impeachment, shall be by jury;" and in the fourth, fifth, and sixth articles of the amendments. . . .

Time has proven the discernment of our ancestors; for even these provisions, expressed in such plain English words, that it would seem the ingenuity of man could not evade them, are now, after the lapse of more than seventy years, sought to be avoided. Those great and good men foresaw that troublous times would arise, when rulers and people would become restive under restraint, and seek by sharp and decisive measures to accomplish ends deemed just and proper; and that the principles of constitutional liberty would be in peril, unless established by irrepealable law. The history of the world had taught them that what was done in the past might be attempted in the future. The Constitution of the United States is a law for rulers and people, equally in war and in peace, and covers with the shield of its protection all classes of men, at all times, and under all circumstances. No doctrine involving more pernicious consequences, was ever invented by the wit of man than that any of its provisions can be suspended during any of the great exigencies of government. Such a doctrine leads directly to anarchy or despotism, but the theory of necessity on which it is based is false; for the government, within the Constitution, has all the powers granted to it which are necessary to preserve its existence, as has been happily proved by the result of the great effort to throw off its just authority.

Have any of the rights guaranteed by the Constitution been violated in the case of Milligan? and if so, what are they?

Every trial involves the exercise of judicial power; and from what source did the Military Commission that tried him derive their authority? Certainly no part of the judicial power of the country was conferred on them; because the Constitution expressly vests it "in one Supreme Court and such inferior courts as the Congress may from time to time ordain and establish," and it is not pretended that the commission was a court ordained and established by Congress. They cannot justify on the mandate of the President; because he is controlled by law, and has his appropriate sphere of duty, which is to execute, not to make, the laws; and there is "no unwritten criminal code to which resort can be had as a source of jurisdiction."

But it is said that the jurisdiction is complete under the "laws and usages of war."

It can serve no useful purpose to inquire what those laws and usages are, whence they originated, where found, and on whom they operate; they can never be applied to citizens in states which have upheld the authority of the government, and where the courts are open and their process unobstructed. This court has judicial knowledge that in Indiana the Federal authority was always unopposed, and its courts always open to hear criminal accusations and redress grievances; and no usage of war could sanction a military trial there for any offense whatever of a citizen in civil life, in nowise connected with the military service. Congress could grant no such power; and to the honor of our national legislature be it said, it has never been provoked by the state of the country even to attempt its exercise. One of the plainest constitutional provisions was, therefore, infringed when Milligan was tried by a court not ordained and established by Congress, and not composed of judges appointed during good behavior.

Why was he not delivered to the circuit court of Indiana to be proceeded against according to law? No reason of necessity could be urged against it; because Congress had declared penalties against the offenses charged, provided for their punishment, and directed that court to hear and determine them. And soon after this military tribunal was ended, the circuit court met, peacefully transacted its business, and adjourned. It needed no bayonets to protect it, and required no military aid to execute its judgments. It was held in a state, eminently distinguished for patriotism, by judges commissioned during the Rebellion who were provided with juries, upright, intelligent, and selected by a marshal appointed by the President. The government had no right to conclude that Milligan, if guilty, would not receive in that court merited punishment; for its records disclose that it was constantly engaged in the trial of similar offenses, and was never interrupted in its administration of criminal justice. If it was dangerous, in the distracted condition of affairs, to leave Milligan unrestrained of his liberty, because he "conspired against the government, afforded aid and comfort to rebels, and incited the people to insurrection," the law said arrest him, confine him closely, render him powerless to do further mischief; and then present his case to the grand jury of the district, with proofs of his guilt and, if indicted, try him according to the course of the common law. If this had been done, the Constitution would have been vindicated, the law of 1863 enforced, and the securities for personal liberty preserved and defended.

Another guarantee of freedom was broken when Milligan was denied a trial by jury. The great minds of the country have differed on the correct interpretation to be given to various provisions of the Federal Constitution; and judicial decision has been often invoked to settle their true meaning; but until recently no one ever doubted that the right of trial by jury was fortified in the organic law against the power of attack. It is now assailed; but if ideas can be expressed in words, and language has any meaning, this right—one of the most valuable in a free country—is preserved to every one accused of crime who is not attached to the Army, or Navy, or Militia in actual service. The sixth amendment affirms that "in all criminal prosecutions the accused shall enjoy the right to a speedy and public trial by an impartial jury," language broad enough to embrace all persons and cases; but the fifth, recognizing the necessity of an indictment, or presentment, before any one can be held to answer for high crimes, "except cases arising in the land or naval forces, or in the militia, when in actual service, in time of war or public danger;" and the framers of the Constitution, doubtless, meant to limit the right to trial by jury, in the Sixth Amendment, to those persons who were subject to indictment or presentment in the Fifth.

The discipline necessary to the efficiency of the army and navy, required other and swifter modes of trial than are furnished by the common law courts; and, in pursuance of the power conferred by the Constitution, Congress has declared the kinds of trial and the manner in which they shall be conducted, for offenses committed while the party is in the military or naval service. Every one connected with these branches of public service is amenable to the jurisdiction which Congress has created for their government, and, while thus serving, surrenders his right to be tried by the civil courts. All other persons, citizens of states where the courts are open, if charged with crime, are guaranteed the inestimable privilege of trial by jury. . . .

It is claimed that martial law covers with its broad mantle the proceedings of this Military Commission. The proposition is this: That in a time of war the commander of an armed force (if in his opinion the exigencies of the country demand it, and of which he is to judge) has the power, within the lines of his military district, to suspend all civil rights and their remedies, and subject citizens as well as soldiers to the rule of his will; and in the exercise of his lawful authority cannot be restrained, except by his superior officer or the President of the United States.

If this position is sound to the extent claimed, then when war exists, foreign or domestic, and the country is subdivided into military departments for mere convenience, the commander of one of them can, if he chooses, within the limits, on the plea of necessity, with the approval of the Executive, substitute military force for and [to] the exclusion of the laws, and punish all persons, as he thinks right and proper, without fixed or certain rules.

The statement of this proposition shows its importance; for, if true, republican government is a failure, and there is an end of liberty regulated by law. Martial law, established on such a basis, destroys every guarantee of the Constitution, and effectually renders the "military independent of and superior to the civil power"—the attempt to do which by the King of Great Britain was deemed by our fathers such an offense, that they assigned it to the world as one of the causes which impelled them to declare their independence. Civil liberty and this kind of martial law cannot endure together; the antagonism is irreconcilable and, in the conflict, one or the other must perish.

This nation, as experience has proved, cannot always remain at peace, and has no right to expect that it will always have wise and humane rulers, sincerely attached to the principles of the Constitution. Wicked men, ambitious of power, with hatred of liberty and contempt of law, may fill the place once occupied by Washington and Lincoln; and if this right is conceded, and the calamities of war again befall us, the dangers to human liberty are frightful to contemplate. If our fathers had failed to provide for just such a contingency, they would have been false to the trust reposed in them. They knew—the history of the world told them—the nation they were founding, be its existence short or long, would be involved in war; how often or how long continued, human foresight could not tell; and that unlimited power, wherever lodged at such a time, was especially hazardous to freemen. For this, and other equally weighty reasons, they secured the inheritance they had fought to maintain, by incorporating in a written Constitution the safeguards which time had proved were essential to its preservation. Not one of these safeguards can the President or Congress or the Judiciary disturb, except the one concerning the writ of habeas corpus.

It is essential to the safety of every government that, in a great crisis, like the one we have just passed through, there should be a power somewhere of suspending the writ of habeas corpus. In every war, there are men of previously good character, wicked enough to counsel their fellow citizens to resist the measures deemed necessary by a good government to sustain its just authority and overthrow its enemies; and their influence may lead to dangerous combinations. In the emergency of the times, an immediate public investigation according to law may not be possible; and yet, the peril to the country may be too imminent to suffer such persons to go at large. Unquestionably, there is then an exigency which demands that the government, if it should see fit, in the exercise of a proper discretion, to make arrests, should not be required to produce the person arrested in answer to a writ of habeas corpus. The Constitution goes no further. It does not say after a writ of habeas corpus is denied a citizen, that he shall be tried otherwise than by the course of common law. If it had intended this result, it was easy by the use of direct words to have accomplished it. The illustrious men who framed that instrument were guarding the foundations of civil liberty against the abuses of unlimited power; they were full of wisdom, and the lessons of history informed them that a trial by an established court, assisted by an impartial jury, was the only sure way of protecting the citizen against oppression and wrong. Knowing this, they limited the suspension to one great right, and left the rest to remain forever inviolable. But, it is insisted that the safety of the country in time of war demands that this broad claim for martial law shall be sustained. If this were true, it could be well said that a country, preserved at the sacrifice of all the cardinal principles of liberty, is not worth the cost of preservation. Happily, it is not so.

It will be borne in mind that this is not a question of the power to proclaim martial law, when war exists in a community and the courts and civil authorities are overthrown. Nor is it a question what rule a military commander, at the head of his army, can impose on States in rebellion to cripple their resources and quell the insurrection. The jurisdiction claimed is much more extensive. The necessities of the service, during the late Rebellion, required that the loyal states should be placed within the limits of certain military districts and commanders appointed in them; and, it is urged, that this, in a military sense, constituted them the theatre of military operations; and, as in this case, Indiana had been and was again threatened with invasion by the enemy, the occasion was furnished to establish martial law. The conclusion does not follow from the premises. If armies were collected in Indiana, they were to be employed in another locality, where the laws were obstructed and the national authority disputed. On her soil there was no hostile foot; if once invaded, that invasion was at an end, and with it all pretext for martial law. Martial law cannot arise from a threatened invasion. The necessity must be actual and present; the invasion real, such as effectually closes the courts and deposes the civil administration.

It is difficult to see how the safety of the country required martial law in Indiana. If any of her citizens were plotting treason, the power of arrest could secure them, until the government was prepared for their trial, when the courts were open and ready to try them. It was as easy to protect witnesses before a civil as a military tribunal; and as there could be no wish to convict, except on sufficient legal evidence, surely an ordained and established court were better able to judge of this than a military tribunal composed of gentlemen not trained to the profession of the law.

It follows, from what has been said on this subject, that there are occasions when martial rule can be properly applied. If, in foreign invasion or civil war, the courts are actually closed, and it is impossible to administer criminal justice according to law, then, on the theatre of actual military operations, where war really prevails, there is a necessity to furnish a substitute for the civil authority, thus overthrown, to preserve the safety of the army and society; and as no power is left but the military, it is allowed to govern by martial rule until the laws can have their free course. As necessity creates the rule, so it limits its duration; for, if this government is continued after the courts are reinstated, it is a gross usurpation of power. Martial rule can never exist where the courts are open, and in the proper and unobstructed exercise of their jurisdiction. It is also confined to the locality of actual war. Because, during the late Rebellion it could have been enforced in Virginia, where the national authority was overturned and the courts driven out, it does not follow that it should obtain in Indiana, where that authority was never disputed, and justice was always administered. And so in the case of a foreign invasion, martial rule may become a necessity, in one state, when, in another, it would be "mere lawless violence." . . .

The two remaining questions in this case must be answered in the affirmative. The suspension of the privilege of the writ of habeas corpus does not suspend the writ itself. The writ issues as a matter of course; and on the return made to it the court decides whether the party applying is denied the right of proceeding any further with it.

If the military trial of Milligan was contrary to law, then he was entitled, on the facts stated in his petition, to be discharged from custody by the terms of the act of Congress of March 3d, 1863. The provisions of this law having been considered in a previous part of this opinion, we will not restate the views there presented. Milligan avers he was a citizen of Indiana, not in the military or naval service, and was detained in close confinement, by order of the President, from the 5th day of October, 1864, until the 2d day of January, 1865, when the circuit court for the district of Indiana, with a grand jury, convened in session at Indianapolis; and afterwards, on the 27th day of the same month, adjourned without finding an indictment or presentment against him. If these averments were true (and their truth is conceded for the purposes of this case), the court was required to liberate him on taking certain oaths prescribed by the law, and entering into recognizance for his good behavior.

But it is insisted that Milligan was a prisoner of war, and, therefore, excluded from the privileges of the statute. It is not easy to see how he can be treated as a prisoner of war, when he lived in Indiana for the past twenty years, was arrested there, and had not been, during the late troubles, a resident of any of the states in rebellion. If in Indiana he conspired with bad men to assist the enemy, he is punishable for it in the courts of Indiana; but, when tried for the offense, he cannot plead the rights of war; for he was not engaged in legal acts of hostility against the government, and only such persons, when captured, are prisoners of war. If he cannot enjoy the immunities attaching to the character of a prisoner of war, how can he be subject to their pains and penalties? . . .

Mr. Chief Justice Chase, for himself and Mr. Justice Wayne, Mr. Justice Swayne, and Mr. Justice Miller, delivered an opinion in which he differed from the Court in several important points, but concurred in the judgment in the case.

KOREMATSU v. UNITED STATES

323 U. S. 214; 65 S. Ct. 193; 89 L. Ed. 194 (1944)

World War I was fought in Europe, brought no serious menace to our domestic national security, and produced no significant clashes between military and civil authority. With World War II, however, the story was very different. This was in every sense a "total" war; its successful outcome was by no means assured, and danger of external attack and internal treachery was at times very real. Military leaders faced unprecedented situations and met them by resort to unprecedented extensions of military authority. Congress, in turn, reinforced these military judgments in cases where such support was needed.

The spectacular case of the Nazi saboteurs, Ex parte Quirin (1942), appeared at first to reopen the major issue settled by the Milligan case. In June, 1942, eight saboteurs landed in this country from a German submarine. They brought with them explosives, incendiaries, fuses, detonators, timing devices, and acids. They had about $175,000 in American money for expenses and bribes, and they carried elaborate lists of American factories, railroad centers, bridges, power plants, and other key war facilities. They were all born in Germany, had previously lived in this country, and had, upon returning to Germany, been trained in a special school for saboteurs. About ten days after they landed, they were arrested by the FBI. Thereupon President Roosevelt issued two proclamations. The first denied to enemies who enter this country to commit sabotage or other hostile acts the right of access to the civil courts and directed that they be tried by military tribunals in accordance with the law of war. The second created a military commission of eight army officers to try the saboteurs, ordered the Attorney General and the Judge Advocate General to prosecute them, and designated two army officers to act as defense counsel. Four charges were filed against the saboteurs, all stating offenses under the law of war. At the outset of the trial, defense counsel attacked the constitutionality of the President's proclamation and the jurisdiction of the military commission, but the trial proceeded. Late in July the country was startled by the announcement that the Supreme Court (then in summer recess) would reconvene in two days to permit the filing of petitions for writs of habeas corpus on behalf of the prisoners. After proceedings that lasted two days, the Court denied the petitions and adjourned. The trial continued and the saboteurs were convicted. Six were executed and two imprisoned. In October, the Court handed down its opinion in the case. It held that the President had the authority to establish the military commission by virtue of statutes passed by Congress, and that the offenses charged were offenses against the law of war. It held that the grand jury indictment and the jury trial provisions of the Fifth and Sixth Amendments are not applicable to trials before military tribunals for crimes against the law of war. The Court then commented upon the Milligan case; it pointed out that Milligan was a citizen and resident of Indiana, had never lived in a rebellious state, was not an enemy belligerent, and was therefore not subject to the law of war. The Court said: "We construe the Court's statement as to the *applicability of the law of war to Milligan's case as having particular reference to the facts before it." The most important point about the case is that the Supreme Court did examine into the right of the military authorities to try the saboteurs. It upheld the military tribunal, but not until it satisfied itself that the tribunal had jurisdiction and was proceeding according to law.*

In December, 1945, the Court scrutinized the authority of an American military commission in the Philippines to try Japanese General Yamashita for offenses against the law of war comprising his failure to restrain his troops from committing atrocities against Americans and Filipinos; see In re Yamashita (1946). Again the Court recognized the right to challenge the military proceedings by a petition for a writ of habeas corpus. It held that the military commission had been properly set up in accordance with federal statutes which provided for trial, by such commissions, of enemy combatants charged with violating the law of war. It found the authority of the military is not ended by the cessation of hostilities but only by the formal establishment of peace by the political departments of the government through proclamation or treaty. It held, further, that the offenses charged against General Yamashita constituted violations of the law of war. It declared that the procedure and rules of evidence employed by the military commission are not subject to judicial scrutiny but are reviewable only by higher military authorities. This meant that the use by the prosecution against General Yamashita of depositions (written testimony) and hearsay evidence (neither of which could validly be introduced in a trial in a civil court) did not violate the due process clause of the Fifth Amendment. A military commission does not have to observe due process of law in trying an enemy combatant. The ruling on this last point elicited vigorous dissents by Justices Murphy and Rutledge.

The present case involved perhaps the most alarming use of executive military authority in our nation's history. Following the bombing of Pearl Harbor in December, 1941, the anti-Japanese sentiment on the West Coast brought the residents of that area to a state of near hysteria; and in February, 1942, President Roosevelt issued an executive order authorizing the creation of military areas from which any or all persons might be excluded as the military authorities might decide. On March 2, the entire West Coast to a depth of about 40 miles was designated by the commanding general as Military Area No. 1, and he thereupon proclaimed a curfew in that area for all persons of Japanese ancestry. Later he ordered the compulsory evacuation from the area of all persons of Japanese ancestry, and by the middle of the summer most of these people had been moved inland to "war relocation centers," the American equivalent of concentration camps. Congress subsequently made it a crime to violate these military orders. Of the 112,000 persons of Japanese ancestry involved, about 70,000 were native-born American citizens, none of whom had been specifically accused of disloyalty. Three cases were brought to the Supreme Court challenging the right of the government to override in this manner the customary civil rights of these citizens. In Hirabayashi v. United States (1943) the Court upheld the curfew regulations as a valid military measure to prevent espionage and sabotage. "Whatever views we may entertain regarding the loyalty to this country of the citizens of Japanese ancestry, we cannot reject as unfounded the judgment of the military authorities and of Congress that there were disloyal members of that population, whose number and strength could not be precisely and quickly ascertained. We cannot say that the war-making branches of the Government did not have ground for believing that in a critical hour such persons could not readily be isolated and separately dealt with, and constituted a menace to the national defense and safety. . . ." While emphasizing that distinctions based on ancestry were "by their very nature odious to a free people" the Court nonetheless felt "that in time of war residents having ethnic affiliations with an invading enemy may be a greater source of danger than those of a different ancestry."

While the Court, in the present case, held valid the discriminatory mass evacuation of all persons of Japanese descent, it also held in Ex parte Endo (1944), that an American citizen of Japanese ancestry whose loyalty to this country had been established could not constitutionally be held in a War Relocation Center but must be unconditionally released. The government had allowed persons to leave the Relocation Centers under conditions and restrictions which aimed to guarantee that there should not be "a dangerously disorderly migration of unwanted people to unprepared communities." Permission to leave was granted only if the applicant had the assurance of a job and a place to live, and wanted to go to a place "approved" by the War Relocation Authority. The Court held that the sole purpose of the evacuation and detention program was to protect the war effort against sabotage and espionage. "A person who is concededly loyal presents no problem of espionage or sabotage. . . . He who is loyal is by definition not a spy or a saboteur." It therefore follows that the authority to detain a citizen of Japanese ancestry ends when his loyalty is established. To hold otherwise would be to justify his detention not on grounds of military necessity but purely on grounds of race.

Although no case reached the Court squarely challenging the right of the government to incarcerate citizens of Japanese ancestry pending a determination of their loyalty, the tenor of the opinions leaves little doubt that such action would have been sustained. The present case involved only the right of the military to evacuate such persons from the West Coast. Mr. Justice Murphy, one of three dissenters, attacked the qualifications of the military to make sociological judgments about the effects of ancestry, and *pointed out that the time consumed in evacuating these persons (11 months) was ample for making an orderly inquiry into their individual loyalty.*

Mr. Justice Black delivered the opinion of the Court, saying in part:

The petitioner, an American citizen of Japanese descent, was convicted in a Federal district court for remaining in San Leandro, California, a "Military Area," contrary to Civilian Exclusion Order No. 34 of the Commanding General of the Western Command, U.S. Army, which directed that after May 9, 1942, all persons of Japanese ancestry should be excluded from that area. No question was raised as to petitioner's loyalty to the United States. The Circuit Court of Appeals affirmed, and the importance of the constitutional question involved caused us to grant certiorari.

It should be noted, to begin with, that all legal restrictions which curtail the civil rights of a single racial group are immediately suspect. That is not to say that all such restrictions are unconstitutional. It is to say that courts must subject them to the most rigid scrutiny. Pressing public necessity may sometimes justify the existence of such restrictions; racial antagonism never can.

In the instant case prosecution of the petitioner was begun by information charging violation of an Act of Congress, of March 21, 1942, which provides that "... whoever shall enter, remain in, leave, or commit any act in any military area or military zone prescribed, under the authority of an Executive order of the President, by the Secretary of War, or by any military commander designated by the Secretary of War, contrary to the restrictions applicable to any such area or zone or contrary to the order of the Secretary of War or any such military commander, shall, if it appears that he knew or should have known of the existence and extent of the restrictions or order and that his act was in violation thereof, be guilty of a misdemeanor and upon conviction shall be liable to a fine of not to exceed $5,000 or to imprisonment for not more than one year, or both, for each offense."

Exclusion Order No. 34, which the petitioner knowingly and admittedly violated was one of a number of military orders and proclamations, all of which were substantially based upon Executive Order No. 9066. That order, issued after we were at war with Japan, declared that "the successful prosecution of the war requires every possible protection against espionage and against sabotage to national-defense material, national-defense premises, and national-defense utilities. . . ."

One of the series of orders and proclamations, a curfew order, which like the exclusion order here was promulgated pursuant to Executive Order 9066, subjected all persons of Japanese ancestry in prescribed West Coast military areas to remain in their residences from 8 p.m. to 6 a.m. As is the case with the exclusion order here, that prior curfew order was designed as a "protection against espionage and against sabotage." In Hirabayashi v. United States [1943], we sustained a conviction obtained for violation of the curfew order. The Hirabayashi conviction and this one thus rest on the same 1942 Congressional Act and the same basic executive and military orders, all of which orders were aimed at the twin dangers of espionage and sabotage.

The 1942 Act was attacked in the Hirabayashi Case as an unconstitutional delegation of power; it was contended that the curfew order and other orders on which it rested were beyond the war powers of the Congress, the military authorities and of the President, as Commander in Chief of the Army; and finally that to apply the curfew order against none but citizens of Japanese ancestry amounted to a constitutionally prohibited discrimination solely on account of race. To these questions, we gave the serious consideration which their importance justified. We upheld the curfew order as an exercise of the power of the government to take steps necessary to prevent espionage and sabotage in an area threatened by Japanese attack.

In the light of the principles we announced in the Hirabayashi Case, we are unable to conclude that it was beyond the war power of Congress and the Executive to exclude those of Japanese ancestry from the West Coast war area at the time they did. True, exclusion from the area in which one's home is located is a far greater deprivation than constant confinement to the home from 8 p.m. to 6 a.m. Nothing short of apprehension by the proper military authorities of the gravest imminent danger to the public safety can constitutionally justify either. But exclusion from a threatened area, no less than curfew, has a definite and close relationship to the prevention of espionage and sabotage. The military authorities, charged with the primary responsibility of defending our shores, concluded that curfew provided inadequate protection and ordered exclusion. They did so, as pointed out in our Hirabayashi opinion, in accordance with Congressional authority to the military to say who should, and who should not, remain in the threatened areas.

In this case the petitioner challenges the assumptions upon which we rested our conclusions in the Hirabayashi Case. He also urges that by May 1942, when Order No. 34 was promulgated, all danger of Japanese invasion of the West Coast had disappeared. After careful consideration of these contentions we are compelled to reject them.

Here, as in the Hirabayashi Case, "we cannot reject as unfounded the judgment of the military authorities and of Congress that there were disloyal members of that population, whose number and strength could not be precisely and quickly ascertained. We cannot say that the war-making branches of the Government did not have ground for believing that in a critical hour such persons could not readily be isolated and separately dealt with, and constituted a menace to the national defense and safety, which demanded that prompt and adequate measures be taken to guard against it."

Like curfew, exclusion of those of Japanese origin was deemed necessary because of the presence of an unascertained number of disloyal members of the group, most of whom we have no doubt were loyal to this country. It was because we could not reject the finding of the military authorities that it was impossible to bring about an immediate segregation of the disloyal from the loyal that we sustained the validity of the curfew order as applying to the whole group. In the instant case, temporary exclusion of the entire group was rested by the military on the same ground. The judgment that exclusion of the whole group was for the same reason a military imperative answers the contention that the exclusion was in the nature of group punishment based on antagonism of those of Japanese origin. That there were members of the group who retained loyalties to Japan has been confirmed by investigations made subsequent to the exclusion. Approximately five thousand American citizens of Japanese ancestry refused to swear unqualified allegiance to the United States and to renounce allegiance to the Japanese Emperor, and several thousand evacuees requested repatriation to Japan.

We uphold the exclusion order as of the time it was made and when the petitioner violated it. . . . In doing so, we are not unmindful of the hardships imposed by it upon a large group of American citizens. . . . But hardships are part of war, and war is an aggregation of hardships. All citizens alike, both in and out of uniform, feel the impact of war in greater or lesser measure. Citizenship has its responsibilities as well as its privileges, and in time of war the burden is always heavier. Compulsory exclusion of large groups of citizens from their homes, except under circumstances of direst emergency and peril, is inconsistent with our basic governmental institution. But when under conditions of modern warfare our shores are threatened by hostile forces, the power to protect must be commensurate with the threatened danger. . . .

[The Court dealt at some length with a technical complication which arose in the case. On May 30, the date on which Korematsu was charged with remaining unlawfully in the prohibited area, there were two conflicting military orders outstanding, one forbidding him to remain in the area, the other forbidding him to leave but ordering him to report to an assembly center. Thus, he alleged, he was punished for doing what it was made a crime to fail to do. The Court held the orders not to be contradictory, since the requirement to report to the assembly center was merely a step in an orderly program of compulsory evacuation from the area.]

It is said that we are dealing here with the case of imprisonment of a citizen in a concentration camp solely because of his ancestry, without evidence or inquiry concerning his loyalty and good disposition towards the United States. Our task would be simple, our duty clear, were this a case involving the imprisonment of a loyal citizen in a concentration camp because of racial prejudice. Regardless of the true nature of the assembly and relocation centers —and we deem it unjustifiable to call them concentration camps with all the ugly connotations that term implies—we are dealing specifically with nothing but an exclusion order. To cast this case into outlines of racial prejudice, without reference to the real military dangers which were presented, merely confuses the issue. Korematsu was not excluded from the Military Area because of hostility to him or his race. He *was* excluded because we are at war with the Japanese Empire, because the properly constituted military authorities feared an invasion of our West Coast and felt constrained to take proper security measures, because they decided that the military urgency of the situation demanded that all citizens of Japanese ancestry be segregated from the West Coast temporarily, and finally, because Congress, reposing its confidence in this time of war in our military leaders—as inevitably it must—determined that they should have the power to do just this. There was evidence of disloyalty on the part of some, the military authorities considered that the need for action was great, and time was short. We cannot—by availing ourselves of the calm perspective of hindsight—now say that at that time these actions were unjustified.

Affirmed.

Mr. Justice Frankfurter wrote a concurring opinion. Justice Roberts, Murphy, and Jackson each wrote a dissenting opinion.

6

The Nationalization
of the Bill of Rights

BARRON v. BALTIMORE
7 Peters 243; 8 L. Ed. 672 (1833)

One of the bitter criticisms urged against our federal Constitution as it came from the hands of the Convention was that it contained no bill of rights. It was feared that without specific guarantees the civil rights and liberties of the people and the states would be at the mercy of the proposed national government. Ratification was secured, but with a tacit understanding that a bill of rights should promptly be added which should restrict the national government in behalf of individual liberty. That the early statesmen thought of a federal bill of rights only in terms of restrictions on national power is emphasized by Hamilton's ingenious argument in The Federalist *(No. 84) that since the proposed central government was one which possessed only the powers delegated to it, it would be not only unnecessary but unwise to prohibit it from doing things which were clearly outside the scope of its delegated authority.*

When the First Congress convened, the House of Representatives proposed seventeen amendments in the nature of a bill of rights. One of these, the fourteenth, provided that "no state should infringe the right of trial by jury in criminal cases, nor the rights of conscience, nor the freedom of speech or of the press." This amendment, which was the only one restricting the powers of the states, was rejected by the Senate. The substance of the others was consolidated into twelve amendments, ten of which were finally ratified by the states.

The First Amendment indicates by its own language that it is directed only against the federal government, for it begins, "Congress shall make no law...." The other amendments are couched in terms of general prohibition; and in spite of the perfectly clear historical evidence as to the intention of those who framed them, it came to be argued that these guarantees of civil liberty ought to be construed as restrictions upon state and federal governments alike. Whether this view is correct is the issue involved in Barron v. Baltimore, the last constitutional decision in which Mr. Chief Justice Marshall participated.

While paving its streets, the city of Baltimore had diverted from their natural courses certain streams, with the result that sand and gravel were deposited near Barron's wharf. The wharf, which had previously enjoyed the deepest water in the harbor, was rendered practically useless, for the deposits prevented the approach of vessels. A verdict of $4500 for Barron had been reversed by the state court of appeals, and a writ of error was taken to the Supreme Court of the United States. It was alleged by Barron that this action upon the part of the city constituted a violation of that clause of the Fifth Amendment which forbids taking private property for public use without just compensation. He insisted that this amendment, being a guarantee in behalf of individual liberty, ought to be construed to restrain the states as well as the national government.

The decision in Barron v. Baltimore has left an indelible impression on the development of civil rights in this country. While today Barron would have brought his case under the due process clause of the Fourteenth Amendment (which does restrict the states), the process of change by which parts of the Bill of Rights have come to be applicable to the states has been slow, uncertain, and confusing. While most rights in the Bill of Rights now do apply to the states, they do so only because they are essential to due process of law. The ruling in the present case that the Bill of Rights does not apply directly to the states has never been overruled.

Mr. Chief Justice Marshall delivered the opinion of the court:

The judgment brought up by this writ of error having been rendered by the court of a State, this tribunal can exercise no jurisdiction over it unless it be shown to come within the provisions of the twenty-fifth section of the Judicial Act.

The plaintiff in error contends that it comes within that clause in the fifth amendment to the Constitution which inhibits the taking of private property for public use without just compensation. He insists that this amendment, being in favor of the liberty of the citizen, ought to be so construed as to restrain the legislative power of a State, as well as that of the United States. If this proposition be untrue, the court can take no jurisdiction of the cause.

The question thus presented is, we think, of great importance, but not of much difficulty.

The Constitution was ordained and established by the people of the United States for themselves, for their own government, and not for the government of the individual States. Each State established a constitution for itself, and in that constitution provided such limitations and restrictions on the powers of its particular government as its judgment dictated. The people of the United States framed such a government for the United States as they supposed best adapted to their situation, and best calculated to promote their interests. The powers they conferred on this government were to be exercised by itself; and the limitations on power, if expressed in general terms, are naturally, and, we think, necessarily applicable to the government created by the instrument. They are limitations of power granted in the instrument itself; not of distinct governments, framed by different persons and for different purposes.

If these propositions be correct, the fifth amendment must be understood as restraining the power of the general government, not as applicable to the States. In their several constitutions they have imposed such restrictions on their respective governments as their own wisdom suggested; such as they deemed most proper for themselves. It is a subject on which they judge exclusively, and with which others interfere no farther than they are supposed to have a common interest.

The counsel for the plaintiff in error insists that the Constitution was intended to secure the people of the several States against the undue exercise of power by their respective State governments; as well as against that which might be attempted by their general government. In support of this argument he relies on the inhibitions contained in the tenth section of the first article.

We think that section affords a strong if not a conclusive argument in support of the opinion already indicated by the court.

The preceding section contains restrictions which are obviously intended for the exclusive purpose of restraining the exercise of power by the departments of the general government. Some of them use language applicable only to Congress, others are expressed in general terms. The third clause, for example, declares that "no bill of attainder or ex post facto law shall be passed." No language can be more general; yet the demonstration is complete that it applies solely to the government of the United States. In addition to the general arguments furnished by the instrument itself, some of which have been already suggested, the succeeding section, the avowed purpose of which is to restrain State legislation, contains in terms the very prohibition. It declares that "no State shall pass any bill of attainder or ex post facto law." This provision, then, of the ninth section, however comprehensive its language, contains no restriction on State legislation.

The ninth section having enumerated, in the nature of a bill of rights, the limitations intended to be imposed on the powers of the general government, the tenth proceeds to enumerate those which were to operate on the State legislatures. These restrictions are brought together in the same section, and are by express words applied to the States. "No State shall enter into any treaty," etc. Perceiving that in a Constitution framed by the people of the United States for the government of all, no limitation of the action of government on the people would apply to the State government unless expressed in terms; the restrictions contained in the tenth section are in direct words so applied to the States.

It is worthy of remark, too, that these inhibitions generally restrain State legislation on subjects intrusted to the general government, or in which the people of all the States feel an interest.

A State is forbidden to enter into any treaty, alliance or confederation. If these compacts are with foreign nations, they interfere with the treaty-making power which is conferred entirely on the general government; if with each other, for political purposes, they can scarcely fail to interfere with the general purpose and intent of the Constitution. To grant letters of marque and reprisal would lead directly to war, the power of declaring which is expressly given to Congress. To coin money is also the exercise of a power conferred on Congress. It would be tedious to recapitulate the several limitations on the powers of the States which are contained in this section. They will be found, generally, to restrain State legislation on subjects intrusted to the government of the Union, in which the citizens of all the States are interested. In these alone were the whole people concerned. The question of their application to States is not left to construction. It is averred in positive words.

If the original Constitution, in the ninth and tenth sections of the first article, draws this plain and marked line of discrimination between the limitations it imposes on the powers of the general government and on those of the States; if in every inhibition intended to act on State power, words are employed which directly express that intent, some strong reason must be assigned for departing from this safe and judicious course in framing the amendments, before that departure can be assumed.

We search in vain for that reason.

Had the people of the several States, or any of them, required changes in their constitutions; had they required additional safeguards to liberty from the apprehended encroachments of their particular governments, the remedy was in their own hands, and would have been applied by themselves. A convention would have been assembled by the discontented State, and the required improvements would have been made by itself. The unwieldy and cumbrous machinery of procuring a recommendation from two-thirds of Congress and the assent of three-fourth of their sister States, could never have occurred to any human being as a mode of doing that which might be effected by the State itself. Had the framers of these amendments intended them to be limitations on the powers of the State governments they would have imitated the framers of the original Constitution, and have expressed that intention. Had Congress engaged in the extraordinary occupation of improving the constitutions of the several States by affording the people additional protection from the exercise of power by their own governments in matters which concerned themselves alone, they would have declared this purpose in plain and intelligible language.

But it is universally understood, it is a part of the history of the day, that the great revolution which established the Constitution of the United States was not effected without immense opposition. Serious fears were extensively entertained that those powers which the patriot statesmen who then watched over the interests of our country, deemed essential to union, and to the attainment of those invaluable objects for which union was sought, might be exercised in a manner dangerous to liberty. In almost every convention by which the Constitution was adopted, amendments to guard against the abuse of power were recommended. These amendments demanded security against the apprehended encroachments of the general government—not against those of the local governments.

In compliance with a sentiment thus generally expressed, to quiet fears thus extensively entertained, amendments were proposed by the required majority in Congress, and adopted by the States. These amendments contain no expression indicating an intention to apply them to the State governments. This court cannot so apply them.

We are of opinion that the provision in the fifth amendment to the Constitution, declaring that private property shall not be taken for public use without just compensation, is intended solely as a limitation on the exercise of power by the government of the United States, and is not applicable to the legislation of the States. We are therefore of opinion that there is no repugnancy between the several acts of the General Assembly of Maryland, given in evidence by the defendants at the trial of this cause in the court of that State, and the Constitution of the United States.

This court, therefore, has no jurisdiction of the cause, and [it] is dismissed.

THE SLAUGHTER-HOUSE CASES
16 Wallace 36; 21 L. Ed. 394 (1873)

In the years prior to the Civil War the individual relied almost entirely on the constitution of his state for the protection of his rights and liberties. The Supreme Court had ruled in Barron v. Baltimore (1833) that the Bill of

Rights limited only the national government, and with the exception of the Alien and Sedition Acts, Congress had passed no law which anyone seriously believed had violated these limitations. The ordinary citizen looked to the state legislature to protect his person and property from private interference, and to the state bill of rights for protection against injury by his state government. Certainly he did not, and could not, expect the national government to step in and protect him either from his neighbor or from his state government.

At the close of the Civil War it seemed clear that without the intervention of the federal government the Southern states would by legislative restrictions strip the newly freed Negro of most of the ordinary rights and immunities of free citizens. To place the civil rights of the Negro upon a firm basis Congress proposed the Fourteenth Amendment authorizing the national government to step in and protect the Negro against actions by his own state government. The states were forbidden to take life, liberty, or property without due process of law, or to deny anyone the equal protection of the laws. The amendment defined United States citizenship in terms which included the Negro, and the states were forbidden to make laws abridging the privileges and immunities of that citizenship.

Exactly what the framers of the amendment intended to include in the phrase "privileges and immunities of citizens of the United States" is not altogether clear, and there is evidence to indicate that it was not clear even to the framers. Some apparently believed that the clause would include within its protection those basic rights enjoyed by all persons—such as the right to marry, to own property, to do business, and to move about freely. Others thought that it would include all or part of the protections listed in the federal Bill of Rights. In the Slaughter-House Cases the Court held that the privileges and immunities clause protected none of these rights, and from this decision the Court has never retreated.

The Slaughter-House Cases were the first cases brought under the Fourteenth Amendment, and they had nothing whatever to do with the rights of freedmen. The case arose on the following facts: the Reconstruction or "carpetbag" government in Louisiana, unquestionably under corrupt influence, had granted a monopoly of the slaughterhouse business to a single concern, thus preventing over one thousand other persons and firms from continuing in that business. The validity of the law was attacked under the Fourteenth Amendment. The case was argued before the Supreme Court twice and was decided by a majority of five to four.

The importance of the case can hardly be overestimated. By distinguishing between state citizenship and national citizenship, and by emphasizing that the rights and privileges of federal citizenship do not include the protection of ordinary civil liberties such as freedom of speech and press, religion, etc., but only the privileges which one enjoys by virtue of his federal citizenship, the Court averted, for the time being at least, the revolution in our constitutional system apparently intended by the framers of the amendment and reserved to the states the responsibility for protecting civil rights generally. Nor has the Court been willing to expand the scope of the privileges and immunities clause beyond this early, limited interpretation. Five years before the Slaughter-House Cases the Supreme Court had held void, in Crandall v. Nevada (1868), a state tax on transporting persons out of the state, on the ground that such a tax would obstruct the citizen in his inherent federal right to come to the seat of his government. Two members of the Court, while concurring in the judgment, held the tax to be a violation of the commerce clause. In his opinion in the Slaughter-House Cases, Mr. Justice Miller cites this freedom of movement as an example of the privileges and immunities of United States citizens, and in 1941 in Edwards v. California, four members of the Court strongly urged that the California "anti-Okie" law should be held invalid on this ground. The majority had rested their decision, as had the minority in the Crandall case, upon the commerce power.

The Slaughter-House Cases held that the privileges and immunities of United States citizenship did not include the right to engage in a business of one's choice since such a privilege did not owe its existence to the national Constitution or laws. But it did not deal with the question whether such privileges include the rights listed in the Bill of Rights—rights which were certainly extended by the Constitution to United States citizens. The Court in the case of Maxwell v. Dow (1900), held that they did not, reasoning that such privileges were those enjoyed only by citizens, and since all persons enjoyed the protection of the Bill of Rights, its guarantees could not be considered privileges and immunities of that citizenship.

Had the Slaughter-House Cases been decided 25 years later, the Louisiana statute would in all probability have been invalidated as a deprivation of liberty and property without due process of law and a denial of the equal protection of the laws. But the majority of the Court disposed rather summarily of these clauses by holding in substance that the due process of law clause was not a limitation on the state's police power and that the equal protection of the laws clause, equally inapplicable, would probably never be invoked except for the protection of the Negro. It is important to bear in mind that Mr. Justice Miller's comments about the due process and equal protection clauses no longer state the law. The Court has long since given those clauses the broadest possible applicability. There have, in fact, been more cases interpreting the Fourteenth Amendment than on any other phrase of constitutional law.

It looked for a time (1935–1940) as though the Court might also broaden the scope and applicability of the privileges and immunities clause of the Fourteenth Amendment. In Colgate v. Harvey (1935) the Court held void a provision of a Vermont income tax law which taxed income from money loaned outside the state at a higher rate than that loaned inside the state. Besides denying the equal protection of the laws, this act was held to abridge the privileges and immunities of citizens of the United States. The right to carry on business freely across state lines was declared to be a privilege or immunity of federal citizenship, a doctrine sharply differing from the rule of Slaughter-House Cases. In 1939, in Hague v. CIO, involving the validity under the Fourteenth Amendment of various repressions of free speech, assembly, etc., in Jersey City, two justices of the Supreme Court from the majority held that the right of citizens to assemble and discuss their rights under the National Labor Relations Act was a privilege or immunity of citizens of the United States within the meaning of the Fourteenth Amendment. There was also speculation as to whether protection against unreasonable searches and seizures was also a privilege and immunity of federal citizenship, but no decision was made on that point. There was sharp dissent in both cases against this tendency to enlarge the scope of the privileges and immunities clause; and in Madden v. Kentucky (1940), in a case similar to Colgate v. Harvey, the Court specifically overruled that case and returned to the time-worn narrow construction of the privileges and immunities clause embodied in the Slaughter-House Cases.

It is not possible to list with certainty the rights protected by the privileges and immunities clause, since, except in Colgate v. Harvey, the Supreme Court has never held the clause to be violated. The Court's interpretation indicates, however, that a privilege or immunity of federal citizenship must meet two tests. First, it must be a right which the federal government itself confers by its Constitution or its laws. Second, as indicated in Maxwell v. Dow, it must be a right which is enjoyed solely because one is a citizen, and is not enjoyed, as a matter of constitutional right, by those who are not citizens. This would include such things as the right to become a citizen of a state (guaranteed by the Fourteenth Amendment itself), the right to settle a homestead on federal land, and the right to take a United States Civil Service examination. It also includes the right to vote in a federal election, which owes its existence to the federal government (see Ex parte Yarbrough, 1884), although the states under their authority to establish suffrage qualifications could extend the right to aliens, and in the past have done so. The federal voter must meet, however, the valid voting qualifications of the state.

Mr. Justice Miller delivered the opinion of the Court, saying in part:

The plaintiffs in error accepting this issue, allege that the statute is a violation of the Constitution of the United States in these several particulars:

That it creates an involuntary servitude forbidden by the 13th article of amendment;

That it abridges the privileges and immunities of citizens of the United States;

That it denies to the plaintiffs the equal protection of the laws; and,

That it deprives them of their property without due process of law; contrary to the provisions of the 1st section of the 14th article of amendment.

This court is thus called upon for the first time to give construction to these articles. . . .

Twelve articles of amendment were added to the Federal Constitution soon after the original organization of the government under it in 1789. Of these all but the last were adopted so soon afterwards as to justify the statement that they were practically contemporaneous with the adoption of the original; and the twelfth, adopted in eighteen hundred and three, was so nearly so as to have become, like the others, historical and of another age. But within the last eight years three other articles of amendment of vast importance have been added, by the voice of the people, to that now venerable instrument.

The most cursory glance at these articles discloses a unity of purpose, when taken in connection with the history of the times, which cannot fail to have an important bearing on any question of doubt concerning their true meaning. . . . Fortunately that history is fresh within the memory of us all, and its leading features, as they bear upon the matter before us, free from doubt. . . . [Here follows a discussion of the Thirteenth and Fifteenth Amendments.]

The 1st section of the 14th article, to which our attention is more specially invited, opens with a definition of citizenship—not only citizenship of the United States, but citizenship of the states. No such definition was previously found in the Constitution, nor had any attempt been made to define it by act of Congress. It had been the occasion of much discussion in the courts, by the executive departments and in the public journals. It had been said by eminent judges that no man was a citizen of the United States except as he was a citizen of one of the states composing the Union. Those, therefore, who had been born and resided always in the District of Columbia or in the territories, though within the United States, were not citizens. Whether this proposition was sound or not had never been judicially decided. But it had been held by this court, in the celebrated Dred Scott Case, only a few years before the outbreak of the Civil War, that a man of African descent, whether a slave or not, was not and could not be a citizen of a state or of the United States. This decision, while it met the condemnation of some of the ablest statesmen and constitutional lawyers of the country, had never been overruled; and, if it was to be accepted as a constitutional limitation of the right of citizenship, then all the negro race who had recently been made freemen were still, not only not citizens, but were incapable of becoming so by anything short of an amendment to the Constitution.

To remove this difficulty primarily, and to establish a clear and comprehensive definition of citizenship which should declare what should constitute citizenship of the United States and also citizenship of a state, the 1st clause of the 1st section was framed:

"All persons born or naturalized in the United States and subject to the jurisdiction thereof are citizens of the United States and of the state wherein they reside."

The first observation we have to make on this clause is that it puts at rest both the questions which we stated to have been the subject of differences of opinion. It declares that persons may be citizens of the United States without regard to their citizenship of a particular state, and it overturns the Dred Scott decision by making all persons born within the United States and subject to its jurisdiction citizens of the United States. That its main purpose was to establish the citizenship of the negro can admit of no doubt. The phrase "subject to its jurisdiction" was intended to exclude from its operation children of ministers, consuls and citizens or subjects of foreign states born within the United States.

The next observation is more important in view of the arguments of counsel in the present case. It is that the distinction between citizenship of the United States and citizenship of a state is clearly recognized and established. Not only may a man be a citizen of the United States without being a citizen of a state, but an important element is necessary to convert the former into the latter. He must reside within the state to make him a citizen of it, but it is only necessary that he should be born or naturalized in the United States to be a citizen of the Union.

It is quite clear, then, that there is a citizenship of the United States and a citizenship of a state, which are distinct from each other and which depend upon different characteristics or circumstances in the individual.

We think this distinction and its explicit recognition in this Amendment of great weight in this argument, because the next paragraph of this same section, which is the one mainly relied on by the plaintiffs in error, speaks only of privileges and immunities of citizens of the United States, and does not speak of those of citizens of the several states. The argument, however, in favor of the plaintiffs, rests wholly on the assumption that the citizenship is the same and the privileges and immunities guaranteed by the clause are the same.

The language is: "No state shall make or enforce any law which shall abridge the privileges or immunities of citizens of the United States." It is a little remarkable, if this clause was intended as a protection to the citizen of a state against the legislative power of his own state, that the words "citizen of the state" should be left out when it is so carefully used, and used in contradistinction to "citizens of the United States" in the very sentence which precedes it.

It is too clear for argument that the change in phraseology was adopted understandingly and with a purpose.

Of the privileges and immunities of the citizens of the United States, and of the privileges and immunities of the citizen of the state, and what they respectively are, we will presently consider; but we wish to state here that it is only the former which are placed by this clause under the protection of the Federal Constitution, and that the latter, whatever they may be, are not intended to have any additional protection by this paragraph of the Amendment.

If, then, there is a difference between the privileges and immunities belonging to a citizen of the United States as such, and those belonging to the citizen of the state as such, the latter must rest for their security and protection where they have heretofore rested; for they are not embraced by this paragraph of the Amendment.

The first occurence of the words "privilege and immunities" in our constitutional history is to be found in the fourth of the Articles of the old Confederation.

It declares "That, the better to secure and perpetuate mutual friendship and intercourse among the people of the different states in this Union, the free inhabitants of each of these states, paupers, vagabonds, and fugitives from justice excepted, shall be entitled to all the privileges and immunities of free citizens in the several states; and the people of each state shall have free ingress and regress to and from any other state, and shall enjoy therein all the privileges of trade and commerce, subject to the same duties, impositions, and restrictions as the inhabitants thereof respectively."

In the Constitution of the United States, which superseded the Articles of Confederation, the corresponding provision is found in section two of the 4th article, in the following words: The citizens of each state shall be entitled to all the privileges and immunities of citizens of the several states.

There can be but little question that the purpose of both these provisions is the same, and that the privileges and immunities intended are the same in each. In the Article[s] of the Confederation we have some of these specifically mentioned, and enough perhaps to give some general idea of the class of civil rights meant by the phrase.

Fortunately we are not without judicial construction of this clause of the Constitution. The first and the leading case on the subject is that of Corfield v. Coryell, decided by Mr. Justice Washington in the circuit court for the district of Pennsylvania in 1823.

"The inquiry," he says, "is, what are the privileges and immunities of citizens of the several states? We feel no hesitation in confining these expressions to those privileges and immunities which are fundamental; which belong of right to the citizens of all free governments, and which have at all times been enjoyed by citizens of the several states which compose this Union, from the time of their becoming free, independent, and sovereign. What these fundamental principles are, it would be more tedious than difficult to enumerate." "They may all, however, be comprehended under the following general heads: protection by the government, with the right to acquire and possess property of every kind, and to pursue and obtain happiness and safety, subject, nevertheless, to such restraints as the government may prescribe for the general good of the whole."

This definition of the privileges and immunities of citizens of the states is adopted in the main by this court in the recent case of Ward v. Maryland [1871], while it declines to undertake an authoritative definition beyond what was necessary to that decision. The description, when taken to include others not named, but which are of the same general character, embraces nearly every civil right for the establishment and protection of which organized government is instituted. They are, in the language of Judge Washington, those rights which are fundamental. Throughout his opinion, they are spoken of as rights belonging to the individual as a citizen of a state. They are so spoken of in the constitutional provision which he was construing. And they have always been held to be the class of rights which the state governments were created to establish and secure. . . .

The constitutional provision there alluded to did not create those rights, which it called privileges and immunities of citizens of the states. It threw around them in that clause no security for the citizen of the state in which they were claimed or exercised. Nor did it profess to control the power of the state governments over the rights of its own citizens.

Its sole purpose was to declare to the several states, that whatever those rights, as you grant or establish them to your own citizens, or as you limit or qualify, or impose restrictions on their exercise, the same, neither more nor less, shall be the measure of the rights of citizens of other states within your jurisdiction.

It would be the vainest show of learning to attempt to prove by citations of authority, that up to the adoption of the recent Amendments, no claim or pretense was set up that those rights depended on the Federal government for their existence or protection, beyond the very few express limitations which the Federal Constitution imposed upon the states—such, for instance, as the prohibition against ex post facto laws, bills of attainder, and laws impairing the obligation of contracts. But with the exception of these and a few other restrictions, the entire domain of the privileges and immunities of citizens of the states, as above defined, lay within the constitutional and legislative power of the states, and without that of the Federal government. Was it the purpose of the 14th Amendment, by the simple declaration that no state should make or enforce any law which shall abridge the privileges and immunities of citizens of the United States, to transfer the security and protection of all the civil rights which we have mentioned, from the states to the Federal government? And where it is declared that Congress shall have the power to enforce that article, was it intended to bring within the power of Congress the entire domain of civil rights heretofore belonging exclusively to states?

All this and more must follow, if the proposition of the plaintiffs in error be sound. For not only are these rights subject to the control of Congress whenever in its discretion any of them are supposed to be abridged by state legislation, but that body may also pass laws in advance, limiting and restricting the exercise of legislative power by the states, in their most ordinary and usual functions, as in its judgment it may think proper on all such subjects. And still further, such a construction followed by the reversal of the judgments of the supreme court of Louisiana in these cases would constitute this court a perpetual censor upon all legislation of the states, on the civil rights of their own citizens, with authority to nullify such as it did not approve as consistent with those rights, as they existed at the time of the adoption of this Amendment. The argument, we admit, is not always the most conclusive which is drawn from the consequences urged against the adoption of a particular construction of an instrument. But when, as in the case before us, these consequences are so serious, so far reaching and pervading, so great a departure from the structure and spirit of our institutions; when the effect is to fetter and degrade the state governments by subjecting them to the control of Congress, in the exercise of powers heretofore universally conceded to them of the most ordinary and fundamental character; when in fact it radically changes the whole theory of the relations of the state and Federal governments to each other and of both these governments to the people; the argument has a force that is irresistible, in the absence of language which expresses such a purpose too clearly to admit of doubt.

We are convinced that no such results were intended by the Congress which proposed these amendments, nor by the legislatures of the states, which ratified them.

Having shown that the privileges and immunities relied on in the argument are those which belong to citizens of the states as such, and that they are left to the state governments for security and protection, and not by this article placed under the special care of the Federal government, we may hold ourselves excused from defining the privileges and immunities of citizens of the United States which no state can abridge, until some case involving those privileges may make it necessary to do so.

But lest it should be said that no such privileges and immunities are to be found if those we have been considering are excluded, we venture to suggest some which owe their existence to the Federal government, its national character, its Constitution, or its laws.

One of these is well described in the case of Crandall v. Nevada [1868]. It is said to be the right of the citizen of this great country, protected by implied guarantees of its Constituion, "to come to the seat of government to assert any claim he may have upon that government, to transact any business he may have with it, to seek its protection, to share its offices, to engage in administering its functions. He has the right of free access to its seaports, through which all operations of foreign commerce are conducted, to the subtreasuries, land-offices, and courts of justice in the several states." . . .

Another privilege of a citizen of the United States is to demand the care and protection of the Federal government over his life, liberty, and property when on the high seas or within the jurisdiction of a foreign government. Of this there can be no doubt, nor that the right depends upon his character as a citizen of the United States. The right to peaceably assemble and petition for redress of grievances, the privilege of the writ of habeas corpus, are rights of the citizen guaranteed by the Federal Constitution. The right to use the navigable waters of the United States, however they may penetrate the territory of the several states, and all rights secured to our citizens by treaties with foreign nations, are dependent upon citizenship of the United States, and not citizenship of a state. One of these privileges is conferred by the very article under consideration. It is that a citizen of the United States can, of his own volition, become a citizen of any state of the Union by a bona fide residence therein, with the same rights as other citizens of that state. To these may be added the rights secured by the 13th and 15th articles of Amendment, and by the other clause of the Fourteenth, next to be considered.

But it is useless to pursue this branch of the inquiry, since we are of opinion that the rights claimed by these plaintiffs in error, if they have any existence, are not privileges and immunities of citizens of the United States within the meaning of the clause of the 14th Amendment under consideration.

"All persons born or naturalized in the United States, and subject to the jurisdiction thereof, are citizens of the United States and of the state, wherein they reside. No state shall make or enforce any law which shall abridge the privileges or immunities of citizens of the United States; nor shall any state deprive any person of life, liberty or property without due process of law, nor deny to any person within its jurisdiction the equal protection of its laws."

The argument has not been much pressed in these cases that the defendant's charter deprives the plaintiffs of their property without due process of law, or that it denies to them the equal protection of the law. The first of these paragraphs has been in the Constitution since the adoption of the 5th Amendment, as a restraint upon the Federal power. It is also to be found in some form of expression in the constitutions of nearly all the states, as a restraint upon the power of the states. This law, then, has practically been the same as it now is during the existence of the government, except so far as the present Amendment may place the restraining power over the states in this matter in the hands of the Federal government.

We are not without judicial interpretation, therefore, both state and national, of the meaning of this clause. And it is sufficient to say that under no construction of that provision that we have ever seen, or any that we deem admissible, can the restraint imposed by the state of Louisiana upon the exercise of their trade by the butchers of New Orleans be held to be a deprivation of property within the meaning of that provision.

"Nor shall any state deny to any person within its jurisdiction the equal protection of the laws."

In the light of the history of these amendments, and the pervading purpose of them, which we have already discussed, it is not difficult to give a meaning to this clause. The existence of laws in the states where the newly emancipated negroes resided, which discriminated with gross injustice and hardship against them as a class, was the evil to be remedied by this clause, and by it such laws are forbidden.

If, however, the states did not conform their laws to its requirements, then by the 5th section of the article of amendment Congress was authorized to enforce it by suitable legislation. We doubt very much whether any action of a state not directed by way of discrimination against the negroes as a class, or on account of their race, will ever be held to come within the purview of this provision. It is so clearly a provision for that race and that emergency, that a strong case would be necessary for its application to any other. But as it is a state that is to be dealt with, and not alone the validity of its laws, we may safely leave that matter until Congress shall have exercised its power, or some case of state oppression, by denial of equal justice in its courts, shall have claimed a decision at our hands. We find no such case in the one before us, and we do not deem it necessary to go over the argument again, as it may have relation to this particular clause of the Amendment. . . .

The judgments of the Supreme Court of Louisiana in these cases are affirmed.

Mr. Justice Field, with whom Mr. Chief Justice Chase, Mr. Justice Swayne, and Mr. Justice Bradley concurred, dissented, saying in part:

The Amendment does not attempt to confer any new privileges or immunities upon citizens or to enumerate or define those already existing. It assumes that there are such privileges and immunities which belong of right to citizens as such, and ordains that they shall not be abridged by state legislation. If this inhibition has no reference to privileges and immunities of this character, but only refers, as held by the majority of the court in their opinion, to such privileges and immunities as were before its adoption specially designated in the Constitution or necessarily implied as belonging to citizens of the United States, it was a vain and idle enactment, which accomplished nothing, and most unnecessarily excited Congress and the people on its passage. With privileges and immunities thus designated no state could ever have interfered by its laws, and no new constitutional provision was required to inhibit such interference. The supremacy of the Constitution and the laws of the United

States always controlled any state legislation of that character. But if the Amendment refers to the natural and inalienable rights which belong to all citizens, the inhibition has a profound significance and consequence. . . .

Mr. Justice Swayne and Mr. Justice Bradley filed separate dissenting opinions.

LOCHNER v. NEW YORK
198 U. S. 45; 25 S. Ct. 539; 49 L. Ed. 937 (1905)

At the time the Fourteenth Amendment was adopted the due process clause of the Fifth Amendment had been in effect against the federal government for three-quarters of a century. During that entire period the Supreme Court had decided only four or five cases interpreting the clause, but from Coke and Blackstone the ancient lineage and narrow meaning of the clause were abundantly clear. The clause traces its beginning to the guarantee embodied in Magna Charta that "no freeman shall be taken or imprisoned or deprived of his freehold or his liberties or free customs, or outlawed or exiled, or in any manner destroyed, nor shall we come upon him or send against him, except by a legal judgment of his peers or by the law of the land." With the reaffirmation of these guarantees in the Statute of Westminster (1354) Ed. III, "per legem terrae" became "due process of the law," although at the time of the adoption of the Bill of Rights the eight state constitutions providing such protection used the term "law of the land." Whichever words were used, the guarantee involved was the same: the government was forbidden to limit in any way the individual's personal or property rights unless it did so through proper procedures. In short, it was a check not on what the government could do but on the process it had to follow in order to do it.

This "procedural" due process was the only kind of due process there was until after the middle of the nineteenth century, when pressure from important property interests for a "substantive" content to the due process clause began to make itself felt. Among the leading purposes for which the United States Constitution had been framed was the protection of private property from the irresponsible attacks of the "too popular" state governments. Hence those with vested property rights looked from the beginning to the judicially enforceable Constitution to protect them from legislation, particularly state legislation. They turned first to the protection against bills of attainder and ex post facto laws, but in Calder v. Bull (1798) the

Supreme Court held that the ex post facto clause applied only to criminal legislation. Better luck was had with the contract clause, and in such cases as Fletcher v. Peck (1810) and the Dartmouth College Case (1819) the Court held that a vested right implied a contract not to divest it or interfere with its exercise. But with the passing of Mr. Chief Justice Marshall the strength of even this doctrine began to wane. In Charles River Bridge v. Warren Bridge (1837) the Court under Taney made clear that henceforth contracts would be strictly construed in favor of the people and against the vested interests; and much later, in Stone v. Mississippi (1880), the Court held that the police power to legislate in the public interest could not be limited by the contract clause.

So it was natural that pressure should mount to persuade the courts that the guarantee of due process of law should provide constitutional protection to the vested interests. In 1856 in Wynhammer v. New York a state court finally struck down a provision of a state prohibition statute as a denial of due process of law because the law provided for the confiscation of stocks of liquor in possession when the law took effect. The court's basic premise was that liquor was property which could not be transformed into a nuisance merely by the whim of the legislature; hence a statute providing for its confiscation was void, even though the procedures by which the confiscation took place followed "the forms which belong to due process of law." The court said, "The act . . . itself pronounces the sentence of condemnation, and the judicial machinery, such as it is, which it provides are agencies merely to insure the execution of the sentence."

This theory that the substance of a law itself could be held void for want of due process made its way slowly into the Supreme Court. In 1857, Mr. Chief Justice Taney in the Dred Scott case, after holding the Missouri Compromise Act void on a number of grounds, added that "an act of Congress which deprives a citizen of the United States of his liberty or property merely because he came himself or brought his property into a particular territory of the United States and who had committed no offense against the laws could hardly be dignified with the name of due process of law." But the Court was not yet ready to receive the doctrine. Mr. Justice Miller rejected it in the Slaughter-House Cases (1873); and in 1875 in Loan Association v. Topeka, the Court, completely ignoring the due process clause, held bad the expenditure of public money for a private purpose on the ground that this was a violation of those limits on governmental power "which grow out of the essential nature of all free governments; implied reservations of individual rights, without which the social compact could not exist. . . ." Again in 1878 in Davidson v. New Orleans, the Court made clear its attitude toward due process, going so far as to scold the bar for pressing upon them this new concept of due process. "There is here abundant evidence that there exists some strange misconception of the scope of this provision as found in the Fourteenth Amendment. In fact, it would seem, from the character of many of the cases before us, and the arguments made in them, that the clause under consideration is looked upon as a means of bringing to the test of the decision of this court the abstract opinions of every unsuccessful litigant in a State court of the justice of the decision against him, and of the merits of the legislation on which such a decision may be founded."

In 1877 there came before the Supreme Court a group of cases known as the "Granger Cases," in which the Court faced for the first time the right of a state legislature to regulate private business. The close of the Civil War ushered in a period of rapid railroad expansion. In the East, where industrial development tended to keep pace with the multiplication of transportation facilities, railroad building proved satisfactorily profitable. In the West, however, where new country was being opened up and population was sparse, the railroads had difficulty in paying dividends and frequently yielded to the temptation to indulge in stock-watering, questionable manipulation of credits, and doubtful practices in respect to grants of lands; to rebating and discrimination; and to other objectionable practices. Pitted against the desperate efforts of the railroads to make profits was the Western farmer, who wished to enjoy adequate railroad facilities at reasonable rates in order to facilitate the movement of crops in sparsely settled communities and who resented the unfair or dishonest methods of which some of the roads were known to be guilty. Out of this conflict of interests grew the Granger Movement, an organized effort on the part of the Western farmers which finally culminated in state legislation designed to cure the worst abuses. Starting in Illinois in 1871, the movement spread to other states; and soon railroads and warehousemen in Minnesota, Iowa, and Wisconsin found themselves subject to severe regulation with respect to rates and services. It was these laws which were challenged in the Granger Cases.

The first of these cases, Munn v. Illinois (1877), did not relate to railroad rate legislation but dealt rather with the question of the validity of an Illinois statute providing for the fixing of maximum charges for the storage of grain, in Chicago and other places having not less than one hundred thousand population, in warehouses "in which grain is stored in bulk, and in which the grain of different owners is mixed together, or in which grain is stored in such a manner that the identity of different lots or parcels cannot be accurately preserved." Here, as in the Slaughter-House Cases, an attempt was made to convince the Court that the legislation in question was in violation of the Fourteenth Amendment. It was urged that it involved a deprivation of property without due process of law and a denial of the equal protection of the laws. But here again the attempt failed. The Court decided that terminal grain elevators were businesses sufficiently affected with a public interest to enable the legislature to regulate the charges which they made. It then went on to point out that the Fourteenth Amendment provided no restriction upon burdensome or confiscatory rates; in cases where the legislature could regulate rates at all the degree of regulation was a matter of legislative discretion, and "for protection aganst abuses by legislatures the people must resort to the polls, not to the courts."

The acceptance by the Supreme Court of this "substantive" due process, in addition to the earlier exclusively "procedural" due process, took place gradually over a period of nearly 20 years as cases involving the validity of state laws came before it. The change came first in the area of rate controls. Within a decade after the Munn case the Court started to backtrack from Mr. Chief Justice Waite's dictum in that case—that the only appeal from an unjust rate was to elect a new legislature to enact a just one. In the Railroad Commission Cases (Stone v. Farmers' Loan & Trust Co., 1886) the Court, while confirming the legislature's power to regulate rates, added that "this power to regulate is not a power to destroy, and limitation is not the equivalent of confiscation. Under pretense of regulating fares and freights, the State cannot require a railroad corporation to carry persons or property without reward; neither can it do that which in law amounts to taking of private property for public use without just compensation, or without due process of law." Thus the legislature is apparently forbidden by due process to enact a regulatory measure which in substance is unreasonable. In Chicago, M. & St. P. R. Co. v. Minnesota (1890), the Court, abandoning the dictum of the Munn case, held that only by providing judicial review of the reasonableness of a rate, in contrast to an appeal to the legislature, could the requirement of due process of law be met.

For over 40 years the Supreme Court supervised with jealous care the rate regulation, whether by regulatory commission or by the legislature itself, of the nation's public utilities. Any rate which did not produce a fair return on a fair evaluation of the property was a denial of due process of law, and both the evaluation and the fairness of the return were subject, ultimately, to judicial review. It was not until 1944 in Federal Power Commission v. Hope Natural Gas Co. that the Court, noting that the value of a company depends on the rates it is allowed to charge, indicated that henceforth it would look to the overall reasonableness of the rate in terms of its general effect on the business, and leave to the proper agency the method by which the rate was to be set.

In Munn v. Illinois and the cases which followed it, the Court established the doctrine that the government could regulate prices and control terms of service (within limits) only of businesses which were "affected with a public interest." To impose these regulations upon a business not affected with a public interest was to deprive it of its liberty and property without due process of law. This doctrine seemed fair on its face and comported with the tradition of American individualism. But what is a business "affected with a public interest"? The Court found it difficult to answer this question because as cases involving it arose, it became obvious that there was no single characteristic by which a business so affected with a public interest could invariably be identified. Furthermore, even those businesses so affected could not necessarily be regulated in their entirety, but only in those aspects demanded by the need to protect the public interest. Thus, in the years in which the Court applied this elusive and difficult doctrine, it held void efforts to control wages in the meat packing business, the resale price of theater tickets, the price of gasoline, the rates charged by an employment agency, and the licensing of ice dealers. When, during the financial depression of the 1930's, New York undertook to improve the lot of the dairy industry by setting a minimum price for milk, it was generally expected the Court would hold the price-fixing statute void. By none of the definitions in use could the milk industry be described as "affected with a public interest," and hence subject to price controls.

In Nebbia v. New York (1934), the Court held the New York statute valid. "The phrase 'affected with a public interest' can," said the Court, "in the nature of things, mean no more than that an industry, for adequate reason, is subject to control for the public good." Many facets of the milk industry were already subject to state regulation, and the Court saw no reason why prices should be "peculiarly sacrosanct." "So far as the requirement of due process is concerned, and in the absence of other constitutional restriction, a state is free to adopt whatever economic policy may reasonably be deemed to promote public welfare, and to enforce that policy by legislation adapted to its purpose. The courts are without authority either to declare such policy, or, when it is declared by the legislature, to override it. ..."

What persuaded the Supreme Court, toward the end of the 19th century, to assert a supervisory power over the substance of state legislation which they had so carefully rejected in the Slaughter-House Cases is not difficult to surmise. During the two decades involved, the entire personnel of the Court, with the exception of Mr. Justice Field, had changed; and Field, who had dissented in the Slaughter-House Cases, had always been an apostle of the new faith. The new members coming on the Court tended to reflect the social and economic pressures of the post-Civil War period: the tremendous expansion of the railroads and industry, the brawling struggle between management and labor with the growth of the trade union movement, and the increasing use of political power by the working-man to secure the enactment of protective labor legislation. Naturally, organized industry looked upon legislative efforts to ameliorate factory *conditions and hours of labor as intolerable interferences with the employer's private affairs and a deprivation of his liberty and property. A generation of judges steeped in the individualism of the common law tended to share this view. Due process of law came to seem the completely appropriate and adequate constitutional weapon with which to combat the onward march of the new social control—the new police power.*

This individualistic interpretation by the courts of due process of law found finally a definite basis in the development during the 1880's of the doctrine of "liberty of contract." The first case turning upon this doctrine was decided by the supreme court of Pennsylvania in 1886, Godcharles v. Wigeman, but the theory was ultimately incorporated into the doctrine of due process of law as applied by both state and federal courts. The concept of "liberty of contract" was both plausible and alluring. It asserted in substance that when two parties, neither of whom was under any legal disability, came together to make a contract which was not contrary to public policy, the legislature had no right to interfere and dictate the terms of the agreement. The application of this doctrine to the problem of protective labor legislation produced, however, some very startling results, due in large measure to the naïve assumption by the courts that the individual employee of a great industrial corporation possessed full liberty of contract and could dicker with his employer upon equal terms. Naturally, as time went on the courts found frequently that this vaunted liberty of contract was infringed by the laws regulating hours of labor, method and time of wage payment, employer's liability, factory conditions, and similar matters.

Sir Henry Maine's statement that "the movement of the progressive societies has hitherto been a movement from status to contract" marked this as a liberal doctrine which emancipated the individual, especially the laborer, from governmental controls and allowed him to bargain freely about his affairs. Hence it was only natural that it should receive a preferred place in the constitutional scheme. The normal presumption that a state statute is constitutional gradually gave way, and the burden of proof was placed upon those who would sustain a law alleged to limit such liberty of contract. The Court's insistence in Mugler v. Kansas (1887) that a state statute purporting to protect the public health, safety, and morals must bear a "real or substantial relation to those objects" meant that the Court had to be shown that such was the case before the act could be upheld.

The difficulty came in showing that such a relationship did in fact exist. In the Mugler case the Court had taken judicial notice of the evils of drink and had upheld the validity of a state prohibition statute; but the judges themselves had no knowledge of the social and economic conditions which led to the passage of laws regulating the hours of labor and working conditions. Nor was the bar, if it had such knowledge, in a position to transmit it to the bench, since the traditional method of arguing cases was to cite case precedents and attempt to show by rational analysis how the case at bar was similar. Thus the protagonists of protective labor laws found themselves with a strong presumption against the validity of the laws and no effective way to rebut the presumption.

If the burden of proof on those defending labor and social welfare legislation was unusually heavy, it was ultimately assumed in a novel and telling way. When Muller v. Oregon (1908), involving the validity of the Oregon ten-hour law for women, was argued in the Supreme Court, the justices had before them the first of the famous "Brandeis briefs." This brief, prepared by Mr. Louis D. Brandeis (later Mr. Justice Brandeis) set out very little in the way of strictly legal argument, but at great length presented documentary evidence of the social and economic facts and conditions which had led the legislature to pass the law. The Court was impressed, and while insisting that constitutional questions "are not settled by even a consensus of present public opinion . . . ," held that "at the same time, when a question of fact is debated and debatable, and the extent to which a special constitutional limitation goes is affected by the truth in respect to that fact, a widespread and long continued belief concerning it is worthy of consideration. We take judicial cognizance of all matters of general knowledge." The Court unanimously sustained the act.

A second break in the doctrine of the Lochner case came in 1917 in the case of Bunting v. Oregon, a case involving an Oregon statute providing a ten-hour day for all industrial workers. In a five-to-three decision the Court sustained the act and in doing so made it plain that the burden of proof had shifted to those who attacked its validity. "But we need not cast about for reasons for the legislative judgment. We are not required to be sure of the precise reasons for its exercise, or be convinced of the wisdom of its exercise. . . . It is enough for our decision if the legislation under review was passed in the exercise of an admitted power of government. . . . 'There is a contention made that the law . . . is not either necessary or useful 'for preservation of the health of employees . . . .' The record contains no facts to support the contention, and against it is the judgment of the legislature and the supreme court. . . ." The same day the Court divided four to four to sustain the Oregon minimum wage law in Stettler v. O'Hara (1917). Mr. Justice Brandeis took no part in the decision of either of these cases. He had been counsel in the cases in the beginning, and with his appointment to the Supreme Court his place on the briefs had been taken by Felix Frankfurter, a professor in the Harvard Law School.

While the Court decided the Bunting case without any mention of the Lochner decision, it was widely assumed that the Lochner doctrine had been permanently abandoned. But in 1922 George Sutherland and Pierce

Butler were appointed to the Court, and the following year the minimum wage statute of the District of Columbia was held void as a denial of due process of law. This was the case of Adkins v. Children's Hospital (1923). The Court divided five to three. Again Mr. Justice Brandeis did not sit, this time because his daughter was a member of the minimum wage commission. The majority opinion of Mr. Justice Sutherland reads like the opinion of the Court in the Lochner case, from which it quotes at length with approval. It held that there is no such connection between the wages women receive and their health, morals, or welfare as to justify destroying by law the freedom of contract of employers and the women who work for them. Furthermore, the Court said, the act does not guarantee that the minimum wage fixed shall not exceed the fair value of the service for which it is paid. Thus the Court returned to the old presumption of the invalidity of the statute and announced that while the materials in Professor Frankfurter's brief were useful enough to the legislature in passing the law, "they reflect no legitimate light upon the question of its validity." In 1925 and in 1927 the Court without opinion ruled that the Adkins case rendered invalid the state minimum wage laws of Arizona and Arkansas respectively.

In 1933 New York passed a minimum wage law for women and children. Its framers sought to escape the ban of the Adkins decision by providing that the wages fixed should be based on the fair value of the labor paid for. The attempt failed. In Morehead v. New York ex rel. Tipaldo (1936) the Supreme Court in a five-to-four decision held the New York statute invalid. In the majority opinion Mr. Justice Butler stated that the statute was like the one held void in the Adkins case, but further said in substance that any minimum wage law, regardless of its provisions, would be invalid as a denial of due process of law. In a dissenting opinion Mr. Justice Stone observed: "It is difficult to imagine any grounds, other than our own personal economic predilections, for saying that the contract of employment is any the less an appropriate subject of legislation than are scores of others, in dealing with which this Court has held that legislatures may curtail individual freedom in the public interest."

During all this time a Washington minimum wage statute passed in 1913 had been in force, and the case of West Coast Hotel Co. v. Parrish challenging its validity was on the docket at the time the Tipaldo case was decided. At the opening of the new term in October, 1936, the Court refused to rehear the Tipaldo case, and the West Coast Hotel case was argued in December. On February 5, 1937, President Roosevelt, then at the height of his popularity and with a clear mandate to effectuate the regulatory policies of the New Deal, announced his famous "Court Packing Plan." Relying on the specious argument that the justices were too old to keep up with their work load, the plan called for adding one new (and presumably young) justice for each justice over 70 who refused to retire within six months.

The country was thunderstruck by this obvious attack on the Court itself, and even staunch New Dealers rallied to its support. It is not likely that the plan would have passed even if the Court had stood its ground, but on March 29, Mr. Justice Roberts having switched his vote, the Court overruled Adkins v. Children's Hospital and Tipaldo and sustained the Washington statute. Justices Sutherland, Van Devanter, McReynolds, and Butler dissented. To the chant of "a switch in time saves nine," the country watched with relief as one New Deal statute after another was held valid. The Supreme Court, in a philosophical about-face, had returned to the political branches of government the power to regulate the nation's economy.

The Lochner case is printed here because it is, in a sense, a museum piece. The archaic opinion of Mr. Justice Peckham for the majority expresses with accuracy the dominant judicial doctrine of that period, with its reliance upon the concept of "liberty of contract," a doctrine which was widely believed to be essential to stability and good order in our economic and social life. The classic dissenting opinion of Mr. Justice Holmes, however, laid down the challenge which was to revolutionize judicial thinking with respect to the state's power to legislate in behalf of the economic and social welfare of its citizens.

Lochner was convicted of violating a New York statute called the Labor Law, which provided that no employee should be "required or permitted to work in a biscuit, bread or cake bakery or confectionery establishment more than sixty hours in any one week, or more than ten hours in any one day unless for the purpose of making a shorter day on the last day of the week." The legislature had proceeded upon the assumption that the conditions in the baking industry were such as to demand the intervention of the state in behalf of the employees. The majority of the Supreme Court did not agree that such protection was reasonably necessary and accordingly held that there was no adequate justification for this infringement of the private rights of the employer. Four justices dissented on the ground that there was sufficient support for the view of the legislature to make it a debatable question whether the law was arbitrary or not and that when such was the case, the courts should not override the legislative judgment. The dissenting opinion of Mr. Justice Holmes has become almost a classic as a statement of the more liberal judicial attitude toward the question of the validity of social and economic legislation under the Fourteenth Amendment.

Mr. Justice Peckham delivered the opinion of the Court, saying in part:

The statute necessarily interferes with the right of contract between the employer and employees, concerning the number of hours in which the latter may labor in the bakery of the employer. The general right to make a contract in relation to his business is part of the liberty of the individual protected by the 14th Amendment of the Federal Constitution. . . . Under that provision no state can deprive any person of life, liberty, or property without due process of law. The right to purchase or to sell labor is part of the liberty protected by this amendment, unless there are circumstances which exclude the right. There are, however, certain powers, existing in the sovereignty of each state in the Union, somewhat vaguely termed police powers, the exact description and limitation of which have not been attempted by the courts. Those powers, broadly stated, and without, at present, any attempt at a more specific limitation, relate to the safety, health, morals, and general welfare of the public. Both property and liberty are held on such reasonable conditions as may be imposed by the governing power of the state in the exercise of those powers, and with such conditions the 14th Amendment was not designed to interfere. . . .

The state, therefore, has power to prevent the individual from making certain kinds of contracts, and in regard to them the Federal Constitution offers no protection. If the contract be one which the state, in the legitimate exercise of its police power, has the right to prohibit, it is not prevented from prohibiting it by the 14th Amendment. Contracts in violation of a statute, either of the Federal or state government, or a contract to let one's property for immoral purposes, or to do any other unlawful act, could obtain no protection from the Federal Constitution, as coming under the liberty of person or of free contract. Therefore, when the state, by its legislature, in the assumed exercise of its police powers, has passed an act which seriously limits the right to labor or the right of contract in regard to their means of livelihood between persons who are sui juris (both employer and employee), it becomes of great importance to determine which shall prevail,—the right of the individual to labor for such time as he may choose, or the right of the state to prevent the individual from laboring, or from entering into any contract to labor, beyond a certain time prescribed by the state. . . .

It must, of course, be conceded that there is a limit to the valid exercise of the police power by the state. There is no dispute concerning this general proposition. Otherwise the 14th Amendment would have no efficacy and the legislatures of the states would have unbounded power, and it would be enough to say that any piece of legislation was enacted to conserve the morals, the health, or the safety of the people; such legislation would be valid, no matter how absolutely without foundation the claim might be. The claim of the police power would be a mere pretext,—become another and delusive name for the supreme sovereignty of the state to be exercised free from constitutional restraint. This is not contended for. In every case that comes before this court, therefore, where legislation of this character is concerned, and where the protection of the Federal Constitution is sought, the question necessarily arises: Is this a fair, reasonable, and appropriate exercise of the police power of the state, or is it an unreasonable, unnecessary, and arbitrary interference with the right of the individual to his personal liberty, or to enter into those contracts in relation to labor which may seem to him appropriate or necessary for the support of himself and his family? Of course the liberty of contract relating to labor includes both parties to it. The one has as much right to purchase as the other to sell labor.

This is not a question of substituting the judgment of the court for that of the legislature. If the act be within the power of the state it is valid, although the judgment of the court might be totally opposed to the enactment of such a law. But the question would still remain: Is it within the police power of the state? and that question must be answered by the court.

The question whether this act is valid as a labor law, pure and simple, may be dismissed in a few words. There is no reasonable ground for interfering with the liberty of person or the right of free contract, by determining the hours of labor, in the occupation of a baker. There is no contention that bakers as a class are not equal in intelligence and capacity to men in other trades or manual occupations, or that they are not able to assert their rights and care for themselves without the protecting arm of the state, interfering with their independence of judgment and of action. They are in no sense wards of the state. Viewed in the light of a purely labor law, with no reference whatever to the question of health, we think that a law like the one before us involves neither the safety, the morals, nor the welfare, of the public, and that the interest of the public is not in the slightest degree affected by such an act. The law must be upheld, if at all, as a law pertaining to the health of the individual engaged in the occupation of a baker. It does not affect any other portion of the public than those who are engaged in that occupation. Clean and wholesome bread does not depend upon whether the baker works but ten hours per day or only sixty hours a week. The limitation of the hours of labor does not come within the police power on that ground.

It is a question of which of two powers or rights shall prevail,—the power of the state to legislate or the right of the individual to liberty of person and freedom of contract. The mere assertion that the subject relates, though but in a remote degree, to the public health, does not necessarily render the enactment valid. The act must have a more direct relation, as a means to an end, and the end itself must be appropriate and legitimate, before an act can be held to be valid which interferes with the general right of an individual to be free in his person and in his power to contract in relation to his own labor. . . .

We think the limit of the police power has been reached and passed in this case. There is, in our judgment, no reasonable foundation for holding this to be necessary or appropriate as a health law to safeguard the public health, or the health of the individuals who are following the trade of a baker. If this statute be valid, and if, therefore, a proper case is made out in which to deny the right of an individual, sui juris, as employer or employee, to make contracts for the labor of the latter under the protection of the provisions of the Federal Constitution, there would seem to be no length to which legislation of this nature might not go. . . .

We think that there can be no fair doubt that the trade of a baker, in and of itself, is not an unhealthy one to that degree which would authorize the legislature to interfere with the right to labor, and with the right of free contract on the part of the individual, either as employer or employee. In looking through statistics regarding all trades and occupations, it may be true that the trade of a baker does not appear to be as healthy as some other trades, and is also vastly more healthy than still others. To the common understanding the trade of a baker has never been regarded as an unhealthy one. Very likely physicians would not recommend the exercise of that or of any other trade as a remedy for ill health. Some occupations are more healthy than others, but we think there are none which might not come under the power of the legislature to supervise and control the hours of working therein, if the mere fact that the occupation is not absolutely and perfectly healthy is to confer that right upon the legislative department of the government. It might be safely affirmed that almost all occupations more or less affect the health. There must be more than the mere fact of the possible existence of some small amount of unhealthiness to warrant legislative interference with liberty. It is unfortunately true that labor, even in any department, may possibly carry with it the seeds of unhealthiness. But are we all, on that account, at the mercy of legislative majorities? A printer, a tinsmith, a locksmith, a carpenter, a cabinetmaker, a dry goods clerk, a bank's, a lawyer's, or a physician's clerk, or a clerk in almost any kind of business, would all come under the power of the legislature, on this assumption. No trade, no occupation, no mode of earning one's living, could escape this all-pervading power, and the acts of the legislature in limiting the hours of labor in all employments would be valid, although such limitation might seriously cripple the ability of the laborer to support himself and his family. In our large cities there are many buildings into which the sun penetrates for but a short time in each day, and these buildings are occupied by people carrying on the business of bankers, brokers, lawyers, real estate, and many other kinds of business, aided by many clerks, messengers, and other employees. Upon the assumption of the validity of this act under review, it is not possible to say that an act, prohibiting lawyers' or bank clerks, or others, from contracting to labor for their employers more than eight hours a day would be invalid. It might be said that it is unhealthy to work more than that number of hours in an apartment lighted by artificial light during the working hours of the day; that the occupation of the bank clerk, the lawyer's clerk, the real-estate clerk, or the broker's clerk, in such offices is therefore unhealthy, and the legislature, in its paternal wisdom, must, therefore, have the right to legislate on the subject of and to limit, the hours for such labor; and, if it exercises that power, and its validity be questioned, it is sufficient to say, it has reference to the public health; it has reference to the health of the employees condemned to labor day after day in buildings where the sun never shines; it is a health law, and therefore it is valid, and cannot be questioned by the courts.

It is also urged, pursuing the same line of argument, that it is to the interest of the state that its population should be strong and robust, and therefore any legislation which may be said to tend to make people healthy must be valid as health laws, enacted under the police power. If this be a valid argument and a justification for this kind of legislation, it follows that the protection of the Federal Constitution from undue interference with liberty of person and freedom of contract is visionary, wherever the law is sought to be justified as a valid exercise of the police power. Scarcely any law but might find shelter under such assumptions, and conduct, properly so called, as well as contract, would come under the restrictive sway of the legislature. Not only the hours of employees, but the hours of employers, could be regulated, and doctors, lawyers, scientists, all professional men, as well as athletes and artisans, could be forbidden to fatigue their brains and bodies by prolonged hours of exercise, lest the fighting strength of the state be impaired. We mention these extreme cases because the contention is extreme. We do not believe in the soundness of the views which uphold this law. On the contrary, we think that such a law as this, although passed in the assumed exercise of the police power, and as relating to the public health, or the health of the employees named, is not within that power, and is invalid. The act is not, within any fair meaning of the term, a health law, but is an illegal interference with the rights of individuals, both employers and employees, to make contracts regarding labor upon such terms as they may think best, or which they may agree upon with the other parties to such contracts. Statutes of the nature of that under review, limiting the hours in which grown and intelligent men may labor to earn their living, are mere meddlesome interferences with the rights of the individual, and they are not saved from condemnation by the claim that they are passed in the exercise of the police power and upon the subject of the health of the individual whose rights are interfered with, unless there be some fair ground, reasonable in and of itself, to say that there is material danger to the public health, or to the health of the employees, if the hours of labor are not curtailed. . . .

It was further urged on the argument that restricting the hours of labor in the case of bakers was valid because it tended to cleanliness on the part of the workers, as a man was more apt to be cleanly when not overworked, and if cleanly then his "output" was also more likely to be so. . . . The connection, if any exist, is too shadowy and thin to build any argument for the interference of the legislature. If the man works ten hours a day it is all right, but if ten and a half or eleven his health is in danger and his bread may be unhealthy, and, therefore, he shall not be permitted to do it. This, we think, is unreasonable and entirely arbitrary. . . .

. . . It seems to us that the real object and purpose were simply to regulate the hours of labor between the master and his employees (all being men, sui juris), in a private business, not dangerous in any degree to morals, or in any real and substantial degree to the health of the employees. Under such circumstances the freedom of master and employee to contract with each other in relation to their employment, and in defining the same, cannot be prohibited or interfered with, without violating the Federal Constitution.

The judgment . . . must be reversed. . . .

Mr. Justice Harlan, with whom Mr. Justice White and Mr. Justice Day concurred, wrote a dissenting opinion.

Mr. Justice Holmes dissenting:

I regret sincerely that I am unable to agree with the judgment in this case, and I think it my duty to express my dissent.

This case is decided upon an economic theory which a large part of the country does not entertain. If it were a question whether I agreed with that theory, I should desire to study it further and long before making up my mind. But I do not conceive that to be my duty, because I strongly believe that my agreement or disagreement has nothing to do with the right of a majority to embody their opinions in law. It is settled by various decisions of this court that state constitutions and state laws may regulate life in many ways which we as legislators might think as injudicious, or if you like as tyrannical, as this, and which, equally with this, interfere with the liberty to contract. Sunday laws and usury laws are ancient examples. A more modern one is the prohibition of lotteries. The liberty of the citizen to do as he likes so long as he does not interfere with the liberty of others to do the same, which has been a shibboleth for some well-known writers, is interfered with by school laws, by the Postoffice, by every state or municipal institution which takes his money for purposes thought desirable, whether he likes it or not. The 14th Amendment does not enact Mr. Herbert Spencer's Social Statics. The other day we sustained the Massachusetts vaccination law. Jacobson v. Massachusetts [1905]. United States and state statutes and decisions cutting down the liberty to contract by way of combination are familiar to this court. Northern Securities Co. v. United States [1904]. Two years ago we upheld the prohibition of sales of stock on margins, or for future delivery, in the Constitution of California. . . . The decision sustaining an eight-hour law for miners is still recent. Holden v. Hardy [1898]. Some of these laws embody convictions or prejudices which judges are likely to share. Some may not. But a Constitution is not intended to embody a particular economic theory, whether of paternalism and the organic relation of the citizen to the state or of laissez faire. It is made for people of fundamentally differing views, and the accident of our finding certain opinions natural and familiar, or novel, and even shocking, ought not to conclude our judgment upon the question whether statutes embodying them conflict with the Constitution of the United States.

General propositions do not decide concrete cases. The decision will depend on a judgment or intuition more subtle than any articulate major premise. But I think that the proposition just stated, if it is accepted, will carry us far toward the end. Every opinion tends to become a law. I think that the word "liberty" in the 14th Amendment, is perverted when it is held to prevent the natural outcome of a dominant opinion, unless it can be said that a rational and fair man necessarily would admit that the statute proposed would infringe fundamental principles as they have been understood by the traditions of our people and our law. It does not need research to show that no such sweeping condemnation can be passed upon the statute before us. A reasonable man might think it a proper measure on the score of health. Men whom I certainly could not pronounce unreasonable would uphold it as a first installment of a general regulation of the hours of work. Whether in the latter aspect it would be open to the charge of inequality I think it unnecessary to discuss.

HURTADO v. CALIFORNIA
110 U. S. 516; 4 S. Ct. 111; 28 L. Ed. 232 (1884)

While the due process clauses of the Fifth and Fourteenth Amendments came to be restrictions by which the validity of the substance of legislation was tested in the courts, it should not be forgotten that originally due process was construed only as a limitation on governmental procedure. Whatever the government did, it had to do in accordance with the "process" which was "due" under the law of the land. But what, concretely, did such process include? To the layman, thinking in terms of criminal procedure, it undoubtedly included the common-law procedures with which he was familiar—procedures spelled out in detail in the Bill of Rights. The Supreme Court, however, rejected the idea that due process required adherence to a fixed list of prescribed procedures, and in David-son v. New Orleans (1878) it explained that the meaning of the clause would be determined "by the gradual process of judicial inclusion and exclusion, as the cases presented for decision shall require, with the reasoning on which such decisions may be founded."

The Court had already decided, in the case of Murray's Lessee v. Hoboken Land and Improvement Co. (1856), that "due" process did not always mean "judicial" process; and an administrative agency could employ procedures which had the sanction of long-established custom. In this case an administrative warrant authorizing the seizure of a man's property to satisfy a debt to the government was found to be a well-established procedure and hence due process of law.

But if old established procedures were due process of law, then surely those common-law procedures listed in the Bill of Rights were due process of law. And if this were the case, why were they not guaranteed by the Fourteenth Amendment in state criminal cases? This was the argument of Hurtado in the present case. He had been convicted of murder by the state of California and sentenced to be hanged. He claimed a denial of due process because instead of a grand jury indictment, to which he would have been entitled under the common law, he had been charged by an information prepared by the prosecuting attorney—a form of charge authorized by the state of California, but limited at common law to misdemeanors.

Mr. Justice Matthews delivered the opinion of the Court, saying in part:

. . . The proposition of law we are asked to affirm is, that an indictment or presentment by a grand jury, as known to the common law of England, is essential to that "due process of law," when applied to prosecutions for felonies, which is secured and guaranteed by this provision of the Constitution of the United States, and which accordingly it is forbidden to the States respectively to dispense with in the administration of criminal law.

. . . It is maintained on behalf of the plaintiff in error that the phrase "due process of law" is equivalent to "law of the land," as found in the [thirty-]ninth chapter of Magna Charta; that, by immemorial usage, it has acquired a fixed, definite and technical meaning; that it refers to and includes, not only the general principles of public liberty and private right, which lie at the foundation of all free government, but the very institutions which, venerable by time and custom, have been tried by experience and found fit and necessary for the preservation of those principles, and which, having been the birthright and inheritance of every English subject, crossed the Atlantic with the colonists and were transplanted and established in the fundamental laws of the State; that, having been originally introduced into the Constitution of the United

States as a limitation upon the powers of the government, brought into being by that instrument, it has now been added as an additional security to the individual against oppression by the States themselves; that one of these institutions is that of the grand jury, an indictment or presentment by which against the accused in cases of alleged felonies is an essential part of due process of law, in order that he may not be harassed or destroyed by prosecutions founded only upon private malice or popular fury. . . .

It is urged upon us, however, in argument, that the claim made in behalf of the plaintiff in error is supported by the decision of this court in Murray's Lessee v. Hoboken Land & Improvement Company [1856]. There, Mr. Justice Curtis delivering the opinion of the court, after showing that due process of law must mean something more than the actual existing law of the land, for otherwise it would be no restraint upon legislative power, proceeds as follows: "To what principle, then, are we to resort to ascertain whether this process, enacted by Congress, is due process? To this the answer must be twofold. We must examine the Constitution itself to see whether this process be in conflict with any of its provisions. If not found to be so, we must look to those settled usages and modes of proceeding existing in the common and statute law of England before the emigration of our ancestors, and which are shown not to have been unsuited to their civil and political condition by having been acted on by them after the settlement of this country."

This, it is argued, furnishes an indispensable test of what constitutes "due process of law"; that any proceeding otherwise authorized by law, which is not thus sanctioned by usage, or which supersedes and displaces one that is, cannot be regarded as due process of law.

But this inference is unwarranted. The real syllabus of the passage quoted is, that a process of law, which is not otherwise forbidden, must be taken to be due process of law, if it can show the sanction of settled usage both in England and in this country; but it by no means follows, that nothing else can be due process of law. The point in the case cited arose in reference to a summary proceeding, questioned on that account, as not due process of law. The answer was: however exceptional it may be, as tested by definitions and principles of ordinary procedure, nevertheless, this, in substance, has been immemorially the actual law of the land, and, therefore, is due process of law. But to hold that such a characteristic is essential to due process of law, would be to deny every quality of the law but its age, and to render it incapable of progress or improvement. It would be to stamp upon our jurisprudence the unchangeableness attributed to the laws of the Medes and Persians.

This would be all the more singular and surprising, in this quick and active age, when we consider that, owing to the progressive development of legal ideas and institutions in England, the words of Magna Charta stood for very different things at the time of the separation of the American Colonies from what they represented originally. . . .

The Constitution of the United States was ordained, it is true, by descendants of Englishmen, who inherited the traditions of English law and history; but it was made for an undefined and expanding future, and for a people gathered and to be gathered from many Nations and of many tongues. And while we take just pride in the principles and institutions of the common law, we are not to forget that in lands where other systems of jurisprudence prevail, the ideas and processes of civil justice are also not unknown. Due process of law, in spite of the absolutism of continental governments, is not alien to that Code which survived the Roman Empire as the foundation of modern civilization in Europe, and which has given us that fundamental maxim of distributive justice, *Suum cuique tribuere.* There is nothing in Magna Charta, rightly construed as a broad charter of public right and law, which ought to exclude the best ideas of all systems and of every age; and as it was the characteristic principle of the common law to draw its inspiration from every fountain of justice, we are not to assume that the sources of its supply have been exhausted. On the contrary, we should expect that the new and various experiences of our own situation and system will mold and shape it into new and not less useful forms. . . .

We are to construe this phrase in the 14th Amendment by the usus loquendi of the Constitution itself. The same words are contained in the 5th Amendment. That article makes specific and express provision for perpetuating the institution of the grand jury, so far as relates to prosecutions, for the more aggravated crimes under the laws of the United States. It declares that "No person shall be held to answer for a capital or otherwise infamous crime, unless on a presentment or indictment of a grand jury, except in cases arising in the land or naval forces, or in the militia when in actual service in time of war or public danger; nor shall any person be subject for the same offense to be twice put in jeopardy of life or limb; nor shall he be compelled in any criminal case to be a witness against himself." It then immediately adds: "nor be deprived of life, liberty or property, without due process of law." According to a recognized canon of interpretation, especially applicable to formal and solemn instruments of constitutional law, we are forbidden to assume, without clear reason to the contrary, that any part of this most important Amendment is superfluous. The natural and obvious inference is, that in the sense of the Constitution, "due process of law" was not meant or intended to include, ex vi termini, the institution and procedure of a grand jury in any case. The conclusion is equally irresistible, that when the same phrase was employed in the 14th Amendment to restrain the action of the States, it was used in the same sense and with no great extent; and that if in the adoption of that Amendment it had been part of its purpose to perpetuate the institution of the grand jury in all the States, it would have embodied, as did the 5th Amendment, express declarations to that effect. Due process of law in the latter refers to that law of the land, which derives its authority from the legislative powers conferred upon Congress by the Constitution of the United States, exercised within the limits therein prescribed, and interpreted according to the principles of the common law. In the 14th Amendment, by parity of reason, it refers to that law of the land in each State, which derives its authority from the inherent and reserved powers of the State, exerted within the limits of those fundamental principles of liberty and justice which lie at the base of all our civil and political institutions, and the greatest security for which resides in the right of the people to make their own laws, and alter them at their pleasure. "The 14th Amendment," as was said by Mr. Justice Bradley in Mo. v. Lewis [1880], "does not profess to secure to all persons in the United States the benefit of the same laws and the same remedies. Great diversities in these respects may exist in two States separated only by an imaginary line. On one side of this line there may be a right of trial by jury, and on the other side no such right. Each State prescribes its own modes of judicial proceeding."

But it is not to be supposed that these legislative powers are absolute and despotic, and that the Amendment prescribing due process of law is too vague and indefinite to operate as a practical restraint. It is not every Act, legislative in form, that is law. Law is something more than mere will exerted as an act of power. . . . Arbitrary power, enforcing its edicts to the injury of the persons and property of its subjects, is not law, whether manifested as the decree of a personal monarch or of an impersonal multitude. And the limitations imposed by our constitutional law upon the action of the governments, both state and national, are essential to the preservation of public and private rights, notwithstanding the representative character of our political institutions. . . .

It follows that any legal proceeding enforced by public authority, whether sanctioned by age and custom, or newly devised in the discretion of the legislative power, in furtherance of the general public good, which regards and preserves these principles of liberty and justice, must be held to be due process of law. . . .

Tried by these principles, we are unable to say that the substitution for a presentment or indictment by a grand jury of the proceeding by information, after examination and commitment by a magistrate, certifying to the probable guilt of the defendant, with the right on his part to the aid of counsel, and to the cross-examination of the witnesses produced for the prosecution, is not due process of law. It is, as we have seen, an ancient proceeding at common law, which might include every case of an offense of less grade than a felony, except misprision of treason; and in every circumstance of its administration, as authorized by the Statute of California, it carefully considers and guards the substantial interest of the prisoner. It is merely a preliminary proceeding, and can result in no final judgment, except as the consequence of a regular judicial trial, conducted precisely as in cases of indictments. . . .

For these reasons, finding no error therein, the judgment of the Supreme Court of California is affirmed.

Mr. Justice Harlan, dissenting, said in part:

... I cannot agree that the State may, consistently with due process of law, require a person to answer for a capital offense, except upon the presentment or indictment of a grand jury. ...

... To what principles are we to resort to ascertain whether this process ... is due process? To this the answer must be twofold. We must examine the Constitution itself to see whether this process be in conflict with any of its provisions. If not found to be so, we must look *"to those settled usages and modes of proceeding existing in the common and statute law of England before the emigration of our ancestors, and which are shown not to have been unsuited to their civil and political condition by having been acted on by them after the settlement of this country."* ...

... Let us inquire (and no other inquiry is at all pertinent) whether according to the settled usages and modes of proceeding to which, this court has said, reference must be had, an information for a capital offense was, prior to the adoption of our Constitution, regarded as due process of law. [Justice Harlan here reviews the authorities and finds it was not.]

My brethren concede that there are principles of liberty and justice, lying at the foundation of our civil and political institutions, which no State can violate consistently with that due process of law required by the 14th Amendment in proceedings involving life, liberty or property. Some of these principles are enumerated in the opinion of the court. But, for reasons which do not impress my mind as satisfactory, they exclude from that enumeration the exemption from prosecution, by information, for a public offense involving life. By what authority is that exclusion made? Is it justified by the settled usages and modes of procedure, existing under the common and statute law of England at the emigration of our ancestors or at the foundation of our government? Does not the fact that the people of the original States required an amendment of the National Constitution, securing exemption from prosecution, for a capital offense, except upon the indictment or presentment of a grand jury, prove that, in their judgment, such an exemption was essential to protection against accusation and unfounded prosecution and, therefore, was a fundamental principle in liberty and justice? ...

But it is said that the framers of the Constitution did not suppose that due process of law necessarily required for a capital offense the institution and procedure of a grand jury, else they would not in the same amendment prohibiting the deprivation of life, liberty or property without due process of law, have made specific and express provision for a grand jury where the crime is capital or otherwise infamous; therefore, it is argued, the requirement by the 14th Amendment, of due process of law in all proceedings involving life, liberty and property, without specific reference to grand juries in any case whatever, was not intended as a restriction upon the power which it is claimed the States previously had, so far as the express restrictions of the National Constitution are concerned, to dispense altogether with grand juries.

This line of argument, it seems to me, would lead to results which are inconsistent with the vital principles of republican government. If the presence in the 5th Amendment of a specific provision for grand juries in capital cases, alongside the provision for due process of law in proceedings involving life, liberty or property, is held to prove that due process of law did not, in the judgment of the framers of the Constitution, necessarily require a grand jury in capital cases, inexorable logic would require it to be, likewise, held that the right not to be put twice in jeopardy of life and limb for the same offense, nor compelled in a criminal case to testify against one's self (rights and immunities also specifically recognized in the 5th Amendment) were not protected by that due process of law required by the settled usages and proceedings existing under the common and statute law of England at the settlement of this country. More than that, other Amendments of the Constitution proposed at the same time, expressly recognize the right of persons to just compensation for private property taken for public use; their right, when accused of crime, to be informed of the nature and cause of the accusation against them, and to a speedy and public trial, by an impartial jury of the State and district wherein the crime was committed; to be confronted by the witnesses against them; and to have compulsory process for obtaining witnesses in their favor. Will it be claimed that these rights were not secured by the "law of the land" or by "due process of law," as declared and established at the foundation of our government? Are they to be excluded from the enumeration of the fundamental principles of liberty and justice and, therefore, not embraced by "due process of law?" . . .

It seems to me that too much stress is put upon the fact that the framers of the Constitution made express provision for the security of those rights which at common law were protected by the requirement of due process of law and, in addition, declared, generally, that no person shall "be deprived of life, liberty or property without due process of law." The rights, for the security of which these express provisions were made, were of a character so essential to the safety of the people that it was deemed wise to avoid the possibility that Congress, in regulating the processes of law, would impair or destroy them. Hence their specific enumeration in the earlier Amendments of the Constitution. . . .

POWELL v. ALABAMA
287 U. S. 45; 53 S. Ct. 55; 77 L. Ed. 158 (1932)

The Court in the Hurtado case not only rejected the idea that the protections listed in the Bill of Rights are included in due process, but the reasoning on which the decision was based seemed to make impossible such inclusion in the future. In 1897, however, with the advent of the concept of substantive due process, the Court held that due process forbade a state to seize private property without just compensation; see Chicago, B. & Q. R. Co. v. Chicago. Mr. Justice Harlan, who had dissented in Hurtado, wrote the opinion of the Court without alluding to that case or calling attention to the fact that the right was one listed in the Bill of Rights. He held, simply, that the right to compensation was a right "founded in natural equity" and "laid down as a principle of universal law. Indeed, in a free government almost all other rights would become worthless if the government possessed an uncontrollable power over the private fortune of every citizen." He emphasized that "in determining what is due process of law regard must be had to substance, not to form," and pointed out that while "the legislature may prescribe a form of procedure to be observed in the taking of private property for public use, . . . it is not due process of law if provision be not made for compensation."

The C. B. & Q. decision had not overruled Hurtado, but since the two cases were in some ways incompatible, it seemed plausible to suppose that some of the Bill of Rights guarantees for persons accused of crime might also be found essential to due process. In the case of Twining v. New Jersey (1908), the Court refused to apply any such notion to the right against compulsory self-incrimination. The Court conceded that it was "possible that some of the personal rights safeguarded by the first eight Amendments against national action may also be safeguarded against state action, because a denial of them would be a denial of due process of law. Chicago, B. & Q. R. Co. v. Chicago. If this is so, it is not because those rights are enumerated in the first eight Amendments, but because they are of such a nature that they are included in the conception of due process of law. . . ." It reviewed the historical development of the protection against self-incrimination and concluded it was not really thought of as an "immutable principle of justice," but merely as a "just and useful principle of law." Certainly it did not rank "with the right to hearing before condemnation, the immunity from arbitrary power not acting by general laws, and the inviolability of private property." The Court noted further that, with the exception of requiring jurisdiction, notice, and hearing, it had uniformly "sustained all state laws, statutory or judicially declared, regulating procedure, evidence, and methods of trial, and held them to be consistent with due process of law. ...." The decision stands in sharp contrast to the decisions in Lochner v. New York (1905) and Adkins v. Children's Hospital (1923). Clearly, the rights protected by due process were property rights—not rights involving criminal procedure. It was not until 1964, in Malloy v. Hogan, that the Court overruled Twining and held the protection against self-incrimination essential to due process.

With the rise of the doctrine of substantive due process it was increasingly urged on the Court that the "liberty" protected by the due process clause of the Fourteenth Amendment should include, at the very least, the freedom of speech and press mentioned in the First Amendment. The pressure was not only from members of the bar, but from the Court itself. In 1907 Mr. Justice Harlan, in a dissenting opinion in Patterson v. Colorado, declared "I go further and hold that the privileges of free speech and a free press, belonging to every citizen of the United States, constitute essential parts of every man's liberty, and are protected against violation by that clause of the Fourteenth Amendment forbidding a state to deprive any person of his liberty without due process of law." Essentially the same view was expressed by Mr. Justice Brandeis in his dissenting opinion in Gilbert v. Minnesota (1920), a case in which the Court assumed for the sake of argument that freedom of speech was "a natural and inherent" right but held that it had not been violated. Although in Prudential Insurance Co. v. Cheek (1920) the Court insisted that "neither the Fourteenth Amendment nor any other provision of the Constitution of the United States imposes upon the states any restrictions about 'freedom of speech,'" the following year it began to show signs of conversion to a broader conception of the term "liberty." In Meyer v. Nebraska (1923) Mr. Justice McReynolds, in an opinion holding invalid a Nebraska statute forbidding the teaching of any subject in any language but English in any private, parochial, or public school, defined the "liberty" protected by the due process clause as follows: "Without doubt, it denotes not merely freedom from bodily restraint, but also the right of the individual to contract, to engage in any of the common occupations of life, to acquire useful knowledge, to marry, establish a home and bring up children, to worship God according to the dictates of his own conscience, and, generally, to enjoy those privileges long recognized at common law as essential to the orderly pursuit of happiness by free men."

Two years later, in what was in fact a constitutional revolution, the Court, in Gitlow v. New York (1925), reversed its stand. Gitlow had challenged a state statute as violating his freedom of speech and thereby denying him due process; the Supreme Court took jurisdiction under the due process clause, declaring that "For present purposes we may and do assume that freedom of speech and of the press—which are protected by the First Amendment from abridgment by Congress—are among the fundamental personal rights and 'liberties' protected by the due process clause of the Fourteenth Amendment from impairment by the states." In Gitlow's case the Court held the state statute valid and upheld Gitlow's conviction; but in 1931, in Near v. Minnesota, the Court held a state statute void on the ground that it denied due process by unreasonably restricting freedom of speech and press. With these two cases these important liberties became effectively "nationalized," and the states came under federal judicial scrutiny and discipline in dealing with freedom of speech and press.

The other liberties mentioned in the First Amendment followed in due course. In Hamilton v. Board of Regents of the University of California (1934) freedom of religion was held to be protected by the Fourteenth Amendment, although the Court held that Hamilton's religious liberty was not abridged by making him take military drill as a condition of attending the state university. In De Jonge v. Oregon (1937) freedom of assembly was added to the list. The assimilation of the First Amendment into the Fourteenth was completed in Everson v. Board of Education (1947). The preceding cases were decided on the theory that the due process clause protects "liberty" and that "liberty" includes freedom of speech, press, religion, and assembly. The Everson case, however, which involved state aid to parochial school pupils, raised no question of "freedom" of religion but the question whether the state action amounted to an "establishment" of religion. It could be argued that a state-supported religion does not abridge freedom of religion and hence is not an abridgment of "liberty" protected by due process of law, but the Supreme Court in the Everson case did not argue the point; it simply declared that "the First Amendment, as made applicable to the states by the Fourteenth ... commands that a state 'shall make no law respecting an establishment of religion. ...' "

With the incorporation of First Amendment rights into the due process clause of the Fourteenth, pressure was again brought on the Court to reconsider its stand in Hurtado and Twining, to find other rights in the Bill of Rights to be "essential to due process" and hence applicable to the states. The present case, one of the famous Scottsboro Cases, raises the question whether the right to counsel, guaranteed against federal infringement by the Sixth Amendment, is applicable to the states through the Fourteenth.

Mr. Justice Sutherland delivered the opinion of the Court, saying in part:

The petitioners, hereinafter referred to as defendants, are negroes charged with the crime of rape, committed upon the persons of two white girls. The crime is said to have been committed on March 25, 1931. The indictment was returned in a state court of first instance on March 31, and the record recites that on the same day the defendants were arraigned and entered pleas of not guilty. There is a further recital to the effect that upon the arraignment they were represented by counsel. But no counsel had been employed, and aside from a statement made by the trial judge several days later during a colloquy immediately preceding the trial, the record does not disclose when, or under what circumstances, an appointment of counsel was made, or who was appointed. During the colloquy referred to, the trial judge, in response to a question, said that he had appointed all the members of the bar for the purpose of arraigning the defendants and then of course anticipated that the members of the bar would continue to help the defendants if no counsel appeared. Upon the argument here both sides accepted that as a correct statement of the facts concerning the matter.

There was a severance upon the request of the state, and the defendants were tried in three several groups, as indicated above. As each of the three cases was called for trial, each defendant was arraigned, and, having the indictment read to him, entered a plea of not guilty. Whether the original arraignment and pleas were regarded as ineffective is not shown. Each of the three trials was completed within a single day. Under the Alabama statute the punishment for rape is to be fixed by the jury, and in its discretion may be from ten years' imprisonment to death. The juries found defendants guilty and imposed the death penalty upon all. The trial court overruled motions for new trials and sentenced the defendants in accordance with the verdicts. The judgments were affirmed by the state supreme court. Chief Justice Anderson thought the defendants had not been accorded a fair trial and strongly dissented.

In this court the judgments are assailed upon the grounds that the defendants, and each of them, were denied due process of law and the equal protection of the laws, in contravention of the Fourteenth Amendment, specifically as follows: (1) They were not given a fair, impartial and deliberate trial; (2) they were denied the right of counsel, with the accustomed incidents of consultation and opportunity of preparation for trial; and (3) they were tried before juries from which qualified members of their own race were systematically excluded. These questions were properly raised and saved in the courts below.

The only one of the assignments which we shall consider is the second, in respect of the denial of counsel; and it becomes unnecessary to discuss the facts of the case or the circumstances surrounding the prosecution except in so far as they reflect light upon that question.

The record shows that on the day when the offense is said to have been committed, these defendants, together with a number of other negroes, were upon a freight train on its way through Alabama. On the same train were seven white boys and two white girls. A fight took place between the negroes and the white boys, in the course of which the white boys, with the exception of one named Gilley, were thrown off the train. A message was sent ahead, reporting the fight and asking that every negro be gotten off the train. The participants in the fight, and the two girls, were in an open gondola car. The two girls testified that each of them was assaulted by six different negroes in turn, and they identified the seven defendants as having been among the number. None of the white boys was called to testify, with the exception of Gilley, who was called in rebuttal.

Before the train reached Scottsboro, Alabama, a sheriff's posse seized the defendants and two other negroes. Both girls and the negroes then were taken to Scottsboro, the county seat. Word of their coming and of the alleged assault had preceded them, and they were met at Scottsboro by a large crowd. It does not sufficiently appear that the defendants were seriously threatened with, or that they were actually in danger of, mob violence; but it does appear that the attitude of the community was one of great hostility. The sheriff thought it necessary to call for the militia to assist in safeguarding the prisoners. Chief Justice Anderson pointed out in his opinion that every step taken from the arrest and arraignment to the sentence was accompanied by the military. Soldiers took the defendants to Gadsden for safekeeping, brought them back to Scottsboro for arraignment, returned them to Gadsden for safekeeping while awaiting trial, escorted them to Scottsboro for trial a few days later, and guarded the courthouse and grounds at every stage of the proceedings. It is perfectly apparent that the proceedings, from beginning to end, took place in an atmosphere of tense, hostile and excited public sentiment. During the entire time, the defendants were closely confined or were under military guard. The record does not disclose their ages, except that one of them was nineteen; but the record clearly indicates that most, if not all, of them were youthful, and they are constantly referred to as "the boys." They were ignorant and illiterate. All of them were residents of other states, where alone members of their families or friends resided.

However guilty defendants, upon due inquiry, might prove to have been, they were, until convicted, presumed to be innocent. It was the duty of the court having their cases in charge to see that they were denied no necessary incident of a fair trial. With any error of the state court involving alleged contravention of the state statutes or constitution we, of course, have nothing to do. The sole inquiry which we are permitted to make is whether the federal Constitution was contravened ... and as to that, we confine ourselves, as already suggested to the inquiry whether the defendants were in substance denied the right of counsel, and if so, whether such denial infringes the due process clause of the Fourteenth Amendment.

First. The record shows that immediately upon the return of the indictment defendants were arraigned and pleaded not guilty. Apparently they were not asked whether they had, or were able to employ counsel, or wished to have counsel appointed; or whether they had friends or relatives who might assist in that regard if communicated with. That it would not have been an idle ceremony to have given the defendants reasonable opportunity to communicate with their families and endeavor to obtain counsel is demonstrated by the fact that very soon after conviction able counsel appeared in their behalf. . . .

It is hardly necessary to say that the right to counsel being conceded, a defendant should be afforded a fair opportunity to secure counsel of his own choice. Not only was that not done here, but such designation of counsel as was attempted was either so indefinite or so close upon the trial as to amount to a denial of effective and substantial aid in that regard. This will be amply demonstrated by a brief review of the record.

April 6, six days after indictment, the trials began. When the first case was called, the court inquired whether the parties were ready for trial. The state's attorney replied that he was ready to proceed. No one answered for the defendants or appeared to represent or defend them. Mr. Roddy, a Tennessee lawyer not a member of the local bar, addressed the court, saying that he had not been employed, but that people who were interested had spoken to him about the case. He was asked by the court whether he intended to appear for the defendants, and answered that he would like to appear along with counsel that the court might appoint. . . .

It thus will be seen that until the very morning of the trial no lawyer had been named or definitely designated to represent the defendants. Prior to that time, the trial judge had "appointed all the members of the bar" for the limited "purpose of arraigning the defendants." Whether they would represent the defendants thereafter if no counsel appeared in their behalf, was a matter of speculation only, or, as the judge indicated, of mere anticipation on the part of the court. Such a designation, even if made for all purposes, would, in our opinion, have fallen far short of meeting, in any proper sense, a requirement for the appointment of counsel. How many lawyers were members of the bar does not appear; but, in the very nature of things, whether many or few, they would not, thus collectively named, have been given that clear appreciation of responsibility or impressed with that individual sense of duty which should and naturally would accompany the appointment of a selected member of the bar, specifically named and assigned. . . .

. . . In any event, the circumstance lends emphasis to the conclusion that during perhaps the most critical period of the proceedings against these defendants, that is to say, from the time of their arraignment until the beginning of their trial, when consultation, thorough-going investigation and preparation were vitally important, the defendants did not have the aid of counsel in any real sense, although they were as much entitled to such aid during that period as at the trial itself. . . .

Second. The Constitution of Alabama provides that in all criminal prosecutions the accused shall enjoy the right to have the assistance of counsel; and a state statute requires the court in a capital case, where the defendant is unable to employ counsel, to appoint counsel for him. The state supreme court held that these provisions had not been infringed, and with that holding we are powerless to interfere. The question, however, which it is our duty, and within our power, to decide, is whether the denial of the assistance of counsel contravenes the due process clause of the Fourteenth Amendment to the federal Constitution. . . .

One test which has been applied to determine whether due process of law has been accorded in given instances is to ascertain what were the settled usages and modes of proceeding under the common and statute law of England before the Declaration of Independence, subject, however, to the qualification that they be shown not to have been suited to the civil and political conditions of our ancestors by having been followed in this country after it became a nation. . . . Plainly, as appears from the foregoing, this test, as thus qualified, has not been met in the present case.

We do not overlook the case of Hurtado v. California [1884], where this court determined that due process of law does not require an indictment by a grand jury as a prerequisite to prosecution by a state for murder. In support of that conclusion the court referred to the fact that the Fifth Amendment, in addition to containing the due process of law clause, provides in explicit terms that "No person shall be held to answer for a capital, or otherwise infamous crime, unless on a presentment or indictment of a grand jury," and said that since no part of this important amendment could be regarded as superfluous, the obvious inference is that in the sense of the Constitution due process of law was not intended to include, ex vi termini, the institution and procedure of a grand jury in any case; and that the same phrase, employed in the Fourteenth Amendment to restrain the action of the states, was to be interpreted as having been used in the same sense and with no greater extent; and that if it had been the purpose of that Amendment to perpetuate the institution of the grand jury in the states, it would have embodied, as did the Fifth Amendment, an express declaration to that effect.

The Sixth Amendment, in terms, provides that in all criminal prosecutions the accused shall enjoy the right "to have the assistance of counsel for his defense." In the face of the reasoning of the Hurtado Case, if it stood alone, it would be difficult to justify the conclusion that the right to counsel, being thus specifically granted by the Sixth Amendment, was also within the intendment of the due process of law clause. But the Hurtado Case does not stand alone. In the later case of Chicago, B. & Q. R. Co. v. Chicago [1897], this court held that a judgment of a state court, even though authorized by statute, by which private property was taken for public use without just compensation, was in violation of the due process of law required by the Fourteenth Amendment, notwithstanding that the Fifth Amendment explicitly declares that private property shall not be taken for public use without just compensation. . . .

Likewise, this court has considered that freedom of speech and of the press are rights protected by the due process clause of the Fourteenth Amendment, although in the First Amendment, Congress is prohibited in specific terms from abridging the right. Gitlow v. New York [1925]. . . .

These later cases establish that notwithstanding the sweeping character of the language in the Hurtado Case, the rule laid down is not without exceptions. The rule is an aid to construction, and in some instances may be conclusive; but it must yield to more compelling considerations whenever such considerations exist. The fact that the right involved is of such a character that it cannot be denied without violating those "fundamental principles of liberty and justice which lie at the base of all our civil and political institutions" (Hebert v. Louisiana, [1926]), is obviously one of those compelling considerations which must prevail in determining whether it is embraced within the due process clause of the Fourteenth Amendment, although it be specifically dealt with in another part of the federal Constitution. Evidently this court, in the later cases enumerated, regarded the rights there under consideration as of this fundamental character. That some such distinction must be observed is foreshadowed in Twining v. New Jersey [1908], where Mr. Justice Moody, speaking for the court, said that ". . . it is possible that some of the personal rights safeguarded by the first eight Amendments against national action may also be safeguarded against state action, because a denial of them would be a denial of due process of law. Chicago, B. & Q. R. Co. v. Chicago [1897]. If this is so, it is not because those rights are enumerated in the first eight Amendments, but because they are of such a nature that they are included in the conception of due process of law." While the question has never been categorically determined by this court, a consideration of the nature of the right and a review of the expressions of this and other courts, make it clear that the right to the aid of counsel is of this fundamental character.

It never has been doubted by this court, or any other so far as we know, that notice and hearing are preliminary steps essential to the passing of an enforceable judgment, and that they, together with a legally competent tribunal having jurisdiction of the case, constitute basic elements of the constitutional requirement of due process of law. . . .

What, then, does a hearing include? Historically and in practice, in our own country at least, it has always included the right to the aid of counsel when desired and provided by the party asserting the right. The right to be heard would be, in many cases, of little avail if it did not comprehend the right to be heard by counsel. Even the intelligent and educated layman has small and sometimes no skill in the science of law. If charged with crime, he is incapable, generally, of determining for himself whether the indictment is good or bad. He is unfamiliar with the rules of evidence. Left without the aid of counsel he may be put on trial without a proper charge, and convicted upon incompetent evidence, or evidence irrelevant to the issue or otherwise inadmissible. He lacks both the skill and knowledge adequately to prepare his defense, even though he have a perfect one. He requires the guiding hand of counsel at every step in the proceedings against him. Without it, though he be not guilty, he faces the danger of conviction because he does not know how to establish his innocence. If that be true of men of intelligence, how much more true is it of the ignorant and illiterate, or those of feeble intellect. If in any case, civil or criminal, a state or federal court were arbitrarily to refuse to hear a party by counsel, employed by and appearing for him, it reasonably may not be doubted that such a refusal would be a denial of a hearing, and, therefore, of due process in the constitutional sense.

The decisions all point to that conclusion. . . . In Ex parte Chin Loy You (D.C.) 223 Fed. 833, also a deportation case, the district judge held that under the particular circumstances of the case the prisoner, having seasonably made demand, was entitled to confer with and have the aid of counsel. Pointing to the fact that the right to counsel as secured by the Sixth Amendment relates only to criminal prosecutions, the judge said, "But it is equally true that the provision was inserted in the Constitution because the assistance of counsel was recognized as essential to any fair trial of a case against a prisoner." . . .

In the light of the facts outlined in the forepart of this opinion—the ignorance and illiteracy of the defendants, their youth, the circumstances of public hostility, the imprisonment and the close surveillance of the defendants by the military forces, the fact that their friends and families were all in other states and communication with them necessarily difficult, and above all that they stood in deadly peril of their lives—we think the failure of the trial court to give them reasonable time and opportunity to secure counsel was a clear denial of due process.

But passing that, and assuming their inability, even if opportunity had been given, to employ counsel, as the trial court evidently did assume, we are of opinion that, under the circumstances just stated, the necessity of counsel was so vital and imperative that the failure of the trial court to make an effective appointment of counsel was likewise a denial of due process within the meaning of the Fourteenth Amendment. Whether this would be so in other criminal prosecutions, or under other circumstances, we need not determine. All that it is necessary now to decide, as we do decide, is that in a capital case, where the defendant is unable to employ counsel, and is incapable adequately of making his own defense because of ignorance, feeblemindedness, illiteracy, or the like, it is the duty of the court, whether requested or not, to assign counsel for him as a necessary requisite of due process of law; and that duty is not discharged by an assignment at such a time or under such circumstances as to preclude the giving of effective aid in the preparation and trial of the case. To hold otherwise would be to ignore the fundamental postulate, already adverted to, "that there are certain immutable principles of justice which inhere in the very idea of free government which no member of the Union may disregard." . . . In a case such as this, whatever may be the rule in other cases, the right to have counsel appointed, when necessary, is a logical corollary from the constitutional right to be heard by counsel. . . .

The United States by statute and every state in the Union by express provision of law, or by the determination of its courts, make it the duty of the trial judge, where the accused is unable to employ counsel, to appoint counsel for him. In most states the rule applies broadly to all criminal prosecutions, in others it is limited to the more serious crimes, and in a very limited number, to capital cases. A rule adopted with such unanimous accord reflects, if it does not establish the inherent right to have counsel appointed at least in cases like the present, and lends convincing support to the conclusion we have reached as to the fundamental nature of that right.

The judgments must be reversed and the causes remanded for further proceedings not inconsistent with this opinion.

Judgments reversed.

Mr. Justice Butler wrote a dissenting opinion in which Mr. Justice McReynolds concurred.

PALKO v. CONNECTICUT
302 U. S. 319; 58 S. Ct. 149; 82 L. Ed. 288 (1937)

With the decision in Powell v. Alabama it appeared that the long struggle to nationalize the Bill of Rights might at last be bearing fruit. The Court had acknowledged that it no longer felt bound by the Hurtado reasoning; the application to the states of the Fifth Amendment right to just compensation and the First Amendment rights of free speech, press, religion, and assembly showed that some of the Bill of Rights guarantees could be applied to the states through due process of law. And now, in Powell, the Court for the first time had found one of the rights of persons accused of crime to be essential to due process.

The Palko case, printed below, made clear that the Court was not prepared to abandon earlier decisions such as Hurtado and Twining. Instead, it undertook to explain why some rights, such as the rights to counsel and free speech, are absorbed into due process; and why others, like jury trial and grand jury indictment, are not. It should be emphasized that the cases "absorbing" rights into the Fourteenth Amendment do not overrule Barron v. Baltimore (1833). The provisions of the federal Bill of Rights still limit directly only the federal government; it is the Fourteenth Amendment which limits the states. What the Court has done is to reverse the practical effect of the rule in Barron v. Baltimore with respect to part, but not all, of the Bill of Rights. Some of these rights are still not considered by the Court to be so fundamental as to be required by due process of law. The Court in case after case has been classifying the provisions of the Bill of Rights into those which are essential to due process of law and thus bind the states through the operation of the Fourteenth Amendment and those which are not essential to due process and by which the states are not bound. In effect, the Court has established an "honor roll" of superior rights which bind both state and national governments. The opinion in the present case is important since it gives an official summary of this classification up to 1937 and states clearly the principles upon which the classification rests.

One question which the Palko case failed to answer satisfactorily was what was meant by "absorption" or "incorporation" of a Bill of Rights guarantee into due process. Did it mean that the right, as listed in the Bill of Rights and interpreted by the Supreme Court in federal cases, was made applicable to the states? Or was the right as applied to the states a more general right, less clearly defined and permitting more leeway and discretion on the part of the states? Clearly, incorporation of the First Amendment has meant its application to the states exactly as it is applied to the national government. Justices Brandeis and Holmes, in their dissent in the Gitlow case, suggested that the free speech applicable to the states perhaps "may be accepted with a somewhat larger latitude of interpretation than is allowed to Congress by the sweeping language that governs or ought to govern the laws of the United States." The Court, however, has never acknowledged such a distinction, and the same rules for deciding such cases are applied to the state and the nation alike. With the gradual extension of due process to include other rights, however, an important controversy developed as to how these rights would apply to the states.

Mr. Justice Cardozo delivered the opinion of the Court, saying in part:

... Appellant was indicted ... for the crime of murder in the first degree. A jury found him guilty of murder in the second degree, and he was sentenced to confinement in the state prison for life. Thereafter the state of Connecticut, with the permission of the judge presiding at the trial, gave notice of appeal to the Supreme Court of Errors. This it did pursuant to an act adopted in 1886 which is printed in the margin.* . . . Upon such appeal, the Supreme Court of Errors reversed the judgment and ordered a new trial. . . . It found that there had been error of law to the prejudice of the state. . . .

. . . [The] defendant was brought to trial again. Before a jury was impaneled and also at later stages of the case he made the objection that the effect of the new trial was to place him twice in jeopardy for the same offense, and in so doing to violate the Fourteenth Amendment of the Constitution of the United States. Upon the overruling of the objection the trial proceeded. The jury returned a verdict of murder in the first degree, and the court sentenced the defendant to the punishment of death. . . . The case is here upon appeal.

1. The execution of the sentence will not deprive appellant of his life without the process of law assured to him by the Fourteenth Amendment of the Federal Constitution.

The argument for appellant is that whatever is forbidden by the Fifth Amendment is forbidden by the Fourteenth also. The Fifth Amendment, which is not directed to the states, but solely to the federal government, creates immunity from double jeopardy. No person shall be "subject for the same offense to be twice put in jeopardy of life or limb." The Fourteenth Amendment ordains, "nor shall any state deprive any person of life, liberty, or property, without due process of law." To retry a defendant, though under one indictment and only one, subjects him, it is said, to double jeopardy in violation of the Fifth Amendment, if the prosecution is one on behalf of the United States. From this the consequence is said to follow that there is a denial of life or liberty without due process of law, if the prosecution is one on behalf of the People of a State. . . .

We have said that in appellant's view the Fourteenth Amendment is to be taken as embodying the prohibitions of the Fifth. His thesis is even broader. Whatever would be a violation of the original bill of rights (Amendments 1 to 8) if done by the federal government is now equally unlawful by force of the Fourteenth Amendment if done by a state. There is no such general rule.

The Fifth Amendment provides, among other things, that no person shall be held to answer for a capital or otherwise infamous crime unless on present-ment or indictment of a grand jury. This court has held that, in prosecutions by a state, presentment or indictment by a grand jury may give way to informa-tions at the instance of a public officer. Hurtado v. California [1884]. . . . The Fifth Amendment provides also that no person shall be compelled in any criminal case to be a witness against himself. This court has said that, in

---

*"Sec. 6494. *Appeals by the state in criminal cases.* Appeals from the rulings and decisions of the superior court or of any criminal court of common pleas, upon all questions of law arising on the trial of criminal cases, may be taken by the state, with the permission of the presiding judge, to the supreme court of errors, in the same manner and to the same effect as if made by the accused." . . .

prosecutions by a state, the exemption will fail if the state elects to end it. Twining v. New Jersey [1908]. . . . The Sixth Amendment calls for a jury trial in criminal cases and the Seventh for a jury trial in civil cases at common law where the value in controversy shall exceed twenty dollars. This court has ruled that consistently with those amendments trial by jury may be modified by a state or abolished altogether. Walker v. Sauvinet [1876]; Maxwell v. Dow [1900]. . . . As to the Fourth Amendment, one should refer to Weeks v. United States [1914] and as to other provisions of the Sixth, to West v. Louisiana [1904].

On the other hand, the due process clause of the Fourteenth Amendment may make it unlawful for a state to abridge by its statutes the freedom of speech which the First Amendment safeguards against encroachment by the Congress (De Jonge v. Oregon [1937]) or the like freedom of the press (Near v. Minnesota [1931]), or the free exercise of religion (Hamilton v. University of California [1934]; . . .), or the right of peaceable assembly, without which speech would be unduly trammeled (De Jonge v. Oregon), or the right of one accused of crime to the benefit of counsel (Powell v. Alabama [1932]). In these and other situations immunities that are valid as against the federal government by force of the specific pledges of particular amendments have been found to be implicit in the concept of ordered liberty, and thus, through the Fourteenth Amendment, become valid as against the states.

The line of division may seem to be wavering and broken if there is a hasty catalogue of the cases on the one side and the other. Reflection and analysis will induce a different view. There emerges the perception of a rationalizing principle which gives to discrete instances a proper order and coherence. The right to trial by jury and the immunity from prosecution except as the result of an indictment may have value and importance. Even so, they are not of the very essence of a scheme of ordered liberty. To abolish them is not to violate a "principle of justice so rooted in the traditions and conscience of our people as to be ranked as fundamental.". . . Few would be so narrow or provincial as to maintain that a fair and enlightened system of justice would be impossible without them. What is true of jury trials and indictments is true also, as the cases show, of the immunity from compulsory self-incrimination. Twining v. New Jersey. This too might be lost, and justice still be done. Indeed, today as in the past there are students of our penal system who look upon the immunity as a mischief rather than a benefit, and who would limit its scope or destroy it altogether. . . . The exclusion of these immunities and privileges from the privileges and immunities protected against the action of the states has not been arbitrary or casual. It has been dictated by a study and appreciation of the meaning, the essential implications, of liberty itself.

We reach a different plane of social and moral values when we pass to the privileges and immunities that have been taken over from the earlier articles of the federal bill of rights and brought within the Fourteenth Amendment by a process of absorption. These in their origin were effective against the federal government alone. If the Fourteenth Amendment has absorbed them, the process of absorption has had its source in the belief that neither liberty nor justice would exist if they were sacrificed. Twining v. New Jersey. This is true, for illustration, of freedom of thought and speech. Of that freedom one may say that it is the matrix, the indispensable condition, of nearly every other form of freedom. With rare aberrations a pervasive recognition of that truth can be traced in our history, political and legal. So it has come about that the domain of liberty, withdrawn by the Fourteenth Amendment from encroachment by the states, has been enlarged by latter-day judgments to include liberty of the mind as well as liberty of action. . . . Fundamental too in the concept of due process, and so in that of liberty, is the thought that condemnation shall be rendered only after trial. . . . The hearing, moreover, must be a real one, not a sham or a pretense. Moore v. Dempsey [1923]. . . . For that reason, ignorant defendants in a capital case were held to have been condemned unlawfully when in truth, though not in form, they were refused the aid of counsel. Powell v. Alabama. The decision did not turn upon the fact that the benefit of counsel would have been guaranteed to the defendants by the provisions of the Sixth Amendment if they had been prosecuted in a federal court. The decision turned upon the fact that in the particular situation laid before us in the evidence the benefit of counsel was essential to the substance of a hearing.

Our survey of the cases serves, we think, to justify the statement that the dividing line between them, if not unfaltering throughout its course, has been true for the most part to a unifying principle. On which side of the line the case made out by the appellant has appropriate location must be the next inquiry and the final one. Is that kind of double jeopardy to which the statute has subjected him a hardship so acute and shocking that our polity will not endure it? Does it violate those "fundamental principles of liberty and justice which lie at the base of all our civil and political institutions?". . . The answer surely must be "no." What the answer would have to be if the state were permitted after a trial free from error to try the accused over again or to bring another case against him, we have no occasion to consider. We deal with the statute before us and no other. The state is not attempting to wear the accused out by a multitude of cases with accumulated trials. It asks no more than this, that the case against him shall go on until there shall be a trial free from the corrosion of substantial legal error. . . . This is not cruelty at all, nor even vexation in any immoderate degree. If the trial had been infected with error adverse to the accused, there might have been review at his instance, and as often as necessary to purge the vicious taint. A reciprocal privilege, subject at all times to the discretion of the presiding judge . . . , has now been granted to the state. There is here no seismic innovation. The edifice of justice stands, in its symmetry, to many, greater than before.

2. The conviction of appellant is not in derogation of any privileges or immunities that belong to him as a citizen of the United States. . . .

Maxwell v. Dow [1900], gives all the answer that is necessary.

The judgment is affirmed.

Mr. Justice Butler dissents.

ROCHIN v. CALIFORNIA

342 U. S. 165; 72 S. Ct. 205; 96 L. Ed. 183 (1952)

Despite its obvious reluctance to incorporate the specific guarantees of the Bill of Rights, the Court did take increasing interest in state procedures and machinery, and grew more watchful lest they not meet the requirements of fundamental fairness. Such insistence on fundamental fairness, especially for persons accused of crime, was bound to bring before the Court the widest variety of state activities. In 1927, for instance, the Court in Tumey v. Ohio reversed the conviction of a bootlegger who had been tried before the mayor of a small town. An ordinance provided that the mayor should retain the court costs as payment for his judicial work, but no costs were paid if the defendant were acquitted. Tumey had been fined $100, and the costs involved were $12. The Supreme Court held it to be a denial of due process to "subject his liberty or property to the judgment of a court, the judge of which has a direct, personal, substantial pecuniary interest in reaching a conclusion against him in his case. . . . There are doubtless mayors," the Court conceded, "who would not allow such a consideration as $12 costs in each case to affect their judgment in it, but the requirement of due process of law in judicial procedure is not satisfied by the argument that men of the highest honor and the greatest self-sacrifice could carry it on without danger of injustice. Every procedure which would offer a possible temptation to the average man as a judge to forget the burden of proof required to convict the defendant, or which might lead him not to hold the balance nice, clear and true between the state and the accused denies the latter due process of law." In 1972, this doctrine was applied to hold void a traffic conviction by the mayor of an Ohio village who was not only the officer responsible for village finances, but who, sitting as a mayor's court, collected fines and fees which regularly provided between one-third and one-half of the village revenues: see Ward v. Monroeville.

Nor are jurymen expected to be persons of unrestrained self-sacrifice, and a trial conducted in an atmosphere of mob violence is inherently unfair. In Moore v. Dempsey (1923) five Negroes were convicted in an Arkansas court of the murder of a white man and sentenced to death. The Court described the trial in these words: "The court and the neighborhood were thronged with an adverse crowd that threatened the most dangerous consequences to any one interfering with the desired result. The counsel did not venture to demand delay or a change of venue, to challenge a juryman, or to ask for separate trials. He had had no preliminary consultation with the accused, called no witness for the defense, although they could have been produced, and did not put the defendants on the stand. The trial lasted about three quarters of an hour, and in less than five minutes the jury brought in a verdict of murder in the first degree. According to the allegations and affidavits there never was a chance for the petitioners to be acquitted; no juryman could have voted for an acquittal and continued to live in Phillips County, and if any prisoner, by any chance, had been acquitted by a jury, he could not have escaped the mob." Under these conditions no trial in the true sense was possible and the defendants were denied due process of law.

The Supreme Court has made it clear that due process is denied by an attempt to punish a person for a crime which is not clearly defined. In Winters v. New York (1948) it held void for vagueness a statue making it a crime to issue a publication which so masses stories of bloodshed and lust "as to become vehicles for inciting violent and depraved crimes against the person." The Court conceded the "impossibility of defining the precise line between permissible uncertainty in statutes caused by describing crimes by words well understood through long use in the criminal law—obscene, lewd, lascivious, filthy, indecent or disgusting—and the unconstitutional vagueness that leaves a person uncertain as to the kind of prohibited conduct—massing stories to incite crime..." but concluded that "an honest distributor of publications could [not] know when he might be held to have ignored such a prohibition. Collections of tales of war horrors, otherwise unexceptionable, might well be found to be 'massed' so as to become 'vehicles for exciting violent and depraved crimes.' Where a statute is so vague as to make criminal an innocent act, a conviction under it cannot be sustained. ..."

In 1972 the Supreme Court struck down a Jacksonville vagrancy ordinance which, in the archaic language of the Elizabethan Poor Law, defines as vagrants (among others) "rogues and vagabonds, or dissolute persons who go about begging, ... common night walkers, ... common railers and brawlers, persons wandering or strolling around from place to place without any lawful purpose or object, habitual loafers, [and] ... persons able to work but habitually living upon the earnings of their wives or minor *children. . . . " Two white girls and their black dates were arrested on the main thoroughfare in Jacksonville and convicted of "prowling by auto." In Papachristou v. Jacksonville (1972) a unanimous Court found the ordinance void for vagueness both in the sense that it "fails to give a person of ordinary intelligence fair notice that his contemplated conduct is forbidden by the statute, ". . . and because it encourages arbitrary arrests and convictions." Not only does it "make criminal activities which by modern standards are normally innocent," but it puts "unfettered discretion in the hands of the Jacksonville police." "Those generally implicated by the imprecise terms of the ordinance—poor people, nonconformists, dissenters, idlers—may be required to comport themselves according to the life-style deemed appropriate by the Jacksonville police and the courts. Where, as here, there are no standards governing the exercise of the discretion granted by the ordinance, the scheme permits and encourages an arbitrary and discriminatory enforcement of the law . . . It results in a regime in which the poor and unpopular are permitted to 'stand on a public sidewalk . . . only at the whim of any police officer.' Shuttlesworth v. Birmingham [1969]."*

Among the things a state cannot do is knowingly permit a conviction to rest upon perjured testimony. In Mooney v. Holohan (1935) the Court held that "depriving a defendant of liberty through a deliberate deception of court and jury by the presentation of testimony known to be perjured . . . is as inconsistent with the rudimentary demands of justice as is the obtaining of a like result by intimidation." The state must also provide "corrective judicial process by which a conviction so obtained may be set aside."

Nor can a state through its criminal procedure favor the wealthy over the poor. In order to carry an appeal to the supreme court of Illinois in a criminal case it is necessary to have a stenographic transcript of the trial proceedings. Only an indigent defendant who had been sentenced to death was provided with a free transcript; all other defendants had to buy it. As a result, a poor man convicted of a noncapital crime and therefore not entitled to a free transcript would be deprived of the right to appeal his case because of his poverty—a right easily available to the well-to-do convict. In Griffin v. Illinois, (1956) the Supreme Court held this to be a violation of due process and equal protection of the laws. "In criminal trials," the Court said, "a State can no more discriminate on account of poverty than on account of religion, race, or color. Plainly the ability to pay costs in advance bears no rational relationship to a defendant's guilt or innocence and could not be used as an excuse to deprive a defendant of a fair trial. . . . There is no meaningful distinction between a rule which would deny the poor the right to defend themselves in a trial court and one which effectively denies the poor an adequate appellate review accorded to all who have money enough to pay the costs in advance." In Mayer v. Chicago (1972) the Court extended the rule to include persons charged with a

*misdemeanor and liable only to a fine. "Griffin," it emphasized, ". . . is
a flat protection against pricing indigent defendants out of as effective an
appeal as would be available to others able to pay their own way."*

Mr. Justice Frankfurter delivered the opinion of the Court, saying in part:

Having "some information that [the petitioner here] was selling narcotics,"
three deputy sheriffs of the County of Los Angeles, on the morning of July 1,
1949, made for the two-story dwelling house in which Rochin lived with his
mother, common-law wife, brothers and sisters. Finding the outside door open,
they entered and then forced open the door to Rochin's room on the second
floor. Inside they found petitioner sitting partly dressed on the side of the bed,
upon which his wife was lying. On a "night stand" beside the bed the deputies
spied two capsules. When asked "Whose stuff is this?" Rochin seized the
capsules and put them in his mouth. A struggle ensued, in the course of which
the three officers "jumped upon him" and attempted to extract the capsules.
The force they applied proved unavailing against Rochin's resistance. He was
handcuffed and taken to a hospital. At the direction of one of the officers a
doctor forced an emetic solution through a tube into Rochin's stomach against
his will. This "stomach pumping" produced vomiting. In the vomited matter
were found two capsules which proved to contain morphine.

Rochin was brought to trial before a California Superior Court, sitting
without a jury, on the charge of possessing "a preparation of morphine" in
violation of the California Health and Safety Code. Rochin was convicted and
sentenced to sixty days' imprisonment. The chief evidence against him was the
two capsules. They were admitted over petitioner's objection, although the
means of obtaining them was frankly set forth in the testimony by one of the
deputies, substantially as here narrated. . . .

. . . Regard for the requirements of the Due Process Clause "inescapably
imposes upon this Court an exercise of judgment upon the whole course of the
proceedings [resulting in a conviction] in order to ascertain whether they
offend those canons of decency and fairness which express the notions of justice
of English-speaking people even toward those charged with the most heinous
offenses." Malinski v. New York [1945]. These standards of justice are not
authoritatively formulated anywhere as though they were specifics. Due process of law is a summarized constitutional guarantee of respect for those
personal immunities which, as Mr. Justice Cardozo twice wrote for the Court,
are "so rooted in the traditions and conscience of our people as to be ranked
as fundamental," Snyder v. Massachusetts [1934], or are "implicit in the
concept of ordered liberty." Palko v. Connecticut [1937].

The Court's function in the observance of this settled conception of the Due

Process Clause does not leave us without adequate guides in subjecting State criminal procedures to constitutional judgment. In dealing not with the machinery of government but with human rights, the absence of formal exactitude, or want of fixity of meaning, is not an unusual or even regrettable attribute of constitutional provisions. Words being symbols do not speak without a gloss. On the one hand the gloss may be the deposit of history, whereby a term gains technical content. Thus the requirements of the Sixth and Seventh Amendments for trial by jury in the Federal courts have a rigid meaning. No changes or chances can alter the content of the verbal symbol of "jury"—a body of twelve men who must reach a unanimous conclusion if the verdict is to go against the defendant. On the other hand, the gloss of some of the verbal symbols of the Constitution does not give them a fixed technical content. It exacts a continuing process of application.

When the gloss has thus not been fixed but is a function of the process of judgment, the judgment is bound to fall differently at different times and differently at the same time through different judges. Even more specific provisions, such as the guaranty of freedom of speech and the detailed protection against unreasonable searches and seizures, have inevitably evoked as sharp divisions in this Court as the least specific and most comprehensive protection of liberties, the Due Process Clause.

The vague contours of the Due Process Clause do not leave judges at large. We may not draw on our merely personal and private notions and disregard the limits that bind judges in their judicial function. Even though the concept of due process of law is not final and fixed, these limits are derived from considerations that are fused in the whole nature of our judicial process. See Cardozo, The Nature of the Judicial Process; The Growth of the Law; The Paradoxes of Legal Science. These are considerations deeply rooted in reason and in the compelling traditions of the legal profession. The Due Process Clause places upon this Court the duty of exercising a judgment, within the narrow confines of judicial power in reviewing State convictions, upon interests of society pushing in opposite directions.

Due process of law thus conceived is not to be derided as resort to a revival of "natural law." To believe that this judicial exercise of judgment could be avoided by freezing "due process of law" at some fixed stage of time or thought is to suggest that the most important aspect of constitutional adjudication is a function for inanimate machines and not for judges, for whom the independence safeguarded by Article 3 of the Constitution was designed and who are presumably guided by established standards of judicial behavior. Even cybernetics has not yet made that haughty claim. To practice the requisite detachment and to achieve sufficient objectivity no doubt demands of judges the habit of self-discipline and self-criticism, incertitude that one's own views are incontestable and alert tolerance toward views not shared. But these are precisely the presuppositions of our judicial process. They are precisely the qualities society has a right to expect from those entrusted with ultimate judicial power.

Restraints on our jurisdiction are self-imposed only in the sense that there is from our decisions no immediate appeal short of impeachment or constitutional amendment. But that does not make due process of law a matter of judicial caprice. The faculties of the Due Process Clause may be indefinite and vague, but the mode of their ascertainment is not self-willed. In each case "due process of law" requires an evaluation based on a disinterested inquiry pursued in the spirit of science, on a balanced order of facts exactly and fairly stated, on the detached consideration of conflicting claims, . . . on a judgment not ad hoc and episodic but duly mindful of reconciling the needs both of continuity and of change in a progressive society.

Applying these general considerations to the circumstances of the present case, we are compelled to conclude that the proceedings by which this conviction was obtained do more than offend some fastidious squeamishness or private sentimentalism about combatting crime too energetically. This is conduct that shocks the conscience. Illegally breaking into the privacy of the petitioner, the struggle to open his mouth and remove what was there, the forcible extraction of his stomach's contents—this course of proceeding by agents of government to obtain evidence is bound to offend even hardened sensibilities. They are methods too close to the rack and the screw to permit of constitutional differentiation.

It has long since ceased to be true that due process of law is heedless of the means by which otherwise relevant and credible evidence is obtained. This was not true even before the series of recent cases enforced the constitutional principle that the States may not base convictions upon confessions, however much verified, obtained by coercion. These decisions are not arbitrary exceptions to the comprehensive right of States to fashion their own rules of evidence for criminal trials. They are not sports in our constitutional law but applications of a general principle. They are only instances of the general requirement that States in their prosecutions respect certain decencies of civilized conduct. Due process of law, as a historic and generative principle, precludes defining, and thereby confining, these standards of conduct more precisely than to say that convictions cannot be brought about by methods that offend "a sense of justice." See Mr. Chief Justice Hughes, speaking for a unanimous Court in Brown v. Mississippi [1936]. It would be a stultification of the responsibility which the course of constitutional history has cast upon this Court to hold that in order to convict a man the police cannot extract by force what is in his mind but can extract what is in his stomach.

To attempt in this case to distinguish what lawyers call "real evidence" from verbal evidence is to ignore the reasons for excluding coerced confessions. Use of involuntary verbal confessions in State criminal trials is constitutionally obnoxious not only because of their unreliability. They are inadmissible under the Due Process Clause even though statements contained in them may be independently established as true. Coerced confessions offend the community's sense of fair play and decency. So here, to sanction the brutal conduct which naturally enough was condemned by the court whose judgment is before us, would be to afford brutality the cloak of law. Nothing would be more calculated to discredit law and thereby to brutalize the temper of a society. . . .

On the facts of this case the conviction of the petitioner has been obtained by methods that offend the Due Process Clause. The judgment below must be Reversed.

Mr. Justice Minton took no part in the consideration or decision of this case.

Mr. Justice Black, concurring, said in part:

Adamson v. California [1947] sets out reasons for my belief that state as well as federal courts and law enforcement officers must obey the Fifth Amendment's command that "No person . . . shall be compelled in any criminal case to be a witness against himself." I think a person is compelled to be a witness against himself not only when he is compelled to testify, but also when as here, incriminating evidence is forcibly taken from him by a contrivance of modern science. . . .

Mr. Justice Douglas wrote a concurring opinion.

IRVINE v. CALIFORNIA
347 U. S. 128; 74 S. Ct. 381; 98 L. Ed. 561 (1954)

While it is clear that rights not mentioned in the Bill of Rights must be protected, if at all, through due process of law, what of those rights listed in the Bill of Rights which are not (as are the First Amendment rights) incorporated into due process? The decision in Powell v. Alabama (1932) was widely regarded as incorporating the Sixth Amendment right to counsel into due process, and this assumption was bolstered by its inclusion in Palko in the list of rights "that have been taken over from the earlier articles of the federal Bill of Rights and brought within the Fourteenth Amendment by a process of absorption." In 1942, however, the Supreme Court made it clear that this was not the case. In Betts v. Brady, it emphasized that "the due process clause of the Fourteenth Amendment does not incorporate, as such, the specific guarantees found in the Sixth Amendment although a denial by a state of rights or privileges specifically embodied in that and others of the first eight amendments may, in certain circumstances, or in connection with other elements, operate, in a given case, to deprive a litigant of due process of law. . . . That which may, in one setting, constitute a denial of fundamental fairness, shocking to the universal sense of justice, may, in other circumstances, and in the light of other considerations, fall short of such denial."

There thus appeared a sharp distinction between the two kinds of rights. Rights like those in the First Amendment were apparently "incorporated" or "absorbed" into due process so that they were applied against the states exactly as they were against the federal government, and state and federal cases served interchangeably as precedent. Rights not so incorporated were protected by the more flexible rule that any state conduct which is grossly unfair denies due process of law.

Important as the distinction was, however, disagreement on the Court both over the implications of incorporation and what language was needed to accomplish it, made it difficult to tell when a right had, in fact, been incorporated. In Louisiana ex rel. Francis v. Resweber (1947), for instance, the Court held it was not a cruel and unusual punishment to try a second time to electrocute a person after the first attempt had failed to kill him. But while four members of the majority stated somewhat ambiguously that the "Fourteenth [Amendment] would prohibit by its due process clause execution by a state in a cruel manner," Mr. Justice Frankfurter wrote a concurring opinion to explain that in his view "the penology of a state is not to be tested by the scope of the Eighth Amendment."

In 1949 the Court appeared to incorporate into due process the protection in the Fourth Amendment against unreasonable searches and seizures. In Wolf v. Colorado (1949) it held that "The security of one's privacy against arbitrary intrusion by the police—which is at the core of the Fourth Amendment—is basic to a free society. It is therefore implicit in 'the concept of ordered liberty' and as such enforceable against the States through the Due Process Clause." Despite Mr. Justice Frankfurter's later protestation that this did not result in incorporation, it was clear that at least four members of the Court assumed it did. Whatever the merits of this, the Court in Wolf effectively nullified such protection as it had extended by refusing to apply a rule, developed years before in Weeks v. United States (1914), that forbade the admission in court of evidence gotten by unreasonable searches and seizures. This rule, concededly the only real deterrent to unlawful police searches, was held to be merely a rule of evidence, and not a requirement of the Fourth Amendment.

While the Court was being equivocal about the question of incorporation, certain theoretical and practical difficulties plagued its attempts to enforce the essential fairness—or "shock the conscience" doctrine, as it came to be known after the Rochin case. What is essentially fair, or *shocking, tends to be a matter of individual judgment reflecting the background and personality of the judge. Moreover, the lack of clear guidelines as to what is fair and what is not makes it difficult for police and prosecutors, however well intentioned, to know what conduct on their part is prohibited. While Mr. Justice Frankfurter's opinion in the Rochin case is a masterful analysis and defense of the doctrine in its purest form, it does not provide completely satisfactory answers on these two points.*

In the present case the California police had broken into the home of a suspected bookmaker and placed a microphone in several rooms of the house, including the bedroom. For over a month police officers eavesdropped in this way, and on the basis of information thus obtained Irvine was tried and convicted. Mr. Justice Jackson, speaking for four members of the Court, conceded that "few police measures have come to our attention that more flagrantly, deliberately, and persistently violated the fundamental principle declared by the Fourth Amendment," but the Court refused to declare the evidence inadmissible although two members of the majority urged the Attorney General of the United States to determine whether the state officials might not be prosecuted under § 242 of the Criminal Code for violating rights guaranteed by the Constitution.

Mr. Justice Jackson announced the judgment of the Court and an opinion in which The Chief Justice [Warren], Mr. Justice Reed, and Mr. Justice Minton join, saying in part:

... The decision in Wolf v. Colorado [1949], for the first time established that "[t]he security of one's privacy against arbitrary intrusion by the police" is embodied in the concept of due process found in the Fourteenth Amendment.

But Wolf, for reasons set forth therein, declined to make the subsidiary procedural and evidentiary doctrines developed by the federal courts limitations on the states. On the contrary, it declared, "We hold, therefore, that in a prosecution in a State court for a State crime the Fourteenth Amendment does not forbid the admission of evidence obtained by an unreasonable search and seizure." ... That holding would seem to control here.

An effort is made, however, to bring this case under the sway of Rochin v. California [1952]. That case involved, among other things, an illegal search of the defendant's person. But it also presented an element totally lacking here —coercion ... applied by a physical assault upon his person to compel submission to the use of a stomach pump. This was the feature which led to a result in Rochin contrary to that in Wolf. Although Rochin raised the search-and-seizure question, this Court studiously avoided it and never once mentioned the Wolf Case. Obviously, it thought that illegal search and seizure alone did not call for reversal. However obnoxious are the facts in the case before us, they do not involve coercion, violence or brutality to the person, but rather a trespass to property, plus eavesdropping.

It is suggested, however, that although we affirmed the conviction in Wolf, we should reverse here because this invasion of privacy is more shocking, more offensive, than the one involved there. The opinions in Wolf were written entirely in the abstract and did not disclose the details of the constitutional violation. Actually, the search was offensive to the law in the same respect, if not the same degree, as here. A deputy sheriff and others went to a doctor's office without a warrant and seized his appointment book, searched through it to learn the names of all his patients, looked up and interrogated certain of them, and filed an information against the doctor on the information that the District Attorney had obtained from the books. The books also were introduced in evidence against the doctor at his trial.

We are urged to make inroads upon Wolf by holding that it applies only to searches and seizures which produce on our minds a mild shock, while if the shock is more serious, the states must exclude the evidence or we will reverse the conviction. We think that the Wolf decision should not be overruled, for the reasons so persuasively stated therein. We think, too, that a distinction of the kind urged would leave the rule so indefinite that no state court could know what it should rule in order to keep its processes on solid constitutional ground. . . .

Judgment affirmed.

Mr. Justice Clark, concurring.

Had I been here in 1949 when Wolf was decided, I would have applied the doctrine of Weeks v. United States [1914] to the states. But the Court refused to do so then, and it still refuses today. Thus Wolf remains the law and, as such, is entitled to the respect of this Court's membership.

Of course, we could sterilize the rule announced in Wolf by adopting a case-by-case approach to due process in which inchoate notions of propriety concerning local police conduct guide our decisions. But this makes for such uncertainty and unpredictability that it would be impossible to foretell—other than by guesswork—just how brazen the invasion of the intimate privacies of one's home must be in order to shock itself into the protective arms of the Constitution. In truth, the practical result of this ad hoc approach is simply that when five Justices are sufficiently revolted by local police action, a conviction is overturned and a guilty man may go free. Rochin bears witness to this. We may thus vindicate the abstract principle of due process, but we do not shape the conduct of local police one whit; unpredictable reversals on dissimilar fact situations are not likely to curb the zeal of those police and prosecutors who may be intent on racking up a high percentage of successful prosecutions. I do not believe that the extension of such a vacillating course beyond the clear cases of physical coercion and brutality, such as Rochin, would serve a useful purpose.

In light of the "incredible" activity of the police here, it is with great reluctance that I follow Wolf. Perhaps strict adherence to the tenor of that decision may produce needed converts for its extinction. Thus I merely concur in the judgment of affirmance.

Mr. Justice Black, with whom Mr. Justice Douglas concurs, wrote a dissenting opinion.

Mr. Justice Frankfurter, whom Mr. Justice Burton joins, dissenting, said in part:

In the Wolf Case, the Court rejected one absolute. In Rochin, it rejected another. . . .

Rochin decided that the Due Process Clause of the Fourteenth Amendment does not leave States free in their prosecutions for crime. The Clause puts limits on the wide discretion of a State in the process of enforcing its criminal law. The holding of the case is that a State cannot resort to methods that offend civilized standards of decency and fairness. The conviction in the Rochin Case was found to offend due process not because evidence had been obtained through an unauthorized search and seizure or was the fruit of compulsory self-incrimination. Neither of these concepts, relevant to federal prosecutions, was invoked by the Court in Rochin, so of course the Wolf Case was not mentioned. While there is in the case before us as there was in Rochin, an element of unreasonable search and seizure, what is decisive here, as in Rochin, is additional aggravating conduct which the Court finds repulsive. . . .

There was lacking here physical violence, even to the restricted extent employed in Rochin. We have here, however, a more powerful and offensive control over the Irvines' life than a single, limited physical trespass. Certainly the conduct of the police here went far beyond a bare search and seizure. The police devised means to hear every word that was said in the Irvine household for more than a month. Those affirming the conviction find that this conduct, in its entirety, is "almost incredible if it were not admitted." Surely the Court does not propose to announce a new absolute, namely, that even the most reprehensible means for securing a conviction will not taint a verdict so long as the body of the accused was not touched by State officials. . . .

Since due process is not a mechanical yardstick it does not afford mechanical answers. In applying the Due Process Clause judicial judgment is involved in an empiric process in the sense that results are not predetermined or mechanically ascertainable. But that is a very different thing from conceiving the results as ad hoc decisions in the opprobrious sense of ad hoc. Empiricism implies judgment upon variant situations by the wisdom of experience. Ad hocness in adjudication means treating a particular case by itself and not in relation to the meaning of a course of decisions and the guides they serve for the future. There is all the difference in the world between disposing of a case as though it were a discrete instance and recognizing it as part of the process of judgment, taking its place in relation to what went before and further cutting a channel for what is to come.

The effort to imprison due process within tidy categories misconceives its nature and is a futile endeavor to save the judicial function from the pains of judicial judgment. It is pertinent to recall how the Court dealt with this craving for unattainable certainty in the Rochin Case:

"The vague contours of the Due Process Clause do not leave judges at large. We may not draw on our merely personal and private notions and disregard the limits that bind judges in their judicial function. Even though the concept of due process of law is not final and fixed, these limits are derived from considerations that are fused in the whole nature of our judicial process. See Cardozo, The Nature of the Judicial Process; The Growth of the Law; The Paradoxes of Legal Science. These are considerations deeply rooted in reason and in the compelling traditions of the legal profession. The Due Process Clause places upon this Court the duty of exercising a judgment, within the narrow confines of judicial power in reviewing State convictions, upon interests of society pushing in opposite directions." . . .

GIDEON v. WAINWRIGHT
372 U. S. 335; 83 S. Ct. 792; 9 L. Ed. 2d 799
(1963)

The attitude of judicial self-restraint under which the states had been shaping their own standards of fair criminal procedure came to an abrupt halt in 1961. In Mapp v. Ohio, the Court overruled Wolf v. Colorado (1949) and clearly made the Fourth Amendment, together with its exclusionary rule, applicable to the states. Then in 1962 it removed all doubt about the "incorporation" of cruel and unusual punishments when it used the formula, made familiar by First Amendment cases, that the state had violated the "Eighth and Fourteenth Amendments"; see Robinson v. California. The following year any lingering doubts about the meaning of "incorporation" were dispelled when eight members of the Court in Ker v. California (1963) agreed that federal constitutional standards of reasonableness of searches "is the same under the Fourth and Fourteenth Amendments." Only Mr. Justice Harlan clung to the view that "the more flexible concept of 'fundamental' fairness" should apply to the states.

The incorporation of other rights came rapidly. In 1964, following the decision in the present case, the Court in Malloy v. Hogan incorporated the Fifth Amendment privilege against self-incrimination. This was followed in 1965 by the right to confront one's accusers (Pointer v. Texas) and in 1967 by speedy trial (Klopfer v. North Carolina), an impartial jury (Parker v. Gladden), and the right to subpoena defense witnesses (Washington v. Texas). In 1968, the Court added the Sixth Amendment right to a jury trial in a criminal case (Duncan v. Louisiana) and in 1969, in Benton v. Maryland, it finally overruled Palko v. Connecticut (1937) and incorporated the protection against double jeopardy. "Palko's roots," the Court explained, "had been cut away years ago. We today only recognize the inevitable."

The decision in Duncan v. Louisiana inaugurated an unforeseen development in the doctrine of incorporation. Incorporation had long been viewed as a way of forcing the states to adhere to a higher standard of conduct than was required by mere "fundamental fairness," and was hence a step in the civilizing process of treating more fairly those who were accused of crime. But following the Duncan case two decisions by the Supreme Court began reducing the requirements traditionally thought of as part of the jury trial. In Williams v. Florida (1970) the Court held a six-man jury met the requirements of the Sixth Amendment, and in Apodaca v. Oregon (1972) it held the Amendment did not require a unanimous verdict. The decisions were reached by reviewing the history of the Amendment's adoption, but while eight justices agreed that it had been incorporated into the Fourteenth and therefore applied to the states, four of them dissented on the ground that it required 12 men and unanimous verdict.

Justice Powell, who had replaced Justice Harlan in 1971, agreed with Justices White, Burger, Blackmun and Rehnquist that "a defendant in a state court may constitutionally be convicted by less than a unanimous verdict." He agreed with his predecessor, however, that not "all of the elements of jury trial within the meaning of the Sixth Amendment are necessarily embodied in or incorporated into the Due Process Clause of the Fourteenth Amendment," and added "that unanimity is one of the indispensible features of federal jury trial." Thus, while eight members agreed that the Sixth Amendment requires the same standards of both state and nation, because of a difference as to what those standards are, the Court may, in fact, require a different standard of each. The effect of Justice Powell's philosophical position is to disincorporate the Sixth Amendment.

Following the reversal of his conviction in the present case, Gideon was retried by the state of Florida in the same courtroom, before the same judge, with the same witnesses, but with a lawyer appointed by the court at Gideon's request. This time he was acquitted.

Mr. Justice Black delivered the opinion of the Court, saying in part:

Petitioner was charged in a Florida state court with having broken and entered a poolroom with intent to commit a misdemeanor. This offense is a felony under Florida law. Appearing in court without funds and without a lawyer, petitioner asked the court to appoint counsel for him, whereupon the following colloquy took place:

"The Court: Mr. Gideon, I am sorry, but I cannot appoint Counsel to represent you in this case. Under the laws of the State of Florida, the only time the Court can appoint Counsel to represent a Defendant is when that person is charged with a capital offense. I am sorry, but I will have to deny your request to appoint Counsel to defend you in this case.

"The Defendant: The United States Supreme Court says I am entitled to be represented by Counsel."

Put to trial before a jury, Gideon conducted his defense about as well as could be expected from a layman. He made an opening statement to the jury, cross-examined the State's witnesses, presented witnesses in his own defense, declined to testify himself, and made a short argument "emphasizing his innocence to the charge contained in the Information filed in this case." The jury returned a verdict of guilty, and petitioner was sentenced to serve five years in the state prison. . . . Since 1942, when Betts v. Brady was decided by a divided Court, the problem of a defendant's federal constitutional right to counsel in a state court has been a continuing source of controversy and litigation in both state and federal courts. To give this problem another review here, we granted certiorari. Since Gideon was proceeding in forma pauperis, we appointed counsel to represent him and requested both sides to discuss in their briefs and oral arguments the following: "Should this Court's holding in Betts v. Brady be reconsidered?"

I.

The facts upon which Betts claimed that he had been unconstitutionally denied the right to have counsel appointed to assist him are strikingly like the facts upon which Gideon here bases his federal constitutional claim. Betts was indicted for robbery in a Maryland state court. On arraignment, he told the trial judge of his lack of funds to hire a lawyer and asked the court to appoint one for him. Betts was advised that it was not the practice in that county to appoint counsel for indigent defendants except in murder and rape cases. He then pleaded not guilty, had witnesses summoned, cross-examined the State's witnesses, examined his own, and chose not to testify himself. He was found guilty by the judge, sitting without a jury, and sentenced to eight years in prison. Like Gideon, Betts sought release by habeas corpus, alleging that he had been denied the right to assistance of counsel in violation of the Fourteenth Amendment. Betts was denied any relief, and on review this Court affirmed. It was held that a refusal to appoint counsel for an indigent defendant charged with a felony did not necessarily violate the Due Process Clause of the Fourteenth Amendment, which for reasons given the Court deemed to be the only applicable federal constitutional provision. The Court said:

"Asserted denial [of due process] is to be tested by an appraisal of the totality of facts in a given case. That which may, in one setting, constitute a denial of fundamental fairness, shocking to the universal sense of justice, may, in other circumstances, and in the light of other considerations, fall short of such denial."

Treating due process as "a concept less rigid and more fluid than those envisaged in other specific and particular provisions of the Bill of Rights," the Court held that refusal to appoint counsel under the particular facts and circumstances in the Betts Case was not so "offensive to the common and fundamental ideas of fairness" as to amount to a denial of due process. Since the facts and circumstances of the two cases are so nearly indistinguishable, we think the Betts v. Brady holding if left standing would require us to reject Gideon's claim that the Constitution guarantees him the assistance of counsel. Upon full reconsideration we conclude that Betts v. Brady should be overruled.

II.

The Sixth Amendment provides, "In all criminal prosecutions, the accused shall enjoy the right . . . to have the Assistance of Counsel for his defense." We have construed this to mean that in federal courts counsel must be provided for defendants unable to employ counsel unless the right is competently and intelligently waived. Betts argued that this right is extended to indigent defendants in state courts by the Fourteenth Amendment. In response the Court stated that, while the Sixth Amendment laid down "no rule for the conduct of the States, the question recurs whether the constraint laid by the Amendment upon the national courts expresses a rule so fundamental and essential to a fair trial, and so, to due process of law, that it is made obligatory upon the States by the Fourteenth Amendment." In order to decide whether the Sixth Amendment's guarantee of counsel is of this fundamental nature, the Court in Betts set out and considered "[r]elevant data on the subject ... afforded by constitutional and statutory provisions subsisting in the colonies and the States prior to the inclusion of the Bill of Rights in the national Constitution, and in the constitutional, legislative, and judicial history of the States to the present date." On the basis of this historical data the Court concluded that "appointment of counsel is not a fundamental right, essential to a fair trial." It was for this reason the Betts Court refused to accept the contention that the Sixth Amendment's guarantee of counsel for indigent federal defendants was extended to or, in the words of that Court, "made obligatory upon the States by the Fourteenth Amendment." Plainly, had the Court concluded that appointment of counsel for an indigent criminal defendant was "a fundamental right, essential to a fair trial," it would have held that the Fourteenth Amendment requires appointment of counsel in a state court, just as the Sixth Amendment requires in a federal court.

We think the Court in Betts had ample precedent for acknowledging that those guarantees of the Bill of Rights which are fundamental safeguards of liberty immune from federal abridgment are equally protected against state invasion by the Due Process Clause of the Fourteenth Amendment. This same principle was recognized, explained and applied in Powell v. Alabama (1932), a case upholding the right of counsel, where the Court held that despite sweeping language to the contrary in Hurtado v. California (1884), the Fourteenth Amendment "embraced" those " 'fundamental principles of liberty and justice which lie at the base of all our civil and political institutions,' " even though they had been "specifically dealt with in another part of the federal Constitution." In many cases other than Powell and Betts, this Court has looked to the fundamental nature of original Bill of Rights guarantees to decide whether the Fourteenth Amendment makes them obligatory on the States. Explicitly recognized to be of this "fundamental nature" and therefore made immune from state invasion by the Fourteenth, or some part of it, are the First Amendment's freedoms of speech, press, religion, assembly, association, and petition for redress of grievances. For the same reason, though not always in precisely the same terminology, the Court has made obligatory on the States the Fifth Amendment's command that private property shall not be taken for public use without just compensation, the Fourth Amendment's prohibition of unreasonable searches and seizures, and the Eighth's ban on cruel and unusual punishment. On the other hand, this Court in Palko v. Connecticut (1937), refused to hold that the Fourteenth Amendment made the double jeopardy provision of the Fifth Amendment obligatory on the States. In so refusing, however, the Court, speaking through Mr. Justice Cardozo, was careful to emphasize that "immunities that are valid as against the federal government by force of the specific pledges of particular amendments have been found to be implicit in the concept of ordered liberty, and thus, through the Fourteenth Amendment, become valid as against the states" and that guarantees "in their origin . . . effective against the federal government alone" had by prior cases "been taken over from the earlier articles of the federal bill of rights and brought within the Fourteenth Amendment by a process of absorption."

We accept Betts v. Brady's assumption, based as it was on our prior cases, that a provision of the Bill of Rights which is "fundamental and essential to a fair trial" is made obligatory upon the States by the Fourteenth Amendment. We think the Court in Betts was wrong, however, in concluding that the Sixth Amendment's guarantee of counsel is not one of these fundamental rights. Ten years before Betts v. Brady, this Court, after full consideration of all the historical data examined in Betts, had unequivocally declared that "the right to the aid of counsel is of this fundamental character." . . . While the court at the close of its Powell opinion did by its language, as this Court frequently does, limit its holding to the particular facts and circumstances of that case, its conclusions about the fundamental nature of the right to counsel are unmistakable. Several years later, in 1936, the Court reemphasized what it had said about the fundamental nature of the right to counsel in this language:

"We concluded that certain fundamental rights, safeguarded by the first eight amendments against federal action, were also safeguarded against state action by the due process of law clause of the Fourteenth Amendment, and among them the fundamental right of the accused to the aid of counsel in a criminal prosecution." Grosjean v. American Press Co. (1936).

And again in 1938 this Court said:

"[The assistance of counsel] is one of the safeguards of the Sixth Amendment deemed necessary to insure fundamental human rights of life and liberty. . . . The Sixth Amendment stands as a constant admonition that if the constitutional safeguards it provides be lost, justice will not 'still be done.' " Johnson v. Zerbst (1938). . . .

In light of these and many other prior decisions of this Court, it is not surprising that the Betts Court, when faced with the contention that "one charged with crime, who is unable to obtain counsel, must be furnished counsel by the State," conceded that "[e]xpressions in the opinions of this court lend color to the argument . . . ." The fact is that in deciding as it did—that "appointment of counsel is not a fundamental right, essential to a fair trial"—the Court in Betts v. Brady made an abrupt break with its own well-considered precedents. In returning to these old precedents, sounder we believe than the new, we but restore constitutional principles established to achieve a fair system of justice. Not only these precedents but also reason and reflection require us to recognize that in our adversary system of criminal justice, any person haled into court, who is too poor to hire a lawyer, cannot be assured a fair trial unless counsel is provided for him. This seems to us to be an obvious truth. Governments, both state and federal, quite properly spend vast sums of money to establish machinery to try defendants accused of crime. Lawyers to prosecute are everywhere deemed essential to protect the public's interest in an orderly society. Similarly, there are few defendants charged with crime, few indeed, who fail to hire the best lawyers they can get to prepare and present their defenses. That government hires lawyers to prosecute and defendants who have the money hire lawyers to defend are the strongest indications of the widespread belief that lawyers in criminal courts are necessities, not luxuries. The right of one charged with crime to counsel may not be deemed fundamental and essential to fair trials in some countries, but it is in ours. From the very beginning, our state and national constitutions and laws have laid great emphasis on procedural and substantive safeguards designed to assure fair trials before impartial tribunals in which every defendant stands equal before the law. This noble ideal cannot be realized if the poor man charged with crime has to face his accusers without a lawyer to assist him. A defendant's need for a lawyer is nowhere better stated than in the moving words of Mr. Justice Sutherland in Powell v. Alabama:

"The right to be heard would be, in many cases, of little avail if it did not comprehend the right to be heard by counsel. Even the intelligent and educated layman has small and sometimes no skill in the science of law. If charged with crime, he is incapable, generally, of determining for himself whether the indictment is good or bad. He is unfamiliar with the rules of evidence. Left without the aid of counsel he may be put on trial without a proper charge, and convicted upon incompetent evidence, or evidence irrelevant to the issue or otherwise inadmissible. He lacks both the skill and knowledge adequately to prepare his defense, even though he have a perfect one. He requires the guiding hand of counsel at every step in the proceedings against him. Without it, though he be not guilty, he faces the danger of conviction because he does not know how to establish his innocence."

The Court in Betts v. Brady departed from the sound wisdom upon which the Court's holding in Powell v. Alabama rested. Florida, supported by two other States, has asked that Betts v. Brady be left intact. Twenty-two States, as friends of the Court, argue that Betts was "an anachronism when handed down" and that it should now be overruled. We agree.

The judgment is reversed and the cause is remanded to the Supreme Court of Florida for further action not inconsistent with this opinion.

Reversed.

Mr. Justice Douglas, while joining the opinion of the Court, wrote a separate opinion, saying in part:

My Brother Harlan is of the view that a guarantee of the Bill of Rights that is made applicable to the States by reason of the Fourteenth Amendment is a lesser version of that same guarantee as applied to the Federal Government. Mr. Justice Jackson shared that view. But that view has not prevailed and rights protected against state invasion by the Due Process Clause of the Fourteenth Amendment are not watered-down versions of what the Bill of Rights guarantees.

Mr. Justice Clark, concurring in the result, wrote a separate opinion.

Mr. Justice Harlan, concurring, said in part:

I agree that Betts v. Brady should be overruled, but consider it entitled to a more respectful burial than has been accorded, at least on the part of those of us who were not on the Court when that case was decided.

I cannot subscribe to the view that Betts v. Brady represented "an abrupt break with its own well-considered precedents." In 1932, in Powell v. Alabama, a capital case, this Court declared that under the particular facts there presented—"the ignorance and illiteracy of the defendants, their youth, the circumstances of public hostility . . . and above all that they stood in deadly peril of their lives"—the state court had a duty to assign counsel for the trial as a necessary requisite of due process of law. It is evident that these limiting facts were not added to the opinion as an afterthought; they were repeatedly emphasized, and were clearly regarded as important to the result.

Thus when this Court, a decade later, decided Betts v. Brady, it did no more than to admit of the possible existence of special circumstances in noncapital as well as capital trials, while at the same time insisting that such circumstances be shown in order to establish a denial of due process. The right to appointed counsel had been recognized as being considerably broader in federal prosecutions, see Johnson v. Zerbst [1938], but to have imposed these requirements on the States would indeed have been "an abrupt break" with the almost immediate past. The declaration that the right to appointed counsel in state prosecutions, as established in Powell v. Alabama, was not limited to capital cases was in truth not a departure from, but an extension of, existing precedent. . . .

[Mr. Justice Harlan here notes the "troubled journey" of the Powell and Betts doctrines and concedes that since 1950 no "special circumstances" have been found to justify the absence of counsel.]

. . . The Court has come to recognize, in other words, that the mere existence of a serious criminal charge constituted in itself special circumstances requiring the services of counsel at trial. In truth the Betts v. Brady rule is no longer a reality.

This evolution, however, appears not to have been fully recognized by many state courts, in this instance charged with the front-line responsibility for the enforcement of constitutional rights. To continue a rule which is honored by this Court only with lip service is not a healthy thing and in the long run will do disservice to the federal system. . . .

In agreeing with the Court that the right to counsel in a case such as this should now be expressly recognized as a fundamental right embraced in the Fourteenth Amendment, I wish to make a further observation. When we hold a right or immunity, valid against the Federal Government, to be "implicit in the concept of ordered liberty" and thus valid against the States, I do not read our past decisions to suggest that by so holding, we automatically carry over an entire body of federal law and apply it in full sweep to the States. Any such concept would disregard the frequently wide disparity between the legitimate interests of the States and of the Federal Government, the divergent problems that they face, and the significantly different consequences of their actions. . . . In what is done today I do not understand the Court to depart from the principles laid down in Palko v. Connecticut, or to embrace the concept that the Fourteenth Amendment "incorporates" the Sixth Amendment as such.

On these premises I join in the judgment of the Court.

ROE v. WADE
410 U. S. 113; 93 S. Ct. 705; 35 L. Ed. 2d 147
(1973)

While the Constitution prescribes certain limits on governmental power, these limits are in a continual state of change. As the Court engages in the endless process of interpreting the constitutional guarantees, certain protections are withdrawn and others are added. Ordinarily this process occurs so slowly and subtly that only a careful observer can detect that a real change is actually taking place. While apparently applying the same principles to a new set of facts, the Court is in reality altering the principle by an almost indistinguishable increment. Now and again the Court will find this process incapable of producing the results that it wants; a former interpretation of principle no longer fills what the Court sees as the needs of society, so that principle must be rejected and another put in its place. On such occasions the Court will overrule its previous interpretation of the Constitution and substitute another interpretation—usually one which has been long clamoring for acceptance. This is what the Court did when, starting in the early 1960's, it began in a serious way to incorporate Bill of Rights guarantees into the due process clause of the Fourteenth Amendment.

On very rare occasions, when what seems to the Court to be an important right cannot be brought comfortably under any existing constitutional guarantee, the Court is forced to draw upon what it conceives to be the general or fundamental principles of the Constitution to supply the necessary protection. In the early days little effort was made to tie such protection to specific parts of the document: in Loan Association v. Topeka (1875), for example, the Court forbade spending tax money for private purposes on the ground that it violated limits on governmental power that "grow out of the essential nature of all free governments." With the evolution of the due process clause, this right and the celebrated "liberty of contract" became elements of due process of law. See the note to Lochner v. New York (1905).

In Griswold v. Connecticut (1965), the Supreme Court raised the right of privacy to constitutional status by drawing on a "penumbra" cast by a number of constitutional provisions. "Privacy in one's association" had been protected in NAACP v. Alabama (1958), and the Third, Fourth and Fifth Amendments had all created a zone of privacy which the government might not violate. This newly created right, the Court held, included a right of marital privacy with an attendant right to use contraceptives and receive birth-control information. In Eisenstadt v. Baird (1972) the Court held that equal protection required that unmarried women, too, be allowed birth control information and articles. "The Court today does not pick out particular human activities, characterize them as 'fundamental,' and give them added protection. . . . To the contrary, the Court simply recognizes, as it must, an established constitutional right, and gives to that right no less protection than the Constitution itself demands."

Although this quotation from Justice Stewart by the Court in San Antonio v. Rodriguez (1973) states the orthodox view of the Court's role, few scholars today would subscribe to it. While in theory all rights in the Constitution are of equal value (the Constitution nowhere suggests that some rights are more important than others), over the years the Court has always cherished certain rights which it considered more important than other rights and hence entitled to greater constitutional protection. The rights so honored have changed from time to time as the Court perceived changes in basic social values. In the early days private property was given special consideration, and later this came to include the rights of businessmen and "liberty of contract." Then in the 1930's and 1940's, while the economic rights fell from grace, the rights listed in the First Amendment rose to favor. In recent years the rights of privacy and the right to vote have joined the ranks of the elite.

Since the ranking of these rights is a matter of value judgment, it has been comdemned by those who disapproved the particular ranking as "judicial legislation," "substituting judicial values for those of the commu-

nity," a "violation of the democratic process," and a "lack of proper judicial restraint." While such attacks seem to challenge the role of the Court in this area, in fact few justices have rejected philosophically the idea that some rights are better than others. The classic example is Justice Holmes, who condemned the judicial favoritism shown to economic rights (see Lochner v. New York, 1905) while insisting that speech could be curtailed only if it presented a "clear and present danger," (see his dissent in Gitlow v. New York, 1925).

Perhaps the easiest method of giving added protection to a right, once it is identified, is to clothe it in language that nullifies the normal presumption in favor of legislative acts and forces the government to show that its laws are reasonable and necessary. Such language abounds in the areas of the First Amendment: the "clear and present danger" test, the statement that First Amendment rights are in a "preferred position" (see Murdock v. Pennsylvania, 1943) and the rule (since modified) that publications cannot be condemned as obscene unless they are utterly without redeeming social value all serve to tip the scales in favor of the right and against the government wishing to suppress or regulate it.

In 1960 in Bates v. Little Rock a new phrase made its appearance. The Court held bad the demand of the city of Little Rock for the publication of the membership lists of the NAACP on the ground that it would destroy the group's organizational privacy and impair its operations. "Where there is a significant encroachment upon personal liberty, the State may prevail only upon showing a subordinating interest which is compelling." This "compelling state interest" phrase appeared again in several cases in 1963 (see Gibson v. Florida Investigating Committee), where its impact was to make the state produce evidence that it had a compelling interest which could be met only by infringing a claimed right of association. In none of the cases was sufficient interest shown.

In 1969 the "compelling state interest" doctrine was applied to the equal protection clause. The Court in this area had long granted favored status to certain bases of classification, such as race and religion, holding that legislative distinctions based on them were, if not "invidious," at least "inherently suspect." But with Shapiro v. Thompson and Kramer v. U.S.F.D. (1969) the Court looked not at the bases of classification alone, but at the aims sought to be achieved by these bases. In striking down the requirement of a year's residence to receive welfare and the requirement of taxpayer (or parental) status to vote in school board elections, the Court found that where a classification limits the right to move freely across state lines or the right to vote, it could only be justified by a compelling state interest.

In the case below, the phrase is moved again—this time into the area of privacy protected by the Constitution. Here the Court not only upholds *the right of a mother to decide, in consultation with her doctor, whether or not to have an abortion, but spells out the "compelling points" at which the state's "compelling interest" permits it to undertake regulation of abortions.*

While the case below in effect holds invalid the statutes of some 30 states which forbid abortions except to save the life of the mother, in Doe v. Bolton, decided the same day, the Court dealt with a Georgia statute patterned after the American Law Institute's Penal Code and followed in about a dozen states. The Georgia statute permitted abortions if it was necessary to the preservation of the health of the mother, if the fetus was likely to be born with a serious defect, or if the pregnancy resulted from rape. Although the Court held that the validity of these provisions was not properly before it, the questions they raise are clearly answered in the Texas case below. In addition, the Georgia law required a number of procedural conditions, such as that the woman's doctor and two other doctors put in writing the judgment that an abortion was needed, that the abortion be performed in a hospital accredited by the nongovernmental Joint Committee on Accreditation of Hospitals, and that the abortion be approved in advance by three members of the hospital's abortion committee. All these requirements were held invalid since they were not required in any surgical procedure other than abortion. The law also limited abortions to state residents, and this the Court struck down as a denial of the "privileges and immunities of citizens in the several states." "Just as the Privileges and Immunities Clause, Const. Art. IV § 2, protects persons who enter other states to ply their trade . . . so must it protect persons who enter Georgia seeking the medical services that are available there. . . . A contrary holding would mean that a state could limit to its own residents the general medical care available within its borders. This we could not approve."

Mr. Justice Blackmun delivered the opinion of the Court, saying in part:

V.

The principal thrust of appellant's attack on the Texas statutes is that they improperly invade a right, said to be possessed by the pregnant woman, to choose to terminate her pregnancy. Appellant would discover this right in the concept of personal "liberty" embodied in the Fourteenth Amendment's Due

Process Clause; or in personal, marital, familial, and sexual privacy said to be protected by the Bill of Rights or its penumbras, see Griswold v. Connecticut (1965); Eisenstadt v. Baird (1972); (White, J., concurring in result); or among those rights reserved to the people by the Ninth Amendment, Griswold v. Connecticut (Goldberg, J., concurring). Before addressing this claim, we feel it desirable briefly to survey, in several aspects, the history of abortion, for such insight as that history may afford us, and then to examine the state purposes and interests behind the criminal abortion laws.

VI.

It perhaps is not generally appreciated that the restrictive criminal abortion laws in effect in a majority of States today are of relatively recent vintage. Those laws, generally proscribing abortion or its attempt at any time during pregnancy except when necessary to preserve the pregnant woman's life, are not of ancient or even of common-law origin. Instead, they derive from statutory changes effected, for the most part, in the latter half of the 19th century.
. . .

[The Court here reviews the history of attitudes toward abortion and abortion laws since ancient times.]

VII.

Three reasons have been advanced to explain historically the enactment of criminal abortion laws in the 19th century and to justify their continued existence.

It has been argued occasionally that these laws were the product of a Victorian social concern to discourage illicit sexual conduct. Texas, however, does not advance this justification in the present case, and it appears that no court or commentator has taken the argument seriously. The appellants and amici contend, moreover, that this is not a proper state purpose at all and suggest that, if it were, the Texas statutes are overbroad in protecting it since the law fails to distinguish between married and unwed mothers.

A second reason is concerned with abortion as a medical procedure. When most criminal abortion laws were first enacted, the procedure was a hazardous one for the woman. This was particularly true prior to the development of antisepsis. Antiseptic techniques, of course, were based on discoveries by Lister, Pasteur, and others first announced in 1867, but were not generally accepted and employed until about the turn of the century. Abortion mortality was high. Even after 1900, and perhaps until as late as the development of antibiotics in the 1940's, standard modern techniques such as dilation and curettage were not nearly so safe as they are today. Thus, it has been argued that a State's real concern in enacting a criminal abortion law was to protect the pregnant woman, that is, to restrain her from submitting to a procedure that placed her life in serious jeopardy.

Modern medical techniques have altered this situation. Appellants and various amici refer to medical data indicating that abortion in early pregnancy, that is, prior to the end of first trimester, although not without its risk, is now relatively safe. Mortality rates for women undergoing early abortions, where the procedure is legal, appear to be as low as or lower than the rates for normal childbirth. Consequently, any interest of the State in protecting the woman from an inherently hazardous procedure, except when it would be equally dangerous for her to forego it, has largely disappeared. Of course, important state interests in the area of health and medical standards do remain.

The State has a legitimate interest in seeing to it that abortion, like any other medical procedure, is performed under circumstances that insure maximum safety for the patient. This interest obviously extends at least to the performing physician and his staff, to the facilities involved, to the availability of after-care, and to adequate provision for any complication or emergency that might arise. The prevalence of high mortality rates at illegal "abortion mills" strengthens, rather than weakens, the State's interest in regulating the conditions under which abortions are performed. Moreover, the risk to the woman increases as her pregnancy continues. Thus, the State retains a definite interest in protecting the woman's own health and safety when an abortion is proposed at a late stage of pregnancy.

The third reason is the State's interest—some phrase it in terms of duty— in protecting prenatal life. Some of the argument for this justification rests on the theory that a new human life is present from the moment of conception. The State's interest and general obligation to protect life then extends, it is argued, to prenatal life. Only when the life of the pregnant mother herself is at stake, balanced against the life she carries within her, should the interest of the embryo or fetus not prevail. Logically, of course, a legitimate state interest in this area need not stand or fall on acceptance of the belief that life begins at conception or at some other point prior to live birth. In assessing the State's interest, recognition may be given to the less rigid claim that as long as at least *potential* life is involved, the State may assert interests beyond the protection of the pregnant woman alone.

Parties challenging state abortion laws have sharply disputed in some courts the contention that a purpose of these laws, when enacted, was to protect prenatal life. . . .

It is with these interests, and the weight to be attached to them, that this case is concerned.

VIII.

The Constitution does not explicitly mention any right of privacy. In a line of decisions, however, going back perhaps as far as Union Pacific R. Co. v. Botsford (1891), the Court has recognized that a right of personal privacy, or a guarantee of certain areas or zones of privacy, does exist under the Constitution. In varying contexts the Court or individual Justices have, indeed, found at least the roots of that right in the First Amendment, Stanley v. Georgia (1969); in the Fourth and Fifth Amendments, Terry v. Ohio (1968), Katz v. United States (1967) . . . ; in the penumbras of the Bill of Rights, Griswold v. Connecticut (1965); in the Ninth Amendment; or in the concept of liberty guaranteed by the first section of the Fourteenth Amendment, see Meyer v. Nebraska (1923). These decisions make it clear that only personal rights that can be deemed "fundamental" or "implicit in the concept of ordered liberty," Palko v. Connecticut (1937), are included in this guarantee of personal privacy. They also make it clear that the right has some extension to activities relating to marriage, Loving v. Virginia (1967); procreation, Skinner v. Oklahoma (1942); contraception, Eisenstadt v. Baird (1972). . . .

This right of privacy, whether it be founded in the Fourteenth Amendment's concept of personal liberty and restrictions upon state action, as we feel it is, or, as the District Court determined, in the Ninth Amendment's reservation of rights to the people, is broad enough to encompass a woman's decision whether or not to terminate her pregnancy. The detriment that the State would impose upon the pregnant woman by denying this choice altogether is apparent. Specific and direct harm medically diagnosable even in early pregnancy may be involved. Maternity, or additional offspring, may force upon the woman a distressful life and future. Psychological harm may be imminent. Mental and physical health may be taxed by child care. There is also the distress, for all concerned, assocated with the unwanted child, and there is the problem of bringing a child into a family already unable, psychologically and otherwise, to care for it. In other cases, as in this one, the additional difficulties and continuing stigma of unwed motherhood may be involved. All these are factors the woman and her responsible physician necessarily will consider in consultation.

On the basis of elements such as these, appellant and some amici argue that the woman's right is absolute and that she is entitled to terminate her pregnancy at whatever time, in whatever way, and for whatever reason she alone chooses. With this we do not agree. Appellant's arguments that Texas either has no valid interest at all in regulating the abortion decision, or no interest strong enough to support any limitation upon the woman's sole determination, is unpersuasive. The Court's decisions recognizing a right of privacy also acknowledge that some state regulation in areas protected by that right is appropriate. As noted above, a State may properly assert important interests in safeguarding health, in maintaining medical standards, and in protecting potential life. At some point in pregnancy, these respective interests become sufficiently compelling to sustain regulation of the factors that govern the abortion decision. The privacy right involved, therefore, cannot be said to be absolute. In fact, it is not clear to us that the claim asserted by some amici that one has an unlimited right to do with one's body as one pleases bears a close relationship to the right of privacy previously articulated in the Court's decisions. The Court has refused to recognize an unlimited right of this kind in the past. Jacobson v. Massachusetts (1905) (vaccination); Buck v. Bell (1927) (sterilization).

We therefore conclude that the right of personal privacy includes the abortion decision, but that this right is not unqualified and must be considered against important state interests in regulation. . . .

Where certain "fundamental rights" are involved, the Court has held that regulation limiting these rights may be justified only by a "compelling state interest," Kramer v. Union Free School District (1969); Shapiro v. Thompson (1969); . . . and that legislative enactments must be narrowly drawn to express only the legitimate state interests at stake. Griswold v. Connecticut (1965). . . .

IX.

The District Court held that the appellee failed to meet his burden of demonstrating that the Texas statute's infringement upon Roe's rights was necessary to support a compelling state interest. . . . Appellee argues that the State's determination to recognize and protect prenatal life from and after conception consitutes a compelling state interest. As noted above, we do not agree fully with either formulation.

A. The appellee and certain amici argue that the fetus is a "person" within the language and meaning of the Fourteenth Amendment. In support of this, they outline at length and in detail the well-known facts of fetal development. If this suggestion of personhood is established, the appellant's case, of course, collapses, for the fetus' right to life is then guaranteed specifically by the Amendment. The appellant conceded as much on reargument. On the other hand, the appellee conceded on reargument that no case could be cited that holds that a fetus is a person within the meaning of the Fourteenth Amendment.

The Constitution does not define "person" in so many words. Section 1 of the Fourteenth Amendment contains three references to "person." The first, in defining "citizens," speaks of "persons born or naturalized in the United States." The word also appears both in the Due Process Clause and in the

Equal Protection Clause. "Person" is used in other places in the Constitution.
. . . But in nearly all these instances, the use of the word is such that it has
application only postnatally. None indicates, with any assurance, that it has
any possible prenatal application.*

All this, together with our observation, that throughout the major portion
of the 19th century prevailing legal abortion practices were far freer than they
are today, persuades us that the word "person," as used in the Fourteenth
Amendment, does not include the unborn. . . .

B. The pregnant woman cannot be isolated in her privacy. She carries an
embryo and, later, a fetus, if one accepts the medical definitions of the developing young in the human uterus. . . . The situation therefore is inherently
different from marital intimacy, or bedroom possession of obscene material,
or marriage, or procreation, or education, with which Eisenstadt, Griswold,
Stanley, Loving, Skinner, Pierce, and Meyer were respectively concerned. As
we have intimated above, it is reasonable and appropriate for a State to decide
that at some point in time another interest, that of health of the mother or that
of potential human life, becomes significantly involved. The woman's privacy
is no longer sole and any right of privacy she possesses must be measured
accordingly.

Texas urges that, apart from the Fourteenth Amendment, life begins at
conception and is present throughout pregnancy, and that, therefore, the State
has a compelling interest in protecting that life from and after conception. We
need not resolve the difficult question of when life begins. When those trained
in the respective disciplines of medicine, philosophy, and theology are unable
to arrive at any consensus, the judiciary, at this point in the development of
man's knowledge, is not in a position to speculate as to the answer.

It should be sufficient to note briefly the wide divergence of thinking on this
most sensitive and difficult question. . . .

X.

In view of all this, we do not agree that, by adopting one theory of life, Texas
may override the rights of the pregnant woman that are at stake. We repeat,

*When Texas urges that a fetus is entitled to Fourteenth Amendment protection as
a person, it faces a dilemma. Neither in Texas nor in any other State are all abortions
prohibited. Despite broad proscription, an exception always exists. The exception
contained in Art. 1196, for an abortion procured or attempted by medical advice for
the purpose of saving the life of the mother, is typical. But if the fetus is a person who
is not to be deprived of life without due process of law, and if the mother's condition
is the sole determinant, does not the Texas exception appear to be out of line with the
Amendment's command? . . .

however, that the State does have an important and legitimate interest in preserving and protecting the health of the pregnant woman, whether she be a resident of the State or a nonresident who seeks medical consultation and treatment there, and that it has still *another* important and legitimate interest in protecting the potentiality of human life. These interests are separate and distinct. Each grows in substantiality as the woman approaches term and, at a point during pregnancy, each becomes "compelling."

With respect to the State's important and legitimate interest in the health of the mother, the "compelling" point, in the light of present medical knowledge, is at approximately the end of the first trimester. This is so because of the now established medical fact, referred to above . . . that until the end of the first trimester mortality in abortion may be less than mortality in normal childbirth. It follows that, from and after this point, a State may regulate the abortion procedure to the extent that the regulation reasonably relates to the preservation and protection of maternal health. Examples of permissible state regulation in this area are requirements as to the qualifications of the person who is to perform the abortion; as to the licensure of that person; as to the facility in which the procedure is to be performed, that is, whether it must be a hospital or may be a clinic or some other place of less-than-hospital status; as to the licensing of the facility; and the like.

This means, on the other hand, that, for the period of pregnancy prior to this "compelling" point, the attending physician, in consultation with his patient, is free to determine, without regulation by the State, that in his medical judgment the patient's pregnancy should be terminated. If that decision is reached, the judgment may be effectuated by an abortion free of interference by the State.

With respect to the State's important and legitimate interest in potential life, the "compelling" point is at viability. This is so because the fetus then presumably has the capability of meaningful life outside the mother's womb. State regulation protective of fetal life after viability thus has both logical and biological justifications. If the State is interested in protecting fetal life after viability, it may go so far as to proscribe abortion during that period except when it is necessary to preserve the life or health of the mother.

Measured against these standards, the Texas Penal Code, in restricting legal abortions to those "procured or attempted by medical advice for the purpose of saving the life of the mother," sweeps too broadly. The statute makes no distinction between abortions performed early in pregnancy and those performed later, and it limits to a single reason, "saving" the mother's life, the legal justification for the procedure. The statute, therefore, cannot survive the constitutional attack made upon it here. . . .

XI.

To summarize and to repeat:

1. A state criminal abortion statute of the current Texas type, that excepts from criminality only a *lifesaving* procedure on behalf of the mother, without regard to pregnancy stage and without recognition of the other interests involved, is violative of the Due Process Clause of the Fourteenth Amendment.

(a) For the stage prior to approximately the end of the first trimester, the abortion decision and its effectuation must be left to the medical judgment of the pregnant woman's attending physician.

(b) For the stage subsequent to approximately the end of the first trimester, the State, in promoting its interest in the health of the mother, may, if it chooses, regulate the abortion procedure in ways that are reasonably related to maternal health.

(c) For the stage subsequent to viability the State in promoting its interest in the potentiality of human life may, if it chooses, regulate, and even proscribe, abortion except where it is necessary, in appropriate medical judgment, for the preservation of the life or health of the mother.

2. The State may define the term "physician," as it has been employed in the preceding numbered paragraphs of this Part XI of this opinion, to mean only a physician currently licensed by the State, and may proscribe any abortion by a person who is not a physician as so defined.

In Doe v. Bolton, procedural requirements contained in one of the modern abortion statutes are considered. That opinion and this one, of course, are to be read together. . . .

Mr. Chief Justice Burger concurred.

Mr. Justice Douglas concurred.

Mr. Justice Stewart, concurring said in part:

In 1963, this Court, in Ferguson v. Skrupa, purported to sound the death knell for the doctrine of substantive due process, a doctrine under which many state laws had in the past been held to violate the Fourteenth Amendment. As Mr. Justice Black's opinion for the Court in Skrupa put it: "We have returned to the original constitutional proposition that courts do not substitute their social and economic beliefs for the judgment of legislative bodies, who are elected to pass laws."

Barely two years later, in Griswold v. Connecticut, the Court held a Connecticut birth control law unconstitutional. In view of what had been so recently said in Skrupa, the Court's opinion in Griswold understandably did its best to avoid reliance on the Due Process Clause of the Fourteenth Amendment as the ground for decision. Yet, the Connecticut law did not violate any provision of the Bill of Rights, nor any other specific provision of the Constitution. So it was clear to me then, and it is equally clear to me now, that the Griswold decision can be rationally understood only as a holding that the Connecticut statute substantively invaded the "liberty" that is protected by the Due Process Clause of the Fourteenth Amendment. As so understood, Griswold stands as one in a long line of pre-Skrupa cases decided under the doctrine of substantive due process, and I now accept it as such.

"In a Constitution for a free people, there can be no doubt that the meaning of 'liberty' must be broad indeed." ... The Constitution nowhere mentions a specific right of personal choice in matters of marriage and family life, but the "liberty" protected by the Due Process Clause of the Fourteenth Amendment covers more than those freedoms explicitly named in the Bill of Rights. ...

Several decisions of this Court make clear that freedom of personal choice in matters of marriage and family life is one of the liberties protected by the Due Process Clause of the Fourteenth Amendment. Loving v. Virginia, Griswold v. Connecticut . . . . That right necessarily includes the right of a woman to decide whether or not to terminate her pregnancy. "Certainly the interests of a woman in giving of her physical and emotional self during pregnancy and the interests that will be affected throughout her life by the birth and raising of a child are of a far greater degree of significance and personal intimacy than the right to send a child to private school protected in Pierce v. Society of Sisters (1925), or the right to teach a foreign language protected in Meyer v. Nebraska (1923)." . . .

Mr. Justice Rehnquist, dissenting, said in part:

. . . I have difficulty in concluding, as the Court does, that the right of "privacy" is involved in this case. Texas, by the statute here challenged, bars the performance of a medical abortion by a licensed physician on a plaintiff such as Roe. A transaction resulting in an operation such as this is not "private" in the ordinary usage of that word. . . .

If the Court means by the term "privacy" no more than that the claim of a person to be free from unwanted state regulation of consensual transactions may be a form of "liberty" protected by the Fourteenth Amendment, there is no doubt that similar claims have been upheld in our earlier decisions on the basis of that liberty. I agree with the statement of Mr. Justice Stewart in his concurring opinion that the "liberty," against deprivation of which without due process the Fourteenth Amendment protects, embraces more than the rights found in the Bill of Rights. But that liberty is not guaranteed absolutely against deprivation, but only against deprivation without due process of law. The test traditionally applied in the area of social and economic legislation is whether or not a law such as that challenged has a rational relation to a valid state objective. . . . But the Court's sweeping invalidation of any restrictions on abortion during the first trimester is impossible to justify under that standard, and the conscious weighing of competing factors that the Court's opinion apparently substitutes for the established test is far more appropriate to a legislative judgment than to a judicial one.

The Court eschews the history of the Fourteenth Amendment in its reliance on the "compelling state interest" test. . . . But the Court adds a new wrinkle to this test by transposing it from the legal considerations associated with the Equal Protection Clause of the Fourteenth Amendment to this case arising under the Due Process Clause of the Fourteenth Amendment. Unless I misapprehend the consequences of this transplanting of the "compelling state interest test," the Court's opinion will accomplish the seemingly impossible feat of leaving this area of the law more confused than it found it.

While the Court's opinion quotes from the dissent of Mr. Justice Holmes in Lochner v. New York (1905), the result it reaches is more closely attuned to the majority opinion of Mr. Justice Peckham in that case. As in Lochner and similar cases applying substantive due process standards to economic and social welfare legislation, the adoption of the compelling state interest standard will inevitably require this Court to examine the legislative policies and pass on the wisdom of these policies in the very process of deciding whether a particular state interest put forward may or may not be "compelling." . . .

The fact that a majority of the States reflecting, after all, the majority sentiment in those States, have had restrictions on abortions for at least a century is a strong indication, it seems to me, that the asserted right to an abortion is not "so rooted in the traditions and conscience of our people as to be ranked as fundamental," Snyder v. Massachusetts (1934). . . .

Mr. Justice White, with whom Mr. Justice Rehnquist joins, dissented.

7

First Amendment Rights

GITLOW v. NEW YORK
268 U. S. 652; 45 S. Ct. 625; 69 L. Ed. 1138
(1925)

Freedom of speech and press are not absolute rights and were never intended to be so. They are relative, in the sense that they are limited by the coexisting rights of others (as in the matter of libel) and by the demands of national security and public decency. As Mr. Justice Holmes put it in the Schenck case (below), "The most stringent protection of free speech would not protect a man in falsely shouting fire in a theatre and causing a panic." Free speech and press cases present to the courts difficult questions of degree: questions involved in drawing the line that separates the speech and publication which government must suppress in order to be safe and decent from that which it must allow and protect in order to be free and democratic.

What was perhaps the most conspicuous and interesting instance of interference with freedom of expression in our history never came before the Supreme Court of the United States. The Sedition Act of 1798 provided among other things for the severe punishment of false, scandalous, and malicious writings against the government, either house of Congress, or the President if published with intent to defame any of them, or to excite against them the hatred of the people, or to stir up sedition. It was limited in operation to two years. Ten persons were convicted under it, and many others were indicted but not tried. Its enactment and enforcement called forth great popular indignation, and President Jefferson upon assuming office pardoned all persons still imprisoned under its provisions. Many years later Congress refunded with interest the fines which had been imposed.

The relative character of the right of free speech and press becomes particularly obvious in time of war. Where is the line to be drawn between legitimate and salutary freedom of discussion and utterances which, by reason of their disloyal or seditious character, must be deemed incompatible with the public safety? This is a delicate and important question. During the Civil War such interferences with freedom of speech and press as occurred were perpetrated by military officers under the sanction of martial law, and no question of the validity of these acts of repression ever came squarely before the Supreme Court. World War I brought forth a large grist of restrictive legislation, both state and federal, and numerous judicial questions arose as to the validity of these acts and their application to specific cases. Most conspicuous of these laws were the Espionage Act of 1917—which penalized any circulation of false statements made with intent to interfere with military success, as well as any attempt to cause disloyalty in the Army or Navy or to obstruct recruiting—and the Sedition Act of 1918—which made it a crime to say or do anything which could obstruct the sale of government bonds, or to utter or publish words intended to bring into contempt or disrepute the form of government of the United States, the Constitution, flag, uniform, etc., or to incite resistance to the government or promote the cause of its enemies. Nearly a thousand persons were convicted under these two acts. Their validity was sustained in six cases coming to the Supreme Court after the close of the war. Schenck v. United States (1919) was the first of these cases, and in it Mr. Justice Holmes announced the now famous "clear and present danger" test: "The question in every case is whether the words used are used in such circumstances and are of such a nature as to create a clear and present danger that they will bring about the substantive evils that Congress has a right to prevent. It is a question of proximity and degree." Schenck had been convicted of circulating pamphlets urging resistance to the draft, and the Court found that they presented a clear and present danger of achieving this result. A week later the Court decided two more cases, Frohwerk v. United States (1919), involving a pro-German newspaper man, and Debs v. United States (1919), involving the famous Socialist leader. Holmes wrote the opinions sustaining the convictions of the two men on the grounds that their writings and speeches met the test of clear and present danger.

The Espionage Act of 1917 forbade certain kinds of action, such as causing or attempting to cause insubordination or obstructing the draft. It did not expressly limit freedom of speech; it limited it only when speech amounted to the kind of action forbidden by the statute. In order to determine when a particular speech became "action" and thus punishable under the statute, the Court resorted to two tests, the "bad tendency" test and the "clear and present danger" test.

The "bad tendency" test was designed, as Professor Chafee put it, "to kill the serpent in the egg" by preventing all speech which had a tendency, however remote, to bring about acts in violation of the law. It had its roots in the doctrine of constructive treason, so infamous in English history, under which criticism of the government was construed as an attempt to accomplish the overthrow of that government and was punished as treason. The "clear and present danger" test, devised by Mr. Justice Holmes in the Schenck case, held that speech becomes punishable as action only when there is a danger, clear and present, that it will bring the action about. If there is no clear and present danger the speech does not amount to action, and the statute forbidding the action has not been violated. Holmes's doctrine was not intended as a test of the validity of the statute itself, since presumably the "action" which the statute forbids is, like obstructing the draft, something Congress could legitimately prohibit.

The clear and present danger test is not simple to apply. It is, for instance, difficult to apply to a statute which by its language forbids certain kinds of speech. If a person makes the kind of speech thus forbidden, then he has violated the statute; in other words, once the legislature has decided for itself what kind of speech is dangerous and forbidden it, the courts can hold the statute unconstitutional but they cannot say it has not been violated. Holmes and Brandeis apparently felt that statutes of this kind could not constitutionally be applied to cases in which there was no clear and present danger of serious substantive evil. See their concurring opinion in Whitney v. California (1927).

In the present case Benjamin Gitlow was prosecuted under the New York Criminal Anarchy Act of 1902 for distributing a document similar to the Communist Manifesto of Marx and Engels (1848). This statute, which formed the model for the federal Smith Act, punishes certain kinds of speech and publication regardless of the intent of the speaker or publisher.

Mr. Justice Sanford delivered the opinion of the Court, saying in part:

Benjamin Gitlow was indicted in the supreme court of New York, with three others, for the statutory crime of criminal anarchy. . . .

The contention here is that the statute, by its terms and as applied in this case, is repugnant to the due process clause of the 14th Amendment. Its material provisions are:

"§ 160. Criminal anarchy defined.—Criminal anarchy is the doctrine that organized government should be overthrown by force or violence, or by assassination of the executive head or of any of the executive officials of government, or by any unlawful means. The advocacy of such doctrine either by word of mouth or writing is a felony.

"§ 161. Advocacy of criminal anarchy.—Any person who:

"1. By word of mouth or writing advocates, advises or teaches the duty, necessity or propriety of overthrowing or overturning organized government by force or violence, or by assassination of the executive head or of any of the executive officials of government, or by any unlawful means; or,

"2. Prints, publishes, edits, issues or knowingly circulates, sells, distributes or publicly displays any book, paper, document, or written or printed matter in any form, containing or advocating, advising or teaching the doctrine that organized government should be overthrown by force, violence or any unlawful means . . .,

"Is guilty of a felony and punishable" by imprisonment or fine, or both.

The indictment was in two counts. The first charged that the defendant had advocated, advised, and taught the duty, necessity, and propriety of overthrowing and overturning organized government by force, violence, and unlawful means, by certain writings therein set forth, entitled, "The Left Wing Manifesto;" the second, that he had printed, published, and knowingly circulated and distributed a certain paper called "The Revolutionary Age," containing the writings set forth in the first count, advocating, advising, and teaching the doctrine that organized government should be overthrown by force, violence, and unlawful means.

. . . It was admitted that the defendant signed a card subscribing to the Manifesto and Program of the Left Wing, which all applicants were required to sign before being admitted to membership; that he went to different parts of the state to speak to branches of the Socialist party about the principles of the Left Wing, and advocated their adoption; and that he was responsible [as business manager] for the Manifesto as it appeared, that "he knew of the publication, in a general way, and he knew of its publication afterwards, and is responsible for its circulation."

There was no evidence of any effect resulting from the publication and circulation of the Manifesto.

No witnesses were offered in behalf of the defendant.

Extracts from the Manifesto are set forth in the margin. Coupled with a review of the rise of Socialism, it condemned the dominant "moderate Socialism" for its recognition of the necessity of the democratic parliamentary state; repudiated its policy of introducing Socialism by legislative measures; and advocated, in plain and unequivocal language, the necessity of accomplishing the "Communist Revolution" by a militant and "revolutionary Socialism," based on "the class struggle" and mobilizing the "power of the proletariat in action," through mass industrial revolts developing into mass political strikes and "revolutionary mass action" for the purpose of conquering and destroying the parliamentary state and establishing in its place, through a "revolutionary dictatorship of the proletariat," the system of Communist Socialism. The then recent strikes in Seattle and Winnipeg were cited as instances of a development already verging on revolutionary action and suggestive of proletarian dictatorship, in which the strike workers were "trying to usurp the functions of municipal government;" and Revolutionary Socialism, it was urged, must use these mass industrial revolts to broaden the strike, make it general and militant, and develop it into mass political strikes and revolutionary mass action for the annihilation of the parliamentary state.

. . . The sole contention here is, essentially, that, as there was no evidence of any concrete result flowing from the publication of the Manifesto, or of circumstances showing the likelihood of such result, the statute as construed and applied by the trial court penalizes the mere utterance, as such, of "doctrine" having no quality of incitement, without regard either to the circumstances of its utterance or to the likelihood of unlawful sequences; and that, as the exercise of the right of free expression with relation to government is only punishable "in circumstances involving likelihood of substantive evil," the statute contravenes the due process clause of the 14th Amendment. The argument in support of this contention rests primarily upon the following propositions: 1st, that the "liberty" protected by the 14th Amendment includes the liberty of speech and of the press; and 2d, that while liberty of expression "is not absolute," it may be restrained "only in circumstances where its exercise bears a causal relation with some substantive evil, consummated, attempted, or likely;" and as the statute "takes no account of circumstances," it unduly restrains this liberty, and is therefore unconstitutional.

The precise question presented, and the only question which we can consider under this writ of error, then, is whether the statute, as construed and applied in this case by the state courts, deprived the defendant of his liberty of expression, in violation of the due process clause of the 14th Amendment.

The statute does not penalize the utterance or publication of abstract "doctrine" or academic discussion having no quality of incitement to any concrete action. It is not aimed against mere historical or philosophical essays. It does not restrain the advocacy of changes in the form of government by constitutional and lawful means. What it prohibits is language advocating, advising, or teaching the overthrow of organized government by unlawful means. These words imply urging to action. Advocacy is defined in the Century Dictionary as: "1. The act of pleading for, supporting, or recommending; active espousal." It is not the abstract "doctrine" of overthrowing organized government by unlawful means which is denounced by the statute, but the advocacy of action for the accomplishment of that purpose. . . .

The Manifesto, plainly, is neither the statement of abstract doctrine nor, as suggested by counsel, mere prediction that industrial disturbances and revolutionary mass strikes will result spontaneously in an inevitable process of evolution in the economic system. It advocates and urges in fervent language mass action which shall progressively foment industrial disturbances, and, through political mass strikes and revolutionary mass action, overthrow and destroy organized parliamentary government. It concludes with a call to action in these words: "The proletariat revolution and the Communist reconstruction of society—*the struggle for these*—is now indispensable. . . . The Communist International calls the proletariat of the world to the final struggle!" This is not the expression of philosophical abstraction, the mere prediction of future events: it is the language of direct incitement.

The means advocated for bringing about the destruction of organized parliamentary government, namely, mass industrial revolts usurping the functions of municipal government, political mass strikes directed against the parliamentary state, and revolutionary mass action for its final destruction, necessarily imply the use of force and violence, and in their essential nature are inherently unlawful in a constitutional government of law and order. That the jury were warranted in finding that the Manifesto advocated not merely the abstract doctrine of overwhelming organized government by force, violence, and unlawful means, but action to that end, is clear.

For present purposes we may and do assume that freedom of speech and of the press—which are protected by the 1st Amendment from abridgment by Congress—are among the fundamental personal rights and "liberties" protected by the due process clause of the 14th Amendment from impairment by the states. . . .

It is a fundamental principle, long established, that the freedom of speech and of the press which is secured by the Constitution does not confer an absolute right to speak or publish, without responsibility, whatever one may choose, or an unrestricted and unbridled license that gives immunity for every possible use of language, and prevents the punishment of those who abuse this freedom. 2 Story, Const. 5th ed. § 1580, p. 634 . . . . Reasonably limited, it was said by Story in the passage cited, this freedom is an inestimable privilege in a free government; without such limitation, it might become the scourge of the Republic.

That a state, in the exercise of its police power, may punish those who abuse this freedom by utterances inimical to the public welfare, tending to corrupt public morals, incite to crime, or disturb the public peace, is not open to question. . . . Thus it was held by this court in the Fox Case, that a state may punish publications advocating and encouraging a breach of its criminal laws; and, in the Gilbert Case, that a state may punish utterances teaching or advocating that its citizens should not assist the United States in prosecuting or carrying on war with its public enemies.

And, for yet more imperative reasons, a state may punish utterances endangering the foundations of organized government and threatening its overthrow by unlawful means. These imperil its own existence as a constitutional state. Freedom of speech and press, said Story (supra), does not protect disturbances of the public peace or the attempt to subvert the government. It does not protect publications or teachings which tend to subvert or imperil the government or to impede or hinder it in the performance of its governmental duties. ... It does not protect publications prompting the overthrow of government by force; the punishment of those who publish articles which tend to destroy organized society being essential to the security of freedom and stability of the state. ... And a state may penalize utterances which openly advocate the overthrow of the representative and constitutional form of government of the United States and the several states, by violence or other unlawful means. ... In short, this freedom does not deprive a state of the primary and essential right of self-preservation, which, so long as human governments endure, they cannot be denied. ...

By enacting the present statute the state has determined, through its legislative body, that utterances advocating the overthrow of organized government by force, violence, and unlawful means, are so inimical to the general welfare, and involve such danger of substantive evil, that they may be penalized in the exercise of its police power. That determination must be given great weight. Every presumption is to be indulged in favor of the validity of the statute. ... That utterances inciting to the overthrow of organized government by unlawful means present a sufficient danger of substantive evil to bring their punishment within the range of legislative discretion is clear. Such utterances, by their very nature, involve danger to the public peace and to the security of the state. They threaten breaches of the peace and ultimate revolution. And the immediate danger is none the less real and substantial because the effect of a given utterance cannot be accurately foreseen. The state cannot reasonably be required to measure the danger from every such utterance in the nice balance of a jeweler's scale. A single revolutionary spark may kindle a fire that, smoldering for a time, may burst into a sweeping and destructive conflagration. It cannot be said that the state is acting arbitrarily or unreasonably when, in the exercise of its judgment as to the measures necessary to protect the public peace and safety, it seeks to extinguish the spark without waiting until it has enkindled the flame or blazed into the conflagration. It cannot reasonably be required to defer the adoption of measures for its own peace and safety until the revolutionary utterances lead to actual disturbances of the public peace or imminent and immediate danger of its own destruction; but it may, in the exercise of its judgment, suppress the threatened danger in its incipiency. ...

We cannot hold that the present statute is an arbitrary or unreasonable exercise of the police power of the state, unwarrantably infringing the freedom of speech or press; and we must and do sustain its constitutionality.

This being so it may be applied to every utterance—not too trivial to be beneath the notice of the law—which is of such a character and used with such intent and purpose as to bring it within the prohibition of the statute. . . . In other words, when the legislative body has determined generally, in the constitutional exercise of its discretion, that utterances of a certain kind involve such danger of substantive evil that they may be punished, the question whether any specific utterance coming within the prohibited class is likely, in and of itself, to bring about the substantive evil, is not open to consideration. It is sufficient that the statute itself be constitutional, and that the use of the language comes within its prohibition.

It is clear that the question in such cases is entirely different from that involved in those cases where the statute merely prohibits certain acts involving the danger of substantive evil, without any reference to language itself, and it is sought to apply its provisions to language used by the defendant for the purpose of bringing about the prohibited results. There, if it be contended that the statute cannot be applied to the language used by the defendant because of its protection by the freedom of speech or press, it must necessarily be found, as an original question, without any previous determination by the legislative body, whether the specific language used involved such likelihood of bringing about the substantive evil as to deprive it of the constitutional protection. In such cases it has been held that the general provisions of the statute may be constitutionally applied to the specific utterance of the defendant if its natural tendency and probable effect were to bring about the substantive evil which the legislative body might prevent. Schenck v. United States [1919]; Debs v. United States [1919]. And the general statement in the Schenck Case that the "question in every case is whether the words are used in such circumstances and are of such a nature as to create a clear and present danger that they will bring about the substantive evils,"—upon which great reliance is placed in the defendant's argument,—was manifestly intended, as shown by the context, to apply only in cases of this class, and has no application to those like the present, where the legislative body itself has previously determined the danger of substantive evil arising from utterances of a specified character. . . .

And finding, for the reasons stated, that the statute is not in itself unconstitutional, and that it has not been applied in the present case in derogation of any constitutional right, the judgment of the Court of Appeals is affirmed.

Mr. Justice Holmes dissented:

Mr. Justice Brandeis and I are of opinion that this judgment should be reversed. The general principle of free speech, it seems to me, must be taken to be included in the 14th Amendment, in view of the scope that has been given to the word "liberty" as there used, although perhaps it may be accepted with a somewhat larger latitude of interpretation than is allowed to Congress by the sweeping language that governs, or ought to govern, the laws of the United

States. If I am right, then I think that the criterion sanctioned by the full court in Schenck v. United States, applies: "The question in every case is whether the words used are used in such circumstances and are of such a nature as to create a clear and present danger that they will bring about the substantive evils that [the state] has a right to prevent." It is true that in my opinion this criterion was departed from in Abrams v. United States [1919] but the convictions that I expressed in that case are too deep for it to be possible for me as yet to believe that it and Schaefer v. United States [1920] have settled the law. If what I think the correct test is applied, it is manifest that there was no present danger of an attempt to overthrow the government by force on the part of the admittedly small minority who shared the defendant's views. It is said that this Manifesto was more than a theory, that it was an incitement. Every idea is an incitement. It offers itself for belief, and, if believed, it is acted on unless some other belief outweighs it, or some failure of energy stifles the movement at its birth. The only difference between the expression of an opinion and an incitement in the narrower sense is the speaker's enthusiasm for the result. Eloquence may set fire to reason. But whatever may be thought of the redundant discourse before us, it had no chance of starting a present conflagration. If, in the long run, the beliefs expressed in proletarian dictatorship are destined to be accepted by the dominant forces of the community, the only meaning of free speech is that they should be given their chance and have their way.

If the publication of this document had been laid as an attempt to induce an uprising against government at once, and not at some indefinite time in the future, it would have presented a different question. The object would have been one with which the law might deal, subject to the doubt whether there was any danger that the publication could produce any result; or, in other words, whether it was not futile and too remote from possible consequences. But the indictment alleges the publication and nothing more.

DENNIS v. UNITED STATES

341 U. S. 494; 71 S. Ct. 857; 95 L. Ed. 1137
(1951)

The Smith Act of 1940, which in 1948 became § 2385 of Title 18 of the United States Code, directs a five-pronged attack against subversion. First, it punishes anyone who "knowingly or willfully advocates . . . or teaches the duty . . . or propriety of overthrowing . . . the government of the United

States . . . by force or violence. . . . Second, it punishes the dissemination of literature advocating such overthrow "with intent to cause such overthrow." Third, it punishes anyone who "organizes . . . any society, group or assembly of persons to teach, advocate or encourage" such overthrow. Fourth, it punishes anyone who "becomes or is a member of . . . any such society, group or assembly . . . knowing the purposes thereof." Finally, it makes it a separate offense to conspire to do any of the above things.

The validity of the act was considered by the Supreme Court for the first time in the Dennis case below. In 1948, the 11 top leaders of the American Communist party were indicted under the act for willfully and knowingly conspiring to teach and advocate the overthrow of government by force and violence, and to organize the Communist party for the purpose of so doing. The trial in District Judge Medina's court in New York ran from January 20 to September 23, 1949, and resulted in conviction. Judge Medina's charge to the jury included two important interpretations of the law. First, he ruled out the possibility that "teaching" or "conspiring to teach" alone would violate the statute. "You must be satisfied from the evidence beyond a reasonable doubt that the defendants had an intent to cause the overthrow or destruction of the Government of the United States by force and violence, and that it was with this intent and for the purpose of furthering that objective that they conspired both (1) to organize the Communist Party . . . and (2) to teach and advocate. . . ." Second, should the jury find that the statute as so construed had been violated, it was their duty to find the defendants guilty. "I find as a matter of law that there is sufficient danger of a substantive evil that the Congress has a right to prevent to justify the application of the statute under the First Amendment. . . ."

Both the conviction and this charge to the jury were upheld by the Court of Appeals in an opinion by Judge Learned Hand. The Supreme Court limited the scope of its review to the constitutional questions raised, chief of which was the First Amendment question of free speech. It did not review the sufficiency of the evidence to support the verdict.

In the five opinions written in the Dennis case, there are four interpretations of the clear and present danger test. Mr. Chief Justice Vinson, speaking for four members of the Court, paid allegiance to Holmes's statement and application of the test, but in reality adopted in its place Judge Hand's test of "clear and probable danger." The danger need not be imminent; it is enough that there is a group willing to attempt the overthrow of government if and when possible. The Chief Justice read the time element out of clear and present danger.

Mr. Justice Frankfurter had always rejected the idea that a law which on its face invades free speech must be presumed to be unconstitutional, or that the First Amendment occupies any "preferred position." See Thomas v. Collins (1945). He felt that free speech cases call for the weighing of competing interests, and that the legislative judgment embodied in the Smith Act, that the Communist threat to the security of the country justifies punitive action, is amply supported by evidence.

In an incisive concurring opinion Mr. Justice Jackson bluntly declared that the test of clear and present danger has no applicability to a criminal conspiracy such as that carried on by the Communist party. It was never intended to be applied in a case like this, and should be reserved for cases involving restrictions upon speeches and publications.

Justices Black and Douglas, dissenting, felt that the clear and present danger test had been destroyed. Justice Douglas emphasized that the defendants were charged with no overt acts, only with speeches and publications. He also felt that the question of clear and present danger should be decided by the jury and not by the court.

The decision in the Dennis case provided for the first time a legal basis for the idea that the Communist party is a criminal conspiracy dedicated to overthrowing the government of the United States by force and violence. It therefore seemed logical to suppose that any official of the party, and probably any member who was familiar with the aims of the party, could be convicted for his part in the conspiracy. Acting upon this assumption the government moved against 14 second-string Communist leaders, and in Yates v. United States (1957) the Supreme Court reversed their convictions, acquitting five of them outright and remanding the other nine for retrial. The district court, it explained, had failed to charge the jury that in order to convict it must find the defendants guilty of advocating "action" in the "language of incitement." "The essence of the Dennis holding," the Court said, "was that indoctrination of a group in preparation for future violent action, as well as exhortation to immediate action, by advocacy found to be directed to 'action for the accomplishment' of forcible overthrow, to violence 'as a rule or principle of action,' and employing 'language of incitement,' is not constitutionally protected when the group is of sufficient size and cohesiveness, is sufficiently oriented towards action, and other circumstances are such as reasonably to justify apprehension that action will occur. This is quite a different thing from the view of the District Court here that mere doctrinal justification of forcible overthrow, if engaged in with the intent to accomplish overthrow, is punishable per se under the Smith Act. That sort of advocacy, even though uttered with the hope that it may ultimately lead to violent revolution, is too remote from concrete action to be regarded as the kind of indoctrination preparatory to action which was condemned in Dennis."

Although Mr. Justice Harlan stresses that he is merely applying the doctrine of the Dennis case, it seems apparent that in insisting in Yates that advocacy amount to incitement to action, he is, without actually using the well-known phrase, moving back toward the clear and present danger rule of Holmes and Brandeis. The Dennis case was widely believed to have modified and weakened that rule.

Four years later, in Scales v. United States (1961), the Supreme Court passed on the validity of the membership section for the first time, and in a five-to-four decision held it valid as applied to Scales. It stated that this was not mere "guilt by association." The guilt was personal and punishable under the act if it was "active membership in an organization [in this case the Communist party] engaged in illegal advocacy by one having guilty knowledge and intent." Scales had been convicted first in 1955, and after a second trial and two full arguments before the Court his case was finally heard and considered in conjunction with Communist Party v. Subversive Activities Control Board (1961). Scales argued that the membership section of the Smith Act had been repealed by the section of the Subversive Activities Control Act of 1950 (requiring registration of Communists), which provides that: "Neither the holding of office nor membership in any Communist organization by any person shall constitute per se a violation of subsection (a) or subsection (c) of this section or any other criminal statute." Mr. Justice Harlan's opinion for the majority held that the section quoted from the act of 1950 clarified, rather than repealed, the membership section of the Smith Act; and he emphasized the difference between punishing a man for membership per se and punishing him for membership with guilty knowledge and with intent to aid in the violent overthrow of government. In the dissenting opinions it was urged that the act of 1950 had repealed the Smith Act provision and that the membership section violated the First Amendment.

On the same day Noto v. United States (1961) set aside Noto's conviction under the Smith Act for membership in the Communist party. The Court was unanimous. The evidence against Noto showed that the Communist organization to which he belonged had not advocated the violent overthrow of government but had merely engaged in the "abstract teaching of Communist theory." The decision rests upon the doctrine of the Yates case, and the facts distinguished it from the Scales case. Scales, who had broken with the party four years before he went to prison, was given a Christmas Day pardon by President Kennedy in 1962 after serving 15 months of a six-year sentence.

In Brandenberg v. Ohio (1969), the Supreme Court held void Ohio's criminal syndicalism act—an act passed in the 1920's and patterned after that of California which had been held valid in Whitney v. California (1927). Without actually using the words "clear and present danger," the Court held the act void as forbidding mere advocacy of violence or sabotage, whether or not it would incite the hearers to lawless action. The Court overruled Whitney v. California.

Mr. Chief Justice Vinson announced the judgment of the Court and an opinion in which Mr. Justice Reed, Mr. Justice Burton, and Mr. Justice Minton joined, saying in part:

I.

It will be helpful in clarifying the issues to treat next the contention that the trial judge improperly interpreted the statute by charging that the statute required an unlawful intent before the jury could convict. . . .

. . . The structure and purpose of the statute demand the inclusion of intent as an element of the crime. Congress was concerned with those who advocate and organize for the overthrow of the Government. Certainly those who recruit and combine for the purpose of advocating overthrow intend to bring about that overthrow. We hold that the statute requires as an essential element of the crime proof of the intent of those who are charged with its violation to overthrow the Government by force and violence. . . .

II.

The obvious purpose of the statute is to protect existing Government, not from change by peaceable, lawful and constitutional means, but from change by violence, revolution and terrorism. That it is within the *power* of the Congress to protect the Government of the United States from armed rebellion is a proposition which requires little discussion. Whatever theoretical merit there may be to the argument that there is a "right" to rebellion against dictatorial governments is without force where the existing structure of the government provides for peaceful and orderly change. We reject any principal of governmental helplessness in the face of preparation for revolution, which principle, carried to its logical conclusion, must lead to anarchy. No one could conceive that it is not within the power of Congress to prohibit acts intended to overthrow the Government by force and violence. The question with which we are concerned here is not whether Congress has such *power*, but whether the *means* which it has employed conflict with the First and Fifth Amendments to the Constitution.

One of the bases for the contention that the means which Congress has employed are invalid takes the form of an attack on the face of the statute on the grounds that by its terms it prohibits academic discussion of the merits of Marxism-Leninism, that it stifles ideas and is contrary to all concepts of a free speech and a free press. Although we do not agree that the language itself has that significance, we must bear in mind that it is the duty of the federal courts to interpret federal legislation in a manner not inconsistent with the demands of the Constitution. . . . This is a federal statute which we must interpret as well as judge. . . .

The very language of the Smith Act negates the interpretation which petitioners would have us impose on that Act. It is directed at advocacy, not discussion. Thus, the trial judge properly charged the jury that they could not convict if they found that petitioners did "no more than pursue peaceful studies and discussions or teaching and advocacy in the realm of ideas." He further charged that it was not unlawful "to conduct in an American college and university a course explaining the philosophical theories set forth in the books which have been placed in evidence." Such a charge is in strict accord with the statutory language, and illustrates the meaning to be placed on those words. Congress did not intend to eradicate the free discussion of political theories, to destroy the traditional rights of Americans to discuss and evaluate ideas without fear of governmental sanction. Rather Congress was concerned with the very kind of activity in which the evidence showed these petitioners engaged.

III.

But although the statute is not directed at the hypothetical cases which petitioners have conjured, its application in this case has resulted in convictions for the teaching and advocacy of the overthrow of the Government by force and violence, which, even though coupled with the intent to accomplish that overthrow, contains an element of speech. For this reason, we must pay special heed to the demands of the First Amendment marking out the boundaries of speech.

We pointed out in [American Communications Ass'n v. Douds, 1950] that the basis of the First Amendment is the hypothesis that speech can rebut speech, propaganda will answer propaganda, free debate of ideas will result in the wisest governmental policies. It is for this reason that this Court has recognized the inherent value of free discourse. An analysis of the leading cases in this Court which have involved direct limitations on speech, however, will demonstrate that both the majority of the Court and the dissenters in particular cases have recognized that this is not an unlimited, unqualified right, but that the societal value of speech must, on occasion, be subordinated to other values and considerations.

No important case involving free speech was decided by this Court prior to Schenck v. United States (1919). . . . Writing for a unanimous Court, Justice Holmes stated that the "question in every case is whether the words used are used in such circumstances and are of such a nature as to create a clear and present danger that they will bring about the substantive evils that Congress has a right to prevent." . . . The fact is inescapable, too, that the phrase bore no connotation that the danger was to be any threat to the safety of the Republic. The charge was causing and attempting to cause insubordination in the military forces and obstruct recruiting. The objectionable document denounced conscription and its most inciting sentence was, "You must do your share to maintain, support and uphold the rights of the people of this country." Fifteen thousand copies were printed and some circulated. This insubstantial gesture toward insubordination in 1917 during war was held to be a clear and present danger of bringing about the evil of military insubordination.

In several later cases involving convictions under the Criminal Espionage Act, the nub of the evidence the Court held sufficient to meet the "clear and present danger" test enunciated in Schenck was as follows: [Five cases, 1919–1920, are here discussed.] . . .

The rule we deduce from these cases is that where an offense is specified by a statute in nonspeech or nonpress terms, a conviction relying upon speech or press as evidence of violation may be sustained only when the speech or publication created a "clear and present danger" of attempting or accomplishing the prohibited crime, e.g., interference with enlistment. The dissents, we repeat, in emphasizing the value of speech, were addressed to the argument of the sufficiency of the evidence.

The next important case before the Court in which free speech was the crux of the conflict was Gitlow v. New York (1925). There New York had made it a crime to "advocate . . . the necessity or propriety of overthrowing . . . the government by force. . . ." The evidence of violation of the statute was that the defendant had published a Manifesto attacking the Government and capitalism. The convictions were sustained, Justices Holmes and Brandeis dissenting. The majority refused to apply the "clear and present danger" test to the specific utterance. Its reasoning was as follows: The "clear and present danger" test was applied to the utterance itself in Schenck because the question was merely one of sufficiency of evidence under an admittedly constitutional statute. Gitlow, however, presented a different question. There a legislature had found that a certain kind of speech was, itself, harmful and unlawful. The constitutionality of such a state statute had to be adjudged by this Court just as it determined the constitutionality of any state statute, namely, whether the statute was "reasonable." Since it was entirely reasonable for a state to attempt to protect itself from violent overthrow, the statute was perforce reasonable. The only question remaining in the case became whether there was evidence to support the conviction, a question which gave the majority no difficulty. Justices Holmes and Brandeis refused to accept this approach, but insisted that wherever speech was the evidence of the violation, it was necessary to show that the speech created the "clear and present danger" of the substantive evil which the legislature had the right to prevent. Justices Holmes and Brandeis, then, made no distinction between a federal statute which made certain acts unlawful, the evidence to support the conviction being speech, and a statute which made speech itself the crime. This approach was emphasized in Whitney v. California (1927), where the Court was confronted with a conviction under the California Criminal Syndicalist statute. The Court sustained the conviction, Justices Brandeis and Holmes concurring in the result. In their concurrence they repeated that even though the legislature had designated certain speech as criminal, this could not prevent the defendant from showing that there was no danger that the substantive evil would be brought about.

Although no case subsequent to Whitney and Gitlow has expressly overruled the majority opinions in those cases, there is little doubt that subsequent opinions have inclined toward the Holmes-Brandeis rationale. And in American Communications Ass'n v. Douds, supra . . . we pointed out that Congress did not intend to punish belief, but rather intended to regulate the conduct of union affairs. We therefore held that any indirect sanction on speech which might arise from the oath requirement did not present a proper case for the "clear and present danger" test, for the regulation was aimed at conduct rather than speech. In discussing the proper measure of evaluation of this kind of legislation, we suggested that the Holmes-Brandeis philosophy insisted that where there was a direct restriction upon speech, a "clear and present danger" that the substantive evil would be caused was necessary before the statute in question could be constitutionally applied. And we stated, "[The First] Amendment requires that one be permitted to believe what he will. It requires that one be permitted to advocate what he will unless there is a clear and present danger that a substantial public evil will result therefrom." But we further suggested that neither Justice Holmes nor Justice Brandeis ever envisioned that a shorthand phrase should be crystallized into a rigid rule to be applied inflexibly without regard to the circumstances of each case. Speech is not an absolute, above and beyond control by the legislature when its judgment, subject to review here, is that certain kinds of speech are so undesirable as to warrant criminal sanction. Nothing is more certain in modern society than the principal that there are no absolutes, that a name, a phrase, a standard has meaning only when associated with the considerations which gave birth to the nonmenclature. . . . To those who would paralyze our Government in the face of impending threat by encasing it in a semantic straitjacket we must reply that all concepts are relative.

In this case we are squarely presented with the application of the "clear and present danger" test, and must decide what that phrase imports. We first note that many of the cases in which this Court has reversed convictions by use of this or similar tests have been based on the fact that the interest which the State was attempting to protect was itself too insubstantial to warrant restriction of speech. . . . Overthrow of the Government by force and violence is certainly a substantial enough interest for the Government to limit speech. Indeed, this is the ultimate value of any society, for if a society cannot protect its very structure from armed internal attack, it must follow that no subordinate value can be protected. If, then, this interest may be protected, the literal problem which is presented is what has been meant by the use of the phrase "clear and present danger" of the utterances bringing about the evil within the power of Congress to punish.

Obviously, the words cannot mean that before the Government may act, it must wait until the putsch is about to be executed, the plans have been laid and the signal is awaited. If Government is aware that a group aiming at its overthrow is attempting to indoctrinate its members and to commit them to a course whereby they will strike when the leaders feel the circumstances permit, action by the Government is required. The argument that there is no need for Government to concern itself, for Government is strong, it possesses ample powers to put down a rebellion, it may defeat the revolution with ease needs no answer. For that is not the question. Certainly an attempt to overthrow the Government by force, even though doomed from the outset because of inadequate numbers or power of the revolutionists, is a sufficient evil for Congress to prevent. The damage which such attempts create both physically and politically to a nation makes it impossible to measure the validity in terms of the probability of success, or the immediacy of a successful attempt. In the instant case the trial judge charged the jury that they could not convict unless they found that petitioners intended to overthrow the Government "as speedily as circumstances would permit." This does not mean, and could not properly mean, that they would not strike until there was certainty of success. What was meant was that the revolutionists would strike when they thought the time was ripe. We must therefore reject the contention that success or probability of success is the criterion.

The situation with which Justices Holmes and Brandeis were concerned in Gitlow was a comparatively isolated event, bearing little relation in their minds to any substantial threat to the safety of the community. . . . They were not confronted with any situation comparable to the instant one—the development of an apparatus designed and dedicated to the overthrow of the Government, in the context of world crisis after crisis.

Chief Judge Learned Hand, writing for the majority below, interpreted the phrase as follows: "In each case [courts] must ask whether the gravity of the 'evil,' discounted by its improbability, justifies such invasion of free speech as is necessary to avoid the danger." We adopt this statement of the rule. As articulated by Chief Judge Hand, it is as succinct and inclusive as any other we might devise at this time. It takes into consideration those factors which we deem relevant, and relates their significances. More we cannot expect from words.

Likewise, we are in accord with the court below, which affirmed the trial court's finding that the requisite danger existed. The mere fact that from the period 1945 to 1948 petitioners' activities did not result in an attempt to overthrow the Government by force and violence is of course no answer to the fact that there was a group that was ready to make the attempt. The formation by petitioners of such a highly organized conspiracy, with rigidly disciplined members subject to call when the leaders, these petitioners, felt that the time had come for action, coupled with the inflammable nature of world conditions, similar uprisings in other countries, and the touch-and-go nature of our relations with countries with whom petitioners were in the very least ideologically attuned, convince us that their convictions were justified on this score. And this analysis disposes of the contention that a conspiracy to advocate, as distinguished from the advocacy itself, cannot be constitutionally restrained, because it comprises only the preparation. It is the existence of the conspiracy which creates the danger. . . . If the ingredients of the reaction are present, we cannot bind the Government to wait until the catalyst is added.

IV.

[The Court here considers whether the trial court was correct in not submitting to the jury the question of the existence of clear and present danger.]

. . . The argument that the action of the trial court is erroneous, in declaring as a matter of law that such violation shows sufficient danger to justify the punishment despite the First Amendment, rests on the theory that a jury must decide a question of the application of the First Amendment. We do not agree.

When facts are found that establish the violation of a statute, the protection against conviction afforded by the First Amendment is a matter of law. The doctrine that there must be a clear and present danger of a substantive evil that Congress has a right to prevent is a judicial rule to be applied as a matter of law by the courts. The guilt is established by proof of facts. Whether the First Amendment protects the activity which constitutes the violation of the statute must depend upon a judicial determination of the scope of the First Amendment applied to the circumstances of the case. . . .

V.

There remains to be discussed the question of vagueness—whether the statute as we have interpreted it is too vague, not sufficiently advising those who speak of the limitations upon their activity. . . .

We hold that §§ 2(a) (1), (2)(a) (3) and 3 of the Smith Act, do not inherently, or as construed or applied in the instant case, violate the First Amendment and other provisions of the Bill of Rights, or the First and Fifth Amendments because of indefiniteness. Petitioners intended to overthrow the Government of the United States as speedily as the circumstances would permit. Their conspiracy to organize the Communist Party and to teach and advocate the

overthrow of the Government of the United States by force and violence created a "clear and present danger" of an attempt to overthrow the Government by force and violence. They were properly and constitutionally convicted for violation of the Smith Act. The judgments of conviction are
Affirmed.

Mr. Justice Clark took no part in this case.

Mr. Justice Frankfurter wrote a concurring opinion.

Mr. Justice Jackson wrote a concurring opinion.

Mr. Justice Black wrote a dissenting opinion.

Mr. Justice Douglas wrote a dissenting opinion.

UNITED STATES v. ROBEL
389 U. S. 258; 88 S. Ct. 419; 19 L. Ed. 2d 508
(1967)

The clear and present danger test was described by Justice Brandeis as a "rule of reason" (Schaefer v. United States, 1920), and it is used by the Court to determine that point at which speech becomes so entwined with action, or so likely to bring about action, as to be punishable under a statute which forbids such action. It was for this reason that the Court refused to apply it in the Gitlow case, where the statute forbade speech, rather than action.

But some social interests are relatively of such slight value that the right of free speech apparently outweighs them even though there is a clear and present danger, and in Schneider v. Irvington (1939) the Court said that keeping the streets clean was such a value. "We are of opinion that the purpose to keep the streets clean and of good appearance is insufficient to justify an ordinance which prohibits a person rightfully on a public street from handing literature to one willing to receive it." The Court assumed there was a clear and present danger the streets would be littered. Thus the Court not only must find a speech presents a clear and present danger, but under what has come to be known as the "balancing of interests"

doctrine, must weigh the social value of the restriction against the serious-
ness of the threat to free speech.

One of the difficulties involved in applying the "balancing of interests"
doctrine is the determination of exactly what interests are at stake. When
the Supreme Court decides a case arising under the First Amendment, it
is deciding between the right of the government to protect some social value
from attack, and the right of an individual to attack it. It is easy to argue,
in such circumstances, that the interest of the one should yield to the
interests of the many—overlooking the fact that there is a vital social value
in the right of the individual to make his challenge. Such an argument
is especially persuasive where the social value involved is, or can be made
to appear to be, the very security of the nation itself. In this situation the
individual interest is bound to yield.

To avoid this almost inevitable result in cases where both the public and
individual interests are important ones, the Court has devised a new
approach which, for the sake of convenience, we will call the "minimum
infringement" doctrine. Under this doctrine the government has an obliga-
tion to achieve its social goals with the least possible infringement of First
Amendment rights, and where it appears to the Court that this standard
has not been met, the statute will be held void.

Following a wave of draft-card burning episodes by antiwar demonstra-
tors, an outraged Congress in 1965 made it a crime to "knowingly destroy"
a draft card. The following year a Boston University philosophy student
publicly burned his draft card as part of a "demonstration against the war
and against the draft." In United States v. O'Brien (1968) the Supreme
Court sustained his conviction under the act. While it rejected the idea that
"an apparently limitless variety of conduct can be labelled 'speech' when-
ever the person engaging in the conduct intends thereby to express an
idea," it proceeded to decide the case "on the assumption that the alleged
communicative element in O'Brien's conduct is sufficient to bring into play
the First Amendment." The Court applied the balancing of interests and
minimum infringement doctrines phrased in these terms: ". . . We think
it clear that a government regulation is sufficiently justified if it is within
the constitutional power of the government; if it furthers an important or
substantial governmental interest; if the governmental interest is unrelated
to the suppression of free expression; and if the incidental restriction on
alleged First Amendment freedom is no greater than is essential to the
furtherance of that interest." Judged by these standards, "the many func-
tions performed by the Selective Service certificates establish beyond doubt
that Congress has a legitimate and substantial interest in preventing their
wanton and unrestrained destruction." Unlike the "red flag" law held void
in Stromberg v. California (1931), which was aimed at suppressing com-

munication, the thrust of the present law was to prevent the destruction of draft cards. "We perceive no alternative means that would more precisely and narrowly assure the continuing availability of issued Selective Service certificates than a law which prohibits their wilful mutilation or destruction. . . . The governmental interest and the scope of the 1956 Amendment are limited to preventing a harm to the smooth and efficient functioning of the Selective Service System."

The case printed below also involves weighing a governmental measure designed for the national security against an individual's First Amendment rights. The Subversive Activities Control Act of 1950 makes it a crime, when a Communist-action organization is under a final order to register, "for any member of that organization to engage in any employment in any defense facility." Robel was a member of the Communist party and a machinist in a West Coast shipyard at the time the Communist party was ordered to register (1961) and the yard was declared a "defense facility" (1962). He continued to work, and was indicted for violating the act. The United States district court dismissed the indictment on the ground that, to be constitutional, the statute had to be read as requiring "active membership and specific intent," and there was no allegation that Robel's membership was of this quality. The Court affirmed the district court judgment but on the ground that the section violated the First Amendment. It stressed that Congress was in no way barred from achieving these same ends "under narrowly drawn legislation."

Mr. Chief Justice Warren delivered the opinion of the Court, saying in part:

We cannot agree with the District Court that § 5(a) (1) (D) can be saved from constitutional infirmity by limiting its application to active members of Communist-action organizations who have the specific intent of furthering the unlawful goals of such organizations. The District Court relied on Scales v. United States (1961) in placing its limiting construction on § 5(a) (1) (D). It is true that in Scales we read the elements of active membership and specific intent into the membership clause of the Smith Act. However, in Aptheker v. Secretary of State (1964) we noted that the Smith Act's membership clause required a defendant to have knowledge of the organization's illegal advocacy, a requirement that "was intimately connected with the construction limiting membership to 'active' members." Aptheker involved a challenge to § 6 of the Subversive Activities Control Act, which provides that, when a Communist organization is registered or under a final order to register, it shall be unlawful for any member thereof with knowledge or notice thereof to apply for a passport. We held that "[t]he clarity and preciseness of the provision in question make it impossible to narrow its indiscriminately cast and overly broad scope without substantial rewriting." We take the same view of § 5(a) (1) (D). It is precisely because that statute sweeps indiscriminately across all types of associations with Communist-action groups, without regard to the quality and degree of membership, that it runs afoul of the First Amendment.

In Aptheker, we held § 6 unconstitutional because it too broadly and indiscriminately infringed upon constitutionally protected rights. The Government has argued that, despite the overbreadth which is obvious on the face of § 5(a) (1) (D), Aptheker is not controlling in this case because the right to travel is a more basic freedom than the right to be employed in a defense facility. We agree Aptheker is not controlling since it was decided under the Fifth Amendment. But we cannot agree with the Government's characterization of the essential issue in this case. It is true the specific disability imposed by § 5(a) (1) (D) is to limit the employment opportunities of those who fall within its coverage, and such a limitation is not without serious constitutional implications. See Greene v. McElroy (1958). But the operative fact upon which the job disability depends is the exercise of an individual's right of association, which is protected by the provisions of the First Amendment. Wherever one would place the right to travel on a scale of constitutional values, it is clear that those rights protected by the First Amendment are no less basic in our democratic scheme.

The Government seeks to defend the statute on the ground that it was passed pursuant to Congress' war power. The Government argues that this Court has given broad deference to the exercise of that constitutional power by the national legislature. That argument finds support in a number of decisions of this Court. However, the phrase "war power" cannot be invoked as a talismanic incantation to support any exercise of congressional power which can be brought within its ambit. "[E]ven the war power does not remove constitutional limitations safeguarding essential liberties." Home Bldg. & Loan Assn. v. Blaisdell (1934). More specifically in this case, the Government asserts that § 5(a) (1) (D) is an expression "of the growing concern shown by the executive and legislative branches of government over the risks of internal subversion in plants on which the national defense depend[s]." Yet, this concept of "national defense" cannot be deemed an end in itself, justifying any exercise of legislative power designed to promote such a goal. Implicit in the term "national defense" is the notion of defending those values and ideals which set this Nation apart. For almost two centuries, our country has taken singular pride in the democratic ideals enshrined in its Constitution, and the most cherished of those ideals have found expression in the First Amendment. It would indeed be ironic if, in the name of national defense, we would sanction the subversion of one of those liberties—the freedom of association—which makes the defense of the Nation worthwhile.

When Congress' exercise of one of its enumerated powers clashes with those individual liberties protected by the Bill of Rights, it is our "delicate and difficult task" to determine whether the resulting restriction on freedom can be tolerated. .... The Government emphasizes that the purpose of § 5(a) (1) (D) is to reduce the threat of sabotage and espionage in the Nation's defense plants. The Government's interest in such a prophylactic measure is not insubstantial. But it cannot be doubted that the means chosen to implement that governmental purpose in this instance cut deeply into the right of association. Section 5(a) (1) (D) put appellee to the choice of surrendering his organizational affiliation, regardless of whether his membership threatened the security of a defense facility, or giving up his job. When appellee refused to make that choice, he became subject to a possible criminal penalty of five years' imprisonment and a $10,000 fine. The statute quite literally establishes guilt by association alone, without any need to establish that an individual's association poses the threat feared by the Government in proscribing it. The inhibiting effect on the exercise of First Amendment rights is clear.

It has become axiomatic that "[p]recision of regulation must be the touchstone in an area so closely touching our most precious freedoms." NAACP v. Button (1963) .... Such precision is notably lacking in § 5(a) (1) (D). That statute casts its net across a broad range of associational activities, indiscriminately trapping membership which can be constitutionally punished and membership which cannot be so proscribed. It is made irrelevant to the statute's operation that an individual may be a passive or inactive member of a designated organization, that he may be unaware of the organization's unlawful aims, or that he may disagree with those unlawful aims. It is also made irrelevant that an individual who is subject to the penalties of § 5(a) (1) (D) may occupy a nonsensitive position in a defense facility. Thus, § 5(a) (1) (D) contains the fatal defect of overbreadth because it seeks to bar employment both for association which may be proscribed and for association which may not be proscribed consistently with First Amendment rights. See Elfbrandt v. Russell [1966]; Aptheker v. Secretary of State .... This the Constitution will not tolerate.

We are not unmindful of the congressional concern over the danger of sabotage and espionage in national defense industries, and nothing we hold today should be read to deny Congress the power under narrowly drawn legislation to keep from sensitive positions in defense facilities those who would use their positions to disrupt the Nation's production facilities. We have recognized that, while the Constitution protects against invasions of individual rights, it does not withdraw from the Government the power to safeguard its vital interests. Kennedy v. Mendoza-Martinez (1963). Spies and saboteurs do exist, and Congress can, of course, prescribe criminal penalties for those who engage in espionage and sabotage. The Government can deny access to its secrets to those who would use such information to harm the Nation. And

Congress can declare sensitive positions in national defense industries off limits to those who would use such positions to disrupt the production of defense materials. The Government has told us that Congress, in passing § 5(a) (1) (D), made a considered judgment that one possible alternative to that statute—an industrial security screening program—would be inadequate and ineffective to protect against sabotage in defense facilities. It is not our function to examine the validity of that congressional judgment. Neither is it our function to determine whether an industrial security screening program exhausts the possible alternatives to the statute under review. We are concerned solely with determining whether the statute before us has exceeded the bounds imposed by the Constitution when First Amendment rights are at stake. The task of writing legislation which will stay within those bounds has been committed to Congress. Our decision today simply recognizes that, when legitimate legislative concerns are expressed in a statute which imposes a substantial burden on protected First Amendment activities, Congress must achieve its goal by means which have a "less drastic" impact on the continued vitality of First Amendment freedoms.* Sheldon v. Tucker [1960], United States v. Brown (1965). The Constitution and the basic position of First Amendment rights in our democratic fabric demands nothing less.

Affirmed.

Mr. Justice Marshall took no part in the consideration or decision of this case.

Mr. Justice Brennan wrote a concurring opinion.

*It has been suggested that this case should be decided by "balancing" the governmental interests expressed in § 5(a) (1) (D) against the First Amendment rights asserted by the appellee. This we decline to do. We recognize that both interests are substantial, but we deem it inappropriate for this Court to label one as being more important or more substantial than the other. Our inquiry is more circumscribed. Faced with a clear conflict between a federal statute enacted in the interests of national security and an individual's exercise of his First Amendment rights, we have confined our analysis to whether Congress has adopted a constitutional means in achieving its concededly legitimate legislative goal. In making this determination we have found it necessary to measure the validity of the means adopted by Congress against both the goal it has sought to achieve and the specific prohibitions of the First Amendment. But we have in no way "balanced" those respective interests. We have ruled only that the Constitution requires that the conflict between congressional power and individual rights be accommodated by legislation drawn more narrowly to avoid the conflict. There is, of course, nothing novel in that analysis. Such a course of adjudication was enunciated by Chief Justice Marshall when he declared: "Let the end be legitimate, let it be within the scope of the constitution, and all means which are appropriate, which are plainly adapted to that end, *which are not prohibited, but consist with the letter and spirit of the constitution,* are constitutional." M'Culloch v. Maryland (1819) (emphasis added). In this case, the means chosen by Congress are contrary to the "letter and spirit" of the First Amendment.

Mr. Justice White, with whom Mr. Justice Harlan joined, dissented, saying in part:

. . . Apparently "active" members of the Communist Party who have demonstrated their commitment to the illegal aims of the Party may be barred from defense facilities. This exclusion would have the same deterrent effect upon associational rights as the statute before us, but the governmental interest in security would override that effect. Also, the Court would seem to permit barring appellee, although not an "active" member of the Party, from employment in "sensitive" positions in the defense establishment. Here, too, the interest in anticipating and preventing espionage or sabotage would outweigh the deterrent impact of job disqualification. If I read the Court correctly, associating with the Communist Party may at times be deterred by barring members from employment and nonmembership may at times be imposed as a condition of engaging in defense work. In the case before us the Court simply disagrees with the Congress and the Defense Dapartment, ruling that Robel does not present a sufficient danger to the national security to require him to choose between membership in the Communist Party and his employment in a defense facility. Having less confidence than the majority in the prescience of this remote body when dealing with threats to the security of the country, I much prefer the judgment of Congress and the Executive Branch that the interest of appellee in remaining a member of the Communist Party, knowing that it has been adjudicated a Communist-action organization, is less substantial than the public interest in excluding him from employment in critical defense industries.

NEAR v. MINNESOTA

283 U. S. 697; 51 S. Ct. 625; 75 L. Ed. 1357
(1931)

The struggle to achieve freedom of the press has been long and difficult. Once the invention of the printing press made possible the dissemination of information to the people generally, it became painfully clear to the monarchs of Europe that here lay a serious threat to their absolute powers. Their first reaction was to outlaw and destroy this new engine of seditious propaganda. Failing in this, they resorted to a system of licensing under which all publications, before being released to the public, had to be submitted to the King's Licenser. Serious penalties were meted out to those whose publications did not bear the official "imprimatur." Obviously no criticism of the sovereign or government, whether just or unjust, could be published under such a system; and the long fight against the official licenser was a major part of the fight to establish democratic institutions.

It is against this background that the case of Near v. Minnesota must be read. The law involved had been dubbed the "Minnesota gag law." It provided for the "padlocking," by injunctive process, of a newspaper for printing matter which was scandalous, malicious, defamatory or obscene. Such a "padlock" injunction, enforceable by the customary process of summary punishment for contempt of court, could be lifted only by convincing the judge who issued it that the publication would, in the future, be unobjectionable. This, in the judgment of the majority of the Court, amounted to previous censorship of publication and a violation of long-established canons of free speech and press.

The present case represents the climax of a striking evolution in our constitutional law whereby freedom of speech and press was at last effectively "nationalized" or confided to the protection of the federal courts against both national and state impairment. The steps in that evolution are traced in the note to Powell v. Alabama. The case of Near v. Minnesota was the first case in which a state law was held unconstitutional as violating that freedom of press protected by the due process clause of the Fourteenth Amendment.

Mr. Chief Justice Hughes delivered the opinion of the Court, saying in part:

Chapter 285 of the Session Laws of Minnesota for the year 1925 provides for the abatement, as a public nuisance, of a "malicious, scandalous and defamatory newspaper, magazine or other periodical." Section one of the act is as follows:

"Section 1: Any person who, as an individual, or as a member or employee of a firm, or association or organization, or as an officer, director, member or employee of a corporation, shall be engaged in the business of regularly or customarily producing, publishing or circulating, having in possession, selling or giving away,

(a) an obscene, lewd and lascivious newspaper, magazine, or other periodical, or

(b) a malicious, scandalous and defamatory newspaper, magazine or other periodical, is guilty of a nuisance, and all persons guilty of such nuisance may be enjoined, as hereinafter provided.

"Participation in such business shall constitute a commission of such nuisance and render the participant liable and subject to the proceedings, orders and judgments provided for in this act. Ownership, in whole or in part, directly or indirectly, of any such periodical, or of any stock or interest in any corporation or organization which owns the same in whole or in part, or which publishes the same, shall constitute such participation. . . ."

Section two provides that whenever any such nuisance is committed or exists, the county attorney of any county where any such periodical is published or circulated, or, in case of his failure or refusal to proceed upon written request in good faith of a reputable citizen, the attorney general, or upon like failure or refusal of the latter, any citizen of the county, may maintain an action in the district court of the county in the name of the state to enjoin perpetually the persons committing or maintaining any such nuisance from further committing or maintaining it. Upon such evidence as the court shall deem sufficient, a temporary injunction may be granted. The defendants have the right to plead by demurrer or answer, and the plaintiff may demur or reply as in other cases.

The action, by section three, is to be "governed by the practice and procedure applicable to civil actions for injunctions," and after trial the court may enter judgment permanently enjoining the defendants found guilty of violating the act from continuing the violation and, "in and by such judgment, such nuisance may be wholly abated." The court is empowered, as in other cases of contempt, to punish disobedience to a temporary or permanent injunction by fine of not more than $1000 or by imprisonment in the county jail for not more than twelve months.

Under this statute, (section one, clause (b)), the county attorney of Hennepin county brought this action to enjoin the publication of what was described as a "malicious, scandalous and defamatory newspaper, magazine and periodical," known as "The Saturday Press," published by the defendants in the city of Minneapolis. . . .

Without attempting to summarize the contents of the voluminous exhibits attached to the complaint, we deem it sufficient to say that the articles charged in substance that a Jewish gangster was in control of gambling, bootlegging and racketeering in Minneapolis, and that law enforcing officers and agencies were not energetically performing their duties. Most of the charges were directed against the chief of police; he was charged with gross neglect of duty, illicit relations with gangsters, and with participation in graft. The county attorney was charged with knowing the existing conditions and with failure to take adequate measures to remedy them. The mayor was accused of inefficiency and dereliction. One member of the grand jury was stated to be in sympathy with the gangsters. A special grand jury and a special prosecutor were demanded to deal with the situation in general, and, in particular, to investigate an attempt to assassinate one Guilford, one of the original defendants, who, it appears from the articles, was shot by gangsters after the first issue of the periodical had been published. There is no question but that the articles made serious accusations against the public officers named and others in connection with the prevalence of crimes and the failure to expose and punish them. . . .

[Upon complaint the state court ordered Near to show cause why a temporary injunction should not be issued and forbade, meanwhile, further publication of the periodical. Near demurred on constitutional grounds. The district court certified the question of the constitutionality of the statute to the state supreme court, which held it valid. Near then answered the complaint but presented no evidence, and a permanent injunction was issued.]

From the judgment as thus affirmed, the defendant Near appeals to this court.

This statute, for the suppression as a public nuisance of a newspaper or periodical, is unusual, if not unique, and raises questions of grave importance transcending the local interests involved in the particular action. It is no longer open to doubt that the liberty of the press and of speech is within the liberty safeguarded by the due process clause of the 14th Amendment from invasion by state action. . . . In maintaining this guaranty, the authority of the State to enact laws to promote the health, safety, morals and general welfare of its people is necessarily admitted. The limits of this sovereign power must always be determined with appropriate regard to the particular subject of its exercise. . . . Liberty of speech and of the press is also not an absolute right, and the state may punish its abuse. . . . Liberty, in each of its phases, has its history and connotation and, in the present instance, the inquiry is as to the historic conception of the liberty of the press and whether the statute under review violates the essential attributes of that liberty. . . .

With respect to these contentions it is enough to say that in passing upon constitutional questions the court has regard to substance and not to mere matters of form, and that, in accordance with familiar principles, the statute must be tested by its operation and effect. . . . That operation and effect we think are clearly shown by the record in this case. We are not concerned with mere errors of the trial court, if there be such, in going beyond the direction of the statute as construed by the supreme court of the state. It is thus important to note precisely the purpose and effect of the statute as the state court has construed it.

First. The statute is not aimed at the redress of individual or private wrongs. Remedies for libel remain available and unaffected. The statute, said the state court, "is not directed at threatened libel but at an existing business which, generally speaking, involves more than libel." It is aimed at the distribution of scandalous matter as "detrimental to public morals and to the general welfare," tending "to disturb the peace of the community" and "to provoke assaults and the commission of crime." . . . Men who are the victims of such assaults seldom resort to the courts. This is especially true if their sins are exposed and the only question relates to whether it was done with good motives and for justifiable ends. This law is not for the protection of the person attacked nor to punish the wrongdoer. It is for the protection of the public welfare."

Second. The statute is directed not simply at the circulation of scandalous and defamatory statements with regard to private citizens, but at the continued publication by newspapers and periodicals of charges against public officers of corruption, malfeasance in office, or serious neglect of duty. Such charges by their very nature create a public scandal. They are scandalous and defamatory within the meaning of the statute, which has its normal operation in relation to publications dealing prominently and chiefly with the alleged derelictions of public officers.

Third. The object of the statute is not punishment, in the ordinary sense, but suppression of the offending newspaper or periodical. The reason for the enactment, as the state court has said, is that prosecutions to enforce penal statutes for libel do not result in "efficient repression or suppression of the evils of scandal." . . . In the present instance, the proof was that nine editions of the newspaper or periodical in question were published on successive dates, and that they were chiefly devoted to charges against public officers and in relation to the prevalence and protection of crime. In such a case, these officers are not left to their ordinary remedy in a suit for libel, or the authorities to a prosecution for criminal libel. Under this statute, a publisher of a newspaper or periodical, undertaking to conduct a campaign to expose and to censure official derelictions, and devoting his publication principally to that purpose, must face not simply the possibility of a verdict against him in a suit or prosecution for libel, but a determination that his newspaper or periodical is a public nuisance to be abated, and that this abatement and suppression will follow unless he is prepared with legal evidence to prove the truth of the charges and also to satisfy the court that, in addition to being true, the matter was published with good motives and for justifiable ends.

This suppression is accomplished by enjoining publications and that restraint is the object and effect of the statute.

Fourth. The statute not only operates to suppress the offending newspaper or periodical but to put the publisher under an effective censorship. When a newspaper or periodical is found to be "malicious, scandalous and defamatory," and is suppressed as such, resumption of publication is punishable as a contempt of court by fine or imprisonment. Thus, where a newspaper or periodical has been suppressed because of the circulation of charges against public officers of official misconduct, it would seem to be clear that the renewal of the publication of such charges would constitute a contempt and that the judgment would lay a permanent restraint upon the publisher, to escape which he must satisfy the court as to the character of a new publication. Whether he would be permitted again to publish matter deemed to be derogatory to the same or other public officers would depend upon the court's ruling. In the present instance the judgment restrained the defendants from "publishing, circulating, having in their possession, selling or giving away any publication whatsoever which is a malicious, scandalous or defamatory newspaper, as defined by law." The law gives no definition except that covered by the words "scandalous and defamatory," and publications charging official misconduct are of that class. While the court, answering the objection that the judgment was too broad, saw no reason for construing it as restraining the defendants "from operating a newspaper in harmony with the public welfare to which all must yield," and said that the defendants had not indicated "any desire to conduct their business in the usual and legitimate manner," the manifest inference is that, at least with respect to a new publication directed against official misconduct, the defendant would be held, under penalty of punishment for contempt as provided in the statute, to a manner of publication which the court considered to be "usual and legitimate" and consistent with the public welfare.

If we cut through mere details of procedure, the operation and effect of the statute in substance is that public authorities may bring the owner or publisher of a newspaper or periodical before a judge upon a charge of conducting a business of publishing scandalous and defamatory matter—in particular that the matter consists of charges against public officers of official dereliction—and unless the owner or publisher is able and disposed to bring competent evidence to satisfy the judge that the charges are true and are published with good motives and for justifiable ends, his newspaper or periodical is suppressed and further publication is made punishable as a contempt. This is of the essence of censorship.

The question is whether a statute authorizing such proceedings in restraint of publication is consistent with the conception of the liberty of the press as historically conceived and guaranteed. In determining the extent of the constitutional protection, it has been generally, if not universally, considered that it is the chief purpose of the guaranty to prevent previous restraints upon publication. The struggle in England, directed against the legislative power of the licenser, resulted in renunciation of the censorship of the press. The liberty deemed to be established was thus described by Blackstone: "The liberty of the press is indeed essential to the nature of a free state; but this consists in laying no *previous* restraints upon publications, and not in freedom from censure for criminal matter when published. Every freeman has an undoubted right to lay what sentiments he pleases before the public; to forbid this, is to destroy the freedom of the press; but if he publishes what is improper, mischievous or illegal, he must take the consequence of his own temerity." 4 Bl. Com. 151, 152; see Story on the Constitution, §§ 1884, 1889. . . .

The criticism upon Blackstone's statement has not been because immunity from previous restraint upon publication has not been regarded as deserving of special emphasis, but chiefly because that immunity cannot be deemed to exhaust the conception of the liberty guaranteed by state and Federal constitutions. The point of criticism has been "that the mere exemption from previous restraints cannot be all that is secured by the constitutional provisions;" and that "the liberty of the press might be rendered a mockery and a delusion, and the phrase itself a by-word, if, while every man was at liberty to publish what he pleased, the public authorities might nevertheless punish him for harmless publications." 2 Cooley, Const. Lim. 8th ed., p. 885. But it is recognized that punishment for the abuse of the liberty accorded to the press is essential to the protection of the public, and that the common law rules that subject the libeler to responsibility for the public offense, as well as for the private injury, are not abolished by the protection extended in our constitutions. . . . In the present case, we have no occasion to inquire as to the permissible scope of subsequent punishment: For whatever wrong the appellant has committed or may commit, by his publications, the state appropriately affords both public and private redress by its libel laws. As has been noted, the statute in question does not deal with punishments; it provides for no punishment, except in case of contempt for violation of the court's order, but for suppression and injunction, that is, for restraint upon publication.

The objection has also been made that the principle as to immunity from previous restraint is stated too broadly, if every such restraint is deemed to be prohibited. That is undoubtedly true; the protection even as to previous restraint is not absolutely unlimited. But the limitation has been recognized only in exceptional cases. "When a nation is at war many things that might be said in time of peace are such a hindrance to its effort that their utterance will not be endured so long as men fight and that no court could regard them as protected by any constitutional right." Schenck v. United States. No one would question but that a government might prevent actual obstruction to its recruiting service or the publication of the sailing dates of transports or the number and location of troops. On similar grounds, the primary requirements of decency may be enforced against obscene publications. The security of the community life may be protected against incitements to acts of violence and the overthrow by force of orderly government. The constitutional guaranty of free speech does not "protect a man from an injunction against uttering words that may have all the effect of force. . . ."

The exceptional nature of its limitations places in a strong light the general conception that liberty of the press, historically considered and taken up by the Federal Constitution, has meant, principally, although not exclusively, immunity from previous restraints or censorship. The conception of the liberty of the press in this country had broadened with the exigencies of the colonial period and with the efforts to secure freedom from oppressive administration. That liberty was especially cherished for the immunity it afforded from previous restraint of the publication of censure of public officers and charges of official misconduct. . . .

The importance of this immunity has not lessened. While reckless assaults upon public men, and efforts to bring obloquy upon those who are endeavoring faithfully to discharge official duties, exert a baleful influence and deserve the severest condemnation in public opinion, it cannot be said that this abuse is greater, and it is believed to be less, than that which characterized the period in which our institutions took shape. Meanwhile, the administration of government has become more complex, the opportunities for malfeasance and corruption have multiplied, crime has grown to most serious proportions, and the danger of its protection by unfaithful officials and of the impairment of the fundamental security of life and property by criminal alliances and official neglect, emphasizes the primary need of a vigilant and courageous press, especially in great cities. The fact that the liberty of the press may be abused by miscreant purveyors of scandal does not make any the less necessary the immunity of the press from previous restraint in dealing with official misconduct. Subsequent punishment for such abuses as may exist is the appropriate remedy, consistent with constitutional privilege. . . .

The statute in question cannot be justified by reason of the fact that the publisher is permitted to show, before injunction issues, that the matter published is true and is published with good motives and for justifiable ends. If such a statute, authorizing suppression and injunction on such a basis, is constitutionally valid, it would be equally permissible for the legislature to provide that at any time the publisher of any newspaper could be brought before a court, or even an administrative officer (as the constitutional protection may not be regarded as resting on mere procedural details) and required to produce proof of the truth of his publication, or of what he intended to publish, and of his motives, or stand enjoined. If this can be done, the legislature may provide machinery for determining in the complete exercise of its discretion what are justifiable ends and restrain publication accordingly. And it would be but a step to a complete system of censorship. The recognition of authority to impose previous restraint upon publication in order to protect the community against the circulation of charges of misconduct, and especially of official misconduct, necessarily would carry with it the admission of the authority of the censor against which the constitutional barrier was erected. The preliminary freedom, by virtue of the very reason for its existence, does not depend, as this court has said, on proof of truth. . . .

Equally unavailing is the insistence that the statute is designed to prevent the circulation of scandal which tends to disturb the public peace and to provoke assaults and the commission of crime. Charges of reprehensible conduct, and in particular of official malfeasance, unquestionably create a public scandal, but the theory of the constitutional guaranty is that even a more serious public evil would be caused by authority to prevent publication. . . .

For these reasons we hold the statute, so far as it authorized the proceedings in this action under clause (b) of section one, to be an infringement of the liberty of the press guaranteed by the 14th Amendment. We should add that this decision rests upon the operation and effect of the statute, without regard to the question of the truth of the charges contained in the particular periodical. The fact that the public officers named in this case, and those associated with the charges of official dereliction, may be deemed to be impeccable, cannot affect the conclusion that the statute imposes an unconstitutional restraint upon publication.

Judgment reversed.

Mr. Justice Butler dissented in an opinion in which Justices Van Devanter, McReynolds, and Sutherland concurred.

NEW YORK TIMES CO. v. UNITED STATES

403 U. S. 713; 91 S. Ct. 2140; 29 L. Ed. 2d 820
(1971)

On Sunday morning, June 13, 1971, The New York Times ran on its front page a modest headline spanning columns five, six, and seven:

*Vietnam Archive: Pentagon Study Traces
3 Decades of Growing U.S. Involvement*

A small box underneath said, "Three pages of documentary material from the Pentagon study begin on page 35."

In this unobtrusive way, the reading public was introduced to what was to become one of the most dramatic and sensational cases ever to reach the Supreme Court. The study, tracing the deliberate involvement of the United States in Vietnam during the administrations of four presidents, was based on a 7000-word top secret study made by the Pentagon and was turned over to the Times *by Daniel Ellsberg, a Pentagon employee, as an act of conscience.*

The following Monday night, just as the third in the series was about to appear, the Justice Department called the Times *and asked them to desist from further publication on the ground that publication violated the Espionage Act. The* Times *refused, and Tuesday afternoon the Attorney General filed a motion for an injunction in the district court in New York. That afternoon District Judge Gurfein, who just that day had started work as a federal judge, issued the first federal injunction against a newspaper publication in the history of the nation.*

Three days later the district court in Washington refused to enjoin the publication of the "Pentagon Papers" by the Washington Post, and the following day Judge Gurfein abolished his restraining order. Both orders freeing the newspapers were set aside by courts of appeal within hours and on Wednesday of the following week the Boston Globe was added to the list.

Following the decision in the present case, Ellsberg, and his assistant, Anthony Russo, were indicted by a federal grand jury for stealing and releasing the papers. The trial jury had been no more than sworn in the case when Justice Douglas, sitting as a circuit justice, stayed the trial pending a determination of whether the defendants were entitled to hear the tapes of unwarranted government eavesdropping involving one of the defense attorneys. The case ultimately resumed, only to be plagued by the disclosures that the FBI had tapped Ellsberg's telephone in 1969 and 1970 (before the Pentagon Papers were published), that investigators under the direction of White House staff members broke into the office of Ellsberg's psychiatrist, and that the presiding judge, W. Matthew Byrne, Jr., had twice been offered the directorship of the FBI by presidential aide John Ehrlichman while the trial was in progress. In mid-May 1973, clearly angered by the government's overzealous behavior, Judge Byrne dismissed all charges against Ellsberg and Russo and ordered that they not be brought to trial again.

While it is perhaps true, as Justice Holmes said, that great cases make bad law, the importance of the Supreme Court's decision in the present case would be hard to overstate. Over the past forty years, the growing complexity and pervasiveness of government have resulted in a steady increase in presidential power at the expense of congressional power. Nowhere is this more apparent than in the areas of foreign affairs and national defense, in which the President has special constitutional authority, and it is widely assumed that constitutional limitations on presidential prerogatives in these areas should bow to presidential determinations of what the national security requires. The Supreme Court has apparently agreed, and not since Ex parte Milligan (1866), except for the Steel Seizure Case in 1952, has the Supreme Court said "no" to the President on matters of this kind. It thus came as a shock to those who approve such presidential authority that the Court should refuse to prevent the publication of material which the government deemed harmful to the national interest despite the refusal of Congress to provide such a remedy.

While Justice Black was probably right in saying that the First Amendment was drafted to prevent just such assumptions of governmental power over the press, his contention that the Amendment should be applied absolutely literally was so at odds with its judicial development that it attracted few adherents. Far more impressive were the votes of Justices

Stewart and White, who felt that the publication was certainly wrong and might even be a crime, but refused to enjoin it because the "heavy burden" borne by the government under the First Amendment had not been met.

In a far less spectacular case decided some six weeks before the Pentagon Papers case the Court also held void an injunction against publication —in this case the distribution of pamphlets in the home neighborhood of an Illinois realtor accused of "block-busting." The leaflets were designed to let "his neighbors know what he was doing to us" in the hope he would agree to stop such tactics. Rejecting the argument that the purpose of the leaflets was to force "rather than inform" and that the injunction was a valid protection for the realtor's right of privacy, the Court held it void as a previous restraint on speech and publication. "The claim that the expressions were intended to exercise a coercive impact on respondent does not remove them from the reach of the First Amendment. Petitioners plainly intended to influence respondent's conduct by their activities; this is not fundamentally different from the function of a newspaper. . . . But so long as the means are peaceful, the communication need not meet standards of acceptability." See Organization for a Better Austin v. Keefe (1971).

In Branzburg v. Hayes (1972) the Supreme Court refused to create a constitutional privilege under the First Amendment for newsmen to withhold confidential sources of information from a grand jury investigating crime. The case involved newspaper reporters who had won the confidence of drug users and of the Black Panther Party and had written behind-the-scenes stories about them. Grand juries investigating these matters subpoenaed the reporters to testify and they refused on the ground that to do so would dry up their news sources and obstruct the free flow of news protected by the First Amendment. A five-man majority rejected their claim, holding that "the First Amendment does not guarantee the press a constitutional right of special access to information not available to the public generally." Nor was there any evidence that there would be "a significant constriction of the flow of news to the public" if newsmen had to testify like anyone else, and it was clear that the state's interest in "extirpating the traffic in illegal drugs, in forestalling assassination attempts on the President, and in preventing the community from being disrupted" were "compelling" enough to justify this indirect burden on the press. Justice Stewart, speaking for three of the four dissenters, argued that the Court has now shifted the burden to those trying to defend their First Amendment rights, and notes that the victory of the grand jury is a Pyrrhic one at best. "The sad paradox of the Court's position is that when a grand jury may exercise an unbridled subpoena power, and sources involved in sensitive matters become fearful of disclosing information, the newsman will not only cease to be a useful grand jury witness; he will cease to investigate and publish information about issues of public import."

Per Curiam.

We granted certiorari in these cases in which the United States seeks to enjoin the New York Times and the Washington Post from publishing the contents of a classified study entitled "History of U.S. Decision-Making Process on Viet Nam Policy."

"Any system of prior restraints of expression comes to this Court bearing a heavy presumption against its constitutional validity." Bantam Books, Inc. v. Sullivan (1963); see also Near v. Minnesota (1931). The Government "thus carries a heavy burden of showing justification for the imposition of such a restraint." Organization for a Better Austin v. Keefe (1971). The District Court for the Southern District of New York in the New York Times case and the District Court for the District of Columbia and the Court of Appeals for the District of Columbia Circuit in the Washington Post case held that the Government had not met that burden. We agree.

The judgment of the Court of Appeals for the District of Columbia Circuit is therefore affirmed. The order of the Court of Appeals for the Second Circuit is reversed and the case is remanded with directions to enter a judgment affirming the judgment of the District Court for the Southern District of New York. The stays entered June 25, 1971, by the Court are vacated. The judgments shall issue forthwith.

So ordered.

Mr. Justice Black, with whom Mr. Justice Douglas joins, concurring, said in part:

. . . I agree completely that we must affirm the judgment of the Court of Appeals for the District of Columbia Circuit and reverse the judgment of the Court of Appeals for the Second Circuit for the reasons stated by my Brothers Douglas and Brennan. In my view it is unfortunate that some of my Brethren are apparently willing to hold that the publication of news may sometimes be enjoined. Such a holding would make a shambles of the First Amendment. . . .

In seeking injunctions against these newspapers and its presentation to the Court, the Executive Branch seems to have forgotten the essential purpose and history of the First Amendment. When the Constitution was adopted, many people strongly opposed it because the document contained no Bill of Rights to safeguard certain basic freedoms. They especially feared that the new powers granted to a central government might be interpreted to permit the government to curtail freedom of religion, press, assembly, and speech. In response to an overwhelming public clamor, James Madison offered a series of amendments to satisfy citizens that these great liberties would remain safe and beyond the power of government to abridge. . . . The amendments were offered to *curtail* and *restrict* the general powers granted to the Executive, Legislative, and Judicial Branches two years before in the original Constitution. The Bill of Rights changed the original Constitution into a new charter under which no branch of government could abridge the people's freedoms of press, speech, religion, and assembly. Yet the Solicitor General argues and some members of the Court appear to agree that the general powers of the Government adopted in the original Constitution should be interpreted to limit and restrict the specific and emphatic guarantees of the Bill of Rights adopted later. I can imagine no greater perversion of history. Madison and the other Framers of the First Amendment, able men that they were, wrote in language they earnestly believed could never be misunderstood: "Congress shall make no law . . . abridging the freedom . . . of the press . . . ." Both the history and language of the First Amendment support the view that the press must be left free to publish news, whatever the source, without censorship, injunctions, or prior restraints.

In the First Amendment the Founding Fathers gave the free press the protection it must have to fulfill its essential role in our democracy. The press was to serve the governed, not the governors. The Government's power to censor the press was abolished so that the press would remain forever free to censure the Government. The press was protected so that it could bare the secrets of government and inform the people. Only a free and unrestrained press can effectively expose deception in government. And paramount among the responsibilities of a free press is the duty to prevent any part of the government from deceiving the people and sending them off to distant lands to die of foreign fevers and foreign shot and shell. In my view, far from deserving condemnation for their courageous reporting, the New York Times, the Washington Post, and other newspapers should be commended for serving the purpose that the Founding Fathers saw so clearly. In revealing the workings of government that led to the Viet Nam war, the newspapers nobly did precisely that which the Founders hoped and trusted they would do. . . .

Mr. Justice Douglas wrote a concurring opinion in which Mr. Justice Black joined.

Mr. Justice Brennan, concurring, said in part:

I write separately in these cases only to emphasize what should be apparent: that our judgments in the present cases may not be taken to indicate the propriety, in the future, of issuing temporary stays and restraining orders to block the publication of material sought to be suppressed by the government. So far as I can determine, never before has the United States sought to enjoin a newspaper from publishing information in its possession. . . .

II.

The error which has pervaded these cases from the outset was the granting of any injunctive relief whatsoever, interim or otherwise. The entire thrust of the Government's claim throughout these cases has been that publication of the material sought to be enjoined "could," or "might," or "may" prejudice the national interest in various ways. But the First Amendment tolerates absolutely no prior judicial restraints of the press predicated upon surmise or conjecture that untoward consequences may result. Our cases, it is true, have indicated that there is a single, extremely narrow class of cases in which the First Amendment's ban on prior judicial restraint may be overridden. Our cases have thus far indicated that such cases may arise only when the Nation "is at war," Schenck v. United States (1919), during which times "[n]o one would question but that a government might prevent actual obstruction to its recruiting service or the publication of the sailing dates of transports or the number and location of troops." Near v. Minnesota (1931). Even if the present world situation were assumed to be tantamount to a time of war, or if the power of presently available armaments would justify even in peacetime the suppression of information that would set in motion a nuclear holocaust, in neither of these actions has the Government presented or even alleged that publication of items from or based upon the material at issue would cause the happening of an event of that nature. "[T]he chief purpose of [the First Amendment's] guarantee [is] to prevent previous restraints upon publication." Near v. Minnesota. Thus, only governmental allegation and proof that publication must inevitably, directly, and immediately cause the occurrence of an event kindred to imperiling the safety of a transport already at sea can support even the issuance of an interim restraining order. In no event may mere conclusions be sufficient: for if the Executive Branch seeks judicial aid in preventing the publication, it must inevitably submit the basis upon which that aid is sought to scrutiny by the judiciary. And therefore, every restraint issued in this case, whatever its form, has violated the First Amendment—and not less so because that restraint was justified as necessary to afford the courts an opportunity to examine the claim more thoroughly. Unless and until the Government has clearly made out its case, the First Amendment commands that no injunction may issue.

Mr. Justice Stewart, with whom Mr. Justice White joins, concurring, said in part:

In the absence of the governmental checks and balances present in other areas of our national life, the only effective restraint upon executive policy and power in the areas of national defense and international affairs may lie in an enlightened citizenry—in an informed and critical public opinion which alone can here protect the values of democratic government. For this reason, it is perhaps here that a press that is alert, aware, and free most vitally serves the basic purpose of the First Amendment. For without an informed and free press there cannot be an enlightened people.

Yet it is elementary that the successful conduct of international diplomacy and the maintenance of an effective national defense require both confidentiality and secrecy. Other nations can hardly deal with this Nation in an atmosphere of mutual trust unless they can be assured that their confidences will be kept. And within our own executive departments, the development of considered and intelligent international policies would be impossible if those charged with their formulation could not communicate with each other freely, frankly, and in confidence. In the area of basic national defense the frequent need for absolute secrecy is, of course, self-evident.

I think there can be but one answer to this dilemma, if dilemma it be. The responsibility must be where the power is. If the Constitution gives the Executive a large degree of unshared power in the conduct of foreign affairs and the maintenance of our national defense, then under the Constitution the Executive must have the largely unshared duty to determine and preserve the degree of internal security necessary to exercise that power successfully. It is an awesome responsibility, requiring judgment and wisdom of a high order. I should suppose that moral, political, and practical considerations would dictate that a very first principle of that wisdom would be an insistence upon avoiding secrecy for its own sake. . . . But be that as it may, it is clear to me that it is the constitutional duty of the Executive—as a matter of sovereign prerogative and not as a matter of law as the courts know law—through the promulgation and enforcement of executive regulations, to protect the confidentiality necessary to carry out its responsibilities in the fields of international relations and national defense. . . .

But in the cases before us we are asked neither to construe specific regulations nor to apply specific laws. We are asked, instead, to perform a function that the Constitution gave to the Executive, not the Judiciary. We are asked, quite simply, to prevent the publication by two newspapers of material that the Executive Branch insists should not, in the national interest, be published. I am convinced that the Executive is correct with respect to some of the documents involved. But I cannot say that disclosure of any of them will surely result in direct, immediate, and irreparable damage to our Nation or its people. That being so, there can under the First Amendment be but one judicial resolution of the issues before us. I join the judgments of the Court.

Mr. Justice White, with whom Mr. Justice Stewart joins, concurring, said in part:

I concur in today's judgments, but only because the concededly extraordinary protection against prior restraints enjoyed by the press under our constitutional system. I do not say that in no circumstances would the First Amendment permit an injunction against publishing information about government plans or operations. Nor, after examining the materials the Government characterizes as the most sensitive and destructive, can I deny that revelation of these documents will do substantial damage to public interests. Indeed, I am confident that their disclosure will have that result. But I nevertheless agree that the United States has not satisfied the very heavy burden that it must meet to warrant an injunction against publication in these cases, at least in the absence of express and appropriately limited congressional authorization for prior restraints in circumstances such as these.

The Government's position is simply stated: The responsibility of the Executive for the conduct of the foreign affairs and for the security of the Nation is so basic that the President is entitled to an injunction against publication of a newspaper story whenever he can convince a court that the information to be revealed threatens "grave and irreparable" injury to the public interest; and the injunction should issue whether or not the material to be published is classified, whether or not publication would be lawful under relevant criminal statutes enacted by Congress, and regardless of the circumstances by which the newspaper came into possession of the information.

At least in the absence of legislation by Congress, based on its own investigations and findings, I am quite unable to agree that the inherent powers of the Executive and the courts reach so far as to authorize remedies having such sweeping potential for inhibiting publications by the press. . . .

When the Espionage Act was under consideration in 1917, Congress eliminated from the bill a provision that would have given the President broad powers in time of war to proscribe, under threat of criminal penalty, the publication of various categories of information related to the national defense. Congress at that time was unwilling to clothe the President with such far-reaching powers to monitor the press . . . . However, these same members of Congress appeared to have little doubt that newspapers would be subject to criminal prosecution if they insisted on publishing information of the type Congress had itself determined should not be revealed. . . .

. . . If any of the material here at issue is of this nature, the newspapers are presumably now on full notice of the position of the United States and must face the consequences if they publish. I would have no difficulty in sustaining convictions under these sections on facts that would not justify the intervention of equity and the imposition of a prior restraint. . . .

Mr. Justice Marshall, concurring, said in part:

It would, however, be utterly inconsistent with the concept of separation of power for this Court to use its power of contempt to prevent behavior that Congress has specifically declined to prohibit. There would be a similar damage to the basic concept of these co-equal branches of Government if when the Executive Branch has adequate authority granted by Congress to protect "national security" it can choose instead to invoke the contempt power of a court to enjoin the threatened conduct. . . .

Mr. Chief Justice Burger, dissenting.

So clear are the constitutional limitations on prior restraint against expression, that from the time of Near v. Minnesota (1931), until recently in Organization for a Better Austin v. Keefe (1971), we have had little occasion to be concerned with cases involving prior restraints against news reporting on matters of public interest. There is, therefore, little variation among the members of the Court in terms of resistance to prior restraints against publication. Adherence to this basic constitutional principle, however, does not make these cases simple. In these cases, the imperative of a free and unfettered press comes into collision with another imperative, the effective functioning of a complex modern government and specifically the effective exercise of certain constitutional powers of the Executive. Only those who view the First Amendment as an absolute in all circumstances—a view I respect, but reject—can find such cases as these to be simple or easy.

These cases are not simple for another and more immediate reason. We do not know the facts of the cases. No District Judge knew all the facts. No Court of Appeals judge knew all the facts. No member of this Court knows all the facts.

Why are we in this posture, in which only those judges to whom the First Amendment is absolute and permits of no restraint in any circumstances or for any reason, are really in a position to act?

I suggest we are in this posture because these cases have been conducted in unseemly haste. Mr. Justice Harlan covers the chronology of events demonstrating the hectic pressures under which these cases have been processed and I need not restate them. The prompt setting of these cases reflects our universal abhorrence of prior restraint. But prompt judicial action does not mean unjudicial haste.

Here, moreover, the frenetic haste is due in large part to the manner in which the Times proceeded from the date it obtained the purloined documents. . . .

The consequence of all this melancholy series of events is that we literally do not know what we are acting on. As I see it we have been forced to deal with litigation concerning rights of great magnitude without an adequate record, and surely without time for adequate treatment either in the prior proceedings or in this Court. It is interesting to note that counsel on both sides in oral argument before this Court, were frequently unable to respond to questions on factual points. Not surprisingly they pointed out that they had been working literally "around the clock" and simply were unable to review the documents that give rise to these cases and were not familiar with them. This Court is in no better posture. I agree generally with Mr. Justice Harlan and Mr. Justice Blackmun but I am not prepared to reach the merits.*

I would affirm the Court of Appeals for the Second Circuit and allow the District Court to complete the trial aborted by our grant of certiorari, meanwhile preserving the status quo in the Post case. I would direct that the District Court on remand give priority to the Times case to the exclusion of all other business of that court but I would not set arbitrary deadlines.

I should add that I am in general agreement with much of what Mr. Justice White has expressed with respect to penal sanctions concerning communication or retention of documents or information relating to the national defense.

We all crave speedier judicial processes but when judges are pressured as in these cases the result is a parody of the judicial function.

Mr. Justice Harlan, with whom the Chief Justice and Mr. Justice Blackmun join, dissenting, said in part:

These cases forcefully call to mind the wise admonition of Mr. Justice Holmes, dissenting in Northern Securities Co. v. United States (1904):

"Great cases like hard cases make bad law. For great cases are called great, not by reason of their real importance in shaping the law of the future, but because of some accident of immediate overwhelming interest which appeals to the feelings and distorts the judgment. These immediate interests exercise a kind of hydraulic pressure which makes what previously was clear seem doubtful, and before which even well settled principles of law will bend." With all respect, I consider that the Court has been almost irresponsibly feverish in dealing with these cases. . . .

Forced as I am to reach the merits of these cases, I dissent from the opinion and judgments of the Court. Within the severe limitations imposed by the time constraints under which I have been required to operate, I can only state my reasons in telescoped form . . . .

. . . It is plain to me that the scope of the judicial function in passing upon the activities of the Executive Branch of the Government in the field of foreign

*With respect to the question of inherent power of the Executive to classify papers, records, and documents as secret, or otherwise unavailable for public exposure, and to secure aid of the courts for enforcement, there may be an analogy with respect to this Court. No statute gives this Court express power to establish and enforce the utmost security measures for the secrecy of our deliberations and records. Yet I have little doubt as to the inherent power of the Court to protect the confidentiality of its internal operations by whatever judicial measures may be required.

affairs is very narrowly restricted. This view is, I think, dictated by the concept of separation of powers upon which our constitutional system rests.

In a speech on the floor of the House of Representatives, Chief Justice John Marshall, then a member of that body, stated: "The President is the sole organ of the nation in its external relations, and its sole representative with foreign nations." . . .

From that time, shortly after the founding of the Nation, to this, there has been no substantial challenge to this description of the scope of executive power. See United States v. Curtiss-Wright Export Corp. (1936), collecting authorities. . . .

The power to evaluate the "pernicious influence" of premature disclosure is not, however, lodged in the Executive alone. I agree that, in performance of its duty to protect the values of the First Amendment against political pressures, the judiciary must review the initial Executive determination to the point of satisfying itself that the subject matter of the dispute does lie within the proper compass of the President's foreign relations power. Constitutional considerations forbid "a complete abandonment of judicial control." . . . Moreover, the judiciary may properly insist that the determination that disclosure of the subject matter would irreparably impair the national security be made by the head of the Executive Department concerned—here the Secretary of State or the Secretary of Defense—after actual personal consideration by that officer. This safeguard is required in the analogous area of executive claims of privilege for secrets of state. . . .

But in my judgment the judiciary may not properly go beyond these two inquiries and redetermine for itself the probable impact of disclosure on the national security.

"[T]he very nature of executive decisions as to foreign policy is political, not judicial. Such decisions are wholly confided by our Constitution to the political departments of the government, Executive and Legislative. They are delicate, complex, and involve large elements of prophecy. They are and should be undertaken only by those directly responsible to the people whose welfare they advance or imperil. They are decisions of a kind for which the Judiciary has neither aptitude, facilities nor responsibility and which has long been held to belong in the domain of political power not subject to judicial intrusion or inquiry." Chicago & Southern Air Lines v. Waterman Steamship Corp. (1948) (Jackson, J.). . . .

Pending further hearings in each case conducted under the appropriate ground rules, I would continue the restraints on publication. I cannot believe that the doctrine prohibiting prior restraints reaches to the point of preventing courts from maintaining the status quo long enough to act responsibly in matters of such national importance as those involved here.

Mr. Justice Blackmun dissenting, said in part:

I join Mr. Justice Harlan in his dissent. I also am in substantial accord with much that Mr. Justice White says, by way of admonition, in the latter part of his opinion. . . .

Two federal district courts, two United States courts of appeals, and this Court—within a period of less than three weeks from inception until today—have been pressed into hurried decision of profound constitutional issues on inadequately developed and largely assumed facts without the careful delibera- tion that, one could hope, should characterize the American judicial process. There has been much writing about the law and little knowledge and less digestion of the facts. In the New York case the judges, both trial and appel- late, had not yet examined the basic material when the case was brought here. In the District of Columbia case, little more was done, and what was accom- plished in this respect was only on required remand, with the Washington Post, on the excuse that it was trying to protect its source of information, initially refusing to reveal what material it actually possessed, and with the District Court forced to make assumptions as to that possession.

With such respect as may be due to the contrary view, this, in my opinion, is not the way to try a lawsuit of this magnitude and asserted importance. It is not the way for federal courts to adjudicate, and to be required to adjudicate, issues that allegedly concern the Nation's vital welfare. The country would be none the worse off were the cases tried quickly, to be sure, but in the customary and properly deliberative manner. The most recent of the material, it is said, dates no later than 1968, already about three years ago, and the Times itself took three months to formulate its plan of procedure and, thus, deprived its public for that period. . . .

PARIS ADULT THEATER I v. SLATON
413 U. S. 49; 93 S. Ct. 2628; 37 L. Ed. 2d 446
(1973)

In contrast to experience in Europe where books and periodicals had been the subject of censorship, the only focus of overt and systematic censorship in the United States was the motion picture. Early movies were largely thought of as entertainment subject to the same police control as stage shows and a number of cities and states censored them for anti-social content. It was not until 1952 that the Supreme Court finally held them to be part of the press of the country protected by the First Amendment, and even then it refused to outlaw their censorship entirely. In Burstyn v. Wilson (1952) it held void New York's censorship of The Miracle *for being sacrilegious, and while it made clear that "the state has no legitimate interest in protecting any or all religions from views distasteful to them," it also emphasized that "it does not follow that the Constitution requires absolute freedom to exhibit every motion picture of every kind at all times and places."*

For nearly a decade after Burstyn the Court held void all challenged exercises of censorship without forbidding censorship in theory but without saying what kind of censorship would be upheld. Doubts arose as to whether any *censorship would be approved, until finally a case came to the Court where the film was not submitted to the censor and a direct challenge was made to the censorship as censorship. In Times Film Corp. v. Chicago (1961) the Court held the censorship valid. A five-man majority pointed out that "one of the exceptional cases" mentioned in Near v. Minnesota (1931) where prior censorship might be permitted included " 'the primary requirements of decency [that] may be enforced against obscene publications,' " and refused to hold, under "petitioner's broadside attack," that "the State is stripped of all constitutional power to prevent, in the most effective fashion, the utterance of this class of speech." The dissenting justices complained that the Court was abandoning the restraints on prior censorship "without requiring any demonstration that this is an exceptional case, whatever that might be, and without any indication that Chicago has sustained the 'heavy burden' which was supposed to have been placed upon it. Clearly, this is neither an exceptional case nor has Chicago sustained any burden. . . ."*

Closely allied to the problem of movie censorship is the problem presented by the publication of obscene material generally, and the constitutional theories involved are closely intertwined. Although a state may not resort to prior censorship of the press, it does have authority to punish the publication of matter offensive to public morals and decency. While it had long been assumed that clearly obscene publications could validly be punished, the question was never squarely decided by the Supreme Court until 1957 in the case of Roth v. United States involving the prosecution of Roth by the federal government for sending obscene matter through the mails. On historical grounds the Court decided that the First Amendment was not intended to protect obscenity, and therefore the question whether an obscene publication presented a clear and present danger of "antisocial conduct" was entirely irrelevant.

The states, however, have experienced great difficulty in drafting legislation under which the publication of such material can validly be punished. In the first place, the problem of finding a sufficiently clear definition of crime in this area has proved to be an extremely challenging one. The state may, of course, properly forbid the publication of "lewd, lascivious, sala-cious, obscene and filthy" matter. These are words with which the courts are familiar; and despite the diverse results obtained in their interpreta-tions, they constitute valid definitions of crime.

In the second place, such machinery as the state provides for enforce-ment must be so designed that publications which are protected by the First Amendment are not suppressed along with those that enjoy no such protec-tion. In Butler v. Michigan (1957) the Supreme Court held unconstitu-tional a Michigan statute which forbade "any person" to sell or give away anything "containing obscene, immoral, lewd or lascivious language . . . tending to incite minors to violent or depraved or immoral acts, manifestly tending to the corruption of the morals of youth. . . ." The Court set aside the conviction of an adult who sold such a book to another adult, in this case a policeman, on the ground that the state could not, under its police power, quarantine "the general reading public against books not too rugged for grown men and women in order to shield juvenile innocence. . . ." This, the Court decided, was "legislation not reasonably restricted to the evil with which it is said to deal. The incidence of this enactment is to reduce the adult population of Michigan to reading only what is fit for children. It thereby arbitrarily curtails one of those liberties of the individ-ual, now enshrined in the Due Process Clause. . . ." The Court noted that Michigan had a statute which forbade selling or giving such books to children, and in 1968, in Ginsberg v. New York, the Court held valid a statute forbidding the sale to children under 17 of " 'girlie' picture-maga-zines" which would not be obscene for adults.

Although the Court had insisted as early as Near v. Minnesota (1931) that "the protection even as to previous restraint is not absolutely unlim-ited," no scheme of previous censorship had ever been found valid and the Court had never undertaken to explain just what this dictum meant. It had spoken of "exceptional" circumstances that might justify such censor-ship, but it had defined them, not in terms of when or how the state could censor, but in terms of the kinds of ideas that could be suppressed. But how, without resorting to a general scheme of censorship and licensing, were these suppressible ideas to be located? How was a state to identify and suppress "utterances creating a hindrance to the . . . war effort," or which offended "the primary requirements of decency," without examining all utterances before they were published? Since it was this very "examining" before publication that the Court had held void in the Near case, the theory underlying the dictum seemed incompatible with the holding of the case. By holding valid previous censorship in the Times Film case while citing this incompatible dictum in Near as authority, the Court raised serious doubts whether or not the basic holding of the Near case had been aban-doned.

In Kingsley Books v. Brown (1957), decided the same day as the Roth case, the Court had found a procedure that met the requirements of the First Amendment. New York law provides a municipality with a "limited injunctive remedy" under which the government requests in court an injunction against the sale of an allegedly obscene book until the matter of obscenity can be determined judicially. The bookseller against whom the injunction is sought is "entitled to a trial of the issues within one day after joinder of issue and a decision shall be rendered by the court within two days of the conclusion of the trial." Only a person disobeying an injunction issued after such a trial would be subject to criminal penalty. The Court pointed out that the procedure had marked advantages over the simple criminal prosecution for selling obscene matter. It advances the public interest by preventing the sale of something already adjudged obscene, at the same time it enables a bookseller to avoid selling a book which may "without prior warning subject him to a criminal prosecution with the hazard of imprisonment." Moreover, since the act "studiously withholds restraint upon matters not already published and not yet found to be offensive," it avoids any limitation on the sale of nonobscene material.

In Freedman v. Maryland (1965) the Court brought the business of movie censorship under the Kingsley Books doctrine. While it did not actually overrule Times Film, it noted that "there is no statutory provision for judicial participation in the procedure which bars a film, nor even assurance of prompt judicial review. Risk of delay is built into the Maryland procedure." All censorship schemes then in effect, including that of Chicago, failed to meet the constitutional test.

Obscene matter, like libellous utterance, is not protected by the First Amendment; see Roth v. United States (1957). Therefore, the government has no obligation, as it does with seditious publications, to show that some punishable evil is likely to result from its dissemination; and hence there is no occasion to apply either the clear and present danger test or the "bad tendency" test. But while the punishment of both sedition and criminal libel is justified on the ground that some serious and tangible harm to society will result, there is no apparent agreement that reading pornography increases sex crimes or has any other injurious effect. Such material is suppressed here, not because it produces injurious results, but because many people find it offensive, and especially do they not want their children exposed to it. By deciding to judge obscenity by its distastefulness rather than by its potential for tangible harm, the Court has made it almost impossible to judge the validity of censorship in terms of the purpose to be served.

In the Roth case, five members of the Court agreed that obscene material was that "which deals with sex in a manner appealing to prurient interest." Such material, it was emphasized, does not enjoy constitutional protection because it is "utterly without social importance." The Court in Roth found that the jury had been properly instructed on the standard, so the conviction was valid.

In Jacobellis v. Ohio (1964) the Court again applied the Roth rule and reversed the Ohio court finding that the movie The Lovers *was obscene. The Court divided badly on the reasoning for its decision, no more than two justices agreeing on the test to be applied. Justices Brennan and Goldberg reaffirmed the Roth test, but added that "community standards" meant national not local, standards; and the question whether something was obscene could not be left solely to a jury, but must ultimately be decided by the Supreme Court itself. They also raised the "redeeming social importance" phrase to the level of an independent test, holding that any material having such importance, however slightly, could not be banned. Justices Black and Douglas joined in the judgment on the ground that punishing any publication was unconstitutional, and Justice Stewart held that the First Amendment forbids only hard core pornography "and the motion picture involved in this case is not that."*

In Memoirs v. Massachusetts (1966), six members of the Court joined in overruling a Massachusetts court decision that the book Fanny Hill, *was obscene—still without agreeing on a definition of obscenity. Justices Brennan, Warren, and Fortas reiterated the Roth rule that "(a) the dominant theme of the material taken as a whole appeals to a prurient interest in sex; (b) the material is patently offensive because it affronts contemporary community standards relating to the description or representation of sexual matters; and (c) the material is utterly without redeeming social value." They held the Massachusetts court had misapplied this test when they weighed the obscenity of* Fanny Hill *against its limited social value. "A book can not be proscribed unless it is found to be utterly without redeeming social value. This is so even though the book is found to possess the requisite prurient appeal and to be patently offensive."*

In Miller v. California (1973), a companion to the case below, the Court reaffirmed that obscenity was outside the First Amendment, but abandoned the "redeeming social value" test and substituted another: "The basic guidelines for the trier of fact must be: (a) whether 'the average person, applying contemporary community standards' would find that the work, taken as a whole, appeals to the prurient interest. . . . (b) whether the work depicts or describes, in a patently offensive way, sexual conduct specifically defined by the applicable state law; and (c) whether the work, taken as a whole, lacks serious literary, artistic, political, or scientific value. We do not adopt as a constitutional standard the 'utterly without redeeming social value' test of Memoirs v. Massachusetts; that concept has never commanded the adherence of more than three Justices at one time. If a state law that regulates obscene material is thus limited, as written or construed, the First Amendment values applicable to the States through the Fourteenth Amendment are adequately protected by the ultimate power of appellate courts to conduct an independent review of constitutional claims when necessary. . . .

"We emphasize that it is not our function to propose regulatory schemes for the States. That must await their concrete legislative efforts. It is possible, however, to give a few plain examples of what a state statute could define for regulation under the second part (b) of the standard announced in this opinion, supra: (a) Patently offensive representations or descriptions of ultimate sexual acts, normal or perverted, actual or simulated. (b) Patently offensive representations or descriptions of masturbation, excretory functions, and lewd exhibition of the genitals."

In 1974, a unanimous Court reversed the conviction of a theater operator for showing a movie which dealt with sex, but without showing "hard core" explicit sexual conduct. "Our own view of the film satisfies us that 'Carnal Knowledge' could not be found under the Miller standards to depict sexual conduct in a patently offensive way." See Jenkins v. Georgia.

In Paris Adult Theater I, the Court rejects Justice Brennan's contention that "consenting adults" should be able to see "dirty movies" if they wish. Here the city of Atlanta, Georgia, had moved, under procedures that met the test of Freedman v. Maryland (1965), to suppress two "adult" movies shown only to adults in a theater devoid of offensive advertising. The trial court agreed the movies were obscene but refused to enjoin their exhibition. The Georgia Supreme Court reversed.

Mr. Chief Justice Burger delivered the opinion of the Court, saying in part:

II.

We categorically disapprove the theory, apparently adopted by the trial judge, that obscene, pornographic films acquire constitutional immunity from state regulation simply because they are exhibited for consenting adults only. This holding was properly rejected by the Georgia Supreme Court. Although we have often pointedly recognized the high importance of the state interest in regulating the exposure of obscene materials to juveniles and unconsenting adults, . . . this Court has never declared these to be the only legitimate state interests permitting regulation of obscene material. The States have a long-recognized legitimate interest in regulating the use of obscene material in local commerce and in all places of public accommodation, as long as these regulations do not run afoul of specific constitutional prohibitions. . . .

In particular, we hold that there are legitimate state interests at stake in stemming the tide of commercialized obscenity, even assuming it is feasible to enforce effective safeguards against exposure to juveniles and to the passerby.* Rights and interests "other than those of the advocates are involved." . . . These include the interest of the public in the quality of life and the total community environment, the tone of commerce in the great city centers, and, possibly, the public safety itself. The Hill-Link Minority Report of the Commission on Obscenity and Pornography indicates that there is at least an arguable correlation between obscene material and crime. Quite apart from sex crimes, however, there remains one problem of large proportions aptly described by Professor Bickel:

"It concerns the tone of the society, the mode, or to use terms that have perhaps greater currency, the style and quality of life, now and in the future. A man may be entitled to read an obscene book in his room, or expose himself indecently there . . . . We should protect his privacy. But if he demands a right to obtain the books and pictures he wants in the market, and to foregather in public places—discreet, if you will, but accessible to all—with others who share his tastes, *then to grant him his right is to affect the world about the rest of us, and to impinge on other privacies.* Even supposing that each of us can, if he wishes, effectively avert the eye and stop the ear (which, in truth, we cannot), what is commonly read and seen and heard and done intrudes upon us all, want it or not." 22 The Public Interest 25–26 (Winter 1971). (Emphasis added.) As Mr. Chief Justice Warren stated there is a "right of the nation and of the states to maintain a decent society . . . ." Jacobellis v. Ohio (1964) (dissenting opinion). . . .

But, it is argued, there are no scientific data which conclusively demonstrate that exposure to obscene materials adversely affects men and women or their society. It is urged on behalf of the petitioner that, absent such a demonstration, any kind of state regulation is "impermissible." We reject this argument. It is not for us to resolve empirical uncertainties underlying state legislation, save in the exceptional case where that legislation plainly impinges upon rights protected by the Constitution itself. . . . Although there is no conclusive proof of a connection between antisocial behavior and obscene material, the legisla-

---

*It is conceivable that an "adult" theatre can—if it really insists—prevent the exposure of its obscene wares to juveniles. An "adult" bookstore, dealing in obscene books, magazines, and pictures, cannot realistically make this claim. The Hill-Link Minority Report of the Commission on Obscenity and Pornography emphasizes evidence (the Abelson National Survey of Youth and Adults) that, although most pornography may be bought by elders, "the heavy users and most highly exposed people to pornography are adolescent females (among women) and adolescent and young adult males (among men)." The legitimate interest in preventing exposure of juveniles to obscene materials cannot be fully served by simply barring juveniles from the immediate physical premises of "adult" bookstores, when there is a flourishing "outside business" in these materials.

ture of Georgia could quite reasonably determine that such a connection does or might exist. In deciding Roth, this Court implicitly accepted that a legislature could legitimately act on such a conclusion to protect *"the social interest in order and morality."* Roth v. United States quoting Chaplinsky v. New Hampshire (1942) (emphasis added in Roth).

From the beginning of civilized societies, legislators and judges have acted on various unprovable assumptions. Such assumptions underlie much lawful state regulation of commercial and business affairs. . . . On the basis of these assumptions both Congress and state legislatures have, for example, drastically restricted associational rights by adopting antitrust laws, and have strictly regulated public expression by issuers of and dealers in securities, profit sharing "coupons," and "trading stamps," commanding what they must and must not publish and announce. . . . Understandably those who entertain an absolutist view of the First Amendment find it uncomfortable to explain why rights of association, speech, and press should be severely restrained in the marketplace of goods and money, but not in the marketplace of pornography. . . .

If we accept the unprovable assumption that a complete education requires certain books, see Bd. of Education v. Allen (1968), . . . and the well nigh universal belief that good books, plays, and art lift the spirit, improve the mind, enrich the human personality and develop character, can we then say that a state legislature may not act on the corollary assumption that commerce in obscene books, or public exhibitions focused on obscene conduct, have a tendency to exert a corrupting and debasing impact leading to antisocial behavior? . . .

It is argued that individual "free will" must govern, even in activities beyond the protection of the First Amendment and other constitutional guarantees of privacy, and that government cannot legitimately impede an individual's desire to see or acquire obscene plays, movies, and books. We do indeed base our society on certain assumptions that people have the capacity for free choice. Most exercises of individual free choice—those in politics, religion, and expression of ideas—are explicitly protected by the Constitution. Totally unlimited play for free will, however, is not allowed in our or any other society. We have just noted, for example, that neither the First Amendment nor "free will" precludes States from having "blue sky" laws to regulate what sellers of securities may write or publish about their wares. Such laws are to protect the weak, the uninformed, the unsuspecting, and the gullible from the exercise of their own volition. Nor do modern societies leave disposal of garbage and sewage up to the individual "free will," but impose regulation to protect both public health and the appearance of public places. . . .

. . . This Court, has, on numerous occasions, refused to hold that commercial ventures such as a motion-picture house are "private" for the purpose of civil rights litigation and civil rights statutes. . . .

. . . The idea of a "privacy" right and a place of public accommodation are, in the context, mutually exclusive. Conduct or depictions of conduct that the state police power can prohibit on a public street do not become automatically protected by the Constitution merely because the conduct is moved to a bar or a "live" theatre stage, any more than a "live" performance of a man and woman locked in a sexual embrace at high noon in Times Square is protected by the Constitution because they simultaneously engage in a valid political dialogue.

... The States have the power to make a morally neutral judgment that public exhibition of obscene material, or commerce in such material, has a tendency to injure the community as a whole, to endanger the public safety, or to jeopardize, in Mr. Chief Justice Warren's words, the States' "right . . . to maintain a decent society." Jacobellis v. Ohio [1964] (dissenting opinion). . . .

Vacated and remanded.

Mr. Justice Douglas wrote a dissenting opinion.

Mr. Justice Brennan, with whom Mr. Justice Stewart and Mr. Justice Marshall joined, dissenting, said in part:

III.

Our experience with the Roth approach has certainly taught us that the outright suppression of obscenity cannot be reconciled with the fundamental principles of the First and Fourteenth Amendments. For we have failed to formulate a standard that sharply distinguishes protected from unprotected speech, and out of necessity, we have resorted to the Redrup approach, which resolves cases as between the parties, but offers only the most obscure guidance to legislation, adjudication by other courts, and primary conduct. By disposing of cases through summary reversal or denial of certiorari we have deliberately and effectively obscured the rationale underlying the decisions. It comes as no surprise that judicial attempts to follow our lead conscientiously have often ended in hopeless confusion.

Of course, the vagueness problem would be largely of our own creation if it stemmed primarily from our failure to reach a consensus on any one standard. But after 16 years of experimentation and debate I am reluctantly forced to the conclusion that none of the available formulas, including the one announced today, can reduce the vagueness to a tolerable level while at the same time striking an acceptable balance between the protections of the First and Fourteenth Amendments, on the one hand, and on the other the asserted state interest in regulating the dissemination of certain sexually oriented materials. Any effort to draw a constitutionally acceptable boundary on state power must resort to such indefinite concepts as "prurient interest," "patent offensive-ness," "serious literary value," and the like. The meaning of these concepts necessarily varies with the experience, outlook, and even idiosyncracies of the person defining them. Although we have assumed that obscenity does exist and that we "know it when [we] see it," Jacobellis v. Ohio [1964] (Stewart, J., concurring), we are manifestly unable to describe it in advance except by reference to concepts so elusive that they fail to distinguish clearly between protected and unprotected speech. . . .

The problems of fair notice and chilling protected speech are very grave standing alone. But it does not detract from their importance to recognize that a vague statute in this area creates a third, although admittedly more subtle, set of problems. These problems concern the institutional stress that inevitably results where the line separating protected from unprotected speech is exces-sively vague. . . .

. . . The problem is, rather, that one cannot say with certainty that material is obscene until at least five members of this Court, applying inevitably obscure standards, have pronounced it so. The number of obscenity cases on our docket gives ample testimony to the burden that has been placed upon this Court.

But the sheer number of the cases does not define the full extent of the institutional problem. For quite apart from the number of cases involved and the need to make a fresh constitutional determination in each case, we are tied to the "absurd business of perusing and viewing the miserable stuff that pours into the Court . . . ." . . . While the material may have varying degrees of social importance, it is hardly a source of edification to the members of this Court who are compelled to view it before passing on its obscenity. . . .

. . . In addition, the uncertainty of the standards creates a continuing source of tension between the state and federal courts, since the need for an indepen-dent determination by this Court seems to render superfluous even the most conscientious analysis by state tribunals. And our inability to justify our decisions with a persuasive rationale—or indeed, any rationale at all—neces-sarily created the impression that we are merely second-guessing state court judges.

The severe problems arising from the lack of fair notice, from the chill on protected expression, and from the stress imposed on the state and federal judicial machinery persuade me that a significant change in direction is ur-gently required. I turn, therefore, to the alternatives that are now open.

IV.

1. The approach requiring the smallest deviation from our present course would be to draw a new line between protected and unprotected speech, still permitting the States to suppress all material on the unprotected side of the

line. In my view, clarity cannot be obtained pursuant to this approach except by drawing a line that resolves all doubts in favor of state power and against the guarantees of the First Amendment. We could hold, for example, that any depiction or description of human sexual organs, irrespective of the manner or purpose of the portrayal, is outside the protection of the First Amendment and therefore open to suppression by the States. . . .

2. The alternative adopted by the Court today recognizes that a prohibition against any depiction or description of human sexual organs could not be reconciled with the guarantees of the First Amendment. But the Court does retain the view that certain sexually oriented material can be considered obscene and therefore unprotected by the First and Fourteenth Amendments. To describe that unprotected class of expression, the Court adopts a restatement of the Roth-Memoirs definition of obscenity . . . .

The differences between this formulation and the three-pronged Memoirs test are, for the most part, academic.* . . .

Although the Court's restatement substantially tracks the three-part test announced in Memoirs v. Massachusetts, it does purport to modify the "social value" component of the test. Instead of requiring, as did Roth and Memoirs, that state suppression be limited to materials utterly lacking in social value, the Court today permits suppression if the government can prove that the materials lack "*serious* literary, artistic, political or scientific value." But the definition of "obscenity" as expression utterly lacking in social importance is the key to the conceptual basis of Roth and our subsequent opinions. In Roth we held that certain expression is obscene, and thus outside the protection of the First Amendment, precisely *because* it lacks even the slightest redeeming social value. . . . The Court's approach necessarily assumes that some works will be deemed obscene—even though they clearly have *some* social value— because the State was able to prove that the value, measured by some unspecified standard, was not sufficiently "serious" to warrant constitutional protection. That result is not merely inconsistent with our holding in Roth; it is nothing less than a rejection of the fundamental First Amendment premises and rationale of the Roth opinion and an invitation to widespread suppression

---

*While the Court's modification of the Memoirs test is small, it should still prove sufficient to invalidate virtually every state law relating to the suppression of obscenity. For, under the Court's restatement, a statute must specifically enumerate certain forms of sexual conduct, the depiction of which is to be prohibited. It seems highly doubtful to me that state courts will be able to construe state statutes so as to incorporate a carefully itemized list of various forms of sexual conduct, and thus to bring them into conformity with the Court's requirements. . . . The statutes of at least one State should, however, escape the wholesale invalidation. Oregon has recently revised its statute to prohibit only the distribution of obscene materials to juveniles or unconsenting adults. The enactment of this principle is, of course, a choice constitutionally open to every State even under the Court's decision.

of sexually oriented speech. Before today, the protections of the First Amendment have never been thought limited to expression of *serious* literary or political value. See ... Cohen v. California (1971); Terminiello v. Chicago (1949).

Although the Court concedes that "Roth presumed 'obscenity' to be 'utterly without redeeming social importance,' " it argues that Memoirs produced "a drastically altered test that called on the prosecution to prove a negative, i.e., that the material was 'utterly without redeeming social value'—a burden virtually impossible to discharge under our criminal standards of proof." One should hardly need to point out that under the third component of the Court's test the prosecution is still required to "prove a negative"—i.e., that the material lacks serious literary, artistic, political, or scientific value. Whether it will be easier to prove that material lacks "serious" value than to prove that it lacks any value at all remains, of course, to be seen.

In any case, even if the Court's approach left undamaged the conceptual framework of Roth, and even if it clearly barred the suppression of works with at least some social value, I would nevertheless be compelled to reject it. For it is beyond dispute that the approach can have no ameliorative impact on the cluster of problems that grow out of the vagueness of our current standards.
. . .

V.

Our experience since Roth requires us not only to abandon the effort to pick out obscene materials on a case-by-case basis, but also to reconsider a fundamental postulate of Roth: that there exists a definable class of sexually oriented expression that may be totally suppressed by the Federal and State governments. Assuming that such a class of expression does in fact exist, I am forced to conclude that the concept of "obscenity" cannot be defined with sufficient specificity and clarity to provide fair notice to persons who create and distribute sexually oriented materials, to prevent substantial erosions of protected speech as a by-product of the attempt to suppress unprotected speech, and to avoid very costly institutional harms. Given these inevitable side effects of state efforts to suppress what is assumed to be *unprotected* speech, we must scrutinize with care the state interest that is asserted to justify the suppression. For in the absence of some very substantial interest in suppressing such speech, we can hardly condone the ill effects that seem to flow inevitably from the effort.
. . .

If, as the Court today assumes, "a state legislature may ... act on the ... assumption that commerce in obscene books, or public exhibitions focused on obscene conduct, have a tendency to exert a corrupting and debasing impact leading to antisocial behavior," [Paris Adult Theatre v. Slaton] then it is hard to see how state-ordered regimentation of our minds can ever be forestalled. For if a State may, in an effort to maintain or create a particular moral tone, prescribe what its citizens cannot read or cannot see, then it would seem to follow that in pursuit of that same objective a State could decree that its citizens must read certain books or must view certain films. . . . However laudable its goal—and that is obviously a question on which reasonable minds may differ—the State cannot proceed by means that violate the Constitution. . . .

. . . Even a legitimate, sharply focused state concern for the morality of the community cannot, in other words, justify an assault on the protections of the First Amendment. . . . Where the state interest in regulation of morality is vague and ill defined, interference with the guarantees of the First Amendment is even more difficult to justify.

. . . I would hold, therefore, that at least in the absence of distribution to juveniles or obtrusive exposure to unconsenting adults, the First and Fourteenth Amendments prohibit the State and Federal Governments from attempting wholly to suppress sexually oriented materials on the basis of their allegedly "obscene" contents. Nothing in this approach precludes those governments from taking action to serve what may be strong and legitimate interests through regulation of the manner of distribution of sexually oriented material.

Two terms ago we noted that "there is developing sentiment that adults should have complete freedom to produce, deal in, possess and consume whatever communicative materials may appeal to them and that the law's involvement with obscenity should be limited to those situations where children are involved or where it is necessary to prevent imposition on unwilling recipients of whatever age . . . ." United States v. Reidel [1971]. Nevertheless, we concluded that "the task of restructuring the obscenity laws lies with those who pass, repeal, and amend statutes and ordinances." But the law of obscenity has been fashioned by this Court—and necessarily so under our duty to enforce the Constitution. It is surely the duty of this Court, as expounder of the Constitution, to provide a remedy for the present unsatisfactory state of affairs. I do not pretend to have found a complete and infallible answer to what Mr. Justice Harlan called "the intractable obscenity problem." Interstate Circuit, Inc. v. Dallas [1968] (separate opinion) . . . . Difficult questions must still be faced, notably in the areas of distribution to juveniles and offensive exposure to unconsenting adults. Whatever the extent of state power to regulate in those areas, it should be clear that the view I expose today would introduce a large measure of clarity to this troubled area, would reduce the institutional pressure on this Court and the rest of the State and Federal Judiciary, and would guarantee fuller freedom of expression while leaving room for the protection of legitimate governmental interests . . . .

WALKER V. BIRMINGHAM

388 U. S. 307; 87 S. Ct. 1824; 18 L. Ed. 2d 1210
(1967)

During the late 1950's and early 1960's Southern Negroes, led by such people as Martin Luther King, Jr., undertook to bring an end to segregation by nonviolent means. This was to be done by attracting public attention to segregation policies in the hope that the public conscience would be aroused and demand their abolition.

Against these efforts the Southern communities rolled out a battery of legal field pieces, some of them dating back to the early days of the common law. One of these was a prosecution for criminal trespass. Among the techniques employed to publicize segregation was the "sit-in" demonstration, in which Negroes, sometimes accompanied by sympathetic whites, would enter a restaurant or lunch counter with a WHITE ONLY sign in the window and ask to be served. When service was denied, they refused to leave, and the police would be called to arrest them for trespass.

In five cases decided in 1964 the Supreme Court reversed on nonconstitutional grounds convictions for sit-in demonstrations. Although the Court carefully avoided the issue whether state enforcement of trespass laws to effect private discrimination made the state a party to the discrimination, six justices in separate opinions indicated their stand on this issue. Justices Black, Harlan, and White argued that in the absence of a statute forbidding such discrimination, the impartial enforcement of trespass statutes does not make the state a party to the discrimination and hence does not deny equal protection, while Justices Warren, Goldberg, and Douglas argued that the framers of the Fourteenth Amendment had assumed the continued existence of the right of all citizens to enter places of public accommodation, and the refusal of the state to enforce that right as to Negroes denies them the equal protection of the law. See Bell v. Maryland, Bouie v. Columbia, Griffin v. Maryland, Robinson v. Florida, and Barr v. Columbia.

The final chapter in the sit-in cases was written in Hamm v. Rock Hill (1964), decided the same day as Heart of Atlanta Motel v. United States. Again the Court failed to reach the constitutional issue but concluded that the Civil Rights Act of 1964, by making sit-ins no longer a crime, had abated sit-in prosecutions then in progress, since the states no longer had a policy to be served by such prosecutions. Federal statutes would decree this result as far as federal crimes were concerned, and the Supremacy Clause dictated the same result for state crimes. The effect of the decision was to stop the prosecution of some 3,000 sit-in demonstrators.

A second technique relied upon by the Southern communities was the well-established right of any organized community to protect itself from a breach of the peace. Such a breach is "a substantive evil which the state can prevent" through the exercise of its police power; therefore a speech which presents a "clear and present danger" of causing a breach of the peace is punishable. Although the use of such statutes against demonstrations and "marches" presented some novel features, the general rules regarding them had been laid down years before. The Supreme Court, in reviewing cases which allege a violation of freedom of speech on this ground must determine (1) that the statute, as interpreted by the state court or by the judge in his charge to the jury, really defines a breach of the peace, and (2) that a clear and present danger of such breach actually exists.

In Chaplinsky v. New Hampshire (1942) a Jehovah's Witness called a police officer "a God damned racketeer" and "a damned Fascist," in violation of a state statute whose purpose, the state court said, was to forbid words "such as have a direct tendency to cause acts of violence by the persons to whom, individually, the remark is addressed." The Court agreed that such speech could constitutionally be punished: "There are certain well-defined and narrowly limited classes of speech, the prevention and punishment of which have never been thought to raise any constitutional problem. These include the lewd and obscene, the profane, the libelous, and the insulting or 'fighting' words—those which by their very utterance inflict injury or tend to incite an immediate breach of the peace. . . . 'Resort to epithets or personal abuse is not in any proper sense communication of information or opinion safeguarded by the Constitution. . . .' "
There was, moreover, a clear and present danger: ". . . the appellations 'damned racketeer' and 'damned Fascist' are epithets likely to provoke the average person to retaliation, and thereby cause a breach of the peace."

Another case in which the making of a speech was punished by the city as a breach of the peace is Terminiello v. Chicago (1949), a case which remains bitterly controversial. Terminiello (who denied he was a Fascist) was introduced by Gerald L. K. Smith and spoke in an auditorium in Chicago to a crowd of about 800 persons, under the sponsorship of the Christian Veterans of America. Outside, a protesting crowd of over a thousand (who denied they were Communist-led) milled about, yelling and throwing stones at the windows. Inside Terminiello spoke despite the tumult, linking Democrats, Jews, and Communists together in a speech filled with race hatred. A cordon of policemen assigned to the meeting was unable to prevent several outbreaks of violence, including the smashing of doors and windows.

Terminiello was found guilty of inciting a breach of the peace and fined $100. The trial court charged the jury that " 'breach of the peace' consists

*of any 'misbehavior which violates the public peace and decorum'; and that
the 'misbehavior may constitute a breach of the peace if it stirs the public
to anger, invites dispute, brings about a condition of unrest, or creates a
disturbance. ...'" The Supreme Court never reached the question
whether the speech itself might be punishable, because it found that the
statute as interpreted by the trial judge permitted the punishment of speech
that was protected by the Constitution: ". . . A function of free speech
under our system of government is to invite dispute. It may indeed best
serve its high purpose when it induces a condition of unrest, creates dissatisfaction with conditions as they are, or even stirs people to anger. Speech
is often provocative and challenging. It may strike at prejudices and
preconceptions and have profound unsettling effects as it presses for acceptance of an idea. . . . The ordinance as construed by the trial court seriously
invaded this province."*

*In contrast to the Terminiello decision, the Court in Feiner v. New York
(1951) upheld the disorderly conduct conviction of a Syracuse University
student for a street-corner speech in which he was apparently "endeavoring
to arouse the Negro people against the whites, urging that they rise up in
arms and fight for equal rights." The two policemen present later testified
that the mixed crowd of 75 to 80 persons "was restless and there was some
pushing, shoving, and milling around." Fearful that they could not control
the crowd if violence erupted, they asked Feiner to stop speaking and
arrested him when he refused. The Court held the trial court justified in
finding a clear and present danger of causing a riot.*

*In 1963 in Edwards v. South Carolina the Court upheld the right to
demonstrate on public property. A group of Negro students had gathered
on the statehouse lawn to protest state segregation policies. The pickets
listened to a religious harangue, sang, stamped their feet, and clapped.
They refused to disperse when ordered and were arrested for a breach of
the peace. The Court held that "the Fourteenth Amendment does not
permit a State to make criminal the peaceful expression of unpopular
views . . ." and the breach of the peace statute was so vague as to "permit
punishment of the fair use of this opportunity." In this case "there was no
violence or threat of violence on their part, or on the part of any member
of the crowd watching them. Police protection was ample. . . . And the
record is barren of any evidence of 'fighting words.'"*

*The courageous efforts of the Southern Negro to achieve racial equality
through nonviolent means won widespread admiration and support from
the liberal white community and strong encouragement was given the
National Association for the Advancement of Colored People (NAACP) in
its efforts to win recognition for Negro rights in the courts. Since the
average victim of race discrimination was ill equipped to fight for his legal
rights, the NAACP shouldered his financial burden and provided him with*

legal assistance, with the result that a number of Southern states made serious efforts to oust or cripple the organization. The result was a series of Supreme Court holdings that the organization need not divulge its membership lists either as a condition of doing business in the state (NAACP v. Alabama, 1958), or to a legislative committee investigating Communism in civil rights organizations (Gibson v. Florida Investigation Committee, 1963). Nor was its bringing of test cases punishable as barratry (NAACP v. Button, 1963), and it could not be forbidden to do business in the state (NAACP v. Alabama, 1964). All of these decisions rested on a freedom of association held to be protected by the First Amendment and made applicable to the states by the Fourteenth.

With the outbreak of racial violence in Northern cities in the summer of 1965 and with the breach between the conservative, law-oriented NAACP on the one hand and the more militant Congress of Racial Equality (CORE) and Student Nonviolent Coordinating Committee (SNCC) on the other, Northern white support for the civil rights movement fell off sharply. The 1966 civil rights bill with provisions against anticivil rights terrorism and an open housing provision failed to pass Congress, and in the fall elections of that year a number of congressional candidates and advocates of referendum measures exploited the fear of "black power" and looked, in some cases successfully, to a "white backlash" for support.

In 1966, in Adderley v. Florida, the Supreme Court for the first time held valid a state criminal trespass statute against Negro demonstrators. A group of some 200 students from Florida A&M had marched to the jail in Tallahassee to protest the arrest of some of their body for trying to integrate public theaters, as well as against segregation policies generally. Over 100 remained after being ordered to leave, and were arrested for trespass. In contrast to Edwards and Cox, the Court held the trespass statute was not too broad to be valid. "It is aimed at conduct of one limited kind, that is for one person or persons to trespass upon the property of another with a malicious and mischievous intent. There is no lack of notice in this law, nothing to entrap or fool the unwary." Moreover, the demonstration was found to be on "that part of the jail grounds reserved for jail uses," and "the State, no less than a private owner of property, has power to preserve the property under its control for the use to which it is lawfully dedicated. . . . The United States Constitution does not forbid a State to control the use of its own property for its own lawful nondiscriminatory purpose."

The difficulties that confront a state in imposing those "reasonable" limits on free speech which the Constitution allows are illustrated by cases involving the suppression of public nuisances. The Supreme Court held that a statute which forbade entirely the distribution of literature was unconstitutional. In Jamison v. Texas (1943) an ordinance forbade the *distribution of handbills on the streets of Dallas. Mrs. Jamison, a member of Jehovah's Witnesses, was convicted of violating the ordinance and fined $5.00. The Court held that "one who is rightfully on a street which the state has left open to the public carries with him there as elsewhere the constitutional right to express his views in an orderly fashion. . . . The right to distribute handbills concerning religious subjects on the streets may not be prohibited at all times, at all places, and under all circumstances."*

The state may, on the other hand, place freedom of speech under reasonable police regulations for the protection of the recognized social interests of the community. In Kovacs v. Cooper (1949) the Court upheld a Trenton, New Jersey, ordinance which forbade the use on the streets of a sound-truck which emitted "loud and raucous noises." The Court found that "loud and raucous" was a sufficiently clear definition of the crime, since it has "through daily use acquired a content that conveys to any interested person a sufficiently accurate concept of what is forbidden." Moreover, the restriction was a reasonable one, since "the unwilling listener is not like the passerby who may be offered a pamphlet in the street but cannot be made to take it. In his home or on the street he is practically helpless to escape this interference with his privacy by loud speakers except through the protection of the municipality." Here the Court was striking a balance between the right to quiet and privacy and the right to free speech.

What a state may not limit directly by statute, it may not permit a policeman or other officer to limit under a grant of administrative discretion which amounts to censorship. Many municipalities have used the device of requiring a license for all public modes of expression, and making it a crime to violate the license requirement. The Supreme Court has almost uniformly held these ordinances to be unconstitutional limitations on freedom of speech and press. If the licensing officer has authority to pass on the desirability of the intended speech, or has authority broad enough to forbid a speech protected by the First Amendment, the ordinance is void on its face because it establishes previous censorship, condemned by the Court in Near v. Minnesota (1931). Thus in Saia v. New York (1948) the Court held void an ordinance which forbade the use of a sound-truck on the streets without the permission of the chief of police: "There are no standards prescribed for the exercise of his discretion. The statute is not narrowly drawn to regulate the hours or places of use of loud-speakers, or the volume of sound. . . ."

What the state may do directly by statute it may also do through the device of administrative discretion provided the discretion is so narrow that the administrator may not censor speech or press. In Cox v. New Hampshire (1941) the Court sustained an ordinance that required a permit from a license board in order to parade in the streets. A group of Jehovah's

Witnesses staged an "information march" without applying for a permit and were convicted of violating the ordinance; the state court held that any other form of expression was open to them, and "the defendants, separately, or collectively in groups not constituting a parade or procession" were "under no contemplation of the Act." Furthermore, the discretion of the license board had to be exercised with "uniformity of method of treatment upon the facts of each application, free from improper or inappropriate considerations and from unfair discrimination." The statutory mandate was held to be a "systematic, consistent and just order of treatment, with reference to the convenience of public use of the highways." This, the Supreme Court found, was a valid use of the authority to "control the use of its public streets for parades or processions."

But if a state may not deny a person a license to speak, may it, nevertheless, enjoin a person from speaking and then punish him when he violates the injunction? This problem first arose in the case of Thomas v. Collins (1945). A Texas statute required every labor union organizer operating in the state to secure from the secretary of state an organizer's card before soliciting any members for his union. In order to get the card he had to give his name and his union affiliations and show his credentials. The secretary of state had no discretion to refuse to register such an organizer if he met these requirements. When registered, he was given a card which he was required to carry with him and show to any person whom he solicited for membership. R. J. Thomas, president of the United Automobile Workers, went to Texas after the passage of this act for the express purpose of contesting its validity. He announced his intention to address a labor union meeting, and this plan was widely advertised in advance. He did not apply for registration as a labor organizer as required by the statute. He addressed a meeting of union men and he specifically invited any nonunion person present to join the union. Prior to the meeting, a restraining order was served on Thomas, forbidding him to address the meeting in the capacity of an organizer since he had not registered; and he was later cited for contempt for a deliberate and willful violation of the order.

The Court held the statute void on two grounds. First, the statute was so broad as to make possible the punishment of legitimate speech. It forbade soliciting members, and "how," the Court said, "one might 'laud unionism,' as the State and the State Supreme Court conceded Thomas was free to do, yet in these circumstances not imply an invitation, is hard to conceive. . . . The restriction's effect, as applied, in a very practical sense was to prohibit Thomas not only to solicit members and memberships, but also to speak in advocacy of the cause of trade unionism. . . ." In the second place, there was not a clear and present danger of bringing about a sufficiently substantial injury to the public to justify the restriction: "We *cannot say that 'solicit' in this setting is such a dangerous word. So far as free speech alone is concerned, there can be no ban or restriction or burden placed on the use of such a word except on showing of exceptional circumstances where the public safety, morality or health is involved or some other substantial interest of the community is at stake. . . . A restriction so destructive of the right of public discussion, without greater or more imminent danger to the public interest than existed in this case, is incompatible with the freedoms secured by the First Amendment. . . . If the exercise of the rights of free speech and free assembly cannot be made a crime, we do not think this can be accomplished by the device of requiring previous registration as a condition for exercising them and making such a condition the foundation for restraining in advance their exercise and for imposing a penalty for violating such a restraining order."*

A similar problem was presented in Poulos v. New Hampshire (1953), which arose under a different section of an ordinance like the one involved in the Cox case. Poulos, a Jehovah's Witness, applied for a permit to speak in Goodwin Park in Portsmouth on a particular Sunday and was refused; Poulos spoke without the permit and was arrested. The state court interpreted the statute as it had in the Cox case, as requiring uniformity and impartiality of treatment. It found that Poulos had not received such treatment, and that the denial of the license had been arbitrary and unreasonable. It held, however, that Poulos was properly convicted; he had no right to violate the ordinance, but should have brought a civil suit in the courts to compel the issuance of a license.

The Supreme Court sustained the conviction on the ground that the ordinance was valid and the state could validly require that arbitrary administrative action be corrected by orderly court procedure: "It must be admitted that judicial correction of arbitrary refusal by administrators to perform official duties under valid laws is exulcerating and costly. But to allow applicants to proceed without the required permits to run businesses, erect structures, purchase firearms, transport or store explosives or inflammatory products, hold public meetings without prior safety arrangements or take other unauthorized action is apt to cause breaches of the peace or create public dangers. The valid requirements of license are for the good of the applicants and the public. It would be unreal to say that such official failures to act in accordance with the state law, redressable by state judicial procedures, are state acts violative of the Federal Constitution. Delay is unfortunate, but the expense and annoyance of litigation is a price citizens must pay for life in an orderly society where the rights of the First Amendment have a real and abiding meaning. Nor can we say that a state's requirement that redress must be sought through appropriate judicial procedure violates due process." The Court distinguished this case from Thomas v. Collins, holding that there the statute was void on its face, while here the ordinance was valid.

While Thomas v. Collins suggests that a person is free to ignore a judicial restraining order if the statute under which it is issued is void on its face, recent decisions cast serious doubt upon the vitality of this holding. In April of 1963, Martin Luther King, Jr. and two other ministers announced plans for a "march" on Good Friday to protest alleged civil rights violations in the city of Birmingham. They requested, and were denied, a permit for the march under § 1159 of the Birmingham city code which provided that the city commission "shall grant a written permit for such parade, procession or other public demonstration, prescribing the streets or other public ways which may be used therefor, unless in its judgment the public welfare, peace, safety, health, decency, good order, morals or convenience require that it be refused."

Apparently fearing the march would take place without a permit, city officials applied the Wednesday before Good Friday for an injunction against "participating in or encouraging mass street parades or mass processions without a permit." The injunction was served the following day, and that night a meeting was held at which one of the petitioners announced that "injunction or no injunction we are going to march tomorrow." No attempt was made to seek judicial review of the injunction, and the petitioners marched both on Good Friday and again on Easter Sunday, leading a group of 50 to 60 followers each time.

The petitioners were convicted both of disobeying the injunction and of marching without a license, receiving sentences of five days in jail and a $50 fine for the first and 90 days at hard labor (plus 48 days at hard labor in default of payment of a $75 fine and $24 costs) for the second. Because of their different rates of movement through the judicial labyrinth, the two cases reached the Supreme Court almost two years apart. It is interesting to speculate what the outcomes might have been had Shuttlesworth been decided before Walker, rather than the other way around.

Mr. Justice Stewart delivered the opinion of the Court, saying in part:

. . . On Easter Sunday, April 14, a crowd of between 1,500 and 2,000 people congregated in the midafternoon in the vicinity of Seventh Avenue and Eleventh Street North in Birmingham. One of the petitioners was seen organizing members of the crowd in formation. A group of about 50, headed by three other petitioners, started down the sidewalk two abreast. At least one other petitioner was among the marchers. Some 300 or 400 people from among the onlookers followed in a crowd that occupied the entire width of the street and overflowed onto the sidewalks. Violence occurred. Members of the crowd threw rocks that injured a newspaperman and damaged a police motorcycle. The next day the city officials who had requested the injunction applied to the state circuit court for an order to show cause why the petitioners should not be held in contempt for violating it. At the ensuing hearing the petitioners sought to attack the constitutionality of the injunction on the ground that it was vague and overbroad, and restrained free speech. They also sought to attack the Birmingham parade ordinance upon similar grounds, and upon the further ground that the ordinance had previously been administered in an arbitrary and discriminatory manner.

The circuit judge refused to consider any of these contentions, pointing out that there had been neither a motion to dissolve the injunction, nor an effort to comply with it by applying for a permit from the city commission before engaging in the Good Friday and Easter Sunday parades. Consequently, the court held that the only issues before it were whether it had jurisdiction to issue the temporary injunction, and whether thereafter the petitioners had knowingly violated it. Upon these issues the court found against the petitioners, and imposed upon each of them a sentence of five days in jail and a $50 fine, in accord with an Alabama statute.

The Supreme Court of Alabama affirmed. . . .

Howat v. Kansas [1922] was decided by this Court almost 50 years ago. That was a case in which people had been punished by a Kansas trial court for refusing to obey an anti-strike injunction issued under the state industrial relations act. They had claimed a right to disobey the court's order upon the ground that the state statute and the injunction based upon it were invalid under the Federal Constitution. The Supreme Court of Kansas had affirmed the judgment, holding that the trial court "had general power to issue injunctions in equity and that, even if its exercise of the power was erroneous, the injunction was not void, and the defendants were precluded from attacking it in this collateral proceeding . . . that, if the injunction was erroneous, jurisdiction was not thereby forfeited, that the error was subject to correction only by the ordinary method of appeal, and disobedience to the order constituted contempt."

This Court, in dismissing the writ of error, not only unanimously accepted but fully approved the validity of the rule of state law upon which the judgment of the Kansas court was grounded:

"An injunction duly issuing out of a court of general jurisdiction with equity powers upon pleadings properly invoking its action, and served upon persons made parties therein and within the jurisdiction, must be obeyed by them however erroneous the action of the court may be, even if the error be in the assumption of the validity of a seeming but void law going to the merits of the case. It is for the court of first instance to determine the question of the validity of the law, and until its decision is reversed for error by orderly review, either by itself or by a higher court, its orders based on its decision are to be respected, and disobedience of them is contempt of its lawful authority, to be punished."

The rule of state law accepted and approved in Howat v. Kansas is consistent with the rule of law followed by the federal courts.

In the present case, however, we are asked to hold that this rule of law, upon which the Alabama courts relied, was constitutionally impermissible. We are asked to say that the Constitution compelled Alabama to allow the petitioners to violate this injunction, to organize and engage in these mass street parades and demonstrations, without any previous effort on their part to have the injunction dissolved or modified, or any attempt to secure a parade permit in accordance with its terms. Whatever the limits of Howat v. Kansas, we cannot accept the petitioners' contentions in the circumstances of this case.

Without question the state court that issued the injunction had, as a court of equity, jurisdiction over the petitioners and over the subject matter of the controversy. And this is not a case where the injunction was transparently invalid or had only a frivolous pretense to validity. We have consistently recognized the strong interest of state and local governments in regulating the use of their streets and other public places. Cox v. New Hampshire [1941]; Kovacs v. Cooper [1949]; Poulos v. New Hampshire [1953]; Adderley v. Florida [1966]. When protest takes the form of mass demonstrations, parades, or picketing on public streets and sidewalks, the free passage of traffic and the prevention of public disorder and violence become important objects of legitimate state concern. As the Court stated, in Cox v. Louisiana, "We emphatically reject the notion . . . that the First and Fourteenth Amendments afford the same kind of freedom to those who would communicate ideas by conduct such as patrolling, marching, and picketing on streets and highways, as these amendments afford to those who communicate ideas by pure speech." . . .

The generality of the language contained in the Birmingham parade ordinance upon which the injunction was based would unquestionably raise substantial constitutional issues concerning some of its provisions. . . . The petitioners, however, did not even attempt to apply to the Alabama courts for an authoritative construction of the ordinance. Had they done so, those courts might have given the licensing authority granted in the ordinance a narrow and precise scope, as did the New Hampshire courts in Cox v. New Hampshire and Poulos v. New Hampshire. . . . Here, just as in Cox and Poulos, it could not be assumed that this ordinance was void on its face.

The breadth and vagueness of the injunction itself would also unquestionably be subject to substantial constitutional question. But the way to raise that question was to apply to the Alabama courts to have the injunction modified or dissolved. The injunction in all events clearly prohibited mass parading without a permit, and the evidence shows that the petitioners fully understood that prohibition when they violated it.

The petitioners also claim that they were free to disobey the injunction because the parade ordinance on which it was based had been administered in the past in an arbitrary and discriminatory fashion. In support of this claim they sought to introduce evidence that, a few days before the injunction issued, requests for permits to picket had been made to a member of the city commission. One request had been rudely rebuffed, and this same official had later made clear that he was without power to grant the permit alone, since the issuance of such permits was the responsibility of the entire city commission. Assuming the truth of this proffered evidence, it does not follow that the parade ordinance was void on its face. The petitioners, moreover, did not apply for a permit either to the commission itself or to any commissioner after the injunction issued. Had they done so, and had the permit been refused, it is clear that their claim of arbitrary or discriminatory administration of the ordinance would have been considered by the state circuit court upon a motion to dissolve the injunction.

This case would arise in quite a different constitutional posture if the petitioners, before disobeying the injunction, had challenged it in the Alabama courts, and had been met with delay or frustration of their constitutional claims. But there is no showing that such would have been the fate of a timely motion to modify or dissolve the injunction. There was an interim of two days between the issuance of the injunction and the Good Friday march. The petitioners give absolutely no explanation of why they did not make some application to the state court during that period. The injunction had issued ex parte; if the court had been presented with the petitioners' contentions, it might well have dissolved or at least modified its order in some respects. If it had not done so, Alabama procedure would have provided for an expedited process of appellate review. It cannot be presumed that the Alabama courts would have ignored the petitioners' constitutional claims. Indeed, these contentions were accepted in another case by an Alabama appellate court that struck down on direct review the conviction under this very ordinance of one of these same petitioners. . . .

The rule of law that Alabama followed in this case reflects a belief that in the fair administration of justice no man can be judge in his own case, however exalted his station, however righteous his motives, and irrespective of his race, color, politics, or religion. This Court cannot hold that the petitioners were constitutionally free to ignore all the procedures of the law and carry their battle to the streets. One may sympathize with the petitioners' impatient commitment to their cause. But respect for judicial process is a small price to pay for the civilizing hand of law, which alone can give abiding meaning to constitutional freedom.

Affirmed.

Mr. Chief Justice Warren, whom Mr. Justice Brennan and Mr. Justice Fortas join, dissenting, said in part:

Petitioners in this case contend that they were convicted under an ordinance that is unconstitutional on its face because it submits their First and Fourteenth Amendment rights to free speech and peaceful assembly to the unfettered discretion of local officials. They further contend that the ordinance was unconstitutionally applied to them because the local officials used their discretion to prohibit peaceful demonstrations by a group whose political viewpoint the officials opposed. The Court does not dispute these contentions, but holds that petitioners may nonetheless be convicted and sent to jail because the patently unconstitutional ordinance was copied into an injunction—issued ex parte without prior notice or hearing on the request of the Commissioner of Public Safety—forbidding all persons having notice of the injunction to violate the ordinance without any limitation of time. I dissent because I do not believe that the fundamental protections of the Constitution were meant to be so easily evaded, or that "the civilizing hand of law" would be hampered in the slightest by enforcing the First Amendment in this case.

The salient facts can be stated very briefly. Petitioners are Negro ministers who sought to express their concern about racial discrimination in Birmingham, Alabama, by holding peaceful protest demonstrations in that city on Good Friday and Easter Sunday, 1963. For obvious reasons, it was important for the significance of the demonstrations that they be held on those particular dates. A representative of petitioners' organization went to the City Hall and asked "to see the person or persons in charge to issue permits, permits for parading, picketing, and demonstrating." She was directed to Public Safety Commissioner Connor, who denied her request for a permit in terms that left no doubt that petitioners were not going to be issued a permit under any circumstances. "He said, 'No, you will not get a permit in Birmingham, Alabama to picket. I will picket you over to the City Jail,' and he repeated that twice." A second, telegraphic request was also summarily denied, in a telegram signed by "Eugene 'Bull' Connor," with the added information that permits could be issued only by the full City Commission, a three-man body consisting of Commissioner Connor and two others.* According to petitioners' offer of proof, the truth of which is assumed for purposes of this case, parade permits had uniformly been issued for all other groups by the city clerk on the request of the traffic bureau of the police department, which was under Commissioner

---

*. . . The attitude of the city administration in general and of its Public Safety Commissioner in particular are a matter of public record, of course, and are familiar to this Court from previous litigation. See Shuttlesworth v. City of Birmingham (1965); Shuttlesworth v. City of Birmingham (1964); Shuttlesworth v. City of Birmingham (1963); Gober v. City of Birmingham (1963); In Re Shuttlesworth (1962). The United States Commission on Civil Rights found continuing abuse of civil rights protestors by the Birmingham police, including use of dogs, clubs, and firehoses . . . Commissioner Eugene "Bull" Connor, a self-proclaimed white supremacist. . . . made no secret of his personal attitude toward the rights of Negroes and the decisions of this Court. He vowed that racial integration would never come to Birmingham, and wore a button inscribed "Never" to advertise that vow. Yet the Court indulges in speculation that these civil rights protesters might have obtained a permit from this city and this man had they made enough repeated applications.

Connor's direction. The requirement that the approval of the full Commission be obtained was applied only to this one group.

Understandably convinced that the City of Birmingham was not going to authorize their demonstrations under any circumstances, petitioners proceeded with their plans despite Commissioner Connor's orders. On Wednesday, April 10, at 9 in the evening, the city filed in a state circuit court a bill of complaint seeking an ex parte injunction. . . . The Circuit Court issued the injunction in the form requested, and in effect ordered petitioners and all other persons having notice of the order to refrain for an unlimited time from carrying on any demonstrations without a permit. A permit, of course, was clearly unobtainable; the city would not have sought this injunction if it had any intention of issuing one.

Petitioners were served with copies of the injunction at various times on Thursday and on Good Friday. Unable to believe that such a blatant and broadly drawn prior restraint on their First Amendment rights could be valid, they announced their intention to defy it and went ahead with the planned peaceful demonstrations on Easter weekend. On the following Monday, when they promptly filed a motion to dissolve the injunction, the court found them in contempt, holding that they had waived all their First Amendment rights by disobeying the court order.

These facts lend no support to the court's charges that petitioners were presuming to act as judges in their own case, or that they had a disregard for the judicial process. They did not flee the jurisdiction or refuse to appear in the Alabama courts. Having violated the injunction, they promptly submitted themselves to the courts to test the constitutionality of the injunction and the ordinance it parroted. They were in essentially the same positions as persons who challenge the constitutionality of a statute by violating it, and then defend the ensuing criminal prosecution on constitutional grounds. It has never been thought that violation of a statute indicated such a disrespect for the legislature that the violator always must be punished even if the statute was unconstitutional. . . .

I do not believe that giving this Court's seal of approval to such a gross misuse of the judicial process is likely to lead to greater respect for the law any more than it is likely to lead to greater protection for First Amendment freedoms. The ex parte temporary injunction has a long and odious history in this country, and its susceptibility to misuse is all too apparent from the facts of the case. As a weapon against strikes, it proved so effective in the hands of judges friendly to employers that Congress was forced to take the drastic step of removing from federal district courts the jurisdiction to issue injunctions in labor disputes. The labor injunction fell into disrepute largely because it was abused in precisely the same way that the injunctive power was abused in this case. Judges who were not sympathetic to the union cause commonly issued, without notice or hearing, broad restraining orders addressed to large numbers of persons and forbidding them to engage in acts that were either legally permissible or, if illegal, that could better have been left to the regular course of criminal prosecution. The injunctions might later be dissolved, but in the meantime strikes would be crippled because the occasion on which concerted activity might have been effective had passed. Such injunctions, so long discredited as weapons against concerted labor activities, have now been given new life by this Court as weapons against the exercise of First Amendment freedoms. Respect for the courts and for judicial process was not increased by the history of the labor injunction. . . .

. . . The majority opinion in this case rests essentially on a single precedent, and that a case the authority of which has clearly been undermined by subsequent decisions. Howat v. Kansas (1922), was decided in the days when the labor injunction was in fashion. . . .

It is not necessary to question the continuing validity of the holding in Howat v. Kansas, however, to demonstrate that neither it nor the Mine Workers [United States v. United Mine Workers (1947)] case supports the holding of the majority in this case. In Howat the subpoena and injunction were issued to enable the Kansas Court of Industrial Relations to determine an underlying labor dispute. In the Mine Workers case, the District Court issued a temporary anti-strike injunction to preserve existing conditions during the time it took to decide whether it had authority to grant the Government relief in a complex and difficult action of enormous importance to the national economy. In both cases the orders were of questionable legality, but in both cases they were reasonably necessary to enable the court or administrative tribunal to decide an underlying controversy of considerable importance before it at the time. This case involves an entirely different situation. The Alabama Circuit Court did not issue this temporary injunction to preserve existing conditions while it proceeded to decide some underlying dispute. There was no underlying dispute before it, and the court in practical effect merely added a judicial signature to a pre-existing criminal ordinance. Just as the court had no need to issue the injunction to perserve its ability to decide some underlying dispute, the city had no need of an injunction to impose a criminal penalty for demonstrating on the streets without a permit. The ordinance already accomplished that. In point of fact, there is only one apparent reason why the city sought this injunction and why the court issued it: to make it possible to punish petitioners for contempt rather than for violating the ordinance, and thus to immunize the unconstitutional statute and its unconstitutional application from any attack. I regret that this strategy has been so successful. . . .

Mr. Justice Douglas, with whom The Chief Justice, Mr. Justice Brennan, and Mr. Justice Fortas concur, dissenting, said in part:

The right to defy an unconstitutional statute is basic in our scheme. Even when an ordinance requires a permit to make a speech, to deliver a sermon, to picket, to parade, or to assemble, it need not be honored when it is invalid on its face. Lovell v. Griffin [1938] . . . Thomas v. Collins [1945]. . . .

Mr. Justice Brennan, with whom The Chief Justice, Mr. Justice Douglas, and Mr. Justice Fortas joined, wrote a dissenting opinion.

SHUTTLESWORTH v. BIRMINGHAM
394 U. S. 147; 89 S. Ct. 935; 22 L. Ed. 2d 162
(1969)

Mr. Justice Stewart delivered the opinion of the Court, saying in part:

The petitioner stands convicted for violating an ordinance of Birmingham, Alabama, making it an offense to participate in any "parade or procession or other public demonstration" without first obtaining a permit from the City Commission. The question before us is whether that conviction can be squared with the Constitution of the United States. . . .

The petitioner was convicted for violation of § 1159 and was sentenced to 90 days' imprisonment at hard labor and an additional 48 days at hard labor in default of payment of a $75 fine and $24 costs. The Alabama Court of Appeals reversed the judgment of conviction, holding the evidence was insufficient "to show a procession which would require, under the terms of § 1159, the getting of a permit," that the ordinance had been applied in a discriminatory fashion, and that it was unconstitutional in imposing an "invidious prior restraint" without ascertainable standards for the granting of permits. The Supreme Court of Alabama, however, giving the language of § 1159 an extraordinarily narrow construction, reversed the judgment of the Court of Appeals and reinstated the conviction. We granted certiorari to consider the petitioner's constitutional claims.

There can be no doubt that the Birmingham ordinance, as it was written, conferred upon the City Commission virtually unbridled and absolute power to prohibit any "parade," "procession," or "demonstration" on the city's streets or public ways. For in deciding whether or not to withhold a permit, the members of the Commission were to be guided only by their own ideas of "public welfare, peace, safety, health, decency, good order, morals or convenience." This ordinance as it was written, therefore, fell squarely within the ambit of the many decisions of this Court over the last 30 years, holding that a law subjecting the exercise of First Amendment freedoms to the prior restraint of a license, without narrow, objective, and definite standards to guide the licensing authority, is unconstitutional. "It is settled by a long line of recent decisions of this Court that an ordinance which, like this one, makes the peaceful enjoyment of freedoms which the Constitution guarantees contingent upon the uncontrolled will of an official—as by requiring a permit or license which may be granted or withheld in the discretion of such official—is an unconstitutional censorship or prior restraint upon the enjoyment of those freedoms." Staub v. Baxley [1958]. And our decisions have made clear that a person faced with such an unconstitutional licensing law may ignore it, and engage with impunity in the exercise of the right of free expression for which the law purports to require a license. "The Constitution can hardly be thought to deny to one subjected to the restraints of such an ordinance the right to attack its constitutionality, because he has not yielded to its demands." Jones v. Opelika [1942]. (Stone, C. J., dissenting)

It is argued, however, that what was involved here was not "pure speech," but the use of public streets and sidewalks, over which a municipality must rightfully exercise a great deal of control in the interest of traffic regulation and public safety. That, of course, is true. We have emphasized before this that "the First and Fourteenth Amendments [do not] afford the same kind of freedom to those who would communicate ideas by conduct such as patrolling, marching, and picketing on streets and highways, as these amendments afford to those who communicate ideas by pure speech." Cox v. Louisiana [1965]. "Governmental authorities have the duty and responsibility to keep their streets open and available for movement."

But our decisions have also made clear that picketing and parading may nonetheless constitute methods of expression, entitled to First Amendment protection. Cox v. Louisiana; Edwards v. South Carolina [1963]; Thornhill v. Alabama [1940]. "Wherever the title of streets and parks may rest, they have immemorially been held in trust for the use of the public and, time out of mind, have been used for purposes of assembly, communicating thoughts between citizens, and discussing public questions. Such use of the streets and public places has, from ancient times, been a part of the privileges, immunities, rights, and liberties of citizens. . . ." Hague v. C. I. O. [1939] (opinion of Mr. Justice Roberts, joined by Mr. Justice Black).

Accordingly, "[a]lthough this Court has recognized that a statute may be enacted which prevents serious interference with normal usage of streets and parks, . . . we have consistently condemned licensing systems which vest in an administrative official discretion to grant or withhold a permit upon broad criteria unrelated to proper regulation of public places." Kunz v. New York [1951]. . . . Even when the use of its public streets and sidewalks is involved, therefore, a municipality may not empower its licensing officials to roam essentially at will, dispensing or withholding permission to speak, assemble, picket, or parade, according to their own opinions regarding the potential effect of the activity in question on the "welfare," "decency," or "morals" of the community.

Understandably, under these settled principles, the Alabama Court of Appeals was unable to reach any conclusion other than that § 1159 was unconstitutional. The terms of the Birmingham ordinance clearly gave the City Commission extensive authority to issue or refuse to issue parade permits on the basis of broad criteria entirely unrelated to legitimate municipal regulation of the public streets and sidewalks.

It is said, however, that no matter how constitutionally invalid the Birmingham ordinance may have been as it was written, nonetheless the authoritative construction that has now been given it by the Supreme Court of Alabama has so modified and narrowed its terms as to render it constitutionally acceptable. It is true that in affirming the petitioner's conviction in the present case, the Supreme Court of Alabama performed a remarkable job of plastic surgery upon the face of the ordinance. The court stated that when § 1159 provided that the City Commission could withhold a permit whenever "in its judgment the public welfare, peace, safety, health, decency, good order, morals or convenience require," the ordinance really meant something quite different:

"[W]e do not construe this [language] as vesting in the Commission an unfettered discretion in granting or denying permits, but, in view of the purpose of the ordinance, one to be exercised in connection with the safety, comfort and convenience in the use of the streets by the general public. . . . The members of the Commission may not act as censors of what is to be said or displayed in any parade. . . .

". . . [We] do not construe § 1159 as conferring upon the 'commission' of the City of Birmingham the right to refuse an application for a permit to carry on a parade, procession or other public demonstration solely on the ground that such activities might tend to provoke disorderly conduct. . . .

"We also hold that under § 1159 the Commission is without authority to act in an arbitrary manner or with unfettered discretion in regard to the issuance of permits. Its discretion must be exercised with uniformity of method of treatment upon the facts of each application, free from improper or inappropriate considerations and from unfair discrimination. A systematic, consistent and just order of treatment with reference to the convenience of public use of the streets and sidewalks must be followed. Applications for permits to parade must be granted if, after an investigation it is found that the convenience of the public in the use of the streets or sidewalks would not thereby be unduly disturbed."

In transforming § 1159 into an ordinance authorizing no more than the objective and even-handed regulation of traffic on Birmingham's streets and public ways, the Supreme Court of Alabama made a commendable effort to give the legislation "a field of operation within constitutional limits." We may

assume that this exercise was successful, and that the ordinance as now authoritatively construed would pass constitutional muster.* It does not follow,
however, that the severely narrowing construction put upon the ordinance by
the Alabama Supreme Court in November of 1967 necessarily serves to restore
constitutional validity to a conviction that occurred in 1963 under the ordinance as it was written. . . .

. . . In April of 1963 the ordinance that was on the books in Birmingham
contained language that affirmatively conferred upon the members of the
Commission absolute power to refuse a parade permit whenever they thought
"the public welfare, peace, safety, health, decency, good order, morals or
convenience require that it be refused." It would have taken extraordinary
clairvoyance for anyone to perceive that this language meant what the Supreme Court of Alabama was destined to find that it meant more than four
years later; and, with First Amendment rights hanging in the balance, we
would hesitate long before assuming that either the members of the Commission or the petitioner possessed any such clairvoyance at the time of the Good
Friday march.

But we need not deal in assumptions. For, as the respondent in this case has
reminded us, in assessing the constitutional claims of the petitioner, "[i]t is less
than realistic to ignore the surrounding relevant circumstances. These include
not only facts developed in the Record in this case, but also those shown in
the opinions in the related case of Walker v. City of Birmingham (1967) . . . ."

Uncontradicted testimony was offered in Walker to show that over a week
before the Good Friday march petitioner Shuttlesworth sent a representative
to apply for a parade permit. She went to the City Hall and asked "to see the
person or persons in charge to issue permits, permits for parading, picketing
and demonstrating." She was directed to Commissioner Connor, who denied
her request in no uncertain terms. "He said, 'No, you will not get a permit in
Birmingham, Alabama to picket. I will picket you over to the City Jail,' and
he repeated that twice."

Two days later petitioner Shuttlesworth himself sent a telegram to Commission Connor requesting, on behalf of his organization, a permit to picket
"against the injustices of segregation and discrimination." His request specified
the sidewalks where the picketing would take place, and stated that "the
normal rules of picketing" would be obeyed. In reply, the Commissioner sent
a wire stating that permits were the responsibility of the entire Commission

---

*The validity of this assumption would depend upon, among other things, the
availability of expeditious judicial review of the Commission's refusal of a permit. Cf.
Poulos v. New Hampshire [1953] (Frankfurter, J., concurring); Freedman v. Maryland
[1965]. See also the concurring opinion of Mr. Justice Harlan, post.

rather than of a single Commissioner, and closing with the blunt admonition: "I insist that you and your people do not start any picketing on the streets in Birmingham, Alabama."*

These "surrounding relevant circumstances" make it indisputably clear, we think, that in April of 1963—at least with respect to this petitioner and his organization[†]—the city authorities thought the ordinance meant exactly what it said. The petitioner was clearly given to understand that under no circumstances would he and his group be permitted to demonstrate in Birmingham, not that a demonstration would be approved if a time and place were selected that would minimize traffic problems. There is no indication whatever that the authorities considered themselves obligated—as the Alabama Supreme Court more than four years later said that they were—to issue a permit "if, after an investigation [they] found that the convenience of the public in the use of the streets or sidewalks would not thereby be unduly disturbed."

This case, therefore, is a far cry from Cox v. New Hampshire [1941], where it could be said that there was nothing to show "that the statute has been administered otherwise than in the ... manner which the state court has construed it to require." Here, by contrast, it is evident that the ordinance was administered so as, in the words of Chief Justice Hughes, "to deny or unwarrantedly abridge the right of assembly and the opportunities for the communication of thought ... immemorially associated with resort to public places." The judgment is
Reversed.

Mr. Justice Black concurs in the result.

Mr. Justice Marshall took no part in the consideration or decision of this case.

Mr. Justice Harlan, concurring.

The Alabama Supreme Court's opinion makes it clear that if petitioner Shuttlesworth had carried his efforts to obtain a parade permit to the highest state court, he could have required the city authorities to grant permission for

---

*The legal and constitutional issues involved in the Walker case were quite different from those involved here. The Court recently summarized the Walker decision as follows:
"In that case, the Court held that demonstrators who had proceeded with their protest march in face of the prohibition of an injunctive order against such a march, could not defend contempt charges by asserting the unconstitutionality of the injunction. The proper procedure, it was held, was to seek judicial review of the injunction and not to disobey it, no matter how well-founded their doubts might be as to its validity." ...

[†]In Walker the petitioner made an offer of proof that parade permits had been issued to other groups by the city clerk at the request of the traffic bureau of the police department.

his march, so long as his proposals were consistent with Birmingham's interest in traffic control. Thus, the difficult question this case presents is whether the Fourteenth Amendment ever bars a State from punishing a citizen for marching without a permit which could have been procured if all available remedies had been pursued.

The Court answers that a citizen is entitled to rely on the statutory construction adopted by the state officials who are on the frontline, administering the permit scheme. If these officials construe a vague statute unconstitutionally, the citizen may take them at their word, and act on the assumption that the statute is void. The Court's holding seems to me to carry seeds of mischief that may impair the conceded ability of the authorities to regulate the use of public thoroughfares in the interests of all. The right to ignore a permit requirement should, in my view, be made to turn on something more substantial than a minor official's view of his authority under the governing statute.

Simply because an inferior state official indicates his view as to a statute's scope, it does not follow that the State's judiciary will come to the same conclusion. Situations do exist, however, in which there can be no effective review of the decision of an inferior state official. In the present case, for example, the decision of Commissioner Connor had the practical effect of the decision of a court of last resort. One week before the Good Friday march, Shuttlesworth learned from Connor that he, as Commissioner of Public Safety, would not issue parade permits, and that the marchers would have to apply to the entire City Commission. But Birmingham's ordinances did not require a prompt decision by the City Commission.* Nor did the State of Alabama provide for a speedy court review of the denial of a parade permit.†

Given the absence of speedy procedures, the Reverend Shuttlesworth and his associates were faced with a serious dilemma when they received their notice from Mr. Connor. If they attempted to exhaust the administrative and judicial remedies provided by Alabama law, it was almost certain that no effective relief could be obtained by Good Friday. Since the right to engage in peaceful and orderly political demonstrations is, under appropriate conditions, a fundamental aspect of the "liberty" protected by the Fourteenth Amendment, . . . the petitioner was not obliged to invoke procedures which could not give him effective relief. With fundamental rights at stake, he was entitled to adopt the more probable meaning of the ordinance and act on his belief that

---

*Section 1159 does not require the City Commission to act on an application within any fixed amount of time. Indeed, by the time Connor definitively declared that he could not issue parade permits, it is not at all clear that petitioner could even have made a timely permit application to the City Commission at its only remaining regular session set before the scheduled Good Friday march. . . .

†Although Shuttlesworth could have petitioned for a writ of mandamus in the Alabama Circuit Court if the City Commission denied his application, that state court is not obliged to render a decision within any fixed period of time.

the city's permit regulations were unconstitutional.

It may be suggested, however, that Shuttlesworth's dilemma was of his own making. He could have requested a permit months in advance of Good Friday, thereby allowing Alabama's administrative and judicial machinery the necessary time to operate fully before the date set for the march. But such a suggestion ignores the principle established in Freedman v. Maryland (1965), which prohibits the States from requiring persons to invoke unduly cumbersome and time-consuming procedures before they may exercise their constitutional right of expression. Freedman holds that if the State is to protect the public from obscene movies, it must afford exhibitors a speedy administrative or judicial right of review, lest "the victorious exhibitor might find the most propitious opportunity for exhibition [passed]." The Freedman principle is applicable here. . . .

I do not mean to suggest that a State or city may not reasonably require that parade permit applications be submitted early enough to allow the authorities and the judiciary to determine whether the parade proposal is consistent with the important interests respecting the use of the streets which local authority may legitimately protect. But such applications must be handled on an expedited basis so that rights of political expression will not be lost in a maze of cumbersome and slow-moving procedures.

WALZ v. TAX COMMISSION
397 U. S. 664; 90 S. Ct. 1409; 25 L. Ed. 2d 697
(1970)

In its first one hundred and fifty years the Supreme Court decided but one important case which dealt with freedom of religion. In 1878 the case of Reynolds v. United States reached the conclusion that the religious liberty protected by the First Amendment does not include the right to commit immoral or criminal acts even though these are sanctioned by religious doctrine. Thus Reynolds, a Mormon in the Territory of Utah, was held properly convicted of the crime of polygamy in spite of the fact that the Mormon religion held polygamy to be proper and desirable. Supreme Court cases involving religious liberty were rare because the First Amendment, which protects freedom of religion, applied only to Congress and not to the states. See Barron v. Baltimore (1833). Congress had little opportunity and less inclination to violate the First Amendment, and what the states did by way of dealing with religious matters was their own business so far as the federal Constitution was concerned.

By the 1930's this situation began to change, and the Supreme Court has long held that freedom of religion in the First Amendment, like freedom of speech and press, is part of the liberty which the due process clause of the Fourteenth Amendment forbids the states to abridge. The first case decided on this theory was Hamilton v. Regents of University of California (1934), which held that a student with religious scruples against bearing arms could be compelled, under penalty of expulsion from the university, to take military drill. The alleged invasion of his religious liberty did not deny him due process of law, since he was not compelled to attend the university and could assert no constitutional right to do so without complying with the state's requirement of military training.

In the early 1930's a religious group called Jehovah's Witnesses began a militant, nation-wide campaign to spread their religious tenets, which include virulent condemnation of all organized religions and churches, especially the Roman Catholic Church. They spread their teachings by personal appeals, by the sale or giving away of literature, and by going from house to house asking permission to play phonograph records, one of which, called "Enemies," is a bitter attack on religious organizations. Community resentment against the Witnesses and their methods was often intense; it expressed itself in a variety of legal measures designed to discourage the Witnesses and curb their more unpopular activities. With fanatical zeal the Witnesses fought every legal attempt to restrict their freedom of action. As a result they have brought to the Supreme Court many cases involving religious liberty issues. In a majority of these they were successful. These decisions have done much to clarify our constitutional law relating to freedom of religion.

The most spectacular issue of religious liberty to be raised by the Jehovah's Witnesses was that of the compulsory flag salute. The Witnesses refuse to salute the flag or permit their children to do so, because they believe that this violates the First Commandment. This refusal caused bitter resentment, and some seventeen states passed statutes requiring all school children to salute the flag and providing for the expulsion of those who refused. The question whether these acts unconstitutionally restricted freedom of religion came to the Court in Minersville School District v. Gobitis (1940). With one judge dissenting the Court held that it did not. In an opinion by Mr. Justice Frankfurter it was stated that freedom of religion is not absolute, and that some compromises may be necessary in order to secure the national unity which is the basis of national security. The flag salute contributes to that national unity, or at least the question whether it does or not is "an issue of educational policy for which the courtroom is not the proper arena." For the Court to hold the requirement void as abridging religious liberty "would amount to no less than the pronouncement of a pedagogical and psychological dogma in a field where courts possess no marked and certainly no controlling competence." The Court seemed content to assume that the Minersville school board was more competent to settle the flag salute issue than the Supreme Court, and it allowed the board's judgment to prevail. Justice Stone wrote a powerful dissenting opinion. The decision came as a shock and was widely and sharply criticized. Members of the Court who had participated in it began to have misgivings. When Jones v. Opelika was decided in 1942, Justices Black, Douglas, and Murphy dissented, and went further to state that they had become convinced that the Gobitis case was "wrongly decided." With Justice Stone, this made four members of the Court who no longer supported the Gobitis decision. When, in February, 1943, Justice Rutledge replaced Justice Byrnes on the bench, he joined with these four to overrule the Gobitis case by the decision in West Virginia State Board of Education v. Barnette (1943).

Although most of the Court's early cases involved the free exercise clause of the First Amendment, a number of difficult problems have arisen in recent years under the provision that "Congress shall make no law respecting an establishment of religion." Perhaps the most challenging and controversial of these problems have been by-products of the tremendous expansion in public education, to which parents are abdicating an increasing share of the child's social development. One is the extent to which the state may aid religious schools. The other is the extent to which religion may be fostered by the public schools.

Early education in America was religious education, supported by the civil government in the Bible-commonwealth of Massachusetts, and by the various church groups in the middle and southern colonies. In the early nineteenth century the demand for free public education resulted in a system of public schools free from religious control and largely free from any sectarian influence, a situation wholly satisfactory to an overwhelmingly Protestant nation. Waves of Catholic immigration injected a new element into the picture. The Catholic Church regards the teaching of religion as a primary function of education. Unwilling to send their children to the public schools, which they regarded as either devoid of all religious influence or tainted with Protestantism, the Catholics felt obliged to build and maintain a system of parochial schools at their own expense. When these parochial schools met the state's educational standards they were accredited as schools in which the requirements of the compulsory education laws could be satisfied. In 1922 the state of Oregon passed a law requiring all parents to send their children to the public schools of the state. The Supreme Court, in Pierce v. Society of Sisters (1925), held that the statute denied due process of law by taking from parents their freedom to "direct the upbringing and education" of their children by sending them either to parochial or to private nonsectarian schools of approved educational standards. It is not surprising that Catholic citizens, who paid taxes to support public schools which they did not use, should try to secure some public aid for the parochial schools; and they exerted a good deal of pressure to bring this about. Opposition to this was, however, bitter and widespread; and by the end of the nineteenth century practically every state had adopted some kind of prohibition against the use of state funds for the support of religious education. In numerous cases the state courts held void attempts to extend direct or indirect aid to parochial schools.

Since the 1930's new and varied services and benefits have been offered by the states to pupils in the public schools. These include free textbooks, free bus transportation, free lunches, and free medical service. Can the state, if it desires, also give these benefits to children attending parochial or private schools? It was argued on the one hand that to do so would not only violate the constitutional clauses which forbid the use of public money in aid of religion or religious education, but would violate also the clause of the First Amendment which forbids "an establishment of religion," a clause now carried over into the Fourteenth Amendment as a limitation on the states. It was argued on the other side that in providing these services and benefits the state was aiding the child and not the school which he attends. Most state courts accepted this latter reasoning, which came to be known as the "child benefit theory" and the Supreme Court applied it in Everson v. Board of Education (1947), discussed in the opinion below, to hold valid the provision of free bus transportation to children attending parochial schools.

Unfortunately, the child benefit theory, while giving a plausible explanation for the results reached, does not provide any real test for reaching those results in the first place. If the fact that a child is benefited makes an expenditure valid, it is hard to see why the state cannot build and support religious schools. On the other hand, if anything that aids religion is forbidden by the First Amendment, why are not fire and police protection for churches unconstitutional? What the Constitution demands is state neutrality toward religion, but what constitutes neutrality in a society where governmental aid and supervision are almost ubiquitous? How is the line to be drawn between neutrality and impermissible state aid to religion?

In Abington School Dist. v. Schempp (1963), a case holding void the required reading in school of "at least ten verses from the Holy Bible," the Court undertook to clarify this distinction: "The test may be stated as follows: what are the purpose and the primary effect of the enactment? If either is the advancement or inhibition of religion then the enactment exceeds the scope of legislative power as circumscribed by the Constitution. That is to say that to withstand the strictures of the Establishment Clause there must be a secular legislative purpose and a primary effect that neither advances nor inhibits religion." In Board of Education v. Allen (1968), this doctrine was applied to hold valid a New York law providing for the loan of textbooks to parochial school pupils.

One of the main difficulties encountered in challenging alleged aid to religious schools has been a rule of the Supreme Court dating back to 1923 that a person could not contest in federal court the expenditure of tax money solely on the ground that he was a taxpayer and had an interest in how the money was spent. See Massachusetts v. Mellon (1923). Not only was the share of the interested taxpayer in the money too small to deserve judicial notice, but the Court clearly viewed with concern the spectre of millions of taxpayers in a position to challenge in the courts every expenditure of federal funds. The result of this ruling was to make virtually impregnable to judicial attack any distribution of federal funds to religious groups. With the passage of Titles I and II of the Elementary and Secondary Education Act of 1965, under which funds could be used to finance secular education in religious schools, the attack on the "no taxpayer suits" rule was reopened. In Flast v. Cohen, decided the same day as the Allen case, the Court eased the rule as applied to challenges brought under the establishment clause of the First Amendment. The Court held that "the taxpayer must show that the challenged enactment exceeds specific constitutional limitations imposed upon the exercise of the congressional taxing and spending power and not simply that the enactment is generally beyond the powers delegated to Congress by Art. I, § 8." Since one of the reasons for adopting the establishment clause was to prevent using the tax power to aid religion, this clause was such a "specific limitation."

The free exercise and no establishment clauses of the First Amendment were the framers' answer to the place of religion in the highly pluralistic social structures of the time. Religion was to be a private affair; the heavy thumb of the government was to be used neither to aid nor hinder, lest man's freedom to worship as he chose and the right to support only the church of his choice be jeopardized. But even as the framers wrote, many of the practices of the time made clear that the "separation of church and state" would not entail the government ignoring the existence of religion. Both houses of the Congress employed a chaplain; "In God We Trust" was embossed on our coins; and the help and understanding of God were exhorted on all public occasions. In general the people thought of themselves as religious, mostly Christian, and a government recognition of that fact did not seem in any way inconsistent with the doctrines of the First Amendment.

With the gradual diversification of religious belief many well-accepted religious practices and manifestations were challenged in the courts, and with the application to the states of the religion clauses of the First Amendment, these challenges raised potential federal questions.

The Supreme Court has shown considerable reluctance to review many of these activities. In November 1964, it left untouched a New York decision upholding the words "under God" in the pledge of allegiance; in 1971 it let stand the rejection by a district court of an effort to stop the astronauts from praying over television on their way to the moon (O'Hair v. Paine, 1971) and as recently as 1966 (Murray v. Goldstein) it declined to review a Maryland case upholding the validity of tax exemption for church buildings.

The present case was brought by a reclusive New York attorney who is a Christian, but not a member of any religious organization. He owned a 22 X 29-foot plot of land on Staten Island which, with neither buildings nor street access, was assessed by the City of New York at $100. Walz refused to pay the $5.24 a year property tax on the ground he was being forced to support churches and synogogues, which pay no taxes.

Mr. Chief Justice Burger delivered the opinion of the Court, saying in part:

Appellant, owner of real estate in Richmond County, New York, sought an injunction in the New York courts to prevent the New York City Tax Commission from granting property tax exemptions to religious organizations for religious properties used solely for religious worship. The exemption from state taxes is authorized by Art. 16, § 1, of the New York Constitution, which provides in relevant part: "Exemptions from taxation may be granted only by general laws. Exemptions may be altered or repealed except those exempting real or personal property used exclusively for religious, educational or charitable purposes as defined by law and owned by any corporation or association organized or conducted exclusively for one or more of such purposes and not operating for profit."

The essence of appellant's contention was that the New York City Tax Commission's grant of an exemption to church property indirectly requires the appellant to make a contribution to religious bodies and thereby violates provisions prohibiting establishment of religion under the First Amendment which under the Fourteenth Amendment is binding on the States.

I. . . .

The Establishment and Free Exercise Clauses of the First Amendment are not the most precisely drawn portions of the Constitution. The sweep of the absolute prohibitions in the Religion Clauses may have been calculated; but the purpose was to state an objective, not to write a statute. In attempting to articulate the scope of the two Religious Clauses, the Court's opinions reflect the limitations inherent in formulating general principles on a case-by-case basis. The considerable internal inconsistency in the opinions of the Court derives from what, in retrospect, may have been too sweeping utterances on aspects of these clauses that seemed clear in relation to the particular cases but have limited meaning as general principles.

The Court has struggled to find a neutral course between the two Religion Clauses, both of which are cast in absolute terms, and either of which, if expanded to a logical extreme, would tend to clash with the other. . . .

The course of constitutional neutrality in this area cannot be an absolutely straight line; rigidity could well defeat the basic purpose of these provisions, which is to insure that no religion be sponsored or favored, none commanded, and none inhibited. The general principle deducible from the First Amendment and all that has been said by the Court is this: that we will not tolerate either governmentally established religion or governmental interference with religion. Short of those expressly proscribed governmental acts there is room for play in the joints productive of a benevolent neutrality which will permit religious exercise to exist without sponsorship and without interference.

Each value judgment under the Religion Clauses must therefore turn on whether particular acts in question are intended to establish or interfere with religious beliefs and practices or have the effect of doing so. Adherence to the policy of neutrality that derives from an accommodation of the Establishment and Free Exercise Clauses has prevented the kind of involvement that would tip the balance toward government control of churches or governmental restraint on religious practice.

Adherents of particular faiths and individual churches frequently take strong positions on public issues including, as this case reveals in the several briefs amici, vigorous advocacy of legal or constitutional positions. Of course, churches as much as secular bodies and private citizens have that right. No perfect or absolute separation is really possible; the very existence of the Religion Clauses is an involvement of sorts—one that seeks to mark boundaries to avoid excessive entanglement.

The hazards of placing too much weight on a few words or phrases of the Court is abundantly illustrated within the pages of the Court's opinion in Everson [1947]. Mr. Justice Black, writing for the Court's majority, said the First Amendment "means at least this: Neither a state nor the Federal Government can . . . pass laws which aid one religion, aid all religions, or prefer one religion over another," yet he had no difficulty in holding that: "Measured by these standards, we cannot say that the First Amendment prohibits New Jersey from spending tax-raised funds to pay the bus fares of parochial school pupils as a part of a general program under which it pays the fares of pupils attending public and other schools. *It is undoubtedly true that children are helped to get to church schools. There is even a possibility that some of the children might not be sent to the church schools if the parents were compelled to pay their children's bus fares out of their own pockets....* " (Emphasis added.)

The Court did not regard such "aid" to schools teaching a particular religious faith as any more a violation of the Establishment Clause than providing "state-paid policemen, detailed to protect children . . . [at the schools] from the very real hazards of traffic...."

Mr. Justice Jackson, in perplexed dissent in Everson, noted that "the undertones of the opinion, advocating complete and uncompromising separation . . . seem utterly discordant with its conclusion. . . ." Perhaps so. One can sympathize with Mr. Justice Jackson's logical analysis but agree with the Court's eminently sensible and realistic application of the language of the Establishment Clause. In Everson the Court declined to construe the religion clauses with a literalness that would undermine the ultimate constitutional objective as illuminated by history. Surely, bus transportation and police protection to pupils who receive religious instruction "aid" that particular religion to maintain schools that plainly tend to assure future adherents to a particular faith by having control of their total education at an early age. No religious body that maintains schools would deny this as an affirmative if not dominant policy of church schools. But if as in Everson buses can be provided to carry and policemen to protect church school pupils, we fail to see how a broader range of police and fire protection given equally to all churches, along with nonprofit hospitals, art galleries, and libraries receiving the same tax exemption, is different for purposes of the Religion Clauses.

Similarly, making textbooks available to pupils in parochial schools in common with public schools was surely an "aid" to the sponsoring churches because it relieved those churches of an enormous aggregate cost for those books. Supplying of costly teaching materials was not seen either as manifesting a legislative purpose to aid or as having a primary effect of aid contravening the First Amendment. Board of Education v. Allen (1968). In so holding the Court was heeding both its own prior decisions and our religious tradition. Mr. Justice Douglas, in Zorach v. Clauson [1952] after recalling that we "are a religious people whose institutions presuppose a Supreme Being," went on to say: "We make room for as wide a variety of beliefs and creeds as the spiritual needs of man deem necessary. . . . *When the state encourages religious instruction . . . it follows the best of our traditions.* For it then respects the religious nature of our people and accommodates the public service to their spiritual needs." (Emphasis added.)

With all the risks inherent in programs that bring about administrative relationships between public education bodies and church-sponsored schools, we have been able to chart a course that preserved the autonomy and freedom of religious bodies while avoiding any semblance of established religion. This is a "tight rope" and one we have successfully traversed.

II.

The legislative purpose of a property tax exemption is neither the advancement nor the inhibition of religion; it is neither sponsorship nor hostility. New York, in common with the other States, has determined that certain entities that exist in a harmonious relationship to the community at large, and that foster its "moral or mental improvement," should not be inhibited in their activities by property taxation or the hazard of loss of those properties for nonpayment of taxes. It has not singled out one particular church or religious group or even churches as such; rather, it has granted exemption to all houses of religious worship within a broad class of property owned by nonprofit, quasi-public corporations which include hospitals, libraries, playgrounds, scientific, professional, historical, and patriotic groups. The State has an affirmative policy that considers these groups as beneficial and stabilizing influences in community life and finds this classification useful, desirable, and in the public interest. Qualification for tax exemption is not perpetual or immutable; some tax-exempt groups lose that status when their activities take them outside the classification and new entities can come into being and qualify for exemption.

Governments have not always been tolerant of religious activity, and hostility toward religion has taken many shapes and forms—economic, political, and sometimes harshly oppressive. Grants of exemption historically reflect the concern of authors of constitutions and statutes as to the latent dangers inherent in the imposition of property taxes; exemption constitutes a reasonable and balanced attempt to guard against those dangers. The limits of permissible state accommodation to religion are by no means co-extensive with the noninterference mandated by the Free Exercise Clause. To equate the two would be to deny a national heritage with roots in the Revolution itself. . . . We cannot read New York's statute as attempting to establish religion; it is simply sparing the exercise of religion from the burden of property taxation levied on private profit institutions. . . .

Determining that the legislative purpose of tax exemption is not aimed at establishing, sponsoring, or supporting religion does not end the inquiry, however. We must also be sure that the end result—the effect—is not an excessive government entanglement with religion. The test is inescapably one of degree. Either course, taxation of churches or exemption, occasions some degree of involvement with religion. Elimination of exemption would tend to expand the involvement of government by giving rise to tax valuation of church property, tax liens, tax foreclosures, and the direct confrontations and conflicts that follow in the train of those legal processes.

Granting tax exemptions to churches necessarily operates to afford an indirect economic benefit and also gives rise to some, but yet a lesser, involvement than taxing them. In analyzing either alternative the questions are whether the involvement is excessive, and whether it is a continuing one calling for official and continuing surveillance leading to an impermissible degree of entanglement. Obviously a direct money subsidy would be a relationship pregnant with involvement and, as with most governmental grant programs, could encompass sustained and detailed administrative relationships for enforcement of statutory or administrative standards, but that is not this case. The hazards of churches supporting government are hardly less in their potential than the hazards of governments supporting churches; each relationship carries some involvement rather than the desired insulation and separation. We cannot ignore the instances in history when church support of government led to the kind of involvement we seek to avoid.

The grant of a tax exemption is not sponsorship since the government does not transfer part of its revenue to churches but simply abstains from demanding that the church support the state. No one has ever suggested that tax exemption has converted libraries, art galleries, or hospitals into arms of the state or put employees "on the public payroll." There is no genuine nexus between tax exemption and establishment of religion. As Mr. Justice Holmes commented in a related context "a page of history is worth a volume of logic." New York Trust Co. v. Eisner (1921). The exemption creates only a minimal and remote involvement between church and state and far less than taxation of churches. It restricts the fiscal relationship between church and state, and tends to complement and reinforce the desired separation insulating each from the other. . . .

All of the 50 States provide for tax exemption of places of worship, most of them doing so by constitutional guarantees. For so long as federal income taxes have had any potential impact on churches—over 75 years—religious organizations have been expressly exempt from the tax. . . .

It is significant that Congress, from its earliest days, has viewed the Religion Clauses of the Constitution as authorizing statutory real estate tax exemption to religious bodies. . . .

It is obviously correct that no one acquires a vested or protected right in violation of the Constitution by long use, even when that span of time covers our entire national existence and indeed predates it. Yet an unbroken practice of according the exemption to churches, openly and by affirmative state action, not covertly or by state inaction, is not something to be lightly cast aside. . . .

Nothing in this national attitude toward religious tolerance and two centuries of uninterrupted freedom from taxation has given the remotest sign of leading to an established church or religion and on the contrary it has operated affirmatively to help guarantee the free exercise of all forms of religious beliefs. Thus, it is hardly useful to suggest that tax exemption is but the "foot in the door" or the "nose of the camel in the tent" leading to an established church. If tax exemption can be seen as this first step toward "establishment" of religion, as Mr. Justice Douglas fears, the second step has been long in coming.

Any move that realistically "establishes" a church or tends to do so can be dealt with "while this Court sits.". . .

Affirmed.

Mr. Justice Brennan and Mr. Justice Harlan each wrote a concurring opinion.

Mr. Justice Douglas wrote a dissenting opinion.

ZORACH v. CLAUSON
343 U. S. 306; 72 S. Ct. 679; 96 L. Ed. 954 (1952)

"Well, in *our* country," said Alice, still panting a little, "You'd generally get to somewhere else—if you ran very fast for a long time as we've been doing."
"A slow sort of country!" said the Queen. "Now, *here*, you see, it takes all the running *you* can do, to keep in the same place."
—Lewis Carroll, *Through the Looking Glass*

This sums up the plight of religious education in the United States. Born in an era when school teachers were poorly paid, school facilities simple and inexpensive, and extracurricular activities virtually nonexistent, the religious school had little difficulty keeping up with its public counterpart. But time has seen marked changes in the public schools. The curriculum, once limited to the three "R's," now includes a wide and sophisticated group of "cultural" subjects; organized athletics has replaced the simple playground games; pupils are transported to school, fed lunch in school, and transported home again; expensive electronic teaching devices have replaced or supplemented the traditional classroom teacher, and even that teacher comes to his job more completely and expensively educated, asking and receiving more money. The religious school must compete with all of this if it is to "keep in the same place." An additional difficulty for the Roman Catholic Church, which operates most religious schools, is the falling enrollment in those religious orders whose members were called to teaching and who received no personal compensation.
Prolonged political efforts to obtain aid for parochial schools have not been wholly unsuccessful. More than 20 states provide bus transportation

for nonpublic school pupils, while a handful provide textbooks, health services, school lunches, and the like. While this indirect aid helped, it did not solve the problem of the rising cost of labor, and since 1968 a number of states have undertaken to provide direct financial help for the secular segment of the religious school curriculum. New York, Ohio, Pennsylvania and Rhode Island undertook to pay from the state treasury part of the cost of teachers' salaries, while Minnesota provided a tax credit for parents with children in nonpublic schools.

In Lemon v. Kurtzman (1971) the Pennsylvania and Rhode Island plans were held void. Conceding that it could "only dimly perceive the lines of demarcation in this extraordinarily sensitive area of constitutional law," the Court identified three tests to be applied. "First, the statute must have a secular legislative purpose; second, its principal or primary effect must be one that neither advances nor inhibits religion, Board of Education v. Allen (1968); finally, the statute must not foster 'an excessive government entanglement with religion.' Walz [1970]. . . ." It was the last of these tests which the Court found to be violated by the teacher payment plans. Since the money was to be used to pay only for secular teaching, "a comprehensive, discriminating, and continuing state surveillance will inevitably be required to ensure that these restrictions are obeyed and the First Amendment otherwise respected. Unlike a book, a teacher cannot be inspected once so as to determine the extent and intent of his or her personal beliefs and subjective acceptance of the limitations imposed by the First Amendment. These prophylactic contacts will involve excessive and enduring entanglement between state and church. . . ." In Pennsylvania the entanglement was increased by a system of post-audit of school records "to determine which expenditures are religious and which are secular."

The Court found an even "broader base of entanglement . . . presented by the divisive political potential of these state programs." "Political division along religious lines was one of the principal evils against which the First Amendment was intended to protect," and in this case the inevitable religious divisiveness would be aggravated by "the need for continuing annual appropriations and the likelihood of larger and larger demands as costs and populations grow."

Efforts to provide aid to religious schools which did not entail such entanglement have not been notably successful. An elaborate New York scheme for paying the cost of state-mandated functions, "maintenance and repair" costs, and tuition money for parents was held void in Levitt v. Committee for Public Education and Committee for Public Education v. Nyquist in 1973, and in Sloan v. Lemon (1973) a similar tuition plan passed by Pennsylvania was struck down. In Meek v. Pittenger (1975), while the Court upheld Pennsylvania's loan of textbooks to religious school pupils, it struck down the loan of other instructional equipment made to the school and not the pupil, and a provision for professional personnel was held bad because it involved both an "entangling" degree of supervision and a potential for political entanglement and divisiveness.

In 1963, in response to a demand for federal help for higher education, Congress passed the Higher Education Facilities Act, which provided building grants and loans to colleges and universities. The act expressly excluded "any facility used or to be used for sectarian instructions or as a place of worship . . ." or "any part of the program of a school or department of divinity," but did not otherwise rule out denominational schools. The interest of the government was to last only 20 years, after which the school was allowed to do what it pleased with the buildings.

In Tilton v. Richardson (1971), decided the same day as Lemon, the Court upheld the validity of the grants to religious colleges, except that the interest of the United States could not end at the end of 20 years. Chief Justice Burger, speaking for himself and Justices Harlan, Stewart, and Blackmun, found that the purpose of the act was to aid education, not religion; that the schools in this case had apparently quite separable secular and religious activities, and the buildings were devoted solely to the former. He refused to deal with the case in terms of a "composite profile" of sectarian institutions, which "imposes religious restrictions on admissions, requires attendance at religious activities, compels obedience to the doctrines and dogmas of the faith . . . and does everything it can to propagate a particular religion." He noted that a number of institutions had been denied aid, and at least one had had its funds withdrawn. "Individual projects can be properly evaluated if and when challenges arise with respect to particular recipients and some evidence is then presented to show that the institution does in fact possess these characteristics. We cannot, however, strike down an Act of Congress on the basis of a hypothetical profile. He agreed, however, that unless the restriction on the use of the buildings were maintained, the grant might become an aid to religion and hence violate the First Amendment.

The four justices found that the Tilton case did not violate the "excessive entanglement" test under which the aid in Lemon had been stricken down. First, it was not the dominant purpose of these colleges, as it was the secondary schools, to inculcate religious values in their students "to assure future adherents to a particular faith." Not only were the courses taught with the normal internal self-discipline and academic freedom, but "the skepticism of the college student is not an inconsiderable barrier to any attempt or tendency to subvert the congressional objectives and limitations." In addition, both the one-shot nature of the aid and the fact it was in the form of buildings rather than teachers tended to reduce the entanglement.

Mr. Justice White, the fifth member of the majority, concurred with the

Chief Justice on the theory that since the purpose of all the aid was secular, the fact it aided religion did not make it unconstitutional.

While the Everson case held valid certain kinds of aid to children attending religious schools, it did not answer the needs of parents whose children were getting what was viewed as a "Godless" education in the public schools. Churches, whose success in competing for the time and interest of children has never been outstanding, and parents who wanted their child to have religious training but could no longer get him to go to Sunday School finally devised a scheme of "released time," whereby the child could get such religious training during his "working day" rather than after school or on weekends. One such program was set up in Champaign, Illinois. Public school pupils whose parents signed "request cards" attended religious-instruction classes conducted during regular school hours in the school building, but taught by outside teachers (chosen by a religious council representing the various faiths) who were subject to the approval and supervision of the superintendent of schools. These teachers were not paid from public funds. Records of attendance at these classes were kept and reported to the school authorities, and pupils who did not attend them spent their time on their ordinary studies. The Supreme Court held the plan void in Illinois ex rel. McCollum v. Board of Education (1948). The facts stated, the Court said, "show the use of tax-supported property for religious instruction and the close cooperation between the school authorities and the religious council in promoting religious education. The operation of the State's compulsory education system thus assists and is integrated with the program of religious instruction carried on by separate religious sects. Pupils compelled by law to go to school for secular education are released in part from their legal duty upon the condition that they attend the religious classes. This is beyond all question a utilization of the tax-established and tax-supported public school system to aid religious groups to spread their faith."

Although the justices in both Everson and McCollum agreed unanimously that the First Amendment set up a complete separation of church and state, they differed sharply in each case on whether aid to religion was in fact shown. They did not question that if it had been, it would have been bad. Religious leaders, both Catholic and Protestant, together with some lay critics, have challenged the basic rule which the Court has announced. They urge that the framers did not intend by the First Amendment to forbid completely all government aid to religion, but only such aid as favors one religion over another.

They argue, first, that there is no really persuasive historical ground for holding that the framers had in mind an absolute separation of church and state; the "establishment" clause was intended merely to prevent the establishment of a state church, such as the Church of England. Second, the historical material mustered by Mr. Justice Black in the Everson case to show that what the framers intended was, in Jefferson's phrase, a wall of separation between church and state has been sharply criticized by a number of historical scholars as presenting an incomplete and distorted picture. Third, the Supreme Court had itself recognized some aid to religion. In Bradfield v. Roberts (1899) it had held valid federal aid to a Roman Catholic hospital, although on the technical ground that the hospital corporation was a secular body which served patients without regard to denomination. Also, weight has been attached to the fact that in 1844 in the Girard will case, Vidal v. Girard's Executors, Justice Story had announced (though by way of dictum) that the "Christian religion is part of the common law."

Those who were arguing that state and national governments should be permitted to give impartial aid to religion were encouraged by the Court's decision in the Zorach case. There seemed little doubt that the Court, in holding that "the First Amendment . . . does not say that in every and all respects there shall be a separation of Church and State" and government need not show a "callous indifference" to religious groups, had backed away sharply from its position in the Everson and McCollum cases.

Mr. Justice Douglas delivered the opinion of the Court, saying in part:

New York City has a program which permits its public schools to release students during the school day so that they may leave the school buildings and school grounds and go to religious centers for religious instruction or devotional exercises. A student is released on written request of his parents. Those not released stay in the classrooms. The churches make weekly reports to the schools, sending a list of children who have been released from public school but who have not reported for religious instruction.

This "released time" program involves neither religious instruction in public school classrooms nor the expenditure of public funds. All costs, including the application blanks, are paid by the religious organizations. The case is therefore unlike McCollum v. Board of Education [1948] which involved a "released time" program from Illinois. In that case the classrooms were turned over to religious instructors. We accordingly held that the program violated the First Amendment which (by reason of the Fourteenth Amendment) prohibits the states from establishing religion or prohibiting its free exercise.

Appellants, who are taxpayers and residents of New York City and whose children attend its public schools, challenge the present law, contending it is in essence not different from the one involved in the McCollum Case. Their argument, stated elaborately in various ways, reduces itself to this: the weight and influence of the school is put behind a program for religious instruction; public school teachers police it, keeping tab on students who are released; the classroom activities come to a halt while the students who are released for religious instruction are on leave; the school is a crutch on which the churches are leaning for support in their religious training; without the cooperation of the schools this "released time" program, like the one in the McCollum Case, would be futile and ineffective. The New York Court of Appeals sustained the law against this claim of unconstitutionality. The case is here on appeal. . . .

It takes obtuse reasoning to inject any issue of the "free exercise" of religion into the present case. No one is forced to go to the religious classroom and no religious exercise or instruction is brought to the classrooms of the public schools. A student need not take religious instruction. He is left to his own desires as to the manner or time of his religious devotions, if any.

There is a suggestion that the system involves the use of coercion to get public school students into religious classrooms. There is no evidence in the record before us that supports that conclusion. The present record indeed tells us that the school authorities are neutral in this regard and do no more than release students whose parents so request. If in fact coercion were used, if it were established that any one or more teachers were using their office to persuade or force students to take the religious instruction, a wholly different case would be presented. Hence we put aside that claim of coercion both as respects the "free exercise" of religion and "an establishment of religion" within the meaning of the First Amendment.

Moreover, apart from that claim of coercion, we do not see how New York by this type of "released time" program has made a law respecting an establishment of religion within the meaning of the First Amendment. There is much talk of the separation of Church and State in the history of the Bill of Rights and in the decisions clustering around the First Amendment. See Everson v. Board of Education [1947]; McCollum v. Board of Education. There cannot be the slightest doubt that the First Amendment reflects the philosophy that Church and State should be separated. And so far as interference with the "free exercise" of religion and an "establishment" of religion are concerned, the separation must be complete and unequivocal. The First Amendment within the scope of its coverage permits no exception; the prohibition is absolute. The First Amendment, however, does not say that in every and all respects there shall be a separation of Church and State. Rather, it studiously defines the manner, the specific ways, in which there shall be no concert or union or dependency one on the other. That is the common sense of the matter. Otherwise, the state and religion would be aliens to each other—hostile, suspicious, and even unfriendly. Churches could not be required to pay even property taxes. Municipalities would not be permitted to render police or fire protection to religious groups. Policemen who helped parishioners into their places of worship would violate the Constitution. Prayers in our legislative halls; the appeals to the Almighty in the messages of the Chief Executive; the proclamations making Thanksgiving Day a holiday; "so help me God" in our courtroom oaths—these and all other references to the Almighty that run through our laws, our public rituals, our ceremonies would be flouting the First Amendment. A fastidious atheist or agnostic could even object to the supplication with which the Court opens each session: "God save the United States and this Honorable Court."

We would have to press the concept of separation of Church and State to these extremes to condemn the present law on constitutional grounds. The nullification of this law would have wide and profound effects. A Catholic student applies to his teacher for permission to leave the school during hours on a Holy Day of Obligation to attend a mass. A Jewish student asks his teacher for permission to be excused for Yom Kippur. A Protestant wants the afternoon off for a family baptismal ceremony. In each case the teacher requires parental consent in writing. In each case the teacher, in order to make sure the student is not a truant, goes further and requires a report from the priest, the rabbi, or the minister. The teacher in other words cooperates in a religious program to the extent of making it possible for her students to participate in it. Whether she does it occasionally for a few students, regularly for one, or pursuant to a systematized program designed to further the religious needs of all the students does not alter the character of the act.

We are a religious people whose institutions presuppose a Supreme Being. We guarantee the freedom to worship as one chooses. We make room for as wide a variety of beliefs and creeds as the spiritual needs of man deem necessary. We sponsor an attitude on the part of government that shows no partiality to any one group and that lets each flourish according to the zeal of its adherents and the appeal of its dogma. When the state encourages religious instruction or cooperates with religious authorities by adjusting the schedule of public events to sectarian needs, it follows the best of our traditions. For it then respects the religious nature of our people and accommodates the public service to their spiritual needs. To hold that it may not would be to find in the Constitution a requirement that the government show a callous indifference to religious groups. That would be preferring those who believe in no religion over those who do believe. Government may not finance religious groups nor undertake religious instruction nor blend secular and sectarian education nor use secular institutions to force one or some religion on any person. But we find no constitutional requirement which makes it necessary for government to be hostile to religion and to throw its weight against efforts to widen the effective scope of religious influence. The government must be neutral when it comes to competition between sects. It may not thrust any sect on any person. It may not make a religious observance compulsory. It may not coerce anyone to attend church, to observe a religious holiday, or to take religious instruction. But it can close its doors or suspend its operations as to those who want to repair to their religious sanctuary for worship or instruction. No more than that is undertaken here. . . .

In the McCollum Case the classrooms were used for religious instruction and the force of the public school was used to promote that instruction. Here, as we have said, the public schools do no more than accommodate their schedules to a program of outside religious instruction. We follow the McCollum Case. But we cannot expand it to cover the present released time program unless separation of Church and State means that public institutions can make no adjustments of their schedules to accommodate the religious needs of the people. We cannot read into the Bill of Rights such a philosophy of hostility to religion.

Affirmed.

Justices Black and Frankfurter wrote dissenting opinions.

Mr. Justice Jackson, dissenting, said in part:

This released time program is founded upon a use of the State's power of coercion, which, for me, determines its unconstitutionality. Stripped to its essentials, the plan has two stages, first, that the State compel each student to yield a large part of his time for public secular education and, second, that some of it be "released" to him on condition that he devote it to sectarian religious purposes.

No one suggests that the Constitution would permit the State directly to require this "released" time to be spent "under the control of a duly constituted religious body." This program accomplishes that forbidden result by indirection. If public education were taking so much of the pupils' time as to injure the public or the students' welfare by encroaching upon their religious opportunity, simply shortening everyone's school day would facilitate voluntary and optional attendance at Church classes. But that suggestion is rejected upon the ground that if they are made free many students will not go to the Church. Hence, they must be deprived of freedom for this period, with Church attendance put to them as one of the two permissible ways of using it.

The greater effectiveness of this system over voluntary attendance after school hours is due to the truant officer who, if the youngster fails to go to the Church school, dogs him back to the public schoolroom. Here schooling is more or less suspended during the "released time" so the nonreligious attendants will not forge ahead of the churchgoing absentees. But it serves as a temporary jail for a pupil who will not go to Church. It takes more subtlety of mind than I possess to deny that this is governmental constraint in support of religion. It is as unconstitutional, in my view, when exerted by indirection as when exercised forthrightly.

As one whose children, as a matter of free choice, have been sent to privately supported Church schools, I may challenge the Court's suggestion that opposition to this plan can only be antireligious, atheistic, or agnostic. My evangelistic brethren confuse an objection to compulsion with an objection to religion. It is possible to hold a faith with enough confidence to believe that what should be rendered to God does not need to be decided and collected by Caesar.

The day that this country ceases to be free for irreligion it will cease to be free for religion—except for the sect that can win political power. The same epithetical jurisprudence used by the Court today to beat down those who oppose pressuring children into some religion can devise as good epithets tomorrow against those who object to pressuring them into a favored religion. And, after all, if we concede to the State power and wisdom to single out "duly constituted religious" bodies as exclusive alternatives for compulsory secular instruction, it would be logical to also uphold the power and wisdom to choose the true faith among those "duly constituted." We start down a rough road when we begin to mix compulsory public education with compulsory godliness.

A number of Justices just short of a majority of the majority that promulgates today's passionate dialectics joined in answering them in Illinois ex rel. McCollum v. Board of Education. The distinction attempted between that case and this is trivial, almost to the point of cynicism, magnifying its nonessential details and disparaging compulsion which was the underlying reason for invalidity. A reading of the Court's opinion in that case along with its opinion in this case will show such difference of overtones and undertones as to make clear that the McCollum Case has passed like a storm in a teacup. The wall which the Court was professing to erect between Church and State has become even more warped and twisted than I expected. Today's judgment will be more interesting to students of psychology and of the judicial processes than to students of constitutional law.

8

Rights of Persons Accused of Crime

UNITED STATES v. ROBINSON
414 U. S. 218; 94 S. Ct. 467; 38 L. Ed. 2d 427
(1973)

One of the areas in which the Supreme Court has had the most difficulty agreeing on a consistent philosophy is that of unreasonable searches and seizures. In part, this is merely a reflection of the conflicting values in the country as a whole, but it is also the result of the methods by which the guarantee is enforced. Individual rights can be divided into two types. Those like free speech and religion have intrinsic value to the individual and are thought of as "substantive" rights, while those like the right to counsel and a jury trial are termed "procedural" because their purpose is to insure that one will only be convicted of crime on the basis of true evidence fairly presented and impartially appraised. Appellate courts will normally enforce the substantive rights by ordering the government either to stop interfering with their exercise or to grant those which are being withheld. The procedural rights, on the otherhand, are usually policed by ordering a new, untainted trial to take the place of the unfair one.

The guarantee against unreasonable searches and seizures, like the protection against compulsory self-incrimination, is in the anomalous position of being a substantive *right, of value to the individual for its own sake, but enforceable by the courts only through the procedural technique of ordering excluded at a new trial the evidence gotten by its violation. The result in those cases where the tainted evidence was essential to conviction is the release of a person who has been found guilty on the basis of probative evidence fairly appraised, not because he might be innocent, but because the police have violated his rights. In Justice Cardozo's famous phrase, "the criminal is to go free because the constable has blundered." People v. Defore, 242 N.Y. 13 (1926). While Supreme Court justices are not supposed to be influenced in constitutional judgments by the apparent guilt or innocence of a particular defendant, it is hard to escape the conclusion that a more consistent concern for the rights of the accused might emerge if the price were not the freeing of so many obviously guilty defendants.*

The technique of judicial interpretation employed by the Court in reaching its decisions in this area is the use of what have become known as talismanic tests—words and phrases originally used as shorthand for a constitutional theory, but which have since become substitutes for the theory itself. The basic constitutional theory underlying the Fourth Amendment is that a magistrate, not a policeman, should decide when a person's privacy should yield to a search, and a search without a magistrate's warrant is "unreasonable" unless it can be justified by some "exigent circumstance" *that makes getting a warrant impractical. Two examples of such exceptions are the warrantless search of an automobile before it can flee the jurisdiction and thus escape search entirely, and the warrantless search of a person by an arresting officer to protect both himself and the evidence of the crime. In both situations it would be impossible to stop and get a warrant and still make the arrest. However, since probable cause is necessary to get a search warrant, there must be probable cause to search without a warrant; and the arresting officer must be prepared to satisfy the court that the probable cause to search existed* before *the search was made.*

The talismans that have evolved from these two exceptions to the warrant requirement are the "Carroll" and the "search incident" doctrines. Carroll v. United States (1925) involved the stopping and searching without a warrant of a bootlegger's car, but while the Supreme Court upheld the search it emphasized that "where the securing of a warrant is reasonably practicable it must be used. . . . In cases where seizure is impossible except without a warrant, the seizing officer acts unlawfully and at his peril unless he can show the court probable cause." In its talismanic form, these last requirements are forgotten and the Carroll doctrine becomes the right to search a car without the usual requirement of a warrant.

The common law authorized a policeman to conduct a limited search, or "frisk," at the time of a lawful arrest. The obvious justification was that an arrested person might have on his person either a weapon with which he could effect his escape, or evidence which he might find an opportunity to destroy. On this theory, the extent of a search, both in time and space, is limited to what is necessary to protect the arresting officer or the evidence. But the talismanic "search incident" doctrine, divorced as it is from the theory, becomes simply an independent right to search an arrested person and the question then is what, if any, limits there are to such a search.

In the past half-century the Supreme Court has wandered back and forth between the theory and the talismans like a restless ghost. In Agnello v. United States (1925) it said that a search incident could extend "to the place where the arrest is made," but held it could not extend to another house several blocks away, and in Harris v. United States (1947), it upheld the search of Harris's four room apartment because it was "under his immediate control." A year later, in Trupiano v. United States (1948), the talismanic approach was abandoned. Revenue agents had watched an illegal still being constructed and put into operation for a period of several weeks, during which they could have obtained both search and arrest warrants. When they finally closed in, one man was engaged in running the still and the Court sustained his arrest. But returning to the basic theory, it held that the "fortuitous circumstance" that he was in the building rather than out in the yard did not justify seizing the still without a warrant as incident to lawful arrest, since there had been plenty of time to get one. In McDonald v. United States (1948), after a two-month surveillance of McDonald in connection with a numbers racket investigation, the police broke into McDonald's room, arrested him, and seized an adding machine and other lottery paraphernalia. Without discussing the question of lawful arrest, the Court held the search unreasonable. "Where, as here, officers are not responding to an emergency, there must be compelling reasons to justify the absence of a search warrant. A search without a warrant demands exceptional circumstances. . . ."

Two years later, in United States v. Rabinowitz (1950), the Court abruptly overruled Trupiano and held valid a widespread search of the defendant's property on the strength of his lawful arrest alone. Noting that the Constitution required only that a search be reasonable, not that it be made with a warrant if practicable, the Court found that, considering all the circumstances, this search was reasonable. The impact of this holding was to make possible a much broader search in conjunction with lawful arrest than could be made under a search warrant—as long as the arrest took place on the premises to be searched—since there was no limit as to "places to be searched" or "things to be seized." This was so much easier that in some communities the traditional search warrant became virtually extinct.

After nearly 20 years of this approach, the Supreme Court overruled Harris and Rabinowitz and returned to the underlying theory. In Chimel v. California (1969), the police had, as incident to arrest, searched an entire house including a garage and workshop, but the Court declined to draw distinguishing lines between this search and that of the single room *involved in Rabinowitz or the four rooms in Harris. "The only reasoned distinction is one between a search of the person arrested and the area within his reach on the one hand, and more extensive searches on the other." Furthermore, the theory justifying the search incident to arrest, the Court explained, itself marks its proper extent. "When an arrest is made, it is reasonable for the arresting officer to search the person arrested in order to remove any weapons that the latter might seek to use in order to resist arrest or effect his escape. Otherwise, the officer's safety might well be endangered, and the arrest itself frustrated. In addition, it is entirely reasonable for the arresting officer to search for and seize any evidence on the arrestee's person in order to prevent its concealment or destruction. And the area into which an arrestee might reach in order to grab a weapon or evidentiary items must, of course, be governed by a like rule. A gun on a table or in a drawer in front of one who is arrested can be as dangerous to the arresting officer as one concealed in the clothing of the person arrested. There is ample justification, therefore, for a search of the arrestee's person and the area "within his immediate control"—construing that phrase to mean the area from within which he might gain possession of a weapon or destructible evidence.*

"There is no comparable justification, however, for routinely searching rooms other than that in which an arrest occurs—or, for that matter, for searching through all the desk drawers or other closed or concealed areas in that room itself. Such searches, in the absence of well-recognized exceptions, may be made only under the authority of a search warrant. The 'adherence to judicial processes' mandated by the Fourth Amendment requires no less."

Although the talismanic "search incident" doctrine, unfettered by the need to show "exigency," would seem to permit arguing over how close in time a search must be to be "incident," until the present case the Court has not raised this point. In Preston v. United States (1964) the Court held void the search of a car in which the defendant had been riding, after it had been towed away to the police garage. "Once an accused is under arrest and in custody, then a search made at another place, without a warrant, is simply not incident to the arrest." Some of the force of this decision was lost in 1967 when the Court, in Cooper v. California, held that such a car could be searched without a warrant if the purpose of seizing it and the later search of it were "closely related" to the reason for the defendant's arrest. Narcotics had been found in both cars, but while Cooper had been arrested on a narcotics charge and his car impounded as contraband, Preston had been merely arrested for vagrancy and his car taken to the police garage to get it off the street.

In Chambers v. Maroney (1970), the Court reaffirmed Preston, but extended the Carroll *doctrine to justify a later search. There the police had* been given a description of a car, its occupants, and the clothing they wore, seen near the scene of a nighttime holdup. Within an hour a car answering the description, and containing the described occupants and clothing was stopped. The occupants were arrested and the car driven to the police station where it was searched and incriminating evidence discovered. The Court agreed unanimously that the evidence was properly admitted. Speaking for seven members of the Court, Justice White conceded that the "search incident" doctrine could not apply because the search was not made at the time and place of arrest.

But while the right to search incident to lawful arrest expired when the car was moved, the right to search under the Carroll doctrine did not. In view of the facts, the police had probable cause to search the car for guns and loot before it escaped their jurisdiction. Since it was impractical to follow it around, either they had to search it on the spot without a warrant, or they had to seize it without a warrant and detain it until a search warrant could be obtained. Conceding that arguably the search was the greater infringement and should only be made with a warrant, the Court found that "for constitutional purposes, we see no difference between on the one hand seizing and holding a car before presenting the probable cause issue to a magistrate and on the other hand carrying out an immediate search without a warrant."

In Coolidge v. New Hampshire (1971), the Court again applied the exigency theory to hold void a search of a suspect's car which was parked in his yard when the police came to arrest him. Since he was in the house, the Court held the search incident doctrine did not justify searching the car, and it rejected the argument "that under Carroll v. United States the police may make a warrantless search of an automobile whenever they have probable cause to do so. . . .

"The word 'automobile' is not a talisman in whose presence the Fourth Amendment fades away and disappears. And surely there is nothing in this case to invoke the meaning and purpose of the rule of Carroll v. United States—no alerted criminal bent on flight, no fleeting opportunity on an open highway after a hazardous chase, no contraband or stolen goods or weapons, no confederates waiting to move the evidence, not even the inconvenience of a special police detail to guard the immobilized automobile. In short, by no possible stretch of the legal imagination can this be made into a case where 'it is not practicable to secure a warrant,' Carroll, and the 'automobile exception,' despite its label, is simply irrelevant."

In United States v. Edwards (1974) the defendant had been arrested for burglarizing a United States post office by jimmying a window—an operation which had chipped the paint on the windowsill. The next day the police came to his cell, gave him new clothes, and without a warrant took his *clothes and searched them for evidence of paint chips (which they found). In upholding the validity of the search, the Court, dividing five to four, argued that the mere fact of a full "custodial" arrest justified a complete warrantless search of his clothing, and since they could have searched him that night, it was not unreasonable to wait until the next morning when substitute clothes could be made available. Referring with approval to Cooper v. California (1967), the Court noted that "it was no answer [in that case] to say that the police could have obtained a search warrant, for the Court held the test to be not whether it was reasonable to procure a search warrant, but whether the search itself was reasonable, which it was."*

Four dissenting justices pointed out that this language had been expressly rejected in Chimel v. California (1969) and that, in view of the time-lapse, "the considerations that typically justify a warrantless search incident to a lawful arrest were wholly absent here. . . . The police had ample time to seek a warrant, and no exigent circumstances were present to excuse their failure to do so."

Cardwell v. Lewis (1974) involved the warrantless seizure of the defendant's car from a public parking lot after he was in police custody. The car was impounded by the police and tire imprints and paint scrapings were taken to compare with information found at the scene of a murder. Justice Blackmun, writing for himself and Justices Burger, White and Rehnquist, argued that a search of the outside of the car was not really a breach of privacy and that in any event, cars were not entitled to as "stringent warrant requirements" as other places. Not only were they mobile, but "one has a lesser expectation of privacy in a motor vehicle because its function is transportation and it seldom serves as one's residence or as the repository of personal effects. A car has little capacity for escaping public scrutiny. It travels public thoroughfares where both its occupants and its contents are in plain view." Repeating the Court's statement in Katz v. United States (1967) that "what a person knowingly exposes to the public, even in his own home or office, is not a subject of Fourth Amendment protection," he added, "this is not to say that no part of the interior of an automobile has Fourth Amendment protection; the exercise of a desire to be mobile does not, of course, waive one's right to be free of unreasonable government intrusion. But insofar as Fourth Amendment protection extends to a motor vehicle, it is the right to privacy that is the touchstone of our inquiry." Justice Powell concurred on the ground that such questions, if fairly litigated in the state courts, should not be subject to federal court review. Justices Stewart, Douglas, Brennan and Marshall dissented, pointing out that the Carroll doctrine did not apply since the car was immobilized, and while "the plurality opinion suggests that other 'exigent circumstances' might have excused the failure of the

*police to procure a warrant, . . . the opinion nowhere states what these
mystical exigencies might have been, and counsel for the petitioner has not
been so inventive as to suggest any.''*

*While in the present case the law required a full "custodial arrest" for
the crime involved, in the companion case of Gustafson v. Florida, Gustafson was stopped at two a.m. and arrested when he could not produce his
driver's license. Although he could have given him a summons, the officer
decided to take him to the station house and searched him before putting
him into the patrol car. A "pat-down" search turned up a cigarette box
which was found to contain marijuana cigarettes. As in Robinson, the
Court rejected the argument that "there could be no evidentiary purpose
for the search," and held that "upon arresting petitioner for the offense
of driving his automobile without a valid operator's license, and taking
him into custody, the officer was entitled to make a full search of petitioner's person incident to that lawful arrest.''*

Mr. Justice Rehnquist delivered the opinion of the Court, saying in part:

On April 23, 1968, at approximately 11 p.m., Officer Richard Jenks, a
15-year veteran of the District of Columbia Metropolitan Police Department,
observed the respondent driving a 1965 Cadillac near the intersection of 8th
and C Streets, N.E., in the District of Columbia. Jenks, as a result of previous
investigation following a check of respondent's operator's permit four days
earlier, determined there was reason to believe that respondent was operating
a motor vehicle after the revocation of his operator's permit. This is an offense
defined by statute in the District of Columbia which carries a mandatory
minimum jail term, a mandatory minimum fine, or both.

Jenks signaled respondent to stop the automobile, which respondent did,
and all three of the occupants emerged from the car. At that point Jenks
informed respondent that he was under arrest for "operating after revocation
and obtaining a permit by misrepresentation." It was assumed by the Court
of Appeals, and is conceded by the respondent here, that Jenks had probable
cause to arrest respondent, and that he effected a full-custody arrest.

In accordance with procedures prescribed in police department instructions,
Jenks then began to search respondent. He explained at a subsequent hearing
that he was "face to face" with the respondent, and "placed [his] hands on [the
respondent], my right hand to his left breast like this (demonstrating) and
proceeded to pat him down thus [with the right hand]." During this patdown,
Jenks felt an object in the left breast pocket of the heavy coat respondent was

wearing, but testified that he "couldn't tell what it was" also that he "couldn't actually tell the size of it." Jenks then reached into the pocket and pulled out the object, which turned out to be a "crumpled up cigarette package." Jenks testified that at this point he still did not know what was in the package: "As I felt the package I could feel objects in the package but I couldn't tell what they were. . . . I knew they weren't cigarettes."

The officer then opened the cigarette pack and found 14 gelatin capsules of white powder which he thought to be, and which later analysis proved to be, heroin. Jenks then continued his search of respondent to completion, feeling around his waist and trouser legs, and examining the remaining pockets. The heroin seized from the respondent was admitted into evidence at the trial which resulted in his conviction in the District Court. . . .

I.

It is well settled that a search incident to a lawful arrest is a traditional exception to the warrant requirement of the Fourth Amendment. This general exception has historically been formulated into two distinct propositions. The first is that a search may be made of the *person* of the arrestee by virtue of the lawful arrest. The second is that a search may be made of the area within the control of the arrestee.

Examination of this Court's decisions shows that these two propositions have been treated quite differently. The validity of the search of a person incident to a lawful arrest has been regarded as settled from its first enunciation, and has remained virtually unchallenged until the present case. The validity of the second proposition, while likewise conceded in principle, has been subject to differing interpretations as to the extent of the area which may be searched.

Because the rule requiring exclusion of evidence obtained in violation of the Fourth Amendment was first enunciated in Weeks v. United States (1914), it is understandable that virtually all of this Court's search-and-seizure law has been developed since that time. In Weeks, the Court made clear its recognition of the validity of a search incident to a lawful arrest:

"What then is the present case? Before answering that inquiry specifically, it may be well by a process of exclusion to state what it is not. It is not an assertion of the right on the part of the Government, always recognized under English and American law, to search the person of the accused when legally arrested to discover and seize the fruits or evidences of crime. This right has been uniformly maintained in many cases. . . ."

Agnello v. United States (1925), decided 11 years after Weeks, repeats the categorical recognition of the validity of a search incident to lawful arrest: "The right without a search warrant contemporaneously to search persons lawfully arrested while committing crime and to search the place where the arrest is made in order to find and seize things connected with the crime as the fruits or as the means by which it was committed, as well as weapons and other things to effect an escape from custody, is not to be doubted."

Throughout the series of cases in which the Court has addressed the second proposition relating to a search incident to a lawful arrest—the permissible area beyond the person of the arrestee which such a search may cover—no doubt has been expressed as to the unqualified authority of the arresting authority to search the person of the arrestee. E.g., . . . Harris v. United States (1947); Trupiano v. United States (1948); United States v. Rabinowitz (1950); Chimel v. California (1969). In Chimel, where the Court overruled Rabinowitz and Harris as to the area of permissible search incident to a lawful arrest, full recognition was again given to the authority to search the person of the arrestee: "When an arrest is made, it is reasonable for the arresting officer to search the person arrested in order to remove any weapons that the latter might seek to use in order to resist arrest or effect his escape. Otherwise, the officer's safety might well be endangered, and the arrest itself frustrated. In addition, it is entirely reasonable for the arresting officer to search for and seize any evidence on the arrestee's person in order to prevent its concealment or destruction." . . . Last Term in Cupp v. Murphy (1973), we again reaffirmed the traditional statement of the authority to search incident to a valid arrest.

Thus the broadly stated rule, and the reasons for it, have been repeatedly affirmed in the decisions of this Court since Weeks v. United States nearly 60 years ago. Since the statements in the cases, speak not simply in terms of an exception to the warrant requirement, but in terms of an affirmative authority to search, they clearly imply that such searches also meet the Fourth Amendment's requirement of reasonableness.

II.

In its decision of this case, the Court of Appeals decided that even after a police officer lawfully places a suspect under arrest for the purpose of taking him into custody, he may not ordinarily proceed to fully search the prisoner. He must instead conduct a limited frisk of the outer clothing and remove such weapons that he may, as a result of that limited frisk, reasonably believe and ascertain that the suspect has in his possession. While recognizing that Terry v. Ohio (1968), dealt with a permissible "frisk" incident to an investigative stop based on less than probable cause to arrest, the Court of Appeals felt that the principles of that case should be carried over to this probable-cause arrest for driving while one's license is revoked. Since there would be no further evidence of such a crime to be obtained in a search of the arrestee, the court held that only a search for weapons could be justified.

Terry v. Ohio did not involve an arrest for probable cause, and it made quite clear that the "protective frisk" for weapons which it approved might be conducted without probable cause. This Court's opinion explicitly recognized that there is a "distinction in purpose, character, and extent between a search incident to an arrest and a limited search for weapons." "The former, although justified in part by the acknowledged necessity to protect the arresting officer from assault with a concealed weapon, . . . is also justified on other grounds, and can therefore involve a relatively extensive exploration of the person. A search for weapons in the absence of probable cause to arrest, however, must, like any other search, be strictly circumscribed by the exigencies which justify its initiation. . . . Thus it must be limited to that which is necessary for the discovery of weapons which might be used to harm the officer or others nearby, and may realistically be characterized as something less than a 'full' search even though it remains a serious intrusion.

". . . An arrest is a wholly different type of intrusion upon the individual freedom from a limited search for weapons, and the interests each is designed to serve are likewise quite different. An arrest is the initial stage of a criminal prosecution. It is intended to vindicate society's interest in having its laws obeyed, and it is inevitably accompanied by future interference with the individual's freedom of movement, whether or not trial or conviction ultimately follows. . . . Terry, therefore, affords no basis to carry over to a probable-cause arrest the limitations this court placed on a stop-and-frisk search permissible without probable cause.

The Court of Appeals also relied on language in Peters v. New York (1968), a companion case to Terry. There the Court held that the police officer had authority to search Peters because he had probable cause to arrest him, and went on to say: "[T]he incident search was obviously justified 'by the need to seize weapons and other things which might be used to assault an officer or effect an escape, as well as by the need to prevent the destruction of evidence of the crime.' Preston v. United States (1964). Moreover, it was reasonably limited in scope by these purposes. Officer Laskey did not engage in an unrestrained and thorough-going examination of Peters and his personal effects." . . .

We do not believe that the Court in Peters intended in one unexplained and unelaborated sentence to impose a novel and far-reaching limitation on the authority to search the person of an arrestee incident to his lawful arrest. While the language from Peters was quoted with approval in Chimel v. California, it is preceded by a full exposition of the traditional and unqualified authority of the arresting officer to search the arrestee's person. We do not believe that either Terry or Peters, when considered in the light of the previously discussed statements of this Court, justified the sort of limitation upon that authority which the Court of Appeals fashioned in this case.

III.

Virtually all of the statements of this Court affirming the existence of an unqualified authority to search incident to a lawful arrest are dicta. We would not therefore be foreclosed by principles of stare decisis from further examination into history and practice in order to see whether the sort of qualifications imposed by the Court of Appeals in this case were in fact intended by the Framers of the Fourth Amendment or recognized in cases decided prior to Weeks. Unfortunately such authorities as exist are sparse. Such common-law treatises as Blackstone's Commentaries and Holmes' Common Law are simply silent on the subject. Pollock and Maitland, in their History of English Law, describe the law of arrest as "rough and rude" before the time of Edward I, but do not address the authority to search incident to arrest. . . .

[The Court here quotes from a number of early English and state court cases.]

While these earlier authorities are sketchy, they tend to support the broad statement of the authority to search incident to arrest found in the successive decisions of this Court, rather than the restrictive one which was applied by the Court of Appeals in this case. The scarcity of case law before Weeks is doubtless due in part to the fact that the exclusionary rule there enunciated had been first adopted only 11 years earlier in Iowa; but it would seem to be also due in part to the fact that the issue was regarded as well settled.

The Court of Appeals in effect determined that the *only* reason supporting the authority for a *full* search incident to lawful arrest was the possibility of discovery of evidence or fruits.* Concluding that there could be no evidence or fruits in the case of an offense such as that with which respondent was charged, it held that any protective search would have to be limited by the conditions laid down in Terry for a search upon less than probable cause to arrest. Quite apart from the fact that Terry clearly recognized the distinction between the two types of searches, and that a different rule governed one than governed the other, we find additional reason to disagree with the Court of Appeals.

The justification or reason for the authority to search incident to a lawful arrest rests as much on the need to disarm the suspect in order to take him into custody as it does on the need to preserve evidence on his person for later use at trial. . . . The standards traditionally governing a search incident to lawful arrest are not, therefore, commuted to the stricter Terry standards by

---

*Where the arrest is made for a crime for which it is reasonable to believe that evidence exists, the Court of Appeals recognizes that "warrantless intrusion into the pockets of the arrestee to discover such evidence is reasonable under the 'search incident' exception." . . .

the absence of probable fruits or further evidence of the particular crime for which the arrest is made.

Nor are we inclined, on the basis of what seems to us to be a rather speculative judgment, to qualify the breadth of the general authority to search incident to a lawful custodial arrest on an assumption that persons arrested for the offense of driving while their licenses have been revoked are less likely to be possessed of dangerous weapons than are those arrested for other crimes.* It is scarcely open to doubt that the danger to an officer is far greater in the case of the extended exposure which follows the taking of a suspect into custody and transporting him to the police station than in the case of the relatively fleeting contact resulting from the typical Terry-type stop. This is an adequate basis for treating all custodial arrests alike for purposes of search justification.

But quite apart from these distinctions, our more fundamental disagreement with the Court of Appeals arises from its suggestion that there must be litigated in each case the issue of whether or not there was present one of the reasons supporting the authority for a search of the person incident to a lawful arrest. We do not think the long line of authorities of this Court dating back to Weeks, nor what we can glean from the history of practice in this country and in England, requires such a case-by-case adjudication. A police officer's determination as to how and where to search the person of a suspect whom he has arrested is necessarily a quick ad hoc judgment which the Fourth Amendment does not require to be broken down in each instance into an analysis of each step in the search. The authority to search the person incident to a lawful custodial arrest, while based upon the need to disarm and to discover evidence, does not depend on what a court may later decide was the probability in a particular arrest situation that weapons or evidence would in fact be found upon the person of the suspect. A custodial arrest of a suspect based on probable cause is a reasonable intrusion under the Fourth Amendment; that intrusion being lawful, a search incident to the arrest requires no additional justification. It is the fact of the lawful arrest which establishes the authority to search, and we hold that in the case of a lawful custodial arrest a full search

---

*Such an assumption appears at least questionable in light of the available statistical data concerning assaults onpolice officers who are in the course of making arrests. The danger to the police officer flows from the fact of the arrest, and its attendant proximity, stress and uncertainty, and not from the grounds for arrest. One study concludes that approximately 30% of the shooting of police officers occur when an officer stops a person in an automobile. Bristow, Police Officer Shootings—A Tactical Evaluation, . . . cited in Adams v. Williams (1972). The Government in its brief notes that the Uniform Crime Reports, prepared by the Federal Bureau of Investigation, indicate that a significant percentage of murdered police officers occurs when the officers are making traffic stops. Brief for the United States 23. Those reports indicate that during January–March, 1973, 35 police officers were murdered; 11 of those officers were killed while engaged in traffic stops.

of the person is not only an exception to the warrant requirement of the Fourth Amendment, but is also a "reasonable" search under that Amendment.

IV.

. . . Since it is the fact of custodial arrest which gives rise to the authority to search,* it is of no moment that Jenks did not indicate any subjective fear of the respondent or that he did not himself suspect that respondent was armed.** Having in the course of a lawful search come upon the crumpled package of cigarettes, he was entitled to inspect it; and when his inspection revealed the heroin capsules, he was entitled to seize them as "fruits, instrumentalities, or contraband" probative of criminal conduct. Harris v. United States. . . . The judgment of the Court of Appeals holding otherwise is

Reversed.

Mr. Justice Powell, concurring, said in part:

Although I join the opinions of the Court, I write briefly to emphasize what seems to me to be the essential premise of our decisions.

The Fourth Amendment safeguards the right of "the people to be secure in their persons, houses, papers, and effects, against unreasonable searches and seizures . . . ." These are areas of an individual's life about which he entertains legitimate expectations of privacy. I believe that an individual lawfully subjected to a custodial arrest retains no significant Fourth Amendment interest in the privacy of his person. Under this view the custodial arrest is the significant intrusion of state power into the privacy of one's person. If the arrest is lawful, the privacy interest guarded by the Fourth Amendment is subordinated to a legitimate and overriding governmental concern. No reason then exists to frustrate law enforcement by requiring some independent justification for a search incident to a lawful custodial arrest. This seems to me the reason that

---

*The opinion of the Court of Appeals also discussed its understanding of the law where the police officer makes what the court characterized as "a routine traffic stop," i.e., where the officer would simply issue a notice of violation and allow the offender to proceed. Since in this case the officer did make a full-custody arrest of the violator, we do not reach the question discussed by the Court of Appeals.

**The United States concedes that "in searching respondent, [Officer Jenks] was not motivated by a feeling of imminent danger and was not specifically looking for weapons." Brief for the United States 34, Officer Jenks testified, "I just searched him [Robinson]. I didn't think about what I was looking for. I just searched him." Officer Jenks also testified that upon removing the cigarette package from the respondent's custody, he was still unsure what was in the package, but that he knew it was not cigarettes.

a valid arrest justifies a full search of the person, even if that search is not narrowly limited by the twin rationales of seizing evidence and disarming the arrestee. The search incident to arrest is reasonable under the Fourth Amendment because the privacy interest protected by the constitutional guarantee is legitimately abated by the fact of arrest.*

Mr. Justice Marshall, with whom Mr. Justice Douglas and Mr. Justice Brennan join, dissenting, said in part:

II.

Mr. Justice Jackson, writing for the Court in Johnson v. United States (1948), explained that: "The point of the Fourth Amendment, which often is not grasped by zealous officers, is not that it denies law enforcement the support of the usual inferences which reasonable men draw from evidence. Its protections consist in requiring that those inferences be drawn by a neutral and detached magistrate instead of being judged by the officer engaged in the often competitive enterprise of ferreting out crime. . . . When the right of privacy must reasonably yield to the right of search is, as a rule, to be decided by a judicial officer, not by a policeman or government enforcement agent.". . . The majority's fear of overruling the "quick ad hoc judgment" of the police officer is thus inconsistent with the very function of the Amendment—to ensure that the quick ad hoc judgments of police officers are subject to review and control by the judiciary. . . .

The requirement that the police seek prior approval of a search from a judicial officer is, no doubt, subject to "a few specifically established and well-delineated exceptions.". . . But because an exception is invoked to justify a search without a warrant does not preclude further judicial inquiry into the reasonableness of that search. . . . Exceptions to warrant requirement are not talismans precluding further judicial inquiry whenever they are invoked, see Coolidge v. New Hampshire, but rather are "jealously and carefully drawn.". . .

Carrying out our mandate of delineating the proper scope of the search-incident-to-arrest exception requires consideration of the purposes of that exception as they apply to the particular search that occurred in this case. . . .

The majority . . . suggests that the Court of Appeals reached a novel and unprecedented result by imposing qualifications on the historically recognized authority to conduct a full search incident to a lawful arrest. Nothing could

---

*In Gustafson, the petitioner conceded the validity of the custodial arrest, although that conclusion was not as self-evident as in Robinson. Gustafson would have presented a different question if the petitioner could have proved that he was taken into custody only to afford a pretext for a search actually undertaken for collateral objectives. But no such question is before us.

be further from the truth, as the Court of Appeals itself was so careful to point out.

One need not go back to Blackstone's Commentaries, Holmes' Common Law, or Pollock & Maitland in search of precedent for the approach adopted by the Court of Appeals. Indeed, given the fact that mass production of the automobile did not begin until the early decades of the present century, I find it somewhat puzzling that the majority even looks to these sources for guidance on the only question presented in this case: the permissible scope of a search of the person incident to a lawful arrest for violation of a motor vehicle regulation. The fact is that this question has been considered by several state and federal courts, the vast majority of which have held that absent special circumstances a police officer has no right to conduct a full search of the person incident to a lawful arrest for violation of a motor vehicle regulation. . . .

[Justice Marshall here reviews a series of state and federal cases dealing with searches following arrests for traffic violations.]

Accordingly, I think it disingenuous for the Court to now pronounce that what precedents exist on the question "tend to support the broad statement of the authority to search incident to arrest found in the successive decisions of this Court, rather than the restrictive one which was applied by the Court of Appeals in this case." It is disquieting, to say the least, to see the Court at once admit that "[v]irtually all of the statements of this Court affirming the existence of an unqualified authority to search incident to a lawful arrest are dicta" and concede that we are presented with an open question on which "further examination into history and practice" would be helpful, yet then conduct an examination into prior practice which is not only wholly superficial, but totally inaccurate and misleading.

The majority's attempt to avoid case-by-case adjudication of Fourth Amendment issues is not only misguided as a matter of principle, but is also doomed to fail as a matter of practical application. . . . There is always the possibility that a police officer, lacking probable cause to obtain a search warrant, will use a traffic arrest as a pretext to conduct a search. . . . I suggest this possibility not to impugn the integrity of our police, but merely to point out that case-by-case adjudication will always be necessary to determine whether a full arrest was effected for purely legitimate reasons or, rather, as a pretext for searching the arrestee. . . .

III. . . .

The underlying rationale of a search incident to arrest of a traffic offender initially suggests as reasonable a search whose scope is similar to the protective weapons frisk permitted in Terry. A search incident to arrest, as the majority indicates, has two basic functions: the removal of weapons the arrestee might use to resist arrest or effect an escape, and the seizure of evidence or fruits of the crime for which the arrest is made, so as to prevent its concealment or destruction. . . .

The Government does not now contend that the search of respondent's pocket can be justified by any need to find and seize evidence in order to prevent its concealment or destruction, for, as the Court of Appeals found, there is no evidence or fruits of the offense with which respondent was charged. The only rationale for a search in this case, then, is the removal of weapons which the arrestee might use to harm the officer and attempt an escape. This rationale, of course, is identical to the rationale of the search permitted in Terry. As we said there, "The sole justification of the search in the present situation is the protection of the police officers and others nearby, and it must therefore be confined in scope to an intrusion reasonably designed to discover guns, knives, clubs, or other hidden instruments for the assault of the police officer." Terry v. Ohio. Since the underlying rationale of a Terry search and the search of a traffic violator are identical, the Court of Appeals held that the scope of the searches must be the same. And in view of its conclusion that the removal of the object from respondent's coat pocket exceeded the scope of a lawful Terry frisk, a conclusion not disputed by the Government or challenged by the majority here, the plurality of the Court of Appeals held that the removal of the package exceeded the scope of a lawful search incident to arrest of a traffic violator.

The problem with this approach, however, is that it ignores several significant differences between the context in which a search incident to arrest for a traffic violation is made, and the situation presented in Terry. . . .

. . . As the Court of Appeals noted, a crucial feature distinguishing the in-custody arrest from the Terry context " 'is not the greater likelihood that a person taken into custody is armed, but rather the increased likelihood of danger to the officer *if* in fact the person is armed.' " . . . A Terry stop involves a momentary encounter between officer and suspect, while an in-custody arrest places the two in close proximity for a much longer period of time. If the individual happens to have a weapon on his person, he will certainly have much more opportunity to use it against the officer in the in-custody situation. . . .

The majority relies on statistics indicating that a significant percentage of murders of police officers occurs when the officers are making traffic stops. But these statistics only confirm what we recognized in Terry—that "American criminals have a long tradition of armed violence, and every year in this country many law enforcement officers are killed in the line of duty, and thousands more are wounded." As the very next sentence in Terry recognized, however, "Virtually all of these deaths and a substantial portion of the injuries are inflicted with guns and knives." The statistics relied on by the Government in this case support this observation. Virtually all of the killings are caused by guns and knives, the very type of weapons which will not go undetected in a properly conducted weapons frisk.* It requires more than citation to these statistics, then, to support the proposition that it is reasonable for police officers to conduct more than a Terry-type frisk for weapons when seeking to disarm a traffic offender who is taken into custody.

C.

The majority opinion fails to recognize that the search conducted by Officer Jenks did not merely involve a search of respondent's person. It also included a separate search of effects found on his person. And even were we to assume, arguendo, that it was reasonable for Jenks to remove the object he felt in respondent's pocket, clearly there was no justification consistent with the Fourth Amendment which would authorize his opening the package and looking inside. . . .

It is suggested, however, that since the custodial arrest itself represents a significant intrusion into the privacy of the person, any additional intrusion by way of opening or examining effects found on the person is not worthy of constitutional protection. But such an approach was expressly rejected by the Court in Chimel. . . . "[W]e can see no reason why, simply because some interference with an individual's privacy and freedom of movement has lawfully taken place, further intrusions should automatically be allowed despite the absence of a warrant that the Fourth Amendment would otherwise require.". . .

The Government argues that it is difficult to see what constitutionally protected "expectation of privacy" a prisoner has in the interior of a cigarette pack. One wonders if the result in this case would have been the same were respondent a businessman who was lawfully taken into custody for driving without a license and whose wallet was taken from him by the police. . . .

UNITED STATES v. UNITED STATES DISTRICT COURT
407 U. S. 297; 92 S. Ct. 2125; 32 L. Ed. 2d 752
(1972)

No area of Fourth Amendment rights stirs both political and constitutional disputes as does the question of electronic surveillance. Law enforcement

---

*The Uniform Crime Reports prepared by the Federal Bureau of Investigation which are relied on by the majority . . . indicate that 112 police officers were killed nationwide in 1972. Of these, 108 were killed by firearms. Two of the remaining four were killed with knives, and the last two cases involved a bomb and an automobile.

and security agencies tend to view the technical advance in eavesdropping equipment as heaven-sent tools in their battle against organized crime and the foreign and domestic enemies of the country. What better way to catch criminals and subversives than to listen to their telephone conversations and "bug" a room in which their nefarious plans are laid. The difficulty lies in the necessarily clandestine nature of such work and the consequent inability of the public to judge how much and against whom the techniques are being used. The realization that everyone must be watched, if the evildoers are to be identified, and that many innocent conversations may rise up to haunt one disturbs many persons who approve of the suppression of crime and subversion. Evidence that the military was collecting information on private citizens (see Laird v. Tatum, 1972), and the dramatic exposures of widespread eavesdropping by government security agencies do nothing to reassure a person who feels these powers may be misused.

Among the most challenging tasks faced by the Supreme Court in recent years has been the extension of the Fourth Amendment protection to cover the threat of privacy posed by electronic eavesdropping. The Fourth Amendment was drafted in an age when all one needed to do to communicate in private was to whisper, or go into the house and shut the door. The amendment does not speak of privacy. It speaks of the security of "persons, houses, papers and effects," and the warrant needed to search has to describe the "persons or things" to be seized. Thus it was a protection only against the physical invasion of a person or his house and the seizure of tangible things belonging to him. What could be heard by the eavesdropper under the window or seen by peeping at the keyhole was not being seized, and the search of a defendant's open field which resulted in the finding of a whiskey bottle was held to be neither a search nor a seizure. See Hester v. United States (1924). It was this interpretation that led the Court, in Olmstead v. United States (1918), to hold that tapping a telephone wire outside the premises of the defendant did not constitute an unreasonable search and seizure. The Court argued first that since the wire-tap itself had not been made on Olmstead's premises, there was no physical trespass. Second, Olmstead had not intended that his voice should reach only the ears of those present in the room—he had intended "to project his voice to those quite outside." And third, what had been seized from Olmstead was his spoken word. Nothing tangible had been taken that would make applicable the constitutional injunction requiring a warrant describing "things to be seized." Justice Brandeis's prophetic warning of the evils of electronic eavesdropping was considered irrelevant largely because the Fourth Amendment was not viewed by the Court as a general protection of the right of private communication. With the passage of the Federal Communications Act of 1934 Congress provided that "no person not being authorized by the sender shall intercept any communication and divulge or publish the existence, contents, substance . . . of such intercepted communication to any person." In Nardone v. United States (1937) the Court held that this section forbade wire tapping by federal officers as well as by others, and that the evidence secured by them by this now unlawful practice could not be used in a federal prosecution of the victim of the wire-tap. In the second Nardone case (1939) the ban was extended to evidence discovered as a result of wire tapping. The Nardone rule has not prevented official wire tapping, but has prevented the use of wire-tap evidence in Court, although it may be used even there for certain purposes.

The argument in Olmstead that the Fourth Amendment was limited to tangible items was the first to be abandoned by the Court. In Goldman v. United States (1942) the Court held that eavesdropping by means of a detectophone, a sensitive device which could pick up conversations in an adjoining room, was not an unreasonable search and seizure; and in 1952 the rule was reaffirmed in On Lee v. United States, in which an undercover narcotics agent with a hidden pocket transmitter engaged a shopkeeper in conversation and transmitted damaging admissions to an agent in a car outside. In both these cases the Court relied on the absence of trespass to sustain the use of the evidence rather than upon the fact that nothing tangible was being seized. Finally, in Silverman v. United States (1961) the Court held void a search for intangibles where there was trespass. A "spike-mike" had been driven into a hot-air duct in a building wall so that police could overhear conversations within the building. While probably not amounting to trespass under local law, it was considered by the Court to be a "physical intrusion into a constitutionally protected area." The Court emphasized that physical trespass distinguished the case from Olmstead, but simply ignored Olmstead's limitation of the amendment to "things" that were tangible.

While breaking into a home or office, or an obvious physical intrusion however slight (like a spike-mike), could clearly be viewed as trespass, what was the status of the traditional undercover agent who posed as a member of the "gang" in order to gain evidence of crime? In 1921 the Court in Gouled v. United States had held unanimously that "whether entrance to the home or office of a person suspected of crime be obtained by a representative of . . . the government . . . by stealth or through social acquaintance, or in the guise of a business call, and whether the owner be present or not when he enters, any search and seizure subsequently and secretly made in his absence falls within the scope of the Fourth Amendment." Does this mean that planting an informer in a criminal conspiracy violates the Fourth Amendment right of the conspirators? In Hoffa v. United States (1966), the Court held that it did not. Partin, a local teamster official, acted as a paid informer to bring federal officials reports on Hoffa's efforts to bribe the jury in a federal trial in which Hoffa was involved. The Court conceded that a hotel room can be an area protected by the Fourth Amendment, that the amendment can be violated by guile as well as by forceful entry, and that its protection is not limited to tangibles. But Hoffa had no protection in this instance because "what the Fourth Amendment protects is the security a man relies upon when he places himself or his property within a constitutionally protected area." In this case Hoffa "was not relying on the security of the hotel room; he was relying upon his misplaced confidence that Partin would not reveal his wrongdoing." A similar result was reached in Lewis v. United States (1966) where a narcotics pusher had invited a federal agent to his home and sold him narcotics, not knowing what he was. By converting his home into a "commercial center to which outsiders are invited for purposes of transacting unlawful business" the pusher forfeited its sanctity under the Fourth Amendment.

And if serving as an undercover agent to obtain evidence does not violate the Fourth Amendment, neither does carrying electronic equipment to insure that the evidence is accurately reported. On Lee v. United States (1952) had upheld the use of a pocket transmitter carried by an old friend of the accused who had turned informer, and in Lopez v. United States (1963) the Court sustained the use of a pocket tape recorder by an internal revenue agent whom Lopez had attempted to bribe. Without specifically reaffirming On Lee, the Court emphasized in this case that "the Government did not use an electronic device to listen in on conversations it could not otherwise have heard." Lopez had known he was addressing a federal officer, and the only result of excluding the tape would have been to permit Lopez "to rely on flaws in the agent's memory, or to challenge the agent's credibility without being beset by corroborating evidence that is not susceptible of impeachment." Chief Justice Warren concurred, but argued that On Lee should be overruled. Justices Brennan, Douglas, and Goldberg, citing the evils of uncontrolled eavesdropping attacked the decision on the broad ground that electronic eavesdropping posed a threat to privacy and free communication—both essential to our type of society. "If a person must always be on his guard against his auditor's having authorized a secret recording of their conversation, he will be no less reluctant to speak freely than if his risk is that a third party is doing the recording. . . . I believe that there is a grave danger of chilling all private, free, and unconstrained communication if secret recordings, turned over to law enforcement officers by one party to a conversation, are competent evidence of any self-incriminating statements the speaker may have made. In a free society, people ought not have to watch their every word so carefully."

In Osborn v. United States (1966), decided the same day as Hoffa, the Court reaffirmed the validity of such "participant surveillance," in which a participant in a conversation carries an electronic device. Here Osborn, a lawyer for Hoffa, learned that one Vick, a local policeman who had been hired to investigate the backgrounds of potential jurors in the Hoffa trial, was related to one of the potential jurors. He allegedly told Vick to approach his relative about voting to acquit Hoffa if he got on the jury, and Vick went to the federal agents with the story. On the strength of Vick's sworn statements, two federal district judges authorized the FBI to conceal a tape recorder on Vick's person, and a record of the attempt to tamper with the jury was introduced in court against Osborn. The Court, while upholding the use of the recorded evidence, declined to do so on the broad grounds of the Lopez case. Bowing, in part at least, to the dissenters in Lopez, it emphasized that "the issue here . . . is not the permissibility of 'indiscriminate use of such devices in law enforcement,' but the permissibility of using such a device under the most precise and discriminate circumstances, circumstances which fully met the 'requirement of particularity' which the dissenting opinion in Lopez found necessary." The Court noted that only "in response to a detailed factual affidavit alleging the commission of a specific criminal offense directly and immediately affecting the administration of justice in the federal court, the judges of that court jointly authorized the use of a recording device for the narrow and particularized purpose of ascertaining the truth of the affidavit's allegations. . . . There could hardly be a clearer example of the procedure of antecedent justification before a magistrate that is central to the Fourth Amendment as 'a precondition of lawful electronic surveillance.' "

The traditional method of protecting the right of privacy in a simple society was through the use of a search warrant, but the nature of the information to be gotten and the techniques involved in getting it make the ordinary search warrant inapplicable to electronic eavesdropping. In Berger v. New York (1967) the Court indicated that at least prior judicial approval was necessary for wire tapping. There the Court held void the use of electronic eavesdrop evidence obtained by the police under a warrant issued by a New York court. The New York statute authorized the issue of an eavesdrop warrant if the police officer swore that there was reasonable ground to believe "that evidence of crime may thus be obtained" and particularly describing the persons whose communications were sought and why, and the telephone to be tapped. The tapping could take place for up to two months, with a two-month renewal at the request of the police. This, the Court held, did not meet the "requirement of particularity" required by the Fourth Amendment which had been met in Osborn v. United States (1966). There the orders sought had "described the type of conversation sought with particularity," had "authorized one limited intrusion rather than a series or a continuous surveillance," and "probable cause was shown for the succeeding one," and the officer was required to make a return to the court showing how the order had been executed and what had been seized.

In Katz v. United States (1969), such prior authorization was held necessary for the electronic bugging of a telephone booth. Abandoning both the trespass requirement of Olmstead and the "constitutionally protected area" concept of Silverman, the Court announced that "what a person knowingly exposes to the public, even in his own home or office, is not a subject of Fourth Amendment protection. . . . But what he seeks to preserve as private, even in an area accessible to the public, may be constitutionally protected."

Did these new rules apply to the kind of participant surveillance involved in On Lee v. United States (1952) and Lopez v. United States (1963)? In deciding Osborn, the Court had carefully refrained from reaffirming Lopez and had approved the use of the transmitted evidence only because the agents had gotten prior approval and the eavesdropping had been carried out under the vigilant surveillance of the court. This fact, plus the approval of Osborn expressed in both Berger and Katz, suggested that the answer might be "yes."

In United States v. White (1971) this apparent trend of the cases was reversed. The case involved an informer who transmitted conversations to which he was a party (concerning narcotics) to a federal agent outside with a radio receiver. Justice White, joined by Chief Justice Burger and Justices Stewart and Blackmun, reaffirmed On Lee and Lopez, noting that the Katz rule had been held not to be retroactive (see Desist v. United States, 1969), and in any event did not deal with the problem of participant surveillance. Although Katz had extended Fourth Amendment protection to "justifiable" expectations of privacy, Hoffa v. United States (1966), "which was left undisturbed by Katz," had made it clear that the "amendment affords no protection to 'a wrongdoer's misplaced belief that a person to whom he voluntarily confides his wrongdoing will not reveal it.'" Since White's expectation of privacy was based upon just such a belief, it was not "justifiable."

An added complication in the field of electronic surveillance was the distinction between illegally seized evidence and unconstitutionally seized evidence. Following the Olmstead case, Congress outlawed wire tapping by statute, and in Nardone v. United States (1937) the Court held wiretap evidence inadmissible in federal court, not because it was gotten unconstitutionally, but because it was gotten illegally. Since wire tapping was merely illegal, rather than a violation of constitutional rights, the decision in Mapp v. Ohio (1961) that unconstitutionally gotten evidence could not be used in a state court did not seem to apply to wire-tap evidence. The New York courts admitted wire-tap evidence and in Dinan v. New York

(1962) the Court rejected an opportunity to hold that the federal statute forbade such admission. The overruling of Olmstead in the Katz case, however, meant that the Fourth Amendment now applies to wire tapping. Hence, starting with the Katz case, wire-tap evidence could be used in a state court if it met the warrant requirements of the Fourth Amendment, but it could not be used in a federal court because federal law did not permit wire tapping even with a warrant.

Nor was there any apparent way in which this distinction could be abolished, if indeed it was necessary to abolish it. The clear implications of Mapp were that the exclusionary rule was a constitutional one, stemming from the Fourth and Fourteenth Amendments' restrictions on searches and seizures, while the Nardone rule forbade the use of illegal evidence under the Court's power to control the use of evidence in the federal courts, a power not applicable to the states.

In Lee v. Florida, decided in June 1968, the Court did abolish the distinction, and made what it referred to as the "judicially devised exclusionary rule" of the Mapp case applicable to illegal as well as unconstitutional evidence. Referring to the supremacy clause in Article VI, it held that under our Constitution no court, state or federal, may serve as an accomplice in the willful transgression of "the Laws of the United States," by which "the Judges in every State [are] bound. . . ." The result of this decision was to make inadmissible in any court evidence gotten by wire tapping, even under a court order which met all the tests described in the Berger case as meeting Fourth Amendment requirements. Thus, while it was possible with a proper authorization to "bug" the telephone booth itself, it was no longer possible to tap the wire going into the booth.

Three days after the decision in Lee v. Florida this distinction was nullified by the enactment of the Omnibus Crime Control and Safe Streets Act of 1968. The statute in effect repealed § 605 of the Federal Communications Act and, for the first time, permits both state and federal officers to tap telephone wires and intercept "oral communications" under court order in cases involving any in a long list of state and federal crimes, including those dealing with gambling and narcotics. The procedures set out in the statute for authorizing such interception conform closely to those required by Berger, and where an "emergency" requires interception before an order can "with due diligence" be obtained, and "there are grounds upon which an order could be entered," the police may tap or bug for 48 hours before applying for an order. If the order is subsequently denied, or never asked for, neither the contents of the communication "nor evidence derived therefrom" may be used in any trial court or other hearing. If the President, however, in exercising his constitutional powers to protect the national security, intercepts wire or oral communications, their contents "may be received in evidence in any trial hearing, or other proceeding only where such interception was reasonable, and shall not be otherwise used or disclosed except as is necessary to implement that power."

The present case arose out of the efforts of one Plamondon to find out whether wire-tap evidence that would be used against him on a charge of bombing a CIA office in Ann Arbor, Michigan, had been gotten illegally and should be made available to him. The government conceded it had not obtained a warrant, but argued that the surveillance was lawful under the President's power to protect the national security. The district court held the evidence illegally gotten, and the government filed for a writ of mandamus to set aside the court's order.

Mr. Justice Powell delivered the opinion of the Court, saying in part:

I.

Title III of the Omnibus Crime Control and Safe Streets Act authorizes the use of electronic surveillance for classes of crimes carefully specified in 18 U.S.C. § 2516. Such surveillance is subject to prior court order. Section 2518 sets forth the detailed and particularized application necessary to obtain such an order as well as carefully circumscribed conditions for its use. The Act represents a comprehensive attempt by Congress to promote more effective control of crime while protecting the privacy of individual thought and expression. Much of Title III was drawn to meet the constitutional requirements for electronic surveillance enunciated by this Court in Berger v. New York (1967) and Katz v. United States (1967).

Together with the elaborate surveillance requirements in Title III, there is the following proviso, 18 U.S.C. § 2511 (3):

"Nothing contained in this chapter or in section 605 of the Communications Act of 1934 shall limit the constitutional power of the President to take such measures as he deems necessary to protect the Nation against actual or potential attack or other hostile acts of a foreign power, to obtain foreign intelligence information deemed essential to the security of the United States, or to protect national security information against foreign intelligence activities. *Nor shall anything contained in this chapter be deemed to limit the constitutional power of the President to take such measures as he deems necessary to protect the United States against the overthrow of the Government by force or other unlawful means, or against any other clear and present danger to the structure or existence of the Government.* The contents of any wire or oral communication intercepted by authority of the President in the exercise of the foregoing powers may be received in evidence in any trial, hearing, or other proceeding only where such interception was reasonable, and shall not be otherwise used or disclosed except as is necessary to implement that power." (Emphasis supplied.)

The Government relies on §2511 (3). It argues that "in excepting national security surveillances from the Act's warrant requirement Congress recognized the President's authority to conduct such surveillances without prior judicial approval." The section thus is viewed as a recognition or affirmance of a constitutional authority in the President to conduct warrantless domestic security surveillance such as that involved in this case.

We think the language of §2511 (3), as well as the legislative history of the statute, refutes this interpretation. The relevant language is that: "Nothing contained in this chapter . . . shall limit the constitutional power of the President to take such measures as he deems necessary to protect . . ." against the dangers specified. At most, this is an implicit recognition that the President does have certain powers in the specified areas. Few would doubt this, as the section refers—among other things—to protection "against actual or potential attack or other hostile acts of a foreign power." But so far as the use of the President's electronic surveillance power is concerned, the language is essentially neutral.

Section 2511 (3) certainly confers no power, as the language is wholly inappropriate for such a purpose. It merely provides that the Act shall not be interpreted to limit or disturb such power as the President may have under the Constitution. In short, Congress simply left presidential powers where it found them. This view is reinforced by the general context of Title III. Section 2511 (1) broadly prohibits the use of electronic surveillance "[e]xcept as otherwise specifically provided in this chapter." Subsection (2) thereof contains four specific exceptions. In each of the specified exceptions, the statutory language is as follows: "It shall not be unlawful . . . to intercept" the particular type of communication described.

The language of subsection (3), here involved, is to be contrasted with the language of the exceptions set forth in the preceding subsection. Rather than stating that warrantless presidential uses of electronic surveillance "shall not be unlawful" and thus employing the standard language of exception, subsection (3) merely disclaims any intention to "limit the constitutional power of the President.". . .

The legislative history of § 2511 (3) supports this interpretation. . . .

. . . If we could accept the Government's characterization of § 2511 (3) as a congressionally prescribed exception to the general requirement of a warrant, it would be necessary to consider the question of whether the surveillance in this case came within the exception and, if so, whether the statutory exception was itself constitutionally valid. But viewing § 2511 (3) as a congressional disclaimer and expression of neutrality, we hold that the statute is not the measure of the executive authority asserted in this case. Rather, we must look to the constitutional powers of the President.

II.

It is important at the outset to emphasize the limited nature of the question before the Court. This case raises no constitutional challenge to electronic surveillance as specifically authorized by Title III of the Omnibus Crime Control and Safe Streets Act of 1968. Nor is there any question or doubt as to the necessity of obtaining a warrant in the surveillance of crimes unrelated to the national security interest. Katz v. United States (1967); Berger v. New York (1967). Further, the instant case requires no judgment on the scope of the President's surveillance power with respect to the activities of foreign powers, within or without this country. The Attorney General's affidavit in this case states that the surveillances were "deemed necessary to protect the nation from attempts of *domestic organizations* to attack and subvert the existing structure of Government" (emphasis supplied). There is no evidence of any involvement, directly or indirectly, of a foreign power.

Our present inquiry, though important, is therefore a narrow one. It addresses a question left open by Katz: "Whether safeguards other than prior authorization by a magistrate would satisfy the Fourth Amendment in a situation involving the national security . . . ." The determination of this question requires the essential Fourth Amendment inquiry into the "reasonableness" of the search and seizure in question, and the way in which that "reasonableness" derives content and meaning through reference to the warrant clause. Coolidge v. New Hampshire (1971).

We begin the inquiry by noting that the President of the United States has the fundamental duty, under Art. II, § 1, of the Constitution, "to preserve, protect, and defend the Constitution of the United States." Implicit in that duty is the power to protect our Government against those who would subvert or overthrow it by unlawful means. In the discharge of this duty, the President —through the Attorney General—may find it necessary to employ electronic surveillance to obtain intelligence information on the plans of those who plot unlawful acts against the Government. The use of such surveillance in internal security cases has been sanctioned more or less continuously by various Presidents and Attorneys General since July 1946. Herbert Brownell, Attorney General under President Eisenhower, urged the use of electronic surveillance both in internal and international security matters on the grounds that those acting against the Government "turn to the telephone to carry on their intrigue. The success of their plans frequently rests upon piecing together shreds of information received from many sources and many nests. The participants in the conspiracy are often dispersed and stationed in various strategic positions in government and industry throughout the country."

Though the Government and respondents debate their seriousness and magnitude, threats and acts of sabotage against the Government exist in sufficient number to justify investigative powers with respect to them. The covertness and complexity of potential unlawful conduct against the Government and the necessary dependency of many conspirators upon the telephone make electronic surveillance an effective investigatory instrument in certain circumstances. The marked acceleration in technological developments and sophistication in their use have resulted in new techniques for the planning, commission and concealment of criminal activities. It would be contrary to the public interest for Government to deny to itself the prudent and lawful employment of those very techniques which are employed against the Government and its law-abiding citizens.

It has been said that "[t]he most basic function of any government is to provide for the security of the individual and of his property." Miranda v. Arizona, (1966) (White, J., dissenting). And unless Government safeguards its own capacity to function and to preserve the security of its people, society itself could become so disordered that all rights and liberties would be endangered.
. . .

But a recognition of these elementary truths does not make the employment by Government of electronic surveillance a welcome development—even when employed with restraint and under judicial supervision. There is, understandably, a deep-seated uneasiness and apprehension that this capability will be used to intrude upon cherished privacy of law-abiding citizens. We look to the Bill of Rights to safeguard this privacy. Though physical entry of the home is the chief evil against which the wording of the Fourth Amendment is directed, its broader spirit now shields private speech from unreasonable surveillance. . . . Our decision in Katz refused to lock the Fourth Amendment into instances of actual physical trespass. Rather, the Amendment governs "not only the seizure of tangible items, but extends as well to the recording of oral statements . . . without any 'technical trespass under . . . local property law.' " That decision implicitly recognized that the broad and unsuspected governmental incursions into conversational privacy which electronic surveillance entails necessitate the application of Fourth Amendment safeguards.

National security cases, moreover, often reflect a convergence of First and Fourth Amendment values not present in cases of "ordinary" crime. Though the investigative duty of the executive may be stronger in such cases, so also is there greater jeopardy to constitutionally protected speech. "Historically the struggle for freedom of speech and press in England was bound up with the issue of the scope of the search and seizure power," Marcus v. Search Warrant (1961). History abundantly documents the tendency of Government—however benevolent and benign its motives—to view with suspicion those who most fervently dispute its policies. Fourth Amendment protections become the more necessary when the targets of official surveillance may be those suspected of unorthodoxy in their political beliefs. The danger to political dissent is acute where the Government attempts to act under so vague a concept as the power to protect "domestic security." Given the difficulty of defining the domestic security interest, the danger of abuse in acting to protect that interest becomes apparent. Senator Hart addressed this dilemma in the floor debate on § 2511 (3): "As I read it—and this is my fear—we are saying that the President, on his motion, could declare—name your favorite poison—draft dodgers, Black Muslims, the Ku Klux Klan, or civil rights activists to be a clear and present danger to the structure or existence of the Government." The price of lawful public dissent must not be a dread of subjection to an unchecked surveillance power. Nor must the fear of unauthorized official eavesdropping deter vigorous citizen dissent and discussion of Government action in private conversation. For private dissent, no less than open public discourse, is essential to our free society.

III.

As the Fourth Amendment is not absolute in its terms, our task is to examine and balance the basic values at stake in this case: the duty of Government to protect the domestic security, and the potential danger posed by unreasonable surveillance to individual privacy and free expression. If the legitimate need of Government to safeguard domestic security requires the use of electronic surveillance, the question is whether the needs of citizens for privacy and free expression may not be better protected by requiring a warrant before such surveillance is undertaken. We must also ask whether a warrant requirement would unduly frustrate the efforts of Government to protect itself from acts of subversion and overthrow directed against it.

Though the Fourth Amendment speaks broadly of "unreasonable searches and seizures," the definition of "reasonableness" turns, at least in part, on the more specific commands of the warrant clause. Some have argued that "[t]he relevant test is not whether it was reasonable to procure a search warrant, but whether the search was reasonable," United States v. Rabinowitz (1950).* This view, however, overlooks the second clause of the Amendment. The warrant clause of the Fourth Amendment is not dead language. Rather it has been "a valued part of our constitutional law for decades, and it has determined the result in scores and scores of cases in the courts all over this country. It is not

---

*This view has not been accepted. In Chimel v. California (1969) the Court considered the Government's contention that the search be judged on a general "reasonableness" standard without reference to the warrant clause. The Court concluded that argument was "founded on little more than a subjective view regarding the acceptability of certain sorts of police conduct, and not on considerations relevant to Fourth Amendment interests. Under such an unconfined analysis, Fourth Amendment protection in this area would approach the evaporation point."

an inconvenience to be somehow 'weighed' against the claims of police efficiency. It is, or should be, an important working part of our machinery of government, operating as a matter of course to check the 'well-intentioned but mistakenly overzealous executive officers' who are a part of any system of law enforcement." Coolidge v. New Hampshire. . . .

Over two centuries ago, Lord Mansfield held that common-law principles prohibited warrants that ordered the arrest of unnamed individuals whom the *officer* might conclude were guilty of seditious libel. "It is not fit," said Mansfield, "that the receiving or judging of the information should be left to the discretion of the officer. The magistrate ought to judge; and should give certain directions to the officer." Leach v. Three of the King's Messengers (1765).

Lord Mansfield's formulation touches the very heart of the Fourth Amendment directive: that, where practical, a governmental search and seizure should represent both the efforts of the officer to gather evidence of wrongful acts and the judgment of the magistrate that the collected evidence is sufficient to justify invasion of a citizen's private premises or conversation. Inherent in the concept of a warrant is its issuance by a "neutral and detached magistrate." . . . The further requirement of "probable cause" instructs the magistrate that baseless searches shall not proceed.

These Fourth Amendment freedoms cannot properly be guaranteed if domestic security surveillances may be conducted solely within the discretion of the executive branch. The Fourth Amendment does not contemplate the executive officers of Government as neutral and disinterested magistrates. Their duty and responsibility is to enforce the laws, to investigate and to prosecute. . . . But those charged with this investigative and prosecutorial duty should not be the sole judges of when to utilize constitutionally sensitive means in pursuing their tasks. The historical judgment, which the Fourth Amendment accepts, is that unreviewed executive discretion may yield too readily to pressures to obtain incriminating evidence and overlook potential invasions of privacy and protected speech.

It may well be that, in the instant case, the Government's surveillance of Plamondon's conversation was a reasonable one which readily would have gained prior judicial approval. But this Court "has never sustained a search upon the sole ground that officers reasonably expected to find evidence of a particular crime and voluntarily confined their activities to the least intrusive means consistent with that end." Katz. The Fourth Amendment contemplates a prior judicial judgment,* not the risk that executive discretion may be reasonably exercised. This judicial role accords with our basic constitutional doctrine that individual freedoms will best be preserved through a separation of powers and division of functions among the different branches and levels

---

*We use the word "judicial" to connote the traditional Fourth Amendment requirement of a neutral and detached magistrate.

of Government. . . . The independent check upon executive discretion is not satisfied, as the Government argues, by "extremely limited" post-surveillance judicial review.* Indeed, post-surveillance review would never reach the surveillances which failed to result in prosecutions. Prior review by a neutral and detached magistrate is the time tested means of effectuating Fourth Amendment rights. . . .

It is true that there have been some exceptions to the warrant requirement. . . . But those exceptions are few in number and carefully delineated; in general they serve the legitimate needs of law enforcement officers to protect their own well-being and preserve evidence from destruction. Even while carving out those exceptions, the Court has reaffirmed the principle that the "police must, whenever practicable, obtain advance judicial approval of searches and seizures through the warrant procedure," Terry v. Ohio. . . .

The Government argues that the special circumstances applicable to domestic security surveillances necessitate a further exception to the warrant requirement. It is urged that the requirement of prior judicial review would obstruct the President in the discharge of his constitutional duty to protect domestic security. We are told further that these surveillances are directed primarily to the collecting and maintaining of intelligence with respect to subversive forces, and are not an attempt to gather evidence for specific criminal prosecutions. It is said that this type of surveillance should not be subject to traditional warrant requirements which were established to govern investigation of criminal activity, not ongoing intelligence gathering.

The Government further insists that courts "as a practical matter would have neither the knowledge nor the techniques necessary to determine whether there was probable cause to believe that surveillance was necessary to protect national security." These security problems, the Government contends, involve "a large number of complex and subtle factors" beyond the competence of courts to evaluate.

As a final reason for exemption from a warrant requirement, the Government believes that disclosure to a magistrate of all or even a significant portion of the information involved in domestic security surveillances "would create serious potential dangers to the national security and to the lives of informants and agents. . . . Secrecy is the essential ingredient in intelligence gathering; requiring prior judicial authorization would create a greater 'danger of leaks . . . , because in addition to the judge, you have the clerk, the stenographer and

---

*The Government argues that domestic security wiretaps should be upheld by courts in post-surveillance review "[u]nless it appears that the Attorney General's determination that the proposed surveillance relates to a national security matter is arbitrary and capricious, i.e., that it constitutes a clear abuse of the broad discretion that the Attorney General has to obtain all information that will be helpful to the President in protecting the Government . . ." against the various unlawful acts in § 2511 (3).

some other official like a law assistant or bailiff who may be apprised of the nature' of the surveillance."

These contentions in behalf of a complete exemption from the warrant requirement, when urged on behalf of the President and the national security in its domestic implications, merit the most careful consideration. We certainly do not reject them lightly, especially at a time of worldwide ferment and when civil disorders in this country are more prevalent than in the less turbulent periods of our history. There is, no doubt, pragmatic force to the Government's position.

But we do not think a case has been made for the requested departure from Fourth Amendment standards. The circumstances described do not justify complete exemption of domestic security surveillance from prior judicial scrutiny. Official surveillance, whether its purpose be criminal investigation or ongoing intelligence gathering, risks infringement of constitutionally protected privacy of speech. Security surveillances are especially sensitive because of the inherent vagueness of the domestic security concept, the necessarily broad and continuing nature of intelligence gathering, and the temptation to utilize such surveillances to oversee political dissent. We recognize, as we have before, the constitutional basis of the President's domestic security role, but we think it must be exercised in a manner compatible with the Fourth Amendment. In this case we hold that this requires an appropriate prior warrant procedure.

We cannot accept the Government's argument that internal security matters are too subtle and complex for judicial evaluation. Courts regularly deal with the most difficult issues of our society. There is no reason to believe that federal judges will be insensitive to or uncomprehending of the issues involved in domestic security cases. Certainly courts can recognize that domestic security surveillance involves different considerations from the surveillance of "ordinary crime." If the threat is too subtle or complex for our senior law enforcement officers to convey its significance to a court, one may question whether there is probable cause for surveillance.

Nor do we believe prior judicial approval will fracture the secrecy essential to official intelligence gathering. The investigation of criminal activity has long involved imparting sensitive information to judicial officers who have respected the confidentialities involved. Judges may be counted upon to be especially conscious of security requirements in national security cases. . . . Whatever security dangers clerical and secretarial personnel may pose can be minimized by proper administrative measures, possibly to the point of allowing the Government itself to provide the necessary clerical assistance.

Thus, we conclude that the Government's concerns do not justify departure in this case from the customary Fourth Amendment requirement of judicial approval prior to initiation of a search or surveillance. Although some added burden will be imposed upon the Attorney General, this inconvenience is justified in a free society to protect constitutional values. Nor do we think the Government's domestic surveillance powers will be impaired to any significant degree. A prior warrant establishes presumptive validity of the surveillance and will minimize the burden of justification in post-surveillance judicial review. By no means of least importance will be the reassurance of the public generally that indiscriminate wiretapping and bugging of law-abiding citizens cannot occur.

IV.

We emphasize, before concluding this opinion, the scope of our decision. As stated at the outset, this case involves only the domestic aspects of national security. We have not addressed, and express no opinion as to, the issues which may be involved with respect to activities of foreign powers or their agents. . . .

V.

As the surveillance of Plamondon's conversations was unlawful, because conducted without prior judicial approval, the courts below correctly held that Alderman v. United States (1969) is controlling and that it requires disclosure to the accused of his own impermissibly intercepted conversations. As stated in Alderman, "the trial court can and should, where appropriate, place a defendant and his counsel under enforceable orders against unwarranted disclosure of the materials which they may be entitled to inspect."

The judgment of the Court of Appeals is hereby
Affirmed.

The Chief Justice concurs in the result.

Mr. Justice Rehnquist took no part in the consideration or decision of this case.

Mr. Justice Douglas wrote a concurring opinion.

Mr. Justice White, concurring in the judgment, said in part:

. . . Because I conclude that on the record before us the surveillance undertaken by the Government in this case was illegal under the statute itself, I find it unnecessary, and therefore improper, to consider or decide the constitutional questions which the courts below improvidently reached.

MIRANDA v. ARIZONA
384 U. S. 436; 86 S. Ct. 1602; 16 L. Ed. 2d 694
(1966)

In 1963, in the celebrated case of Gideon v. Wainwright, the Supreme Court held applicable to trials in state courts the Sixth Amendment right to counsel; in the years since, the Court has decided a series of cases, some of them highly controversial, extending that right to points both earlier and later in the criminal process. In Hamilton v. Alabama (1961) it held that an accused was entitled to counsel (at state expense, if necessary) at the time of his arraignment, since certain defenses such as insanity had to be plead at that time or completely forfeited. In White v. Maryland (1963) it was pushed back to the preliminary hearing stage, because a guilty plea made at that stage became a permanent part of the record; and in Douglas v. California (1963) it was moved forward to cover the first appeal from a criminal conviction which is normally given by the state as a matter of right. The rationale behind all of these cases was that these were "critical stages" in the criminal process. It was at these points that a person might do or fail to do, or say or fail to say, something that could irrevocably prejudice his chances of acquittal. It was at these points that the "guiding hand of counsel" was vital if his rights were to receive full protection. In United States v. Wade and Gilbert v. California (1967) the Court extended the right of counsel to include that point where an accused is identified as a wanted suspect by being picked out of a police line-up by an eye witness, although it did hold in Gilbert that taking a handwriting sample from a man before he saw his lawyer did not violate his rights. Here, too, the suspect's right to an unprejudiced identification may easily be jeopardized by an excess of police enthusiasm.

While these changes were going on the Court was also struggling with the somewhat unrelated problem of coerced confessions. Although it had held in Brown v. Mississippi (1936) that a confession based on coercion—in this case physical torture—was void, it was continually plagued by the problem of what constituted coercion. While physical violence clearly amounts to coercion, it is apparent that certain types of psychological pressure may do so, too. In Chambers v. Florida (1940) the Court held a denial of due process the "sunrise confessions" of four Negroes which followed five days of interrogation in the absence of "friends, advisors or counselors, and under circumstances calculated to break the strongest nerves and the stoutest resistance." The same result was reached in Ashcraft v. Tennessee (1944), where the prisoner confessed to a murder after 36 hours of continuous questioning under powerful electric lights, though without any physical abuse.

In Lisenba v. California (1941), however, the Court upheld the use of a confession despite the fact that the defendant had been subject to two sleepless days and nights of almost continuous questioning by relays of police officers. The confession took place ten days after this questioning, and the Court concluded that he had not "so lost his freedom of action that the statements made were not his but were the result of the deprivation of his free choice to admit, to deny, or to refuse to answer." A similar result was reached in Stein v. New York (1953), the Reader's Digest *murder case. Here the judge had left to the jury the question of admissibility, and since the jury had delivered a general verdict of guilty the Court faced two problems: (1) could the jury have constitutionally found the confessions voluntary and used them as the basis of the conviction, and (2) if the jury found the confessions inadmissible, could it convict on the basis of other evidence or did the use of the confessions vitiate the entire trial. The Court held the confessions were " 'voluntary,' in the only sense in which confessions to the police by one under arrest and suspicion ever are" and hence were admissible. After prolonged questioning one defendant had confessed after receiving assurances that his father and brother would not be molested by the police; the second had confessed when confronted with the confession of the first. "Of course, these confessions were not voluntary in the sense that petitioners wanted to make them or that they were completely spontaneous, like a confession to a priest, a lawyer, or a psychiatrist. But in this sense no criminal confession is voluntary." The Court made it clear that "the limits in any case depend upon a weighing of the circumstances of pressure against the power of resistance of the person confessing." Neither man, the Court noted, was "young, soft, ignorant or timid." Their will to resist had not been broken by psychological coercion. The Court also found that the jury could convict on other evidence even if it found the confessions to have been coerced.*

It is interesting to note that the Court is not entirely consistent in its reasons for excluding evidence obtained by coercion. The common-law rule against the admission of forced confessions was not based on any theory of fairness, but was a practical one designed to prevent the admission in court of untrustworthy evidence. A confession was rejected if sufficient force was applied in getting it to cast doubt upon its reliability. In Lisenba v. California, however, the Court made clear what was implied in previous cases, that "the aim of the requirement of due process is not to exclude presumptively false evidence, but to prevent fundamental unfairness in the use of evidence whether true or false. . . . Such unfairness exists when a coerced confession is used as a means of obtaining a verdict of guilt." Without mentioning either the Lisenba or Rochin cases, the Court in the Stein case suggested a return to the common-law rationale, noting that forced confessions constitute "illusory and deceptive evidence," while sto-

len or wire-tap evidence "often is of the utmost verity." In Spano v. New York (1959) it was made clear that only where the Court has not found a confession to be involuntary may a jury convict on the basis of other evidence; a forced confession always voids the conviction. And in Rogers v. Richmond (1961) the Court reaffirmed the rule that the truth or falsity of a confession does not determine its admissibility.

A definition of "voluntary" that meant some pressure could be used, but not too much, raised endless difficulties for the Court. Since most confessions are secured before a person is formally charged with crime, the Court had managed to solve much of the problem in the federal courts by requiring that an accused be taken immediately before a committing magistrate. But this ruling rested on the supervisory authority of the Court over the administration of federal justice and so could not be extended to the states. Consequently the Court had to trace a guideline for the states as cases came before it, and as the Court noted in Spano v. New York, as "the methods used to extract confessions become more sophisticated, our duty . . . only becomes more difficult because of the more delicate judgments to be made." In the Spano case the defendant was persuaded to confess by fatigue and the false sympathy aroused by a boyhood friend on the police force, while in subsequent cases the techniques used included threatening to bring the defendant's wife in for questioning (Rogers v. Richmond, 1961), threatening to take her infant children from her and give them to strangers (Lynumn v. Illinois, 1963), injecting "truth serum" into his veins (Townsend v. Sain, 1963), and refusing to let him call his wife or lawyer until he had confessed (Haynes v. Washington, 1963). While in some of these cases the police disputed the defendant's version, in all of them the defendants were denied access to counsel who might have given them moral support and perhaps furnished a dispassionate version of the proceedings. Claims that the right to counsel was being denied were noted by the Court but not reached because the confessions were held to be coerced. Clearly the amount of "pressure" a state could use to invoke a confession was getting less and less.

Then in 1964 the Court moved sharply to merge these two lines of development, extending the right to counsel, but in such a way that would serve also as a protection against forced confessions. In Massiah v. United States the government was forbidden to question an accused, who was under indictment, in the absence of his lawyer, and in Escobedo v. Illinois (1964) it held that where "the investigation is no longer a general inquiry into an unsolved crime but has begun to focus on a particular suspect, the suspect has been taken into police custody, the police carry out a process of interrogations that lends itself to eliciting incriminating statements, the suspect has requested and been denied an opportunity to consult with his lawyer, and the police have not effectively warned him of his absolute constitutional right to remain silent, the accused has been denied 'the Assistance of Counsel' in violation of the Sixth Amendment to the Constitution as 'made obligatory upon the States by the Fourteenth Amendment.' "

The two years following the Escobedo decision (1964) witnessed a nationwide debate on the implications and wisdom of what the Court had done. The case itself had involved only the denial of Danny Escobedo's request to see his attorney and reaffirmed his absolute right to remain silent. But did it imply, in effect, an adoption of the English "Judge's Rule" that a suspect must be warned of his right to silence and cautioned that anything he said could be used against him? Did it require that he be told of his right to counsel? That he be furnished counsel at state expense? Did it, perhaps, outlaw all confessions? All police interrogation?

The Court itself was bitterly attacked for what was considered a gratuitous hamstringing of the police in their efforts to protect society against criminals. It was asserted that between 75 percent and 80 percent of the convictions in major crimes were dependent upon confessions; and police officers and prosecutors across the country, together with some courts, echoed the conviction of New York City's police commissioner, Michael J. Murphy, that "if suspects are told of their rights they will not confess." Certainly a competent lawyer would tell them not to confess, and then this effective method of solving crimes would come to an end.

Meanwhile, public confidence in the reliability of confessions as a substitute for investigatory evidence was badly shaken in early 1965 when George Whitmore, Jr., was conceded to be innocent of the sensational murder of career girls Janice Wylie and Emily Hoffert in their New York apartment. Whitmore had been arrested a year and a half after the murders and during 28 hours of questioning had given a 61-page confession filled with details "which only he, as the killer, could have known." Although Whitmore repudiated his confession to this and two other major crimes, the police contended it had been freely given, and his indictment was not dismissed until eight months later when incontrovertible evidence of his innocence was presented—evidence which the police could have obtained at once had they checked into the truth of his alibi.

The increased number of public defenders and court-appointed counsel, sparked by the Court's decision in the Escobedo and Miranda cases, has raised serious problems concerning the adequacy of the legal service given to indigent defendants. In Griffin v. Illinois (1956) the Court held that to insure equal protection a state may not make the nature of appellate review depend on the amount of money a man has, and in Argersinger v. Hamlin (1972) this was applied to any offense, however petty, for which a person could be imprisoned.

How good a lawyer is needed to bring about equality? Is a man entitled to a counsel of his own choice, or must he settle for whom the court appoints, or a public defender? In 1967 the Court gave a partial answer to these questions. In Anders v. California the defendant wished to appeal from a felony conviction and his court-appointed lawyer, "after a study of the record and consultation with petitioner . . . concluded that there was no merit to the appeal." The court refused to appoint another attorney, so the defendant filed a brief of his own and the appellate court confirmed his conviction. The Supreme Court reversed on the ground that "the constitutional requirement of substantial equality and fair process can only be attained where counsel acts in the role of an active advocate in behalf of his client, as opposed to that of amicus curiae. The no-merit letter and the procedure it triggers does not reach that dignity." Counsel should, if he finds the appeal wholly frivolous, request permission to withdraw and file a brief pointing up anything in the case that might support the appeal. "This requirement would not force appointed counsel to brief his case against his client but would merely afford the latter that advocacy which a nonindigent defendant is able to obtain." In Faretta v. California (1975), the Court held that the Sixth and Fourteenth Amendments guarantee a defendant the right to defend himself in court if he "voluntarily and intelligently elects to do so."

Not until 1971 in Harris v. New York did the Court move to reduce the impact of Miranda by permitting the use in court of evidence gotten in violation of the rule. Harris, on trial for a narcotics violation, took the stand and testified that a bag of powder he had sold to an undercover agent was baking powder rather than heroin. He was asked on cross-examination if this did not contradict statements made to the police at the time of his arrest and without the Miranda warnings and the statements were then read to him. The jury was instructed that they could not be used to determine his guilt, but only his credibility. In a five-to-four decision the Court held this use of the statements valid. Conceding that "some comments in the Miranda opinion can indeed be read as indicating a bar to use of any uncounseled statement for any purpose," they were only dicta and "it does not follow from Miranda that evidence inadmissible against an accused in the prosecution's case in chief is barred for all purposes, provided of course that the trustworthiness of the evidence satisfies legal standards." The Court reaffirmed Walder v. United States (1954) in which a similar decision had been reached with regard to illegally seized evidence and added, "the shield provided by Miranda cannot be perverted into a license to use perjury by way of a defense, free from the risk of confrontation with prior inconsistent utterances."

In Oregon v. Hass (1975), the Court not only reaffirmed Harris but extended it to a defendant who had been given the Miranda warnings and had his request for an attorney ignored. "One might concede that when *proper Miranda warnings have been given, and the officer then continues his interrogation after the suspect asks for an attorney, the officer may be said to have little to lose and perhaps something to gain by way of possibly uncovering impeachment material. . . . In any event, the balance was struck in Harris, and we are not disposed to change it now."*

The case below is a combination of four cases, all raising questions of the admissibility of confessions. Miranda was convicted of kidnapping and rape on the basis of a confession obtained after two hours of questioning in which he was not told of his right to counsel or silence; Vignera was convicted by the state of New York for robbery without being told of his right to counsel or silence. Stewart was similarly convicted by a California trial court of robbery and murder, but the state supreme court reversed, interpreting Escobedo as requiring that the accused be informed of his rights. In the Westover case, the FBI informed Westover of his rights, but they interrogated him in the same Kansas City police station where he had already been in the custody of the city police for 14 hours, during which he had been interrogated without being warned of his rights. From Westover's point of view, the Court said, it was one long interrogation with information about his rights being given only toward the end. "In these circumstances an intelligent waiver of constitutional rights cannot be assumed." In January, 1976, Ernesto Miranda was stabbed to death in a barroom fight over a card game. On his person were a number of "Miranda Cards," one of which was dutifully read to the suspect who was arrested for his murder.

Mr. Chief Justice Warren delivered the opinion of the Court, saying in part:

The cases before us raise questions which go to the roots of our concepts of American criminal jurisprudence: the restraints society must observe consistent with the Federal Constitution in prosecuting individuals for crime. More specifically, we deal with the admissibility of statements obtained from an individual who is subjected to custodial police interrogation and the necessity for procedures which assure that the individual is accorded his privilege under the Fifth Amendment to the Constitution not to be compelled to incriminate himself. . . .

We start here, as we did in Escobedo [v. Illinois, 1964], with the premise that our holding is not an innovation in our jurisprudence, but is an application of principles long recognized and applied in other settings. We have undertaken a thorough re-examination of the Escobedo decision and the principles it announced, and we reaffirm it. That case was but an explication of basic rights that are enshrined in our Constitution—that "No person . . . shall be compelled in any criminal case to be a witness against himself," and that "the accused shall . . . have the Assistance of Counsel"—rights which were put in jeopardy in that case through official overbearing. These precious rights were fixed in our Constitution only after centuries of persecution and struggle. And in the words of Chief Justice Marshall, they were secured "for ages to come and . . . designed to approach immortality as nearly as human institutions can approach it," Cohens v. Virginia (1821). . . .

Our holding will be spelled out with some specificity in the pages which follow but briefly stated it is this: the prosecution may not use statements, whether exculpatory or inculpatory, stemming from custodial interrogation of the defendant unless it demonstrates the use of procedural safeguards effective to secure the privilege against self-incrimination. By custodial interrogation, we mean questioning initiated by law enforcement officers after a person has been taken into custody or otherwise deprived of his freedom of action in any significant way. As for the procedural safeguards to be employed, unless other fully effective means are devised to inform accused persons of their right of silence and to assure a continuous opportunity to exercise it, the following measures are required. Prior to any questioning, the person must be warned that he has a right to remain silent, that any statement he does make may be used as evidence against him, and that he has a right to the presence of an attorney, either retained or appointed. The defendant may waive effectuation of these rights, provided the waiver is made voluntarily, knowingly and intelligently. If, however, he indicates in any manner and at any stage of the process that he wishes to consult with an attorney before speaking there can be no questioning. Likewise, if the individual is alone and indicates in any manner that he does not wish to be interrogated, the police may not question him. The mere fact that he may have answered some questions or volunteered some statements on his own does not deprive him of the right to refrain from answering any further inquiries until he has consulted with an attorney and thereafter consents to be questioned.

I.

The constitutional issue we decide in each of these cases is the admissibility of statements obtained from a defendant questioned while in custody or otherwise deprived of his freedom of action in any significant way. In each, the defendant was questioned by police officers, detectives, or a prosecuting attorney in a room in which he was cut off from the outside world. In none of these cases was the defendant given a full and effective warning of his rights at the outset of the interrogation process. In all the cases, the questioning elicited oral admissions, and in three of them, signed statements as well which were admitted at their trials. They all thus share salient features—incommunicado inter-rogation of individuals in a police-dominated atmosphere, resulting in self-incriminating statements without full warnings of constitutional rights.

An understanding of the nature and setting of this in-custody interrogation is essential to our decisions today. The difficulty in depicting what transpires at such interrogations stems from the fact that in this country they have largely taken place incommunicado. From extensive factual studies undertaken in the early 1930's, including the famous Wickersham Report to Congress by a Presidential Commission, it is clear that police violence and the "third degree" flourished at that time. In a series of cases decided by this Court long after these studies, the police resorted to physical brutality—beating, hanging, whipping—and to sustained and protracted questioning incommunicado in order to extort confessions. The Commission on Civil Rights in 1961 found much evidence to indicate that "some policemen still resort to physical force to obtain confessions.". . . The use of physical brutality and violence is not, unfortunately, relegated to the past or to any part of the country. Only recently in Kings County, New York, the police brutally beat, kicked and placed lighted cigarette butts on the back of a potential witness under interrogation for the purpose of securing a statement incriminating a third party. People v. Portelli, 15 N.Y. 2d 235 (1965).

The examples given above are undoubtedly the exception now, but they are sufficiently widespread to be the object of concern. Unless a proper limitation upon custodial interrogation is achieved—such as these decisions will advance —there can be no assurance that practices of this nature will be eradicated in the foreseeable future. . . .

Again we stress that the modern practice of in-custody interrogation is psychologically rather than physically oriented. As we have stated before, "Since Chambers v. Florida [1940], this Court has recognized that coercion can be mental as well as physical, and that the blood of the accused is not the only hallmark of an unconstitutional inquisition." Blackburn v. Alabama (1960). Interrogation still takes place in privacy. Privacy results in secrecy and this in turn results in a gap in our knowledge as to what in fact goes on in the interrogation rooms. A valuable source of information about present police practices, however, may be found in various police manuals and texts which document procedures employed with success in the past, and which recom-mend various other effective tactics. These texts are used by law enforcement agencies themselves as guides. It should be noted that these texts professedly present the most enlightened and effective means presently used to obtain statements through custodial interrogation. By considering these texts and other data, it is possible to describe procedures observed and noted around the country. . . . [The Court here quotes at length from a number of books on criminal investigation.]

From these representative samples of interrogation techniques, the setting prescribed by the manuals and observed in practice becomes clear. In essence, it is this: To be alone with the subject is essential to prevent distraction and to deprive him of any outside support. The aura of confidence in his guilt undermines his will to resist. He merely confirms the preconceived story the police seek to have him describe. Patience and persistence, at times relentless questioning are employed. To obtain a confession, the interrogator must "patiently maneuver himself or his quarry into a position from which the desired objective may be obtained." When normal procedures fail to produce the needed result, the police may resort to deceptive stratagems such as giving false legal advice. It is important to keep the subject off balance, for example, by trading on his insecurity about himself or his surroundings. The police then persuade, trick, or cajole him out of exercising his constitutional rights.

Even without employing brutality, the "third degree" or the specific stratagems described above, the very fact of custodial interrogation exacts a heavy toll on individual liberty and trades on the weakness of individuals. This fact may be illustrated simply by referring to three confession cases decided by this Court in the Term immediately preceding our Escobedo decision. In Townsend v. Sain (1963), the defendant was a 19-year-old heroin addict, described as a "near mental defective." The defendant in Lynumn v. Illinois (1963), was a woman who confessed to the arresting officer after being importuned to "cooperate" in order to prevent her children from being taken by relief authorities. This Court as in those cases reversed the conviction of a defendant in Haynes v. Washington (1963), whose persistent request during his interrogation was to phone his wife or attorney. In other settings, these individuals might have exercised their constitutional rights. In the incommunicado police-dominated atmosphere, they succumbed.

In the cases before us today, given this background, we concern ourselves primarily with this interrogation atmosphere and the evils it can bring. In No. 759, Miranda v. Arizona, the police arrested the defendant and took him to a special interrogation room where they secured a confession. In No. 760, Vignera v. New York, the defendant made oral admissions to the police after interrogation in the afternoon, and then signed an inculpatory statement upon being questioned by an assistant district attorney later the same evening. In No. 761, Westover v. United States, the defendant was handed over to the Federal Bureau of Investigation by local authorities after they had detained and interrogated him for a lengthy period, both at night and the following morning. After some two hours of questioning, the federal officers had obtained signed statements from the defendant. Lastly, in No. 584, California v. Stewart, the local police held the defendant five days in the station and interrogated him on nine separate occasions before they secured his inculpatory statement.

In these cases, we might not find the defendants' statements to have been involuntary in traditional terms. Our concern for adequate safeguards to protect precious Fifth Amendment rights is, of course, not lessened in the slightest. In each of the cases, the defendant was thrust into an unfamiliar atmosphere and run through menacing police interrogation procedures. The potentiality for compulsion is forcefully apparent, for example, in Miranda, where the indigent Mexican defendant was a seriously disturbed individual with pronounced sexual fantasies, and in Stewart, in which the defendant was an indigent Los Angeles Negro who had dropped out of school in the sixth grade. To be sure, the records do not evince overt physical coercion or patented psychological ploys. The fact remains that in none of these cases did the officers undertake to afford appropriate safeguards at the outset of the interrogation to insure that the statements were truly the product of free choice.

It is obvious that such an interrogation environment is created for no purpose other than to subjugate the individual to the will of his examiner. This atmosphere carries its own badge of intimidation. To be sure, this is not physical intimidation, but it is equally destructive of human dignity. The current practice of incommunicado interrogation is at odds with one of our Nation's most cherished principles—that the individual may not be compelled to incriminate himself. Unless adequate protective devices are employed to dispel the compulsion inherent in custodial surroundings, no statement obtained from the defendant can truly be the product of his free choice.

From the foregoing, we can readily perceive an intimate connection between the privilege against self-incrimination and police custodial questioning. . . .

II.

. . . As a "noble principle often transcends its origins," the privilege has come rightfully to be recognized in part as an individual's substantive right, a "right to a private enclave where he may lead a private life. That right is the hallmark of our democracy." . . . We have recently noted that the privilege against self-incrimination—the essential mainstay of our adversary system— is founded on a complex of values. . . . All these policies point to one overriding thought: the constitutional foundation underlying the privilege is the respect a government—state or federal—must accord to the dignity and integrity of its citizens. To maintain a "fair state-individual balance," to require the government "to shoulder the entire load," . . . to respect the inviolability of the human personality, our accusatory system of criminal justice demands that the government seeking to punish an individual produce the evidence against him by its own independent labors, rather than by the cruel, simple expedient of compelling it from his own mouth. . . . In sum, the privilege is fulfilled only when the person is guaranteed the right "to remain silent unless he chooses to speak in the unfettered exercise of his own will." . . .

The question in these cases is whether the privilege is fully applicable during a period of custodial interrogation. . . . We are satisfied that all the principles embodied in the privilege apply to informal compulsion exerted by law-enforcement officers during in-custody questioning. An individual swept from familiar surroundings into police custody, surrounded by antagonistic forces, and subjected to the techniques of persuasion described above cannot be otherwise than under compulsion to speak. As a practical matter, the compulsion to speak in the isolated setting of the police station may well be greater than in courts or other official investigations, where there are often impartial observers to guard against intimidation or trickery.

This question, in fact, could have been taken as settled in federal courts almost 70 years ago, when, in Bram v. United States (1897), this Court held:

"In criminal trials, in the courts of the United States, wherever a question arises whether a confession is incompetent because not voluntary, the issue is controlled by that portion of the Fifth Amendment . . . commanding that no person 'shall be compelled in any criminal case to be a witness against himself.' " . . .

III.

It is impossible for us to foresee the potential alternatives for protecting the privilege which might be devised by Congress or the States in the exercise of their creative rule-making capacities. Therefore we cannot say that the Constitution necessarily requires adherence to any particular solution for the inherent compulsions of the interrogation process as it is presently conducted. Our decision in no way creates a constitutional straitjacket which will handicap sound efforts at reform, nor is it intended to have this effect. We encourage Congress and the States to continue their laudable search for increasingly effective ways of protecting the rights of the individual while promoting efficient enforcement of our criminal laws. However, unless we are shown other procedures which are at least as effective in apprising accused persons of their right of silence and in assuring a continuous opportunity to exercise it, the following safeguards must be observed. . . .

[The Court here elaborates on and justifies the requirements summarized at the beginning of the opinion.]

Once warnings have been given, the subsequent procedure is clear. If the individual indicates in any manner, at any time prior to or during questioning, that he wishes to remain silent, the interrogation must cease. At this point he has shown that he intends to exercise his Fifth Amendment privilege; any statement taken after the person invokes his privilege cannot be other than the product of compulsion, subtle or otherwise. Without the right to cut off questioning, the setting of in-custody interrogation operates on the individual to overcome free choice in producing a statement after the privilege has been once invoked. If the individual states that he wants an attorney, the interrogation must cease until an attorney is present. At that time, the individual must have an opportunity to confer with the attorney and to have him present during any subsequent questioning. If the individual cannot obtain an attorney and he indicates that he wants one before speaking to police, they must respect his decision to remain silent. . . .

If the interrogation continues without the presence of an attorney and a statement is taken, a heavy burden rests on the government to demonstrate that the defendant knowingly and intelligently waived his privilege against self-incrimination and his right to retained or appointed counsel. . . . This Court has always set high standards of proof for the waiver of constitutional rights, Johnson v. Zerbst (1938), and we re-assert these standards as applied to in-custody interrogation. Since the State is responsible for establishing the isolated circumstances under which the interrogation takes place and has the only means of making available corroborated evidence of warnings given during incommunicado interrogation, the burden is rightly on its shoulders.

An express statement that the individual is willing to make a statement and does not want an attorney followed closely by a statement could constitute a waiver. But a valid waiver will not be presumed simply from the silence of the accused after warnings are given or simply from the fact that a confession was in fact eventually obtained. . . .

. . . Moreover, where in-custody interrogation is involved, there is no room for the contention that the privilege is waived if the individual answers some questions or gives some information on his own prior to invoking his right to remain silent when interrogated.*

Whatever the testimony of the authorities as to waiver of rights by an accused, the fact of lengthy interrogation or incommunicado incarceration before a statement is made is strong evidence that the accused did not validly waive his rights. In these circumstances the fact that the individual eventually made a statement is consistent with the conclusion that the compelling influence of the interrogation finally forced him to do so. It is inconsistent with any notion of a voluntary relinquishment of the privilege. Moreover, any evidence that the accused was threatened, tricked, or cajoled into a waiver will, of course, show that the defendant did not voluntarily waive his privilege. The requirement of warnings and waiver of rights is a fundamental with respect to the Fifth Amendment privilege and not simply a preliminary ritual to existing methods of interrogation.

---

*Although this Court held in Rogers v. United States (1951), over strong dissent, that a witness before a grand jury may not in certain circumstances decide to answer some questions and then refuse to answer others, that decision has no application to the interrogation situation we deal with today. No legislative or judicial fact-finding authority is involved here, nor is there a possibility that the individual might make self-serving statements of which he could make use at trial while refusing to answer incriminating statements.

The warnings required and the waiver necessary in accordance with our opinion today are, in the absence of a fully effective equivalent, prerequisites to the admissibility of any statement made by a defendant. No distinction can be drawn between statements which are direct confessions and statements which amount to "admissions" of part or all of an offense. The privilege against self-incrimination protects the individual from being compelled to incriminate himself in any manner; it does not distinguish degrees of incrimination. Similarly, for precisely the same reason, no distinction may be drawn between inculpatory statements and statements alleged to be merely "exculpatory." If a statement made were in fact truly exculpatory it would, of course, never be used by the prosecution. In fact, statements merely intended to be exculpatory by the defendant are often used to impeach his testimony at trial or to demonstrate untruths in the statement given under interrogation and thus to prove guilt by implication. These statements are incriminating in any meaningful sense of the word and may not be used without the full warnings and effective waiver required for any other statement. In Escobedo itself, the defendant fully intended his accusation of another as the slayer to be exculpatory as to himself.

The principles announced today deal with the protection which must be given to the privilege against self-incrimination when the individual is first subjected to police interrogation while in custody at the station or otherwise deprived of his freedom of action in any significant way. It is at this point that our adversary system of criminal proceedings commences, distinguishing itself at the outset from the inquisitorial system recognized in some countries. Under the system of warnings we delineate today or under any other system which may be devised and found effective, the safeguards to be erected about the privilege must come into play at this point. . . .

In dealing with statements obtained through interrogation, we do not purport to find all confessions inadmissible. Confessions remain a proper element in law enforcement. Any statement given freely and voluntarily without any compelling influences is, of course, admissible in evidence. The fundamental import of the privilege while an individual is in custody is not whether he is allowed to talk to the police without the benefit of warnings and counsel, but whether he can be interrogated. There is no requirement that police stop a person who enters a police station and states that he wishes to confess to a crime, or a person who calls the police to offer a confession or any other statement he desires to make. Volunteered statements of any kind are not barred by the Fifth Amendment and their admissibility is not affected by our holding today. . . .

IV.

A recurrent argument made in these cases is that society's need for interrogation outweighs the privilege. This argument is not unfamiliar to this Court.

... The whole thrust of our foregoing discussion demonstrates that the Constitution has prescribed the rights of the individual when confronted with the power of government when it provided in the Fifth Amendment that an individual cannot be compelled to be a witness against himself. That right cannot be abridged. As Mr. Justice Brandeis once observed:

"Decency, security and liberty alike demand that government officials shall be subjected to the same rules of conduct that are commands to the citizen. In a government of laws, existence of the government will be imperilled if it fails to observe the laws scrupulously. Our Government is the potent, the omnipresent teacher. For good or for ill, it teaches the whole people by its example. Crime is contagious. If the Government becomes a lawbreaker, it breeds contempt for law; it invites every man to become a law unto himself; it invites anarchy. To declare that in the administration of the criminal law the end justifies the means ... would bring terrible retribution. Against that pernicious doctrine this Court should resolutely set its face." Olmstead v. United States (1928) (dissenting opinion). ...

It is also urged that an unfettered right to detention for interrogation should be allowed because it will often redound to the benefit of the person questioned. When police inquiry determines that there is no reason to believe that the person has committed any crime, it is said, he will be released without need for further formal procedures. The person who has committed no offense, however, will be better able to clear himself after warnings with counsel present than without. It can be assumed that in such circumstances a lawyer would advise his client to talk freely to police in order to clear himself. ...

V.

Because of the nature of the problem and because of its recurrent significance in numerous cases, we have to this point discussed the relationship of the Fifth Amendment privilege to police interrogation without specific concentration on the facts of the cases before us. We turn now to these facts to consider the application to these cases of the constitutional principles discussed above. In each instance, we have concluded that statements were obtained from the defendant under circumstances that did not meet constitutional standards for protection of the privilege.

[The Court here reviews in detail the facts of the four cases and concludes either that the defendant did not waive his right to silence, or was not informed that he had a right to silence or to counsel.]

Mr. Justice Clark dissented in part.

Mr. Justice Harlan, whom Mr. Justice Stewart and Mr. Justice White joined, dissented, saying in part:

I believe the decision of the Court represents poor constitutional law and entails harmful consequences for the country at large. How serious these consequences may prove to be only time can tell. But the basic flaws in the Court's justification seem to me readily apparent now once all sides of the problem are considered. . . .

While the fine points of this scheme are far less clear than the Court admits, the tenor is quite apparent. The new rules are not designed to guard against police brutality or other unmistakably banned forms of coercion. Those who use third-degree tactics and deny them in court are equally able and destined to lie as skillfully about warnings and waivers. Rather, the thrust of the new rules is to negate all pressures, to reinforce the nervous or ignorant suspect, and ultimately to discourage any confession at all. The aim in short is toward "voluntariness" in a utopian sense, or to view it from a different angle, voluntariness with a vengeance. . . .

What the Court largely ignores is that its rules impair, if they will not eventually serve wholly to frustrate, an instrument of law enforcement that has long and quite reasonably been thought worth the price paid for it. There can be little doubt that the Court's new code would markedly decrease the number of confessions. To warn the suspect that he may remain silent and remind him that his confession may be used in court are minor obstructions. To require also an express waiver by the suspect and an end to questioning whenever he demurs must heavily handicap questioning. And to suggest or provide counsel for the suspect simply invites the end of the interrogation.

How much harm this decision will inflict on law enforcement cannot fairly be predicted with accuracy. Evidence on the role of confessions is notoriously incomplete, . . . and little is added by the Court's reference to the FBI experience and the resources believed wasted in interrogation. . . . We do know that some crimes cannot be solved without confessions, that ample expert testimony attests to their importance in crime control, and that the Court is taking a real risk with society's welfare in imposing its new regime on the country. The social costs of crime are too great to call the new rules anything but a hazardous experimentation.

While passing over the costs and risks of its experiment, the Court portrays the evils of normal police questioning in terms which I think are exaggerated. Albeit stringently confined by the due process standards interrogation is no doubt often inconvenient and unpleasant for the suspect. However, it is no less so for a man to be arrested and jailed, to have his house searched, or to stand trial in court, yet all this may properly happen to the most innocent given probable cause, a warrant, or an indictment. Society has always paid a stiff price for law and order, and peaceful interrogation is not one of the dark moments of the law.

This brief statement of the competing considerations seems to me ample proof that the Court's preference is highly debatable at best and therefore not to be read into the Constitution. However, it may make the analysis more graphic to consider the actual facts of one of the four cases reversed by the Court. Miranda v. Arizona serves best, being neither the hardest nor easiest of the four under the Court's standards.

On March 3, 1963, an 18-year-old girl was kidnapped and forcibly raped near Phoenix, Arizona. Ten days later, on the morning of March 13, petitioner Miranda was arrested and taken to the police station. At this time Miranda was 23 years old, indigent, and educated to the extent of completing half the ninth grade. He had "an emotional illness" of the schizophrenic type, according to the doctor who eventually examined him; the doctor's report also stated that Miranda was "alert and oriented as to time, place, and person," intelligent within normal limits, competent to stand trial, and sane within the legal definition. At the police station, the victim picked Miranda out of a lineup, and two officers then took him into a separate room to interrogate him, starting about 11:30 a.m. Though at first denying his guilt, within a short time Miranda gave a detailed oral confession and then wrote out in his own hand and signed a brief statement admitting and describing the crime. All this was accomplished in two hours or less without any force, threats or promises and—I will assume this though the record is uncertain—without any effective warnings at all.

Miranda's oral and written confessions are now held inadmissible under the Court's new rules. One is entitled to feel astonished that the Constitution can be read to produce this result. These confessions were obtained during brief, daytime questioning conducted by two officers and unmarked by any of the traditional indicia of coercion. They assured a conviction for a brutal and unsettling crime, for which the police had and quite possibly could obtain little evidence other than the victim's identifications, evidence which is frequently unreliable. There was, in sum, a legitimate purpose, no perceptible unfairness, and certainly little risk of injustice in the interrogation. Yet the resulting confessions, and the responsible course of police practice they represent, are to be sacrificed to the Court's own finespun conception of fairness which I seriously doubt is shared by many thinking citizens in this country.

Mr. Justice White, with whom Mr. Justice Harlan and Mr. Justice Stewart joined, dissented, saying in part:

The proposition that the privilege against self-incrimination forbids in-custody interrogation without the warnings specified in the majority opinion and without a clear waiver of counsel has no significant support in the history of the privilege or in the language of the Fifth Amendment. As for the English authorities and the common-law history, the privilege, firmly established in the second half of the seventeenth century, was never applied except to prohibit compelled judicial interrogations. The rule excluding coerced confessions matured about 100 years later, "[b]ut there is nothing in the reports to suggest that the theory has its roots in the privilege against self-incrimination. And so far as the cases reveal, the privilege, as such, seems to have been given effect only in judicial proceedings, including the preliminary examinations by authorized magistrates."

FURMAN v. GEORGIA
408 U. S. 238; 92 S. Ct. 2726; 33 L. Ed. 2d 346
(1972)

The Eighth Amendment prohibits the infliction of cruel and unusual punishment, but makes no effort to define such punishment. In early England most felonies were punished by hanging, and for certain serious crimes, such as treason, a person could be drawn and quartered. In colonial America the pillory and stocks were a feature of nearly every town square, and flogging was common for many offenses. Many, if not all, of these forms of punishment would be considered uncivilized today, and have long since been abolished. In 1963 the supreme court of Delaware, the last state to permit flogging (except for infraction of prison rules), upheld the sentence of 20 lashes for breaking parole in a car theft case; but the state pardons board freed the man and the sentence was not carried out. In Louisiana ex rel. Francis v. Resweber (1947) the Supreme Court, assuming capital punishment to be valid, rejected the contention that the state's failure to electrocute the defendant on the first try made subsequent tries cruel and unusual. In Wilkerson v. Utah (1879) the Court had held shooting was not cruel and unusual, but suggested the ban would include both drawing and quartering and burning alive.

The idea that punishment could be cruel and unusual, not in the abstract, but because it did not "fit the crime" to which it was attached, was argued as early as 1892 by Justice Field in his dissent in O'Neil v. Vermont, a case in which a New Yorker selling liquor illegally in Vermont stood to serve 19,914 days in jail for 307 separate illegal sales. The Court found that since the Eighth Amendment did not limit the states, no federal question was involved. In reviewing a case arising under the Philippine constitution, whose cruel and unusual punishment clause was identical to the Eighth Amendment's, the Court struck down as cruel and unusual a fifteen-year sentence for knowingly making a false statement in a public document; see Weems v. United States (1910).

It is also cruel to punish a person for being sick or having some affliction over which he has no control. In Robinson v. California (1962) the Court struck down a state statute making it a misdemeanor "to be addicted to the use of narcotics." While the state was free to punish the use of narcotics or prescribe a mandatory program of treatment for addicts, such addiction was an "illness which may be contracted innocently or involuntarily. We hold that a state law which imprisons a person thus afflicted as a criminal, even though he has never touched any narcotic drug within the State or been guilty of any irregular behavior there, inflicts a cruel and unusual punishment in violation of the Fourteenth Amendment. To be sure, imprisonment for ninety days is not, in the abstract, a punishment which is either cruel or unusual. But the question cannot be considered in the abstract. Even one day in prison would be a cruel and unusual punishment for the 'crime' of having a common cold."

Following the Robinson case, a sixty-year-old bootblack with over one hundred convictions for public drunkenness argued that alcoholism, like drug addiction, was a disease and could not be punished. Five members of the Court agreed that his conviction for public drunkenness was not a cruel and unusual punishment. While they were unable to agree on an opinion regarding alcoholism, they did agree that Powell was not being punished for alcoholism, but for being in public while drunk. Four members of the Court dissented on the ground that his affliction was such that he could not resist being drunk in public. See Powell v. Texas (1968).

Unlike most constitutional developments, which take place gradually with the Court hinting broadly at the path it plans to follow, the inclusion of the death penalty in the Eighth Amendment came with startling suddenness. In nearly every case involving cruel and unusual punishment, the Court had discussed the death penalty, and while none of these cases had raised the Eighth Amendment question directly, in each of them the Court had left no doubt that the penalty, as such, was valid. As late as 1958, four members of the majority (Justice Brennan concurred on other grounds) said in Trop v. Dulles that while expatriation was cruel and unusual punishment, the death penalty "cannot be said to violate the constitutional concept of cruelty."

Then in the 1960's an all-out legal attack was launched against the penalty, underwritten largely by the American Civil Liberties Union and the NAACP Legal Defense Fund, which had evidence that most of those executed since 1930 were black. The penalty was challenged on a variety of grounds, and on June 3, 1967, the execution of more than 500 condemned prisoners throughout the country came to a halt while courts and governors waited to see what the Supreme Court would do.

The first of these challenges reached the Supreme Court in Witherspoon v. Illinois (1968), and for the first time the Court gave an indication that the death penalty was in trouble. Illinois permitted a verdict of guilty and a sentence of death to be handed down by a jury from which the state had deliberately excluded all persons with scruples against capital punishment. The Court declined to reverse the verdict of guilty, since the jury would not be necessarily prone to convict, but it held that no jury so constituted could hand down a sentence of death since such a jury "fell woefully short of that impartiality to which the petitioner was entitled under the Sixth and Fourteenth Amendments." "A jury that must choose between life imprisonment and capital punishment can do little more—and must do nothing less—than express the conscience of the community on the ultimate question of life or death. Yet, in a nation less than half of whose people believe in the death penalty, a jury composed exclusively of such people cannot speak for the community. Culled of all who harbor doubts about the wisdom of capital punishment—of all who would be reluctant to pronounce the extreme penalty—such a jury can speak only for a distinct and dwindling minority." Justice Black, dissenting with Justices Harlan and White, pointed up the majority's underlying motives. "If this Court is to hold capital punishment unconstitutional, I think it should do so forthrightly, not by making it impossible for States to get juries that will enforce the death penalty."

The hopes of opponents of the death penalty that it had been abolished by the Witherspoon case proved unduly optimistic, but the moratorium on executions remained in effect while other challenges were readied for Supreme Court review. One such challenge involved the question of whether a jury could constitutionally impose the death penalty without any governing standards, and in McGautha v. California (1971) the Court held that it could. Justice Harlan, writing for a six-man majority, traced the efforts of the states to reduce the rigors of mandatory death sentences, first by introducing "degrees" of murder, and, when juries still took the law into their own hands, finally giving way to reality and providing for complete jury discretion to hang or not to hang.

On the basis of this history the Court concluded that "to identify before the fact those characteristics of criminal homicides and their perpetrators which call for the death penalty, and to express these characteristics in language which can be fairly understood and applied by the sentencing authority, appear to be tasks which are beyond present human ability." It cited the efforts of a British Royal Commission to solve the same problem and its conclusion that "no simple formula can take account of the innumerable degrees of culpability, and no formula which fails to do so can claim to satisfy public opinion." The list of "aggravating and mitigating circumstances" provided in the Model Penal Code for jury consideration, the Court said, "bear witness to the intractable nature of the problem of 'standards'. . . [and] caution against this Court's undertaking to establish such standards itself." . . .

The Court concluded that "in the light of history, experience, and the present limitations of human knowledge, we find it quite impossible to say that committing to the untrammeled discretion of the jury the power to pronounce life or death in capital cases is offensive to anything in the Constitution." At the same time it held that the Ohio system of having the jury decide both guilt and punishment together did not deny due process merely because a defendant who wanted to argue for clemency could hardly do so without incriminating himself. "The criminal process, like the rest of the legal system, is replete with situations requiring 'the making of difficult judgments' as to which course to follow."

In a long and carefully reasoned dissent Justice Brennan, joined by Justices Douglas and Marshall, attacked the discretion of the sentencing jury to kill or not to kill as it wished as amounting to "nothing more than government by whim"—a form totally at odds with the "government of laws" protected by the due process clause. "We are not presented with the slightest attempt to bring the power of reason to bear on the considerations relevant to capital sentencing. We are faced with nothing more than stark legislative abdication. Not once in the history of this Court, until today, have we sustained against a due process challenge such an unguided, unbridled, unreviewable exercise of naked power. Almost a century ago, we found an almost identical California procedure constitutionally inadequate to license a laundry. Yick Wo v. Hopkins (1886). Today we hold it adequate to a license life."

Nor, he argued, is such an abdication either necessary or justified. Granted all the difficulties, there are certain state interests such as retribution, deterrence, rehabilitation or the removal of the criminal from society that can be articulated as guides. "But I can see no reason whatsoever that a State may be excused from declaring what policies it seeks to further by the infliction of capital punishment merely because it may be difficult to determine how those policies should be applied in any particular case. If anything, it would seem that the difficulty of decision in particular cases would support rather than weaken the point that uniform decisionmaking requires that state policy be explicitly articulated." And "finally, even if I shared the Court's view that the rule of law and the power of States to kill are in irreconcilable conflict, I would have no hesitation in concluding that the rule of law must prevail."

The decision in McGautha was widely viewed as the Supreme Court's final word on the death penalty. No more cases involving it were pending before the Court, and with the right of juries to act arbitrarily firmly guaranteed, there seemed little likelihood that an Eighth Amendment argument would prevail. As states made preparations to start executing the now almost 700 prisoners on death row, the Court announced it would hear four cases involving the Eighth Amendment. However, between the hear-

*ing of oral argument in January and the Court's decision in June one of
the four was rendered moot when the California supreme court held the
death penalty a cruel or unusual punishment under its state constitition;
see Akins v. California (1972).*

Per Curiam.

... The Court holds that the imposition and carrying out of the death
penalty in these cases constitutes cruel and unusual punishment in violation
of the Eighth and Fourteenth Amendments. The judgment in each case is
therefore reversed insofar as it leaves undisturbed the death sentence imposed,
and the cases are remanded for further proceedings.

So ordered.

Mr. Justice Brennan, concurring, said in part:

II.

Ours would indeed be a simple task were we required merely to measure a
challenged punishment against those that history has long condemned. That
narrow and unwarranted view of the Clause, however, was left behind with the
19th century. Our task today is more complex. We know "that the words of
the [Clause] are not precise, and that their scope is not static." We know,
therefore, that the Clause "must draw its meaning from the evolving standards
of decency that mark the progress of a maturing society." Trop v. Dulles
[1958]. That knowledge, of course, is but the beginning of the inquiry.

In Trop v. Dulles it was said that "[t]he question is whether [a] penalty
subjects the individual to a fate forbidden by the principle of civilized treatment guaranteed by the [Clause]." It was also said that a challenged punishment must be examined "in light of the basic prohibition against inhuman
treatment" embodied in the Clause. It was said, finally, that: "The basic
concept underlying the [Clause] is nothing less than the dignity of man. While
the State has the power to punish, the [Clause] stands to assure that this power
be exercised within the limits of civilized standards." At bottom, then, the
Cruel and Unusual Punishments Clause prohibits the infliction of uncivilized
and inhuman punishments. The State, even as it punishes, must treat its
members with respect for their intrinsic worth as human beings. A punishment
is "cruel and unusual," therefore, if it does not comport with human dignity. ...

The primary principle is that a punishment must not be so severe as to be degrading to the dignity of human beings. Pain, certainly, may be a factor in the judgment. . . .

More than the presence of pain, however, is comprehended in the judgment that the extreme severity of a punishment makes it degrading to the dignity of human beings. The barbaric punishments condemned by history, "punishments which inflict torture, such as the rack, the thumbscrew, the iron boot, the stretching of limbs and the like," are, of course, "attended with acute pain and suffering." O'Neil v. Vermont (1892) (Field, J., dissenting). When we consider why they have been condemned, however, we realize that the pain involved is not the only reason. The true significance of these punishments is that they treat members of the human race as nonhumans, as objects to be toyed with and discarded. They are thus inconsistent with the fundamental premise of the Clause that even the vilest criminal remains a human being possessed of common human dignity. . . .

In determining whether a punishment comports with human dignity, we are aided also by a second principle inherent in the Clause—that the State must not arbitrarily inflict a severe punishment. This principle derives from the notion that the State does not respect human dignity when, without reason, it inflicts upon some people a severe punishment that it does not inflict upon others. Indeed, the very words "cruel and unusual punishments" imply condemnation of the arbitrary infliction of severe punishments. . . .

A third principle inherent in the Clause is that a severe punishment must not be unacceptable to contemporary society. . . .

The question under this principle, then, is whether there are objective indicators from which a court can conclude that contemporary society considers a severe punishment unacceptable. Accordingly, the judicial task is to review the history of a challenged punishment and to examine society's present practices with respect to its use. Legislative authorization, of course, does not establish acceptance. The acceptability of a severe punishment is measured, not by its availability, for it might become so offensive to society as never to be inflicted, but by its use.

The final principle inherent in the Clause is that a severe punishment must not be excessive. A punishment is excessive under this principle if it is unnecessary: The infliction of a severe punishment by the State cannot comport with human dignity when it is nothing more than the pointless infliction of suffering. If there is a significantly less severe punishment adequate to achieve the purposes for which the punishment is inflicted, . . . the punishment inflicted is unnecessary and therefore excessive.

This principle first appeared in our cases in Mr. Justice Field's dissent in O'Neil v. Vermont. He there took the position that: "[The Clause] is directed, not only against punishments of the character mentioned [torturous punishments], but against all punishments which by their excessive length or severity are greatly disproportioned to the offences charged. The whole inhibition is against that which is excessive either in the bail required, or fine imposed, or punishment inflicted." Although the determination that a severe punishment is excessive may be grounded in a judgment that it is disproportionate to the crime, the more significant basis is that the punishment serves no penal purpose more effectively than a less severe punishment. . . .

III.

. . . There is, first, a textual consideration raised by the Bill of Rights itself. The Fifth Amendment declares that if a particular crime is punishable by death, a person charged with that crime is entitled to certain procedural protections. We can thus infer that the Framers recognized the existence of what was then a common punishment. We cannot, however, make the further inference that they intended to exempt this particular punishment from the express prohibition of the Cruel and Unusual Punishments Clause. Nor is there any indication in the debates on the Clause that a special exception was to be made for death. If anything, the indication is to the contrary . . . . Finally, it does not advance analysis to insist that the Framers did not believe that adoption of the Bill of Rights would immediately prevent the infliction of the punishment of death; neither did they believe that it would immediately prevent the infliction of other corporal punishments that, although common at the time are now acknowledged to be impermissible.

There is also the consideration that this Court has decided three cases involving constitutional challenges to particular methods of inflicting this punishment. [Wilkerson v. Utah (1879), In re Kemmler (1890) and Louisiana ex rel. Francis v. Resweber (1947)]. . . . These three decisions . . . reveal that the Court, while ruling upon various methods of inflicting death, has assumed in the past that death was a constitutionally permissible punishment. Past assumptions, however, are not sufficient to limit the scope of our examination of this punishment today. The constitutionality of death itself under the Cruel and Unusual Punishments Clause is before this Court for the first time; we cannot avoid the question by recalling past cases that never directly considered it.

The question, then, is whether the deliberate infliction of death is today consistent with the command of the Clause that the State may not inflict punishments that do not comport with human dignity. I will analyze the punishment of death in terms of the principles set out above and the cumulative test to which they lead: It is a denial of human dignity for the State arbitrarily to subject a person to an unusually severe punishment that society has indicated it does not regard as acceptable, and that cannot be shown to serve any penal purpose more effectively than a significantly less drastic punishment. Under these principles and this test, death is today a "cruel and unusual" punishment. . . .

The outstanding characteristic of our present practice of punishing criminals by death is the infrequency with which we resort to it. The evidence is conclusive that death is not the ordinary punishment for any crime.

There has been a steady decline in the infliction of this punishment in every decade since the 1930's, the earliest period for which accurate statistics are available. In the 1930's, executions averaged 167 per year; in the 1940's, the average was 128; in the 1950's, it was 72; and in the years 1960–1962, it was 48. There have been a total of 46 executions since then, 36 of them in 1963–1964. Yet our population and the numbers of capital crimes committed have increased greatly over the past four decades. . . .

When a country of over 200 million people inflicts an unusually severe punishment no more than 50 times a year, the inference is strong that the punishment is not being regularly and fairly applied. To dispel it would indeed require a clear showing of nonarbitrary infliction. . . .

When the punishment of death is inflicted in a trivial number of the cases in which it is legally available, the conclusion is virtually inescapable that it is being inflicted arbitrarily. Indeed, it smacks of little more than a lottery system. The States claim, however, that this rarity is evidence not of arbitrariness, but of informed selectivity: Death is inflicted, they say, only in "extreme" cases.

Informed selectivity, of course, is a value not to be denigrated. Yet presumably the States could make precisely the same claim if there were 10 executions per year, or five, or even if there were but one. That there may be as many as 50 per year does not strengthen the claim. When the rate of infliction is at this low level, it is highly implausible that only the worst criminals or the criminals who commit the worst crimes are selected for this punishment. No one has yet suggested a rational basis that could differentiate in those terms the few who die from the many who go to prison. . . .

When there is a strong probability that an unusually severe and degrading punishment is being inflicted arbitrarily, we may well expect that society will disapprove of its infliction. I turn, therefore, to the third principle. An examination of the history and present operation of the American practice of punishing criminals by death reveals that this punishment has been almost totally rejected by contemporary society. . . .

The progressive decline in, and the current rarity of, the infliction of death demonstrate that our society seriously questions the appropriateness of this punishment today. . . . When an unusually severe punishment is authorized for wide-scale application but not, because of society's refusal, inflicted save in a few instances, the inference is compelling that there is a deep-seated reluctance to inflict it. Indeed, the likelihood is great that the punishment is tolerated only because of its disuse. The objective indicator of society's view of an unusually severe punishment is what society does with it, and today society will inflict death upon only a small sample of the eligible criminals. Rejection could hardly be more complete without becoming absolute. At the very least, I must conclude that contemporary society views this punishment with substantial doubt.

The final principle to be considered is that an unusually severe and degrading punishment may not be excessive in view of the purposes for which it is inflicted. This principle, too, is related to the others. When there is a strong probability that the State is arbitrarily inflicting an unusually severe punishment that is subject to grave societal doubts, it is likely also that the punishment cannot be shown to be serving any penal purpose that could not be served equally well by some less severe punishment.

The States' primary claim is that death is a necessary punishment because it prevents the commission of capital crimes more effectively than any less severe punishment. . . .

. . . The argument is not based upon evidence that the threat of death is a superior deterrent. Indeed, as my Brother Marshall establishes, the available evidence uniformly indicates, although it does not conclusively prove, that the threat of death has no greater deterrent effect than the threat of imprisonment. The States argue, however, that they are entitled to rely upon common human experience, and that experience, they say, supports the conclusion that death must be a more effective deterrent than any less severe punishment. Because people fear death the most, the argument runs, the threat of death must be the greatest deterrent.

It is important to focus upon the precise import of this argument. It is not denied that many, and probably most, capital crimes cannot be deterred by the threat of punishment. Thus the argument can apply only to those who think rationally about the commission of capital crimes. . . . The concern, then, is with a particular type of potential criminal, the rational person who will commit a capital crime knowing that the punishment is long-term imprisonment, which may well be for the rest of his life, but will not commit the crime knowing that the punishment is death. On the face of it, the assumption that such persons exist is implausible. . . .

. . . The only other purpose suggested, one that is independent of protection for society, is retribution. Shortly stated, retribution in this context means that criminals are put to death because they deserve it. . . .

. . . Obviously, concepts of justice change; no immutable moral order requires death for murderers and rapists. The claim that death is a just punishment necessarily refers to the existence of certain public beliefs. The claim must be that for capital crimes death alone comports with society's notion of proper punishment. As administered today, however, the punishment of death cannot be justified as a necessary means of exacting retribution from criminals. When the overwhelming number of criminals who commit capital crimes go to prison, it cannot be concluded that death serves the purpose of retribution more effectively than imprisonment. The asserted public belief that murderers and rapists deserve to die is flatly inconsistent with the execution of a random few. . . .

I concur in the judgments of the Court.

Mr. Justice Stewart, concurring, said in part:

The penalty of death differs from all other forms of criminal punishment, not in degree but in kind. It is unique in its total irrevocability. It is unique in its rejection of rehabilitation of the convict as a basic purpose of criminal justice. And it is unique, finally, in its absolute renunciation of all that is embodied in our concept of humanity.

For these and other reasons, at least two of my Brothers have concluded that the infliction of the death penalty is constitutionally impermissible in all circumstances under the Eighth and Fourteenth Amendments. Their case is a strong one. But I find it unnecessary to reach the ultimate question they would decide. . . .

Legislatures—state and federal—have sometimes specified that the penalty of death shall be the mandatory punishment for every person convicted of engaging in certain designated criminal conduct. . . .

If we were reviewing death sentences imposed under these or similar laws, we would be faced with the need to decide whether capital punishment is unconstitutional for all crimes and under all circumstances. . . .

On that score I would say only that I cannot agree that retribution is a constitutionally impermissible ingredient in the imposition of punishment. The instinct for retribution is part of the nature of man, and channeling that instinct in the administration of criminal justice serves an important purpose in promoting the stability of a society governed by law. When people begin to believe that organized society is unwilling or unable to impose upon criminal offenders the punishment they "deserve," then there are sown the seeds of anarchy—of self-help, vigilante justice, and lynch law.

The constitutionality of capital punishment in the abstract is not, however, before us in these cases. . . . Neither State has made a legislative determination that forcible rape and murder can be deterred only by imposing the penalty of death upon all who perpetrate those offenses. As Mr. Justice White so tellingly puts it, the "legislative will is not frustrated if the penalty is never imposed."

Instead, the death sentences now before us are the product of a legal system that brings them, I believe, within the very core of the Eighth Amendment's guarantee against cruel and unusual punishments, a guarantee applicable against the States through the Fourteenth Amendment. . . . In the first place, it is clear that these sentences are "cruel" in the sense that they excessively go beyond, not in degree but in kind, the punishments that the state legislatures have determined to be necessary. . . . In the second place, it is equally clear that these sentences are "unusual" in the sense that the penalty of death is infrequently imposed for murder, and that its imposition for rape is extraordinarily rare. But I do not rest my conclusion upon these two propositions alone.

These death sentences are cruel and unusual in the same way that being struck by lightning is cruel and unusual. For, of all the people convicted of rapes and murders in 1967 and 1968, many just as reprehensible as these, the petitioners are among a capriciously selected random handful upon whom the sentence of death has in fact been imposed . . . . I simply conclude that the Eighth and Fourteenth Amendments cannot tolerate the infliction of a sentence of death under legal systems that permit this unique penalty to be so wantonly and so freakishly imposed.

For these reasons I concur in the judgments of the Court.

Mr. Justice White, concurring, said in part:

. . . In joining the Court's judgments, . . . I do not at all intimate that the death penalty is unconstitutional per se or that there is no system of capital punishment that would comport with the Eighth Amendment. That question, ably argued by several of my Brethren, is not presented by these cases and need not be decided.

The narrow question to which I address myself concerns the constitutionality of capital punishment statutes under which (1) the legislature authorizes the imposition of the death penalty for murder or rape; (2) the legislature does not itself mandate the penalty in any particular class or kind of case (that is, legislative will is not frustrated if the penalty is never imposed), but delegates to judges or juries the decisions as to those cases, if any, in which the penalty will be utilized; and (3) judges and juries have ordered the death penalty with such infrequency that the odds are now very much against imposition and execution of the penalty with respect to any convicted murderer or rapist. It is in this context that we must consider whether the execution of these petitioners would violate the Eighth Amendment.

I begin with what I consider a near truism: that the death penalty could so seldom be imposed that it would cease to be a credible deterrent or measurably to contribute to any other end of punishment in the criminal justice system. It is perhaps true that no matter how infrequently those convicted of rape or murder are executed, the penalty so imposed is not disproportionate to the crime and those executed may deserve exactly what they received. It would also be clear that executed defendants are finally and completely incapacitated from again committing rape or murder or any other crime. But when imposition of the penalty reaches a certain degree of infrequency, it would be very doubtful that any existing general need for retribution would be measurably satisfied. Nor could it be said with confidence that society's need for specific deterrence justifies death for so few when for so many in like circumstances life imprisonment or shorter prison terms are judged sufficient, or that community values are measurably reenforced by authorizing a penalty so rarely invoked.

Most important, a major goal of the criminal law—to deter others by punishing the convicted criminal—would not be substantially served where the penalty is so seldom invoked that it ceases to be the credible threat essential to influence the conduct of others. For present purposes I accept the morality and utility of punishing one person to influence another. I accept also the effectiveness of punishment generally and need not reject the death penalty as a more effective deterrent than a lesser punishment. But common sense and experience tell us that seldom-enforced laws become ineffective measures for controlling human conduct and that the death penalty, unless imposed with sufficient frequency, will make little contribution to deterring those crimes for which it may be exacted.

The imposition and execution of the death penalty are obviously cruel in the dictionary sense. But the penalty has not been considered cruel and unusual punishment in the constitutional sense because it was thought justified by the social ends it was deemed to serve. At the moment that it ceases realistically to further these purposes, however, the emerging question is whether its imposition in such circumstances would violate the Eighth Amendment. It is my view that it would, for its imposition would then be the pointless and needless extinction of life with only marginal contributions to any discernible social or public purposes. A penalty with such negligible returns to the State would be patently excessive and cruel and unusual punishment violative of the Eighth Amendment.

It is also my judgment that this point has been reached with respect to capital punishment as it is presently administered under the statutes involved in these cases. . . .

. . . The short of it is that the policy of vesting sentencing authority primarily in juries—a decision largely motivated by the desire to mitigate the harshness of the law and to bring community judgment to bear on the sentence as well as guilt or innocence—has so effectively achieved its aims that capital punishment within the confines of the statutes now before us has for all practical purposes run its course. . . .

I concur in the judgments of the Court.

Mr. Justice Marshall, concurring, said in part:

V.

In order to assess whether or not death is an excessive or unnecessary penalty, it is necessary to consider the reasons why a legislature might select it as punishment for one or more offenses, and examine whether less severe penalties would satisfy the legitimate legislative wants as well as capital punishment. If they would, then the death penalty is unnecessary cruelty, and, therefore, unconstitutional.

There are six purposes conceivably served by capital punishment: retribution, deterrence, prevention of repetitive criminal acts, encouragement of guilty pleas and confessions, eugenics, and economy. These are considered seriatim below. . . .

. . . It is undoubtedly correct that there is a demand for vengeance on the part of many persons in a community against one who is convicted of a particularly offensive act. At times a cry is heard that morality requires vengeance to evidence society's abhorrence of the act. But the Eighth Amendment is our insulation from our baser selves. . . .

B. The most hotly contested issue regarding capital punishment is whether it is better than life imprisonment as a deterrent to crime. . . .

Thorston Sellin, one of the leading authorities on capital punishment, has urged that if the death penalty deters prospective murderers, the following hypotheses should be true:

"(a) Murders should be less frequent in states that have the death penalty than in those that have abolished it, other factors being equal. . . .

"(b) Murders should increase when the death penalty is abolished and should decline when it is restored.

"(c) The deterrent effect should be greatest and should therefore affect murder rates most powerfully in those communities where the crime occurred and its consequences are most strongly brought home to the population.

"(d) Law enforcement officers would be safer from murderous attacks in states that have the death penalty than in those without it."

Sellin's evidence indicates that not one of these propositions is true. This evidence has its problems, however. One is that there are no accurate figures for capital murders; there are only figures on homicides and they, of course, include noncapital killings. A second problem is that certain murders undoubtedly are misinterpreted as accidental deaths or suicides, and there is no way of estimating the number of such undetected crimes. A third problem is that not all homicides are reported. Despite these difficulties, most authorities have assumed that the proportion of capital murders in a State's or nation's homicide statistics remains reasonably constant, and that the homicide statistics are therefore useful.

Sellin's statistics demonstrate that there is no correlation between the murder rate and the presence or absence of the capital sanction. He compares States that have similar characteristics and finds that irrespective of their position on capital punishment, they have similar murder rates. . . .

Sellin also concludes that abolition and/or reintroduction of the death penalty had no effect on the homicide rates of the various States involved. . . . Despite problems with the statistics, Sellin's evidence has been relied upon in international studies of capital punishment.

Statistics also show that the deterrent effect of capital punishment is no greater in those communities where executions take place than in other communities. In fact, there is some evidence that imposition of capital punishment may actually encourage crime, rather than deter it. And, while police and law enforcement officers are the strongest advocates of capital punishment, the evidence is overwhelming that police are no safer in communities that retain the sanction than in those that have abolished it.

There is also a substantial body of data showing that the existence of the death penalty has virtually no effect on the homicide rate in prisons. Most of the persons sentenced to death are murderers, and murderers tend to be model prisoners. . . .

The United Nations Committee that studied capital punishment found that "[i]t is generally agreed between the retentionists and abolitionists, whatever their opinions about the validity of comparative studies of deterrence, that the data which now exist show no correlation between the existence of capital punishment and lower rates of capital crime." . . .

Regarding discrimination, it has been said that "[i]t is usually the poor, the illiterate, the underprivileged, the member of the minority group—the man who, because he is without means, and is defended by a court-appointed attorney—who becomes society's sacrificial lamb . . . ." Indeed, a look at the bare statistics regarding executions is enough to betray much of the discrimination. A total of 3,859 persons have been executed since 1930, of which 1,751 were White and 2,066 were Negro. Of the executions, 3,334 were for murder; 1,664 of the executed murderers were white and 1,630 were Negro; 455 persons, including 48 whites and 405 Negroes, were executed for rape. It is immediately apparent that Negroes were executed far more often than whites in proportion to their percentage of the population. Studies indicate that while the higher rate of execution among Negroes is partially due to a higher rate of crime, there is evidence of racial discrimination. Racial or other discriminations should not be surprising. In McGautha v. California [1971] this Court held "that committing to the untrammeled discretion of the jury the power to pronounce life or death in capital cases is [not] offensive to anything in the Constitution." This was an open invitation to discrimination.

There is also overwhelming evidence that the death penalty is employed against men and not women. Only 32 women have been executed since 1930, while 3,827 men have met a similar fate. It is difficult to understand why women have received such favored treatment since the purposes allegedly served by capital punishment seemingly are equally applicable to both sexes.

It also is evident that the burden of capital punishment falls upon the poor, the ignorant, and the underprivileged members of society. It is the poor, and the members of minority groups who are least able to voice their complaints against capital punishment. Their impotence leaves them victims of a sanction that the wealthier, better-represented, just-as-guilty person can escape. So long as the capital sanction is used only against the forlorn, easily forgotten members of society, legislators are content to maintain the status quo, because change would draw attention to the problem and concern might develop. Ignorance is perpetuated and apathy soon becomes its mate, and we have today's situation. . . .

I concur in the judgments of the Court.

Mr. Justice Douglas, concurring, said in part:

It would seem to be incontestable that the death penalty inflicted on one defendant is "unusual" if it discriminates against him by reason of his race, religion, wealth, social position, or class, or if it is imposed under a procedure that gives room for the play of such prejudices. . . .

There is increasing recognition of the fact that the basic theme of equal protection is implicit in "cruel and unusual" punishments. "A penalty . . . should be considered 'unusually' imposed if it is administered arbitrarily or discriminatorily." . . . The President's Commission on Law Enforcement and Administration of Justice recently concluded: "Finally there is evidence that the imposition of the death sentence and the exercise of dispensing power by the courts and the executive follow discriminatory patterns. The death sentence is disproportionately imposed and carried out on the poor, the Negro, and the members of unpopular groups."

A study of capital cases in Texas from 1924 to 1968 reached the following conclusions:

"Application of the death penalty is unequal: most of the those executed were poor, young, and ignorant.

"Seventy-five of the 460 cases involved codefendants, who, under Texas law, were given separate trials. In several instances where a white and a Negro were codefendants, the white was sentenced to life imprisonment or a term of years, and the Negro was given the death penalty.

"Another ethnic disparity is found in the type of sentence imposed for rape. The Negro convicted of rape is far more likely to get the death penalty than a term sentence, whereas whites and Latins are far more likely to get a term sentence than the death penalty." . . .

Former Attorney General Ramsey Clark has said, "It is the poor, the sick, the ignorant, the powerless and the hated who are executed." One searches our chronicles in vain for the execution of any member of the affluent strata of this society. The Leopolds and Loebs are given prison terms, not sentenced to death. . . .

The high service rendered by the "cruel and unusual" punishment clause of the Eighth Amendment is to require legislatures to write penal laws that are evenhanded, nonselective, and nonarbitrary, and to require judges to see to it that general laws are not applied sparsely, selectively, and spottily to unpopular groups.

A law that stated that anyone making more than $50,000 would be exempt from the death penalty would plainly fall, as would a law that in terms said that blacks, those who never went beyond the fifth grade in school, those who made less than $3,000 a year, or those who were unpopular or unstable should be the only people executed. A law which in the overall view reaches that result in practice has no more sanctity than a law which in terms provides the same.

Thus, these discretionary statutes are unconstitutional in their operation. They are pregnant with discrimination and discrimination is an ingredient not compatible with the idea of equal protection of the laws that is implicit in the ban on "cruel and unusual" punishments. . . .

I concur in the judgments of the Court.

Mr. Chief Justice Burger, with whom Mr. Justice Blackmun, Mr. Justice Powell, and Mr. Justice Rehnquist join, dissenting, said in part:

At the outset it is important to note that only two members of the Court, Mr. Justice Brennan and Mr. Justice Marshall, have concluded that the Eighth Amendment prohibits capital punishment for all crimes and under all circumstances. Mr. Justice Douglas has also determined that the death penalty contravenes the Eighth Amendment, although I do not read his opinion as necessarily requiring final abolition of the penalty. . . .

Mr. Justice Stewart and Mr. Justice White have concluded that petitioners' death sentences must be set aside because prevailing sentencing practices do not comply with the Eighth Amendment. . . .

I.

If we were possessed of legislative power, I would either join with Mr. Justice Brennan and Mr. Justice Marshall or, at the very least, restrict the use of capital punishment to a small category of the most heinous crimes. Our constitutional inquiry, however, must be divorced from personal feelings as to the morality and efficacy of the death penalty, and be confined to the meaning and applicability of the uncertain language of the Eighth Amendment. . . .

. . . I view these cases as turning on the single question whether capital punishment is "cruel" in the constitutional sense. The term "unusual" cannot be read as limiting the ban on "cruel" punishments or as somehow expanding the meaning of the term "cruel." For this reason I am unpersuaded by the facile argument that since capital punishment has always been cruel in the everyday sense of the word, and has become unusual due to decreased use, it is, therefore, now "cruel and unusual."

II.

Counsel for petitioners properly concede that capital punishment was not impermissibly cruel at the time of the adoption of the Eighth Amendment. . . .

In the 181 years since the enactment of the Eighth Amendment, not a single decision of this Court has cast the slightest shadow of a doubt on the constitutionality of capital punishment. . . .

. . . Nonetheless, the Court has now been asked to hold that a punishment clearly permissible under the Constitution at the time of its adoption and accepted as such by every member of the Court until today, is suddenly so cruel as to be incompatible with the Eighth Amendment.

Before recognizing such an instant evolution in the law, it seems fair to ask what factors have changed that capital punishment should now be "cruel" in the constitutional sense as it has not been in the past. It is apparent that there has been no change of constitutional significance in the nature of the punishment itself. Twentieth century modes of execution surely involve no greater physical suffering than the means employed at the time of the Eighth Amendment's adoption. And although a man awaiting execution must inevitably experience extraordinary mental anguish, no one suggests that this anguish is materially different from that experienced by condemned men in 1791, even though protracted appellate review processes have greatly increased the waiting time on "death row." . . .

I do not suggest that the validity of legislatively authorized punishments presents no justiciable issue under the Eighth Amendment, but rather, that the primacy of the legislative role narrowly confines the scope of judicial inquiry. Whether or not provable, and whether or not true at all times, in a democracy the legislative judgment is presumed to embody the basic standards of decency prevailing in the society. This presumption can only be negated by unambiguous and compelling evidence of legislative default.

III.

There are no obvious indications that capital punishment offends the conscience of society to such a degree that our traditional deference to the legislative judgment must be abandoned. It is not a punishment such as burning at the stake that everyone would ineffably find to be repugnant to all civilized standards. Nor is it a punishment so roundly condemned that only a few aberrant legislatures have retained it on the statute books. Capital punishment is authorized by statute in 40 States, the District of Columbia and in the federal courts for the commission of certain crimes. On four occasions in the last 11 years Congress has added to the list of federal crimes punishable by death. In looking for reliable indicia of contemporary attitude, none more trustworthy has been advanced.

One conceivable source of evidence that legislatures have abdicated their essentially barometric role with respect to community values would be public opinion polls, of which there have been many in the past decade addressed to the question of capital punishment. Without assessing the reliability of such polls, or intimating that any judicial reliance could ever be placed on them, it need only be noted that the reported results have shown nothing approximating the universal condemnation of capital punishment that might lead us to suspect that the legislatures in general have lost touch with current social values.

Counsel for petitioners rely on a different body of empirical evidence. They argue, in effect, that the number of cases in which the death penalty is imposed, as compared with the number of cases in which it is statutorily available, reflects a general revulsion toward the penalty that would lead to its repeal if only it were more generally and widely enforced. It cannot be gainsaid that by the choice of juries—and sometimes judges—the death penalty is imposed in far fewer than half the cases in which it is available. To go further and characterize the rate of imposition as "freakishly rare," as petitioners insist, is unwarranted hyperbole. And regardless of its characterization, the rate of imposition does not impel the conclusion that capital punishment is now regarded as intolerably cruel or uncivilized. . . .

. . . The selectivity of juries in imposing the punishment of death is properly viewed as a refinement on rather than a repudiation of the statutory authorization for that penalty. Legislatures prescribe the categories of crimes for which the death penalty should be available, and, acting as "the conscience of the community," juries are entrusted to determine in individual cases that the ultimate punishment is warranted. . . . But to assume from the mere fact of relative infrequency that only a random assortment of pariahs are sentenced to death, is to cast grave doubt on the basic integrity of our jury system.

. . . There is no empirical basis for concluding that juries have generally failed to discharge in good faith the responsibility described in Witherspoon [v. Illinois, 1968]—that of choosing between life and death in individual cases according to the dictates of community values.

The rate of imposition of death sentences falls far short of providing the requisite unambiguous evidence that the legislatures of 40 States and the Congress have turned their backs on current or evolving standards of decency in continuing to make the death penalty available. For, if selective imposition evidences a rejection of capital punishment in those cases where it is not imposed, it surely evidences a correlative affirmation of the penalty in those cases where it is imposed. Absent some clear indication that the continued imposition of the death penalty on a selective basis is violative of prevailing standards of civilized conduct, the Eighth Amendment cannot be said to interdict its use. . . .

IV.

Capital punishment has also been attacked as violative of the Eighth Amendment on the ground that it is not needed to achieve legitimate penal aims and is thus "unnecessarily cruel." As a pure policy matter, this approach has much to recommend it, but it seeks to give a dimension to the Eighth Amendment that it was never intended to have and promotes a line of inquiry that this Court has never before pursued.

The Eighth Amendment, as I have noted, was included in the Bill of Rights to guard against the use of torturous and inhuman punishments, not those of limited efficacy. . . .

The apparent seed of the "unnecessary cruelty" argument is the following language . . . found in Wilkerson v. Utah: "Difficulty would attend the effort to define with exactness the extent of the constitutional provision which provides that cruel and unusual punishments shall not be inflicted; but it is safe to affirm that punishments of torture . . . *and all others in the same line of unnecessary cruelty,* are forbidden by that amendment to the Constitution." (emphasis added). To lift the italicized phrase from the context of the Wilkerson opinion and now view it as a mandate for assessing the value of punishments in achieving the aims of penology is a gross distortion; nowhere are such aims even mentioned in the Wilkerson opinion. The only fair reading of this phrase is that punishments similar to torture in their extreme cruelty are prohibited by the Eighth Amendment. . . .

Apart from these isolated uses of the word "unnecessary," nothing in the cases suggests that it is for the courts to make a determination of the efficacy of punishments. . . .

By pursuing the necessity approach, it becomes even more apparent that it involves matters outside the purview of the Eighth Amendment. Two of the several aims of punishment are generally associated with capital punishment —retribution and deterrence. It is argued that retribution can be discounted because that, after all, is what the Eighth Amendment seeks to eliminate. There is no authority suggesting that the Eighth Amendment was intended to purge the law of its retributive elements, and the Court has consistently assumed that retribution is a legitimate dimension of the punishment of crimes. . . . Furthermore, responsible legal thinkers of widely varying persuasions have debated the sociological and philosophical aspects of the retribution question for generations, neither side being able to convince the other. It would be reading a great deal into the Eighth Amendment to hold that the punishments authorized by legislatures cannot constitutionally reflect a retributive purpose.

The less esoteric but no less controversial question is whether the death penalty acts as a superior deterrent. Those favoring abolition find no evidence that it does. Those favoring retention start from the intuitive notion that capital punishment should act as the most effective deterrent and note that there is no convincing evidence that it does not. Escape from this empirical stalemate is sought by placing the burden of proof on the States and concluding that they have failed to demonstrate that capital punishment is a more effective deterrent than life imprisonment. . . . In fact, there are some who go so far as to challenge the notion that any punishments deter crime. If the States are unable to adduce convincing proof rebutting such assertions, does it then follow that all punishments are suspect as being "cruel and unusual" within the meaning of the Constitution? On the contrary, I submit that the questions raised by the necessity approach are beyond the pale of judicial inquiry under the Eighth Amendment.

V. . . .

As I have earlier stated, the Eighth Amendment forbids the imposition of punishments that are so cruel and inhumane as to violate society's standards of civilized conduct. The Amendment does not prohibit all punishments the States are unable to prove necessary to deter or control crime. The Amendment is not concerned with the process by which a State determines that a particular punishment is to be imposed in a particular case. And the Amendment most assuredly does not speak to the power of legislatures to confer sentencing discretion on juries, rather than to fix all sentences by statute. . . .

. . . The decisive grievance of the opinions—not translated into Eighth Amendment terms—is that the present system of discretionary sentencing in capital cases has failed to produce evenhanded justice; the problem is not that too few have been sentenced to die, but that the selection process has followed no rational pattern. This claim of arbitrariness is not only lacking in empirical support, but also it manifestly fails to establish that the death penalty is a "cruel and unusual" punishment. The Eighth Amendment was included in the Bill of Rights to assure that certain types of punishments would never be imposed, not to channelize the sentencing process. The approach of these concurring opinions has no antecedent in the Eighth Amendment cases. It is essentially and exclusively a procedural due process argument.

Mr. Justice Blackmun, dissenting, said in part:

I join the respective opinions of The Chief Justice, Mr. Justice Powell, and Mr. Justice Rehnquist, and add only the following, somewhat personal, comments.

1. Cases such as these provide for me an excruciating agony of the spirit. I yield to no one in the depth of my distaste, antipathy, and, indeed, abhorrence, for the death penalty, with all its aspects of physical distress and fear and of moral judgment exercised by finite minds. That distaste is buttressed by a belief that capital punishment serves no useful purpose that can be demonstrated. For me, it violates childhood's training and life's experiences, and is not compatible with the philosophical convictions I have been able to develop. It is antagonistic to any sense of "reverence for life." Were I a legislator, I would vote against the death penalty for the policy reasons argued by counsel for the respective petitioners and expressed and adopted in the several opinions filed by the Justices who vote to reverse these convictions. . . .

I do not sit on these cases, however, as a legislator, responsive, at least in part, to the will of constituents. Our task here, as must so frequently be emphasized and re-emphasized, is to pass upon the constitutionality of legislation that has been enacted and that is challenged. This is the sole task for judges. We should not allow our personal preferences as to the wisdom of legislative and congressional action, or our distaste for such action, to guide our judicial decision in cases such as these. The temptations to cross that policy line are very great. In fact, as today's decision reveals, they are almost irresistible. . . .

9. If the reservations expressed by my Brother Stewart (which, as I read his opinion, my Brother White shares) were to command support, namely, that capital punishment may not be unconstitutional so long as it be mandatorily imposed, the result, I fear, will be that statutes struck down today will be reenacted by the state legislatures to prescribe the death penalty for specified crimes without any alternative for the imposition of a lesser punishment in the discretion of the judge or jury, as the case may be. This approach, it seems to me, encourages legislation that is regressive and of an antique mold, for it eliminates the element of mercy in the imposition of punishment. I thought we had passed beyond that point in our criminology long ago.

Mr. Justice Powell, with whom The Chief Justice, Mr. Justice Blackmun, and Mr. Justice Rehnquist join, dissenting, said in part:

II.

. . . On virtually every occasion that any opinion has touched on the question of the constitutionality of the death penalty, it has been asserted affirmatively, or tacitly assumed, that the Constitution does not prohibit the penalty. No

Justice of the Court, until today, has dissented from this consistent reading of the Constitution. The petitioners in these cases now before the Court cannot fairly avoid the weight of this substantial body of precedent merely by asserting that there is no prior decision precisely in point. Stare decisis, if it is a doctrine founded on principle, surely applies where there exists a long line of cases endorsing or necessarily assuming the validity of a particular matter of constitutional interpretation. . . .

III. . . .

Whether one views the question as one of due process or of cruel and unusual punishment, as I do for convenience in this case, the issue is essentially the same. The fundamental premise upon which either standard is based is that notions of what constitutes cruel and unusual punishment or due process do evolve. Neither the Congress nor any state legislature would today tolerate pillorying, branding, or cropping or nailing of the ears—punishments that were in existence during our colonial era. . . .

The prior opinions of this Court point with great clarity to reasons why those of us who sit on this Court at a particular time should act with restraint before assuming, contrary to a century of precedent, that we now know the answer for all time to come. . . . It is too easy to propound our subjective standards of wise policy under the rubric of more or less universally held standards of decency. . . .

The second consideration dictating judicial self-restraint arises from a proper recognition of the respective roles of the legislative and judicial branches. The designation of punishments for crimes is a matter peculiarly within the sphere of the state and federal legislative bodies. . . .

V.

Petitioners seek to salvage their thesis by arguing that the infrequency and discriminatory nature of the actual resort to the ultimate penalty tend to diffuse public opposition. We are told that the penalty is imposed exclusively on uninfluential minorities—"the poor, and powerless, the personally ugly and socially unacceptable." . . .

Certainly the claim is justified that this criminal sanction falls more heavily on the relatively impoverished and underprivileged elements of society. The "have-nots" in every society always have been subject to greater pressure to commit crimes and to fewer constraints than their more affluent fellow citizens. This is, indeed, a tragic byproduct of social and economic deprivation, but it is not an argument of constitutional proportions under the Eighth or

Fourteenth Amendment. . . . The root causes of the higher incidence of criminal penalties on "minorities and the poor" will not be cured by abolishing the system of penalties. Nor, indeed, could any society have a viable system of criminal justice if sanctions were abolished or ameliorated because most of those who commit crimes happen to be underprivileged. The basic problem results not from the penalties imposed for criminal conduct but from social and economic factors that have plagued humanity since the beginning of recorded history, frustrating all efforts to create in any country at any time the perfect society in which there are no "poor," no "minorities" and no "underprivileged." The causes underlying this problem are unrelated to the constitutional issue before the Court.

Mr. Justice Rehnquist, with whom The Chief Justice, Mr. Justice Blackmun, and Mr. Justice Powell join, dissenting, said in part:

. . . The most expansive reading of the leading constitutional cases does not remotely suggest that this Court has been granted a roving commission, either by the Founding Fathers or by the framers of the Fourteenth Amendment, to strike down laws that are based upon notions of policy or morality suddenly found unacceptable by a majority of this Court. . . .

The task of judging constitutional cases imposed by Art. III cannot for this reason be avoided, but it must surely be approached with the deepest humility and genuine deference to legislative judgment. Today's decision to invalidate capital punishment is, I respectfully submit, significantly lacking in those attributes. For the reasons well stated in the opinions of The Chief Justice, Mr. Justice Blackmun and Mr. Justice Powell, I conclude that this decision holding unconstitutional capital punishment is not an act of judgment, but rather an act of will. . . .

If there can be said to be one dominant theme in the Constitution, perhaps more fully articulated in The Federalist Papers than in the instrument itself, it is the notion of checks and balances. The Framers were well aware of the natural desire of office holders as well as others to seek to expand the scope and authority of their particular office at the expense of others. They sought to provide against success in such efforts by erecting adequate checks and balances in the form of grants of authority to each branch of the government in order to counteract and prevent usurpation on the part of the others. . . .

. . . While overreaching by the Legislative and Executive Branches may result in the sacrifice of individual protections that the Constitution was designed to secure against action of the State, judicial overreaching may result in sacrifice of the equally important right of the people to govern themselves. The Due Process and Equal Protection Clauses of the Fourteenth Amendment were "never intended to destroy the States' power to govern themselves."

9

Right to Equal Protection of the Laws

PLESSY v. FERGUSON
163 U. S. 537; 16 S. Ct. 1138; 41 L. Ed. 256
(1896)

With the passing of the Reconstruction era and the return of "white man's government" to the Southern states, state laws were again adopted reminiscent of the "Black Codes" which had been passed right after the Civil War to "keep the Negro in his place." These laws established, and enforced by criminal penalties, a system of racial segregation under which members of the Negro and white races were required to be separated in the enjoyment of public and semi-public facilities. Separate schools, parks, waiting rooms, bus and railroad accommodations were required by law to be furnished each race; and where completely separate facilities later on proved to be not feasible, as in a dining car, a curtained partition served to separate the races.

Where racial segregation was effected by private action, as in the case of stores or clubs, no constitutional issue could be raised after the decision in the Civil Rights Cases in 1883. Where the segregation was required by law, however, the question arose whether it violated the rights guaranteed to the newly freed Negro by the Fourteenth Amendment. This problem came to the Court for the first time in the present case, 28 years after the Amendment had been adopted. The legislature of Louisiana had passed in 1890 a statute providing "that all railway companies carrying passengers in their coaches in this state shall provide equal but separate accommodations for the white and colored races, by providing two or more *passenger coaches for each passenger train, or by dividing the passenger coaches by a partition so as to secure separate accommodations. . . ." A fine of $25 or 20 days in jail was the penalty for sitting in the wrong compartment. Plessy, a person with one-eighth Negro blood, refused to vacate a seat in the white compartment of a railway car and was arrested for violating the statute.*

The Plessy case made lawful for nearly 60 years the doctrine that the Negro is not denied the equal protection of the laws by compelling him to accept "equal but separate" accommodations. There is a bit of irony in the fact that the majority opinion in the Plessy case was written by Mr. Justice Brown, a Yale man from the state of Michigan, while the eloquent protest against racial discrimination is found in the dissenting opinion of Mr. Justice Harlan, a Southerner from Kentucky.

Mr. Justice Brown delivered the opinion of the Court, saying in part:

The object of the [Fourteenth] amendment was undoubtedly to enforce the absolute equality of the two races before the law, but in the nature of things it could not have been intended to abolish distinctions based upon color, or to enforce social, as distinguished from political, equality, or a commingling of the two races upon terms unsatisfactory to either. Laws permitting, and even requiring their separation in places where they are liable to be brought into contact do not necessarily imply the inferiority of either race to the other, and have been generally, if not universally, recognized as within the competency of the state legislatures in the exercise of their police power. The most common instance of this is connected with the establishment of separate schools for white and colored children, which [has] been held to be a valid exercise of the legislative power even by courts of states where the political rights of the colored race have been longest and most earnestly enforced.

One of the earliest of these cases is that of Roberts v. Boston [1849] in which the supreme judicial court of Massachusetts held that the general school committee of Boston had power to make provision for the instruction of colored children in separate schools established exclusively for them, and to prohibit their attendance upon the other schools. . . . Similar laws have been enacted by Congress under its general power of legislation over the District of Columbia as well as by the legislatures of many of the states, and have been generally, if not uniformly, sustained by the courts. . . .

Laws forbidding the intermarriage of the two races may be said in a technical sense to interfere with the freedom of contract, and yet have been universally recognized as within the police power of the state. . . .

The distinction between laws interfering with the political equality of the negro and those requiring the separation of the two races in schools, theatres, and railway carriages, has been frequently drawn by this court. . . .

In this connection, it is also suggested by the learned counsel for the plaintiff in error that the same argument that will justify the state legislature in requiring railways to provide separate accommodations for the two races will also authorize them to require separate cars to be provided for people whose hair is of a certain color, or who are aliens, or who belong to certain nationalities, or to enact laws requiring colored people to walk upon one side of the street, and white people upon the other, or requiring white men's houses to be painted white, and colored men's black, or their vehicles or business signs to be of different colors, upon the theory that one side of the street is as good as the other, or that a house or vehicle of one color is as good as one of another color. The reply to all this is that every exercise of the police power must be reasonable, and extend only to such laws as are enacted in good faith for the promotion of the public good, and not for the annoyance or oppression of a particular class. . . .

So far, then, as a conflict with the 14th Amendment is concerned, the case reduces itself to the question whether the statute of Louisiana is a reasonable regulation, and with respect to this there must necessarily be a large discretion on the part of the legislature. In determining the question of reasonableness it is at liberty to act with reference to the established usages, customs, and traditions of the people, and with a view to the promotion of their comfort, and the preservation of the public peace and good order. Gauged by this standard, we cannot say that a law which authorizes or even requires the separation of the two races in public conveyances is unreasonable or more obnoxious to the 14th Amendment than the acts of Congress requiring separate schools for colored children in the District of Columbia, the constitutionality of which does not seem to have been questioned, or the corresponding acts of state legislatures.

We consider the underlying fallacy of the plaintiff's argument to consist in the assumption that the enforced separation of the two races stamps the colored race with a badge of inferiority. If this be so, it is not by reason of anything found in the act, but solely because the colored race chooses to put that construction upon it. The argument necessarily assumes that if, as has been more than once the case, and is not unlikely to be so again, the colored race should become the dominant power in the state legislature, and should enact a law in precisely similar terms, it would thereby relegate the white race to an inferior position. We imagine that the white race, at least, would not acquiesce in this assumption. The argument also assumes that social prejudices may be overcome by legislation, and that equal rights cannot be secured to the negro except by an enforced commingling of the two races. We cannot accept this proposition. If the two races are to meet on terms of social equality, it must be the result of natural affinities, a mutual appreciation of each other's merits and a voluntary consent of individuals. . . . Legislation is powerless to eradicate racial instincts or to abolish distinctions based upon physical differences, and the attempt to do so can only result in accentuating the difficulties of the present situation. If the civil and political rights of both races be equal, one cannot be inferior to the other civilly or politically. If one race be inferior to the other socially, the Constitution of the United States cannot put them upon the same plane. . . .

The judgment of the court below is therefore affirmed.

Mr. Justice Brewer took no part in the decision of this case.

Mr. Justice Harlan wrote a dissenting opinion, saying in part:

While there may be in Louisiana persons of different races who are not citizens of the United States, the words in the act, "white and colored races" necessarily include all citizens of the United States of both races residing in that state. So that we have before us a state enactment that compels, under penalties, the separation of the two races in railroad passenger coaches, and makes it a crime for a citizen of either race to enter a coach that has been assigned to citizens of the other race.

Thus the state regulates the use of a public highway by citizens of the United States solely upon the basis of race.

However apparent the injustice of such legislation may be, we have only to consider whether it is consistent with the Constitution of the United States. . . .

In respect of civil rights, common to all citizens, the Constitution of the United States does not, I think, permit any public authority to know the race of those entitled to be protected in the enjoyment of such rights. Every true man has pride of race, and under appropriate circumstances, when the rights of others, his equals before the law, are not to be affected, it is his privilege to express such pride and to take such action based upon it as to him seems proper. But I deny that any legislative body or judicial tribunal may have regard to the race of citizens when the civil rights of those citizens are involved. Indeed such legislation as that here in question is inconsistent, not only with that equality of rights which pertains to citizenship, national and state, but with the personal liberty enjoyed by everyone within the United States. . . .

The white race deems itself to be the dominant race in this country. And so it is, in prestige, in achievements, in education, in wealth, and in power. So, I doubt not that it will continue to be for all time, if it remains true to its great heritage and holds fast to the principles of constitutional liberty. But in view of the Constitution, in the eye of the law, there is in this country no superior, dominant, ruling class of citizens. There is no caste here. Our Constitution is color-blind, and neither knows nor tolerates classes among citizens. In respect of civil rights, all citizens are equal before the law. The humblest is the peer of the most powerful. The law regards man as man, and takes no account of his surroundings or of his color when his civil rights as guaranteed by the supreme law of the land are involved. It is therefore to be regretted that this high tribunal, the final expositor of the fundamental law of the land, has reached the conclusion that it is competent for a state to regulate the enjoyment by citizens of their civil rights solely upon the basis of race.

In my opinion, the judgment this day rendered will, in time, prove to be quite as pernicious as the decision made by this tribunal in the Dred Scott Case. It was adjudged in that case that the descendants of Africans who were imported into this country and sold as slaves were not included nor intended to be included under the word "citizens" in the Constitution, and could not claim any of the rights and privileges which that instrument provided for and secured to citizens of the United States; that at the time of the adoption of the Constitution they were "considered as a subordinate and inferior class of beings, who had been subjugated by the dominant race, and, whether emancipated or not, yet remained subject to their authority, and had no rights or privileges but such as those who held the power and the government might choose to grant them." The recent amendments of the Constitution, it was supposed, had eradicated these principles from our institutions. But it seems that we have yet, in some of the states, a dominant race, a superior class of citizens, which assumes to regulate the enjoyment of civil rights, common to all citizens, upon the basis of race. The present decision, it may well be apprehended, will not [only] stimulate aggressions, more or less brutal and irritating, upon the admitted rights of colored citizens, but will encourage the belief that it is possible, by means of state enactments, to defeat the beneficient purposes which the people of the United States had in view when they adopted the recent amendments of the Constitution, by one of which the blacks of this country were made citizens of the United States and of the states in which they respectively reside and whose privileges and immunities, as citizens, the states are forbidden to abridge. Sixty millions of whites are in no danger from the presence here of eight millions of blacks. The destinies of the two races in this country are indissolubly linked together, and the interests of both require that the common government of all shall not permit the seeds of race hate to be planted under the sanction of law. What can more certainly arouse race hate, what more certainly create and perpetuate a feeling of distrust between these races, than state enactments which in fact proceed on the ground that colored citizens are so inferior and degraded that they cannot be allowed to sit in public coaches occupied by white citizens? That, as all will admit, is the real meaning of such legislation as was enacted in Louisiana.

The sure guarantee of the peace and security of each race is the clear, distinct, unconditional recognition by our governments, national and state, of every right that inheres in civil freedom, and of the equality before the law of all citizens of the United States without regard to race. State enactments, regulating the enjoyment of civil rights, upon the basis of race, and cunningly devised to defeat legitimate results of the war, under the pretense of recognizing equality of rights, can have no other result than to render permanent peace impossible and to keep alive a conflict of races, the continuance of which must do harm to all concerned. This question is not met by the suggestion that social equality cannot exist between the white and black races in this country. That argument, if it can be properly regarded as one, is scarcely worthy of consideration, for social equality no more exists between two races when travelling in a passenger coach or a public highway than when members of the same races sit by each other in a street car or in the jury box, or stand or sit with each other in a political assembly, or when they use in common the streets of a city or town, or when they are in the same room for the purpose of having their names placed on the registry of voters, or when they approach the ballot-box in order to exercise the high privilege of voting. . . .

The arbitrary separation of citizens, on the basis of race, while they are on a public highway, is a badge of servitude wholly inconsistent with the civil freedom and the equality before the law established by the Constitution. It cannot be justified upon any legal grounds.

If evils will result from the commingling of the two races upon public highways established for the benefit of all, they will be infinitely less than those that will surely come from state legislation regulating the enjoyment of civil rights upon the basis of race. We boast of the freedom enjoyed by our people above all other peoples. But it is difficult to reconcile that boast with a state of the law which, practically, puts the brand of servitude and degradation upon a large class of our fellow citizens, our equals before the law. The thin disguise of "equal" accommodations for passengers in railroad coaches will not mislead any one, or atone for the wrong this day done. . . .

I am of opinion that the statute of Louisiana is inconsistent with the personal liberty of citizens, white and black, in that state, and hostile to both the spirit and letter of the Constitution of the United States. If laws of like character should be enacted in the several states of the Union, the effect would be in the highest degree mischievous. Slavery as an institution tolerated by law would, it is true, have disappeared from our country, but there would remain a power in the states, by sinister legislation, to interfere with the full enjoyment of the blessings of freedom; to regulate civil rights, common to all citizens, upon the basis of race; and to place in a condition of legal inferiority a large body of American citizens, now constituting a part of the political community called the people of the United States, for whom and by whom, through representatives, our government is administered. Such a system is inconsistent with the guarantee given by the Constitution to each state of a republican form of government, and may be stricken down by congressional action, or by the courts in the discharge of their solemn duty to maintain the supreme law of the land, anything in the Constitution or laws of any state to the contrary notwithstanding.

For the reasons stated, I am constrained to withhold my assent from the opinion and judgment of the majority.

BROWN v. BOARD OF EDUCATION OF TOPEKA

347 U. S. 483; 74 S. Ct. 686; 98 L. Ed. 873 (1954)

Although Plessy v. Ferguson (1896) involved segregation only in the use of railroad facilities, there was no reason to doubt that the Court would uphold segregation in other areas as well, especially education. This became clear when the Court, in Berea College v. Kentucky (1908), held that the state could validly forbid a college, even though a private institution, to teach whites and blacks at the same time and place. This left no doubt of the validity of the Southern laws requiring the education of white and black children in separate tax-supported schools.

While the segregation of whites and blacks was valid, it was valid only on the theory that the facilities offered were equal, since it is the "equal" protection of the laws that is guaranteed by the Fourteenth Amendment. At first, however, the Supreme Court was extremely lenient in construing what this "equality" required. It held that the term meant, not exact or mathematical equality, but only "substantial" equality. In Cumming v. County Board of Education (1899), it found no denial of "equal" protection of the laws in the failure of a southern county to provide a high school for sixty colored children, although it maintained a high school for white children. The Court seemed satisfied with the county's defense that it could not afford to build a high school for Negro children. In Gong Lum v. Rice (1927), the Court held that a Chinese girl could validly be required to attend a school for colored children in a neighboring school district, rather than be allowed to attend the nearby school for white children. It looked as though the Negro was not only to be segregated, but must also be content with very inferior accommodations and services under that segregation.

In 1914 the Supreme Court began to show signs of requiring a much closer approach to equality under segregation. In McCabe v. Atchison, T. & S. F. Ry. Co. (1914), an Oklahoma law was held not to accord equal accommodations to Negroes and whites when it allowed railroads to haul sleeping, dining, and chair cars for the exclusive use of whites without providing them on demand for the use of Negroes.

The tougher attitude of the Court toward what equality under segregation means was made abundantly clear in 1938 in the leading case of Missouri ex rel. Gaines v. Canada. Gaines, a Negro graduate of Lincoln University and a citizen of Missouri, applied for admission to the University of Missouri law school. Negroes were barred from the law school at the state university; but in order to give them "equal" treatment, the state would pay their tuition in any out-of-state law school (Illinois, Indiana, etc.) which would admit them. Gaines, a Negro, refused to accept this compromise, and Chief Justice Hughes, in a strong opinion, held that Gaines was "entitled to be admitted to the law school of the state university in the absence of other and proper provision for his legal training within the state . . . ."

In Sweatt v. Painter (1950), the state of Texas claimed that its new law school for Negroes afforded educational opportunities essentially equal to those at the University of Texas Law School. The Court rejected this claim of equality on very significant grounds. The law school for white students, it said, "possesses to a far greater degree those qualities which are incapable of objective measurement but which make for greatness in a law school. . . . The law school, the proving ground for legal learning and practice, cannot be effective in isolation from the individuals and institutions with which the law interacts. . . . The [Negro] law school . . . excludes from its student body members of racial groups which number 85% of the population of the State and include most of the lawyers, judges and other officials with whom petitioner will inevitably be dealing when he becomes a member of the Texas bar. With such a substantial and significant segment of society excluded, we cannot conclude that the education offered petitioner is substantially equal to that which he would receive if admitted to the University of Texas Law School." This strongly suggests that no Negro law school could ever be "equal" under segregation.

While Congress has full power to regulate interstate commerce, it had never abolished racial segregation on interstate trains. All it had done was to forbid any interstate common carrier to give any person or group any "unreasonable preference or advantage," or subject them to "any undue or unreasonable prejudice or disadvantage." In practice these restrictions had been interpreted in the light of the "separate but equal" doctrine of Plessy v. Ferguson. The Southern Railway Company segregated Negroes in dining cars by reserving ten tables exclusively for white passengers, and one table exclusively for Negroes. A curtain or partition cut the Negro table off from the others. In Henderson v. United States (1950), the Court held that such segregation subjected Negro passengers to undue prejudice and disadvantage, and in 1961 the Interstate Commerce Commission issued a regulation forbidding interstate motor carriers of passengers to discriminate on grounds of race, color, creed, or national origin in the seating of such passengers, or in the terminal facilities provided for them, such as "waiting room, restroom, eating, drinking, and ticket sales facilities," or to display signs indicating such discrimination.

In the cases dealing with Negro segregation which reached the Supreme Court after Plessy v. Ferguson (1896) the doctrine of that case was followed and never reexamined. The Court seemed content with the "separate but equal" rule of that case, which, as someone aptly put it, guaranteed to the Negro "the equal, but different, protection of the laws." During the 40-year period beginning with the McCabe case in 1914, the Court, applying ever more rigid standards of equality under segregation, found that Negro plaintiffs in each case had in fact been denied equality of treatment; and so the Court, following the rule that it will not decide constitutional issues if it can avoid doing so, continued to grant relief to Negroes not because they were segregated but because they were unequally treated under segregation. While in the Texas Law School case and the dining car case the Court virtually stated that there were circumstances in which segregation in itself resulted in inequality of treatment, the rule of Plessy v. Ferguson remained intact.

In the fall if 1952, however, the Supreme Court had on its docket cases from four states (Kansas, South Carolina, Virginia, and Delaware), and from the District of Columbia, challenging the constitutionality of racial segregation in public schools. In all of these cases the facts showed that "the Negro and white schools involved have been equalized, or are being equalized, with respect to buildings, curricula, qualifications and salaries of teachers, and other 'tangible' factors." After nearly 60 years the Court again had squarely before it the question of the constitutionality of segregation per se—the question whether the doctrine of Plessy v. Ferguson should be affirmed or reversed.

The five cases were argued together in December, 1952, and the country waited with tense interest for the Court's decision. On June 8, 1953, the Court restored the cases to the docket for reargument in the fall and issued a list of questions upon which it wished that argument to turn. The Court asked for enlightenment on two main points. First, is there historical evidence which shows the intentions of those who framed and ratified the Fourteenth Amendment with respect to the impact of that amendment upon racial segregation in the public schools? Second, if the Court finds racial segregation violates the Fourteenth Amendment, what kind of decree could and should be issued to bring about an end of segregation?

The cases were reargued in December, 1953. Elaborate briefs set forth in great detail the background of the Fourteenth Amendment and the intentions of its framers and ratifiers. The negative result of this historical research is commented on in the opinion below. Some of the briefs, includ-ing the one filed by the Attorney General, presented suggestions on the form of the court decree by which segregation might best be ended should the Court hold it to be invalid. Counsel for the National Association for the Advancement of Colored People, who had played a major part in the instigation of these cases, declined to deal with this point. In their view segregation, if held invalid, should be abolished completely and without delay.

Following the rehearing ordered in the opinion below, the Court handed down its decision remanding the cases back to the lower courts, which were directed to fashion decrees in accordance with "equitable principles." While recognizing that to abolish segregation "may call for the elimination of a variety of obstacles in making the transition," the Court declared that the district "courts will require that the defendants make a prompt and reasonable start toward full compliance with our May 17, 1954, ruling. Once such a start has been made, the courts may find that additional time is necessary to carry out the ruling in an effective manner. The burden rests upon the defendants to establish that such time is necessary in the public interest and is consistent with good faith compliance at the earliest practi-cable date. . . . The cases are remanded to the District Courts to take such proceedings and enter such orders and decrees consistent with this opinion as are necessary and proper to admit to public schools on a racially nondiscriminatory basis with all deliberate speed the parties to these cases."

The only persons directly bound by the decision in Brown v. Topeka were the five school boards actually parties to the suit, and the only laws specifically held unconstitutional were those involved in those cases. Nor-mally, and in less controversial cases, a rule of constitutional law an-nounced by the Court in a particular case will be accepted and complied with by all those across the country to whom the rule clearly applies. But this compliance is technically voluntary, since only the parties to the case are immediately bound by the Court's decree. It follows, therefore, that obstinate school boards can be compelled to desegregate their schools only as cases are brought against them in the courts and those courts apply to them the rule of the Brown case. In the 15 years since the Court abandoned the separate but equal doctrine in Brown v. Board of Education of Topeka (1954), little or no actual desegregation has been done voluntarily. Al-though they knew segregated schooling was unconstitutional, most school boards have insisted on being brought into court and forced to take the first reluctant steps. Unlimited ingenuity has been expended in devising tech-niques for thwarting the Court's ruling, and each technique has been defended as long as possible in the courts in an effort to gain time, and in the hope that either Congress would come to the rescue or the Supreme

Court would relent. For example, one of the five districts ordered to desegregate its public schools "with all deliberate speed" was Prince Edward County, Virginia. The response of the Virginia legislature was a program of "massive resistance," which included closing integrated schools, cutting off their funds, paying tuition grants to students in private, nonsectarian schools, and providing state and local financial aid (including teacher retirement benefits) for such schools. In 1959 the supreme court of Virginia held the program void under the Virginia constitution, so the legislature repealed it and enacted instead a program under which school attendance was a matter of local option.

Faced with the desegregation order, Prince Edward County closed its public schools and provided various kinds of financial support for privately operated segregated schools. In Griffin v. School Board of Prince Edward County (1964), the Court held the plan denied equal protection of the law. Noting that "the case has been delayed since 1951 by resistance at the state and county level, by legislation, and by law suits," it emphasized that "there has been entirely too much deliberation and not enough speed." The Court conceded to the state a "wide discretion" in deciding whether state laws should operate statewide or only in some counties, "but the record in the present case could not be clearer that Prince Edward's public schools were closed and private schools operated in their place with state and county assistance, for one reason, and one reason only: to ensure, through measures taken by the county and the State, that white and colored children in Prince Edward County would not, under any circumstances, go to the same school. Whatever nonracial grounds might support a State's allowing a county to abandon public schools, the object must be a constitutional one, and grounds of race and opposition to desegregation do not qualify as consitutional." The district court was told to "enter a decree which will guarantee that these petitioners will get the kind of education that is given in the State's public schools" even if it had to order the Board of Supervisors to levy taxes to do it. After trying in vain to discover what the penalties for refusal would be, the supervisors finally decided to obey, and in the fall of 1964 Prince Edward County reopened its schools on an integrated basis.

The county did not, however, abandon its aid to private segregated schools, and in what Negroes termed "a midnight raid on the treasury," the Board of Supervisors hurriedly paid out $180,000 in tuition grants to white pupils while the issue of the constitutionality of such payments was still being litigated in the United States court of appeals. That court subsequently barred such tuition grants as long as the schools remained segregated, and in 1966, it found the Board in contempt and ordered it to repay the grants. The Supreme Court refused to upset this contempt *ruling, and in the summer of 1967 the Board finally returned the money to the county treasury.*

Meanwhile the political branches of government had taken a hand in speeding integration, and threats to withhold federal aid to segregated schools under the Civil Rights Act of 1964 resulted in widespread token compliance, largely by offering Negroes "freedom of choice" among schools. Yet with the start of the 1965–66 school year fewer than ten percent of the South's Negroes were attending desegregated schools. In March of 1966 the Office of Education announced new guidelines designed to desegregate all 12 grades by the fall of 1967. Protracted litigation, complicated by disputes over the effectiveness of the toughened "freedom of choice" plan, culminated in an announcement by the court of appeals in a Georgia case in December, 1968, that all schools in the states of the fifth circuit—Alabama, Florida, Louisiana, Mississippi, and Texas—be integrated by the fall of 1969 or abandoned.

In July, 1969, it became apparent that some 30 schools in Mississippi would not be ready for integration with the opening of the fall term, and the government suddenly announced that it would no longer try to hold the South to "arbitrary" deadlines for desegregation. At the same time the United States Court of Appeals for the Fifth Circuit reaffirmed its policy and ordered full integration, by September, and the justice department replied by asking for a delay until December 1.

The announced change in policy came as a shock to the lawyers of the NAACP Legal Defense Fund who, after working for many years in partnership with government attorneys for full integration, suddenly found themselves carrying on the fight alone. Even the government attorneys themselves had trouble accepting the sudden switch, and a large number of them signed a statement of protest against the new policy. In spite of this the court of appeals granted the requested delay, and the Legal Defense Fund appealed to the Supreme Court. In a brief per curiam opinion, one of the first in which Chief Justice Berger participated, the Court rejected the government's request for a delay. The "continued operation of segregated schools under a standard of allowing 'all deliberate speed' for desegregation" said the Court, "is no longer constitutionally permissible. Under explicit holdings of this Court the obligation of every school district is to terminate dual school systems at once and to operate now and hereafter only unitary schools." See Alexander v. Holmes County Board of Education (1969).

The extension of the Brown doctrine to other areas of segregation has so far been done by the Court largely through the technique of affirming lower court decisions without opinion. In Baltimore v. Dawson (1955), the desegregation ruling was held applicable to public beaches, and in Holmes v. Atlanta (1955), to public golf courses. In 1963, in deciding Watson v. Memphis, the Court held that recreation facilities, like universities, must be desegregated at once. On the strength of this rule, the city of Jackson, Mississippi desegregated its parks and golf links but decided instead to close its five swimming pools. In Palmer v. Thompson (1971) the Court upheld the move, noting that a statute could not be held void because of the motivations of the legislature which adopted it, and there was no evidence that the city was "now covertly aiding the maintenance and operation of pools which are private in name only. It shows no state action affecting blacks differently from whites." Three of the four dissenting justices argued that the city action was a public stand against desegregating public facilities and the forbidding of Negroes to swim because of their color—both denials of equal protection.

A separate opinion was necessary to invalidate segregation in the schools of the District of Columbia, which is under congressional authority. In Bolling v. Sharpe, the Court holds that the due process clause of the Fifth Amendment forbids racial segregation by the federal government.

Mr. Chief Justice Warren, delivering the opinion of the Court in the Brown case, said in part:

These cases came to us from the States of Kansas, South Carolina, Virginia, and Delaware. They are premised on different facts and different local conditions, but a common legal question justifies their consideration together in this consolidated opinion.

In each of the cases, minors of the Negro race, through their legal representatives, seek the aid of the courts in obtaining admission to the public schools of their community on a nonsegregated basis. In each instance, they had been denied admission to schools attended by white children under laws requiring or permitting segregation according to race. This segregation was alleged to deprive the plaintiffs of the equal protection of the laws under the Fourteenth Amendment. . . .

The plaintiffs contend that segregated public schools are not "equal" and cannot be made "equal," and that hence they are deprived of the equal protection of the laws. Because of the obvious importance of the question presented, the Court took jurisdiction. Argument was heard in the 1952 Term, and reargument was heard this Term on certain questions propounded by the Court.

Reargument was largely devoted to the circumstances surrounding the adoption of the Fourteenth Amendment in 1868. It covered exhaustively consideration of the Amendment in Congress, ratification by the states, then existing practices in racial segregation, and the views of proponents and opponents of the Amendment. This discussion and our own investigation convince us that, although these sources cast some light, it is not enough to resolve the problem with which we are faced. At best, they are inconclusive. The most avid proponents of the post-War Amendments undoubtedly intended them to remove all legal distinctions among "all persons born or naturalized in the United States." Their opponents, just as certainly, were antagonistic to both the letter and the spirit of the Amendments and wished them to have the most limited effect. What others in Congress and the state legislatures had in mind cannot be determined with any degree of certainty.

An additional reason for the inconclusive nature of the Amendment's history, with respect to segregated schools, is the status of public education at that time. In the South, the movement toward free common schools, supported by general taxation, had not yet taken hold. Education of white children was largely in the hands of private groups. Education of Negroes was almost nonexistent, and practically all of the race were illiterate. In fact, any education of Negroes was forbidden by law in some states. Today, in contrast, many Negroes have achieved outstanding success in the arts and sciences as well as in the business and professional world. It is true that public school education at the time of the Amendment had advanced further in the North, but the effect of the Amendment on Northern States was generally ignored in the congressional debates. Even in the North, the conditions of public education did not approximate those existing today. The curriculum was usually rudimentary; ungraded schools were common in rural areas; the school term was but three months a year in many states; and compulsory school attendance was virtually unknown. As a consequence, it is not surprising that there should be so little in the history of the Fourteenth Amendment relating to its intended effect on public education.

In the first cases in this Court construing the Fourteenth Amendment, decided shortly after its adoption, the Court interpreted it as proscribing all state-imposed discriminations against the Negro race. The doctrine of "separate but equal" did not make its appearance in this Court until 1896 in the case of Plessy v. Ferguson involving not education but transportation. American courts have since labored with the doctrine for over half a century. In this Court, there have been six cases involving the "separate but equal" doctrine in the field of public education. In Cumming v. County Board of Education [1899], and Gong Lum v. Rice [1927], the validity of the doctrine itself was not challenged. In more recent cases, all on the graduate school level, inequality was found in that specific benefits enjoyed by white students were denied to Negro students of the same educational qualifications. State of Missouri ex rel. Gaines v. Canada [1938]; Sipuel v. Board of Regents of University of Oklahoma [1948]; Sweatt v. Painter [1950]; McLaurin v. Oklahoma State

Regents [1950]. In none of these cases was it necessary to reexamine the doctrine to grant relief to the Negro plaintiff. And in Sweatt v. Painter the Court expressly reserved decision on the question whether Plessy v. Ferguson should be held inapplicable to public education.

In the instant cases, that question is directly presented. Here, unlike Sweatt v. Painter, there are findings below that the Negro and white schools involved have been equalized, or are being equalized, with respect to buildings, curricula, qualifications and salaries of teachers, and other "tangible" factors. Our decision, therefore, cannot turn on merely a comparison of these tangible factors in the Negro and white schools involved in each of the cases. We must look instead to the effect of segregation itself on public education.

In approaching this problem, we cannot turn the clock back to 1868 when the Amendment was adopted, or even to 1896 when Plessy v. Ferguson was written. We must consider public education in the light of its full development and its present place in American life throughout the Nation. Only in this way can it be determined if segregation in public schools deprives these plaintiffs of the equal protection of the laws.

Today, education is perhaps the most important function of state and local governments. Compulsory school attendance laws and the great expenditures for education both demonstrate our recognition of the importance of education to our democratic society. It is required in the performance of our most basic public responsibilities, even service in the armed forces. It is the very foundation of good citizenship. Today it is a principal instrument in awakening the child to cultural values, in preparing him for later professional training, and in helping him to adjust normally to his environment. In these days, it is doubtful that any child may reasonably be expected to succeed in life if he is denied the opportunity of an education. Such an opportunity, where the state has undertaken to provide it, is a right which must be made available to all on equal terms.

We come then to the question presented: Does segregation of children in public schools solely on the basis of race, even though the physical facilities and other "tangible" factors may be equal, deprive the children of the minority group of equal educational opportunities? We believe that it does.

In Sweatt v. Painter, in finding that a segregated law school for Negroes could not provide them equal educational opportunities, this Court relied in large part on "those qualities which are incapable of objective measurement but which make for greatness in a law school." In McLaurin v. Oklahoma State Regents, the Court, in requiring that a Negro admitted to a white graduate school be treated like all other students, again resorted to intangible considerations: ". . . his ability to study, to engage in discussions and exchange views with other students, and, in general, to learn his profession." Such considerations apply with added force to children in grade and high schools.

To separate them from others of similar age and qualifications solely because of their race generates a feeling of inferiority as to their status in the community that may affect their hearts and minds in a way unlikely ever to be undone. The effect of this separation on their educational opportunities was well stated by a finding in the Kansas case by a court which nevertheless felt compelled to rule against the Negro plaintiffs:

"Segregation of white and colored children in public schools has a detrimental effect upon the colored children. The impact is greater when it has the sanction of the law; for the policy of separating the races is usually interpreted as denoting the inferiority of the Negro group. A sense of inferiority affects the motivation of a child to learn. Segregation with the sanction of law, therefore, has a tendency to [retard] the educational and mental development of Negro children and to deprive them of some of the benefits they would receive in a racial[ly] integrated school system." Whatever may have been the extent of psychological knowledge at the time of Plessy v. Ferguson, this finding is amply supported by modern authority.* Any language in Plessy v. Ferguson contrary to this finding is rejected.

We conclude that in the field of public education the doctrine of "separate but equal" has no place. Separate educational facilities are inherently unequal. Therefore, we hold that the plaintiffs and others similarly situated for whom the actions have been brought are, by reason of the segregation complained of, deprived of the equal protection of the laws guaranteed by the Fourteenth Amendment. This disposition makes unnecessary any discussion whether such segregation also violates the Due Process Clause of the Fourteenth Amendment.

Because these are class actions, because of the wide applicability of this decision, and because of the great variety of local conditions the formulation of decrees in these cases presents problems of considerable complexity. On reargument, the consideration of appropriate relief was necessarily subordinated to the primary question—the constitutionality of segregation in public education. We have now announced that such segregation is a denial of the equal protection of the laws. In order that we may have the full assistance of the parties in formulating decrees, the cases will be restored to the docket, and

*K. B. Clark, Effect of Prejudice and Discrimination on Personality Development (Midcentury White House Conference on Children and Youth, 1950); Witmer and Kotinsky, Personality in the Making (1952), ch VI; Deutscher and Chein, The Psychological Effects of Enforced Segregation: A Survey of Social Science Opinion, 26 J Psychol 259 (1948); Chein, What are the Psychological Effects of Segregation Under Conditions of Equal Facilities? 3 Int J Opinion and Attitude Res 229 (1949); Brameld, Educational Costs, in Discrimination and National Welfare (MacIver, ed, 1949), 44–48; Frazier, The Negro in the United States (1949), 674–681. And see generally Myrdal, An American Dilemma (1944).

the parties are requested to present further argument on Questions 4 and 5 previously propounded by the Court for the reargument this Term.* The Attorney General of the United States is again invited to participate. The Attorneys General of the states requiring or permitting segregation in public education will also be permitted to appear as amici curiae upon request to do so by September 15, 1954, and submission of briefs by October 1, 1954.

It is so ordered.

BOLLING v. SHARPE

347 U. S. 497; 74 S. Ct. 693; 98 L. Ed. 884 (1954)

Mr. Chief Justice Warren delivered the opinion of the Court:

This case challenges the validity of segregation in the public schools of the District of Columbia. The petitioners, minors of the Negro race, allege that such segregation deprives them of due process of law under the Fifth Amendment. They were refused admission to a public school attended by white children solely because of their race. They sought the aid of the District Court for the District of Columbia in obtaining admission. That court dismissed their

---

*"4. Assuming it is decided that segregation in public schools violates the Fourteenth Amendment

"(a) would a decree necessarily follow providing that, within the limits set by normal geographic school districting, Negro children should forthwith be admitted to schools of their choice, or

"(b) may this Court, in the exercise of its equity powers, permit an effective gradual adjustment to be brought about from existing segregated systems to a system not based on color distinctions?

"5. On the assumption on which questions 4(a) and (b) are based, and assuming further that this Court will exercise its equity powers to the end described in question 4(b),

"(a) should this Court formulate detailed decrees in these cases;

"(b) if so, what specific issues should the decrees reach;

"(c) should this Court appoint a special master to hear evidence with a view to recommending specific terms for such decrees;

"(d) should this Court remand to the courts of first instance with directions to frame decrees in these cases, and if so what general directions should the decrees of this Court include and what procedures should the courts of first instance follow in arriving at the specific terms of more detailed decrees?"

complaint. The Court granted a writ of certiorari before judgment in the Court of Appeals because of the importance of the constitutional question presented.

We have this day held that the Equal Protection Clause of the Fourteenth Amendment prohibits the states from maintaining racially segregated public schools. The legal problem in the District of Columbia is somewhat different, however. The Fifth Amendment, which is applicable in the District of Columbia, does not contain an equal protection clause as does the Fourteenth Amendment which applies only to the states. But the concepts of equal protection and due process, both stemming from our American ideal of fairness, are not mutually exclusive. The "equal protection of the laws" is a more explicit safeguard of prohibited unfairness than "due process of law," and, therefore, we do not imply that the two are always interchangeable phrases. But, as this Court has recognized, discrimination may be so unjustifiable as to be violative of due process.

Classifications based solely upon race must be scrutinized with particular care, since they are contrary to our traditions and hence constitutionally suspect. As long ago as 1896, this Court declared the principle "that the Constitution of the United States, in its present form, forbids, so far as civil and political rights are concerned, discrimination by the General Government, or by the States, against any citizen because of his race." And in Buchanan v. Warley [1919], the Court held that a statute which limited the right of a property owner to convey his property to a person of another race was, as an unreasonable discrimination, a denial of due process of law.

Although the Court has not assumed to define "liberty" with any great precision, that term is not confined to mere freedom from bodily restraint. Liberty under law extends to the full range of conduct which the individual is free to pursue, and it cannot be restricted except for a proper governmental objective. Segregation in public education is not reasonably related to any proper governmental objective, and thus it imposes on Negro children of the District of Columbia a burden that constitutes an arbitary deprivation of their liberty in violation of the Due Process Clause.

In view of our decision that the Constitution prohibits the states from maintaining racially segregated public schools, it would be unthinkable that the same Constitution would impose a lesser duty on the Federal Government. We hold that racial segregation in the public schools of the District of Columbia is a denial of the due process of law guaranteed by the Fifth Amendment to the Constitution.

For the reasons set out in Brown v. Board of Education, this case will be restored to the docket for reargument on Questions 4 and 5 previously propounded by the Court.

It is so ordered.

MILLIKEN v. BRADLEY
418 U. S. 717; 94 S. Ct. 3112; 41 L. Ed. 2d 1069
(1974)

With the refusal of the Supreme Court to delay integration in 30 Mississippi school districts (see Alexander v. Holmes County Board of Education, 1969), the Justice Department promptly announced that it would no longer push for more rapid desegregation in over 100 schools in the Deep South. It did not matter much because the Department of Health, Education, and Welfare (HEW) with its authority to withhold funds from schools that were not desegregating effectively had become the principle administrative support for the courts' orders. The Mississippi school districts did integrate, but many whites in heavily black areas transferred to hastily created all white "private academies." HEW promptly urged the Internal Revenue Service (IRS) to withhold tax exemption from such schools, and in July 1970 the IRS complied.

While apparently most rural and small town school districts moved rapidly and peacefully toward integration in 1970, in big cities a new cry was heard. To desegregate urban schools located in the center of black or white neighborhoods, it was necessary to transport students out of their home neighborhoods by school bus. As district courts prepared plans calling for busing between pairs of black and white schools, community voices rose in defense of their "neighborhood schools." In Florida, Governor Claude Kirk seized physically the Bradenton schools to prevent busing and relinquished them only when faced with a $10,000-a-day fine. In both the House and Senate, amendments passed to prevent HEW guidelines from requiring busing, only to have them fail when the act finally passed.

And in Charlotte-Mecklenburg, the country's 43d largest school district, an "antibusing" school board was elected. The district court rejected a plan devised by the Board as not producing sufficient integration at the elementary level and accepted in its place a plan prepared by an outside expert which called for the pairing and grouping of elementary schools and the busing of pupils between them. In Swann v. Charlotte-Mecklenburg Board of Education and Davis v. Board of Commissioners in 1971, the Supreme Court upheld the district court's plan. It approved busing, pairing, and the limited use of mathematical ratios as tools to achieve desegregation and noted that while one-race schools were not outlawed, "the burden upon the school authorities will be to satisfy the court that their racial composition is not the result of present or past discriminatory action on their part." In Nyquist v. Lee (1971), the Court held void without opinion New York's 1969 antibusing statute upon which most of the Southern antibusing statutes had been based.

As the long fight to integrate Southern schools achieved increasing success, attention was turned to Northern cities in which segregation was as complete in many cases as it had ever been in the South. While segregation in the South had its genesis in laws providing separate facilities for the two races (de jure), in the big cities of the North an equally effective segregation (de facto) came about as a by-product of the development of single-race neighborhoods. The creation of these neighborhoods, while in part probably the result of personal preferences, has been fostered by both a tacit unwillingness of whites to sell to blacks and a system of economic zoning that puts the cost of homes in middle-class white communities beyond the financial reach of blacks whose economic opportunities are in turn restricted by both the inferior "ghetto" education afforded them and the hiring policies of business which reserves the best-paid jobs for whites. Thus, while in Charlotte-Mecklenburg only two-thirds of the black pupils were in schools that were 99 percent black and a quarter of them attended schools more than half white, in Chicago three-quarters of the black children went to all-black schools and only three percent went to schools that were mostly white.

Even systematic desegregation, however, does not always provide a permanent solution to the segregation problem. Experience has shown that the migration that tends to follow desegregation orders in big cities merely converts de jure patterns into de facto ones. The most striking illustration is the District of Columbia school system, which integrated in 1956; in subsequent years so many whites with school-age children left the District that only five percent of the pupils in the system are white.

This situation faced the cities of Detroit, Michigan and Richmond, Virginia. The school districts in those cities had such a high concentration of blacks that no amount of line-drawing or busing could change their racial composition. In contrast, the school districts in the surrounding suburban counties were almost entirely white. Despite the fact that the segregated schools were not the product of school board action, the district courts in both cases ordered the black inner-city districts merged with the white suburban districts and pupils bused across county lines to produce integrated schools in both communities. On appeal, the Justice Department sided with the white counties and the court of appeals for the Fourth Circuit, in June 1972, reversed the district court in the Richmond case, while the court of appeals for the Sixth Circuit upheld the district court in the Detroit case. In Richmond School Board v. Virginia Board of Education (1973), the decision of the court of appeals was affirmed by an equally divided Court. Justice Powell, who had been a member of both boards involved in the suit, disqualified himself. Meanwhile the Detroit case was delayed in its efforts to reach the Supreme Court, and in July

1973, a district judge in Indianapolis ordered inter-county transportation of pupils to achieve desegregation.

In contrast to the Detroit and Richmond cases, a number of communities were found to be supporting segregated schools by their deliberate actions and inactions, despite the absence of state laws requiring such segregation. In Pontiac, Michigan and Denver, Colorado, for instance, district courts found that the school boards, by their power to locate new schools and draw attendance lines, had encouraged segregation. In dealing with this problem in Keyes v. School District (1973), the Court held that such conduct constituted de jure segregative action, and the fact that the Denver school board had acted to segregate the Park Hill section of the city created a presumption that heavily segregated parts of the core city were also the product of board action, rather than merely of community social patterns. Justice Powell, in a powerful concurrance, had attacked the de facto-de jure distinction and urged its abolition, pointing out that in the large metropolitan districts, both north and south, the causes of segregation were largely unrelated to government policy, that a pupil has a right not to be compelled by the state to attend a segregated school, and the state has an obligation to operate only integrated schools. Was he, the only southerner on the Court, suggesting the state responsibility for providing desegregated schools made school district lines no more sacred than attendance zones?

In the present case, unlike the Richmond case, both the district court and the court of appeals had found that local school board action in the core city and state action both there and to a limited extent in the suburbs, had contributed to segregation and ordered a plan worked out which would involve both the core city and 53 suburban school districts. That the suburban districts as such might not be engaged in segregation was found immaterial. "(T)he State," said the Court, "has commiteed de jure acts of segregation and . . . the State controls the instrumentalities whose action is necessary to remedy the harmful effects of the State acts." The decision in the present case raises interesting questions regarding state responsibility for desegregation, as opposed to school board responsibility. If a state's obligation to stop segregating can be compartmentalized by district lines, what are its obligations when it decides to alter the size or shape of a district?

Mr. Chief Justice Burger delivered the opinion of the Court, saying in part:

II.

Ever since Brown v. Board of Education (1954), judicial consideration of school desegration cases has begun with the standard that: "[I]n the field of public education the doctrine of 'separate but equal' has no place. Separate educational facilities are inherently unequal." This has been reaffirmed time and again as the meaning of the Constitution and the controlling rule of law.

The target of the Brown holding was clear and forthright: the elimination of state mandated or deliberately maintained dual school systems with certain schools for Negro pupils and others for white pupils. This duality and racial segregation were held to violate the Constitution in the cases subsequent to 1954, including particularly Green v. County School Board of New Kent County, (1968); . . . Swann v. Charlotte-Mecklenburg Board of Education, (1971). . . .

The Swann case, of course, dealt "with the problem of defining in more precise terms than heretofore the scope of the duty of school authorities and district courts in implementing Brown I and the mandate to eliminate dual systems and establish unitary systems at once." In Brown v. Board of Education (1955) (Brown II), the Court's first encounter with the problem of remedies in school desegregation cases, the Court noted: "In fashioning and effectuating the decrees the courts will be guided by equitable principles. Traditionally, equity has been characterized by a practical flexibility in shaping its remedies and by a facility for adjusting and reconciling public and private needs." Brown v. Board of Education. In further refining the remedial process, Swann held, the task is to correct, by a balancing of the individual and collective interests, "the condition that offends the Constitution." A federal remedial power may be exercised "only on the basis of a constitutional violation" and, "[a]s with any equity case, the nature of the violation determines the scope of the remedy."

Proceeding from these basic principles, we first note that in the District Court the complainants sought a remedy aimed at the *condition* alleged to offend the Constitution—the segregation within the Detroit City School District. The Court acted on this theory of the case and in its initial ruling on the "Desegregation Area" stated: "The task before this court, therefore, is now, and . . . has always been, how to desegregate the Detroit public schools." Thereafter, however, the District Court abruptly rejected the proposed Detroit-only plans on the ground that "while [they] would provide a racial mix more in keeping with the Black-White proportions of the student population, [they] would accentuate the racial identifiability of the [Detroit] district as a Black school system, and would not accomplish desegregation." "[T]he racial composition of the student body is such," said the court, "that the plan's implementation would clearly make the entire Detroit public school system racially identifiable," "leav[ing] many of its schools 75 to 90 percent Black." Consequently, the court reasoned, it was imperative to "look beyond the limits of the Detroit school district for a solution to the problem of segregation in the Detroit schools . . ." since "school district lines are simply matters of political convenience and may not be used to deny constitutional rights." Accordingly, the District Court proceeded to redefine the relevant area to include areas of predominantly white pupil population in order to ensure that "upon implementation, no school, grade or classroom [would be] substantially disproportionate to the overall pupil racial composition" of the entire metropolitan area.

While specifically acknowledging that the District Court's findings of a condition of segregation were limited to Detroit, the Court of Appeals approved the use of a metropolitan remedy largely on the grounds that it is "impossible to declare 'clearly erroneous' the District Judge's conclusion that any Detroit only segregation plan will lead directly to a single segregated Detroit school district overwhelmingly black in all of its schools, surrounded by a ring of suburbs and suburban school districts overwhelmingly white in composition in a State in which the racial composition is 87 percent white and 13 percent black."

Viewing the record as a whole it seems clear that the District Court and the Court of Appeals shifted the primary focus from a Detroit remedy to the metropolitan area only because of their conclusion that total desegregation of Detroit would not produce the racial balance which they perceived as desirable. Both courts proceeded on an assumption that the Detroit schools could not be truly desegregated—in their view of what constituted desegregation— unless the racial composition of the student body of each school substantially reflected the racial composition of the population of the metropolitan area as a whole. The metropolitan area was then defined as Detroit plus 53 of the outlying school districts. That this was the approach the District Court expressly and frankly employed is shown by the order which expressed the Court's view of the constitutional standard . . . . In Swann, which arose in the context of a single independent school district, the Court held: "If we were to read the holding of the District Court to require as a matter of substantive constitutional right, any particular degree of racial balance or mixing, that approach would be disapproved and we would be obliged to reverse." The clear import of this language from Swann is that desegregation, in the sense of dismantling a dual school system, does not require any particular racial balance in each "school, grade or classroom."* . . .

*Disparity in the racial composition of pupils within a single district may well constitute a "signal" to a district court at the outset, leading to inquiry into the causes accounting for a pronounced racial identifiability of schools within one school system. In Swann, for example, we were dealing with a large but single independent school system and a unanimous Court noted: "Where the . . . proposed plan for conversion

Here the District Court's approach to what constituted "actual desegregation" raises the fundamental question, not presented in Swann, as to the circumstances in which a federal court may order desegregation relief that embraces more than a single school district. The court's analytical starting point was its conclusion that school district lines are no more than arbitrary lines on a map drawn "for political convenience." Boundary lines may be bridged where there has been a constitutional violation calling for interdistrict relief, but the notion that school district lines may be casually ignored or treated as a mere administrative convenience is contrary to the history of public education in our country. No single tradition in public education is more deeply rooted than local control over the operation of schools; local autonomy has long been thought essential both to the maintenance of community concern and support for public schools and to quality of the educational process. ... Thus, in San Antonio School District v. Rodriguez [1973], we observed that local control over the educational process affords citizens an opportunity to participate in decision-making, permits the structuring of school programs to fit local needs, and encourages "experimentation, innovation and a healthy competition for educational excellence."

The Michigan educational structure involved in this case, in common with most States, provides for a large measure of local control and a review of the scope and character of these local powers indicates the extent to which the interdistrict remedy approved by the two courts could disrupt and alter the structure of public education in Michigan. The metropolitan remedy would require, in effect, consolidation of 54 independent school districts historically administered as separate units into a vast new super school district. Entirely apart from the logistical and other serious problems attending large-scale transportation of students, the consolidation would give rise to an array of other problems in financing and operating this new school system. Some of the more obvious questions would be: What would be the status and authority of the present popularly elected school boards? Would the children of Detroit be within the jurisdiction and operating control of a school board elected by the parents and residents of other districts? What board or boards would levy taxes for school operations in these 54 districts constituting the consolidated metropolitan area? ...

It may be suggested that all of these vital operational problems are yet to

---

from a dual to a unitary system contemplates the continued existence of some schools that are all or predominantly of one race [the school authority has] the burden of showing that such school assignments are genuinely nondiscriminatory." ... However, the use of significant racial imbalance in schools within an autonomous school district as a signal which operates simply to shift the burden of proof, is a very different matter from equating racial imbalance with a constitutional violation calling for a remedy. Keyes [v. Denver School District (1973)] also involved a remedial order within a single autonomous school district.

be resolved by the District Court, and that this is the purpose of the Court of Appeals' proposed remand. But it is obvious from the scope of the interdistrict remedy itself that absent a complete restructuring of the laws of Michigan relating to school districts the District Court will become first, a de facto "legislative authority" to resolve these complex questions, and then the "school superintendent" for the entire area. This is a task which few, if any, judges are qualified to perform and one which would deprive the people of control of schools through their elected representatives.

Of course, no state law is above the Constitution. School district lines and the present laws with respect to local control, are not sacrosanct and if they conflict with the Fourteenth Amendment federal courts have a duty to pre-scribe appropriate remedies. . . . But our prior holdings have been confined to violations and remedies within a single school district. We therefore turn to address, for the first time, the validity of a remedy mandating cross-district or interdistrict consolidation to remedy a condition of segregation found to exist in only one district.

The controlling principle consistently expounded in our holdings is that the scope of the remedy is determined by the nature and extent of the constitutional violation. Swann. Before the boundaries of separate and autonomous school districts may be set aside by consolidating the separate units for remedial purposes or by imposing a cross-district remedy, it must first be shown that there has been a constitutional violation within one district that produces a significant segregative effect in another district. Specifically, it must be shown that racially discriminatory acts of the state or local school districts, or of a single school district have been a substantial cause of interdistrict segregation. Thus an interdistrict remedy might be in order where the racially discriminatory acts of one or more school districts caused racial segregation in an adjacent district, or where district lines have been deliberately drawn on the basis of race. In such circumstances an interdistrict remedy would be appropriate to eliminate the interdistrict segregation directly caused by the constitutional violation. Conversely, without an interdistrict violation and interdistrict effect, there is no constitutional wrong calling for an interdistrict remedy.

The record before us, voluminous as it is, contains evidence of de jure segregated conditions only in the Detroit schools; indeed, that was the theory on which the litigation was initially based and on which the District Court took evidence. With no showing of significant violation by the 53 outlying school districts and no evidence of any interdistrict violation or effect, the court went beyond the original theory of the case as framed by the pleadings and man-dated a metropolitan area remedy. To approve the remedy ordered by the court would impose on the outlying districts, not shown to have committed any constitutional violation, a wholly impermissible remedy based on a stan-dard not hinted at in Brown I and II or any holding of this Court.

In dissent Mr. Justice White and Mr. Justice Marshall undertake to demonstrate that agencies having statewide authority participated in maintaining the dual school system found to exist in Detroit. They are apparently of the view that once such participation is shown, the District Court should have a relatively free hand to reconstruct school districts outside of Detroit in fashioning relief. Our assumption, arguendo, that state agencies did participate in the maintenance of the Detroit system, should make it clear that it is not on this point that we part company. The difference between us arises instead from established doctrine laid down by our cases. Brown, Green, [and] Swann . . . each addressed the issue of constitutional wrong in terms of an established geographic and administrative school system populated by both Negro and white children. In such a context, terms such as "unitary" and "dual" systems, and "racially identifiable schools," have meaning, and the necessary federal authority to remedy the constitutional wrong is firmly established. But the remedy is necessarily designed, as all remedies are, to restore the victims of discriminatory conduct to the position they would have occupied in the absence of such conduct. Disparate treatment of white and Negro students occurred within the Detroit school system, and not elsewhere, and on this record the remedy must be limited to that system. Swann.

The constitutional right of the Negro respondents residing in Detroit is to attend a unitary school system in that district. Unless petitioners drew the district lines in a discriminatory fashion, or arranged for white students residing in the Detroit district to attend schools in Oakland and Macomb Counties, they were under no constitutional duty to make provisions for Negro students to do so. The view of the dissenters, that the existence of a dual system in *Detroit* can be made the basis for a decree requiring cross-district transportation of pupils cannot be supported on the grounds that it represents merely the devising of a suitably flexible remedy for the violation of rights already established by our prior decisions. It can be supported only by drastic expansion of the constitutional right itself, an expansion without any support in either constitutional principle or precedent.

III.

We recognize that the six-volume record presently under consideration contains language and some specific incidental findings thought by the District Court to afford a basis for interdistrict relief. However, these comparatively isolated findings and brief comments concern only one possible interdistrict violation and are found in the context of a proceeding that, as the District Court conceded, included no proof of segregation practiced by any of the 85 suburban school districts surrounding Detroit. The Court of Appeals, for example, relied on five factors which, it held, amounted to unconstitutional state action with respect to the violations found in the Detroit system:

(1) It held the State derivatively responsible for the Detroit Board's violations on the theory that actions of Detroit as a political subdivision of the State were attributable to the State. Accepting, arguendo, the correctness of this finding of state responsibility for the segregated conditions within the city of Detroit, it does not follow that an interdistrict remedy is constitutionally justified or required. With a single exception, discussed later, there has been no showing that either the State or any of the 85 outlying districts engaged in activity that had a cross-district effect. . . . Where the schools of only one district have been affected, there is no constitutional power in the courts to decree relief balancing the racial composition of that district's schools with those of the surrounding districts.

(2) There was evidence introduced at trial that, during the late 1950's, Carver School District, a predominantly Negro suburban district, contracted to have Negro high school students sent to a predominantly Negro school in Detroit. At the time, Carver was an independent school district that had no high school because, according to the trial evidence, "Carver District . . . did not have a place for adequate high school facilities." Accordingly, arrangements were made with Northern High School in the abutting Detroit School District so that the Carver high school students could obtain a secondary school education. In 1960 the Oak Park School District, a predominantly white suburban district, annexed the predominantly Negro Carver School District, through the initiative of local officials. There is, of course, no claim that the 1960 annexation had a segregatory purpose or result or that Oak Park now maintains a duel system.

According to the Court of Appeals, the arrangement during the late 1950's which allowed Carver students to be educated within the Detroit District was dependent upon the "tacit or express" approval of the State Board of Education and was the result of the refusal of the white suburban districts to accept the Carver students. Although there is nothing in the record supporting the Court of Appeals' supposition that suburban white schools refused to accept the Carver students, it appears that this situation, whether with or without the State's consent, may have had a segregative effect on the school populations of the two districts involved. However, since "the nature of the violation determines the scope of the remedy," this isolated instance affecting two of the school districts would not justify the broad metropolitanwide remedy contemplated by the District Court and approved by the Court of Appeals, particularly since it embraced potentially 52 districts having no responsibility for the arrangement and involved 503,000 pupils in addition to Detroit's 276,000 students.

(3) The Court of Appeals cited the enactment of state legislation (Act 48) which had the effect of rescinding Detroit's voluntary desegregation plan (the April 7 Plan). That plan, however, affected only 12 of 21 Detroit high schools and had no causal connection with the distribution of pupils by race between Detroit and the other school districts within the tri-county area.

(4) The court relied on the State's authority to supervise school site selection and to approve building construction as a basis for holding the State responsible for the segregative results of the school construction program in Detroit. Specifically, the Court of Appeals asserted that during the period between 1949 and 1962 the State of Board of Education exercised general authority as overseer of site acquisitions by local boards for new school construction, and suggested that this State-approved school construction "fostered segregation throughout the Detroit Metropolitan area." This brief comment, however, is not supported by the evidence taken at trial since that evidence was specifically limited to proof that school site acquisition and school construction within the city of Detroit produced de jure segregation *within* the city itself. Thus, there was no evidence suggesting that the State's activities with respect to either school construction or site acquisition within Detroit affected the racial composition of the school population outside Detroit or, conversely, that the State's school construction and site acquisition activities within the outlying districts affected the racial composition of the schools within Detroit.

(5) The Court of Appeals also relied upon the District Court's finding that: "This and other financial limitations, such as those on bonding and the working of the state aid formula whereby suburban districts were able to make far larger per pupil expenditures despite less tax effort, have created and perpetuated systematic educational inequalities." However, neither the Court of Appeals nor the District Court offered any indication in the record or in their opinions as to how, if at all, the availability of state-financed aid for some Michigan students outside Detroit, but not for those within Detroit, might have affected the racial character of any of the State's school districts.... This again underscores the crucial fact that the theory upon which the case proceeded related solely to the establishment of Detroit city violations as a basis for desegregating Detroit schools and that, at the time of trial, neither the parties nor the trial judge were concerned with a foundation for interdistrict relief. ...

Mr. Justice Stewart, concurring, said in part:

The opinion of the Court convincingly demonstrates, that traditions of local control of schools, together with the difficulty of a judicially supervised restructuring of local administration of schools, render improper and inequitable such an interdistrict response to a constitutional violation found to have occurred only within a single school district.

This is not to say, however, that an interdistrict remedy of the sort approved by the Court of Appeals would not be proper, or even necessary, in other factual situations. Were it to be shown, for example, that state officials had contributed to the separation of the races by drawing or redrawing school district lines ... by transfer of school units between districts, ... or by purposeful, racially discriminatory use of state housing or zoning laws, then a decree calling for transfer of pupils across district lines or for restructuring of district lines might well be appropriate.

In this case, however, no such interdistrict violation was shown. Indeed, no evidence at all concerning the administration of schools outside the city of Detroit was presented other than the fact that these schools contained a higher proportion of white pupils than did the schools within the city. Since the mere fact of different racial compositions in contiguous districts does not itself imply or constitute a violation of the Equal Protection Clause in the absence of a showing that such disparity was imposed, fostered, or encouraged by the State or its political subdivisions, it follows that no interdistrict violation was shown in this case.* The formulation of an interdistrict remedy was thus simply not responsive to the factual record before the District Court and was an abuse of that court's equitable powers.

Mr. Justice Douglas, dissenting, said in part:

When we rule against the metropolitan area remedy we take a step that will likely put the problems of the blacks and our society back to the period that antedated the "separate but equal" regime of Plessy v. Ferguson [1896]. The reason is simple.

The inner core of Detroit is now rather solidly black; and the blacks, we know, in many instances are likely to be poorer, just as were the Chicanos in San Antonio School District v. Rodriguez [1973]. By that decision the poorer

---

*My Brother Marshall seems to ignore this fundamental fact when he states . . . that "the most essential finding [made by the District Court] was that Negro children in Detroit had been confined by intentional acts of segregation to a growing core of Negro schools surrounded by a receding ring of white schools." This conclusion is simply not substantiated by the record presented in this case. The record here does support the claim made by the respondents that white and Negro students within Detroit who otherwise would have attended school together were separated by acts of the State or its subdivision. However, segregative acts within the city alone cannot be presumed to have produced—and no factual showing was made that they did produce—an increase in the number of Negro students *in the city as a whole.* It is this essential fact of a predominantly Negro school population in Detroit—caused by unknown and perhaps unknowable factors such as in-migration, birth rates, economic changes, or cumulative acts of private racial fears—that accounts for the "growing core of Negro schools," a "core" that has grown to include virtually the entire city. The Constitution simply does not allow federal courts to attempt to change that situation unless and until it is shown that the State, or its political subdivisions, have contributed to cause the situation to exist. No record has been made in this case showing that the racial composition of the Detroit school population or that residential patterns within Detroit and in the surrounding areas were in any significant measure caused by governmental activity, and it follows that the situation over which my dissenting Brothers express concern cannot serve as the predicate for the remedy adopted by the District Court and approved by the Court of Appeals.

school districts must pay their own way. It is therefore a foregone conclusion that we have now given the States a formula whereby the poor must pay their own way.

Today's decision, given Rodriguez, means that there is no violation of the Equal Protection Clause though the schools are segregated by race and though the black schools are not only "separate" but "inferior."

So far as equal protection is concerned we are now in a dramatic retreat from the 7-to-1 decision in 1896 that blacks could be segregated in public facilities provided they received equal treatment.

. . . Given the State's control over the educational system in Michigan, the fact that the black schools are in one district and the white schools are in another is not controlling—either constitutionally or equitably. No specific plan has yet been adopted. We are still at an interlocutory stage of a long drawn-out judicial effort at school desegregation. It is conceivable that ghettos develop on their own without any hint of state action. But since Michigan by one device or another has over the years created black school districts and white schools districts, the task of equity is to provide a unitary system for the affected area where, as here, the State washes its hands of its own creations.

Mr. Justice White, with whom Mr. Justice Douglas, Mr. Justice Brennan, and Mr. Justice Marshall join, dissenting, said in part:

The District Court and the Court of Appeals found that over a long period of years those in charge of the Michigan public schools engaged in various practices calculated to effect the segregation of the Detroit school system. The Court does not question these findings, nor could it reasonably do so. Neither does it question the obligation of the federal courts to devise a feasible and effective remedy. But it promptly cripples the ability of the judiciary to perform this task, which is of fundamental importance to our constitutional system, by fashioning a strict rule that remedies in school cases must stop at the school district line unless certain other conditions are met. As applied here, the remedy for unquestioned violations of the equal protection rights of Detroit's Negroes by the Detroit School Board and the State of Michigan must be totally confined to the limits of the school district and may not reach into adjoining or surrounding districts unless and until it is proved there has been some sort of "interdistrict violation"—unless unconstitutional actions of the Detroit School Board have had a segregative impact on other districts, or unless the segregated condition of the Detroit schools has itself been influenced by segregative practices in those surrounding districts into which it is proposed to extend the remedy.

Regretfully, and for several reasons, I can join neither the Court's judgment nor its opinion. The core of my disagreement is that deliberate acts of segregation and their consequences will go unremedied, not because a remedy would be infeasible or unreasonable in terms of the usual criteria governing school desegregation cases, but because an effective remedy would cause what the Court considers to be undue administrative inconvenience to the State. The result is that the State of Michigan, the entity at which the Fourteenth Amendment is directed, has successfully insulated itself from its duty to provide effective desegregation remedies by vesting sufficient power over its public schools in its local school districts. If this is the case in Michigan, it will be the case in most States.

There are undoubted practical as well as legal limits to the remedial powers of federal courts in school desegregation cases. The Court has made it clear that the achievement of any particular degree of racial balance in the school system is not required by the Constitution; nor may it be the primary focus of a court in devising an acceptable remedy for de jure segregation. A variety of procedures and techniques are available to a district court engrossed in fashioning remedies in a case such as this; but the courts must keep in mind that they are dealing with the process of *educating* the young, including the very young. The task is not to devise a system of pains and penalties to punish constitutional violations brought to light. Rather, it is to desegregate an *educational* system in which the races have been kept apart, without, at the same time, losing sight of the central *educational* function of the schools.

Viewed in this light, remedies calling for school zoning, pairing, and pupil assignments, become more and more suspect as they require that school children spend more and more time in buses going to and from school and that more and more educational dollars be diverted to transportation systems. Manifestly, these considerations are of immediate and urgent concern when the issue is the desegregation of a city school system where residential patterns are predominantly segregated and the respective areas occupied by blacks and whites are heavily populated and geographically extensive. Thus, if one postulates a metropolitan school system covering a sufficiently large area, with the population evenly divided between whites and Negroes and with the races occupying identifiable residential areas, there will be very real practical limits on the extent to which racially identifiable schools can be eliminated within the school district. It is also apparent that the larger the proportion of Negroes in the area, the more difficult it would be to avoid having a substantial number of all-black or nearly all-black schools. . . .

The District Court therefore considered extending its remedy to the suburbs. After hearings, it concluded that a much more effective desegregation plan could be implemented if the suburban districts were included. In proceeding to design its plan on the basis that student bus rides to and from school should not exceed 40 minutes each way as a general matter, the court's express finding was that "[f]or all the reasons stated heretofore—including time, distance, and transportation factors—desegregation within the area described is physically easier and more practicable and feasible, than desegregation efforts limited to the corporate geographic limits of the city of Detroit."

The Court of Appeals agreed with the District Court that the remedy must extend beyond the city limits of Detroit. It concluded that "[i]n the instant case the *only* feasible desegregation plan involves the crossing of the boundary lines between the Detroit School District and adjacent or nearby school districts for the limited purpose of providing an effective desegregation plan." . . .

This Court now reverses the Court of Appeals. It does not question the District Court's findings that *any* feasible Detroit-only plan would leave many schools 75 to 90 percent black and that the district would become progressively more black as whites left the city. Neither does the Court suggest that including the suburbs in a desegregation plan would be impractical or infeasible because of educational considerations, because of the number of children requiring transportation, or because of the length of their rides. Indeed, the Court leaves unchallenged the District Court's conclusion that a plan including the suburbs would be physically easier and more practical and feasible than a Detroit-only plan. Whereas the most promising Detroit-only plan, for example, would have entailed the purchase of 900 buses, the metropolitan plan would involve the acquisition of no more than 350 new vehicles.

Despite the fact that a metropolitan remedy, if the findings of the District Court accepted by the Court of Appeals are to be credited, would more effectively desegregate the Detroit schools, would prevent resegregation, and would be easier and more feasible from many standpoints, the Court fashions out of whole cloth an arbitrary rule that remedies for constitutional violations occurring in a single Michigan school district must stop at the school district line. Apparently, no matter how much less burdensome or more effective and efficient in many respects, such as transportation, the metropolitan plan might be, the school district line may not be crossed. Otherwise, it seems, there would be too much disruption of the Michigan scheme for managing its educational system, too much confusion and too much administrative burden. . . .

I am surprised that the Court, sitting at this distance from the State of Michigan, claims better insight than the Court of Appeals and the District Court as to whether an inter-district remedy for equal protection violations practiced by the State of Michigan would involve undue difficulties for the State in the management of its public schools. . . .

I am even more mystified as to how the Court can ignore the legal reality that the constitutional violations, even if occurring locally, were committed by governmental entities for which the State is responsible and that it is the State that must respond to the command of the Fourteenth Amendment. An inter-district remedy for the infringements that occurred in this case is well within the confines and powers of the State, which is the governmental entity ultimately responsible for desegregating its schools. . . .

It is unnecessary to catalogue at length the various public misdeeds found by the District Court and the Court of Appeals to have contributed to the present segregation of the Detroit public schools. The legislature contributed directly by enacting a statute overriding a partial high school desegregation plan voluntarily adopted by the Detroit Board of Education. Indirectly, the trial court found the State was accountable for the thinly disguised, pervasive acts of segregation committed by the Detroit Board, for Detroit's school construction plans that would promote segregation, and for the Detroit school district' not having funds for pupil transportation within the district. The State was also chargeable with responsibility for the transportation of Negro high school students in the late 1950's from the suburban Ferndale School District, past closer suburban and Detroit high schools with predominantly white student bodies, to a predominantly Negro high school within Detroit. Swann v. Charlotte-Mecklenburg Board of Education and Keyes v. School District No. 1 (1973) make abundantly clear that the tactics employed by the Detroit Board of Education, a local instrumentality of the State, violated the constitutional rights of the Negro students in Detroit's public schools and required equitable relief sufficient to accomplish the maximum, practical desegregation within the power of the political body against which the Fourteenth Amendment directs its proscriptions. No "State" may deny any individual the equal protection of the laws; and if the Constitution and the Supremacy Clause are to have any substance at all, the courts must be free to devise workable remedies against the political entity with the effective power to determine local choice. It is also the case here that the State's legislative interdiction of Detroit's voluntary effort to desegregate its school system was unconstitutional. . . .

The unwavering decisions of this Court over the past 20 years support the assumption of the Court of Appeals that the District Court's remedial power does not cease at the school district line. The Court's first formulation of the remedial principles to be followed in disestablishing racially discriminatory school systems recognized the variety of problems arising from different local school conditions and the necessity for that "practical flexibility" traditionally associated with courts of equity. Brown v. Board of Education (1955) (Brown II). Indeed, the district courts to which the Brown cases were remanded for the formulation of remedial decrees were specifically instructed that they might consider, inter alia, "revision of school districts and attendance areas into compact units to achieve a system of determining admission to the public schools on a nonracial basis. . . ." The malady addressed in Brown II was the statewide policy of requiring or permitting school segregation on the basis of race, while the record here concerns segregated schools only in the city of Detroit. The obligation to rectify the unlawful condition nevertheless rests on the State. The permissible revision of school districts contemplated in Brown II rested on the State's responsibility for desegregating its unlawfully segregated schools, not on any segregative effect which the condition of segregation in one school district might have had on the schools of a neighboring district. The same situation obtains here and the same remedial power is available to the District Court. . . .

Until today, the permissible contours of the equitable authority of the district courts to remedy the unlawful establishment of a dual school system have been extensive, adaptable, and fully responsive to the ultimate goal of achieving "the greatest possible degree of actual desegregation." There are indeed limitations on the equity powers of the federal judiciary, but until now the Court has not accepted the proposition that effective enforcement of the Fourteenth Amendment could be limited by political or administrative boundary lines demarcated by the very State responsible for the constitutional violation and for the disestablishment of the dual system. Until now the Court has instead looked to practical considerations in effectuating a desegregation decree, such as excessive distance, transportation time, and hazards to the safety of the school children involved in a proposed plan. That these broad principles have developed in the context of dual school systems compelled or authorized by state statute at the time of Brown v. Board of Education (1954) (Brown I), does not lessen their current applicability to dual systems found to exist in other contexts, like that in Detroit, where intentional school segregation does not stem from the compulsion of state law, but from deliberate individual actions of local and state school authorities directed at a particular school system. The majority properly does not suggest that the duty to eradicate completely the resulting dual system in the latter context is any less than in the former. But its reason for incapacitating the remedial authority of the federal judiciary in the presence of school district perimeters in the latter context is not readily apparent. . . .

Mr. Justice Marshall, with whom Mr. Justice Douglas, Mr. Justice Brennan, and Mr. Justice White join, dissenting, said in part:

After 20 years of small, often difficult steps toward that great end, the Court today takes a giant step backwards. Notwithstanding a record showing widespread and pervasive racial segregation in the educational system provided by the State of Michigan for children in Detroit, this Court holds that the District Court was powerless to require the State to remedy its constitutional violation in any meaningful fashion. Ironically purporting to base its result on the principle that the scope of the remedy in a desegregation case should be determined by the nature and the extent of the constitutional violation, the Court's answer is to provide no remedy at all for the violation proved in this case, thereby guaranteeing that Negro children in Detroit will receive the same separate and inherently unequal education in the future as they have been unconstitutionally afforded in the past.

I cannot subscribe to this emasculation of our constitutional guarantee of equal protection of the laws and must respectfully dissent. Our precedents, in my view, firmly establish that where, as here, state-imposed segregation has been demonstrated, it becomes the duty of the State to eliminate root and branch all vestiges of racial discrimination and to achieve the greatest possible degree of actual desegregation. I agree with both the District Court and the Court of Appeals that, under the facts of this case, this duty cannot be fulfilled unless the State of Michigan involves outlying metropolitan area school districts in its desegregation remedy. Furthermore, I perceive no basis either in law or in the practicalities of the situation justifying the State's interposition of school district boundaries as absolute barriers to the implementation of an effective desegregation remedy. Under established and frequently used Michigan procedures, school district lines are both flexible and permeable for a wide variety of purposes, and there is no reason why they must now stand in the way of meaningful desegregation relief.

The rights at issue in this case are too fundamental to be abridged on grounds as superficial as those relied on by the majority today. We deal here with the right of all of our children, whatever their race, to an equal start in life and to an equal opportunity to reach their full potential as citizens. Those children who have been denied that right in the past deserve better than to see fences thrown up to deny them that right in the future. Our Nation, I fear, will be ill-served by the Court's refusal to remedy separate and unequal education, for unless our children begin to learn together, there is little hope that our people will ever learn to live together.

I.

The great irony of the Court's opinion and, in my view its most serious analytical flaw may be gleaned from its concluding sentence, in which the Court remands for "prompt formulation of a decree directed to eliminating the segregation found to exist in Detroit city schools, a remedy which has been delayed since 1970." The majority, however, seems to have forgotten the District Court's explicit finding that a Detroit-only decree, the only remedy permitted under today's decision, "would not accomplish desegregation."

Nowhere in the Court's opinion does the majority confront, let alone respond to, the District Court's conclusion that a remedy limited to the city of Detroit would not effectively desegregate the Detroit city schools. I, for one, find the District Court's conclusion well supported by the record and its analysis compelled by our prior cases. Before turning to these questions, however, it is best to begin by laying to rest some mischaracterizations in the Court's opinion with respect to the basis for the District Court's decision to impose a metropolitan remedy.

The Court maintains that while the initial focus of this lawsuit was the condition of segregation within the Detroit city schools, the District Court abruptly shifted focus in mid-course and altered its theory of the case. This new theory, in the majority's words, was "equating racial imbalance with a constitutional violation calling for a remedy." As the following review of the District Court's handling of the case demonstrates, however, the majority's characterization is totally inaccurate. . . .

The District Court's consideration of this case began with its finding, which the majority accepts, that the State of Michigan, through its instrumentality, the Detroit Board of Education, engaged in widespread purposeful acts of racial segregation in the Detroit school district. Without belaboring the details, it is sufficient to note that the various techniques used in Detroit were typical of methods employed to segregate students by race in areas where no statutory dual system of education has existed. See, e.g., Keyes v. School District No. 1 (1973). Exacerbating the effects of extensive residential segregation between Negroes and whites, the school board consciously drew attendance zones along lines which maximized the segregation of the races in schools as well. Optional attendance zones were created for neighborhoods undergoing racial transition so as to allow whites in these areas to escape integration. Negro students in areas with overcrowded schools were transported past or away from closer white schools with available space to more distant Negro schools. Grade structures and feeder-school patterns were created and maintained in a manner which had the foreseeable and actual effect of keeping Negro and white pupils in separate schools. Schools were also constructed in locations and in sizes which ensured that they would open with predominantly one-race student bodies. In sum, the evidence adduced below showed that Negro children had been intentionally confined to an expanding core of virtually all-Negro schools immediately surrounded by a receding band of all-white schools.

Contrary to the suggestions in the Court's opinion, the basis for affording a desegregation remedy in this case was not some perceived racial imbalance either between schools within a single school district or between independent school districts. What we confront here is "a systematic program of segregation affecting a substantial portion of the students, schools . . . and facilities within the school system . . . ." The constitutional violation found here was not some de facto racial imbalance, but rather the purposeful, intentional, massive, de jure segregation of the Detroit city schools, which under our decision in Keyes, forms "a predicate for a finding of the existence of a dual school system," and justifies "all-out desegregation." . . .

In seeking to define the appropriate scope of [an] expanded desegregation area, however, the District Court continued to maintain as its sole focus the condition shown to violate the Constitution in this case—the segregation of the Detroit school district. As it stated, the primary question "remains the determination of the area necessary and practicable effectively to eliminate 'root and branch' the effects of state-imposed and supported segregation and to desegregate the Detroit public schools."

There is simply no foundation in the record, then, for the majority's accusation that the only basis for the District Court's order was some desire to achieve a racial balance in the Detroit metropolitan area. In fact, just the contrary is the case. . . .

The Court also misstates the basis for the District Court's order by suggesting that since the only segregation proved at trial was within the Detroit school district, any relief which extended beyond the jurisdiction of the Detroit Board of Education would be inappropriate because it would impose a remedy on outlying districts "not shown to have committed any constitutional violation." The essential foundation of interdistrict relief in this case was not to correct conditions within outlying districts which themselves engaged in purposeful segregation. Instead, interdistrict relief was seen as a necessary part of any meaningful effort by the State of Michigan to remedy the state-caused segregation within the city of Detroit.

Rather than consider the propriety of interdistrict relief on this basis, however, the Court has conjured up a largely fictional account of what the District Court was attempting to accomplish. With all due respect, the Court, in my view, does a great disservice to the District Judge who labored long and hard with this complex litigation by accusing him of changing horses in midstream and shifting the focus of this case from the pursuit of a remedy for the condition of segregation within the Detroit school district to some unprincipled attempt to impose his own philosophy of racial balance on the entire Detroit metropolitan area. The focus of this case has always been the segregated system of education in the city of Detroit. The District Court determined that interdistrict relief was necessary and appropriate only because it found that the condition of segregation within the Detroit school district could not be cured with a Detroit-only remedy. It is on this theory that the interdistrict relief must stand or fall. Unlike the Court, I perceive my task to be to review the District Court's order for what it is, rather than to criticize it for what it manifestly is not.

II. . . .

Under a Detroit-only decree, Detroit's schools will clearly remain racially identifiable in comparison with neighboring schools in the metropolitan community. Schools with 65% and more Negro students will stand in sharp and obvious contrast to schools in neighboring districts with less than 2% Negro enrollment. Negro students will continue to perceive their schools as segregated educational facilities and this perception will only be increased when whites react to a Detroit-only decree by fleeing to the suburbs to avoid integration. School district lines, however innocently drawn, will surely be perceived as fences to separate the races when, under a Detroit-only decree, white parents withdraw their children from the Detroit city schools and move to the suburbs in order to continue them in all-white schools. The message of this action will not escape the Negro children in the city of Detroit. . . . It will be of scant significance to Negro children who have for years been confined by de jure acts of segregation to a growing core of all-Negro schools surrounded by a ring of all-white schools that the new dividing line between the races is the school district boundary.

Nor can it be said that the State is free from any responsibility for the disparity between the racial makeup of Detroit and its surrounding suburbs. The State's creation, through de jure acts of segregation, of a growing core of all-Negro schools inevitably acted as a magnet to attract Negroes to the areas served by such schools and to deter them from settling either in other areas of the city or in the suburbs. By the same token, the growing core of all-Negro schools inevitably helped drive whites to other areas of the city or to the suburbs. . . .

The State must also bear part of the blame for the white flight to the suburbs which would be forthcoming from a Detroit-only decree and would render such a remedy ineffective. Having created a system where whites and Negroes were intentionally kept apart so that they could not become accustomed to learning together, the State is responsible for the fact that many whites will react to the dismantling of that segregated system by attempting to flee to the suburbs. Indeed, by limiting the District Court to a Detroit-only remedy and allowing that flight to the suburbs to succeed, the Court today allows the State to profit from its own wrong and to perpetuate for years to come the separation of the races it achieved in the past by purposeful state action.

The majority asserts, however, that involvement of outlying districts would do violence to the accepted principle that "the nature of the violation determines the scope of the remedy." Not only is the majority's attempt to find in this single phrase the answer to the complex and difficult questions presented in this case hopelessly simplistic but more important, the Court reads these words in a manner which perverts their obvious meaning. The nature of a violation determines the scope of the remedy simply because the function of any remedy is to cure the violation to which it is addressed. . . . To read this principle as barring a District Court from imposing the only effective remedy for past segregation and remitting the court to a patently ineffective alternative is, in my view, to turn a simple commonsense rule into a cruel and meaningless paradox. Ironically, by ruling out an interdistrict remedy, the only relief which promises to cure segregation in the Detroit public schools, the majority flouts the very principle on which it purports to rely.

Nor should it be of any significance that the suburban school districts were not shown to have themselves taken any direct action to promote segregation of the races. Given the State's broad powers over local school districts, it was well within the State's powers to require those districts surrounding the Detroit school district to participate in a metropolitan remedy. The State's duty should be no different here than in cases where it is shown that certain of a

State's voting districts are malapportioned in violation of the Fourteenth Amendment. See Reynolds v. Sims (1964). Overrepresented electoral districts are required to participate in reapportionment although their only "participation" in the violation was to do nothing about it. Similarly, electoral districts which themselves meet representation standards must frequently be redrawn as part of a remedy for other over- and under-inclusive districts. No finding of fault on the part of each electoral district and no finding of a discriminatory effect on each district is a prerequisite to its involvement in the constitutionally required remedy. By the same logic, no finding of fault on the part of the suburban school districts in this case and no finding of a discriminatory effect on each district should be a prerequisite to their involvement in the constitutionally required remedy. . . .

Desegregation is not and was never expected to be an easy task. Racial attitudes ingrained in our Nation's childhood and adolescence are not quickly thrown aside in its middle years. But just as the inconvenience of some cannot be allowed to stand in the way of the rights of others, so public opposition, no matter how strident, cannot be permittted to divert this Court from the enforcement of the constitutional principles at issue in this case. Today's holding, I fear, is more a reflection of a perceived public mood that we have gone far enough in enforcing the Constitution's guarantee of equal justice than it is the product of neutral principles of law. In the short run, it may seem to be the easier course to allow our great metropolitan areas to be divided up each into two cities—one white, the other black—but it is a course, I predict, our people will ultimately regret. I dissent.

Constitution of the United States

WE THE PEOPLE of the United States, in order to form a more perfect union, establish justice, insure domestic tranquility, provide for the common defense, promote the general welfare, and secure the blessings of liberty to ourselves and our posterity, do ordain and establish this Constitution for the United States of America.

Article I

SECTION 1. All legislative powers herein granted shall be vested in a Congress of the United States, which shall consist of a Senate and House of Representatives.

SECTION 2. (1). The House of Representatives shall be composed of members chosen every second year by the people of the several States, and the electors in each State shall have the qualifications requisite for electors of the most numerous branch of the State legislature.

(2). No person shall be a Representative who shall not have attained to the age of twenty-five years, and been seven years a citizen of the United States and who shall not, when elected, be an inhabitant of that State in which he shall be chosen.

(3). Representatives and direct taxes[1] shall be apportioned among the several States which may be included within this Union, according to their respective numbers, which shall be determined by adding to the whole number

---

[1]Modified as to income taxes by the 16th Amendment.

of free persons, including those bound to service for a term of years, and excluding Indians not taxed, three fifths of all other persons.[2] The actual enumeration shall be made within three years after the first meeting of the Congress of the United States, and within every subsequent term of ten years, in such manner as they shall by law direct. The number of Representatives shall not excede one for every thirty thousand, but each State shall have at least one Representative; and until such enumeration shall be made, the State of New Hampshire shall be entitled to choose three, Massachusetts eight, Rhode Island and Providence Plantations one, Connecticut five, New York six, New Jersey four, Pennsylvania eight, Delaware one, Maryland six, Virginia ten, North Carolina five, South Carolina five, and Georgia three.

(4). When vacancies happen in the representation from any State, the executive authority thereof shall issue writs of election to fill such vacancies.

(5). The House of Representatives shall choose their Speaker and other officers; and shall have the sole power of impeachment.

SECTION 3. (1). The Senate of the United States shall be composed of two Senators from each State, chosen by the legislature thereof,[3] for six years; and each Senator shall have one vote.

(2). Immediately after they shall be assembled in consequence of the first election, they shall be divided as equally as may be into three classes. The seats of the Senators of the first class shall be vacated at the expiration of the second year, of the second class at the expiration of the fourth year, and of the third class at the expiration of the sixth year, so that one third may be chosen every second year; and if vacancies happen by resignation, or otherwise, during the recess of the legislature of any State, the executive thereof may make temporary appointments until the next meeting of the legislature, which[3] shall then fill such vacancies.

(3). No person shall be a Senator who shall not have attained to the age of thirty years, and been nine years a citizen of the United States, and who shall not, when elected, be an inhabitant of that State for which he shall be chosen.

(4). The Vice President of the United States shall be president of the Senate, but shall have no vote, unless they be equally divided.

(5). The Senate shall choose their other officers, and also a president pro tempore, in the absence of the Vice President, or when he shall exercise the office of President of the United States.

(6). The Senate shall have the sole power to try all impeachments. When sitting for that purpose, they shall be on oath or affirmation. When the President of the United States is tried, the Chief Justice shall preside: and no person shall be convicted without the concurrence of two thirds of the members present.

(7). Judgment in cases of impeachment shall not extend further than to removal from office, and disqualification to hold and enjoy any office of honor, trust or profit under the United States: but the party convicted shall nevertheless be liable and subject to indictment, trial, judgment and punishment, according to law.

[2]Replaced by the 14th Amendment.
[3]Modified by the 17th Amendment.
[3]Modified by the 17th Amendment.

SECTION 4. (1). The times, places and manner of holding elections for Senators and Representatives, shall be prescribed in each State by the legislature thereof; but the Congress may at any time by law make or alter such regulations, except as to the places of choosing Senators.

(2). The Congress shall assemble at least once in every year, and such meeting shall be on the first Monday in December, unless they shall by law appoint a different day.

SECTION 5. (1). Each House shall be the judge of the elections, returns and qualifications of its own members, and a majority of each shall constitute a quorum to do business; but a smaller number may adjourn from day to day, and may be authorized to compel the attendance of absent members, in such manner, and under such penalties as each House may provide.

(2). Each House may determine the rules of its proceedings, punish its members for disorderly behavior, and, with the concurrence of two thirds, expel a member.

(3). Each House shall keep a journal of its proceedings, and from time to time publish the same, excepting such parts as may in their judgment require secrecy; and the yeas and nays of the members of either House on any question shall, at the desire of one fifth of those present, be entered on the journal.

(4). Neither House, during the session of Congress, shall, without the consent of the other, adjourn for more than three days, nor to any other place than that in which the two Houses shall be sitting.

SECTION 6. (1). The Senators and Representatives shall receive a compensation for their services, to be ascertained by law, and paid out of the Treasury of the United States. They shall in all cases, except treason, felony and breach of the peace, be privileged from arrest during their attendance at the session of their respective Houses, and in going to and returning from the same; and for any speech or debate in either House, they shall not be questioned in any other place.

(2). No Senator or Representative shall, during the time for which he was elected, be appointed to any civil office under the authority of the United States, which shall have been created, or the emoluments whereof shall have been increased during such time; and no person holding any office under the United States, shall be a member of either House during his continuance in office.

SECTION 7. (1). All bills for raising revenue shall originate in the House of Representatives; but the Senate may propose or concur with amendments as on other bills.

(2). Every bill which shall have passed the House of Representatives and the Senate, shall, before it become a law, be presented to the President of the United States; if he approve he shall sign it, but if not he shall return it, with his objections to that House in which it shall have originated, who shall enter the objections at large on their journal, and proceed to reconsider it. If after such reconsideration two thirds of that House shall agree to pass the bill, it shall be sent, together with the objections, to the other House, by which it shall likewise be reconsidered, and if approved by two thirds of that House, it shall become a law. But in all such cases the votes of both Houses shall be determined by yeas and nays, and the names of the persons voting for and against the bill shall be entered on the journal of each House respectively. If any bill shall not be returned by the President within ten days (Sundays excepted) after it shall have been presented to him, the same shall be a law, in like manner as if he had signed it, unless the Congress by their adjournment prevent its return, in which case it shall not be a law.

(3). Every order, resolution, or vote to which the concurrence of the Senate and House of Representatives may be necessary (except on a question of adjournment) shall be presented to the President of the United States; and before the same shall take effect, shall be approved by him, or being disapproved by him, shall be repassed by two thirds of the Senate and House of Representatives, according to the rules and limitations prescribed in the case of a bill.

SECTION 8. (1). The Congress shall have power to lay and collect taxes, duties, imposts and excises, to pay the debts and provide for the common defense and general welfare of the United States; but all duties, imposts and excises shall be uniform throughout the United States;

(2). To borrow money on the credit of the United States;

(3). To regulate commerce with foreign nations, and among the several States, and with the Indian tribes;

(4). To establish an uniform rule of naturalization, and uniform laws on the subject of bankruptcies throughout the United States;

(5). To coin money, regulate the value thereof, and of foreign coin, and fix the standard of weights and measures;

(6). To provide for the punishment of counterfeiting the securities and current coin of the United States;

(7). To establish post offices and post roads;

(8). To promote the progress of science and useful arts, by securing for limited times to authors and inventors the exclusive right to their respective writings and discoveries;

(9). To constitute tribunals inferior to the Supreme Court;

(10). To define and punish piracies and felonies committed on the high seas, and offenses against the law of nations;

(11). To declare war, grant letters of marque and reprisal, and make rules concerning captures on land and water;

(12). To raise and support armies, but no appropriation of money to that use shall be for a longer term than two years;

(13). To provide and maintain a navy;

(14). To make rules for the government and regulation of the land and naval forces;

(15). To provide for calling forth the militia to execute the laws of the Union, suppress insurrections and repel invasions;

(16). To provide for organizing, arming, and disciplining the militia, and for governing such part of them as may be employed in the service of the United States, reserving to the States respectively, the appointment of the officers, and the authority of training the militia according to the discipline prescribed by Congress;

(17). To exercise exclusive legislation in all cases whatsoever, over such district (not exceeding ten miles square) as may, by cession of particular States, and the acceptance of Congress, become the seat of the government of the

United States, and to exercise like authority over all places purchased by the consent of the legislature of the State in which the same shall be, for the erection of forts, magazines, arsenals, dockyards, and other needful buildings; and

(18). To make all laws which shall be necessary and proper for carrying into execution the foregoing powers, and all other powers vested by this Constitution in the government of the United States, or in any department or officer thereof.

SECTION 9. (1). The migration or importation of such persons as any of the States now existing shall think proper to admit, shall not be prohibited by the Congress prior to the year one thousand eight hundred and eight, but a tax or duty may be imposed on such importation, not exceeding ten dollars for each person.

(2). The privilege of the writ of habeas corpus shall not be suspended, unless when in cases of rebellion or invasion the public safety may require it.

(3). No bill of attainder or ex post facto law shall be passed.

(4). No capitation, or other direct, tax shall be laid, unless in proportion to the census or enumeration herein before directed to be taken.[4]

(5). No tax or duty shall be laid on articles exported from any State.

(6). No preference shall be given by any regulation of commerce or revenue to the ports of one State over those of another: nor shall vessels bound to, or from, one State, be obliged to enter, clear, or pay duties in another.

(7). No money shall be drawn from the Treasury, but in consequence of appropriations made by law; and a regular statement and account of the receipts and expenditures of all public money shall be published from time to time.

(8). No title of nobility shall be granted by the United States: and no person holding any office of profit or trust under them, shall, without the consent of the Congress, accept of any present, emolument, office, or title, of any kind whatever, from any king, prince, or foreign State.

SECTION 10.(1). No State shall enter into any treaty, alliance, or confederation; grant letters of marque and reprisal; coin money; emit bills of credit; make anything but gold and silver coin a tender in payment of debts; pass any bill of attainder, ex post facto law, or law impairing the obligation of contracts, or grant any title of nobility.

(2). No State shall, without the consent of the Congress, lay any imposts or duties on imports or exports, except what may be absolutely necessary for executing its inspection laws; and the net produce of all duties and imposts, laid by any State on imports or exports, shall be for the use of the Treasury of the United States; and all such laws shall be subject to the revision and control of the Congress.

(3). No State shall, without the consent of Congress, lay any duty of tonnage, keep troops, or ships of war in time of peace, enter into any agreement or compact with another State, or with a foreign power, or engage in war, unless actually invaded, or in such imminent danger as will not admit of delay.

[4]Modified by the 16th Amendment.

Article II

SECTION 1. (1). The executive power shall be vested in a President of the United States of America. He shall hold his office during the term of four years, and, together with the Vice President, chosen for the same term, be elected, as follows:

(2). Each State shall appoint, in such manner as the legislature thereof may direct, a number of electors, equal to the whole number of Senators and Representatives to which the State may be entitled in the Congress: but no Senator or Representative, or person holding an office of trust or profit under the United States, shall be appointed an elector.

The electors[5] shall meet in their respective States, and vote by ballot for two persons, of whom one at least shall not be an inhabitant of the same State with themselves. And they shall make a list of all the persons voted for, and of the number of votes for each; which list they shall sign and certify, and transmit sealed to the seat of the government of the United States, directed to the president of the Senate. The president of the Senate shall, in the presence of the Senate and House of Representatives, open all the certificates, and the votes shall then be counted. The person having the greatest number of votes shall be the President, if such number be a majority of the whole number of electors appointed; and if there be more than one who have such majority, and have an equal number of votes, then the House of Representatives shall immediately choose by ballot one of them for President; and if no person have a majority, then from the five highest on the list the said House shall in like manner choose the President. But in choosing the President, the votes shall be taken by States, the representation from each State having one vote; a quorum for this purpose shall consist of a member or members from two thirds of the States, and a majority of all the States shall be necessary to a choice. In every case, after the choice of the President, the person having the greatest number of votes of the electors shall be the Vice President. But if there should remain two or more who have equal votes, the Senate shall choose from them by ballot the Vice President.

(3). The Congress may determine the time of choosing the electors, and the day on which they shall give their votes; which day shall be the same throughout the United States.

(4). No person except a natural born citizen, or a citizen of the United States, at the time of the adoption of this Constitution, shall be eligible to the office of President; neither shall any person be eligible to that office who shall not have attained to the age of thirty five years, and been fourteen years a resident within the United States.

(5). In the case of the removal of the President from office, or of his death, resignation, or inability to discharge the powers and duties of the said office, the same shall devolve on the Vice President, and the Congress may by law provide for the case of removal, death, resignation, or inability, both of the President and Vice President, declaring what officer shall then act as president,

[5]This paragraph was replaced in 1804 by the 12th Amendment.

and such officer shall act accordingly, until the disability be removed, or a President shall be elected.

(6). The President shall, at stated times, receive for his services, a compensation, which shall neither be increased nor diminished during the period for which he shall have been elected, and he shall not receive within that period any other emolument from the United States, or any of them.

(7). Before he enter on the execution of his office, he shall take the following oath or affirmation:—"I do solemnly swear (or affirm) that I will faithfully execute the office of the President of the United States, and will to the best of my ability, preserve, protect and defend the Constitution of the United States."

SECTION 2. (1). The President shall be commander in chief of the army and navy of the United States, and of the militia of the several States, when called into the actual service of the United States; he may require the opinion, in writing, of the principal officer in each of the executive departments, upon any subject relating to the duties of their respective offices, and he shall have power to grant reprieves and pardons for offenses against the United States, except in cases of impeachment.

(2). He shall have power, by and with the advice and consent of the Senate, to make treaties, provided two thirds of the Senators present concur; and he shall nominate, and by and with the advice and consent of the Senate, shall appoint ambassadors, other public ministers and consuls, judges of the Supreme Court, and all other officers of the United States, whose appointments are not herein otherwise provided for, and which shall be established by law: but the Congress may by law vest the appointment of such inferior officers, as they think proper, in the President alone, in the courts of law, or in the heads of departments.

(3). The President shall have power to fill up all vacancies that may happen during the recess of the Senate, by granting commissions which shall expire at the end of their next session.

SECTION 3. He shall from time to time give to the Congress information of the state of the Union, and recommend to their consideration such measures as he shall judge necessary and expedient; he may, on extraordinary occasions, convene both Houses, or either of them, and in case of disagreement between them, with respect to the time of adjournment, he may adjourn them to such time as he shall think proper; he shall receive ambassadors and other public ministers; he shall take care that the laws be faithfully executed, and shall commission all the officers of the United States.

SECTION 4. The President, Vice President and all civil officers of the United States, shall be removed from office on impeachment for, and conviction of, treason, bribery, or other high crimes and misdemeanors.

Article III

SECTION 1. The judicial power of the United States, shall be vested in one Supreme Court, and in such inferior courts as the Congress may from time to time ordain and establish. The judges, both of the Supreme and inferior courts, shall hold their offices during good behavior, and shall, at stated times, receive for their services, a compensation, which shall not be diminished during their continuance in office.

Section 2. (1). The judicial power shall extend to all cases, in law and equity, arising under this Constitution, the laws of the United States, and treaties made, or which shall be made, under their authority;—to all cases affecting ambassadors, other public ministers and consuls;—to all cases of admiralty and maritime jurisdiction;—to controversies to which the United states shall be a party;—to controversies between two or more States;—between a State and citizens of another State;[6] —between citizens of different States;—between citizens of the same State claiming lands under grants of different States, and between a State, or the citizens thereof, and foreign States, citizens or subjects.

(2). In all cases affecting ambassadors, other public ministers and consuls, and those in which a State shall be party, the Supreme Court shall have original jurisdiction. In all the other cases before mentioned, the Supreme Court shall have appellate jurisdiction, both as to law and fact, with such exceptions, and under such regulations as the Congress shall make.

(3). The trial of all crimes, except in cases of impeachment, shall be by jury; and such trial shall be held in the State where the said crimes shall have been committed; but when not committed within any State, the trial shall be at such place or places as the Congress may by law have directed.

Section 3. (1). Treason against the United States, shall consist only in levying war against them, or in adhering to their enemies, giving them aid and comfort. No person shall be convicted of treason unless on the testimony of two witnesses to the same overt act, or on confession in open court.

(2). The Congress shall have power to declare the punishment of treason, but no attainder of treason shall work corruption of blood, or forfeiture except during the life of the person attainted.

Article IV

Section 1. Full faith and credit shall be given in each State to the public acts, records, and judicial proceedings of every other State. And the Congress may by general laws prescribe the manner in which such acts, records and proceedings shall be proved, and the effect thereof.

Section 2. (1). The citizens of each State shall be entitled to all privileges and immunities of citizens in the several States.

(2). A person charged in any State with treason, felony, or other crime, who shall flee from justice, and be found in another State, shall on demand of the executive authority of the State from which he fled, be delivered up, to be removed to the State having jurisdiction of the crime.

(3). No person held to service or labor in one State, under the laws thereof, escaping into another, shall, in consequence of any law or regulation therein, be discharged from such service or labor, but shall be delivered up on claim of the party to whom such service or labor may be due.

[6]Restricted by the 11th Amendment.

SECTION 3. (1). New States may be admitted by the Congress into this Union; but no new State shall be formed or erected within the jursidiction of any other State; nor any State be formed by the junction of two or more States, or parts of States, without the consent of the legislatures of the States concerned as well as of the Congress.

(2). The Congress shall have power to dispose of and make all needful rules and regulations respecting the territory or other property belonging to the United States; and nothing in this Constitution shall be so construed as to prejudice any claims of the United States, or of any particular State.

SECTION 4. The United States shall guarantee to every State in this Union a republican form of government, and shall protect each of them against invasion; and on application of the legislature, or of the executive (when the legislature cannot be convened) against domestic violence.

Article V

The Congress, whenever two thirds of both Houses shall deem it necessary, shall propose amendments to this Constitution, or, on the application of the legislatures of two thirds of the several States, shall call a convention for proposing amendments, which, in either case, shall be valid to all intents and purposes, as part of this Constitution, when ratified by the legislatures of three fourths of the several States, or by conventions in three fourths thereof, as the one or the other mode of ratification may be proposed by the Congress; Provided that no amendment which may be made prior to the year one thousand eight hundred and eight shall in any manner affect the first and fourth clauses in the ninth section of the first article; and that no State, without its consent, shall be deprived of its equal suffrage in the Senate.

Article VI

SECTION 1. All debts contracted and engagements entered into, before the adoption of this Constitution, shall be as valid against the United States under this Constitution, as under the Confederation.

SECTION 2. This Constitution, and the laws of the United States which shall be made in pursuance thereof; and all treaties made, or which shall be made, under the authority of the United States, shall be the supreme law of the land; and the judges in every State shall be bound thereby, anything in the constitution or laws of any State to the contrary notwithstanding.

SECTION 3. The Senators and Representatives before mentioned, and the members of the several State legislatures, and all executive and judicial officers, both of the United States and of the several States, shall be bound by oath or affirmation to support this Constitution; but no religious test shall ever be required as a qualification to any office or public trust under the United States.

Article VII

The ratification of the conventions of nine States, shall be sufficient for the establishment of this Constitution between the States so ratifying the same.

Done in Convention by the unanimous consent of the States present the seventeenth day of September in the year of our Lord one thousand seven hundred and eighty-seven, and of the independence of the United States of America the twelfth. In witness whereof we have hereunto subscribed our names.

Go. Washington—

Presidt. and Deputy from Virginia

Articles in addition to and amendments of the Constitution of the United States of America, proposed by Congress, and ratified by the legislatures of the several States, pursuant to the fifth article of the original Constitution.

Article I[7]

Congress shall make no law respecting an establishment of religion, or prohibiting the free exercise thereof; or abridging the freedom of speech, or of the press; or the right of the people peaceably to assemble, and to petition the government for a redress of grievances.

Article II

A well regulated militia, being necessary to the security of a free State, the right of the people to keep and bear arms, shall not be infringed.

Article III

No soldier shall, in time of peace be quartered in any house, without the consent of the owner, nor in time of war, but in a manner to be prescribed by law.

Article IV

The right of the people to be secure in their persons, houses, papers, and effects, against unreasonable searches and seizures, shall not be violated, and no warrants shall issue, but upon probable cause, supported by oath or affirmation, and particularly describing the place to be searched, and the persons or things to be seized.

Article V

No person shall be held to answer for a capital, or otherwise infamous crime, unless on a presentment or indictment of a grand jury, except in cases arising in the land or naval forces, or in the militia, when in actual service in time of war or public danger; nor shall any person be subject for the same offense to

---

[7]The first ten Amendments were adopted in 1791.

be twice put in jeopardy of life or limb; nor shall be compelled in any criminal case to be a witness against himself, nor be deprived of life, liberty, or property, without due process of law; nor shall private property be taken for public use, without just compensation.

Article VI

In all criminal prosecutions the accused shall enjoy the right to a speedy and public trial, by an impartial jury of the State and district wherein the crime shall have been committed, which district shall have been previously ascertained by law, and to be informed of the nature and cause of the accusation; to be confronted with the witnesses against him; to have compulsory process for obtaining witnesses in his favor, and to have the assistance of counsel for his defense.

Article VII

In suits at common law, where the value in controversy shall exceed twenty dollars, the right of trial by jury shall be preserved, and no fact tried by a jury shall be otherwise reexamined in any court of the United States, than according to the rules of the common law.

Article VIII

Excessive bail shall not be required, nor excessive fines imposed, nor cruel and unusual punishments inflicted.

Article IX

The enumeration in the Constitution, of certain rights, shall not be construed to deny or disparage others retained by the people.

Article X

The powers not delegated to the United States by the Constitution, nor prohibited by it to the States, are reserved to the States respectively, or to the people.

Article XI[8]

The judicial power of the United States shall not be construed to extend to any suit in law or equity, commenced or prosecuted against one of the United States by citizens of another State, or by citizens or subjects of any foreign State.

[8]Ratified in 1795; proclaimed in 1798.

Article XII[9]

The electors shall meet in their respective States and vote by ballot for President and Vice-President, one of whom, at least, shall not be an inhabitant of the same State with themselves; they shall name in their ballots the person voted for as President, and in distinct ballots the person voted for as Vice-President, and they shall make distinct lists of all persons voted for as President, and of all persons voted for as Vice-President, and of the number of votes for each, which lists they shall sign and certify, and transmit sealed to the seat of the government of the United States, directed to the president of the Senate; —The president of the Senate shall, in the presence of the Senate and House of Representatives, open all the certificates and the votes shall then be counted; —The person having the greatest number of votes for President, shall be the President, if such number be a majority of the whole number of electors appointed; and if no person have such majority, then from the persons having the highest numbers not exceeding three on the list of those voted for as President, the House of Representatives shall choose immediately, by ballot, the President. But in choosing the President, the votes shall be taken by States, the representation from each State having one vote; a quorum for this purpose shall consist of a member or members from two thirds of the States, and a majority of all the States shall be necessary to a choice. And if the House of Representatives shall not choose a President whenever the right of choice shall devolve upon them, before the fourth day of March next following, then the Vice-President shall act as President, as in the case of the death or other constitutional disability of the President.—The person having the greatest number of votes as Vice-President, shall be the Vice-President, if such number be a majority of the whole number of electors appointed, and if no person have a majority, then from the two highest numbers on the list, the Senate shall choose the Vice-President; a quorum for the purpose shall consist of two thirds of the whole number of Senators, and a majority of the whole number shall be necessary to a choice. But no person constitutionally ineligible to the office of President shall be eligible to that of Vice-President of the United States.

Article XIII[10]

SECTION 1. Neither slavery nor involuntary servitude, except as a punishment for crime whereof the party shall have been duly convicted, shall exist within the United States, or any place subject to their jurisdiction.

SECTION 2. Congress shall have power to enforce this article by appropriate legislation.

[9]Adopted in 1804.
[10]Adopted in 1865.

Article XIV[11]

SECTION 1. All persons born or naturalized in the United States, and subject to the jurisdiction thereof, are citizens of the United States and of the State wherein they reside. No State shall make or enforce any law which shall abridge the privileges or immunities of citizens of the United States; nor shall any State deprive any person of life, liberty, or property, without due process of law; nor deny any person within its jurisdiction the equal protection of the laws.

SECTION 2. Representatives shall be apportioned among the several States according to their respective numbers, counting the whole number of persons in each State, excluding Indians not taxed. But when the right to vote at any election for the choice of electors for President and Vice President of the United States, Representatives in Congress, the executive and judicial offices of a State, or the members of the legislature thereof, is denied to any of the male inhabitants of such State, being twenty-one years of age, and citizens of the United States, or in any way abridged, except for participation in rebellion, or other crime, the basis of representation therein shall be reduced in the proportion which the number of such male citizens shall bear to the whole number of male citizens twenty-one years of age in such State.

SECTION 3. No person shall be a Senator or Representative in Congress, or elector of President and Vice President, or hold any office, civil or military, under the United States, or under any State, who, having previously taken an oath, as a member of Congress, or as an officer of the United States, or as a member of any State legislature, or as an executive or judicial officer of any State, to support the Constitution of the United States, shall have engaged in insurrection or rebellion against the same, or given aid or comfort to the enemies thereof. But Congress may by a vote of two thirds of each House, remove such disability.

SECTION 4. The validity of the public debt of the United States, authorized by law, including debts incurred for payment of pensions and bounties for services in suppressing insurrection or rebellion, shall not be questioned. But neither the United States nor any State shall assume or pay any debt or obligation incurred in aid of insurrection or rebellion against the United States, or any claim for the loss or emancipation of any slave; but all such debts, obligations and claims shall be held illegal and void.

SECTION 5. The Congress shall have power to enforce, by appropriate legislation, the provision of this article.

Article XV[12]

SECTION 1. The right of citizens of the United States to vote shall not be denied or abridged by the United States or by any State on account of race, color, or previous condition of servitude.

[11]Adopted in 1868.
[12]Adopted in 1870.

SECTION 2. The Congress shall have the power to enforce this article by appropriate legislation.

Article XVI[13]

The Congress shall have the power to lay and collect taxes on incomes, from whatever source derived, without apportionment among the several States, and without regard to any census or enumeration.

Article XVII[13]

The Senate of the United States shall be composed of two Senators from each State, elected by the people thereof, for six years; and each Senator shall have one vote. The electors in each State shall have the qualifications requisite for electors of the most numerous branch of the State legislatures.

When vacancies happen in the representation of any State in the Senate, the executive authority of such State shall issue writs of election to fill such vacancies: *Provided,* That the legislature of any State may empower the executive thereof to make temporary appointments until the people fill the vacancies by election as the legislature may direct.

This amendment shall not be so construed as to affect the election or term of any Senator chosen before it becomes valid as part of the Constitution.

Article XVIII[14]

SECTION 1. After one year from the ratification of this article the manufacture, sale, or transportation of intoxicating liquors within, the importation thereof into, or the exportation thereof from the United States and all territory subject to the jurisdiction thereof for beverage purposes is hereby prohibited.

SECTION 2. The Congress and the several States shall have concurrent power to enforce this article by appropriate legislation.

SECTION 3. This article shall be inoperative unless it shall have been ratified as an amendment to the Constitution by the legislatures of the several States, as provided in the Constitution, within seven years from the date of the submission hereof to the States by the Congress.

[13]Adopted in 1913.
[13]Adopted in 1913.
[14]Adopted in 1919. Repealed by Article XXI.

Article XIX[15]

The right of citizens of the United States to vote shall not be denied or abridged by the United States or by any State on account of sex.

The Congress shall have power to enforce this article by appropriate legislation.

Article XX[16]

SECTION 1. The terms of the President and Vice President shall end at noon on the 20th day of January, and the terms of Senators and Representatives at noon on the 3rd day of January, of the years in which such terms would have ended if this article had not been ratified; and the terms of their successors shall then begin.

SECTION 2. The Congress shall assemble at least once in every year, and such meeting shall begin at noon on the 3rd day of January, unless they shall by law appoint a different day.

SECTION 3. If, at the time fixed for the beginning of the term of the President, the President elect shall have died, the Vice President elect shall become President. If a President shall not have been chosen before the time fixed for the beginning of his term, or if the President elect shall have failed to qualify, then the Vice President elect shall act as President until a President shall have qualified; and the Congress may by law provide for the case wherein neither a President elect nor a Vice President elect shall have qualified, declaring who shall then act as President, or the manner in which one who is to act shall be selected, and such person shall act accordingly until a President or Vice President shall have qualified.

SECTION 4. The Congress may by law provide for the case of the death of any of the persons from whom the House of Representatives may choose a President whenever the right of choice shall have devolved upon them, and for the case of the death of any of the persons from whom the Senate may choose a Vice President whenever the right of choice shall have devolved upon them.

SECTION 5. Sections 1 and 2 shall take effect on the 15th day of October following the ratification of this article.

SECTION 6. This article shall be inoperative unless it shall have been ratified as an amendment to the Constitution by the legislatures of three fourths of the several States within seven years from the date of its submission.

[15]Adopted in 1920.
[16]Adopted in 1933.

Article XXI[17]

SECTION 1. The Eighteenth Article of Amendment to the Constitution of the United States is hereby repealed.

SECTION 2. The transportation or importation into any State, Territory or Possession of the United States for delivery or use therein of intoxicating liquors in violation of the laws thereof is hereby prohibited.

SECTION 3. This article shall be inoperative unless it shall have been ratified as an amendment to the Constitution by conventions in the several States, as provided in the Constitution, within seven years from the date of submission hereof to the States by the Congress.

Article XXII[18]

SECTION 1. No person shall be elected to the office of the President more than twice, and no person who has held the office of President, or acted as President, for more than two years of a term to which some other person was elected President shall be elected to the office of the President more than once. But this Article shall not apply to any person holding the office of President when this Article was proposed by the Congress, and shall not prevent any person who may be holding the office of President, or acting as President, during the term within which the Article becomes operative from holding the office of President or acting as President during the remainder of such term.

SECTION 2. This article shall be inoperative unless it shall have been ratified as an amendment to the Constitution by the legislatures of three-fourths of the several States within seven years from the date of its submission to the States by the Congress.

Article XXIII[19]

SECTION 1. The District constituting the seat of Government of the United States shall appoint in such manner as the Congress may direct:

A number of electors of President and Vice President equal to the whole number of Senators and Representatives in Congress to which the District would be entitled if it were a State, but in no event more than the least populous State; they shall be in addition to those appointed by the States, but they shall be considered, for the purposes of the election of President and Vice President, to be electors appointed by a State; and they shall meet in the District and perform such duties as provided by the twelfth article of amendment.

SECTION 2. The Congress shall have power to enforce this article by appropriate legislation.

[17]Adopted in 1933.
[18]Adopted in 1951.
[19]Adopted in 1961.

Article XXIV[20]

SECTION 1. The right of citizens of the United States to vote in any primary or other election for President or Vice President, for electors for President or Vice President, or for Senator or Representative in Congress, shall not be denied or abridged by the United States or any State by reason of failure to pay any poll tax or other tax.

SECTION 2. The Congress shall have power to enforce this article by appropriate legislation.

Article XXV[21]

SECTION 1. In case of the removal of the President from office or his death or resignation, the Vice President shall become President.

SECTION 2. Whenever there is a vacancy in the office of the Vice President, the President shall nominate a Vice President who shall take the Office upon confirmation by a majority vote of both houses of Congress.

SECTION 3. Whenever the President transmits to the President pro tempore of the Senate and the Speaker of the House of Representatives his written declaration that he is unable to discharge the powers and duties of his office, and until he transmits to them a written declaration to the contrary, such powers and duties shall be discharged by the Vice President as Acting President.

SECTION 4. Whenever the Vice President and a majority of either the principal officers of the executive departments, or of such other body as Congress may by law provide, transmit to the President pro tempore of the Senate and the Speaker of the House of Representatives their written declaration that the President is unable to discharge the powers and duties of his office, the Vice President shall immediately assume the powers and duties of the office as Acting President.

Thereafter, when the President transmits to the President pro tempore of the Senate and the Speaker of the House of Representatives his written declaration that no inability exists, he shall resume the powers and duties of his office unless the Vice President and a majority of either the principal officers of the executive department, or of such other body as Congress may by law provide, transmit within four days to the President pro tempore of the Senate and the Speaker of the House of Representatives their written declaration that the President is unable to discharge the powers and duties of his office. Thereupon Congress shall decide the issue, assembling within 48 hours for that purpose if not in session. If the Congress, within 21 days after receipt of the latter written declaration, or, if Congress is not in session, within 21 days after Congress is required to assemble, determines by two-thirds vote of both houses that the President is unable to discharge the powers and duties of his office,

[20]Adopted in 1964.
[21]Adopted in 1967.

the Vice President shall continue to discharge the same as Acting President; otherwise, the President shall resume the powers and duties of his office.

Article XXVI[22]

SECTION 1. The right of citizens of the United States, who are eighteen years of age, or older, to vote shall not be denied or abridged by the United States or by any state on account of age.

SECTION 2. The Congress shall have the power to enforce this article by appropriate legislation.

Article XXVII[23]

SECTION 1. Equality of rights under the law shall not be denied or abridged by the United States or by any state on account of sex.

SECTION 2. The Congress shall have the power to enforce, by appropriate legislation, the provisions of this article.

SECTION 3. This amendment shall take effect two years after the date of ratification.

[22]Adopted in 1971.
[23]Proposed to states for ratification March 22, 1972.